Blackstone's Statutes on

Media Law

Blackstone's Statutes on
Media Law

4th edition

edited by

Richard Caddell

Senior Lecturer in Law, Swansea University

and

Howard Johnson

LLM Tutor, Cardiff Law School

OXFORD
UNIVERSITY PRESS

OXFORD
UNIVERSITY PRESS

Great Clarendon Street, Oxford, OX2 6DP,
United Kingdom

Oxford University Press is a department of the University of Oxford.
It furthers the University's objective of excellence in research, scholarship,
and education by publishing worldwide. Oxford is a registered trade mark of
Oxford University Press in the UK and in certain other countries

First edition 2006
Second edition 2008
Third edition 2010
Fourth edition 2013

Impression: 1

Published in the United States of America by Oxford University Press
198 Madison Avenue, New York, NY 10016, United States of America

British Library Cataloguing in Publication Data
Data available

ISBN 978–0–19–965633–2

Printed in Great Britain by
Bell & Bain Ltd, Glasgow

Contents

	Editors' preface	*xi*
	New to this edition	*xii*

Part I   Freedom of speech   **1**

Bill of Rights 1688	1
Parliamentary Standards Act 2009	1
European Convention for the Protection of Human Rights and Fundamental Freedoms 1950	1
Protocol to the Convention for the Protection of Human Rights and Fundamental Freedoms	2
Human Rights Act 1998	3
First Amendment to the Constitution of the United States of America 1787	9

Part II   Defamation   **10**

Defamation Act 2013	10
Defamation Act 1952	15
Defamation Act 1996	17
Rehabilitation of Offenders Act 1974	28
Limitation Act 1980	29
Courts and Legal Services Act 1990	32
Access to Justice Act 1999	32
Broadcasting Act 1990	33
Civil Evidence Act 1968	33
Senior Courts Act 1981	35
Criminal Procedure and Investigations Act 1996	35
Copyright, Designs and Patents Act 1988	37
Electronic Commerce (EC Directive) Regulations 2002	41

Part III   Reporting restrictions   **44**

Children and Young Persons Act 1933	44
Youth Justice and Criminal Evidence Act 1999	47
Children Act 1989	55
Children, Schools and Families Act 2010	55
Children's Hearings (Scotland) Act 2011	61
Sexual Offences (Amendment) Act 1976	62
Sexual Offences (Amendment) Act 1992	63
Sexual Offences (Protected Material) Act 1997	68
Crime and Disorder Act 1998	72
Criminal Justice Act 1987	74
Criminal Justice Act 2003	76
Criminal Procedure and Investigations Act 1996	78
Magistrates' Courts Act 1980	82
Judicial Proceedings (Regulation of Reports) Act 1926	84

	Employment Tribunals Act 1996	85
	Inquiries Act 2005	90
	Coroners and Justice Act 2009	92

Part IV   Contempt of court and the media   97

	Contempt of Court Act 1981	97
	Administration of Justice Act 1960	104
	Courts Act 2003	105

Part V   Protection of confidential sources of information   106

| | Recommendation No. R (2000) 7 of the Committee of Ministers to Member States on the Right of Journalists not to Disclose their Sources of Information | 106 |
| | Terrorism Act 2000 | 109 |

Part VI   Freedom of information and data protection   111

	Freedom of Information Act 2000	111
	Data Protection Act 1998	138
	Official Secrets Act 1989	166
	Security Service Act 1989	174
	Criminal Justice and Immigration Act 2008	175

Part VII   Privacy and media intrusion   176

	Protection from Harassment Act 1997	176
	Data Protection Act 1998	184
	Copyright, Designs and Patents Act 1988	190
	Criminal Justice and Immigration Act 2008	190

Part VIII   Self-regulation of the print media   193

	Press Complaints Commission Code of Practice	193
	National Union of Journalists Code of Conduct	196
	Enterprise and Regulatory Reform Act 2013	197
	Crime and Courts Act 2013	197
	Draft Royal Charter on Self-Regulation of the Press	201

Part IX   Broadcasting regulation   214

	Broadcasting Act 1990	214
	Broadcasting Act 1996	233
	Communications Act 2003	251
	Directive 2010/13/EU of the European Parliament and of the Council of 10 March 2010	340
	OFCOM Broadcasting Code	352
	BBC Royal Charter for the Continuance of the British Broadcasting Corporation	366
	BBC Licence Agreement	373
	UN Convention on the Law of the Sea 1982	386

Part X   Proscribed, offensive and indecent materials   387

Obscene Publications Act 1959   387
Obscene Publications Act 1964   390
Video Recordings Act 1984   391
Coroners and Justice Act 2009   395
Racial and Religious Hatred Act 2006   397
Public Order Act 1986   398
Terrorism Act 2006   401
Terrorism Act 2000   406
Criminal Justice and Immigration Act 2008   406

Index   *411*

Chronological contents

1688   Bill of Rights . . . 1
1787   First Amendment to the Constitution
      of the United States of America . . . 9
1926   Judicial Proceedings (Regulation of
      Reports) Act . . . 84
1933   Children and Young Persons Act . . . 44
1950   European Convention for the Protection
      of Human Rights and Fundamental
      Freedoms . . . 1
      Protocol to the Convention for the
      Protection of Human Rights and
      Fundamental Freedoms . . . 2
1952   Defamation Act . . . 15
1959   Obscene Publications Act . . . 387
1960   Administration of Justice Act . . . 104
1964   Obscene Publications Act . . . 390
1968   Civil Evidence Act . . . 33
1974   Rehabilitation of Offenders Act . . . 28
1976   Sexual Offences (Amendment) Act . . . 62
1980   Limitation Act . . . 29
      Magistrates' Courts Act . . . 82
1981   Contempt of Court Act 1981 . . . 97
      Senior Courts Act . . . 35
1982   UN Convention on the Law of
      the Sea . . . 386
1984   Video Recordings Act . . . 391
1986   Public Order Act . . . 398
1987   Criminal Justice Act . . . 74
1988   Copyright, Designs and Patents Act . . . 37,
      190
1989   Children Act . . . 55
      Official Secrets Act . . . 166
      Security Service Act . . . 174
1990   Broadcasting Act . . . 33, 214
      Courts and Legal Services Act . . . 32
1992   Sexual Offences (Amendment) Act . . . 63
1996   Broadcasting Act . . . 233
      Criminal Procedure and Investigations
      Act . . . 35, 78
      Defamation Act . . . 17
      Employment Tribunals Act . . . 85
1997   Protection from Harassment Act . . . 176
      Sexual Offences (Protected Material)
      Act . . . 68
1998   Crime and Disorder Act . . . 72
      Data Protection Act . . . 138, 184

      Human Rights Act . . . 3
1999   Access to Justice Act . . . 32
      Youth Justice and Criminal Evidence
      Act . . . 47
2000   Freedom of Information Act . . . 111
      Recommendation No. R (2000) 7 of
      the Committee of Ministers to
      Member States on the Right of
      Journalists not to Disclose their
      Sources of Information . . . 106
      Terrorism Act . . . 109, 406
2002   Electronic Commerce (EC Directive)
      Regulations . . . 41
2003   Communications Act . . . 251
      Courts Act . . . 105
      Criminal Justice Act . . . 76
2005   Inquiries Act . . . 90
2006   BBC Royal Charter for the
      Continuance of the British
      Broadcasting Corporation . . . 366
      Racial and Religious
      Hatred Act . . . 397
      Terrorism Act . . . 401
2008   Criminal Justice and Immigration
      Act . . . 175, 190, 406
2009   Coroners and Justice Act . . . 92, 395
      Parliamentary Standards Act . . . 1
2010   BBC Licence Agreement . . . 373
      Children, Schools and Families
      Act . . . 55
      Directive 2010/13/EU of the European
      Parliament and of the Council of 10
      March 2010 . . . 340
2011   Children's Hearings (Scotland) Act . . . 61
      National Union of Journalists Code of
      Conduct . . . 196
      Press Complaints Commission Code of
      Practice . . . 193
2013   Crime and Courts Act . . . 197
      Defamation Act . . . 10
      Draft Royal Charter on Self-Regulation of
      the Press . . . 201
      Enterprise and Regulatory Reform
      Act . . . 197
      OFCOM Broadcasting Code . . . 352

Alphabetical contents

A   Access to Justice Act 1999...32
    Administration of Justice
        Act 1960...104
B   BBC Licence Agreement...373
    BBC Royal Charter for the Continuance
        of the British Broadcasting
        Corporation...366
    Bill of Rights 1688...1
    Broadcasting Act 1990...33, 214
    Broadcasting Act 1996...233
C   Children Act 1989...55
    Children and Young Persons Act 1933...44
    Children, Schools and Families Act 2010...55
    Children's Hearings (Scotland) Act 2011...61
    Civil Evidence Act 1968...33
    Communications Act 2003...251
    Contempt of Court Act 1981...97
    Copyright, Designs and Patents Act
        1988...37, 190
    Coroners and Justice Act 2009...92, 395
    Courts Act 2003...105
    Courts and Legal Services Act 1990...32
    Crime and Courts Act 2013...197
    Crime and Disorder Act 1998...72
    Criminal Justice Act 1987...74
    Criminal Justice Act 2003...76
    Criminal Justice and Immigration
        Act 2008 ... 175, 190, 406
    Criminal Procedure and Investigations
        Act 1996...35, 78
D   Data Protection Act 1998...138, 184
    Defamation Act 1952...15
    Defamation Act 1996...17
    Defamation Act 2013...10
    Directive 2010/13/EU of the European
        Parliament and of the Council of 10
        March 2010...340
    Draft Royal Charter on Self-Regulation of the
        Press...201
E   Electronic Commerce (EC Directive)
        Regulations 2002...41
    Employment Tribunals Act 1996...85
    Enterprise and Regulatory Reform
        Act 2013...197
    European Convention for the Protection
        of Human Rights and Fundamental
        Freedoms 1950...1

    Protocol to the Convention for the Protection
        of Human Rights and Fundamental
        Freedoms...2
F   First Amendment to the Constitution of
        the United States of America 1787...9
    Freedom of Information Act 2000...111
H   Human Rights Act 1998...3
I   Inquiries Act 2005...90
J   Judicial Proceedings (Regulation of
        Reports) Act 1926...84
L   Limitation Act 1980...29
M   Magistrates' Courts Act 1980...82
N   National Union of Journalists Code
        of Conduct...196
O   Obscene Publications Act 1959...387
    Obscene Publications Act 1964...390
    OFCOM Broadcasting Code...352
    Official Secrets Act 1989...166
P   Parliamentary Standards Act 2009...1
    Press Complaints Commission Code
        of Practice...193
    Protection from Harassment
        Act 1997...176
    Public Order Act 1986...398
R   Racial and Religious Hatred
        Act 2006...397
    Recommendation No. R (2000) 7 of the
        Committee of Ministers to Member
        States on the Right of Journalists
        not to Disclose their Sources of
        Information...106
    Rehabilitation of Offenders Act
        1974...28
S   Security Service Act 1989...174
    Senior Courts Act 1981...35
    Sexual Offences (Amendment)
        Act 1976...62
    Sexual Offences (Amendment) Act 1992...63
    Sexual Offences (Protected Material)
        Act 1997...68
T   Terrorism Act 2000...109, 406
    Terrorism Act 2006...401
U   UN Convention on the Law of the Sea
        1982...386
V   Video Recordings Act 1984...391
Y   Youth Justice and Criminal Evidence
        Act 1999...47

Editors' preface

It is our great pleasure to welcome you to what is now the fourth edition of *Blackstone's Statutes on Media Law*. As with its predecessors, our aim with this volume is to provide an overview of essential statutory materials within the broad subject of 'media law', which we hope will prove to be a useful guide for undergraduate and postgraduate students, their course directors and practitioners within the fields of media and entertainment law, as well as those working within the industry.

As ever, the variety of statutory materials that may be considered to fall under this most expansive of legal umbrellas continues to grow at an astonishing rate, against the backdrop of unprecedented regulatory reform of the print, broadcast and online media. The confines of space have required us to be especially selective of the materials that we have included within this new edition of the book. The major updates to this particular volume include the traditional amendments to the existing contents, as well as the inclusion of the new Defamation Act 2013, the draft Privy Council Royal Charter relating to Self-Regulation of the press (as it stands as of May 2013), alongside the accompanying legislative 'underpinning' provisions in the Crime and Courts Act 2013 and the Enterprise and Regulatory Reform Act 2013.

Regrettably, in order to accommodate this new sweep of materials, certain other instruments have inevitably had to be omitted. However, we would like to draw the reader's attention to the comprehensive Online Resource Centre that accompanies this volume within which provisions that have fallen victim to the editing process of this edition may be found. The ORC is periodically updated with new developments in policy, legislation and case law, which we hope will provide a helpful resource to accompany this book. Indeed, at the time of compilation a series of major developments were afoot. As the reverberations from the Leveson Inquiry continue to be keenly felt within the media industry, the battle over the form and content of a new Royal Charter continues apace. The various proposals and counter-proposals from the government and the industry will be represented on the ORC as they emerge. Likewise, new proposals concerning the reporting of family proceedings are also expected shortly. Contemporary media law remains as fast-paced as ever and we hope that the online resources will accordingly be of particular benefit to students and commentators in remaining abreast of developments.

In compiling this volume, we would like to express our most heartfelt thanks to Joanna Williams, who has steered the new edition, and to the OUP production, editing and proofreading team. We are also very grateful to all those who have made very helpful suggestions for future content, and we warmly welcome the thoughts of our colleagues for future editions.

Richard Caddell, Swansea
Howard Johnson, Cardiff
May 2013

New to this edition

The fourth edition of *Blackstone's Statutes on Media Law* has been fully revised and updated to include all relevant legislation through to May 2013 including:

- Defamation Act 2013
- Draft Privy Council Royal Charter on Self-Regulation of the Press (as at May 2013)
- Provisions of Crime and Courts Act 2013 and the Enterprise and Regulatory Reform Act 2013 relating to press self-regulation

Part I

Freedom of speech

Bill of Rights 1688

(1 Will and Mary Sess. 2, c. 2)

AND thereupon the said Lords Spirituall and Temporall and Commons pursuant to their respective Letters and Elections being now assembled in a full and free Representative of this nation takeing into their most serious Consideration the best meanes for attaining the Ends aforesaid Doe in the first place (as their Auncestors in like Case have usually done) for the Vindicating and Asserting their auntient Rights and Liberties, Declare:

9.   That the Freedome of Speech and Debates or Proceedings in Parlyament ought not to be impeached or questioned in any Court or Place out of Parlyament.

Parliamentary Standards Act 2009

(2009, c. 13)

1   Bill of Rights
Nothing in this Act shall be construed by any court in the United Kingdom as affecting Article IX of the Bill of Rights 1689.

European Convention for the Protection of Human Rights and Fundamental Freedoms 1950*

(213 UNTS 221)

Article 6   Right to a fair trial
    1. In the determination of his civil rights and obligations or of any criminal charge against him, everyone is entitled to a fair and public hearing within a reasonable time by an independent and impartial tribunal established by law. Judgment shall be pronounced publicly but the press and public may be excluded from all or part of the trial in the interests of morals, public order or national security in a democratic society, where the interests of juveniles or the protection of the private life of the parties so require, or to the extent strictly necessary in the opinion of the court in special circumstances where publicity would prejudice the interests of justice.
        […]

---

* Reproduced with the kind permission of the Council of Europe, https://coe.int/.

Article 8   Right to respect for private and family life

1. Everyone has the right to respect for his private and family life, his home and his correspondence.

2. There shall be no interference by a public authority with the exercise of this right except such as is in accordance with the law and is necessary in a democratic society in the interests of national security, public safety or the economic well-being of the country, for the prevention of disorder or crime, for the protection of health or morals, or for the protection of the rights and freedoms of others.

Article 9   Freedom of thought, conscience and religion

1. Everyone has the right to freedom of thought, conscience and religion; this right includes freedom to change his religion or belief and freedom, either alone or in community with others and in public or private, to manifest his religion or belief, in worship, teaching, practice and observance.

2. Freedom to manifest one's religion or beliefs shall be subject only to such limitations as are prescribed by law and are necessary in a democratic society in the interests of public safety, for the protection of public order, health or morals, or for the protection of the rights and freedoms of others.

Article 10   Freedom of expression

1. Everyone has the right to freedom of expression. This right shall include freedom to hold opinions and to receive and impart information and ideas without interference by public authority and regardless of frontiers. This Article shall not prevent States from requiring the licensing of broadcasting, television or cinema enterprises.

2. The exercise of these freedoms, since it carries with it duties and responsibilities, may be subject to such formalities, conditions, restrictions or penalties as are prescribed by law and are necessary in a democratic society, in the interests of national security, territorial integrity or public safety, for the prevention of disorder or crime, for the protection of health or morals, for the protection of the reputation or rights of others, for preventing the disclosure of information received in confidence, or for maintaining the authority and impartiality of the judiciary.

Article 14   Prohibition of discrimination

The enjoyment of the rights and freedoms set forth in this Convention shall be secured without discrimination on any ground such as sex, race, colour, language, religion, political or other opinion, national or social origin, association with a national minority, property, birth or other status.

Article 16   Restrictions on political activity of aliens

Nothing in Articles 10, 11 and 14 shall be regarded as preventing the High Contracting Parties from imposing restrictions on the political activity of aliens.

Article 17   Prohibition of abuse of rights

Nothing in this Convention may be interpreted as implying for any State, group or person any right to engage in any activity or perform any act aimed at the destruction of any of the rights and freedoms set forth herein or at their limitation to a greater extent than is provided for in the Convention.

Protocol to the Convention for the Protection of Human Rights and Fundamental Freedoms*

(213 UNTS 262)

Article 3   Right to free elections

The High Contracting Parties undertake to hold free elections at reasonable intervals by secret ballot, under conditions which will ensure the free expression of the opinion of the people in the choice of the legislature.

---

* Reproduced with the kind permission of the Council of Europe, https://coe.int/.

Human Rights Act 1998

(1998, c. 42)

1 The Convention Rights

(1) In this Act 'the Convention rights' means the rights and fundamental freedoms set out in—

(a) Articles 2 to 12 and 14 of the Convention,

(b) Articles 1 to 3 of the First Protocol, and

(c) [Article 1 of the Thirteenth Protocol],

as read with Articles 16 to 18 of the Convention.

(2) Those Articles are to have effect for the purposes of this Act subject to any designated derogation or reservation (as to which see sections 14 and 15).

(3) The Articles are set out in Schedule 1.

(4) The Secretary of State may by order make such amendments to this Act as he considers appropriate to reflect the effect, in relation to the United Kingdom, of a protocol.

(5) In subsection (4) 'protocol' means a protocol to the Convention—

(a) which the United Kingdom has ratified; or

(b) which the United Kingdom has signed with a view to ratification.

(6) No amendment may be made by an order under subsection (4) so as to come into force before the protocol concerned is in force in relation to the United Kingdom.

2 Interpretation of Convention rights

(1) A court or tribunal determining a question which has arisen in connection with a Convention right must take into account any—

(a) judgment, decision, declaration or advisory opinion of the European Court of Human Rights,

(b) opinion of the Commission given in a report adopted under Article 31 of the Convention,

(c) decision of the Commission in connection with Article 26 or 27(2) of the Convention, or

(d) decision of the Committee of Ministers taken under Article 46 of the Convention,

whenever made or given, so far as, in the opinion of the court or tribunal, it is relevant to the proceedings in which that question has arisen.

(2) Evidence of any judgment, decision, declaration or opinion of which account may have to be taken under this section is to be given in proceedings before any court or tribunal in such manner as may be provided by rules.

(3) In this section 'rules' means rules of court or, in the case of proceedings before a tribunal, rules made for the purposes of this section—

(a) by the Secretary of State, in relation to any proceedings outside Scotland;

(b) by the Secretary of State, in relation to proceedings in Scotland; or

(c) by a Northern Ireland department, in relation to proceedings before a tribunal in Northern Ireland—

(i) which deals with transferred matters; and

(ii) for which no rules made under paragraph (a) are in force.

3 Interpretation of legislation

(1) So far as it is possible to do so, primary legislation and subordinate legislation must be read and given effect in a way which is compatible with the Convention rights.

(2) This section—

(a) applies to primary legislation and subordinate legislation whenever enacted;

(b) does not affect the validity, continuing operation or enforcement of any incompatible primary legislation; and

(c) does not affect the validity, continuing operation or enforcement of any incompatible subordinate legislation if (disregarding any possibility of revocation) primary legislation prevents removal of the incompatibility.

4   Declaration of incompatibility

(1) Subsection (2) applies in any proceedings in which a court determines whether a provision of primary legislation is compatible with a Convention right.

(2) If the court is satisfied that the provision is incompatible with a Convention right, it may make a declaration of that incompatibility.

(3) Subsection (4) applies in any proceedings in which a court determines whether a provision of subordinate legislation, made in the exercise of a power conferred by primary legislation, is compatible with a Convention right.

(4) If the court is satisfied—

    (a) that the provision is incompatible with a Convention right, and

    (b) that (disregarding any possibility of revocation) the primary legislation concerned prevents removal of the incompatibility,

it may make a declaration of that incompatibility.

(5) In this section 'court' means—

    (a) the Supreme Court

    (b) the Judicial Committee of the Privy Council;

    (c) the Court Martial Appeal Court;

    (d) in Scotland, the High Court of Justiciary sitting otherwise than as a trial court or the Court of Session;

    (e) in England and Wales or Northern Ireland, the High Court or the Court of Appeal;

    [(f) the Court of Protection, in any matter being dealt with by the President of the Family Division, the Vice-Chancellor or a puisne judge of the High Court].

(6) A declaration under this section ('a declaration of incompatibility')—

    (a) does not affect the validity, continuing operation or enforcement of the provision in respect of which it is given; and

    (b) is not binding on the parties to the proceedings in which it is made.

5   Right of Crown to intervene

(1) Where a court is considering whether to make a declaration of incompatibility, the Crown is entitled to notice in accordance with rules of court.

(2) In any case to which subsection (1) applies—

    (a) a Minister of the Crown (or a person nominated by him),

    (b) a member of the Scottish Executive,

    (c) a Northern Ireland Minister,

    (d) a Northern Ireland department,

is entitled, on giving notice in accordance with rules of court, to be joined as a party to the proceedings.

(3) Notice under subsection (2) may be given at any time during the proceedings.

(4) A person who has been made a party to criminal proceedings (other than in Scotland) as the result of a notice under subsection (2) may, with leave, appeal to the [Supreme Court] against any declaration of incompatibility made in the proceedings.

(5) In subsection (4)—

'criminal proceedings' includes all proceedings before the Court Martial Appeal Court; and

'leave' means leave granted by the court making the declaration of incompatibility or by the [Supreme Court].

6   Acts of public authorities

(1) It is unlawful for a public authority to act in a way which is incompatible with a Convention right.

(2) Subsection (1) does not apply to an act if—

    (a) as the result of one or more provisions of primary legislation, the authority could not have acted differently; or

    (b) in the case of one or more provisions of, or made under, primary legislation which cannot be read or given effect in a way which is compatible with the Convention rights, the authority was acting so as to give effect to or enforce those provisions.

(3) In this section 'public authority' includes—
    (a) a court or tribunal, and
    (b) any person certain of whose functions are functions of a public nature,
but does not include either House of Parliament or a person exercising functions in connection with proceedings in Parliament.

(5) In relation to a particular act, a person is not a public authority by virtue only of subsection (3)(b) if the nature of the act is private.

(6) 'An act' includes a failure to act but does not include a failure to—
    (a) introduce in, or lay before, Parliament a proposal for legislation; or
    (b) make any primary legislation or remedial order.

7 Proceedings

(1) A person who claims that a public authority has acted (or proposes to act) in a way which is made unlawful by section 6(1) may—
    (a) bring proceedings against the authority under this Act in the appropriate court or tribunal, or
    (b) rely on the Convention right or rights concerned in any legal proceedings,
but only if he is (or would be) a victim of the unlawful act.

(2) In subsection (1)(a) 'appropriate court or tribunal' means such court or tribunal as may be determined in accordance with rules; and proceedings against an authority include a counterclaim or similar proceeding.

(3) If the proceedings are brought on an application for judicial review, the applicant is to be taken to have a sufficient interest in relation to the unlawful act only if he is, or would be, a victim of that act.

(4) If the proceedings are made by way of a petition for judicial review in Scotland, the applicant shall be taken to have title and interest to sue in relation to the unlawful act only if he is, or would be, a victim of that act.

(5) Proceedings under subsection (1)(a) must be brought before the end of—
    (a) the period of one year beginning with the date on which the act complained of took place; or
    (b) such longer period as the court or tribunal considers equitable having regard to all the circumstances,
but that is subject to any rule imposing a stricter time limit in relation to the procedure in question.

(6) In subsection (1)(b) 'legal proceedings' includes—
    (a) proceedings brought by or at the instigation of a public authority; and
    (b) an appeal against the decision of a court or tribunal.

(7) For the purposes of this section, a person is a victim of an unlawful act only if he would be a victim for the purposes of Article 34 of the Convention if proceedings were brought in the European Court of Human Rights in respect of that act.

(8) Nothing in this Act creates a criminal offence.

(9) In this section 'rules' means—
    (a) in relation to proceedings before a court or tribunal outside Scotland, rules made by the Secretary of State for the purposes of this section or rules of court,
    (b) in relation to proceedings before a court or tribunal in Scotland, rules made by the Secretary of State for those purposes,
    (c) in relation to proceedings before a tribunal in Northern Ireland—
        (i)   which deals with transferred matters; and
        (ii) for which no rules made under paragraph (a) are in force,
    rules made by a Northern Ireland department for those purposes,
and includes provision made by order under section 1 of the Courts and Legal Services Act 1990.

(10) In making rules, regard must be had to section 9.

(11) The Minister who has power to make rules in relation to a particular tribunal may, to the extent he considers it necessary to ensure that the tribunal can provide an appropriate remedy in relation to an act (or proposed act) of a public authority which is (or would be) unlawful as a result of section 6(1), by order add to—

(a) the relief or remedies which the tribunal may grant; or

(b) the grounds on which it may grant any of them.

(12) An order made under subsection (11) may contain such incidental, supplemental, conse-quential or transitional provision as the Minister making it considers appropriate.

(13) 'The Minister' includes the Northern Ireland department concerned.

8   Judicial remedies

(1) In relation to any act (or proposed act) of a public authority which the court finds is (or would be) unlawful, it may grant such relief or remedy, or make such order, within its powers as it considers just and appropriate.

(2) But damages may be awarded only by a court which has power to award damages, or to order the payment of compensation, in civil proceedings.

(3) No award of damages is to be made unless, taking account of all the circumstances of the case, including—

(a) any other relief or remedy granted, or order made, in relation to the act in question (by that or any other court), and

(b) the consequences of any decision (of that or any other court) in respect of that act,

the court is satisfied that the award is necessary to afford just satisfaction to the person in whose favour it is made.

(4) In determining—

(a) whether to award damages, or

(b) the amount of an award,

the court must take into account the principles applied by the European Court of Human Rights in relation to the award of compensation under Article 41 of the Convention.

(5) A public authority against which damages are awarded is to be treated—

(a) in Scotland, for the purposes of section 3 of the Law Reform (Miscellaneous Provisions) (Scotland) Act 1940 as if the award were made in an action of damages in which the authority has been found liable in respect of loss or damage to the person to whom the award is made;

(b) for the purposes of the Civil Liability (Contribution) Act 1978 as liable in respect of damage suffered by the person to whom the award is made.

(6) In this section—

'court' includes a tribunal;

'damages' means damages for an unlawful act of a public authority; and

'unlawful' means unlawful under section 6(1).

9   Judicial acts

(1) Proceedings under section 7(1)(a) in respect of a judicial act may be brought only—

(a) by exercising a right of appeal;

(b) on an application (in Scotland a petition) for judicial review; or

(c) in such other forum as may be prescribed by rules.

(2) That does not affect any rule of law which prevents a court from being the subject of judicial review.

(3) In proceedings under this Act in respect of a judicial act done in good faith, damages may not be awarded otherwise than to compensate a person to the extent required by Article 5(5) of the Convention.

(4) An award of damages permitted by subsection (3) is to be made against the Crown; but no award may be made unless the appropriate person, if not a party to the proceedings, is joined.

(5) In this section—

'appropriate person' means the Minister responsible for the court concerned, or a person or govern-ment department nominated by him;

'court' includes a tribunal;

'judge' includes a member of a tribunal, a justice of the peace [(or, in Northern Ireland, a lay magis-trate)] and a clerk or other officer entitled to exercise the jurisdiction of a court;

'judicial act' means a judicial act of a court and includes an act done on the instructions, or on behalf, of a judge; and

'rules' has the same meaning as in section 7(9).

10 Power to take remedial action

(1) This section applies if—

    (a) a provision of legislation has been declared under section 4 to be incompatible with a Convention right and, if an appeal lies—

        (i) all persons who may appeal have stated in writing that they do not intend to do so;

        (ii) the time for bringing an appeal has expired and no appeal has been brought within that time; or

        (iii) an appeal brought within that time has been determined or abandoned;

or

    (b) it appears to a Minister of the Crown or Her Majesty in Council that, having regard to a finding of the European Court of Human Rights made after the coming into force of this section in proceedings against the United Kingdom, a provision of legislation is incompatible with an obligation of the United Kingdom arising from the Convention.

(2) If a Minister of the Crown considers that there are compelling reasons for proceeding under this section, he may by order make such amendments to the legislation as he considers necessary to remove the incompatibility.

(3) If, in the case of subordinate legislation, a Minister of the Crown considers—

    (a) that it is necessary to amend the primary legislation under which the subordinate legislation in question was made, in order to enable the incompatibility to be removed, and

    (b) that there are compelling reasons for proceeding under this section,

he may by order make such amendments to the primary legislation as he considers necessary.

(4) This section also applies where the provision in question is in subordinate legislation and has been quashed, or declared invalid, by reason of incompatibility with a Convention right and the Minister proposes to proceed under paragraph 2(b) of Schedule 2.

(5) If the legislation is an Order in Council, the power conferred by subsection (2) or (3) is exercisable by Her Majesty in Council.

(6) In this section 'legislation' does not include a Measure of the Church Assembly or of the General Synod of the Church of England.

(7) Schedule 2 makes further provision about remedial orders.

11 Safeguard for existing human rights

A person's reliance on a Convention right does not restrict—

    (a) any other right or freedom conferred on him by or under any law having effect in any part of the United Kingdom; or

    (b) his right to make any claim or bring any proceedings which he could make or bring apart from sections 7 to 9.

12 Freedom of expression

(1) This section applies if a court is considering whether to grant any relief which, if granted, might affect the exercise of the Convention right to freedom of expression.

(2) If the person against whom the application for relief is made ('the respondent') is neither present nor represented, no such relief is to be granted unless the court is satisfied—

    (a) that the applicant has taken all practicable steps to notify the respondent; or

    (b) that there are compelling reasons why the respondent should not be notified.

(3) No such relief is to be granted so as to restrain publication before trial unless the court is satisfied that the applicant is likely to establish that publication should not be allowed.

(4) The court must have particular regard to the importance of the Convention right to freedom of expression and, where the proceedings relate to material which the respondent claims, or which appears to the court, to be journalistic, literary or artistic material (or to conduct connected with such material), to—

(a) the extent to which—
   (i)   the material has, or is about to, become available to the public; or
   (ii) it is, or would be, in the public interest for the material to be published;
(b) any relevant privacy code.
(5) In this section—
'court' includes a tribunal; and
'relief' includes any remedy or order (other than in criminal proceedings).

13   Freedom of thought, conscience and religion

(1) If a court's determination of any question arising under this Act might affect the exercise by a religious organisation (itself or its members collectively) of the Convention right to freedom of thought, conscience and religion, it must have particular regard to the importance of that right.

(2) In this section 'court' includes a tribunal.

21   Interpretation, etc.

(1) In this Act—

'amend' includes repeal and apply (with or without modifications);

'the appropriate Minister' means the Minister of the Crown having charge of the appropriate author-ised government department (within the meaning of the Crown Proceedings Act 1947);

'the Commission' means the European Commission of Human Rights;

'the Convention' means the Convention for the Protection of Human Rights and Fundamental Freedoms, agreed by the Council of Europe at Rome on 4th November 1950 as it has effect for the time being in relation to the United Kingdom;

'declaration of incompatibility' means a declaration under section 4;

'Minister of the Crown' has the same meaning as in the Ministers of the Crown Act 1975;

'Northern Ireland Minister' includes the First Minister and the deputy First Minister in Northern Ireland;

'primary legislation' means any—
(a) public general Act;
(b) local and personal Act;
(c) private Act;
(d) Measure of the Church Assembly;
(e) Measure of the General Synod of the Church of England;
(f) Order in Council—
   (i)   made in exercise of Her Majesty's Royal Prerogative;
   (ii) made under section 38(1)(a) of the Northern Ireland Constitution Act 1973 or the corresponding provision of the Northern Ireland Act 1998; or
   (iii) amending an Act of a kind mentioned in paragraph (a), (b) or (c);
and includes an order or other instrument made under primary legislation (otherwise than by the National Assembly for Wales, a member of the Scottish Executive, a Northern Ireland Minister or a Northern Ireland department) to the extent to which it operates to bring one or more provisions of that legislation into force or amends any primary legislation;

'the First Protocol' means the protocol to the Convention agreed at Paris on 20th March 1952;

'the Eleventh Protocol' means the protocol to the Convention (restructuring the control machinery established by the Convention) agreed at Strasbourg on 11th May 1994;

'the Thirteenth Protocol' means the protocol to the Convention (concerning the abolition of the death penalty in all circumstances) agreed at Vilnius on 3rd May 2002;

'remedial order' means an order under section 10;

'subordinate legislation' means any—
(a) Order in Council other than one—
   (i)   made in exercise of Her Majesty's Royal Prerogative;
   (ii) made under section 38(1)(a) of the Northern Ireland Constitution Act 1973 or the corresponding provision of the Northern Ireland Act 1998; or

(iii) amending an Act of a kind mentioned in the definition of primary legislation;

(b)   Act of the Scottish Parliament;

(ba) Measure of National Assembly for Wales;

(bb) Act of the National Assembly for Wales;

(c)   Act of the Parliament of Northern Ireland;

(d)   Measure of the Assembly established under section 1 of the Northern Ireland Assembly Act 1973;

(e)   Act of the Northern Ireland Assembly;

(f)   order, rules, regulations, scheme, warrant, byelaw or other instrument made under primary legislation (except to the extent to which it operates to bring one or more provisions of that legislation into force or amends any primary legislation);

(g)   order, rules, regulations, scheme, warrant, byelaw or other instrument made under legislation mentioned in paragraph (b), (c), (d) or (e) or made under an Order in Council applying only to Northern Ireland;

(h)   order, rules, regulations, scheme, warrant, byelaw or other instrument made by a member of the Scottish Executive, Welsh Ministers, the First Minister for Wales, the Counsel General to the Welsh Assembly Government, a Northern Ireland Minister or a Northern Ireland department in exercise of prerogative or other executive functions of Her Majesty which are exercisable by such a person on behalf of Her Majesty;

'transferred matters' has the same meaning as in the Northern Ireland Act 1998; and

'tribunal' means any tribunal in which legal proceedings may be brought.

(2) The references in paragraphs (b) and (c) of section 2(1) to Articles are to Articles of the Convention as they had effect immediately before the coming into force of the Eleventh Protocol.

(3) The reference in paragraph (d) of section 2(1) to Article 46 includes a reference to Articles 32 and 54 of the Convention as they had effect immediately before the coming into force of the Eleventh Protocol.

(4) The references in section 2(1) to a report or decision of the Commission or a decision of the Committee of Ministers include references to a report or decision made as provided by paragraphs 3, 4 and 6 of Article 5 of the Eleventh Protocol (transitional provisions).

22   Short title, commencement, application and extent

(1) This Act may be cited as the Human Rights Act 1998.

(2) Sections 18, 20 and 21(5) and this section come into force on the passing of this Act.

(3) The other provisions of this Act come into force on such day as the Secretary of State may by order appoint; and different days may be appointed for different purposes.

(4) Paragraph (b) of subsection (1) of section 7 applies to proceedings brought by or at the instigation of a public authority whenever the act in question took place; but otherwise that subsection does not apply to an act taking place before the coming into force of that section.

(5) This Act binds the Crown.

(6) This Act extends to Northern Ireland.

First Amendment to the Constitution of the United States of America 1787

Amendment I   Freedom of Religion, Press, Expression

Congress shall make no law respecting an establishment of religion, or prohibiting the free exercise thereof; or abridging the freedom of speech, or of the press; or the right of the people peaceably to assemble, and to petition the Government for a redress of grievances.

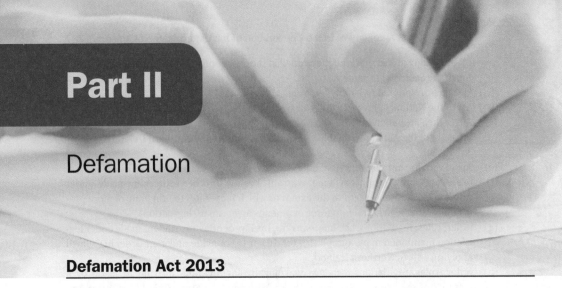

Part II

Defamation

Defamation Act 2013

(2013, c. 26)

(2013, c. 26)

Requirement of serious harm

1 Serious harm

(1) A statement is not defamatory unless its publication has caused or is likely to cause serious harm to the reputation of the claimant.

(2) For the purposes of this section, harm to the reputation of a body that trades for profit is not 'serious harm' unless it has caused or is likely to cause the body serious financial loss.

Defences

2 Truth

(1) It is a defence to an action for defamation for the defendant to show that the imputation conveyed by the statement complained of is substantially true.

(2) Subsection (3) applies in an action for defamation if the statement complained of conveys two or more distinct imputations.

(3) If one or more of the imputations is not shown to be substantially true, the defence under this section does not fail if, having regard to the imputations which are shown to be substantially true, the imputations which are not shown to be substantially true do not seriously harm the claimant's reputation.

(4) The common law defence of justification is abolished and, accordingly, section 5 of the Defamation Act 1952 (justification) is repealed.

3 Honest opinion

(1) It is a defence to an action for defamation for the defendant to show that the following conditions are met.

(2) The first condition is that the statement complained of was a statement of opinion.

(3) The second condition is that the statement complained of indicated, whether in general or specific terms, the basis of the opinion.

(4) The third condition is that an honest person could have held the opinion on the basis of—

(a) any fact which existed at the time the statement complained of was published;

(b) anything asserted to be a fact in a privileged statement published before the statement complained of.

(5) The defence is defeated if the claimant shows that the defendant did not hold the opinion.

(6) Subsection (5) does not apply in a case where the statement complained of was published by the defendant but made by another person ('the author'); and in such a case the defence is defeated if the claimant shows that the defendant knew or ought to have known that the author did not hold the opinion.

(7) For the purposes of subsection (4)(b) a statement is a 'privileged statement' if the person responsible for its publication would have one or more of the following defences if an action for defamation were brought in respect of it—

    (a) a defence under section 4 (publication on matter of public interest);

    (b) a defence under section 6 (peer-reviewed statement in scientific or academic journal);

    (c) a defence under section 14 of the Defamation Act 1996 (reports of court proceedings protected by absolute privilege);

    (d) a defence under section 15 of that Act (other reports protected by qualified privilege).

(8) The common law defence of fair comment is abolished and, accordingly, section 6 of the Defamation Act 1952 (fair comment) is repealed.

4 Publication on matter of public interest

(1) It is a defence to an action for defamation for the defendant to show that—

    (a) the statement complained of was, or formed part of, a statement on a matter of public interest; and

    (b) the defendant reasonably believed that publishing the statement complained of was in the public interest

(2) Subject to subsections (3) and (4), in determining whether the defendant has shown the matters mentioned in subsection (1), the court must have regard to all the circumstances of the case.

(3) If the statement complained of was, or formed part of, an accurate and impartial account of a dispute to which the claimant was a party, the court must in determining whether it was reasonable for the defendant to believe that publishing the statement was in the public interest disregard any omission of the defendant to take steps to verify the truth of the imputation conveyed by it.

(4) In determining whether it was reasonable for the defendant to believe that publishing the statement complained of was in the public interest, the court must make such allowance for editorial judgement as it considers appropriate.

(5) For the avoidance of doubt, the defence under this section may be relied upon irrespective of whether the statement complained of is a statement of fact or a statement of opinion.

(6) The common law defence known as the Reynolds defence is abolished.

5 Operators of websites

(1) This section applies where an action for defamation is brought against the operator of a website in respect of a statement posted on the website.

(2) It is a defence for the operator to show that it was not the operator who posted the statement on the website.

(3) The defence is defeated if the claimant shows that—

    (a) it was not possible for the claimant to identify the person who posted the statement,

    (b) the claimant gave the operator a notice of complaint in relation to the statement, and

    (c) the operator failed to respond to the notice of complaint in accordance with any provision contained in regulations.

(4) For the purposes of subsection (3)(a), it is possible for a claimant to 'identify' a person only if the claimant has sufficient information to bring proceedings against the person.

(5) Regulations may—

    (a) make provision as to the action required to be taken by an operator of a website in response to a notice of complaint (which may in particular include action relating to the identity or contact details of the person who posted the statement and action relating to its removal);

    (b) make provision specifying a time limit for the taking of any such action;

    (c) make provision conferring on the court a discretion to treat action taken after the expiry of a time limit as having been taken before the expiry;

    (d) make any other provision for the purposes of this section.

(6) Subject to any provision made by virtue of subsection (7), a notice of complaint is a notice which—

  (a) specifies the complainant's name,

  (b) sets out the statement concerned and explains why it is defamatory of the complainant,

  (c) specifies where on the website the statement was posted, and

  (d) contains such other information as may be specified in regulations.

(7) Regulations may make provision about the circumstances in which a notice which is not a notice of complaint is to be treated as a notice of complaint for the purposes of this section or any provision made under it.

(8) Regulations under this section—

  (a) may make different provision for different circumstances;

  (b) are to be made by statutory instrument.

(9) A statutory instrument containing regulations under this section may not be made unless a draft of the instrument has been laid before, and approved by a resolution of, each House of Parliament.

(10) In this section 'regulations' means regulations made by the Secretary of State.

(11) The defence under this section is defeated if the claimant shows that the operator of the website has acted with malice in relation to the posting of the statement concerned.

(12) The defence under this section is not defeated by reason only of the fact that the operator of the website moderates the statements posted on it by others.

6 Peer-reviewed statement in scientific or academic journal etc

(1) The publication of a statement in a scientific or academic journal (whether published in electronic form or otherwise) is privileged if the following conditions are met.

(2) The first condition is that the statement relates to a scientific or academic matter.

(3) The second condition is that before the statement was published in the journal an independent review of the statement's scientific or academic merit was carried out by—

  (a) the editor of the journal, and

  (b) one or more persons with expertise in the scientific or academic matter concerned.

(4) Where the publication of a statement in a scientific or academic journal is privileged by virtue of subsection (1), the publication in the same journal of any assessment of the statement's scientific or academic merit is also privileged if—

  (a) the assessment was written by one or more of the persons who carried out the independent review of the statement; and

  (b) the assessment was written in the course of that review.

(5) Where the publication of a statement or assessment is privileged by virtue of this section, the publication of a fair and accurate copy of, extract from or summary of the statement or assessment is also privileged.

(6) A publication is not privileged by virtue of this section if it is shown to be made with malice.

(7) Nothing in this section is to be construed—

  (a) as protecting the publication of matter the publication of which is prohibited by law;

  (b) as limiting any privilege subsisting apart from this section.

(8) The reference in subsection (3)(a) to 'the editor of the journal' is to be read, in the case of a journal with more than one editor, as a reference to the editor or editors who were responsible for deciding to publish the statement concerned.

Single publication rule

8 Single publication rule

(1) This section applies if a person—

  (a) publishes a statement to the public ('the first publication'), and

  (b) subsequently publishes (whether or not to the public) that statement or a statement which is substantially the same.

(2) In subsection (1) 'publication to the public' includes publication to a section of the public.

(3) For the purposes of section 4A of the Limitation Act 1980 (time limit for actions for defamation etc) any cause of action against the person for defamation in respect of the subsequent publication is to be treated as having accrued on the date of the first publication.

(4) This section does not apply in relation to the subsequent publication if the manner of that publication is materially different from the manner of the first publication.

(5) In determining whether the manner of a subsequent publication is materially different from the manner of the first publication, the matters to which the court may have regard include (amongst other matters)—

    (a) the level of prominence that a statement is given;

    (b) the extent of the subsequent publication.

(6) Where this section applies—

    (a) it does not affect the court's discretion under section 32A of the Limitation Act 1980 (discretionary exclusion of time limit for actions for defamation etc), and

    (b) the reference in subsection (1)(a) of that section to the operation of section 4A of that Act is a reference to the operation of section 4A together with this section.

Jurisdiction

9   Action against a person not domiciled in the UK or a Member State etc

(1) This section applies to an action for defamation against a person who is not domiciled—

    (a) in the United Kingdom;

    (b) in another Member State; or

    (c) in a state which is for the time being a contracting party to the Lugano Convention.

(2) A court does not have jurisdiction to hear and determine an action to which this section applies unless the court is satisfied that, of all the places in which the statement complained of has been published, England and Wales is clearly the most appropriate place in which to bring an action in respect of the statement.

(3) The references in subsection (2) to the statement complained of include references to any statement which conveys the same, or substantially the same, imputation as the statement complained of.

(4) For the purposes of this section—

    (a) a person is domiciled in the United Kingdom or in another Member State if the person is domiciled there for the purposes of the Brussels Regulation;

    (b) a person is domiciled in a state which is a contracting party to the Lugano Convention if the person is domiciled in the state for the purposes of that Convention.

(5) In this section—

'the Brussels Regulation' means Council Regulation (EC) No 44/2001 of 22nd December 2000 on jurisdiction and the recognition and enforcement of judgments in civil and commercial matters, as amended from time to time and as applied by the Agreement made on 19th October 2005 between the European Community and the Kingdom of Denmark on jurisdiction and the recognition and enforcement of Judgments in civil and commercial matters (OJ No L299 16.11.2005 at p 62);

'the Lugano Convention' means the Convention on jurisdiction and the recognition and enforcement of judgments in civil and commercial matters, between the European Community and the Republic of Iceland, the Kingdom of Norway, the Swiss Confederation and the Kingdom of Denmark signed on behalf of the European Community on 30th October 2007.

10   Action against a person who was not the author, editor etc

(1) A court does not have jurisdiction to hear and determine an action for defamation brought against a person who was not the author, editor or publisher of the statement complained of unless the court is satisfied that it is not reasonably practicable for an action to be brought against the author, editor or publisher.

(2) In this section 'author', 'editor' and 'publisher' have the same meaning as in section 1 of the Defamation Act 1996.

Summary of court judgment

12   Power of court to order a summary of its judgment to be published

(1) Where a court gives judgment for the claimant in an action for defamation the court may order the defendant to publish a summary of the judgment.

(2) The wording of any summary and the time, manner, form and place of its publication are to be for the parties to agree.

(3) If the parties cannot agree on the wording, the wording is to be settled by the court.

(4) If the parties cannot agree on the time, manner, form or place of publication, the court may give such directions as to those matters as it considers reasonable and practicable in the circumstances.

(5) This section does not apply where the court gives judgment for the claimant under section 8(3) of the Defamation Act 1996 (summary disposal of claims).

Removal, etc of statements

13   Order to remove statement or cease distribution etc

(1) Where a court gives judgment for the claimant in an action for defamation the court may order—

   (a) the operator of a website on which the defamatory statement is posted to remove the statement, or

   (b) any person who was not the author, editor or publisher of the defamatory statement to stop distributing, selling or exhibiting material containing the statement.

(2) In this section 'author', 'editor' and 'publisher' have the same meaning as in section 1 of the Defamation Act 1996.

(3) Subsection (1) does not affect the power of the court apart from that subsection.

Slander

14   Special damage

(1) The Slander of Women Act 1891 is repealed.

(2) The publication of a statement that conveys the imputation that a person has a contagious or infectious disease does not give rise to a cause of action for slander unless the publication causes the person special damage.

General provisions

15   Meaning of 'publish' and 'statement'

In this Act—

   'publish' and 'publication', in relation to a statement, have the meaning they have for the purposes of the law of defamation generally;

   'statement' means words, pictures, visual images, gestures or any other method of signifying meaning.

16   Consequential amendments and savings etc

[. . .]

(4) Nothing in section 1 or 14 affects any cause of action accrued before the commencement of the section in question.

(5) Nothing in sections 2 to 7 or 10 has effect in relation to an action for defamation if the cause of action accrued before the commencement of the section in question.

(6) In determining whether section 8 applies, no account is to be taken of any publication made before the commencement of the section.

(7) Nothing in section 9 or 11 has effect in relation to an action for defamation begun before the commencement of the section in question.

(8) In determining for the purposes of subsection (7)(a) of section 3 whether a person would have a defence under section 4 to any action for defamation, the operation of subsection (5) of this section is to be ignored.

17   Short title, extent and commencement

(1) This Act may be cited as the Defamation Act 2013.

(2) Subject to subsection (3), this Act extends to England and Wales only.

(3) The following provisions also extend to Scotland—

    (a)   section 6;

    (b)   section 7(9);

    (c)   section 15;

    (d)   section 16(5) (in so far as it relates to sections 6 and 7(9));

    (e)   this section.

(4) Subject to subsections (5) and (6), the provisions of this Act come into force on such day as the Secretary of State may by order made by statutory instrument appoint.

(5) Sections 6 and 7(9) come into force in so far as they extend to Scotland on such day as the Scottish Ministers may by order appoint.

(6) Section 15, subsections (4) to (8) of section 16 and this section come into force on the day on which this Act is passed.

Defamation Act 1952

(1952, 15 and 16 Geo. 6 and 1 Eliz. 2, c. 66)

1   [...]

2   Slander affecting official, professional or business reputation

In an action for slander in respect of words calculated to disparage the plaintiff in any office, profession, calling, trade or business held or carried on by him at the time of the publication, it shall not be necessary to allege or prove special damage, whether or not the words are spoken of the plaintiff in the way of his office, profession, calling, trade or business.

3   Slander of title, &c.

(1) In an action for slander of title, slander of goods or other malicious falsehood, it shall not be necessary to allege or prove special damage—

    (a) if the words upon which the action is founded are calculated to cause pecuniary damage to the plaintiff and are published in writing or other permanent form; or

    (b) if the said words are calculated to cause pecuniary damage to the plaintiff in respect of any office, profession, calling, trade or business held or carried on by him at the time of the publication.

(2) Section one of this Act shall apply for the purposes of this section as it applies for the purposes of the law of libel and slander.

4–8   [...]

9   Extension of certain defences to broadcasting

(1) Section three of the Parliamentary Papers Act 1840 (which confers protection in respect of proceedings for printing extracts from or abstracts of parliamentary papers) shall have effect as if the reference to printing included a reference to broadcasting by means of wireless telegraphy.

(2)–(3) [...]

10   Limitation on privilege at elections

A defamatory statement published by or on behalf of a candidate in any election to a local government authority, to the National Assembly for Wales, to the Scottish Parliament or to Parliament shall not be deemed to be published on a privileged occasion on the ground that it is material to a question in issue in the election, whether or not the person by whom it is published is qualified to vote at the election.

11   Agreements for indemnity

An agreement for indemnifying any person against civil liability for libel in respect of the publication of any matter shall not be unlawful unless at the time of the publication that person knows that the matter is defamatory, and does not reasonably believe there is a good defence to any action brought upon it.

12   Evidence of other damages recovered by plaintiff

In any action for libel or slander the defendant may give evidence in mitigation of damages that the plaintiff has recovered damages, or has brought actions for damages, for libel or slander in respect of the publication of words to the same effect as the words on which the action is founded, or has received or agreed to receive compensation in respect of any such publication.

13   Consolidation of actions for slander &c.

Section five of the Law of Libel Amendment Act 1888 (which provides for the consolidation, on the application of the defendants, of two or more actions for libel by the same plaintiff) shall apply to actions for slander and to actions for slander of title, slander of goods or other malicious falsehood as it applies to actions for libel; and references in that section to the same, or substantially the same, libel shall be construed accordingly.

14   Application of Act to Scotland

This Act shall apply to Scotland subject to the following modifications, that is to say:—

(a) sections one, two, eight and thirteen shall be omitted;

(b) for section three there shall be substituted the following section—

'3   Actions for verbal injury

In any action for verbal injury it shall not be necessary for the pursuer to aver or prove special damage if the words on which the action is founded are calculated to cause pecuniary damage to the pursuer.';

(c) subsection (2) of section four shall have effect as if at the end thereof there were added the words 'Nothing in this subsection shall be held to entitle a defender to lead evidence of any fact specified in the declaration unless notice of his intention so to do has been given in the defences.'; and

(d) for any reference to libel, or to libel or slander, there shall be substituted a reference to defamation; the expression 'plaintiff' means pursuer; the expression 'defendant' means defender; for any reference to an affidavit made by any person there shall be substituted a reference to a written declaration signed by that person; for any reference to the High Court there shall be substituted a reference to the Court of Session or, if an action of defamation is depending in the sheriff court in respect of the publication in question, the sheriff; the expression 'costs' means expenses; and for any reference to a defence of justification there shall be substituted a reference to a defence of veritas.

15   [...]

16   Interpretation

(1) Any reference in this Act to words shall be construed as including a reference to pictures, visual images, gestures and other methods of signifying meaning.

(2)–(3) [...]

17   Proceedings affected and saving

(1) This Act applies for the purposes of any proceedings begun after the commencement of this Act, whenever the cause of action arose, but does not affect any proceedings begun before the commencement of this Act.

18   Short title, commencement, extent and repeals

(1) This Act may be cited as the Defamation Act 1952, and shall come into operation one month after the passing of this Act.

(2) This Act […] shall not extend to Northern Ireland.

(3) […]

Defamation Act 1996

(1996, c. 31)

Responsibility for publication

1   Responsibility for publication

(1) In defamation proceedings a person has a defence if he shows that—
  (a) he was not the author, editor or publisher of the statement complained of,
  (b) he took reasonable care in relation to its publication, and
  (c) he did not know, and had no reason to believe, that what he did caused or contributed to the publication of a defamatory statement.

(2) For this purpose 'author', 'editor' and 'publisher' have the following meanings, which are further explained in subsection (3)—

'author' means the originator of the statement, but does not include a person who did not intend that his statement be published at all;

'editor' means a person having editorial or equivalent responsibility for the content of the statement or the decision to publish it; and

'publisher' means a commercial publisher, that is, a person whose business is issuing material to the public, or a section of the public, who issues material containing the statement in the course of that business.

(3) A person shall not be considered the author, editor or publisher of a statement if he is only involved—
  (a) in printing, producing, distributing or selling printed material containing the statement;
  (b) in processing, making copies of, distributing, exhibiting or selling a film or sound recording (as defined in Part I of the Copyright, Designs and Patents Act 1988) containing the statement;
  (c) in processing, making copies of, distributing or selling any electronic medium in or on which the statement is recorded, or in operating or providing any equipment, system or service by means of which the statement is retrieved, copied, distributed or made available in electronic form;
  (d) as the broadcaster of a live programme containing the statement in circumstances in which he has no effective control over the maker of the statement;
  (e) as the operator of or provider of access to a communications system by means of which the statement is transmitted, or made available, by a person over whom he has no effective control.

In a case not within paragraphs (a) to (e) the court may have regard to those provisions by way of analogy in deciding whether a person is to be considered the author, editor or publisher of a statement.

(4) Employees or agents of an author, editor or publisher are in the same position as their employer or principal to the extent that they are responsible for the content of the statement or the decision to publish it.

(5) In determining for the purposes of this section whether a person took reasonable care, or had reason to believe that what he did caused or contributed to the publication of a defamatory statement, regard shall be had to—

(a) the extent of his responsibility for the content of the statement or the decision to publish it,

(b) the nature or circumstances of the publication, and

(c) the previous conduct or character of the author, editor or publisher.

(6) This section does not apply to any cause of action which arose before the section came into force.

Offer to make amends

2   Offer to make amends

(1) A person who has published a statement alleged to be defamatory of another may offer to make amends under this section.

(2) The offer may be in relation to the statement generally or in relation to a specific defamatory meaning which the person making the offer accepts that the statement conveys ('a qualified offer').

(3) An offer to make amends—

(a) must be in writing,

(b) must be expressed to be an offer to make amends under section 2 of the Defamation Act 1996, and

(c) must state whether it is a qualified offer and, if so, set out the defamatory meaning in relation to which it is made.

(4) An offer to make amends under this section is an offer—

(a) to make a suitable correction of the statement complained of and a sufficient apology to the aggrieved party,

(b) to publish the correction and apology in a manner that is reasonable and practicable in the circumstances, and

(c) to pay to the aggrieved party such compensation (if any), and such costs, as may be agreed or determined to be payable.

The fact that the offer is accompanied by an offer to take specific steps does not affect the fact that an offer to make amends under this section is an offer to do all the things mentioned in paragraphs (a) to (c).

(5) An offer to make amends under this section may not be made by a person after serving a defence in defamation proceedings brought against him by the aggrieved party in respect of the publication in question.

(6) An offer to make amends under this section may be withdrawn before it is accepted; and a renewal of an offer which has been withdrawn shall be treated as a new offer.

3   Accepting an offer to make amends

(1) If an offer to make amends under section 2 is accepted by the aggrieved party, the following provisions apply.

(2) The party accepting the offer may not bring or continue defamation proceedings in respect of the publication concerned against the person making the offer, but he is entitled to enforce the offer to make amends, as follows.

(3) If the parties agree on the steps to be taken in fulfilment of the offer, the aggrieved party may apply to the court for an order that the other party fulfil his offer by taking the steps agreed.

(4) If the parties do not agree on the steps to be taken by way of correction, apology and publication, the party who made the offer may take such steps as he thinks appropriate, and may in particular—

(a) make the correction and apology by a statement in open court in terms approved by the court, and

(b) give an undertaking to the court as to the manner of their publication.

(5) If the parties do not agree on the amount to be paid by way of compensation, it shall be determined by the court on the same principles as damages in defamation proceedings.

The court shall take account of any steps taken in fulfilment of the offer and (so far as not agreed between the parties) of the suitability of the correction, the sufficiency of the apology and whether the manner of their publication was reasonable in the circumstances, and may reduce or increase the amount of compensation accordingly.

(6) If the parties do not agree on the amount to be paid by way of costs, it shall be determined by the court on the same principles as costs awarded in court proceedings.

(7) The acceptance of an offer by one person to make amends does not affect any cause of action against another person in respect of the same publication, subject as follows.

(8) In England and Wales or Northern Ireland, for the purposes of the Civil Liability (Contribution) Act 1978—

    (a) the amount of compensation paid under the offer shall be treated as paid in bona fide settlement or compromise of the claim; and

    (b) where another person is liable in respect of the same damage (whether jointly or otherwise), the person whose offer to make amends was accepted is not required to pay by virtue of any contribution under section 1 of that Act a greater amount than the amount of the compensation payable in pursuance of the offer.

(9) In Scotland—

    (a) subsection (2) of section 3 of the Law Reform (Miscellaneous Provisions) (Scotland) Act 1940 (right of one joint wrongdoer as respects another to recover contribution towards damages) applies in relation to compensation paid under an offer to make amends as it applies in relation to damages in an action to which that section applies; and

    (b) where another person is liable in respect of the same damage (whether jointly or otherwise), the person whose offer to make amends was accepted is not required to pay by virtue of any contribution under section 3(2) of that Act a greater amount than the amount of compensation payable in pursuance of the offer.

(10) Proceedings under this section shall be heard and determined without a jury.

4   Failure to accept offer to make amends

(1) If an offer to make amends under section 2, duly made and not withdrawn, is not accepted by the aggrieved party, the following provisions apply.

(2) The fact that the offer was made is a defence (subject to subsection (3)) to defamation proceedings in respect of the publication in question by that party against the person making the offer. A qualified offer is only a defence in respect of the meaning to which the offer related.

(3) There is no such defence if the person by whom the offer was made knew or had reason to believe that the statement complained of—

    (a) referred to the aggrieved party or was likely to be understood as referring to him, and

    (b) was both false and defamatory of that party;

but it shall be presumed until the contrary is shown that he did not know and had no reason to believe that was the case.

(4) The person who made the offer need not rely on it by way of defence, but if he does he may not rely on any other defence. If the offer was a qualified offer, this applies only in respect of the meaning to which the offer related.

(5) The offer may be relied on in mitigation of damages whether or not it was relied on as a defence.

The meaning of a statement

7   Ruling on the meaning of a statement

In defamation proceedings the court shall not be asked to rule whether a statement is arguably capable, as opposed to capable, of bearing a particular meaning or meanings attributed to it.

Summary disposal of claim

8   Summary disposal of claim

(1) In defamation proceedings the court may dispose summarily of the plaintiff's claim in accordance with the following provisions.

(2) The court may dismiss the plaintiff's claim if it appears to the court that it has no realistic prospect of success and there is no reason why it should be tried.

(3) The court may give judgment for the plaintiff and grant him summary relief (see section 9) if it appears to the court that there is no defence to the claim which has a realistic prospect of success, and that there is no other reason why the claim should be tried.

Unless the plaintiff asks for summary relief, the court shall not act under this subsection unless it is satisfied that summary relief will adequately compensate him for the wrong he has suffered.

(4) In considering whether a claim should be tried the court shall have regard to—

    (a) whether all the persons who are or might be defendants in respect of the publication complained of are before the court;

    (b) whether summary disposal of the claim against another defendant would be inappropriate;

    (c) the extent to which there is a conflict of evidence;

    (d) the seriousness of the alleged wrong (as regards the content of the statement and the extent of publication); and

    (e) whether it is justifiable in the circumstances to proceed to a full trial.

(5) Proceedings under this section shall be heard and determined without a jury.

9   Meaning of summary relief

(1) For the purposes of section 8 (summary disposal of claim) 'summary relief' means such of the following as may be appropriate—

    (a) a declaration that the statement was false and defamatory of the plaintiff;

    (b) an order that the defendant publish or cause to be published a suitable correction and apology;

    (c) damages not exceeding £10,000 or such other amount as may be prescribed by order of the Lord Chancellor;

    (d) an order restraining the defendant from publishing or further publishing the matter complained of.

(2) The content of any correction and apology, and the time, manner, form and place of publication, shall be for the parties to agree.

If they cannot agree on the content, the court may direct the defendant to publish or cause to be published a summary of the court's judgment agreed by the parties or settled by the court in accordance with rules of court.

If they cannot agree on the time, manner, form or place of publication, the court may direct the defendant to take such reasonable and practicable steps as the court considers appropriate.

(2A) The Lord Chancellor must consult the Lord Chief Justice of England and Wales before making any order under subsection (1)(c) in relation to England and Wales.

(2B) The Lord Chancellor must consult the Lord Chief Justice of Northern Ireland before making any order under subsection (1) (c) in relation to Northern Ireland.

(2C) The Lord Chief Justice may nominate a judicial officer holder (as defined in section 109(4) of the Constitutional Reform Act 2005) to exercise his functions under this section.

(2D) The Lord Chief Justice of Northern Ireland may nominate any one of the following to exercise his functions under this section—

    (a) the holder of one of the offices listed in Schedule 1 to the Justice (Northern Ireland) Act 2002;

    (b) a Lord Justice of Appeal (as defined in section 88 of the Act).

(3) [Subject to subsection (4) a]ny order under subsection (1)(c) shall be made by statutory instrument which shall be subject to annulment in pursuance of a resolution of either House of Parliament.

(4) Any order made by the Department of Justice in Northern Ireland under subsection (1)(c) shall be made by statutory rule for the purposes of the Statutory Rules (Northern Ireland) Order 1979, and shall be subject to negative resolution within the meaning of section 41(6) of the Interpretation Act (Northern Ireland) 1954.

10   Summary disposal: rules of court

(1) Provision may be made by rules of court as to the summary disposal of the plaintiff's claim in defamation proceedings.

(2) Without prejudice to the generality of that power, provision may be made—
  (a) authorising a party to apply for summary disposal at any stage of the proceedings;
  (b) authorising the court at any stage of the proceedings—
      (i) to treat any application, pleading or other step in the proceedings as an application for summary disposal, or
      (ii) to make an order for summary disposal without any such application;
  (c) as to the time for serving pleadings or taking any other step in the proceedings in a case where there are proceedings for summary disposal;
  (d) requiring the parties to identify any question of law or construction which the court is to be asked to determine in the proceedings;
  (e) as to the nature of any hearing on the question of summary disposal, and in particular—
      (i) authorising the court to order affidavits or witness statements to be prepared for use as evidence at the hearing, and
      (ii) requiring the leave of the court for the calling of oral evidence, or the introduction of new evidence, at the hearing;
  (f) authorising the court to require a defendant to elect, at or before the hearing, whether or not to make an offer to make amends under section 2.

11   Summary disposal: application to Northern Ireland

In their application to Northern Ireland the provisions of sections 8 to 10 (summary disposal of claim) apply only to proceedings in the High Court.

Evidence of convictions

12   Evidence of convictions

(1) In section 13 of the Civil Evidence Act 1968 (conclusiveness of convictions for purposes of defamation actions), in subsections (1) and (2) for 'a person' substitute 'the plaintiff' and for 'that person' substitute 'he'; and after subsection (2) insert—

'(2A) In the case of an action for libel or slander in which there is more than one plaintiff—
  (a) the references in subsections (1) and (2) above to the plaintiff shall be construed as references to any of the plaintiffs, and
  (b) proof that any of the plaintiffs stands convicted of an offence shall be conclusive evidence that he committed that offence so far as that fact is relevant to any issue arising in relation to his cause of action or that of any other plaintiff.'

The amendments made by this subsection apply only where the trial of the action begins after this section comes into force.

(2) In section 12 of the Law Reform (Miscellaneous Provisions) (Scotland) Act 1968 (conclusiveness of convictions for purposes of defamation actions), in subsections (1) and (2) for 'a person' substitute 'the pursuer' and for 'that person' substitute 'he'; and after subsection (2) insert—

'(2A) In the case of an action for defamation in which there is more than one pursuer—
  (a) the references in subsections (1) and (2) above to the pursuer shall be construed as references to any of the pursuers, and

(b) proof that any of the pursuers stands convicted of an offence shall be conclusive evidence that he committed that offence so far as that fact is relevant to any issue arising in relation to his cause of action or that of any other pursuer.'

The amendments made by this subsection apply only for the purposes of an action begun after this section comes into force, whenever the cause of action arose.

(3) In section 9 of the Civil Evidence Act (Northern Ireland) 1971 (conclusiveness of convictions for purposes of defamation actions), in subsections (1) and (2) for 'a person' substitute 'the plaintiff' and for 'that person' substitute 'he'; and after subsection (2) insert—

'(2A) In the case of an action for libel or slander in which there is more than one plaintiff—

(a) the references in subsections (1) and (2) to the plaintiff shall be construed as references to any of the plaintiffs, and

(b) proof that any of the plaintiffs stands convicted of an offence shall be conclusive evidence that he committed that offence so far as that fact is relevant to any issue arising in relation to his cause of action or that of any other plaintiff.'

The amendments made by this subsection apply only where the trial of the action begins after this section comes into force.

Evidence concerning proceedings in Parliament

13   Evidence concerning proceedings in Parliament

(1) Where the conduct of a person in or in relation to proceedings in Parliament is in issue in defamation proceedings, he may waive for the purposes of those proceedings, so far as concerns him, the protection of any enactment or rule of law which prevents proceedings in Parliament being impeached or questioned in any court or place out of Parliament.

(2) Where a person waives that protection—

(a) any such enactment or rule of law shall not apply to prevent evidence being given, questions being asked or statements, submissions, comments or findings being made about his conduct, and

(b) none of those things shall be regarded as infringing the privilege of either House of Parliament.

(3) The waiver by one person of that protection does not affect its operation in relation to another person who has not waived it.

(4) Nothing in this section affects any enactment or rule of law so far as it protects a person (including a person who has waived the protection referred to above) from legal liability for words spoken or things done in the course of, or for the purposes of or incidental to, any proceedings in Parliament.

(5) Without prejudice to the generality of subsection (4), that subsection applies to—

(a) the giving of evidence before either House or a committee;

(b) the presentation or submission of a document to either House or a committee;

(c) the preparation of a document for the purposes of or incidental to the transacting of any such business;

(d) the formulation, making or publication of a document, including a report, by or pursuant to an order of either House or a committee; and

(e) any communication with the Parliamentary Commissioner for Standards or any person having functions in connection with the registration of members' interests.

In this subsection 'a committee' means a committee of either House or a joint committee of both Houses of Parliament.

Statutory privilege

14   Reports of court proceedings absolutely privileged

(1) A fair and accurate report of proceedings in public before a court to which this section applies, if published contemporaneously with the proceedings, is absolutely privileged.

(2) A report of proceedings which by an order of the court, or as a consequence of any statutory provision, is required to be postponed shall be treated as published contemporaneously if it is published as soon as practicable after publication is permitted.

[(3) This section applies to—

(a) any court in the United Kingdom;

(b) any court established under the law of a country or territory outside the United Kingdom;

(c) any international court or tribunal established by the Security Council of the United Nations or by an international agreement;

and in paragraphs (a) and (b) 'court' includes any tribunal or body exercising the judicial power of the State.]

15   Reports, &c. protected by qualified privilege

(1) The publication of any report or other statement mentioned in Schedule 1 to this Act is privileged unless the publication is shown to be made with malice, subject as follows.

(2) In defamation proceedings in respect of the publication of a report or other statement mentioned in Part II of that Schedule, there is no defence under this section if the plaintiff shows that the defendant—

(a) was requested by him to publish in a suitable manner a reasonable letter or statement by way of explanation or contradiction, and

(b) refused or neglected to do so.

For this purpose 'in a suitable manner' means in the same manner as the publication complained of or in a manner that is adequate and reasonable in the circumstances.

(3) This section does not apply to the publication to the public, or a section of the public, of matter which is not of public [interest] and the publication of which is not for the public benefit.

(4) Nothing in this section shall be construed—

(a) as protecting the publication of matter the publication of which is prohibited by law, or

(b) as limiting or abridging any privilege subsisting apart from this section.

Supplementary provisions

17   Interpretation

(1) In this Act—

'publication and' 'publish' , in relation to a statement, have the meaning they have for the purposes of the law of defamation generally, but 'publisher' is specially defined for the purposes of section 1;

'statement' means words, pictures, visual images, gestures or any other method of signifying meaning; and

'statutory provision' means—

(a) a provision contained in an Act or in subordinate legislation within the meaning of the Interpretation Act 1978, or

(aa) a provision contained in an Act of the Scottish Parliament or in an instrument made under such an Act, or

(b) a statutory provision within the meaning given by section 1(f) of the Interpretation Act (Northern Ireland) 1954.

(2) In this Act as it applies to proceedings in Scotland—

'costs' means expenses; and

'plaintiff' and 'defendant' mean pursuer and defender.

General provisions

18   Extent

(1) The following provisions of this Act extend to England and Wales—

section 1 (responsibility for publication),

sections 2 to 4 (offer to make amends), except section 3(9),

section 5 (time limit for actions for defamation or malicious falsehood),

section 7 (ruling on the meaning of a statement),

sections 8 to 10 (summary disposal of claim),

section 12(1) (evidence of convictions),

section 13 (evidence concerning proceedings in Parliament),

sections 14 and 15 and Schedule 1 (statutory privilege),

section 16 and Schedule 2 (repeals) so far as relating to enactments extending to England and Wales,

section 17(1) (interpretation),

this subsection,

section 19 (commencement) so far as relating to provisions which extend to England and Wales, and

section 20 (short title and saving).

(2) The following provisions of this Act extend to Scotland—

section 1 (responsibility for publication),

sections 2 to 4 (offer to make amends), except section 3(8),

section 12(2) (evidence of convictions),

section 13 (evidence concerning proceedings in Parliament),

sections 14 and 15 and Schedule 1 (statutory privilege),

section 16 and Schedule 2 (repeals) so far as relating to enactments extending to Scotland,

section 17 (interpretation),

this subsection,

section 19 (commencement) so far as relating to provisions which extend to Scotland, and

section 20 (short title and saving).

(3) The following provisions of this Act extend to Northern Ireland—

section 1 (responsibility for publication),

sections 2 to 4 (offer to make amends), except section 3(9),

section 6 (time limit for actions for defamation or malicious falsehood),

section 7 (ruling on the meaning of a statement),

sections 8 to 11 (summary disposal of claim),

section 12(3) (evidence of convictions),

section 13 (evidence concerning proceedings in Parliament),

sections 14 and 15 and Schedule 1 (statutory privilege),

section 16 and Schedule 2 (repeals) so far as relating to enactments extending to Northern Ireland,

section 17(1) (interpretation),

this subsection,

section 19 (commencement) so far as relating to provisions which extend to Northern Ireland,

and section 20 (short title and saving).

19   Commencement

(1) Sections 18 to 20 (extent, commencement and other general provisions) come into force on Royal Assent.

(2) The following provisions of this Act come into force at the end of the period of two months beginning with the day on which this Act is passed—

section 1 (responsibility for publication),

sections 5 and 6 (time limit for actions for defamation or malicious falsehood), section 12 (evidence of convictions),

section 13 (evidence concerning proceedings in Parliament),

section 16 and the repeals in Schedule 2, so far as consequential on the above provisions, and

section 17 (interpretation), so far as relating to the above provisions.

(3) The provisions of this Act otherwise come into force on such day as may be appointed—

(a) for England and Wales or Northern Ireland, by order of the Lord Chancellor, or

(b) for Scotland, by order of the Secretary of State,

and different days may be appointed for different purposes.

(4) Any such order shall be made by statutory instrument and may contain such transitional provisions as appear to the Lord Chancellor or Secretary of State to be appropriate.

20   Short title and saving

(1) This Act may be cited as the Defamation Act 1996.

[(2) Nothing in this Act affects the law relating to criminal libel.]

SCHEDULES

SCHEDULE 1   QUALIFIED PRIVILEGE

PART I   STATEMENTS HAVING QUALIFIED PRIVILEGE WITHOUT EXPLANATION OR CONTRADICTION

1. A fair and accurate report of proceedings in public of a legislature anywhere in the world.

2. A fair and accurate report of proceedings in public before a court anywhere in the world.

3. A fair and accurate report of proceedings in public of a person appointed to hold a public inquiry by a government or legislature anywhere in the world.

4. A fair and accurate report of proceedings in public anywhere in the world of an international organisation or an international conference.

5. A fair and accurate copy of or extract from any register or other document required by law to be open to public inspection.

6. A notice or advertisement published by or on the authority of a court, or of a judge or officer of a court, anywhere in the world.

7. A fair and accurate copy of or extract from matter published by or on the authority of a government or legislature anywhere in the world.

8. A fair and accurate copy of or extract from matter published anywhere in the world by an international organisation or an international conference.

PART II   STATEMENTS PRIVILEGED SUBJECT TO EXPLANATION OR CONTRADICTION

[9.—(1) A fair and accurate copy of, extract from or summary of a notice or other matter issued for the information of the public by or on behalf of—

(a)   a legislature or government anywhere in the world;

(b)   an authority anywhere in the world performing governmental functions;

(c)   an international organisation or international conference.

(2) In this paragraph 'governmental functions' includes police functions.]

[10. A fair and accurate copy of, extract from or summary of a document made available by a court anywhere in the world, or by a judge or officer of such a court.]

11. (1) A fair and accurate report of proceedings at any public meeting or sitting in the United Kingdom of—

(a)   a local authority or local authority committee;

    (aa) in the case of a local authority which are operating executive arrangements, the executive of that authority or a committee of that executive;

    (b) a justice or justices of the peace acting otherwise than as a court exercising judicial authority;

    (c) a commission, tribunal, committee or person appointed for the purposes of any inquiry by any statutory provision, by Her Majesty or by a Minister of the Crown, a member of the Scottish Executive, the Welsh Ministers or the Counsel General to the Welsh Assembly Government or a Northern Ireland Department;

    (d) a person appointed by a local authority to hold a local inquiry in pursuance of any statutory provision;

    (e) any other tribunal, board, committee or body constituted by or under, and exercising functions under, any statutory provision.

(1A) In the case of a local authority which are operating executive arrangements, a fair and accurate record of any decision made by any member of the executive where that record is required to be made and available for public inspection by virtue of section 22 of the Local Government Act 2000 or of any provision in regulations made under that section.

(2) In sub-paragraphs (1)(a)[, (1)(aa)] and (1A) —

'local authority' means—

    (a) in relation to England and Wales, a principal council within the meaning of the Local Government Act 1972, any body falling within any paragraph of section 100J(1) of that Act or an authority or body to which the Public Bodies (Admission to Meetings) Act 1960 applies,

    (b) in relation to Scotland, a council constituted under section 2 of the Local Government etc. (Scotland) Act 1994 or an authority or body to which the Public Bodies (Admission to Meetings) Act 1960 applies,

    (c) in relation to Northern Ireland, any authority or body to which sections 23 to 27 of the Local Government Act (Northern Ireland) 1972 apply; and

'local authority committee' means any committee of a local authority or of local authorities, and includes—

    (a) any committee or sub-committee in relation to which sections 100A to 100D of the Local Government Act 1972 apply by virtue of section 100E of that Act (whether or not also by virtue of section 100J of that Act), and

    (b) any committee or sub-committee in relation to which sections 50A to 50D of the Local Government (Scotland) Act 1973 apply by virtue of section 50E of that Act.

(2A) In sub-paragraphs (1) and (1A)—

'executive' and 'executive arrangements' have the same meaning as in Part II of the Local Government Act 2000.

(3) A fair and accurate report of any corresponding proceedings in any of the Channel Islands or the Isle of Man or in another member State.

[11A.—A fair and accurate report of proceedings at a press conference held anywhere in the world for the discussion of a matter of public interest.]

12.—(1) A fair and accurate report of proceedings at any public meeting held [anywhere in the world].

(2) In this paragraph a 'public meeting' means a meeting bona fide and lawfully held for a lawful purpose and for the furtherance or discussion of a matter of public [interest], whether admission to the meeting is general or restricted.

13.—(1) A fair and accurate report of proceedings at a general meeting of a [listed] company.

(2) A fair and accurate copy of, extract from or summary of any document circulated to members of a listed company—

    (a) by or with the authority of the board of directors of the company,

    (b) by the auditors of the company, or

    (c) by any member of the company in pursuance of a right conferred by any statutory provision.

(3) A fair and accurate copy of, extract from or summary of any document circulated to members of a listed company which relates to the appointment, resignation, retirement or dismissal of directors of the company or its auditors.

(4) In this paragraph 'listed company' has the same meaning as in Part 12 of the Corporation Tax Act 2009 (see section 1005 of that Act).

14. A fair and accurate report of any finding or decision of any of the following descriptions of association, formed [anywhere in the world], or of any committee or governing body of such an association—

(a) an association formed for the purpose of promoting or encouraging the exercise of or interest in any art, science, religion or learning, and empowered by its constitution to exercise control over or adjudicate on matters of interest or concern to the association, or the actions or conduct of any person subject to such control or adjudication;

(b) an association formed for the purpose of promoting or safeguarding the interests of any trade, business, industry or profession, or of the persons carrying on or engaged in any trade, business, industry or profession, and empowered by its constitution to exercise control over or adjudicate upon matters connected with that trade, business, industry or profession, or the actions or conduct of those persons;

(c) an association formed for the purpose of promoting or safeguarding the interests of a game, sport or pastime to the playing or exercise of which members of the public are invited or admitted, and empowered by its constitution to exercise control over or adjudicate upon persons connected with or taking part in the game, sport or pastime;

(d) an association formed for the purpose of promoting charitable objects or other objects beneficial to the community and empowered by its constitution to exercise control over or to adjudicate on matters of interest or concern to the association, or the actions or conduct of any person subject to such control or adjudication.

[14A. A fair and accurate—

(a) report of proceedings of a scientific or academic conference held anywhere in the world, or

(b) copy of, extract from or summary of matter published by such a conference.]

15.—[(1) A fair and accurate report or summary of, copy of or extract from, any adjudication, report, statement or notice issued by a body, officer or other person designated for the purposes of this paragraph by order of the Lord Chancellor.

(2) An order under this paragraph shall be made by statutory instrument which shall be subject to annulment in pursuance of a resolution of either House of Parliament.]

PART III SUPPLEMENTARY PROVISIONS

16.—[In this Schedule—

'court' includes—

(a) any tribunal or body established under the law of any country or territory exercising the judicial power of the State;

(b) any international tribunal established by the Security Council of the United Nations or by an international agreement;

(c) any international tribunal deciding matters in dispute between States;

'international conference' means a conference attended by representatives of two or more governments;

'international organisation' means an organisation of which two or more governments are members, and includes any committee or other subordinate body of such an organisation;

'legislature' includes a local legislature; and

'member State' includes any European dependent territory of a member State.]

Rehabilitation of Offenders Act 1974

(1974, c. 53)

8   Defamation actions

(1) This section applies to any action for libel or slander begun after the commencement of this Act by a rehabilitated person and founded upon the publication of any matter imputing that the plaintiff has committed or been charged with or prosecuted for or convicted of or sentenced for an offence which was the subject of a spent conviction.

(2) Nothing in section 4(1) above shall affect an action to which this section applies where the publication complained of took place before the conviction in question became spent, and the following provisions of this section shall not apply in any such case.

(3) Subject to subsections (5) and (6) below, nothing in section 4(1) above shall prevent the defendant in an action to which this section applies from relying on any defence [under section 2 or 3 of the Defamation Act 2013 which is available to him or any defence] of absolute or qualified privilege which is available to him, or restrict the matters he may establish in support of any such defence.

(4) Without prejudice to the generality of subsection (3) above, where in any such action malice is alleged against a defendant who is relying on a defence of qualified privilege, nothing in section 4(1) above shall restrict the matters he may establish in rebuttal of the allegation.

(5) A defendant in any such action shall not by virtue of subsection (3) above be entitled to rely upon [a defence under section 2 of the Defamation Act 2013] if the publication is proved to have been made with malice.

(6) Subject to subsection (7) below a defendant in any such action shall not, by virtue of subsection (3) above, be entitled to rely on any matter or adduce or require any evidence for the purpose of establishing (whether under section 14 of the Defamation Act 1996 or otherwise) the defence that the matter published constituted a fair and accurate report of judicial proceedings if it is proved that the publication contained a reference to evidence which was ruled to be inadmissible in the proceedings by virtue of section 4(1) above.

(7) Subsection (3) above shall apply without the qualifications imposed by subsection (6) above in relation to—

(a) any report of judicial proceedings contained in any bona fide series of law reports which does not form part of any other publication and consists solely of reports of proceedings in courts of law; and

(b) any report or account of judicial proceedings published for bona fide educational, scientific or professional purposes, or given in the course of any lecture, class or discussion given or held for any of those purposes.

(8) In the application of this section to Scotland—

(a) for the reference in subsection (1) to libel and slander there shall be substituted a reference to defamation;

(b) for references to the plaintiff and the defendant there shall be substituted respectively references to the pursuer and the defender; and

(c) for references to the defence of justification there shall be substituted references to the defence of veritas.

8A   Protection afforded to spent cautions

(1) Schedule 2 to this Act (protection for spent cautions) shall have effect.

(2) In this Act 'caution' means—

(a) a conditional caution, that is to say, a caution given under section 22 of the Criminal Justice Act 2003 (c. 44) (conditional cautions for adults) or under section 66A of the Crime and Disorder Act 1998 (c. 37) (conditional cautions for children and young persons);

(b) any other caution given to a person in England and Wales in respect of an offence which, at the time the caution is given, that person has admitted;

(c) [...]

(d) anything corresponding to a caution, reprimand or warning falling within paragraphs (a) [or (b)] (however described) which is given to a person in respect of an offence under the law of a country outside England and Wales [and which is not an alternative to prosecution (within the meaning of section 8AA)].

SCHEDULE 2

3—(1) A person who is given a caution for an offence shall, from the time the caution is spent, be treated for all purposes in law as a person who has not committed, been charged with or prosecuted for, or been given a caution for the offence; and notwithstanding the provisions of any other enactment or rule of law to the contrary—

(a) no evidence shall be admissible in any proceedings before a judicial authority exercising its jurisdiction or functions in England and Wales to prove that any such person has committed, been charged with or prosecuted for, or been given a caution for the offence; and

(b) a person shall not, in any such proceedings, be asked and, if asked, shall not be required to answer, any question relating to his past which cannot be answered without acknowledging or referring to a spent caution or any ancillary circumstances.

Limitation Act 1980

(1980, c. 58)

PART I ORDINARY TIME LIMITS FOR DIFFERENT CLASSES OF ACTION

Actions founded on tort

4A Time limit for actions for defamation or malicious falsehood

The time limit under section 2 of this Act shall not apply to an action for—

(a) libel or slander, or malicious falsehood,

(b) slander of title, slander of goods or other malicious falsehood,

but no such action shall be brought after the expiration of one year from the date on which the cause of action accrued.

28 Extension of limitation period in case of disability

(1) Subject to the following provisions of this section, if on the date when any right of action accrued for which a period of limitation is prescribed by this Act, the person to whom it accrued was under a disability, the action may be brought at any time before the expiration of six years from the date when he ceased to be under a disability or died (whichever first occurred) notwithstanding that the period of limitation has expired.

(2) This section shall not affect any case where the right of action first accrued to some person (not under a disability) through whom the person under a disability claims.

(3) When a right of action which has accrued to a person under a disability accrues, on the death of that person while still under a disability, to another person under a disability, no further extension of time shall be allowed by reason of the disability of the second person.

(4) No action to recover land or money charged on land shall be brought by virtue of this section by any person after the expiration of thirty years from the date on which the right of action accrued to that person or some person through whom he claims.

(4A) If the action is one to which section 4A of this Act applies, subsection (1) above shall have effect—

(a) in the case of an action for libel or slander, as if for the words from 'at any time' to 'occurred' there were substituted the words 'by him at any time (b) before the expiration of one year from the date on which he ceased to be under a disability'; and

(b) in the case of an action for slander of title, slander of goods or other malicious falsehood, as if for the words 'six years' there were substituted the words 'one year'.

(5) If the action is one to which section 10 of this Act applies, subsection (1) above shall have effect as if for the words 'six years' there were substituted the words 'two years'.

(6) If the action is one to which section 11 or 12(2) of this Act applies, subsection (1) above shall have effect as if for the words 'six years' there were substituted the words 'three years'.

(7) If the action is one to which section 11A of this Act applies or one by virtue of section 6(1)(a) of the Consumer Protection Act 1987 (death caused by defective product), subsection (1) above—

(a) shall not apply to the time limit prescribed by subsection (3) of the said section 11A or to that time limit as applied by virtue of section 12(1) of this Act; and

(b) in relation to any other time limit prescribed by this Act shall have effect as if for the word 'six years' there were substituted the words 'three years'.

PART II EXTENSION OR EXCLUSION OF ORDINARY TIME LIMITS

32 Postponement of limitation period in case of fraud, concealment or mistake

(1) Subject to subsections (3) and (4A) below, where in the case of any action for which a period of limitation is prescribed by this Act, either—

(a) the action is based upon the fraud of the defendant; or

(b) any fact relevant to the plaintiff's right of action has been deliberately concealed from him by the defendant; or

(c) the action is for relief from the consequences of a mistake;

the period of limitation shall not begin to run until the plaintiff has discovered the fraud, concealment or mistake (as the case may be) or could with reasonable diligence have discovered it.

References in this subsection to the defendant include references to the defendant's agent and to any person through whom the defendant claims and his agent.

(2) For the purposes of subsection (1) above, deliberate commission of a breach of duty in circumstances in which it is unlikely to be discovered for some time amounts to deliberate concealment of the facts involved in that breach of duty.

(3) Nothing in this section shall enable any action—

(a) to recover, or recover the value of, any property; or

(b) to enforce any charge against, or set aside any transaction affecting, any property;

to be brought against the purchaser of the property or any person claiming through him in any case where the property has been purchased for valuable consideration by an innocent third party since the fraud or concealment or (as the case may be) the transaction in which the mistake was made took place.

(4) A purchaser is an innocent third party for the purposes of this section—

(a) in the case of fraud or concealment of any fact relevant to the plaintiff's right of action, if he was not a party to the fraud or (as the case may be) to the concealment of that fact and did not at the time of the purchase know or have reason to believe that the fraud or concealment had taken place; and

    (b) in the case of mistake, if he did not at the time of the purchase know or have reason to believe that the mistake had been made.

(4A) Subsection (1) above shall not apply in relation to the time limit prescribed by section 11A(3) of this Act or in relation to that time limit as applied by virtue of section 12(1) of this Act.

(5) Sections 14A and 14B of this Act shall not apply to any action to which subsection (1)(b) above applies (and accordingly the period of limitation referred to in that subsection, in any case to which either of those sections would otherwise apply, is the period applicable under section 2 of this Act).

32A Discretionary exclusion of time limit for actions for defamation or malicious falsehood

(1) If it appears to the court that it would be exclusion of time equitable to allow an action to proceed having regard to limit for actions the degree to which—

    (a) the operation of section 4A of this Act prejudices the plaintiff or any person whom he represents, and

    (b) any decision of the court under this subsection would prejudice the defendant or any person whom he represents,

the court may direct that that section shall not apply to the action or shall not apply to any specified cause of action to which the action relates.

(2) In acting under this section the court shall have regard to all the circumstances of the case and in particular to—

    (a) the length of, and the reasons for, the delay on the part of the plaintiff;

    (b) where the reason or one of the reasons for the delay was that all or any of the facts relevant to the cause of action did not become known to the plaintiff until after the end of the period mentioned in section 4A—

      (i) the date on which any such facts did become known to him, and

      (ii) the extent to which he acted promptly and reasonably once he knew whether or not the facts in question might be capable of giving rise to an action; and

    (c) the extent to which, having regard to the delay, relevant evidence is likely—

      (i) to be unavailable, or

      (ii) to be less cogent than if the action had been brought within the period mentioned in section 4A.

(3) In the case of an action for slander of title, slander of goods or other malicious falsehood brought by a personal representative—

    (a) the references in subsection (2) above to the plaintiff shall be construed as including the deceased person to whom the cause of action accrued and any previous personal representative of that person; and

    (b) nothing in section 28(3) of this Act shall be construed as affecting the court's discretion under this section.

(4) In this section 'the court' means the court in which the action has been brought.

36 Equitable jurisdiction and remedies

(1) The following time limits under this Act, that is to say—

    (a) the time limit under section 2 for actions founded on tort;

  (aa) the time limit under section 4A for actions for libel or slander, or for slander of title, slander of goods or other malicious falsehood;

    (b) the time limit under section 5 for actions founded on simple contract;

    (c) the time limit under section 7 for actions to enforce awards where the submission is not by an instrument under seal;

    (d) the time limit under section 8 for actions on a specialty;

(e) the time limit under section 9 for actions to recover a sum recoverable by virtue of any enactment; and

(f) the time limit under section 24 for actions to enforce a judgment;

shall not apply to any claim for specific performance of a contract or for an injunction or for other equitable relief, except in so far as any such time limit may be applied by the court by analogy in like manner as the corresponding time limit under any enactment repealed by the Limitation Act 1939 was applied before 1st July 1940.

(2) Nothing in this Act shall affect any equitable jurisdiction to refuse relief on the ground of acquiescence or otherwise.

Courts and Legal Services Act 1990

(1990, c. 41)

8   Powers of Court of Appeal to award damages

(1) In this section 'case' means any case where the Court of Appeal has power to order a new trial on the ground that damages awarded by a jury are excessive or inadequate.

(2) Rules of court may provide for the Court of Appeal, in such classes of case as may be specified in the rules, to have power, in place of ordering a new trial, to substitute for the sum awarded by the jury such sum as appears to the court to be proper.

(3) This section is not to be read as prejudicing in any way any other power to make rules of court.

Access to Justice Act 1999

(1999, c. 22)

6   Services which may be funded

(6) The Commission may not fund as part of the Community Legal Service any of the services specified in Schedule 2.

(7) Regulations may amend that Schedule by adding new services or omitting or varying any services.

(8) The [Lord Chancellor]—

(a) may by direction require the Commission to fund the provision of any of the services specified in Schedule 2 in circumstances specified in the direction, and

(b) may authorise the Commission to fund the provision of any of those services in specified circumstances or, if the Commission request him to do so, in an individual case.

(8A) The circumstances specified in a direction or authorisation under subsection (8) may be circumstances described by reference to—

(a) one or more areas or localities;

(b) one or more descriptions of court or tribunal.

(8B) A direction or authorisation under subsection (8) may provide that it requires or authorises the Commission to fund the provision of services only for—

(a) one or more specified classes of person;

(b) persons selected—

(i)   by reference to specified criteria; or

(ii) on a sampling basis.

SCHEDULE 2 COMMUNITY LEGAL SERVICE: EXCLUDED SERVICES

The services which may not be funded as part of the Community Legal Service are as follows.

1.   Services consisting of the provision of help (beyond the provision of general information about the law and the legal system and the availability of legal services) in relation to—

(f) defamation or malicious falsehood,

Broadcasting Act 1990

(1990, c. 42)

Defamation

166 Defamatory material

(1) For the purposes of the law of libel and slander the publication of words in the course of any programme included in a programme service shall be treated as publication in permanent form.

(2) Subsection (1) above shall apply for the purposes of section 3 of each of the Defamation Acts (slander of title etc.) as it applies for the purposes of the law of libel and slander.

(4) In this section 'the Defamation Acts' means the Defamation Act 1952 and the Defamation Act (Northern Ireland) 1955.

(5) Subsections (1) and (2) above do not extend to Scotland.

Civil Evidence Act 1968

(1968, c. 64)

PART II MISCELLANEOUS AND GENERAL

Convictions, etc. as evidence in civil proceedings

11 Convictions as evidence in civil proceedings

(1) In any civil proceedings the fact that a person has been convicted of an offence by or before any court in the United Kingdom or by a court-martial there or elsewhere shall (subject to subsection (3) below) be admissible in evidence for the purpose of proving, where to do so is relevant to any issue in those proceedings, that he committed that offence, whether he was so convicted upon a plea of guilty or otherwise and whether or not he is a party to the civil proceedings; but no conviction other than a subsisting one shall be admissible in evidence by virtue of this section.

(2) In any civil proceedings in which by virtue of this section a person is proved to have been convicted of an offence by or before any court in the United Kingdom or by a court-martial there or elsewhere—

(a) he shall be taken to have committed that offence unless the contrary is proved; and

(b) without prejudice to the reception of any other admissible evidence for the purpose of identifying the facts on which the conviction was based, the contents of any document which is admissible as evidence of the conviction, and the contents of the information, complaint, indictment or charge-sheet on which the person in question was convicted, shall be admissible in evidence for that purpose.

(3) Nothing in this section shall prejudice the operation of section 13 of this Act or any other enactment whereby a conviction or a finding of fact in any criminal proceedings is for the purposes of any other proceedings made conclusive evidence of any fact.

(4) Where in any civil proceedings the contents of any document are admissible in evidence by virtue of subsection (2) above, a copy of that document, or of the material part thereof, purporting to be certified or otherwise authenticated by or on behalf of the court or authority having custody of that document shall be admissible in evidence and shall be taken to be a true copy of that document or part unless the contrary is shown.

(5) Nothing in any of the following enactments, that is to say—

(a) section 14 of the Powers of Criminal Courts (Sentencing) Act 2000 (under which a conviction leading to . . . discharge is to be disregarded except as therein mentioned);

(aa) section 187 of the Armed Forces Act 2006 (which makes similar provision in respect of service convictions);

(b) section 191 of the Criminal Procedure (Scotland) Act 1975 (which makes similar provision in respect of convictions on indictment in Scotland); and

(c) section 8 of the Probation Act (Northern Ireland) 1950 (which corresponds to the said section 12) or any corresponding enactment of the Parliament of Northern Ireland for the time being in force,

shall affect the operation of this section; and for the purposes of this section any order made by a court of summary jurisdiction in Scotland under section 383 or section 384 of the said Act of 1975 shall be treated as a conviction.

(7) In this section—

'service offence' has the same meaning as in the Armed Forces Act 2006;

'conviction' includes anything that under section 376(1) and (2) of that Act is to be treated as a conviction, and 'convicted' is to be read accordingly.

13   Conclusiveness of convictions for purposes of defamation actions

(1) In an action for libel or slander in which the question whether the plaintiff did or did not commit a criminal offence is relevant to an issue arising in the action, proof that at the time when that issue falls to be determined, he stands convicted of that offence shall be conclusive evidence that he committed that offence; and his conviction thereof shall be admissible in evidence accordingly.

(2) In any such action as aforesaid in which by virtue of this section the plaintiff is proved to have been convicted of an offence, the contents of any document which is admissible as evidence of the conviction, and the contents of the information, complaint, indictment or charge-sheet on which he was convicted, shall, without prejudice to the reception of any other admissible evidence for the purpose of identifying the facts on which the conviction was based, be admissible in evidence for the purpose of identifying those facts.

(2A) In the case of an action for libel or slander in which there is more than one plaintiff—

(a) the references in subsections (1) and (2) above to the plaintiff shall be construed as references to any of the plaintiffs, and

(b) proof that any of the plaintiffs stands convicted of an offence shall be conclusive evidence that he committed that offence so far as that fact is relevant to any issue arising in relation to his cause of action or that of any other plaintiff.

(3) For the purposes of this section a person shall be taken to stand convicted of an offence if but only if there subsists against him a conviction of that offence by or before a court in the United Kingdom or (in the case of a service offence) a conviction (anywhere) of that service offence.

(4) Subsections (4) to (7) of section 11 of this Act shall apply for the purposes of this section as they apply for the purposes of that section, but as if in the said subsection (4) the reference to subsection (2) were a reference to subsection (2) of this section.

(5) The foregoing provisions of this section shall apply for the purposes of any action begun after the passing of this Act, whenever the cause of action arose, but shall not apply for the purposes of any action begun before the passing of this Act or any appeal or other proceedings arising out of any such action.

Senior Courts Act 1981

(1981, c. 54)

69 Trial by jury

(1) Where, on the application of any party to an action to be tried in the Queen's Bench Division, the court is satisfied that there is in issue—

(a) a charge of fraud against that party; or

(b) a claim in respect of [. . .] malicious prosecution or false imprisonment; or

(c) any question or issue of a kind prescribed for the purposes of this paragraph,

the action shall be tried with a jury, unless the court is of opinion that the trial requires any prolonged examination of documents or accounts or any scientific or local investigation which cannot conveniently be made with a jury.

(2) An application under subsection (1) must be made not later than such time before the trial as may be prescribed.

(3) An action to be tried in the Queen's Bench Division which does not by virtue of subsection (1) fall to be tried with a jury shall be tried without a jury unless the court in its discretion orders it to be tried with a jury.

(4) Nothing in subsections (1) to (3) shall affect the power of the court to order, in accordance with rules of court, that different questions of fact arising in any action be tried by different modes of trial; and where any such order is made, subsection (1) shall have effect only as respects questions relating to any such charge, claim, question or issue as is mentioned in that subsection.

(5) Where for the purpose of disposing of any action or other matter which is being tried in the High Court by a judge with a jury it is necessary to ascertain the law of any other country which is applicable to the facts of the case, any question as to the effect of the evidence given with respect to that law shall, instead of being submitted to the jury, be decided by the judge alone.

Criminal Procedure and Investigations Act 1996

(1996, c. 25)

Derogatory assertions

58 Orders in respect of certain assertions

(1) This section applies where a person has been convicted of an offence and a speech in mitigation is made by him or on his behalf before—

(a) a court determining what sentence should be passed on him in respect of the offence, or

(b) a magistrates' court determining whether he should be committed to the Crown Court for sentence.

(2) This section also applies where a sentence has been passed on a person in respect of an offence and a submission relating to the sentence is made by him or on his behalf before—

(a) a court hearing an appeal against or reviewing the sentence, or

(b) a court determining whether to grant leave to appeal against the sentence.

(3) Where it appears to the court that there is a real possibility that an order under subsection (8) will be made in relation to the assertion, the court may make an order under subsection (7) in relation to the assertion.

(4) Where there are substantial grounds for believing—

(a) that an assertion forming part of the speech or submission is derogatory to a person's character (for instance, because it suggests that his conduct is or has been criminal, immoral or improper), and

(b) that the assertion is false or that the facts asserted are irrelevant to the sentence,
the court may make an order under subsection (8) in relation to the assertion.

(5) An order under subsection (7) or (8) must not be made in relation to an assertion if it appears to the court that the assertion was previously made—

(a) at the trial at which the person was convicted of the offence, or

(b) during any other proceedings relating to the offence.

(6) Section 59 has effect where a court makes an order under subsection (7) or (8).

(7) An order under this subsection—

(a) may be made at any time before the court has made a determination with regard to sentencing;

(b) may be revoked at any time by the court;

(c) subject to paragraph (b), shall cease to have effect when the court makes a determination with regard to sentencing.

(8) An order under this subsection—

(a) may be made after the court has made a determination with regard to sentencing, but only if it is made as soon as is reasonably practicable after the making of the determination;

(b) may be revoked at any time by the court;

(c) subject to paragraph (b), shall cease to have effect at the end of the period of 12 months beginning with the day on which it is made;

(d) may be made whether or not an order has been made under subsection (7) with regard to the case concerned.

(9) For the purposes of subsections (7) and (8) the court makes a determination with regard to sentencing—

(a) when it determines what sentence should be passed (where this section applies by virtue of subsection (1)(a));

(b) when it determines whether the person should be committed to the Crown Court for sentence (where this section applies by virtue of subsection (1)(b));

(c) when it determines what the sentence should be (where this section applies by virtue of subsection (2)(a));

(d) when it determines whether to grant leave to appeal (where this section applies by virtue of subsection (2)(b)).

59   Restriction on reporting of assertions

(1) Where a court makes an order under section 58(7) or (8) in relation to any assertion, at any time when the order has effect the assertion must not—

(a) be published in Great Britain in a written publication available to the public, or

(b) be included in a relevant programme for reception in Great Britain.

(2) In this section—

'relevant programme' means a programme included in a programme service, within the meaning of the Broadcasting Act 1990;

'written publication' includes a film, a soundtrack and any other record in permanent form but does not include an indictment or other document prepared for use in particular legal proceedings.

(3) For the purposes of this section an assertion is published or included in a programme if the material published or included—

(a) names the person about whom the assertion is made or, without naming him, contains enough to make it likely that members of the public will identify him as the person about whom it is made, and

(b) reproduces the actual wording of the matter asserted or contains its substance.

60   Reporting of assertions: offences

(1) If an assertion is published or included in a relevant programme in contravention of section 59, each of the following persons is guilty of an offence—

(a) in the case of publication in a newspaper or periodical, any proprietor, any editor and any publisher of the newspaper or periodical;

    (b) in the case of publication in any other form, the person publishing the assertion;

    (c) in the case of an assertion included in a relevant programme, any body corporate engaged in providing the service in which the programme is included and any person having functions in relation to the programme corresponding to those of an editor of a newspaper.

(2) A person guilty of an offence under this section is liable on summary conviction to a fine of an amount not exceeding level 5 on the standard scale.

(3) Where a person is charged with an offence under this section it is a defence to prove that at the time of the alleged offence—

    (a) he was not aware, and neither suspected nor had reason to suspect, that an order under section 58(7) or (8) had effect at that time, or

    (b) he was not aware, and neither suspected nor had reason to suspect, that the publication or programme in question was of, or (as the case may be) included, the assertion in question.

(4) Where an offence under this section committed by a body corporate is proved to have been committed with the consent or connivance of, or to be attributable to any neglect on the part of—

    (a) a director, manager, secretary or other similar officer of the body corporate, or

    (b) a person purporting to act in any such capacity,

he as well as the body corporate is guilty of the offence and liable to be proceeded against and punished accordingly.

(5) In relation to a body corporate whose affairs are managed by its members 'director' in subsection (4) means a member of the body corporate.

(6) Subsections (2) and (3) of section 59 apply for the purposes of this section as they apply for the purposes of that.

61   Reporting of assertions: commencement and supplementary

(1) Section 58 applies where the offence mentioned in subsection (1) or (2) of that section is committed on or after the appointed day.

(2) The reference in subsection (1) to the appointed day is to such day as is appointed for the purposes of this section by the Secretary of State by order.

(3) Nothing in section 58 or 59 affects any prohibition or restriction imposed by virtue of any other enactment on a publication or on matter included in a programme.

(6) In section 159 of the Criminal Justice Act 1988 (appeal to Court of Appeal against orders restricting reports etc.) in subsection (1) the following paragraph shall be inserted after paragraph (a)—

    '(aa) an order made by the Crown Court under section 58(7) or (8) of the Criminal Procedure and Investigations Act 1996 in a case where the Court has convicted a person on a trial on indictment;'.

Copyright, Designs and Patents Act 1988

(1988, c. 48)

Right to object to derogatory treatment of work

80   Right to object to derogatory treatment of work

(1) The author of a copyright literary, dramatic, musical or artistic work, and the director of a copyright film, has the right in the circumstances mentioned in this section not to have his work subjected to derogatory treatment.

(2) For the purposes of this section—

    (a) 'treatment' of a work means any addition to, deletion from or alteration to or adaptation of the work, other than—

        (i)   a translation of a literary or dramatic work, or

        (ii) an arrangement or transcription of a musical work involving no more than a change of key or register; and

(b) the treatment of a work is derogatory if it amounts to distortion or mutilation of the work or is otherwise prejudicial to the honour or reputation of the author or director;

and in the following provisions of this section references to a derogatory treatment of a work shall be construed accordingly.

(3) In the case of a literary, dramatic or musical work the right is infringed by a person who—

(a) publishes commercially, performs in public, or communicates to the public a derogatory treatment of the work; or

(b) issues to the public copies of a film or sound recording of, or including, a derogatory treatment of the work.

(4) In the case of an artistic work the right is infringed by a person who—

(a) publishes commercially or exhibits in public a derogatory treatment of the work, or broadcasts or includes in a cable programme service a visual image of a derogatory treatment of the work,

(b) shows in public a film including a visual image of a derogatory treatment of the work or issues to the public copies of such a film, or

(c) in the case of—

(i) a work of architecture in the form of a model for a building,

(ii) a sculpture, or

(iii) a work of artistic craftsmanship,

(d) issues to the public copies of a graphic work representing, or of a photograph of, a derogatory treatment of the work.

(5) Subsection (4) does not apply to a work of architecture in the form of a building; but where the author of such a work is identified on the building and it is the subject of derogatory treatment he has the right to require the identification to be removed.

(6) In the case of a film, the right is infringed by a person who—

(a) shows in public, or communicates to the public a derogatory treatment of the film; or

(b) issues to the public copies of a derogatory treatment of the film.

(7) The right conferred by this section extends to the treatment of parts of a work resulting from a previous treatment by a person other than the author or director, if those parts are attributed to, or are likely to be regarded as the work of, the author or director.

(8) This section has effect subject to sections 81 and 82 (exceptions to and qualifications of right).

81   Exceptions to right

(1) The right conferred by section 80 (right to object to derogatory treatment of work) is subject to the following exceptions.

(2) The right does not apply to a computer program or to any computer-generated work.

(3) The right does not apply in relation to any work made for the purpose of reporting current events.

(4) The right does not apply in relation to the publication in—

(a) a newspaper, magazine or similar periodical, or

(b) an encyclopaedia, dictionary, yearbook or other collective work of reference,

of a literary, dramatic, musical or artistic work made for the purposes of such publication or made available with the consent of the author for the purposes of such publication. Nor does the right apply in relation to any subsequent exploitation elsewhere of such a work without any modification of the published version.

(5) The right is not infringed by an act which by virtue of section 57 or 66A (acts permitted on assumptions as to expiry of copyright, &c would not infringe copyright).

(6) The right is not infringed by anything done for the purpose of—

(a) avoiding the commission of an offence,

(b) complying with a duty imposed by or under an enactment, or

(c) in the case of the British Broadcasting Corporation, avoiding the inclusion in a programme broadcast by them of anything which offends against good taste or decency or which is likely to encourage or incite to crime or to lead to disorder or to be offensive to public feeling,

provided, where the author or director is identified at the time of the relevant act or has previously been identified in or on published copies of the work, that there is a sufficient disclaimer.

82 Qualification of right in certain cases

(1) This section applies to—

(a) works in which copyright originally vested in the author's or director's employer by virtue of section 11(2) (works produced in course of employment),

(b) works in which Crown copyright or Parliamentary copyright subsists, and

(c) works in which copyright originally vested in an international organisation by virtue of section 168.

(2) The right conferred by section 80 (right to object to derogatory treatment of work) does not apply to anything done in relation to such a work by or with the authority of the copyright owner unless the author or director—

(a) is identified at the time of the relevant act, or

(b) has previously been identified in or on published copies of the work;

and where in such a case the right does apply, it is not infringed if there is a sufficient disclaimer.

83 Infringement of right by possessing or dealing with infringing article

(1) The right conferred by section 80 (right to object to derogatory treatment of work) is also infringed by a person who—

(a) possesses in the course of a business, or

(b) sells or lets for hire, or offers or exposes for sale or hire, or

(c) in the course of a business exhibits in public or distributes, or

(d) distributes otherwise than in the course of a business so as to affect prejudicially the honour or reputation of the author or director,

an article which is, and which he knows or has reason to believe is, an infringing article.

(2) An 'infringing article' means a work or a copy of a work which—

(a) has been subjected to derogatory treatment within the meaning of section 80, and

(b) has been or is likely to be the subject of any of the acts mentioned in that section in circumstances infringing that right.

False attribution of work

84 False attribution of work

(1) A person has the right in the circumstances mentioned in this section—

(a) not to have a literary, dramatic, musical or artistic work falsely attributed to him as author, and

(b) not to have a film falsely attributed to him as director;

and in this section an 'attribution', in relation to such a work, means a statement (express or implied) as to who is the author or director.

(2) The right is infringed by a person who—

(a) issues to the public copies of a work of any of those descriptions in or on which there is a false attribution, or

(b) exhibits in public an artistic work, or a copy of an artistic work, in or on which there is a false attribution.

(3) The right is also infringed by a person who—

(a) in the case of a literary, dramatic or musical work, performs the work in public, broadcasts it or includes it in a cable programme service as being the work of a person, or

(b) in the case of a film, shows it in public, or communicates it to the public as being directed by a person, knowing or having reason to believe that the attribution is false.

(4) The right is also infringed by the issue to the public or public display of material containing a false attribution in connection with any of the acts mentioned in subsection (2) or (3).

(5) The right is also infringed by a person who in the course of a business—

(a) possesses or deals with a copy of a work of any of the descriptions mentioned in subsection (1) in or on which there is a false attribution, or

(b) in the case of an artistic work, possesses or deals with the work itself when there is a false attribution in or on it,

knowing or having reason to believe that there is such an attribution and that it is false.

(6) In the case of an artistic work the right is also infringed by a person who in the course of a business—

(a) deals with a work which has been altered after the author parted with possession of it as being the unaltered work of the author, or

(b) deals with a copy of such a work as being a copy of the unaltered work of the author,

knowing or having reason to believe that that is not the case.

(7) References in this section to dealing are to selling or letting for hire, offering or exposing for sale or hire, exhibiting in public, or distributing.

(8) This section applies where, contrary to the fact—

(a) a literary, dramatic or musical work is falsely represented as being an adaptation of the work of a person, or

(b) a copy of an artistic work is falsely represented as being a copy made by the author of the artistic work,

as it applies where the work is falsely attributed to a person as author.

Supplementary

86   Duration of rights

(1) The rights conferred by section 77 (right to be identified as author or director), section 80 (right to object to derogatory treatment of work) and section 85 (right to privacy of certain photographs and films) continue to subsist so long as copyright subsists in the work.

(2) The right conferred by section 84 (false attribution) continues to subsist until 20 years after a person's death.

87   Consent and waiver of rights

(1) It is not an infringement of any of the rights conferred by this Chapter to do any act to which the person entitled to the right has consented.

(2) Any of those rights may be waived by instrument in writing signed by the person giving up the right.

(3) A waiver—

(a) may relate to a specific work, to works of a specified description or to works generally, and may relate to existing or future works, and

(b) may be conditional or unconditional and may be expressed to be subject to revocation;

and if made in favour of the owner or prospective owner of the copyright in the work or works to which it relates, it shall be presumed to extend to his licensees and successors in title unless a contrary intention is expressed.

(4) Nothing in this Chapter shall be construed as excluding the operation of the general law of contract or estoppel in relation to an informal waiver or other transaction in relation to any of the rights mentioned in subsection (1).

88   Application of provisions to joint works

(1) The right conferred by section 77 (right to be identified as author or director) is, in the case of a work of joint authorship, a right of each joint author to be identified as a joint author and must be asserted in accordance with section 78 by each joint author in relation to himself.

(2) The right conferred by section 80 (right to object to derogatory treatment of work) is, in the case of a work of joint authorship, a right of each joint author and his right is satisfied if he consents to the treatment in question.

(3) A waiver under section 87 of those rights by one joint author does not affect the rights of the other joint authors.

(4) The right conferred by section 84 (false attribution) is infringed, in the circumstances mentioned in that section—

    (a) by any false statement as to the authorship of a work of joint authorship, and

    (b) by the false attribution of joint authorship in relation to a work of sole authorship;

and such a false attribution infringes the right of every person to whom authorship of any description is, whether rightly or wrongly, attributed.

(5) The above provisions also apply (with any necessary adaptations) in relation to a film which was, or is alleged to have been, jointly directed, as they apply to a work which is, or is alleged to be, a work of joint authorship.

A film is 'jointly directed' if it is made by the collaboration of two or more directors and the contribution of each director is not distinct from that of the other director or directors.

89   Application of provisions to parts of works

(1) The rights conferred by section 77 (right to be identified as author or director) and section 85 (right to privacy of certain photographs and films) apply in relation to the whole or any substantial part of a work.

(2) The rights conferred by section 80 (right to object to derogatory treatment of work) and section 84 (false attribution) apply in relation to the whole or any part of a work.

Remedies for infringement of moral rights

103   Remedies for infringement of moral rights

(1) An infringement of a right conferred by Chapter IV (moral rights) is actionable as a breach of statutory duty owed to the person entitled to the right.

(2) In proceedings for infringement of the right conferred by section 80 (right to object to derogatory treatment of work) the court may, if it thinks it is an adequate remedy in the circumstances, grant an injunction on terms prohibiting the doing of any act unless a disclaimer is made, in such terms and in such manner as may be approved by the court, dissociating the author or director from the treatment of the work.

Electronic Commerce (EC Directive) Regulations 2002

(SI 2002 No 2013)

2.   Interpretation

'information society services' (which is summarised in recital 17 of the Directive as covering 'any service normally provided for remuneration, at a distance, by means of electronic equipment for the processing (including digital compression) and storage of data, and at the individual request of a recipient of a service') has the meaning set out in Article 2(a) of the Directive, (which refers to Article 1(2) of Directive 98/34/EC of the European Parliament and of the Council of 22 June 1998 laying down a procedure for the provision of information in the field of technical standards and regulations, as amended by Directive 98/48/EC of 20 July 1998);

'recipient of the service' means any person who, for professional ends or otherwise, uses an information society service, in particular for the purposes of seeking information or making it accessible;

'service provider' means any person providing an information society service;

17.   Mere conduit

(1)   Where an information society service is provided which consists of the transmission in a communication network of information provided by a recipient of the service or the provision of access to a communication network, the service provider (if he otherwise would) shall not be liable for damages or for any other pecuniary remedy or for any criminal sanction as a result of that transmission where the service provider—

(a) did not initiate the transmission;

(b) did not select the receiver of the transmission; and

(c) did not select or modify the information contained in the transmission.

(2)   The acts of transmission and of provision of access referred to in paragraph (1) include the automatic, intermediate and transient storage of the information transmitted where:

(a) this takes place for the sole purpose of carrying out the transmission in the communication network, and

(b) the information is not stored for any period longer than is reasonably necessary for the transmission.

18.   Caching

Where an information society service is provided which consists of the transmission in a communication network of information provided by a recipient of the service, the service provider (if he otherwise would) shall not be liable for damages or for any other pecuniary remedy or for any criminal sanction as a result of that transmission where—

(a) the information is the subject of automatic, intermediate and temporary storage where that storage is for the sole purpose of making more efficient onward transmission of the information to other recipients of the service upon their request, and

(b) the service provider—

(i)   does not modify the information;

(ii) complies with conditions on access to the information;

(iii) complies with any rules regarding the updating of the information, specified in a manner widely recognised and used by industry;

(iv) does not interfere with the lawful use of technology, widely recognised and used by industry, to obtain data on the use of the information; and

(v)   acts expeditiously to remove or to disable access to the information he has stored upon obtaining actual knowledge of the fact that the information at the initial source of the transmission has been removed from the network, or access to it has been disabled, or that a court or an administrative authority has ordered such removal or disablement.

19.   Hosting

Where an information society service is provided which consists of the storage of information provided by a recipient of the service, the service provider (if he otherwise would) shall not be liable for damages or for any other pecuniary remedy or for any criminal sanction as a result of that storage where—

(a) the service provider—

(i)   does not have actual knowledge of unlawful activity or information and, where a claim for damages is made, is not aware of facts or circumstances from which it would have been apparent to the service provider that the activity or information was unlawful; or

(ii) upon obtaining such knowledge or awareness, acts expeditiously to remove or to disable access to the information, and

(b) the recipient of the service was not acting under the authority or the control of the service provider.

20. Protection of rights

(1) Nothing in regulations 17, 18 and 19 shall—

 (a) prevent a person agreeing different contractual terms; or

 (b) affect the rights of any party to apply to a court for relief to prevent or stop infringement of any rights.

(2) Any power of an administrative authority to prevent or stop infringement of any rights shall continue to apply notwithstanding regulations 17, 18 and 19.

Part III

Reporting restrictions

Children and Young Persons Act 1933

(1933, c. 12)

PART III PROTECTION OF CHILDREN AND YOUNG PERSONS IN RELATION TO CRIMINAL AND SUMMARY PROCEEDINGS

General provisions as to proceedings in court

39 Power to prohibit publication of certain matter in newspapers

(1) In relation to any proceedings in any court [...] the court may direct that—

(a) no newspaper report of the proceedings shall reveal the name, address, or school, or include any particulars calculated to lead to the identification, of any child or young person concerned in the proceedings, either as being the person by or against or in respect of whom the proceedings are taken, or as being a witness therein;

(b) no picture shall be published in any newspaper as being or including a picture of any child or young person so concerned in the proceedings as aforesaid;

except in so far (if at all) as may be permitted by the direction of the court.

(2) Any person who publishes any matter in contravention of any such direction shall on summary conviction be liable in respect of each offence to a fine not exceeding level 5 on the standard scale.

[(2A) Nothing in this section applies in relation to proceedings to which section 11 of the Children, Schools and Families Act 2010 (restriction on publication of information relating to family proceedings) applies.]

[(3) In this section 'proceedings' means proceedings other than criminal proceedings.]

49 Restrictions on reports of proceedings in which children or young persons are concerned

(1) The following prohibitions apply (subject to subsection (5) below) in relation to any proceedings to which this section applies, that is to say—

(a) no report shall be published which reveals the name, address or school of any child or young person concerned in the proceedings or includes any particulars likely to lead to the identification of any child or young person concerned in the proceedings; and

(b) no picture shall be published or included in a programme service as being or including a picture of any child or young person concerned in the proceedings.

(2) The proceedings to which this section applies are—
- (a) proceedings in a youth court;
- (b) proceedings on appeal from a youth court (including proceedings by way of case stated);
- (c) proceedings in a magistrates' court under Schedule 2 to the Criminal Justice and Immigration Act 2008 (proceedings for breach, revocation or amendment of youth rehabilitation orders); and
- (d) proceedings on appeal from a magistrates' court arising out of proceedings mentioned in paragraph (c) (including proceedings by way of case stated).

(3) The reports to which this section applies are reports in a newspaper and reports included in a programme service; and similarly as respects pictures.

(3A) The matters relating to a person in relation to which the restrictions imposed by subsection (1) above apply (if their inclusion in any publication is likely to have the result mentioned in that subsection) include in particular—
- (a) his name,
- (b) his address,
- (c) the identity of any school or other educational establishment attended by him,
- (d) the identity of any place of work, and
- (e) any still or moving picture of him.

(4) For the purposes of this section a child or young person is 'concerned' in any proceedings whether as being the person against or in respect of whom the proceedings are taken or as being a witness in the proceedings if he is—
- (a) a person against or in respect of whom the proceedings are taken, or
- (b) a person called, or proposed to be called, to give evidence in the proceedings.

(4A) If a court is satisfied that it is in the public interest to do so, it may, in relation to a child or young person who has been convicted of an offence, by order dispense to any specified extent with the requirements of this section [restrictions imposed by subsection (1) above in relation to any proceedings before it to which this section applies by virtue of subsection (2)(a) or above, being proceedings relating to—
- (a) the prosecution or conviction of the offender for the offence;
- (b) the manner in which he, or his parent or guardian, should be dealt with in respect of the offence;
- (c) the enforcement, amendment, variation, revocation or discharge of any order made in respect of the offence;
- (d) where an attendance centre order is made in respect of the offence, the enforcement of any rules made under section 222(1)(d) or (e) of the Criminal Justice Act 2003; or
- (e) where a detention and training order is made, the enforcement of any requirements imposed under section 103(6)(b) of the Powers of Criminal Courts (Sentencing) Act 2000.

(4B) A court shall not exercise its power under subsection (4A) above without—
- (a) affording the parties to the proceedings an opportunity to make representations; and
- (b) taking into account any representations which are duly made.

(5) Subject to subsection (7) below, a court may, in relation to proceedings before it to which this section applies, by order dispense to any specified extent with the requirements of this section in relation to a child or young person who is concerned in the proceedings if it is satisfied—
- (a) that it is appropriate to do so for the purpose of avoiding injustice to the child or young person; or
- (b) that, as respects a child or young person to whom this paragraph applies who is unlawfully at large, it is necessary to dispense with those requirements for the purpose of apprehending him and bringing him before a court or returning him to the place in which he was in custody.

(6) Paragraph (b) of subsection (5) above applies to any child or young person who is charged with or has been convicted of—

(a) a violent offence,

(b) a sexual offence, or

(c) an offence punishable in the case of a person aged [18] or over with imprisonment for fourteen years or more.

(7) The court shall not exercise its power under subsection (5)(b) above—

(a) except in pursuance of an application by or on behalf of the Director of Public Prosecutions; and

(b) unless notice of the application has been given by the Director of Public Prosecutions to any legal representative of the child or young person.

(8) The court's power under subsection [(4A) or (5)] above may be exercised by a single justice.

(9) If a report or picture is published or included in a programme service in contravention of subsection (1) above, the following persons, that is to say—

(a) in the case of publication of a written report or a picture as part of a newspaper, any proprietor, editor or publisher of the newspaper;

(b) in the case of the inclusion of a report or picture in a programme service, any body corporate which provides the service and any person having functions in relation to the programme corresponding to those of an editor of a newspaper,

shall be liable on summary conviction to a fine not exceeding level 5 on the standard scale.

(9) If a publication includes any matter in contravention of subsection (1) above, the following persons shall be guilty of an offence and liable on summary conviction to a fine not exceeding level 5 on the standard scale—

(a) where the publication is a newspaper or periodical, any proprietor, any editor and any publisher of the newspaper or periodical;

(b) where the publication is a relevant programme—

(i) any body corporate or Scottish partnership engaged in providing the programme service in which the programme is included; and

(ii) any person having functions in relation to the programme corresponding to those of an editor of a newspaper;

(c) in the case of any other publication, any person publishing it.

[(9A) Where a person is charged with an offence under subsection (9) above it shall be a defence to prove that at the time of the alleged offence he was not aware, and neither suspected nor had reason to suspect, that the publication included the matter in question.

(9B) If an offence under subsection (9) above committed by a body corporate is proved—

(a) to have been committed with the consent or connivance of, or

(b) to be attributable to any neglect on the part of, an officer,

the officer as well as the body corporate is guilty of the offence and liable to be proceeded against and punished accordingly.

(9C) In subsection (9B) above 'officer' means a director, manager, secretary or other similar officer of the body, or a person purporting to act in any such capacity.

(9D) If the affairs of a body corporate are managed by its members, 'director' in subsection (9C) above means a member of that body.

(9E) Where an offence under subsection (9) above is committed by a Scottish partnership and is proved to have been committed with the consent or connivance of a partner, he as well as the partnership shall be guilty of the offence and shall be liable to be proceeded against and punished accordingly.]

(10) In any proceedings under Schedule 2 to the Criminal Justice and Immigration Act 2008 (proceedings for breach, revocation or amendment of youth rehabilitation orders) before a magistrates' court other than a youth court or on appeal from such a court it shall be the duty of the magistrates' court or the appellate court to announce in the course of the proceedings that this section applies to the proceedings; and if the court fails to do so this section shall not apply to the proceedings.

(11) In this section—

'programme' and 'programme service' have the same meaning as in the Broadcasting Act 1990;

['picture' includes a likeness however produced;

'relevant programme' means a programme included in a programme service, within the meaning of the Broadcasting Act 1990;]

'sexual offence' means an offence listed in Part 2 of Schedule 15 to the Criminal Justice Act 2003;

'specified' means specified in an order under this section;

'violent offence' means an offence listed in Part 1 of Schedule 15 to the Criminal Justice Act 2003;

and a person who, having been granted bail, is liable to arrest (whether with or without a warrant) shall be treated as unlawfully at large.

[(12) This section extends to England and Wales, Scotland and Northern Ireland, but no reference in this section to any court includes a court in Scotland.

(13) In its application to Northern Ireland, this section has effect as if—

(a) in subsection (1) for the reference to the age of 18 there were substituted a reference to the age of 17;

(b) subsection (2)(c) and (d) were omitted;

(c) in subsection (4A)—

(i) in paragraph (d) for the reference to section 62(3) of the Powers of Criminal Courts (Sentencing) Act 2000 there were substituted a reference to Article 50(3) of the Criminal Justice (Children) (Northern Ireland) Order 1998; and

(ii) in paragraph (e) for the references to a detention and training order and to section 103(6)(b) of the Powers of Criminal Courts (Sentencing) Act 2000 there were substituted references to a juvenile justice centre order and to Article 40(2) of the Criminal Justice (Children) (Northern Ireland) Order 1998;

(d) in subsection (5) for references to a court (other than the reference in paragraph (b)) there were substituted references to a court or the Secretary of State;

(e) in subsection (7)—

(i) for the references to the Director of Public Prosecutions there were substituted references to the Director of Public Prosecutions for Northern Ireland; and

(ii) in paragraph (b) for the reference to any legal representative of the child or young person there were substituted a reference to any barrister or solicitor acting for the child or young person;

(f) subsections (8) and (10) were omitted; and

(g) in subsection (11)—

(i) the definition of 'legal representative' were omitted; and

(ii) for the references to the Powers of Criminal Courts (Sentencing) Act 2000 there were substituted references to Article 2(2) of the Criminal Justice (Northern Ireland) Order 1996.

(14) References in this section to a young person concerned in proceedings are, where the proceedings are in a court in Northern Ireland, to a person who has attained the age of 14 but is under the age of 17.]

Youth Justice and Criminal Evidence Act 1999

(1999, c. 23)

Chapter IV Reporting Restrictions

Reports relating to persons under 18

44 Restrictions on reporting alleged offences involving persons under 18

(1) This section applies (subject to subsection (3)) where a criminal investigation has begun in respect of—

(a) an alleged offence against the law of—

(i) England and Wales, or

(ii)   Northern Ireland; or
(b) an alleged civil offence (other than an offence falling within paragraph (a)) committed (whether or not in the United Kingdom) by a person subject to service law.

(2) No matter relating to any person involved in the offence shall while he is under the age of 18 be included in any publication if it is likely to lead members of the public to identify him as a person involved in the offence.

(3) The restrictions imposed by subsection (2) cease to apply once there are proceedings in a court (whether a court in England and Wales, a service court or a court in Northern Ireland) in respect of the offence.

(4) For the purposes of subsection (2) any reference to a person involved in the offence is to—
(a) a person by whom the offence is alleged to have been committed; or
(b) if this paragraph applies to the publication in question by virtue of subsection (5)—
(i)   a person against or in respect of whom the offence is alleged to have been committed, or
(ii)   a person who is alleged to have been a witness to the commission of the offence;
except that paragraph (b)(i) does not include a person in relation to whom section 1 of the Sexual Offences (Amendment) Act 1992 (anonymity of victims of certain sexual offences) applies in connection with the offence.

(5) Subsection (4)(b) applies to a publication if—
(a) where it is a relevant programme, it is transmitted, or
(b) in the case of any other publication, it is published,
on or after such date as may be specified in an order made by the Secretary of State.

(5A) In the application of this section to Northern Ireland, the reference in subsection (5) to the Secretary of State shall be construed as a reference to the Department of Justice in Northern Ireland.

(6) The matters relating to a person in relation to which the restrictions imposed by subsection (2) apply (if their inclusion in any publication is likely to have the result mentioned in that subsection) include in particular—
(a) his name,
(b) his address,
(c) the identity of any school or other educational establishment attended by him,
(d) the identity of any place of work, and
(e) any still or moving picture of him.

(7) Any appropriate criminal court may by order dispense, to any extent specified in the order, with the restrictions imposed by subsection (2) in relation to a person if it is satisfied that it is necessary in the interests of justice to do so.

(8) However, when deciding whether to make such an order dispensing (to any extent) with the restrictions imposed by subsection (2) in relation to a person, the court shall have regard to the welfare of that person.

(9) In subsection (7) 'appropriate criminal court' means—
(a) in a case where this section applies by virtue of subsection (1)(a)(i) or (ii), any court in England and Wales or (as the case may be) in Northern Ireland which has any jurisdiction in, or in relation to, any criminal proceedings (but not a service court unless the offence is alleged to have been committed by a person subject to service law);
(b) in a case where this section applies by virtue of subsection (1)(b), any court falling within paragraph (a) or a service court.

(10) The power under subsection (7) of a magistrate's court in England and Wales may be exercised by a single justice.

(11) In the case of a decision of a magistrate's court in England and Wales, or a court of summary jurisdiction in Northern Ireland, to make or refuse to make an order under subsection (7), the following persons, namely—

(a) any person who was a party to the proceedings on the application for the order, and

(b) with the leave of the Crown Court [, or in Northern Ireland a county court], any other person, may, in accordance with [Criminal Procedure Rules in England and Wales, or rules of court in Northern Ireland,] appeal to the Crown Court[, or in Northern Ireland a county court,] against that decision or appear or be represented at the hearing of such an appeal.

(12) On such an appeal the Crown Court [, or in Northern Ireland a county court]—

(a) may make such order as is necessary to give effect to its determination of the appeal; and

(b) may also make such incidental or consequential orders as appear to it to be just.

(13) In this section—

(a) 'civil offence' means an act or omission which, if committed in England and Wales, would be an offence against the law of England and Wales;

(b) any reference to a criminal investigation, in relation to an alleged offence, is to an investigation conducted by police officers, or other persons charged with the duty of investigating offences, with a view to it being ascertained whether a person should be charged with the offence;

(c) any reference to a person subject to service law is to—

(i) [a person subject to service law within the meaning of the Armed Forces Act 2006; or

(ii) a civilian subject to service discipline within the meaning of that Act.]

45 Power to restrict reporting of criminal proceedings involving persons under 18

(1) This section applies (subject to subsection (2)) in relation to—

(a) any criminal proceedings in any court (other than a service court) in England and Wales or Northern Ireland; and

(b) any proceedings (whether in the United Kingdom or elsewhere) in any service court.

(2) This section does not apply in relation to any proceedings to which section 49 of the Children and Young Persons Act 1933 applies.

(3) [The magistrate] may direct that no matter relating to any person concerned in the proceedings shall while he is under the age of 18 be included in any publication if it is likely to lead members of the public to identify him as a person concerned in the proceedings.

(4) [The magistrate] or an appellate court may by direction ('an excepting direction') dispense, to any extent specified in the excepting direction, with the restrictions imposed by a direction under subsection (3) if it is satisfied that it is necessary in the interests of justice to do so.

(5) [The magistrate] or an appellate court may also by direction ('an excepting direction') dispense, to any extent specified in the excepting direction, with the restrictions imposed by a direction under subsection (3) if it is satisfied—

(a) that their effect is to impose a substantial and unreasonable restriction on the reporting of the proceedings, and

(b) that it is in the public interest to remove or relax that restriction;

but no excepting direction shall be given under this subsection by reason only of the fact that the proceedings have been determined in any way or have been abandoned.

(6) When deciding whether to make—

(a) a direction under subsection (3) in relation to a person, or

(b) an excepting direction under subsection (4) or (5) by virtue of which the restrictions imposed by a direction under subsection (3) would be dispensed with (to any extent) in relation to a person,

[the magistrate] or (as the case may be) the appellate court shall have regard to the welfare of that person.

(7) For the purposes of subsection (3) any reference to a person concerned in the proceedings is to a person—

(a) against or in respect of whom the proceedings are taken, or

(b) who is a witness in the proceedings.

(8) The matters relating to a person in relation to which the restrictions imposed by a direction under subsection (3) apply (if their inclusion in any publication is likely to have the result mentioned in that subsection) include in particular—

(a) his name,

(b) his address,

(c) the identity of any school or other educational establishment attended by him,

(d) the identity of any place of work, and

(e) any still or moving picture of him.

(9) A direction under subsection (3) may be revoked by [the magistrate]or an appellate court.

(10) An excepting direction—

(a) may be given at the time the direction under subsection (3) is given or subsequently; and

(b) may be varied or revoked by[the magistrate] or an appellate court.

(11) In this section 'appellate court', in relation to any proceedings in a court, means a court dealing with an appeal (including an appeal by way of case stated) arising out of the proceedings or with any further appeal.

Reports relating to adult witnesses

46   Power to restrict reports about certain adult witnesses in criminal proceedings

(1) This section applies where—

(a) in any criminal proceedings in any court (other than a service court) in England and Wales or Northern Ireland, or

(b) in any proceedings (whether in the United Kingdom or elsewhere) in any service court,

a party to the proceedings makes an application for the court to give a reporting direction in relation to a witness in the proceedings (other than the accused) who has attained the age of 18. In this section 'reporting direction' has the meaning given by subsection (6).

(2) If the[magistrate] determines—

(a) that the witness is eligible for protection, and

(b) that giving a reporting direction in relation to the witness is likely to improve—

(i)   the quality of evidence given by the witness, or

(ii)   the level of co-operation given by the witness to any party to the proceedings in connection with that party's preparation of its case,

the [magistrate] may give a reporting direction in relation to the witness.

(3) For the purposes of this section a witness is eligible for protection if the [magistrate]is satisfied—

(a) that the quality of evidence given by the witness, or

(b) the level of co-operation given by the witness to any party to the proceedings in connection with that party's preparation of its case,

is likely to be diminished by reason of fear or distress on the part of the witness in connection with being identified by members of the public as a witness in the proceedings.

(4) In determining whether a witness is eligible for protection the [magistrate] must take into account, in particular—

(a) the nature and alleged circumstances of the offence to which the proceedings relate;

(b) the age of the witness;

(c) such of the following matters as appear to the [magistrate]to be relevant, namely—

(i)   the social and cultural background and ethnic origins of the witness,

(ii)   the domestic and employment circumstances of the witness, and

(iii) any religious beliefs or political opinions of the witness;

    (d) any behaviour towards the witness on the part of—
        (i) the accused,
        (ii) members of the family or associates of the accused, or
        (iii) any other person who is likely to be an accused or a witness in the proceedings.

(5) In determining that question the [magistrate]must in addition consider any views expressed by the witness.

(6) For the purposes of this section a reporting direction in relation to a witness is a direction that no matter relating to the witness shall during the witness's lifetime be included in any publication if it is likely to lead members of the public to identify him as being a witness in the proceedings.

(7) The matters relating to a witness in relation to which the restrictions imposed by a reporting direction apply (if their inclusion in any publication is likely to have the result mentioned in subsection (6)) include in particular—
    (a) the witness's name,
    (b) the witness's address,
    (c) the identity of any educational establishment attended by the witness,
    (d) the identity of any place of work, and
    (e) any still or moving picture of the witness.

(8) In determining whether to give a reporting direction the[magistrate] shall consider—
    (a) whether it would be in the interests of justice to do so, and
    (b) the public interest in avoiding the imposition of a substantial and unreasonable restriction on the reporting of the proceedings.

(9) The [magistrate or an appellate court] may by direction ('an excepting direction') dispense, to any extent specified in the excepting direction, with the restrictions imposed by a reporting direction if—
    (a) it is satisfied that it is necessary in the interests of justice to do so, or
    (b) it is satisfied—
        (i) that the effect of those restrictions is to impose a substantial and unreasonable restriction on the reporting of the proceedings, and
        (ii) that it is in the public interest to remove or relax that restriction;
but no excepting direction shall be given under paragraph (b) by reason only of the fact that the proceedings have been determined in any way or have been abandoned.

(10) A reporting direction may be revoked by the [magistrate or an appellate court].

(11) An excepting direction—
    (a) may be given at the time the reporting direction is given or subsequently; and
    (b) may be varied or revoked by the [magistrate or an appellate court].

(12) In this section—
    (a) 'appellate court', in relation to any proceedings in a court, means a court dealing with an appeal (including an appeal by way of case stated) arising out of the proceedings or with any further appeal;
    (b) references to the quality of a witness's evidence are to its quality in terms of completeness, coherence and accuracy (and for this purpose 'coherence' refers to a witness's ability in giving evidence to give answers which address the questions put to the witness and can be understood both individually and collectively);
    (c) references to the preparation of the case of a party to any proceedings include, where the party is the prosecution, the carrying out of investigations into any offence at any time charged in the proceedings.

Reports relating to directions under Chapter I or II

47 Restrictions on reporting directions under [Chapter 1, 1A or 2]

(1) Except as provided by this section, no publication shall include a report of a matter falling within subsection (2).

(2) The matters falling within this subsection are—
    (a) a direction under section 19,[33a], or 36 or an order discharging, or (in the case of a direction under section 19) varying, such a direction;

(b) proceedings—
 (i)   on an application for such a direction or order, or
 (ii) where the [magistrate acts of his] own motion to determine whether to give or make
       any such direction or order.

(3) The [magistrate] dealing with a matter falling within subsection (2) may order that subsection (1) is not to apply, or is not to apply to a specified extent, to a report of that matter.

(4) Where—
 (a) there is only one accused in the relevant proceedings, and
 (b) he objects to the making of an order under subsection (3),
the [magistrate] shall make the order if (and only if) satisfied after hearing the representations of the accused that it is in the interests of justice to do so; and if the order is made it shall not apply to the extent that a report deals with any such objections or representations.

(5) Where—
 (a) there are two or more accused in the relevant proceedings, and
 (b) one or more of them object to the making of an order under subsection (3),
the [magistrate] shall make the order if (and only if) satisfied after hearing the representations of each of the accused that it is in the interests of justice to do so; and if the order is made it shall not apply to the extent that a report deals with any such objections or representations.

(6) Subsection (1) does not apply to the inclusion in a publication of a report of matters after the relevant proceedings are either—
 (a) determined (by acquittal, conviction or otherwise), or
 (b) abandoned,
in relation to the accused or (if there is more than one) in relation to each of the accused.

(7) In this section 'the relevant proceedings' means the proceedings to which any such direction as is mentioned in subsection (2) relates or would relate.

(8) Nothing in this section affects any prohibition or restriction by virtue of any other enactment on the inclusion of matter in a publication.

Other restrictions

48   Amendments relating to other reporting restrictions
Schedule 2, which contains amendments relating to reporting restrictions under—
 (a) the Children and Young Persons Act 1933,
 (b) the Sexual Offences (Amendment) Act 1976,
 (c) the Sexual Offences (Northern Ireland) Order 1978,
 (d) the Sexual Offences (Amendment) Act 1992, and
 (e) the Criminal Justice (Northern Ireland) Order 1994,
shall have effect.

Offences

49   Offences under Chapter IV
(1) This section applies if a publication—
 (a) includes any matter in contravention of section 44(2) or of a direction under section 45(3) or 46(2); or
 (b) includes a report in contravention of section 47.

(2) Where the publication is a newspaper or periodical, any proprietor, any editor and any publisher of the newspaper or periodical is guilty of an offence.

(3) Where the publication is a relevant programme—
 (a) any body corporate or Scottish partnership engaged in providing the programme service in which the programme is included, and
 (b) any person having functions in relation to the programme corresponding to those of an editor of a newspaper,
is guilty of an offence.

(4) In the case of any other publication, any person publishing it is guilty of an offence.

(5) A person guilty of an offence under this section is liable on summary conviction to a fine not exceeding level 5 on the standard scale.

(6) Proceedings for an offence under this section in respect of a publication falling within subsection (1)(b) may not be instituted—

(a) in England and Wales otherwise than by or with the consent of the Attorney General, or

(b) in Northern Ireland otherwise than by or with the consent of the Attorney General for Northern Ireland.

50 Defences

(1) Where a person is charged with an offence under section 49 it shall be a defence to prove that at the time of the alleged offence he was not aware, and neither suspected nor had reason to suspect, that the publication included the matter or report in question.

(2) Where—

(a) a person is charged with an offence under section 49, and

(b) the offence relates to the inclusion of any matter in a publication in contravention of section 44(2),

it shall be a defence to prove that at the time of the alleged offence he was not aware, and neither suspected nor had reason to suspect, that the criminal investigation in question had begun.

(3) Where—

(a) paragraphs (a) and (b) of subsection (2) apply, and

(b) the contravention of section 44(2) does not relate to either—

(i) the person by whom the offence mentioned in that provision is alleged to have been committed, or

(ii) (where that offence is one in relation to which section 1 of the Sexual Offences (Amendment) Act 1992 applies) a person who is alleged to be a witness to the commission of the offence,

it shall be a defence to show to the satisfaction of the court that the inclusion in the publication of the matter in question was in the public interest on the ground that, to the extent that they operated to prevent that matter from being so included, the effect of the restrictions imposed by section 44(2) was to impose a substantial and unreasonable restriction on the reporting of matters connected with that offence.

(4) Subsection (5) applies where—

(a) paragraphs (a) and (b) of subsection (2) apply, and

(b) the contravention of section 44(2) relates to a person ('the protected person') who is neither—

(i) the person mentioned in subsection (3)(b)(i), nor

(ii) a person within subsection (3)(b)(ii) who is under the age of 16.

(5) In such a case it shall be a defence, subject to subsection (6), to prove that written consent to the inclusion of the matter in question in the publication had been given—

(a) by an appropriate person, if at the time when the consent was given the protected person was under the age of 16, or

(b) by the protected person, if that person was aged 16 or 17 at that time,

and (where the consent was given by an appropriate person) that written notice had been previously given to that person drawing to his attention the need to consider the welfare of the protected person when deciding whether to give consent.

(6) The defence provided by subsection (5) is not available if—

(a) (where the consent was given by an appropriate person) it is proved that written or other notice withdrawing the consent—

(i) was given to the appropriate recipient by any other appropriate person or by the protected person, and

(ii) was so given in sufficient time to enable the inclusion in the publication of the matter in question to be prevented; or

(b) subsection (8) applies.

(7) Where—

(a) a person is charged with an offence under section 49, and

(b) the offence relates to the inclusion of any matter in a publication in contravention of a direction under section 46(2),

it shall be a defence, unless subsection (8) applies, to prove that the person in relation to whom the direction was given had given written consent to the inclusion of that matter in the publication.

(8) Written consent is not a defence if it is proved that any person interfered—

(a) with the peace or comfort of the person giving the consent, or

(b) (where the consent was given by an appropriate person) with the peace or comfort of either that person or the protected person,

with intent to obtain the consent.

(9) In this section—

'an appropriate person' means (subject to subsections (10) to (12))—

(a) in England and Wales or Northern Ireland, a person who is a parent or guardian of the protected person, or

(b) in Scotland, a person who has parental responsibilities (within the meaning of section 1(3) of the Children (Scotland) Act 1995) in relation to the protected person;

'guardian', in relation to the protected person, means any person who is not a parent of the protected person but who has parental responsibility for the protected person within the meaning of—

(a) (in England and Wales) the Children Act 1989, or

(b) (in Northern Ireland) the Children (Northern Ireland) Order 1995.

(10) Where the protected person is (within the meaning of the Children Act 1989) a child who is looked after by a local authority, 'an appropriate person' means a person who is—

(a) a representative of that authority, or

(b) a parent or guardian of the protected person with whom the protected person is allowed to live.

(11) Where the protected person is (within the meaning of the Children (Northern Ireland) Order 1995) a child who is looked after by an authority, 'an appropriate person' means a person who is—

(a) an officer of that authority, or

(b) a parent or guardian of the protected person with whom the protected person is allowed to live.

(12) Where the protected person is (within the meaning of section 17(6) of the Children (Scotland) Act 1995) a child who is looked after by a local authority, 'an appropriate person' means a person who is—

(a) a representative of that authority, or

(b) a person who has parental responsibilities (within the meaning of section 1(3) of that Act) in relation to the protected person and with whom the protected person is allowed to live.

(13) However, no person by whom the offence mentioned in section 44(2) is alleged to have been committed is, by virtue of subsections (9) to (12), an appropriate person for the purposes of this section.

(14) In this section 'the appropriate recipient', in relation to a notice under subsection (6)(a), means—

(a) the person to whom the notice giving consent was given,

(b) (if different) the person by whom the matter in question was published, or

(c) any other person exercising, on behalf of the person mentioned in paragraph (b), any responsibility in relation to the publication of that matter;

and for this purpose 'person' includes a body of persons and a partnership.

Supplementary

52 Decisions as to public interest for purposes of Chapter IV

(1) Where for the purposes of any provision of this Chapter it falls to a [magistrate] to determine whether anything is (or, as the case may be, was) in the public interest, the [magistrate] must have regard, in particular, to the matters referred to in subsection (2) (so far as relevant).

(2) Those matters are—

(a) the interest in each of the following—

(i) the open reporting of crime,

(ii) the open reporting of matters relating to human health or safety, and

(iii) the prevention and exposure of miscarriages of justice;

(b) the welfare of any person in relation to whom the relevant restrictions imposed by or under this Chapter apply or would apply (or, as the case may be, applied); and

(c) any views expressed—

(i) by an appropriate person on behalf of a person within paragraph (b) who is under the age of 16 ('the protected person'), or

(ii) by a person within that paragraph who has attained that age.

(3) In subsection (2) 'an appropriate person', in relation to the protected person, has the same meaning as it has for the purposes of section 50.

Children Act 1989

(1989, c. 41)

97 Privacy for children involved in certain proceedings

(1) [Family Procedure Rules] may make provision for a magistrates' court to sit in private in proceedings in which any powers under this Act [or the Adoption and Children Act 2002] may be exercised by the court with respect to any child.

[...]

Children, Schools and Families Act 2010

(2010, c. 26)

PART 2   FAMILY PROCEEDINGS

11 Restriction on publication of information relating to family proceedings

(1) This section applies in relation to any relevant family proceedings at which the public are not (or, in the case of proceedings which have already taken place, were not) entitled to be present.

(2) The publication of information relating to the proceedings is a contempt of court committed by the publisher unless the publication of the information is—

(a) an authorised publication of the text, or a summary, of the whole or part of an order made or judgment given by the court in the proceedings (see section 12),

(b) an authorised news publication (see section 13), or

(c) authorised by rules of court.

(3) Nothing in this section makes it a contempt of court to publish information with the permission of the court.

(4) 'Family proceedings' means family proceedings within the meaning of —

(a) section 65 of the Magistrates' Courts Act 1980, or

(b) section 32 of the Matrimonial and Family Proceedings Act 1984.

(5) Where proceedings are family proceedings at the time they are commenced and, but for this subsection, would later cease to be family proceedings, for the purposes of this section they continue to be family proceedings.

(6) 'Relevant family proceedings' means family proceedings other than—

    (a) matrimonial causes and matters;

    (b) applications under Part 3 of the Family Law Act 1986 (declarations of status);

    (c) applications under section 27 of the Matrimonial Causes Act 1973 (financial provision where failure to maintain);

    (d) civil partnership causes and matters;

    (e) applications under section 58 of the Civil Partnership Act 2004 (declarations relating to civil partnerships);

    (f) applications under Part 9 of Schedule 5 to that Act (financial provision where failure to maintain);

    (g) causes and matters relating to non-contentious or common form probate business (within the meaning of section 128 of the Senior Courts Act 1981).

(7) The Lord Chancellor may, by order made by statutory instrument, amend the definition of 'relevant family proceedings' in subsection (6).

(8) An order under subsection (7) may make transitional provision or savings.

(9) A statutory instrument containing an order under subsection (7) may not be made unless a draft of the instrument containing the order has been laid before, and approved by a resolution of, each House of Parliament.

12 Authorised publication of court orders and judgments

(1) A publication of the text, or a summary, of the whole or part of an order made by a court in the proceedings is an authorised publication—

    (a) in a case where the proceedings are adoption proceedings or parental order proceedings or a case where the publication of the text or summary contains identification information relating to an individual involved in the proceedings, to the extent that the publication of the text or summary is permitted by the court for the purposes of this section, and

    (b) in any other case, to the extent that the publication of the text or summary is not prohibited by, and does not breach any restriction imposed by, the court for the purposes of this section.

(2) A publication of the text, or a summary, of the whole or part of a judgment given by a court in the proceedings is an authorised publication to the extent that the publication of the text or summary is permitted by the court for the purposes of this section.

(3) The court may permit, prohibit or restrict publication for the purposes of this section on its own initiative or on the application of any interested person.

(4) The court may permit publication for the purposes of this section subject to conditions specified by the court.

(5) In this section—

'adoption proceedings' means proceedings under the Adoption and Children Act 2002 (other than proceedings on an application for a placement order under section 22 of that Act);

'parental order proceedings' means proceedings for parental orders under section 30 of the Human Fertilisation and Embryology Act 1990 or section 54 of the Human Fertilisation and Embryology Act 2008.

13 Authorised news publications

(1) A publication of information is an authorised news publication if the following conditions are met.

(2) Condition 1 is that the information was obtained by an accredited news representative by observing or listening to the proceedings when attending them in exercise of a right conferred on accredited news representatives by rules of court.

(3) Condition 2 is that the publisher of the information—

(a) is the accredited news representative,

(b) publishes the information with the consent of, or pursuant to a contract or other agreement entered into with, that representative, or

(c) has obtained the information from a publication of information which is an authorised news publication.

(4) Condition 3 is that —

(a) the information is not—

(i) identification information relating to an individual involved in the proceedings,

(ii) [...], or

(iii) restricted adoption information or restricted parental order information,

(b) the information is information within paragraphs (i) to (iii) of paragraph (a) and the publication is permitted by the court for the purposes of this Condition, or

(c) the information is identification information relating to an individual involved in the proceedings (but not restricted adoption information or restricted parental order information) and the individual is a professional witness in the proceedings.

(5) Condition 4 is that if the publication is—

(a) a publication of the text, or a summary, of an order made by a court in adoption proceedings or parental order proceedings, or

(b) a publication of the text, or a summary, of a judgment given by a court in relevant family proceedings, the publication is permitted by the court for the purposes of section 12.

(6) Condition 5 is that the publication is not prohibited by, and does not breach any restriction imposed by, the court for the purposes of this condition or section 12.

(7) The court may permit the publication of information for the purposes of Condition 3 or prohibit or restrict the publication of information for the purposes of Condition 5 on its own initiative or on the application of any interested person.

14 Permitting publication for purposes of section 13: general

(1) This section applies where the court is determining whether to permit the publication of information for the purposes of Condition 3 in section 13 (except where section 15 applies).

(2) The court may not permit the publication of the information unless it is satisfied of one or more of the following matters.

(3) The matters are—

(a) that it is in the public interest to give the permission;

(b) that it is appropriate to give the permission so as to avoid injustice to a person involved in, referred to in or otherwise connected with the proceedings;

(c) that it is necessary to give the permission in the interests of the welfare of a child or vulnerable adult involved in, referred to in or otherwise connected with the proceedings;

(d) that an application for permission has been made by a party to the proceedings, or on behalf of a child who is the subject of the proceedings, and granting the permission is appropriate in all the circumstances.

(4) The court must have regard to any risk which publication of the information would pose to the safety or welfare of any individual involved in, referred to in or otherwise connected with the proceedings.

(5) The court may permit the publication subject to conditions specified by the court.

15 Permitting publication for purposes of section 13: adoption etc.

(1) This section applies where the court is determining whether to permit the publication of restricted adoption information or restricted parental order information for the purposes of Condition 3 in section 13.

(2) 'Restricted adoption information' means information the publication of which is likely to lead one or more persons—

    (a) to identify a person as—
        (i)   a prospective adopter of a child,
        (ii) a person who has adopted a child, or
        (iii) a person who has been, or may be, adopted, or
    (b) to identify the whereabouts of a person identified as a person within sub-paragraph (i),
        (ii) or (iii) of paragraph (a).

(3) 'Restricted parental order information' means information the publication of which is likely to lead one or more persons—
    (a) to identify a person as—
        (i)   a person who has applied for a parental order,
        (ii) a person in respect of whom a parental order has been made, or
        (iii) a child in relation to whom a parental order has been, or may be, made, or
    (b) to identify the whereabouts of a person identified as a person within sub-paragraph (i),
        (ii) or (iii) of paragraph (a).

(4) If the person who has been or may be adopted or in relation to whom a parental order has been or may be made ('the affected person')—
    (a) is a child,
    (b) lacks capacity to consent to the publication, or
    (c) cannot be found,
the court may not permit the publication of the information unless it is satisfied that publication of the information would not prejudice the safety or welfare of the affected person.

(5) In any other case where the affected person is alive, the court may not permit the publication except with the consent of the affected person.

(6) The court must have regard to whether consent to the publication has been given by—
    (a) in the case of restricted adoption information, any prospective adopter of, or person who has adopted, the child in question, and
    (b) in the case of restricted parental order information, any person who applied for the parental order or in respect of whom the parental order has been made.

(7) The court must have regard to any risk which publication of the information would pose to the safety or welfare of any individual involved in, referred to in or otherwise connected with the proceedings.

(8) The court may permit the publication subject to conditions specified by the court.

(9) For the purposes of this section—
'adoption' means adoption under the Adoption Act 1976 or the Adoption and Children Act 2002 (and related terms are to be construed accordingly);
'parental order' means a parental order under section 30 of the Human Fertilisation and Embryology Act 1990 or section 54 of the Human Fertilisation and Embryology Act 2008.

16 Prohibiting or restricting publication for purposes of section 13: adoption etc.

(1) The court may not prohibit or restrict the publication of information for the purposes of Condition 5 in section 13 unless subsection (2) or (3) applies (or both subsections apply).

[(2) This subsection applies if the court considers that, despite the fact the publication satisfies Condition 3 in section 13, there is a real risk that in the absence of the prohibition or restriction the publication would—
    (a) prejudice—
        (i)   the safety of any person,
        (ii) the welfare of a child or vulnerable adult, or
        (iii) the interests of justice in the proceedings in question, or
    (b) be an unreasonable infringement of the privacy of any person].

(3) This subsection applies if the information is identification information relating to a professional witness in the proceedings and—

(a) the information is also identification information relating to—
  (i) another individual involved in the proceedings (other than a professional witness in the proceedings), or
  (ii) an individual otherwise connected with the proceedings,
(b) [...]
(c) the court is satisfied that the professional witness is, has been or will be involved in the care or treatment of an individual involved in, or otherwise connected with, the proceedings, otherwise than for the purpose of being a professional witness in the proceedings.

17   Defences to contempt of court

(1) A person is not guilty of a contempt of court under section 11 by reason of the publication of information relating to relevant family proceedings if subsection (2), (3) or (4) applies.

(2) This subsection applies if the person proves that at the time of the publication the person did not know and had no reason to suspect that the information was information relating to the proceedings.

(3) This subsection applies if the person proves that—
  (a) the person obtained the information from a previous publication, and
  (b) at the time of the person's publication the person did not know and had no reason to suspect that the previous publication was not an authorised news publication.

(4) This subsection applies if the person proves that—
  (a) the publication of the information would be an authorised news publication but for the failure to meet Condition 3 in section 13, and
  (b) at the time of the publication the person did not know and had no reason to suspect that the information was—
    (i) identification information relating to an individual involved in the proceedings,
    (ii) [...]
    (iii) restricted adoption information or restricted parental order information.

18   Appeals against decisions under section 12 or 13

(1) Rules of court—
  (a) may make provision about appeals against decisions within subsection (2) (including provision which modifies provision made by or under any Act as it applies to such appeals), and
  (b) to the extent that provision is not made by or under any Act for appeals against such decisions, must make such provision (including provision about the route of such appeals).

(2) Those decisions are—
  (a) decisions to permit, or refuse to permit, publication of information for the purposes of section 12 or Condition 3 in section 13,
  (b) decisions to impose, or refuse to impose, conditions on permission granted for those purposes, and
  (c) decisions to prohibit or restrict, or refuse to prohibit or restrict, publication of information for the purposes of section 12 or Condition 5 in section 13.

21   Interpretation of Part 2, etc.

(1) In this Part—
'accredited news representative', in relation to any proceedings, means a representative of one or more news organisations who is a member of a class of representatives of news organisations on which rules of court confer a right to attend the proceedings;
'child' means a person under the age of 18;
'court' includes a judge and any person exercising the functions of a court or a judge;

'identification information', in relation to an individual involved in or otherwise connected with proceedings, means—

> (a) information, including in particular information as to any of the matters set out in sub-section (2), the publication of which is likely to lead members of the public to identify the individual as someone who is or has been involved in or otherwise connected with the proceedings, and
>
> (b) in a case where the individual is a child, information the publication of which is likely to lead members of the public to identify the address or school of the individual as being that of an individual who is or has been involved in or otherwise connected with the proceedings;

'judgment' includes a record produced by the court of its reasons for a decision;

'news organisation' means a news gathering or reporting organisation;

'professional witness', in any proceedings, means a person—

> (a) who has given, or whom it is proposed will give, written or oral evidence in the proceedings in exchange for a fee, and
>
> (b) whose instruction by a party to the proceedings has been authorised by the court for the purposes of the proceedings;

'publication' includes disclosure or communication in any form to any person or persons;

'publisher' means—

> (a) where the information is published in a newspaper or periodical, any proprietor, any editor and any publisher of the newspaper or periodical;
>
> (b) where the information is published in a relevant programme—
>
> > (i) any body corporate or Scottish partnership engaged in providing the programme service in which the programme is included, and
> >
> > (ii) any person having functions in relation to the programme corresponding to those of an editor of a newspaper;
>
> (c) in the case of any other publication of information, any person publishing it;

'relevant family proceedings' has the meaning given by section 11;

'relevant programme' means a programme included in a programme service, within the meaning of the Broadcasting Act 1990;

'restricted adoption information' has the meaning given by section 15;

'restricted parental order information' has the meaning given by section 15.

[. . .]

> (2) The matters referred to in the definition of 'identification information' in subsection (1) are—
>
> > (a) the name of the individual or any title, pseudonym or alias of the individual;
> >
> > (b) the address or locality of any place where the individual lives or works or is educated or taken care of;
> >
> > (c) the individual's appearance or style of dress;
> >
> > (d) any employment or other occupation of, or position held by, the individual;
> >
> > (e) the individual's relationship to particular relatives, or association with particular friends or acquaintances, of the individual;
> >
> > (f) the individual's recreational interests;
> >
> > (g) the individual's political, philosophical or religious beliefs or interests;
> >
> > (h) any property (whether real or personal) in which the individual has an interest or with which the individual is otherwise associated.
>
> (3) For the purposes of this Part an individual is 'involved' in proceedings if the individual—
>
> > (a) is or was a party to the proceedings or the subject of the proceedings,
> >
> > (b) is a person called, or whom it is proposed to call, as a witness in the proceedings, or
> >
> > (c) is a person who has given written evidence in connection with the proceedings.
>
> (4) The Lord Chancellor may, by order made by statutory instrument, amend—
>
> > (a) [the definition of 'professional witness' in subsection (1).]

(b) [...]

(5) An order under subsection (4) may make transitional provision or savings.

(6) A statutory instrument containing an order under subsection (4) may not be made unless a draft of the statutory instrument containing the order has been laid before, and approved by a resolution of, each House of Parliament.

(7) Nothing in this Part prejudices any other power a court may have to prevent or restrict the publication of information relating to relevant family proceedings.

(8) No provision of this Part (or of Part 2 of Schedule 3 or Part 2 of Schedule 4) applies in relation to relevant family proceedings concluded before the coming into force of the provision in question.

Children's Hearings (Scotland) Act 2011

(2011, asp 1)

Publishing restrictions

182 Publishing restrictions

(1) A person must not publish protected information if the publication of the information is intended, or is likely, to identify—

(a) a child mentioned in the protected information, or

(b) an address or school as being that of such a child.

(2) A person who contravenes subsection (1) commits an offence and is liable on summary conviction to a fine not exceeding level 4 on the standard scale.

(3) It is a defence for a person ('P') charged with a contravention of subsection (1) to show that P did not know or have reason to suspect that the publication of the protected information was likely to identify a child mentioned in the protected information, or, as the case may be, an address or school of such a child.

(4) In relation to proceedings before a children's hearing, the Scottish Ministers may in the interests of justice—

(a) dispense with the prohibition in subsection (1), or

(b) relax it to such extent as they consider appropriate.

(5) In relation to proceedings before the sheriff under Part 10 or 15, the sheriff may in the interests of justice—

(a) dispense with the prohibition in subsection (1), or

(b) relax it to such extent as the sheriff considers appropriate.

(6) In relation to proceedings in an appeal to the Court of Session under this Act, the Court may in the interests of justice—

(a) dispense with the prohibition in subsection (1), or

(b) relax it to such extent as the Court considers appropriate.

(7) The prohibition in subsection (1) does not apply in relation to the publication by or on behalf of a local authority or an adoption agency of information about a child for the purposes of making arrangements in relation to the child under this Act or the Adoption and Children (Scotland) Act 2007 (asp 4).

(8) In subsection (7), 'adoption agency' has the meaning given by the Adoption and Children (Scotland) Act 2007.

(9) In this section—

'protected information' means—

(a) information in relation to—

(i) a children's hearing,

(ii) an appeal against a decision of a children's hearing,

(iii) proceedings before the sheriff under Part 10 or 15, or

(iv) an appeal from any decision of the sheriff or sheriff principal made under this Act, or

(b) information given to the Principal Reporter in respect of a child in reliance on, or satisfaction of, a provision of this Act or any other enactment,

'publish' includes in particular—

(a) to publish matter in a programme service, as defined by section 201 of the Broadcasting Act 1990 (c.42), and

(b) to cause matter to be published.

Sexual Offences (Amendment) Act 1976

(1976, c. 82)

7   Citation, interpretation, commencement and extent

(1) This Act may be cited as the Sexual Offences (Amendment) Act 1976, and this Act and the Sexual Offences Acts 1956 and 1967 maybe cited together as the Sexual Offences Acts 1956 to 1976.

[(2) In this Act—

(a) 'a rape offence' means any of the following—

(i)   an offence under section 1 of the Sexual Offences Act 2003 (rape);

(ii) an offence under section 2 of that Act (assault by penetration);

(iii) an offence under section 4 of that Act (causing a person to engage in sexual activity without consent), where the activity caused involved penetration within subsection (4)(a) to (d) of that section;

(iv) an offence under section 5 of that Act (rape of a child under 13);

(v)   an offence under section 6 of that Act (assault of a child under 13 by penetration);

(vi) an offence under section 8 of that Act (causing or inciting a child under 13 to engage in sexual activity), where an activity involving penetration within subsection (3)(a) to (d) of that section was caused;

(vii) an offence under section 30 of that Act (sexual activity with a person with a mental disorder impeding choice), where the touching involved penetration within subsection (3)(a) to (d) of that section;

(viii) an offence under section 31 of that Act (causing or inciting a person, with a mental disorder impeding choice, to engage in sexual activity), where an activity involving penetration within subsection (3)(a) to (d) of that section was caused;

(ix) an attempt, conspiracy or incitement to commit an offence within any of paragraphs (i) to (vii);

(x)   aiding, abetting, counselling or procuring the commission of such an offence or an attempt to commit such an offence.

(b) the use in any provision of the word 'man' without the addition of the word 'boy' does not prevent the provision applying to any person to whom it would have applied if both words had been used, and similarly with the words 'woman' and 'girl'.]

(3) [...]

(4) This Act shall come into force on the expiration of the period of one month beginning with the date on which it is passed, [...]

(5) [...]

(6) This Act, except so far as it relates to courts-martial and the Courts-Martial Appeal Court, shall not extend to Scotland[or Northern Ireland].

Sexual Offences (Amendment) Act 1992

(1992, c. 34)

2 Offences to which this Act applies

(1) This Act applies to the following offences against the law of England and Wales—

  (aa) rape;

  (ab) burglary with intent to rape;

  (a) any offence under any of the provisions of the Sexual Offences Act 1956 mentioned in subsection (2);

  (b) any offence under section 128 of the Mental Health Act 1959 (intercourse with mentally handicapped person by hospital staff etc.);

  (c) any offence under section 1 of the Indecency with Children Act 1960 (indecent conduct towards young child);

  (d) any offence under section 54 of the Criminal Law Act 1977 (incitement by man of his grand-daughter, daughter or sister under the age of 16 to commit incest with him);

  (da) any offence under any of the provisions of Part 1 of the Sexual Offences Act 2003 except section 64, 65, 69 or 71;

  (e) any attempt to commit any of the offences mentioned in paragraphs (aa) to (da);

  (f) any conspiracy to commit any of those offences;

  (g) any incitement of another to commit any of those offences;

  (h) aiding, abetting, counselling or procuring the commission of any of the offences mentioned in paragraphs (aa) to (e) and (g).

(2) The provisions of the Act of 1956 are—

  (a) section 2 (procurement of a woman by threats);

  (b) section 3 (procurement of a woman by false pretences);

  (c) section 4 (administering drugs to obtain intercourse with a woman);

  (d) section 5 (intercourse with a girl under the age of 13);

  (e) section 6 (intercourse with a girl between the ages of 13 and 16);

  (f) section 7 (intercourse with a mentally handicapped person);

  (g) section 9 (procurement of a mentally handicapped person);

  (h) section 10 (incest by a man);

  (i) section 11 (incest by a woman);

  (j) section 12 (buggery);

  (k) section 14 (indecent assault on a woman);

  (l) section 15 (indecent assault on a man);

  (m) section 16 (assault with intent to commit buggery);

  (n) section 17 (abduction of woman by force).

(3) This Act applies to the following offences against the law of Northern Ireland—

  (a) rape;

  (b) burglary with intent to rape;

  (c) any offence under any of the following provisions of the Offences against the Person Act 1861—

    (i) section 52 (indecent assault on a female);

    (ii) section 53 so far as it relates to abduction of a woman against her will;

    (iii) section 61 (buggery);

    (iv) section 62 (attempt to commit buggery, assault with intent to commit buggery or indecent assault on a male);

  (d) any offence under any of the following provisions of the Criminal Law Amendment Act 1885—

    (i) section 3 (procuring unlawful carnal knowledge of woman by threats, false pretences or administering drugs);

(ii) section 4 (unlawful carnal knowledge, or attempted unlawful carnal knowledge, of a girl under 14);
(iii) section 5 (unlawful carnal knowledge of a girl under 17);
(e) any offence under any of the following provisions of the Punishment of Incest Act 1908—
  (i) section 1 (incest, attempted incest by males);
  (ii) section 2 (incest by females over 16);
(f) any offence under section 22 of the Children and Young Persons Act (Northern Ireland) 1968 (indecent conduct towards child);
(g) any offence under Article 9 of the Criminal Justice (Northern Ireland) Order 1980 (inciting girl under 16 to have incestuous sexual intercourse);
(h) any offence under any of the following provisions of the Mental Health (Northern Ireland) Order 1986—
  (i) Article 122(1)(a) (unlawful sexual intercourse with a woman suffering from severe mental handicap);
  (ii) Article 122(1)(b) (procuring a woman suffering from severe mental handicap to have unlawful sexual intercourse);
  (iii) Article 123 (unlawful sexual intercourse by hospital staff, etc. with a person receiving treatment for mental disorder);
(hh) any offence under any of the following provisions of the Criminal Justice (Northern Ireland) Order 2003—
  (i) Article 19 (buggery);
  (ii) Article 20 (assault with intent to commit buggery);
  (iii) Article 21 (indecent assault on a male);
(ha) any offence under any of sections 15 to 21, 47 to 53, 57 to 59, 66, 67, 70 and 72 of the Sexual Offences Act 2003;
(i) any attempt to commit any of the offences mentioned in paragraphs (a) to [(ha)];
(j) any conspiracy to commit any of those offences;
(k) any incitement of another to commit any of those offences;
(l) aiding, abetting, counselling or procuring the commission of any of the offences mentioned in paragraphs (a) to (i) and (k).

(4) This Act applies to an offence under section 42 of the Armed Forces Act 2006 if the corresponding offence under the law of England and Wales (within the meaning given by that section) is an offence within a paragraph of subsection (1) above.

3   Power to displace section 1

(1) If, before the commencement of a trial at which a person is charged with an offence to which this Act applies, he or another person against whom the complainant may be expected to give evidence at the trial, applies to the judge for a direction under this subsection and satisfies the judge—
(a) that the direction is required for the purpose of inducing persons who are likely to be needed as witnesses at the trial to come forward; and
(b) that the conduct of the applicant's defence at the trial is likely to be substantially prejudiced if the direction is not given,
the judge shall direct that section 1 shall not, by virtue of the accusation alleging the offence in question, apply in relation to the complainant.

(2) If at a trial the judge is satisfied—
(a) that the effect of section 1 is to impose a substantial and unreasonable restriction upon the reporting of proceedings at the trial, and
(b) that it is in the public interest to remove or relax the restriction,
he shall direct that that section shall not apply to such matter as is specified in the direction.

(3) A direction shall not be given under subsection (2) by reason only of the outcome of the trial.

(4) If a person who has been convicted of an offence and has given notice of appeal against the conviction, or notice of an application for leave so to appeal, applies to the appellate court for a direction under this subsection and satisfies the court—

    (a) that the direction is required for the purpose of obtaining evidence in support of the appeal; and

    (b) that the applicant is likely to suffer substantial injustice if the direction is not given,

the court shall direct that section 1 shall not, by virtue of an accusation which alleges an offence to which this Act applies and is specified in the direction, apply in relation to a complainant so specified.

(5) A direction given under any provision of this section does not affect the operation of section 1 at any time before the direction is given.

(6) In subsections (1) and (2), 'judge' means—

    (a) in the case of an offence which is to be tried summarily or for which the mode of trial has not been determined, any justice of the peace [...]; and

    (b) in any other case, any judge of the Crown Court in England and Wales.

(6A) In its application to Northern Ireland, this section has effect as if—

    (a) in subsections (1) and (2) for any reference to the judge there were substituted a reference to the court; and

    (b) subsection (6) were omitted.

(6B) Where a person is charged with an offence to which this Act applies by virtue of sction 2(4), this section applies as if—

    (a) in subsection (1) and (2) for any reference to the judge there was substituted a reference to the court; and

    (b) subsections (6) and (6A) were omitted.

(7) If, after the commencement of a trial at which a person is charged with an offence to which this Act applies, a new trial of the person for that offence is ordered, the commencement of any previous trial shall be disregarded for the purposes of subsection (1).

4   Special rules for cases of incest or buggery

(1) In this section—

'section 10 offence' means an offence under section 10 of the Sexual Offences Act 1956 (incest by a man) or an attempt to commit that offence;

'section 11 offence' means an offence under section 11 of that Act (incest by a woman) or an attempt to commit that offence;

'section 12 offence' means an offence under section 12 of that Act (buggery) or an attempt to commit that offence.

(2) Section 1 does not apply to a woman against whom a section 10 offence is alleged to have been committed if she is accused of having committed a section 11 offence against the man who is alleged to have committed the section 10 offence against her.

(3) Section 1 does not apply to a man against whom a section 11 offence is alleged to have been committed if he is accused of having committed a section 10 offence against the woman who is alleged to have committed the section 11 offence against him.

(4) Section 1 does not apply to a person against whom a section 12 offence is alleged to have been committed if that person is accused of having committed a section 12 offence against the person who is alleged to have committed the section 12 offence against him.

(5) Subsection (2) does not affect the operation of this Act in relation to anything done at any time before the woman is accused.

(6) Subsection (3) does not affect the operation of this Act in relation to anything done at any time before the man is accused.

(7) Subsection (4) does not affect the operation of this Act in relation to anything done at any time before the person mentioned first in that subsection is accused.

(8) In its application to Northern Ireland, this section has effect as if—

    (a) subsection (1) were omitted;

    (b) for references to a section 10 offence there were substituted references to an offence under section 1 of the Punishment of Incest Act 1908 (incest by a man) or an attempt to commit that offence;

(c) for references to a section 11 offence there were substituted references to an offence under section 2 of that Act (incest by a woman) or an attempt to commit that offence; and

(d) for references to a section 12 offence there were substituted references to an offence under [Article 19 of the Criminal Justice (Northern Ireland) Order 2003] (buggery) or an attempt to commit that offence.

5 Offences

(1) If any matter is published or included in a relevant programme in contravention of section 1, the following persons shall be guilty of an offence and liable on summary conviction to a fine not exceeding level 5 on the standard scale—

(a) in the case of publication in a newspaper or periodical, any proprietor, any editor and any publisher of the newspaper or periodical;

(b) in the case of publication in any other form, the person publishing the matter; and

(c) in the case of matter included in a relevant programme—

(i) any body corporate engaged in providing the service in which the programme is included; and

(ii) any person having functions in relation to the programme corresponding to those in relation to that of an editor of a newspaper.

(2) Where a person is charged with an offence under this section in respect of the publication of any matter or the inclusion of any matter in a relevant programme[inclusion of any matter in a publication], it shall be a defence, subject to subsection (3), to prove that the publication or programme in which the matter appeared was one in respect of which the person against whom the offence mentioned in section 1 is alleged to have been committed had given written consent to the appearance of matter of that description.

(3) Written consent is not a defence if it is proved that any person interfered unreasonably with the peace or comfort of the person giving the consent, with intent to obtain it[, or that person was under the age of 16 at the time when it was given.]

(4) Proceedings for an offence under this section shall not be instituted except by or with the consent of the Attorney General [if the offence is alleged to have been committed in England and Wales or of the Attorney General for Northern Ireland if the offence is alleged to have been committed in Northern Ireland.]

(5) Where a person is charged with an offence under this section it shall be a defence to prove that at the time of the alleged offence he was not aware, and neither suspected nor had reason to suspect, that the publication or programme in question was of, or (as the case may be)[included the matter in question].

(5A) Where—

(a) a person is charged with an offence under this section, and

(b) the offence relates to the inclusion of any matter in a publication in contravention of section 1(1),

it shall be a defence to prove that at the time of the alleged offence he was not aware, and neither suspected nor had reason to suspect, that the allegation in question had been made.

(6) Where an offence under this section committed by a body corporate is proved to have been committed with the consent or connivance of, or to be attributable to any neglect on the part of—

(a) a director, manager, secretary or other similar officer of the body corporate, or

(b) a person purporting to act in any such capacity,

he as well as the body corporate shall be guilty of the offence and liable to be proceeded against and punished accordingly.

(7) In relation to a body corporate whose affairs are managed by its members 'director', in subsection (6), means a member of the body corporate.

[(8) Where an offence under this section is committed by a Scottish partnership and is proved to have been committed with the consent or connivance of a partner, he as well as the partnership shall be guilty of the offence and shall be liable to be proceeded against and punished accordingly.]

6 Interpretation etc.

(1) In this Act—

'complainant' has the meaning given in section 1(2);

'corresponding civil offence', in relation to a service offence, means the civil offence (within the meaning of the Army Act 1955, the Air Force Act 1955 or the Naval Discipline Act 1957) the commission of which constitutes the service offence;

'picture' includes a likeness however produced;

['publication' includes any speech, writing, relevant programme or other communication in whatever form, which is addressed to the public at large or any section of the public (and for this purpose every relevant programme shall be taken to be so addressed), but does not include an indictment or other document prepared for use in particular legal proceedings;]

'relevant programme' means a programme included in a programme service, within the meaning of the Broadcasting Act 1990;

(1A) Section 48 of the Armed Forces Act 2006 (attempts, conspiracy, encouragement and assistance and aiding and abetting outside England and Wales) applies for the purpose of this Act as if the reference in subsection (3)(b) of that section to any of the following provisions of that Act were a reference to any provision of this Act.

(2) For the purposes of this Act—

    (a) where it is alleged that an offence to which this Act applies has been committed, the fact that any person has consented to an act which, on any prosecution for that offence, would fall to be proved by the prosecution, does not prevent that person from being regarded as a person against whom the alleged offence was committed; and

    (b) where a person is accused of an offence of incest or buggery, the other party to the act in question shall be taken to be a person against whom the offence was committed even though he consented to that act.

[(2A) For the purposes of this Act, where it is alleged or there is an accusation—

    (a) that an offence of conspiracy or incitement of another to commit an offence mentioned in section 2(1)(aa) to (d) or (3)(a) to [(hh)] has been committed, or

    (b) that an offence of aiding, abetting, counselling or procuring the commission of an offence of incitement of another to commit an offence mentioned in section 2(1)(aa) to (d) or (3) (a) to [(hh)] has been committed,

the person against whom the substantive offence is alleged to have been intended to be committed shall be regarded as the person against whom the conspiracy or incitement is alleged to have been committed.

In this subsection, 'the substantive offence' means the offence to which the alleged conspiracy or incitement related.

(3) For the purposes of this Act, a person is accused of an offence[, other than an offence under section 42 of the Armed Forces Act 2006,] if—

    (a) an information is laid[, or (in Northern Ireland) a complaint is made,]alleging that he has committed the offence,

    (b) he appears before a court charged with the offence,

    (c) a court before which he is appearing [sends him to the Crown Court] for trial on a new charge alleging the offence, or

    (d) a bill of indictment charging him with the offence is preferred before a court in which he may lawfully be indicted for the offence,

and references in [subsection (2A) and in] section 3 to an accusation alleging an offence shall be construed accordingly.

[(3A) For the purposes of this Act, a person is accused of an offence under section 42 of the Armed Forces Act 2006 if he is charged (under Part 5 of that Act) with the offence, and references in section 3 to an accusation alleging an offence shall be construed accordingly.]

(4) Nothing in this Act affects any prohibition or restriction imposed by virtue of any other enactment upon a publication or upon matter included in a relevant programme.

8   Short title, commencement and extent, etc.

(1) This Act may be cited as the Sexual Offences (Amendment) Act 1992.

(2) This Act and the Sexual Offences Acts 1956 to 1976 may be cited together as the Sexual Offences Acts 1956 to 1992.

(3) This section comes into force on the passing of this Act but otherwise this Act comes into force on such date as may be appointed by order made by the Secretary of State.

(4) The power to make an order under subsection (3) shall be exercisable by statutory instrument.

(5) Different dates may be appointed for different provisions of this Act and for different purposes.

[(6) This Act extends to England and Wales, Scotland and Northern Ireland].

Sexual Offences (Protected Material) Act 1997

(1997, c. 39)

Introductory

1   Meaning of 'protected material'

(1) In this Act 'protected material', in relation to proceedings for a sexual offence, means a copy (in whatever form) of any of the following material, namely—

 (a) a statement relating to that or any other sexual offence made by any victim of the offence (whether the statement is recorded in writing or in any other form),

 (b) a photograph or pseudo-photograph of any such victim, or

 (c) a report of a medical examination of the physical condition of any such victim,

which is a copy given by the prosecutor to any person under this Act.

(2) For the purposes of subsection (1) a person is, in relation to any proceedings for a sexual offence, a victim of that offence if—

 (a) the charge, summons or indictment by which the proceedings are instituted names that person as a person in relation to whom that offence was committed; or

 (b) that offence can, in the prosecutor's opinion, be reasonably regarded as having been committed in relation to that person;

and a person is, in relation to any such proceedings, a victim of any other sexual offence if that offence can, in the prosecutor's opinion, be reasonably regarded as having been committed in relation to that person.

(3) In this Act, where the context so permits (and subject to subsection (4))—

 (a) references to any protected material include references to any part of any such material; and

 (b) references to a copy of any such material include references to any part of any such copy.

(4) Nothing in this Act—

 (a) so far as it refers to a defendant making any copy of—

  (i)   any protected material, or

  (ii) a copy of any such material,

  applies to a manuscript copy which is not a verbatim copy of the whole of that material or copy; or

 (b) so far as it refers to a defendant having in his possession any copy of any protected material, applies to a manuscript copy made by him which is not a verbatim copy of the whole of that material.

2   Meaning of other expressions

(1) In this Act—

'contracted out prison' means a contracted out prison within the meaning of Part IV of the Criminal Justice Act 1991;

'defendant', in relation to any proceedings for a sexual offence, means any person charged with that offence (whether or not he has been convicted);

'governor', in relation to a contracted out prison, means the director of the prison;

'inform' means inform in writing;

'photograph' and 'pseudo-photograph' shall be construed in accordance with section 7(4) and (7) of the Protection of Children Act 1978;

'prison' means any prison, [or young offender institution] which is under the general superintendence of, or is provided by, the Secretary of State under the Prison Act 1952, including a contracted out prison;

'proceedings' means (subject to subsection (2)) criminal proceedings;

'the prosecutor', in relation to any proceedings for a sexual offence, means any person acting as prosecutor (whether an individual or a body);

'relevant proceedings', in relation to any material which has been disclosed by the prosecutor under this Act, means any proceedings for the purposes of which it has been so disclosed or any further proceedings for the sexual offence in question;

'sexual offence' means one of the offences listed in the Schedule to this Act.

(2) For the purposes of this Act references to proceedings for a sexual offence include references to—

    (a) any appeal or application for leave to appeal brought or made by or in relation to a defendant in such proceedings;

    (b) any application made to the Criminal Cases Review Commission for the reference under section 9 or 11 of the Criminal Appeal Act 1995 of any conviction, verdict, finding or sentence recorded or imposed in relation to any such defendant; and

    (c) any petition to the Secretary of State requesting him to recommend the exercise of Her Majesty's prerogative of mercy in relation to any such defendant.

(3) In this Act, in the context of the prosecutor giving a copy of any material to any person—

    (a) references to the prosecutor include references to a person acting on behalf of the prosecutor; and

    (b) where any such copy falls to be given to the defendant's legal representative, references to the defendant's legal representative include references to a person acting on behalf of the defendant's legal representative.

3 Regulation of disclosures to defendant

(1) Where, in connection with any proceedings for a sexual offence, any statement or other material falling within any of paragraphs (a) to (c) of section 1(1) would (apart from this section) fall to be disclosed by the prosecutor to the defendant—

    (a) the prosecutor shall not disclose that material to the defendant; and

    (b) it shall instead be disclosed under this Act in accordance with whichever of subsections (2) and (3) below is applicable.

(2) If—

    (a) the defendant has a legal representative, and

    (b) the defendant's legal representative gives the prosecutor the undertaking required by section 4 (disclosure to defendant's legal representative),

the prosecutor shall disclose the material in question by giving a copy of it to the defendant's legal representative.

(3) If subsection (2) is not applicable, the prosecutor shall disclose the material in question by giving a copy of it to the appropriate person for the purposes of section 5 (disclosure to unrepresented defendant) in order for that person to show that copy to the defendant under that section.

(4) Where under this Act a copy of any material falls to be given to any person by the prosecutor, any such copy—

    (a) may be in such form as the prosecutor thinks fit, and

    (b) where the material consists of information which has been recorded in any form, need not be in the same form as that in which the information has already been recorded.

(5) Once a copy of any material is given to any person under this Act by the prosecutor, the copy shall (in accordance with section 1(1)) be protected material for the purposes of this Act.

4   Regulation of disclosures by prosecutor

(1) For the purposes of this Act the undertaking which a defendant's legal representative is required to give in relation to any protected material given to him under this Act is an undertaking by him to discharge the obligations set out in subsections (2) to (7).

(2) He must take reasonable steps to ensure—

    (a) that the protected material, or any copy of it, is only shown to the defendant in circumstances where it is possible to exercise adequate supervision to prevent the defendant retaining possession of the material or copy or making a copy of it, and

    (b) that the protected material is not shown and no copy of it is given, and its contents are not otherwise revealed, to any person other than the defendant, except so far as it appears to him necessary to show the material or give a copy of it to any such person—

        (i)   in connection with any relevant proceedings, or

        (ii)   for the purposes of any assessment or treatment of the defendant (whether before or after conviction).

(3) He must inform the defendant—

    (a) that the protected material is such material for the purposes of this Act,

    (b) that the defendant can only inspect that material, or any copy of it, in circumstances such as are described in subsection (2)(a), and

    (c) that it would be an offence for the defendant—

        (i)   to have that material, or any copy of it, in his possession otherwise than while inspecting it or the copy in such circumstances, or

        (ii)   to give that material or any copy of it, or otherwise reveal its contents, to any other person.

(4) He must, where the protected material or a copy of it has been shown or given in accordance with subsection (2)(b)(i) or (ii) to a person other than the defendant, inform that person—

    (a) that that person must not give any copy of that material, or otherwise reveal its contents—

        (i)   to any other person other than the defendant, or

        (ii)   to the defendant otherwise than in circumstances such as are described in subsection (2)(a); and

    (b) that it would be an offence for that person to do so.

(5) He must, where he ceases to act as the defendant's legal representative at a time when any relevant proceedings are current or in contemplation—

    (a) inform the prosecutor of that fact, and

    (b) if he is informed by the prosecutor that the defendant has a new legal representative who has given the prosecutor the undertaking required by this section, give the protected material, and any copies of it in his possession, to the defendant's new legal representative.

(6) He must, at the time of giving the protected material to the new legal representative under subsection (5), inform that person—

    (a) that that material is protected material for the purposes of this Act, and

    (b) of the extent to which—

        (i)   that material has been shown by him, and

        (ii)   any copies of it have been given by him, to any other person (including the defendant).

(7) He must keep a record of every occasion on which the protected material was shown, or a copy of it was given, as mentioned in subsection (6)(b).

Supplementary

8 Offences

(1) Where any material has been disclosed under this Act in connection with any proceedings for a sexual offence, it is an offence for the defendant—

    (a) to have the protected material, or any copy of it, in his possession otherwise than while inspecting it or the copy in circumstances such as are described in section 4(2)(a) or 5(4)(a), or

    (b) to give that material or any copy of it, or otherwise reveal its contents, to any other person.

(2) Where any protected material, or any copy of any such material, has been shown or given to any person in accordance with section 4(2)(b)(i) or (ii) or section 5(7) or (8), it is an offence for that person to give any copy of that material or otherwise reveal its contents—

    (a) to any person other than the defendant, or

    (b) to the defendant otherwise than in circumstances such as are described in section 4(2)(a) or 5(4)(a).

(3) Subsections (1) and (2) apply whether or not any relevant proceedings are current or in contemplation (and references to the defendant shall be construed accordingly).

(4) A person guilty of an offence under this section is liable—

    (a) on summary conviction, to imprisonment for a term not exceeding six months or a fine not exceeding the statutory maximum or both;

    (b) on conviction on indictment, to imprisonment for a term not exceeding two years or a fine or both.

(5) Where a person is charged with an offence under this section relating to any protected material or copy of any such material, it is a defence to prove that, at the time of the alleged offence, he was not aware, and neither suspected nor had reason to suspect, that the material or copy in question was protected material or (as the case may be) a copy of any such material.

(6) The court before which a person is tried for an offence under this section may (whether or not he is convicted of that offence) make an order requiring him to return any protected material, or any copy of any such material, in his possession to the prosecutor.

(7) Nothing in subsection (1) or (2) shall be taken to apply to—

    (a) any disclosure made in the course of any proceedings before a court or in any report of any such proceedings, or

    (b) any disclosure made or copy given by a person when returning any protected material, or a copy of any such material, to the prosecutor or the defendant's legal representative;

and accordingly nothing in section 4 or 5 shall be read as precluding the making of any disclosure or the giving of any copy in circumstances falling within paragraph (a) or (as the case may be) paragraph (b) above.

11 Short title, commencement and extent

(1) This Act may be cited as the Sexual Offences (Protected Material) Act 1997.

(2) This Act shall come into force on such day as the Secretary of State may appoint by order made by statutory instrument.

(3) Nothing in this Act applies to any proceedings for a sexual offence where the defendant was charged with the offence before the commencement of this Act.

(4) This Act extends to England and Wales only.

SCHEDULE SEXUAL OFFENCES FOR PURPOSES OF THIS ACT

1.–4. […]

5. Any offence under section 1 of the Protection of Children Act 1978 or section 160 of the Criminal Justice Act 1988 (indecent photographs of children).

5A. Any offence under any provision of Part I of the Sexual Offences Act 2003 except section 64, 65, 69 or 71.

6. Any offence under section 1 of the Criminal Law Act 1977 of conspiracy to commit any of the offences mentioned in paragraphs 1 to 5 and 5A.

7. Any offence under section 1 of the Criminal Attempts Act 1981 of attempting to commit any of those offences.

8. Any offence of inciting another to commit any of those offences.

Crime and Disorder Act 1998

(1998, c. 37)

51   [Sending cases to the Crown Court: adults

(1) Where an adult appears or is brought before a magistrates' court ('the court') charged with an offence and any of the conditions mentioned in subsection (2) below is satisfied, the court shall send him forthwith to the Crown Court for trial for the offence.

(2) Those conditions are—
>   (a) that the offence is an offence triable only on indictment other than one in respect of which notice has been given under section 51B or 51C below;
>   (b) that the offence is an either-way offence and the court is required under section 20(9)(b), 21, 23(4)(b) or (5) or 25(2D) of the Magistrates' Courts Act 1980 to proceed in relation to the offence in accordance with subsection (1) above;
>   (c) that notice is given to the court under section 51B or 51C below in respect of the offence.

(3) Where the court sends an adult for trial under subsection (1) above, it shall at the same time send him to the Crown Court for trial for any either-way or summary offence with which he is charged and which—
>   (a) (if it is an either-way offence) appears to the court to be related to the offence mentioned in subsection (1) above; or
>   (b) (if it is a summary offence) appears to the court to be related to the offence mentioned in subsection (1) above or to the either-way offence, and which fulfils the requisite condition (as defined in subsection (11) below).

(4) Where an adult who has been sent for trial under subsection (1) above subsequently appears or is brought before a magistrates' court charged with an either-way or summary offence which—
>   (a) appears to the court to be related to the offence mentioned in subsection (1) above; and
>   (b) (in the case of a summary offence) fulfils the requisite condition,

the court may send him forthwith to the Crown Court for trial for the either-way or summary offence.

(5) Where—
>   (a) the court sends an adult ('A') for trial under subsection (1) or (3) above;
>   (b) another adult appears or is brought before the court on the same or a subsequent occasion charged jointly with A with an either-way offence; and
>   (c) that offence appears to the court to be related to an offence for which A was sent for trial under subsection (1) or (3) above,

the court shall where it is the same occasion, and may where it is a subsequent occasion, send the other adult forthwith to the Crown Court for trial for the either-way offence.

(6) Where the court sends an adult for trial under subsection (5) above, it shall at the same time send him to the Crown Court for trial for any either-way or summary offence with which he is charged and which—
>   (a) (if it is an either-way offence) appears to the court to be related to the offence for which he is sent for trial; and

(b) (if it is a summary offence) appears to the court to be related to the offence for which he is sent for trial or to the either-way offence, and which fulfils the requisite condition.

(7) Where—

(a) the court sends an adult ('A') for trial under subsection (1), (3) or (5) above; and

(b) a child or young person appears or is brought before the court on the same or a subsequent occasion charged jointly with A with an indictable offence for which A is sent for trial under subsection (1), (3) or (5) above, or an indictable offence which appears to the court to be related to that offence,

the court shall, if it considers it necessary in the interests of justice to do so, send the child or young person forthwith to the Crown Court for trial for the indictable offence.

(8) Where the court sends a child or young person for trial under subsection (7) above, it may at the same time send him to the Crown Court for trial for any indictable or summary offence with which he is charged and which—

(a) (if it is an indictable offence) appears to the court to be related to the offence for which he is sent for trial; and

(b) (if it is a summary offence) appears to the court to be related to the offence for which he is sent for trial or to the indictable offence, and which fulfils the requisite condition.

(9) Subsections (7) and (8) above are subject to sections 24A and 24B of the Magistrates' Courts Act 1980 (which provide for certain cases involving children and young persons to be tried summarily).

(10) The trial of the information charging any summary offence for which a person is sent for trial under this section shall be treated as if the court had adjourned it under section 10 of the 1980 Act and had not fixed the time and place for its resumption.

(11) A summary offence fulfils the requisite condition if it is punishable with imprisonment or involves obligatory or discretionary disqualification from driving.

(12) In the case of an adult charged with an offence—

(a) if the offence satisfies paragraph (c) of subsection (2) above, the offence shall be dealt with under subsection (1) above and not under any other provision of this section or section 51A below;

(b) subject to paragraph (a) above, if the offence is one in respect of which the court is required to, or would decide to, send the adult to the Crown Court under—

(i) subsection (5) above; or

(ii) subsection (6) of section 51A below,

the offence shall be dealt with under that subsection and not under any other provision of this section or section 51A below.

(13) The functions of a magistrates' court under this section, and its related functions under section 51D below, may be discharged by a single justice.]

[52B Offences in connection with reporting

(1) If a report is published or included in a relevant programme in contravention of section 52A above, each of the following persons is guilty of an offence—

(a) in the case of a publication of a written report as part of a newspaper or periodical, any proprietor, editor or publisher of the newspaper or periodical;

(b) in the case of a publication of a written report otherwise than as part of a newspaper or periodical, the person who publishes it;

(c) in the case of the inclusion of a report in a relevant programme, any body corporate which is engaged in providing the service in which the programme is included and any person having functions in relation to the programme corresponding to those of the editor of a newspaper.

(2) A person guilty of an offence under this section is liable on summary conviction to a fine not exceeding level 5 on the standard scale.

(3) Proceedings for an offence under this section shall not, in England and Wales, be instituted otherwise than by or with the consent of the Attorney General.

(4) Proceedings for an offence under this section shall not, in Northern Ireland, be instituted otherwise than by or with the consent of the Attorney General for Northern Ireland.

(5) Subsection (11) of section 52A above applies for the purposes of this section as it applies for the purposes of that section.]

Criminal Justice Act 1987

(1987, c. 38)

PART I FRAUD REPORTING RESTRICTIONS

11 Restrictions on reporting

(1) Except as provided by this section—
  (a) no written report of proceedings falling within subsection (2) below shall be published in the United Kingdom;
  (b) no report of proceedings falling within subsection (2) below shall be included in a relevant programme for reception in the United Kingdom.

(2) The following proceedings fall within this subsection—
  (a) [...]
  (b) a preparatory hearing;
  (c) an application for leave to appeal in relation to such a hearing;
  (d) an appeal in relation to such a hearing.

(3) [...]

(4) The judge dealing with a preparatory hearing may order that subsection (1) above shall not apply, or shall not apply to a specified extent, to a report of—
  (a) the preparatory hearing, or
  (b) an application to the judge for leave to appeal to the Court of Appeal under section 9(11) above in relation to the preparatory hearing.

(5) The Court of Appeal may order that subsection (1) above shall not apply, or shall not apply to a specified extent, to a report of—
  (a) an appeal to the Court of Appeal under section 9(11) above in relation to a preparatory hearing,
  (b) an application to that Court for leave to appeal to it under section 9(11) above in relation to a preparatory hearing, or
  (c) an application to that Court for leave to appeal to the [Supreme Court] under Part II of the Criminal Appeal Act 1968 in relation to a preparatory hearing.

(6) The House of Lords may order that subsection (1) above shall not apply, or shall not apply to a specified extent, to a report of—
  (a) an appeal to that [Supreme Court] under Part II of the Criminal Appeal Act 1968 in relation to a preparatory hearing, or
  (b) an application to that [Supreme Court] for leave to appeal to it under Part II of the Criminal Appeal Act 1968 in relation to a preparatory hearing.

(7) Where there is only one accused and he objects to the making of an order under subsection [...], (4), (5) or (6) above the judge or the Court of Appeal or the [Supreme Court] shall make the order if (and only if) satisfied after hearing the representations of the accused that it is in the interests of justice to do so; and if the order is made it shall not apply to the extent that a report deals with any such objection or representations.

(8) Where there are two or more accused and one or more of them objects to the making of an order under subsection (3), (4), (5) or (6) above the judge or the Court of Appeal or the [Supreme Court] shall make the order if (and only if) satisfied after hearing the representations of each of the

accused that it is in the interests of justice to do so; and if the order is made it shall not apply to the extent that a report deals with any such objection or representations.

(9)–(10) [...]

(11) Subsection (1) above does not apply to—

(a)–(d) [...]

(e) the inclusion in a relevant programme of a report of a preparatory hearing, or

(f) the inclusion in a relevant programme of a report of an appeal in relation to a preparatory hearing or of an application for leave to appeal in relation to such a hearing,

at the conclusion of the trial of the accused or of the last of the accused to be tried.

(12) Subsection (1) above does not apply to a report which contains only one or more of the following matters—

(a) the identity of the court and the name of the judge;

(b) the names, ages, home addresses and occupations of the accused and witnesses;

(c) any relevant business information;

(d) the offence or offences, or a summary of them, with which the accused is or are charged;

(e) the names of counsel and solicitors in the proceedings;

(f) where the proceedings are adjourned, the date and place to which they are adjourned;

(g) any arrangements as to bail;

(h) [whether, for the purposes of the proceedings, representation was provided to the accused or any of the accused under Part 1 of the Legal Aid, Sentencing and Punishment of Offenders Act 2012].

(13) The addresses that may be published or included in a relevant programme under subsection (12) above are addresses—

(a) at any relevant time, and

(b) at the time of their publication or inclusion in a relevant programme;

and 'relevant time' here means a time when events giving rise to the charges to which the proceedings relate occurred.

(14) The following is relevant business information for the purposes of subsection (12) above—

(a) any address used by the accused for carrying on a business on his own account;

(b) the name of any business which he was carrying on on his own account at any relevant time;

(c) the name of any firm in which he was a partner at any relevant time or by which he was engaged at any such time;

(d) the address of any such firm;

(e) the name of any company of which he was a director at any relevant time or by which he was otherwise engaged at any such time;

(f) the address of the registered or principal office of any such company;

(g) any working address of the accused in his capacity as a person engaged by any such company;

and here 'engaged' means engaged under a contract of service or a contract for services, and 'relevant time' has the same meaning as in subsection (13) above.

(15) Nothing in this section affects any prohibition or restriction imposed by virtue of any other enactment on a publication or on matter included in a programme.

(16) In this section—

(a) 'publish', in relation to a report, means publish the report, either by itself or as part of a newspaper or periodical, for distribution to the public;

(b) expressions cognate with 'publish' shall be construed accordingly;

(c) 'relevant programme' means a programme included in a programme service, within the meaning of the Broadcasting Act 1990.

11A   Offences in connection with reporting

(1) If a report is published or included in a relevant programme in contravention of section 11 above each of the following persons is guilty of an offence—

  (a) in the case of a publication of a written report as part of a newspaper or periodical, any proprietor, editor or publisher of the newspaper or periodical;

  (b) in the case of a publication of a written report otherwise than as part of a newspaper or periodical, the person who publishes it;

  (c) in the case of the inclusion of a report in a relevant programme, any body corporate which is engaged in providing the service in which the programme is included and any person having functions in relation to the programme corresponding to those of an editor of a newspaper.

(2) A person guilty of an offence under this section is liable on summary conviction to a fine of an amount not exceeding level 5 on the standard scale.

(3) Proceedings for an offence under this section shall not be instituted in England and Wales otherwise than by or with the consent of the Attorney General.

(3A) Proceedings for an offence under this section shall not be instituted in Northern Ireland otherwise than by or with the consent of the Attorney General for Northern Ireland.

(4) Subsection (16) of section 11 above applies for the purposes of this section as it applies for the purposes of that.

Criminal Justice Act 2003

(2003, c. 44)

71   Restrictions on reporting

(1) Except as provided by this section no publication shall include a report of—

  (a) anything done under section 58, 59, 62, 63 or 64,{relating to prosecution appeals in respect of rulings and evidentiary rulings}

  (b) an appeal under this Part,

  (c) an appeal under Part 2 of the 1968 Act in relation to an appeal under this Part, or

  (d) an application for leave to appeal in relation to an appeal mentioned in paragraph (b) or (c).

(2) The judge may order that subsection (1) is not to apply, or is not to apply to a specified extent, to a report of—

  (a) anything done under section 58, 59, 62, 63 or 64, or

  (b) an application to the judge for leave to appeal to the Court of Appeal under this Part.

(3) The Court of Appeal may order that subsection (1) is not to apply, or is not to apply to a specified extent, to a report of—

  (a) an appeal to the Court of Appeal under this Part,

  (b) an application to that Court for leave to appeal to it under this Part, or

  (c) an application to that Court for leave to appeal to the [Supreme Court] under Part 2 of the 1968 Act.

(4) The [Supreme Court] may order that subsection (1) is not to apply, or is not to apply to a specified extent, to a report of—

  (a) an appeal to[the Supreme Court] under Part 2 of the 1968 Act, or

  (b) an application to[the Supreme Court] for leave to appeal to it under Part 2 of that Act.

(5) Where there is only one defendant and he objects to the making of an order under subsection (2), (3) or (4)—

  (a) the judge, the Court of Appeal [or the Supreme Court] is to make the order if (and only if) satisfied, after hearing the representations of the defendant, that it is in the interests of justice to do so, and

  (b) the order (if made) is not to apply to the extent that a report deals with any such objection or representations.

(6) Where there are two or more defendants and one or more of them object to the making of an order under subsection (2), (3) or (4)—

    (a) the judge, the Court of Appeal or the[Supreme Court] is to make the order if (and only if) satisfied, after hearing the representations of each of the defendants, that it is in the interests of justice to do so, and

    (b) the order (if made) is not to apply to the extent that a report deals with any such objection or representations.

(7) Subsection (1) does not apply to the inclusion in a publication of a report of—

    (a) anything done under section 58, 59, 62, 63 or 64,

    (b) an appeal under this Part,

    (c) an appeal under Part 2 of the 1968 Act in relation to an appeal under this Part, or

    (d) an application for leave to appeal in relation to an appeal mentioned in paragraph (b) or (c),

at the conclusion of the trial of the defendant or the last of the defendants to be tried.

(8) Subsection (1) does not apply to a report which contains only one or more of the following matters—

    (a) the identity of the court and the name of the judge,

    (b) the names, ages, home addresses and occupations of the defendant or defendants and witnesses,

    (c) the offence or offences, or a summary of them, with which the defendant or defendants are charged,

    (d) the names of counsel and solicitors in the proceedings,

    (e) where the proceedings are adjourned, the date and place to which they are adjourned,

    (f) any arrangements as to bail,

    (g) [whether, for the purposes of the proceedings, representation was provided to the defendant or any of the defendants under Part 1 of the Legal Aid, Sentencing and Punishment of Offenders Act 2012].

(9) The addresses that may be included in a report by virtue of subsection (8) are addresses—

    (a) at any relevant time, and

    (b) at the time of their inclusion in the publication.

(10) Nothing in this section affects any prohibition or restriction by virtue of any other enactment on the inclusion of any matter in a publication.

(11) In this section—

'programme service' has the same meaning as in the Broadcasting Act 1990 (c 42),

'publication' includes any speech, writing, relevant programme or other communication in whatever form, which is addressed to the public at large or any section of the public (and for this purpose every relevant programme is to be taken to be so addressed), but does not include an indictment or other document prepared for use in particular legal proceedings,

'relevant time' means a time when events giving rise to the charges to which the proceedings relate are alleged to have occurred,

'relevant programme' means a programme included in a programme service.

72 Offences in connection with reporting

(1) This section applies if a publication includes a report in contravention of section 71.

(2) Where the publication is a newspaper or periodical, any proprietor, editor or publisher of the newspaper or periodical is guilty of an offence.

(3) Where the publication is a relevant programme—

    (a) any body corporate or Scottish partnership engaged in providing the programme service in which the programme is included, and

    (b) any person having functions in relation to the programme corresponding to those of an editor of a newspaper,

is guilty of an offence.

(4) In the case of any other publication, any person publishing it is guilty of an offence.

(5) If an offence under this section committed by a body corporate is proved—

    (a) to have been committed with the consent or connivance of, or

    (b) to be attributable to any neglect on the part of,

an officer, the officer as well as the body corporate is guilty of the offence and liable to be proceeded against and punished accordingly.

(6) In subsection (5), 'officer' means a director, manager, secretary or other similar officer of the body, or a person purporting to act in any such capacity.

(7) If the affairs of a body corporate are managed by its members, 'director' in subsection (6) means a member of that body.

(8) Where an offence under this section is committed by a Scottish partnership and is proved to have been committed with the consent or connivance of a partner, he as well as the partnership shall be guilty of the offence and shall be liable to be proceeded against and punished accordingly.

(9) A person guilty of an offence under this section is liable on summary conviction to a fine not exceeding level 5 on the standard scale.

(10) Proceedings for an offence under this section may not be instituted—

    (a) in England and Wales otherwise than by or with the consent of the Attorney General, or

    (b) in Northern Ireland otherwise than by or with the consent of—

        (i)   before the relevant date, the Attorney General for Northern Ireland, or

        (ii) on or after the relevant date, the Director of Public Prosecutions for Northern Ireland.

(11) In subsection (10) 'the relevant date' means the date on which section 22(1) of the Justice (Northern Ireland) Act 2002 (c 26) comes into force.

Criminal Procedure and Investigations Act 1996

(1996, c. 25)

Reporting restrictions

37   Restrictions on reporting

(1) Except as provided by this section—

    (a) no written report of proceedings falling within subsection (2) shall be published in the United Kingdom;

    (b) no report of proceedings falling within subsection (2) shall be included in a relevant programme for reception in [the United Kingdom].

(2) The following proceedings fall within this subsection—

    (a) a preparatory hearing;

    (b) an application for leave to appeal in relation to such a hearing;

    (c) an appeal in relation to such a hearing.

(3) The judge dealing with a preparatory hearing may order that subsection (1) shall not apply, or shall not apply to a specified extent, to a report of—

    (a) the preparatory hearing, or

    (b) an application to the judge for leave to appeal to the Court of Appeal under section 35(1) in relation to the preparatory hearing.

(4) The Court of Appeal may order that subsection (1) shall not apply, or shall not apply to a specified extent, to a report of—

    (a) an appeal to the Court of Appeal under section 35(1) in relation to a preparatory hearing,

    (b) an application to that Court for leave to appeal to it under section 35(1) in relation to a preparatory hearing, or

    (c) an application to that Court for leave to appeal to the [Supreme Court] under Part II of the Criminal Appeal Act 1968 in relation to a preparatory hearing.

(5) [The Supreme Court] may order that subsection (1) shall not apply, or shall not apply to a specified extent, to a report of—

    (a) an appeal to [the Supreme Court] under Part II of the Criminal Appeal Act 1968 in relation to a preparatory hearing, or

    (b) an application to [the Supreme Court] for leave to appeal to it under Part II of the Criminal Appeal Act 1968 in relation to a preparatory hearing.

(6) Where there is only one accused and he objects to the making of an order under subsection (3), (4) or (5) the judge or the Court of Appeal or the [Supreme Court] shall make the order if (and only if) satisfied after hearing the representations of the accused that it is in the interests of justice to do so; and if the order is made it shall not apply to the extent that a report deals with any such objection or representations.

(7) Where there are two or more accused and one or more of them objects to the making of an order under subsection (3), (4) or (5) the judge or the Court of Appeal or the [Supreme Court] shall make the order if (and only if) satisfied after hearing the representations of each of the accused that it is in the interests of justice to do so; and if the order is made it shall not apply to the extent that a report deals with any such objection or representations.

(8) Subsection (1) does not apply to—

    (a) the publication of a report of a preparatory hearing,

    (b) the publication of a report of an appeal in relation to a preparatory hearing or of an application for leave to appeal in relation to such a hearing,

    (c) the inclusion in a relevant programme of a report of a preparatory hearing, or

    (d) the inclusion in a relevant programme of a report of an appeal in relation to a preparatory hearing or of an application for leave to appeal in relation to such a hearing,

at the conclusion of the trial of the accused or of the last of the accused to be tried.

(9) Subsection (1) does not apply to a report which contains only one or more of the following matters—

    (a) the identity of the court and the name of the judge;

    (b) the names, ages, home addresses and occupations of the accused and witnesses;

    (c) the offence or offences, or a summary of them, with which the accused is or are charged;

    (d) the names of counsel and solicitors in the proceedings;

    (e) where the proceedings are adjourned, the date and place to which they are adjourned;

    (f) any arrangements as to bail;

    (g) whether a right to representation funded by the Legal Services Commission as part of the Criminal Defence Service was granted to the accused or any of the accused.

(10) The addresses that may be published or included in a relevant programme under subsection (9) are addresses—

    (a) at any relevant time, and

    (b) at the time of their publication or inclusion in a relevant programme;

and 'relevant time' here means a time when events giving rise to the charges to which the proceedings relate occurred.

(11) Nothing in this section affects any prohibition or restriction imposed by virtue of any other enactment on a publication or on matter included in a programme.

(12) In this section—

    (a) 'publish', in relation to a report, means publish the report, either by itself or as part of a newspaper or periodical, for distribution to the public;

    (b) expressions cognate with 'publish' shall be construed accordingly;

    (c) 'relevant programme' means a programme included in a programme service, within the meaning of the Broadcasting Act 1990.

38   Offences in connection with reporting

(1) If a report is published or included in a relevant programme in contravention of section 37 each of the following persons is guilty of an offence—

     (a) in the case of a publication of a written report as part of a newspaper or periodical, any proprietor, editor or publisher of the newspaper or periodical;

     (b) in the case of a publication of a written report otherwise than as part of a newspaper or periodical, the person who publishes it;

     (c) in the case of the inclusion of a report in a relevant programme, any body corporate which is engaged in providing the service in which the programme is included and any person having functions in relation to the programme corresponding to those of an editor of a newspaper.

(2) A person guilty of an offence under this section is liable on summary conviction to a fine of an amount not exceeding level 5 on the standard scale.

(3) Proceedings for an offence under this section shall not be instituted in England and Wales otherwise than by or with the consent of the Attorney General.

(3A) Proceedings for an offence under this section shall not be instituted in Northern Ireland otherwise than by or with the consent of the Attorney General for Northern Ireland.

(4) Subsection (12) of section 37 applies for the purposes of this section as it applies for the purposes of that.

PART IV   RULINGS

39   Meaning of pre-trial hearing

(1) For the purposes of this Part a hearing is a pre-trial hearing if it relates to a trial on indictment and it takes place—

     (a) after the accused has been sent for trial for the offence, and

     (b) before the start of the trial.

(2) For the purposes of this Part a hearing is also a pre-trial hearing if—

     (a) it relates to a trial on indictment to be held in pursuance of a bill of indictment preferred under the authority of section 2(2)(b) of the Administration of Justice (Miscellaneous Provisions) Act 1933 (bill preferred by direction of Court of Appeal, or by direction or with consent of a judge), and

     (b) it takes place after the bill of indictment has been preferred and before the start of the trial.

(3) For the purposes of this section the start of a trial on indictment occurs [at the time when a jury is sworn] to consider the issue of guilt or fitness to plead or, if the court accepts a plea of guilty before [the time when a jury is sworn], when that plea is accepted; but this is subject to section 8 of the Criminal Justice Act 1987 and section 30 of this Act (preparatory hearings).

[(4) The references in subsection (3) to the time when a jury is sworn include the time when that jury would be sworn but for the making of an order under Part 7 of the Criminal Justice Act 2003].

40   Power to make rulings

(1) A judge may make at a pre-trial hearing a ruling as to—

     (a) any question as to the admissibility of evidence;

     (b) any other question of law relating to the case concerned.

(2) A ruling may be made under this section—

     (a) on an application by a party to the case, or

     (b) of the judge's own motion.

(3) Subject to subsection (4), a ruling made under this section has binding effect from the time it is made until the case against the accused or, if there is more than one, against each of them is disposed of; and the case against an accused is disposed of if—

     (a) he is acquitted or convicted, or

     (b) the prosecutor decides not to proceed with the case against him.

(4) A judge may discharge or vary (or further vary) a ruling made under this section if it appears to him that it is in the interests of justice to do so; and a judge may act under this subsection—

    (a) on an application by a party to the case, or

    (b) of the judge's own motion.

(5) No application may be made under subsection (4)(a) unless there has been a material change of circumstances since the ruling was made or, if a previous application has been made, since the application (or last application) was made.

(6) The judge referred to in subsection (4) need not be the judge who made the ruling or, if it has been varied, the judge (or any of the judges) who varied it.

(7) For the purposes of this section the prosecutor is any person acting as prosecutor, whether an individual or a body.

41 Restrictions on reporting

(1) Except as provided by this section—

    (a) no written report of matters falling within subsection (2) shall be published in the United Kingdom;

    (b) no report of matters falling within subsection (2) shall be included in a relevant programme for reception in the United Kingdom.

(2) The following matters fall within this subsection—

    (a) a ruling made under section 40;

    (b) proceedings on an application for a ruling to be made under section 40;

    (c) an order that a ruling made under section 40 be discharged or varied or further varied;

    (d) proceedings on an application for a ruling made under section 40 to be discharged or varied or further varied.

(3) The judge dealing with any matter falling within subsection (2) may order that subsection (1) shall not apply, or shall not apply to a specified extent, to a report of the matter.

(4) Where there is only one accused and he objects to the making of an order under subsection (3) the judge shall make the order if (and only if) satisfied after hearing the representations of the accused that it is in the interests of justice to do so; and if the order is made it shall not apply to the extent that a report deals with any such objection or representations.

(5) Where there are two or more accused and one or more of them objects to the making of an order under subsection (3) the judge shall make the order if (and only if) satisfied after hearing the representations of each of the accused that it is in the interests of justice to do so; and if the order is made it shall not apply to the extent that a report deals with any such objection or representations.

(6) Subsection (1) does not apply to—

    (a) the publication of a report of matters, or

    (b) the inclusion in a relevant programme of a report of matters,

at the conclusion of the trial of the accused or of the last of the accused to be tried.

(7) Nothing in this section affects any prohibition or restriction imposed by virtue of any other enactment on a publication or on matter included in a programme.

(8) In this section—

    (a) 'publish', in relation to a report, means publish the report, either by itself or as part of a newspaper or periodical, for distribution to the public;

    (b) expressions cognate with 'publish' shall be construed accordingly;

    (c) 'relevant programme' means a programme included in a programme service, within the meaning of the Broadcasting Act 1990.

42 Offences in connection with reporting

(1) If a report is published or included in a relevant programme in contravention of section 41 each of the following persons is guilty of an offence—

    (a) in the case of a publication of a written report as part of a newspaper or periodical, any proprietor, editor or publisher of the newspaper or periodical;

(b) in the case of a publication of a written report otherwise than as part of a newspaper or periodical, the person who publishes it;

(c) in the case of the inclusion of a report in a relevant programme, any body corporate which is engaged in providing the service in which the programme is included and any person having functions in relation to the programme corresponding to those of an editor of a newspaper.

(2) A person guilty of an offence under this section is liable on summary conviction to a fine of an amount not exceeding level 5 on the standard scale.

(3) Proceedings for an offence under this section shall not be instituted in England and Wales otherwise than by or with the consent of the Attorney General.

(4) Subsection (8) of section 41 applies for the purposes of this section as it applies for the purposes of that.

43   Application of this Part

(1) This Part applies in relation to pre-trial hearings beginning on or after the appointed day.

(2) The reference in subsection (1) to the appointed day is to such day as is appointed for the purposes of this section by the Secretary of State by order.

[...]

Magistrates' Courts Act 1980

(1980, c. 43)

PART I CRIMINAL JURISDICTION AND PROCEDURE

Committal proceedings

8   Restrictions on reports of committal proceedings

(1) Except as provided by subsections (2), (3) and (8) below, it shall not be lawful to publish in Great Britain a written report, or to [include in a relevant programme for reception] in Great Britain a report, of any committal proceedings in England and Wales containing any matter other than that permitted by subsection (4) below.

(2) Subject to subsection (2A) below a magistrates' court shall, on an application for the purpose made with reference to any committal proceedings by the accused or one of the accused, as the case may be, order that subsection (1) above shall not apply to reports of those proceedings.

(2A) Where in the case of two or more accused one of them objects to the making of an order under subsection (2) above, the court shall make the order if, and only if, it is satisfied, after hearing the representations of the accused, that it is in the interests of justice to do so.

(2B) An order under subsection (2) above shall not apply to reports of proceedings under subsection (2A) above, but any decision of the court to make or not to make such an order may be contained in reports published or included in a relevant programme before the time authorised by subsection (3) below.

(3) It shall not be unlawful under this section to publish or include in a relevant programme a report of committal proceedings containing any matter other than that permitted by subsection (4) below—

(a) where the magistrates' court determines not to commit the accused, or determines to commit none of the accused, for trial, after it so determines;

(b) where the court commits the accused or any of the accused for trial, after the conclusion of his trial or, as the case may be, the trial of the last to be tried;

and where at any time during the inquiry the court proceeds to try summarily the case of one or more of the accused under section 25(3) or (7) below, while committing the other accused or one or more of the other accused for trial, it shall not be unlawful under this section to publish or include in a relevant programme as part of a report of the summary trial, after the court determines to proceed as aforesaid, a report of so much of the committal proceedings containing any such matter as takes place before the determination.

(4) The following matters may be contained in a report of committal proceedings published [or included in a relevant programme] without an order under subsection (2) above before the time authorised by subsection (3) above, that is to say—

(a) the identity of the court and the names of the examining justices;

(b) the names, addresses and occupations of the parties and witnesses and the ages of the accused and witnesses;

(c) the offence or offences, or a summary of them, with which the accused is or are charged;

(d) the names of the legal representatives engaged in the proceedings;

(e) any decision of the court to commit the accused or any of the accused for trial, and any decision of the court on the disposal of the case of any accused not committed;

(f) where the court commits the accused or any of the accused for trial, the charge or charges, or a summary of them, on which he is committed and the court to which he is committed;

(g) where the committal proceedings are adjourned, the date and place to which they are adjourned;

(h) any arrangements as to bail on committal or adjournment;

(i) whether a right to representation funded by the Legal Services Commission as part of the Criminal Defence Service was granted to the accused or any of the accused.

(5) If a report is published or included in a relevant programme in contravention of this section, the following persons, that is to say—

(a) in the case of a publication of a written report as part of a newspaper or periodical, any proprietor, editor or publisher of the newspaper or periodical;

(b) in the case of a publication of a written report otherwise than as part of a newspaper or periodical, the person who publishes it;

(c) in the case of the inclusion of a report in a relevant programme, any body corporate which provides the service in which the programme is included and any person having functions in relation to the programme corresponding to those of an editor of a newspaper,

shall be liable on summary conviction to a fine not exceeding level 5 on the standard scale.

(6) Proceedings for an offence under this section shall not, in England and Wales, be instituted otherwise than by or with the consent of the Attorney-General.

(7) Subsection (1) above shall be in addition to, and not in derogation from, the provisions of any other enactment with respect to the publication of reports and proceedings of magistrates' and other courts.

(8) For the purposes of this section committal proceedings shall, in relation to an information charging an indictable offence, be deemed to include any proceedings in the magistrates' court before the court proceeds to inquire into the information as examining justices; but where a magistrates' court which has begun to try an information summarily discontinues the summary trial in pursuance of section 25(2) or (6) below and proceeds to inquire into the information as examining justices, that circumstance shall not make it unlawful under this section for a report of any proceedings on the information which was published [or included in a relevant programme] before the court determined to proceed as aforesaid to have been so published or broadcast.

(9) [...]

(10) In this section—

[...]

'publish', in relation to a report, means publish the report, either by itself or as part of a newspaper or periodical, for distribution to the public;

'relevant programme' means a programme included in a programme service (within the meaning of the Broadcasting Act 1990).

Judicial Proceedings (Regulation of Reports) Act 1926

(1926, c. 61)

1   Restriction on publication of reports of judicial proceedings

(1) It shall not be lawful to print or publish, or cause or procure to be printed or published—

(a) in relation to any judicial proceedings any indecent matter or indecent medical, surgical or physiological details being matter or details the publication of which would be calculated to injure public morals;

(b) in relation to [any proceedings under Part II of the Family Law Act 1996 or otherwise in relation] to any judicial proceedings for dissolution of marriage, for nullity of marriage, or for judicial separation, [or for the dissolution or annulment of a civil partnership or for the separation of civil partners], any particulars other than the following, that is to say—

(i)   the names, addresses and occupations of the parties and witnesses;

(ii)   a concise statement of the charges, defences and counter charges in support of which evidence has been given;

(iii) submissions on any point of law arising in the course of the proceedings, and the decision of the court thereon;

(iv) the summing-up of the judge and the finding of the jury (if any) and the judgment of the court and observations made by the judge in giving judgment:

Provided that nothing in this part of this subsection shall be held to permit the publication of anything contrary to the provisions of paragraph (a) of this subsection.

(2) If any person acts in contravention of the provisions of this Act, he shall in respect of each offence be liable, on summary conviction, to imprisonment for a term not exceeding [51 weeks], or to a fine not exceeding level 5 on the standard scale, or to both such imprisonment and fine:

Provided that no person, other than a proprietor, editor, master printer or publisher, shall be liable to be convicted under this Act.

(3) No prosecution for an offence under this Act shall be commenced in England and Wales by any person without the sanction of the Attorney-General.

(4) Nothing in this section shall apply to the printing of any pleading, transcript of evidence or other document for use in connection with any judicial proceedings or the communication thereof to persons concerned in the proceedings, or to the printing or publishing of any notice or report in pursuance of the directions of the court; or to the printing or publishing of any matter in any separate volume or part of any bona fide series of law reports which does not form part of any other publication and consists solely of reports of proceedings in courts of law, or in any publication of a technical character bona fide intended for circulation among members of the legal or medical professions.

(5) [...]

2   Short title and extent

(1) This Act may be cited as the Judicial Proceedings (Regulation of Reports) Act 1926.

(2) This Act does not extend to Northern Ireland.

Employment Tribunals Act 1996

(1996, c. 17)

PART I EMPLOYMENT TRIBUNALS

Procedure

10A Confidential information

(1) Employment tribunal procedure regulations may enable an employment tribunal to sit in private for the purpose of hearing evidence from any person which in the opinion of the tribunal is likely to consist of—

(a) information which he could not disclose without contravening a prohibition imposed by or by virtue of any enactment,

(b) information which has been communicated to him in confidence or which he has otherwise obtained in consequence of the confidence reposed in him by another person, or

(c) information the disclosure of which would, for reasons other than its effect on negotiations with respect to any of the matters mentioned in section 178(2) of the Trade Union and Labour Relations (Consolidation) Act 1992, cause substantial injury to any undertaking of his or in which he works.

(2) The reference in subsection (1)(c) to any undertaking of a person or in which he works shall be construed—

(a) in relation to a person in Crown employment, as a reference to the national interest,

(b) in relation to a person who is a relevant member of the House of Lords staff, as a reference to the national interest or (if the case so requires) the interests of the House of Lords, and

(c) in relation to a person who is a relevant member of the House of Commons staff, as a reference to the national interest or (if the case so requires) the interests of the House of Commons.

10B Restriction of publicity in cases involving national security

[(1) This section applies where a tribunal has been directed under section 10(5) or has determined under section 10(6)—

(a) to take steps to conceal the identity of a particular witness, or

(b) to take steps to keep secret all or part of the reasons for its decision.

(2) It is an offence to publish—

(a) anything likely to lead to the identification of the witness, or

(b) the reasons for the tribunal's decision or the part of its reasons which it is directed or has determined to keep secret.

(3) A person guilty of an offence under this section is liable on summary conviction to a fine not exceeding level 5 on the standard scale.

(4) Where a person is charged with an offence under this section it is a defence to prove that at the time of the alleged offence he was not aware, and neither suspected nor had reason to suspect, that the publication in question was of, or included, the matter in question.

(5) Where an offence under this section committed by a body corporate is proved to have been committed with the consent or connivance of, or to be attributable to any neglect on the part of—

(a) a director, manager, secretary or other similar officer of the body corporate, or

(b) a person purporting to act in any such capacity,

he as well as the body corporate is guilty of the offence and liable to be proceeded against and punished accordingly.

(6) A reference in this section to publication includes a reference to inclusion in a programme which is included in a programme service, within the meaning of the Broadcasting Act 1990.]

11 Restriction of publicity in cases involving sexual misconduct

(1) [Employment tribunal] procedure regulations may include provision—

    (a) for cases involving allegations of the commission of sexual offences, for securing that the registration or other making available of documents or decisions shall be so effected as to prevent the identification of any person affected by or making the allegation, and

    (b) for cases involving allegations of sexual misconduct, enabling an [employment tribunal], on the application of any party to proceedings before it or of its own motion, to make a restricted reporting order having effect (if not revoked earlier) until the promulgation of the decision of the tribunal.

(2) If any identifying matter is published or included in a relevant programme in contravention of a restricted reporting order—

    (a) in the case of publication in a newspaper or periodical, any proprietor, any editor and any publisher of the newspaper or periodical,

    (b) in the case of publication in any other form, the person publishing the matter, and

    (c) in the case of matter included in a relevant programme—

        (i)   any body corporate engaged in providing the service in which the programme is included, and

        (ii)   any person having functions in relation to the programme corresponding to those of an editor of a newspaper,

shall be guilty of an offence and liable on summary conviction to a fine not exceeding level 5 on the standard scale.

(3) Where a person is charged with an offence under subsection (2) it is a defence to prove that at the time of the alleged offence he was not aware, and neither suspected nor had reason to suspect, that the publication or programme in question was of, or included, the matter in question.

(4) Where an offence under subsection (2) committed by a body corporate is proved to have been committed with the consent or connivance of, or to be attributable to any neglect on the part of—

    (a) a director, manager, secretary or other similar officer of the body corporate, or

    (b) a person purporting to act in any such capacity,

he as well as the body corporate is guilty of the offence and liable to be proceeded against and punished accordingly.

(5) In relation to a body corporate whose affairs are managed by its members 'director', in subsection (4), means a member of the body corporate.

(6) In this section—

'identifying matter', in relation to a person, means any matter likely to lead members of the public to identify him as a person affected by, or as the person making, the allegation,

'relevant programme' has the same meaning as in the Sexual Offences (Amendment) Act 1992,

'restricted reporting order' means an order—

    (a) made in exercise of a power conferred by regulations made by virtue of this section, and

    (b) prohibiting the publication in Great Britain of identifying matter in a written publication available to the public or its inclusion in a relevant programme for reception in Great Britain,

'sexual misconduct' means the commission of a sexual offence, sexual harassment or other adverse conduct (of whatever nature) related to sex, and conduct is related to sex whether the relationship with sex lies in the character of the conduct or in its having reference to the sex or sexual orientation of the person at whom the conduct is directed,

'sexual offence' means any offence to which section 4 of the Sexual Offences (Amendment) Act 1976, the Sexual Offences (Amendment) Act 1992 or section 274(2) of the Criminal Procedure (Scotland) Act 1995 applies (offences under the Sexual Offences Act 1956, Part I of the Criminal Law (Consolidation) (Scotland) Act 1995 and certain other enactments), and

'written publication' has the same meaning as in the Sexual Offences (Amendment) Act 1992.

12   Restriction of publicity in disability cases

(1) This section applies to proceedings on a complaint under [section 17A or 25(8)] of the Disability Discrimination Act 1995 in which evidence of a personal nature is likely to be heard by the [employment tribunal] hearing the complaint.

(2) [Employment tribunal] procedure regulations may include provision in relation to proceedings to which this section applies for—

    (a) enabling an [employment tribunal], on the application of the complainant or of its own motion, to make a restricted reporting order having effect (if not revoked earlier) until the promulgation of the decision of the tribunal, and

    (b) where a restricted reporting order is made in relation to a complaint which is being dealt with by the tribunal together with any other proceedings, enabling the tribunal to direct that the order is to apply also in relation to those other proceedings or such part of them as the tribunal may direct.

(3) If any identifying matter is published or included in a relevant programme in contravention of a restricted reporting order—

    (a) in the case of publication in a newspaper or periodical, any proprietor, any editor and any publisher of the newspaper or periodical,

    (b) in the case of publication in any other form, the person publishing the matter, and

    (c) in the case of matter included in a relevant programme—

        (i) any body corporate engaged in providing the service in which the programme is included, and

        (ii) any person having functions in relation to the programme corresponding to those of an editor of a newspaper,

shall be guilty of an offence and liable on summary conviction to a fine not exceeding level 5 on the standard scale.

(4) Where a person is charged with an offence under subsection (3), it is a defence to prove that at the time of the alleged offence he was not aware, and neither suspected nor had reason to suspect, that the publication or programme in question was of, or included, the matter in question.

(5) Where an offence under subsection (3) committed by a body corporate is proved to have been committed with the consent or connivance of, or to be attributable to any neglect on the part of—

    (a) a director, manager, secretary or other similar officer of the body corporate, or

    (b) a person purporting to act in any such capacity,

he as well as the body corporate is guilty of the offence and liable to be proceeded against and punished accordingly.

(6) In relation to a body corporate whose affairs are managed by its members 'director', in subsection (5), means a member of the body corporate.

(7) In this section—

'evidence of a personal nature' means any evidence of a medical, or other intimate, nature which might reasonably be assumed to be likely to cause significant embarrassment to the complainant if reported,

'identifying matter' means any matter likely to lead members of the public to identify the complainant or such other persons (if any) as may be named in the order,

'promulgation' has such meaning as may be prescribed by regulations made by virtue of this section,

'relevant programme' means a programme included in a programme service, within the meaning of the Broadcasting Act 1990,

'restricted reporting order' means an order—

    (a) made in exercise of a power conferred by regulations made by virtue of this section, and

    (b) prohibiting the publication in Great Britain of identifying matter in a written publication available to the public or its inclusion in a relevant programme for reception in Great Britain, and

'written publication' includes a film, a sound track and any other record in permanent form but does not include an indictment or other document prepared for use in particular legal proceedings.

PART II THE EMPLOYMENT APPEAL TRIBUNAL

Procedure

31   Restriction of publicity in cases involving sexual misconduct

(1) Appeal Tribunal procedure rules may, as respects proceedings to which this section applies, include provision—

    (a) for cases involving allegations of the commission of sexual offences, for securing that the registration or other making available of documents or divisions shall be so effected as to prevent the identification of any person affected by or making the allegation, and

    (b) for cases involving allegations of sexual misconduct, enabling the Appeal Tribunal, on the application of any party to the proceedings before it or of its own motion, to make a restricted reporting order having effect (if not revoked earlier) until the promulgation of the decision of the Appeal Tribunal.

(2) This section applies to—

    (a) proceedings on an appeal against a decision of an [employment tribunal] to make, or not to make, a restricted reporting order, and

    (b) proceedings on an appeal against any interlocutory decision of an [employment tribunal] in proceedings in which the [employment tribunal] has made a restricted reporting order which it has not revoked.

(3) If any identifying matter is published or included in a relevant programme in contravention of a restricted reporting order—

    (a) in the case of publication in a newspaper or periodical, any proprietor, any editor and any publisher of the newspaper or periodical,

    (b) in the case of publication in any other form, the person publishing the matter, and

    (c) in the case of matter included in a relevant programme—

        (i)   any body corporate engaged in providing the service in which the programme is included, and

        (ii) any person having functions in relation to the programme corresponding to those of an editor of a newspaper,

shall be guilty of an offence and liable on summary conviction to a fine not exceeding level 5 on the standard scale.

(4) Where a person is charged with an offence under subsection (3) it is a defence to prove that at the time of the alleged offence he was not aware, and neither suspected nor had reason to suspect, that the publication or programme in question was of, or included, the matter in question.

(5) Where an offence under subsection (3) committed by a body corporate is proved to have been committed with the consent or connivance of, or to be attributable to any neglect on the part of—

    (a) a director, manager, secretary or other similar officer of the body corporate, or

    (b) a person purporting to act in any such capacity,

he as well as the body corporate is guilty of the offence and liable to be proceeded against and punished accordingly.

(6) In relation to a body corporate whose affairs are managed by its members 'director', in subsection (5), means a member of the body corporate.

(7) 'Restricted reporting order' means—

    (a) in subsections (1) and (3), an order—

        (i)   made in exercise of a power conferred by rules made by virtue of this section, and

        (ii) prohibiting the publication in Great Britain of identifying matter in a written publication available to the public or its inclusion in a relevant programme for reception in Great Britain, and

(b) in subsection (2), an order which is a restricted reporting order for the purposes of section 11.

(8) In this section—

'identifying matter', in relation to a person, means any matter likely to lead members of the public to identify him as a person affected by, or as the person making, the allegation,

'relevant programme' has the same meaning as in the Sexual Offences (Amendment) Act 1992,

'sexual misconduct' means the commission of a sexual offence, sexual harassment or other adverse conduct (of whatever nature) related to sex, and conduct is related to sex whether the relationship with sex lies in the character of the conduct or in its having reference to the sex or sexual orientation of the person at whom the conduct is directed,

'sexual offence' means any offence to which section 4 of the Sexual Offences (Amendment) Act 1976, the Sexual Offences (Amendment) Act 1992 or section 274(2) of the Criminal Procedure (Scotland) Act 1995 applies (offences under the Sexual Offences Act 1956, Part I of the Criminal Law (Consolidation) (Scotland) Act 1995 and certain other enactments), and

'written publication' has the same meaning as in the Sexual Offences (Amendment) Act 1992.

32   Restriction of publicity in disability cases

(1) This section applies to proceedings—

    (a) on an appeal against a decision of an [employment tribunal] to make, or not to make, a restricted reporting order, or

    (b) on an appeal against any interlocutory decision of an [employment tribunal] in proceedings in which [the employment tribunal] has made a restricted reporting order which it has not revoked.

(2) Appeal Tribunal procedure rules may, as respects proceedings to which this section applies, include provision for—

    (a) enabling the Appeal Tribunal, on the application of the complainant or of its own motion, to make a restricted reporting order having effect (if not revoked earlier) until the promulgation of the decision of the Appeal Tribunal, and

    (b) where a restricted reporting order is made in relation to an appeal which is being dealt with by the Appeal Tribunal together with any other proceedings, enabling the Appeal Tribunal to direct that the order is to apply also in relation to those other proceedings or such part of them as the Appeal Tribunal may direct.

(3) If any identifying matter is published or included in a relevant programme in contravention of a restricted reporting order—

    (a) in the case of publication in a newspaper or periodical, any proprietor, any editor and any publisher of the newspaper or periodical,

    (b) in the case of publication in any other form, the person publishing the matter, and

    (c) in the case of matter included in a relevant programme—

        (i) any body corporate engaged in providing the service in which the programme is included, and

        (ii) any person having functions in relation to the programme corresponding to those of an editor of a newspaper,

shall be guilty of an offence and liable on summary conviction to a fine not exceeding level 5 on the standard scale.

(4) Where a person is charged with an offence under subsection (3), it is a defence to prove that at the time of the alleged offence he was not aware, and neither suspected nor had reason to suspect, that the publication or programme in question was of, or included, the matter in question.

(5) Where an offence under subsection (3) committed by a body corporate is proved to have been committed with the consent or connivance of, or to be attributable to any neglect on the part of—

    (a) a director, manager, secretary or other similar officer of the body corporate, or

    (b) a person purporting to act in any such capacity,

he as well as the body corporate is guilty of the offence and liable to be proceeded against and punished accordingly.

(6) In relation to a body corporate whose affairs are managed by its members 'director', in subsection (5), means a member of the body corporate.

(7) 'Restricted reporting order' means—

    (a) in subsection (1), an order which is a restricted reporting order for the purposes of section 12, and

    (b) in subsections (2) and (3), an order—

        (i)   made in exercise of a power conferred by rules made by virtue of this section, and

        (ii) prohibiting the publication in Great Britain of identifying matter in a written publication available to the public or its inclusion in a relevant programme for reception in Great Britain.

(8) In this section—

'complainant' means the person who made the complaint to which the proceedings before the Appeal Tribunal relate,

'identifying matter' means any matter likely to lead members of the public to identify the complainant or such other persons (if any) as may be named in the order,

'promulgation' has such meaning as may be prescribed by rules made by virtue of this section,

'relevant programme' means a programme included in a programme service, within the meaning of the Broadcasting Act 1990, and

'written publication' includes a film, a sound track and any other record in permanent form but does not include an indictment or other document prepared for use in particular legal proceedings.

Inquiries Act 2005

(2005, c. 12)

18   Public access to inquiry proceedings and information

(1) Subject to any restrictions imposed by a notice or order under section 19, the chairman must take such steps as he considers reasonable to secure that members of the public (including reporters) are able—

    (a) to attend the inquiry or to see and hear a simultaneous transmission of proceedings at the inquiry;

    (b) to obtain or to view a record of evidence and documents given, produced or provided to the inquiry or inquiry panel.

(2) No recording or broadcast of proceedings at an inquiry may be made except—

    (a) at the request of the chairman, or

    (b) with the permission of the chairman and in accordance with any terms on which permission is given.

Any such request or permission must be framed so as not to enable a person to see or hear by means of a recording or broadcast anything that he is prohibited by a notice under section 19 from seeing or hearing.

19   Restrictions on public access etc.

(1) Restrictions may, in accordance with this section, be imposed on—

    (a) attendance at an inquiry, or at any particular part of an inquiry;

    (b) disclosure or publication of any evidence or documents given, produced or provided to an inquiry.

(2) Restrictions may be imposed in either or both of the following ways—

    (a) by being specified in a notice (a 'restriction notice') given by the Minister to the chairman at any time before the end of the inquiry;

    (b) by being specified in an order (a 'restriction order') made by the chairman during the course of the inquiry.

(3)　A restriction notice or restriction order must specify only such restrictions—

   (a)　as are required by any statutory provision, enforceable Community obligation or rule of law, or

   (b)　as the Minister or chairman considers to be conducive to the inquiry fulfilling its terms of reference or to be necessary in the public interest, having regard in particular to the matters mentioned in subsection (4).

(4)　Those matters are—

   (a)　the extent to which any restriction on attendance, disclosure or publication might inhibit the allaying of public concern;

   (b)　any risk of harm or damage that could be avoided or reduced by any such restriction;

   (c)　any conditions as to confidentiality subject to which a person acquired information that he is to give, or has given, to the inquiry;

   (d)　the extent to which not imposing any particular restriction would be likely—

      (i)　to cause delay or to impair the efficiency or effectiveness of the inquiry, or

      (ii)　otherwise to result in additional cost (whether to public funds or to witnesses or others).

(5)　In subsection (4)(b) 'harm or damage' includes in particular—

   (a)　death or injury;

   (b)　damage to national security or international relations;

   (c)　damage to the economic interests of the United Kingdom or of any part of the United Kingdom;

   (d)　damage caused by disclosure of commercially sensitive information.

20　Further provisions about restriction notices and orders

(5)　Restrictions imposed under section 19 on disclosure or publication of evidence or documents ('disclosure restrictions') continue in force indefinitely, unless—

   (a)　under the terms of the relevant notice or order the restrictions expire at the end of the inquiry, or at some other time, or

   (b)　the relevant notice or order is varied or revoked under subsection (3), (4) or (7). This is subject to subsection (6).

(6)　After the end of the inquiry, disclosure restrictions do not apply to a public authority, or a Scottish public authority, in relation to information held by the authority otherwise than as a result of the breach of any such restrictions.

(7)　After the end of an inquiry the Minister may, by a notice published in a way that he considers suitable—

   (a)　revoke a restriction order or restriction notice containing disclosure restrictions that are still in force, or

   (b)　vary it so as to remove or relax any of the restrictions.

(8)　In this section 'restriction notice' and 'restriction order' have the meaning given by section 19(2).

36　Enforcement by High Court or Court of Session

(1)　Where a person—

   (a)　fails to comply with, or acts in breach of, a notice under section 19 or 21 or an order made by an inquiry, or

   (b)　threatens to do so,

the chairman of the inquiry, or after the end of the inquiry the Minister, may certify the matter to the appropriate court.

(2)　The court, after hearing any evidence or representations on a matter certified to it under subsection (1), may make such order by way of enforcement or otherwise as it could make if the matter had arisen in proceedings before the court.

(3)　In this section 'the appropriate court' means the High Court or, in the case of an inquiry in relation to which the relevant part of the United Kingdom is Scotland, the Court of Session.

Coroners and Justice Act 2009

(2009, c. 25)

PART 3 CRIMINAL EVIDENCE, INVESTIGATIONS AND PROCEDURE

[...]

Chapter 2 Anonymity of witnesses

Witness Anonymity Orders

86 Witness anonymity orders

(1) In this Chapter a 'witness anonymity order' is an order made by a court that requires such specified measures to be taken in relation to a witness in criminal proceedings as the court considers appropriate to ensure that the identity of the witness is not disclosed in or in connection with the proceedings.

(2) The kinds of measures that may be required to be taken in relation to a witness include measures for securing one or more of the following—

(a) that the witness's name and other identifying details may be—
   (i) withheld;
   (ii) removed from materials disclosed to any party to the proceedings;
(b) that the witness may use a pseudonym;
(c) that the witness is not asked questions of any specified description that might lead to the identification of the witness;
(d) that the witness is screened to any specified extent;
(e) that the witness's voice is subjected to modulation to any specified extent.

(3) Subsection (2) does not affect the generality of subsection (1).

(4) Nothing in this section authorises the court to require—

(a) the witness to be screened to such an extent that the witness cannot be seen by—
   (i) the judge or other members of the court (if any), or
   (ii) the jury (if there is one);
(b) the witness's voice to be modulated to such an extent that the witness's natural voice cannot be heard by any persons within paragraph (a)(i) or (ii).

(5) In this section 'specified' means specified in the witness anonymity order concerned.

87 Applications

(1) An application for a witness anonymity order to be made in relation to a witness in criminal proceedings may be made to the court by the prosecutor or the defendant.

(2) Where an application is made by the prosecutor, the prosecutor—

(a) must (unless the court directs otherwise) inform the court of the identity of the witness, but
(b) is not required to disclose in connection with the application—
   (i) the identity of the witness, or
   (ii) any information that might enable the witness to be identified,
   to any other party to the proceedings or his or her legal representatives.

(3) Where an application is made by the defendant, the defendant—

(a) must inform the court and the prosecutor of the identity of the witness, but
(b) (if there is more than one defendant) is not required to disclose in connection with the application—
   (i) the identity of the witness, or
   (ii) any information that might enable the witness to be identified,

to any other defendant or his or her legal representatives.

(4) Accordingly, where the prosecutor or the defendant proposes to make an application under this section in respect of a witness, any relevant material which is disclosed by or on behalf of that party before the determination of the application may be disclosed in such a way as to prevent—

(a) the identity of the witness, or

(b) any information that might enable the witness to be identified,

from being disclosed except as required by subsection (2)(a) or (3)(a).

(5) 'Relevant material' means any document or other material which falls to be disclosed, or is sought to be relied on, by or on behalf of the party concerned in connection with the proceedings or proceedings preliminary to them.

(6) The court must give every party to the proceedings the opportunity to be heard on an application under this section.

(7) But subsection (6) does not prevent the court from hearing one or more parties in the absence of a defendant and his or her legal representatives, if it appears to the court to be appropriate to do so in the circumstances of the case.

(8) Nothing in this section is to be taken as restricting any power to make rules of court.

88   Conditions for making order

(1) This section applies where an application is made for a witness anonymity order to be made in relation to a witness in criminal proceedings.

(2) The court may make such an order only if it is satisfied that Conditions A to C below are met.

(3) Condition A is that the proposed order is necessary—

(a) in order to protect the safety of the witness or another person or to prevent any serious damage to property, or

(b) in order to prevent real harm to the public interest (whether affecting the carrying on of any activities in the public interest or the safety of a person involved in carrying on such activities, or otherwise).

(4) Condition B is that, having regard to all the circumstances, the effect of the proposed order would be consistent with the defendant receiving a fair trial.

(5) Condition C is that the importance of the witness's testimony is such that in the interests of justice the witness ought to testify and—

(a) the witness would not testify if the proposed order were not made, or

(b) there would be real harm to the public interest if the witness were to testify without the proposed order being made.

(6) In determining whether the proposed order is necessary for the purpose mentioned in subsection (3)(a), the court must have regard (in particular) to any reasonable fear on the part of the witness—

(a) that the witness or another person would suffer death or injury, or

(b) that there would be serious damage to property,

if the witness were to be identified.

89   Relevant considerations

(1) When deciding whether Conditions A to C in section 88 are met in the case of an application for a witness anonymity order, the court must have regard to—

(a) the considerations mentioned in subsection (2) below, and

(b) such other matters as the court considers relevant.

(2) The considerations are—

(a) the general right of a defendant in criminal proceedings to know the identity of a witness in the proceedings;

(b) the extent to which the credibility of the witness concerned would be a relevant factor when the weight of his or her evidence comes to be assessed;

(c) whether evidence given by the witness might be the sole or decisive evidence implicating the defendant;

    (d) whether the witness's evidence could be properly tested (whether on grounds of cred-
ibility or otherwise) without his or her identity being disclosed;

    (e) whether there is any reason to believe that the witness—

      (i) has a tendency to be dishonest, or

      (ii) has any motive to be dishonest in the circumstances of the case,

        having regard (in particular) to any previous convictions of the witness and to any rela-
tionship between the witness and the defendant or any associates of the defendant;

    (f) whether it would be reasonably practicable to protect the witness by any means other
than by making a witness anonymity order specifying the measures that are under consideration by the court.

    [. . .]

Discharge and variation

91   Discharge or variation of order

(1) A court that has made a witness anonymity order in relation to any criminal proceedings
may in those proceedings subsequently discharge or vary (or further vary) the order if it appears to
the court to be appropriate to do so in view of the provisions of sections 88 and 89 that apply to the
making of an order.

    (2) The court may do so—

    (a) on an application made by a party to the proceedings if there has been a material change
of circumstances since the relevant time, or

    (b) on its own initiative.

    (3) The court must give every party to the proceedings the opportunity to be heard—

    (a) before determining an application made to it under subsection (2);

    (b) before discharging or varying the order on its own initiative.

    (4) But subsection (3) does not prevent the court hearing one or more of the parties to the pro-
ceedings in the absence of a defendant in the proceedings and his or her legal representatives, if it
appears to the court to be appropriate to do so in the circumstances of the case.

    (5) 'The relevant time' means—

    (a) the time when the order was made, or

    (b) if a previous application has been made under subsection (2), the time when the appli-
cation (or the last application) was made.

92   Discharge or variation after proceedings

(1) This section applies if—

    (a) a court has made a witness anonymity order in relation to a witness in criminal proceed-
ings ('the old proceedings'), and

    (b) the old proceedings have come to an end.

    (2) The court that made the order may discharge or vary (or further vary) the order if it appears
to the court to be appropriate to do so in view of—

    (a) the provisions of sections 88 and 89 that apply to the making of a witness anonymity
order, and

    (b) such other matters as the court considers relevant.

    (3) The court may do so—

    (a) on an application made by a party to the old proceedings if there has been a material
change of circumstances since the relevant time, or

    (b) on an application made by the witness if there has been a material change of circum-
stances since the relevant time.

    (4) The court may not determine an application made to it under subsection (3) unless in the
case of each of the parties to the old proceedings and the witness—

    (a) it has given the person the opportunity to be heard, or

    (b) it is satisfied that it is not reasonably practicable to communicate with the person.

(5) Subsection (4) does not prevent the court hearing one or more of the persons mentioned in that subsection in the absence of a person who was a defendant in the old proceedings and that person's legal representatives, if it appears to the court to be appropriate to do so in the circumstances of the case.

(6) 'The relevant time' means—

(a) the time when the old proceedings came to an end, or

(b) if a previous application has been made under subsection (3), the time when the application (or the last application) was made.

93 Discharge or variation by appeal court

(1) This section applies if—

(a) a court has made a witness anonymity order in relation to a witness in criminal proceedings ('the trial proceedings'), and

(b) a defendant in the trial proceedings has in those proceedings—

(i) been convicted,

(ii) been found not guilty by reason of insanity, or

(iii) been found to be under a disability and to have done the act charged in respect of an offence.

(2) The appeal court may in proceedings on or in connection with an appeal by the defendant from the trial proceedings discharge or vary (or further vary) the order if it appears to the court to be appropriate to do so in view of—

(a) the provisions of sections 88 and 89 that apply to the making of a witness anonymity order, and

(b) such other matters as the court considers relevant.

(3) The appeal court may not discharge or vary the order unless in the case of each party to the trial proceedings—

(a) it has given the person the opportunity to be heard, or

(b) it is satisfied that it is not reasonably practicable to communicate with the person.

(4) But subsection (3) does not prevent the appeal court hearing one or more of the parties to the trial proceedings in the absence of a person who was a defendant in the trial proceedings and that person's legal representatives, if it appears to the court to be appropriate to do so in the circumstances of the case.

(5) In this section a reference to the doing of an act includes a reference to a failure to act.

(6) 'Appeal court' means—

(a) the Court of Appeal,

(b) the Court of Appeal in Northern Ireland, or

(c) the Court Martial Appeal Court.

[. . .]

Interpretation

97 Interpretation of this Chapter

(1) In this Chapter—

'court' means—

(a) in relation to England and Wales, a magistrates' court, the Crown Court or the criminal division of the Court of Appeal,

(b) in relation to Northern Ireland, a magistrates' court, the Crown Court, a county court exercising its criminal jurisdiction, the High Court or the Court of Appeal in Northern Ireland, or

(c) a service court;

'criminal proceedings' means—

(a) in relation to a court within paragraph (a) or (b) above (other than the High Court in

Northern Ireland), criminal proceedings consisting of a trial or other hearing at which evidence falls to be given;

(b) in relation to the High Court in Northern Ireland, proceedings relating to bail in respect of a person charged with or convicted of an offence where the proceedings consist of a hearing at which evidence falls to be given;

(c) in relation to a service court, proceedings in respect of a service offence consisting of a trial or other hearing at which evidence falls to be given;

'the defendant', in relation to any criminal proceedings, means any person charged with an offence to which the proceedings relate (whether or not convicted);

'prosecutor' means any person acting as prosecutor, whether an individual or body;

'service court' means—

(a) the Court Martial established by the Armed Forces Act 2006 (c. 52),

(b) the Summary Appeal Court established by that Act,

(c) the Service Civilian Court established by that Act, or

(d) the Court Martial Appeal Court;

'service offence' has the meaning given by section 50(2) of the Armed Forces Act 2006 (c. 52);

'witness', in relation to any criminal proceedings, means any person called, or proposed to be called, to give evidence at the trial or hearing in question;

'witness anonymity order' has the meaning given by section 86.

(2) In the case of a witness anonymity order made by a magistrates' court in England and Wales or Northern Ireland, a thing authorised or required by section 91 or 92 to be done by the court by which the order was made may be done by any magistrates' court acting in the same local justice area, or for the same petty sessions district, as that court.

Part IV

Contempt of court and the media

Contempt of Court Act 1981

(1981, c. 49)

1 The strict liability rule

In this Act 'the strict liability rule' means the rule of law whereby conduct may be treated as a contempt of court as tending to interfere with the course of justice in particular legal proceedings regardless of intent to do so.

2 Limitation of scope of strict liability

(1) The strict liability rule applies only in relation to publications, and for this purpose 'publication' includes any speech, writing, [programme included in a cable programme service] or other communication in whatever form, which is addressed to the public at large or any section of the public.

(2) The strict liability rule applies only to a publication which creates a substantial risk that the course of justice in the proceedings in question will be seriously impeded or prejudiced.

(3) The strict liability rule applies to a publication only if the proceedings in question are active within the meaning of this section at the time of the publication.

(4) Schedule 1 applies for determining the times at which proceedings are to be treated as active within the meaning of this section.

(5) In this section 'programme service' [has the same meaning as in the Broadcasting Act 1990].

3 Defence of innocent publication or distribution

(1) A person is not guilty of contempt of court under the strict liability rule as the publisher of any matter to which that rule applies if at the time of publication (having taken all reasonable care) he does not know and has no reason to suspect that relevant proceedings are active.

(2) A person is not guilty of contempt of court under the strict liability rule as the distributor of a publication containing any such matter if at the time of distribution (having taken all reasonable care) he does not know that it contains such matter and has no reason to suspect that it is likely to do so.

(3) The burden of proof of any fact tending to establish a defence afforded by this section to any person lies upon that person.

(4) [...]

4 Contemporary reports of proceedings

(1) Subject to this section a person is not guilty of contempt of court under the strict liability rule in respect of a fair and accurate report of legal proceedings held in public, published contemporaneously and in good faith.

(2) In any such proceedings the court may, where it appears to be necessary for avoiding a substantial risk of prejudice to the administration of justice in those proceedings, or in any other proceedings pending or imminent, order that the publication of any report of the proceedings, or any part of the proceedings, be postponed for such period as the court thinks necessary for that purpose.

(2A) Where in proceedings for any offence which is an administration of justice offence for the purposes of section 54 of the Criminal Procedure and Investigations Act 1996 (acquittal tainted by an administration of justice offence) it appears to the court that there is a possibility that (by virtue of that section) proceedings may be taken against a person for an offence of which he has been acquitted, subsection (2) of this section shall apply as if those proceedings were pending or imminent.

(3) For the purposes of subsection (1) of this section [...] a report of proceedings shall be treated as published contemporaneously—

    (a) in the case of a report of which publication is postponed pursuant to an order under subsection (2) of this section, if published as soon as practicable after that order expires;

    (b) in the case of a report of committal proceedings of which publication is permitted by virtue only of subsection (3) of section 8 of the Magistrates' Courts Act 1980, if published as soon as practicable after publication is so permitted.

5   Discussion of public affairs

A publication made as or as part of a discussion in good faith of public affairs or other matters of general public interest is not to be treated as a contempt of court under the strict liability rule if the risk of impediment or prejudice to particular legal proceedings is merely incidental to the discussion.

6   Savings

Nothing in the foregoing provisions of this Act—

    (a) prejudices any defence available at common law to a charge of contempt of court under the strict liability rule;

    (b) implies that any publication is punishable as contempt of court under that rule which would not be so punishable apart from those provisions;

    (c) restricts liability for contempt of court in respect of conduct intended to impede or prejudice the administration of justice.

7   Consent required for institution of proceedings

Proceedings for a contempt of court under the strict liability rule (other than Scottish proceedings) shall not be instituted except by or with the consent of the Attorney General or on the motion of a court having jurisdiction to deal with it.

Other aspects of law and procedure

8   Confidentiality of jury's deliberations

(1) Subject to subsection (2) below, it is a contempt of court to obtain, disclose or solicit any particulars of statements made, opinions expressed, arguments advanced or votes cast by members of a jury in the course of their deliberations in any legal proceedings.

(2) This section does not apply to any disclosure of any particulars—

    (a) in the proceedings in question for the purpose of enabling the jury to arrive at their verdict, or in connection with the delivery of that verdict, or

    (b) in evidence in any subsequent proceedings for an offence alleged to have been committed in relation to the jury in the first mentioned proceedings,

or to the publication of any particulars so disclosed.

(3) Proceedings for a contempt of court under this section (other than Scottish proceedings) shall not be instituted except by or with the consent of the Attorney General or on the motion of a court having jurisdiction to deal with it.

9   Use of tape recorders

(1) Subject to subsection (4) below, it is a contempt of court—

    (a) to use in court, or bring into court for use, any tape recorder or other instrument for recording sound, except with the leave of the court;

    (b) to publish a recording of legal proceedings made by means of any such instrument, or any recording derived directly or indirectly from it, by playing it in the hearing of the public or any section of the public, or to dispose of it or any recording so derived, with a view to such publication;

(c) to use any such recording in contravention of any conditions of leave granted under paragraph (a).

(2) Leave under paragraph (a) of subsection (1) may be granted or refused at the discretion of the court, and if granted may be granted subject to such conditions as the court thinks proper with respect to the use of any recording made pursuant to the leave; and where leave has been granted the court may at the like discretion withdraw or amend it either generally or in relation to any particular part of the proceedings.

(3) Without prejudice to any other power to deal with an act of contempt under paragraph (a) of subsection (1), the court may order the instrument, or any recording made with it, or both, to be forfeited; and any object so forfeited shall (unless the court otherwise determines on application by a person appearing to be the owner) be sold or otherwise disposed of in such manner as the court may direct.

(4) This section does not apply to the making or use of sound recordings for purposes of official transcripts of proceedings.

10 Sources of information

No court may require a person to disclose, nor is any person guilty of contempt of court for refusing to disclose, the source of information contained in a publication for which he is responsible, unless it be established to the satisfaction of the court that disclosure is necessary in the interests of justice or national security or for the prevention of disorder or crime.

11 Publication of matters exempted from disclosure in court

In any case where a court (having power to do so) allows a name or other matter to be withheld from the public in proceedings before the court, the court may give such directions prohibiting the publication of that name or matter in connection with the proceedings as appear to the court to be necessary for the purpose for which it was so withheld.

12 Offences of contempt of magistrates' courts

(1) A magistrates' court has jurisdiction under this section to deal with any person who—

(a) wilfully insults the justice or justices, any witness before or officer of the court or any solicitor or counsel having business in the court, during his or their sitting or attendance in court or in going to or returning from the court; or

(b) wilfully interrupts the proceedings of the court or otherwise misbehaves in court.

(2) In any such case the court may order any officer of the court, or any constable, to take the offender into custody and detain him until the rising of the court; and the court may, if it thinks fit, commit the offender to custody for a specified period not exceeding one month or impose on him a fine not exceeding £2,500, or both.

(2A) A fine imposed under subsection (2) above shall be deemed, for the purposes of any enactment, to be a sum adjudged to be paid by a conviction.

(4) A magistrates' court may at any time revoke an order of committal made under subsection (2) and, if the offender is in custody, order his discharge.

(5) [Section 135 of the Powers of Criminal Courts (Sentencing) Act 2000 (limit on fines in respect of young persons) and the] following provisions of the Magistrates' Courts Act 1980 apply in relation to an order under this section as they apply in relation to a sentence on conviction or finding of guilty of an offence; and those provisions of the Magistrates' Courts Act 1980 are section 36 (restriction on fines in respect of young persons); sections 75 to 91 (enforcement); section 108 (appeal to Crown Court); section 136 (overnight detention in default of payment); and section 142(1) (power to rectify mistakes).

13 [. . .]

Penalties for contempt and kindred offences

14   Proceedings in England and Wales

(1) In any case where a court has power to commit a person to prison for contempt of court and (apart from this provision) no limitation applies to the period of committal, the committal shall (without prejudice to the power of the court to order his earlier discharge) be for a fixed term, and that term shall not on any occasion exceed two years in the case of committal by a superior court, or one month in the case of committal by an inferior court.

(2) In any case where an inferior court has power to fine a person for contempt of court and (apart from this provision) no limit applies to the amount of the fine, the fine shall not on any occasion exceed £2,500.

(2A) In the exercise of jurisdiction to commit for contempt of court or any kindred offence the court shall not deal with the offender by making an order under [section 60 of the Powers of Criminal Courts (Sentencing) Act 2000] (an attendance centre order) if it appears to the court, after considering any available evidence, that he is under 17 years of age.

(2A) A fine imposed under subsection (2) above shall be deemed, for the purposes of any enactment, to be a sum adjudged to be paid by a conviction.

(4) Each of the superior courts shall have the like power to make a hospital order or guardianship order under section 37 of the Mental Health Act 1983 or an interim hospital order under section 38 of that Act in the case of a person suffering from mental disorder within the meaning of that Act who could otherwise be committed to prison for contempt of court as the Crown Court has under that section in the case of a person convicted of an offence.

(4A) Each of the superior courts shall have the like power to make an order under section 35 of the said Act of 1983 (remand for report on accused's mental condition) where there is reason to suspect that a person who could be committed to prison for contempt of court is suffering from mental disorder within the meaning of that Act as the Crown Court has under that section in the case of an accused person within the meaning of that section.

(4A) For the purposes of the preceding provisions of this section a county court shall be treated as a superior court and not as an inferior court.

15   Penalties for contempt of court in Scottish proceedings

(1) In Scottish proceedings, when a person is committed to prison for contempt of court the committal shall (without prejudice to the power of the court to order his earlier discharge) be for a fixed term.

(2) The maximum penalty which may be imposed by way of imprisonment or fine for contempt of court in Scottish proceedings shall be two years' imprisonment or a fine or both, except that—

   (a) where the contempt is dealt with by the sheriff in the course of or in connection with proceedings other than criminal proceedings on indictment, such penalty shall not exceed three months' imprisonment or a fine of level 4 on the standard scale or both; and

   (b) where the contempt is dealt with by the district court, such penalty shall not exceed sixty days' imprisonment or a fine of level 4 on the standard scale or both.

(3) The following provisions of the Criminal Procedure (Scotland) Act 1995 shall apply in relation to persons found guilty of contempt of court in Scottish proceedings as they apply in relation to persons convicted of offences—

   (a) in every case, section 207 (restrictions on detention of young offenders);

   (b) in any case to which paragraph (b) of subsection (2) above does not apply, sections 58, 59 and 61 (persons suffering from mental disorder); and in any case to which the said paragraph (b) does apply, subsection (5) below shall have effect.

(5) Where a person is found guilty by a district court of contempt of court and it appears to the court that he may be suffering from mental disorder, it shall remit him to the sheriff in the manner provided by [section 7(9) and (10) of the Criminal Procedure (Scotland) Act 1995] and the sheriff shall, on such remit being made, have the like power to make an order under [section 58(1)] of the

said Act in respect of him as if he had been convicted by the sheriff of an offence, or in dealing with him may exercise the like powers as the court making the remit.

16   Enforcement of fines imposed by certain superior courts

(1) Payment of a fine for contempt of court imposed by a superior court, other than the Crown Court or one of the courts specified in subsection (4) below, may be enforced upon the order of the court—

(a) in like manner as a judgment of the High Court for the payment of money; or

(b) in like manner as a fine imposed by the Crown Court.

(2) Where payment of a fine imposed by any court falls to be enforced as mentioned in paragraph (a) of subsection (1)—

(a) the court shall, if the fine is not paid in full forthwith or within such time as the court may allow, certify to Her Majesty's Remembrancer the sum payable;

(b) Her Majesty's Remembrancer shall thereupon proceed to enforce payment of that sum as if it were due to him as a judgment debt.

(3) Where payment of a fine imposed by any court falls to be enforced as mentioned in paragraph (b) of subsection (1), the provisions of [sections 139 and 140 of the Powers of Criminal Courts (Sentencing) Act 2000] shall apply as they apply to a fine imposed by the Crown Court.

(4) Subsection (1) of this section does not apply to fines imposed by the criminal division of the Court of Appeal or by the Supreme Court on appeal from that division.

(5) The Fines Act 1833 shall not apply to a fine to which subsection (1) of this section applies.

17   Disobedience to certain orders of magistrates' courts

(1) The powers of a magistrates' court under subsection (3) of section 63 of the Magistrates' Courts Act 1980 (punishment by fine or committal for disobeying an order to do anything other than the payment of money or to abstain from doing anything) may be exercised either of the court's own motion or by order on complaint.

(2) In relation to the exercise of those powers the provisions of the Magistrates' Court Act 1980 shall apply subject to the modifications set out in Schedule 3 to this Act.

Supplemental

18   Northern Ireland

(1) In the application of this Act to Northern Ireland references to the Attorney General shall be construed as references to the Attorney General for Northern Ireland.

(2) In their application to Northern Ireland, sections 12, 13, 14 and 16 of this Act shall have effect as set out in Schedule 4.

19   Interpretation

In this Act—

'court' includes any tribunal or body exercising the judicial power of the State, and 'legal proceedings' shall be construed accordingly;

'publication' has the meaning assigned by subsection (1) of section 2, and 'publish' (except in section 9) shall be construed accordingly;

'Scottish proceedings' means proceedings before any court, including the Court Martial Appeal Court, the Restrictive Practices Court and the Employment Appeal Tribunal, sitting in Scotland, and includes proceedings before the Supreme Court in the exercise of any appellate jurisdiction over proceedings in such a court;

'the strict liability rule' has the meaning assigned by section 1;

'superior court' means Supreme Court, the Court of Appeal, the High Court, the Crown Court, the Court Martial Appeal Court, the Restrictive Practices Court, the Employment Appeal Tribunal and any other court exercising in relation to its proceedings powers equivalent to those of the High Court.

20   Tribunals of Inquiry

(1) In relation to any tribunal to which the Tribunals of Inquiry (Evidence) Act 1921 applies, and the proceedings of such a tribunal, the provisions of this Act (except subsection (3) of section 9) apply as they apply in relation to courts and legal proceedings; and references to the course of justice or the administration of justice in legal proceedings shall be construed accordingly.

(2) The proceedings of a tribunal established under the said Act shall be treated as active within the meaning of section 2 from the time when the tribunal is appointed until its report is presented to Parliament.

21   Short title, commencement and extent

(1) This Act may be cited as the Contempt of Court Act 1981.

(2) The provisions of this Act relating to legal aid in England and Wales shall come into force on such day as the Lord Chancellor may appoint by order made by statutory instrument; and the provisions of this Act relating to legal aid in Scotland and Northern Ireland shall come into force on such day or days as the Secretary of State may so appoint. Different days may be appointed under this subsection in relation to different courts.

(3) Subject to subsection (2), this Act shall come into force at the expiration of the period of one month beginning with the day on which it is passed.

(4) Sections 7, 8(3), 12, 13(1) to (3), 14, 16, 17 and 18, Parts I and III of Schedule 2 and Schedules 3 and 4 of this Act do not extend to Scotland.

(5) This Act, except sections 15 and 17 and Schedules 2 and 3, extends to Northern Ireland.

SCHEDULE ONE TIMES WHEN PROCEEDINGS ARE ACTIVE FOR PURPOSES OF SECTION 2

Preliminary

1. In this Schedule 'criminal proceedings' means proceedings against a person in respect of an offence, not being appellate proceedings or proceedings commenced by motion for committal or attachment in England and Wales or Northern Ireland; and 'appellate proceedings' means proceedings on appeal from or for the review of the decision of a court in any proceedings.

1A. In paragraph 1 the reference to an offence includes a service offence within the meaning of the Armed Forces Act 2006.

[1ZA. Proceedings under the Double Jeopardy (Scotland) Act 2011 (asp 16) are criminal proceedings for the purposes of this Schedule.]

2. Criminal, appellate and other proceedings are active within the meaning of section 2 at the times respectively prescribed by the following paragraphs of this Schedule; and in relation to proceedings in which more than one of the steps described in any of those paragraphs is taken, the reference in that paragraph is a reference to the first of those steps.

Criminal proceedings

3. Subject to the following provisions of this Schedule, criminal proceedings are active from the relevant initial step specified in paragraph 4 until concluded as described in paragraph 5.

4. The initial steps of criminal proceedings are—

(a) arrest without warrant;

(b) the issue, or in Scotland the grant, of a warrant for arrest;

(c) the issue of a summons to appear, or in Scotland the grant of a warrant to cite;

(d) the service of an indictment or other document specifying the charge;

(e) except in Scotland, oral charge.

[(f) the making of an application under section 2(2) (tainted acquittals), 3(3)(b) (admission made or becoming known after acquittal), 4(3)(b) (new evidence), 11(3) (eventual death of injured person) or 12(3) (nullity of previous proceedings) of the Double Jeopardy (Scotland) Act 2011 (asp 16).]

[4A. Where as a result of an order under section 54 of the Criminal Procedure and Investigations Act 1996 (acquittal tainted by an administration of justice offence) proceedings are brought against a person for an offence of which he has previously been acquitted, the initial step of the proceedings is a certification under subsection (2) of that section; and paragraph 4 has effect subject to this.]

5. Criminal proceedings are concluded—

    (a) by acquittal or, as the case may be, by sentence;

    (b) by any other verdict, finding, order or decision which puts an end to the proceedings;

    (c) by discontinuance or by operation of law.

    [(d) where the initial steps of the proceedings are as mentioned in paragraph 4(f)—

        (i) by refusal of the application;

        (ii) if the application is granted and within the period of 2 months mentioned in section 6(3) of the Double Jeopardy (Scotland) Act 2011 (asp 16) a new prosecution is brought, by acquittal or, as the case may be, by sentence in the new prosecution.]

6. The reference in paragraph 5(a) to sentence includes any order or decision consequent on conviction or finding of guilt which disposes of the case, either absolutely or subject to future events, and a deferment of sentence under [section 1 of the Powers of Criminal Courts (Sentencing) Act 2000], section 219 or 432 of the Criminal Procedure (Scotland) Act 1975 or Article 14 of the Treatment of Offenders (Northern Ireland) Order 1976.

7. Proceedings are discontinued within the meaning of paragraph 5(c)—

    (a) in England and Wales or Northern Ireland, if the charge or summons is withdrawn or a *nolle prosequi* entered;

    [(aa) in England and Wales, if they are discontinued by Virtue of section 23 of the Prosecution of Offences Act 1985;]

    (b) in Scotland, if the proceedings are expressly abandoned by the prosecutor or are deserted *simpliciter;*

    (c) in the case of proceedings in England and Wales or Northern Ireland commenced by arrest without warrant, if the person arrested is released, otherwise than on bail, without having been charged.

    [(d) where the initial steps of the proceedings are as mentioned in paragraph 4(f) and the application is granted, if no new prosecution is brought within the period of 2 months mentioned in section 6(3) of the Double Jeopardy (Scotland) Act 2011 (asp 16).]

9. Criminal proceedings in England and Wales or Northern Ireland cease to be active if an order is made for the charge to lie on the file, but become active again if leave is later given for the proceedings to continue.

[9A. Where proceedings in England and Wales have been discontinued by virtue of section 23 of the Prosecution of Offences Act 1985, but notice is given by the accused under subsection (7) of that section to the effect that he wants the proceedings to continue, they become active again with the giving of that notice.]

10. Without prejudice to paragraph 5(b) above, criminal proceedings against a person cease to be active—

    (a) if the accused is found to be under a disability such as to render him unfit to be tried or unfit to plead or, in Scotland, is found to be insane in bar of trial; or

    (b) if a hospital order is made in his case under section 51(5) of the Mental Health Act 1983 or paragraph (b) of subsection (2) of section 62 of the Mental Health Act (Northern Ireland) 1961 or, in Scotland, where [an assessment order or a treatment order ceases to have effect by virtue of sections 52H or 52R respectively of the Criminal Procedure (Scotland) Act 1995],

but become active again if they are later resumed.

11. Criminal proceedings against a person which become active on the issue or the grant of a warrant for his arrest cease to be active at the end of the period of twelve months beginning with the date of the warrant unless he has been arrested within that period, but become active again if he is subsequently arrested.

Other proceedings at first instance

12. Proceedings other than criminal proceedings and appellate proceedings are active from the time when arrangements for the hearing are made or, if no such arrangements are previously made, from the time the hearing begins, until the proceedings are disposed of or discontinued or withdrawn; and for the purposes of this paragraph any motion or application made in or for the purposes of any proceedings, and any pre-trial review in the county court, is to be treated as a distinct proceeding.

13. In England and Wales or Northern Ireland arrangements for the hearing of proceedings to which paragraph 12 applies are made within the meaning of that paragraph—

    (a) in the case of proceedings in the High Court for which provision is made by rules of court for setting down for trial, when the case is set down;

    (b) in the case of any proceedings, when a date for the trial or hearing is fixed.

14. In Scotland arrangements for the hearing of proceedings to which paragraph 12 applies are made within the meaning of that paragraph—

    (a) in the case of an ordinary action in the Court of Session or in the sheriff court, when the Record is closed;

    (b) in the case of a motion or application, when it is enrolled or made;

    (c) in any other case, when the date for a hearing is fixed or a hearing is allowed.

Appellate proceedings

15. Appellate proceedings are active from the time when they are commenced—

    (a) by application for leave to appeal or apply for review, or by notice of such an application;

    (b) by notice of appeal or of application for review;

    (c) by other originating process, until disposed of or abandoned, discontinued or withdrawn.

16. Where, in appellate proceedings relating to criminal proceedings, the court—

    (a) remits the case to the court below; or

    (b) orders a new trial or a *venire de novo,* or in Scotland grants authority to bring a new prosecution, any further or new proceedings which result shall be treated as active from the conclusion of the appellate proceedings.

Administration of Justice Act 1960

(8 and 9 Eliz. 2, c. 65)

12   Publication of information relating to proceedings in private

(1) The publication of information relating to proceedings before any court sitting in private shall not of itself be contempt of court except in the following cases, that is to say—

    (a) [. . .]

    (b) where the proceedings are brought under the Mental Capacity Act 2005, or under any provision of the Mental Health Act 1983 authorising an application or reference to be made to the First-Tier Tribunal, the Mental Health Review Tribunal for Wales or to a county court;

    (c) where the court sits in private for reasons of national security during that part of the proceedings about which the information in question is published;

    (d) where the information relates to a secret process, discovery or invention which is in issue in the proceedings;

    (e) where the court (having power to do so) expressly prohibits the publication of all information relating to the proceedings or of information of the description which is published.

(2) Without prejudice to the foregoing subsection, the publication of the text or a summary of the whole or part of an order made by a court sitting in private shall not of itself be contempt of court except where the court (having power to do so) expressly prohibits the publication.

(3) In this section references to a court shall include references to a judge and to a tribunal and to any person exercising the functions of a court, a judge or a tribunal; and references to a court sitting in private include references to a court sitting in camera or in chambers.

(4) Nothing in this section shall be construed as implying that any publication is punishable as contempt of court which would not be so punishable apart from this section (and in particular where the publication is not so punishable by reason of being authorised by rules of court).

[(5) Subsection (1) is subject to Part 2 of the Children Schools and Families Act 2010 (family proceedings) and nothing in subsection (2) applies in relation to a contempt of court under section 11 of that Act (restriction on publication of information relating to family proceedings).]

Courts Act 2003

(2003, c. 39)

93   Award of costs against third parties
After section 19A of the Prosecution of Offences Act 1985 (c. 23) insert—

'19B   Provision for award of costs against third parties
(1) The Lord Chancellor may by regulations make provision empowering magistrates' courts, the Crown Court and the Court of Appeal to make a third party costs order if the condition in subsection (3) is satisfied.

(2) A 'third party costs order' is an order as to the payment of costs incurred by a party to criminal proceedings by a person who is not a party to those proceedings ('the third party').

(3) The condition is that—
  (a) there has been serious misconduct (whether or not constituting a contempt of court) by the third party, and
  (b) the court considers it appropriate, having regard to that misconduct, to make a third party costs order against him.

(4) Regulations made under this section may, in particular—
  (a) specify types of misconduct in respect of which a third party costs order may not be made;
  (b) allow the making of a third party costs order at any time;
  (c) make provision for any other order as to costs which has been made in respect of the proceedings to be varied on, or taken account of in, the making of a third party costs order;
  (d) make provision for account to be taken of any third party costs order in the making of any other order as to costs in respect of the proceedings.

(5) Regulations made under this section in relation to magistrates' courts must provide that the third party may appeal to the Crown Court against a third party costs order made by a magistrates' court.

(6) Regulations made under this section in relation to the Crown Court must provide that the third party may appeal to the Court of Appeal against a third party costs order made by the Crown Court.'

Part V

Protection of confidential sources of information

Recommendation No. R (2000) 7 of the Committee of Ministers to Member States on the Right of Journalists not to Disclose their Sources of Information*

(Adopted by the Committee of Ministers on 8 March 2000 at the 701st meeting of the Ministers' Deputies)

The Committee of Ministers, under the terms of Article 15.b of the Statute of the Council of Europe,

Considering that the aim of the Council of Europe is to achieve greater unity between its members for the purpose of safeguarding and realising the ideals and principles which are their common heritage;

Recalling the commitment of the member states to the fundamental right to freedom of expression as guaranteed by Article 10 of the Convention for the Protection of Human Rights and Fundamental Freedoms;

Reaffirming that the right to freedom of expression and information constitutes one of the essential foundations of a democratic society and one of the basic conditions for its progress and the development of every individual, as expressed in the Declaration on the Freedom of Expression and Information of 1982;

Reaffirming the need for democratic societies to secure adequate means of promoting the development of free, independent and pluralist media;

Recognising that the free and unhindered exercise of journalism is enshrined in the right to freedom of expression and is a fundamental prerequisite to the right of the public to be informed on matters of public concern;

Convinced that the protection of journalists' sources of information constitutes a basic condition for journalistic work and freedom as well as for the freedom of the media;

Recalling that many journalists have expressed in professional codes of conduct their obligation not to disclose their sources of information in case they received the information confidentially;

Recalling that the protection of journalists and their sources has been established in the legal systems of some member states;

Recalling also that the exercise by journalists of their right not to disclose their sources of information carries with it duties and responsibilities as expressed in Article 10 of the Convention for the Protection of Human Rights and Fundamental Freedoms;

Aware of the Resolution of the European Parliament of 1994 on confidentiality for journalists' sources and the right of civil servants to disclose information;

Aware of Resolution No. 2 on journalistic freedoms and human rights of the 4th European Ministerial Conference on Mass Media Policy held in Prague in December 1994, and recalling Recommendation No. R (96) 4 on the protection of journalists in situations of conflict and tension,

Recommends to the governments of member states:

1. to implement in their domestic law and practice the principles appended to this recommendation,
2. to disseminate widely this recommendation and its appended principles, where appropriate accompanied by a translation, and
3. to bring them in particular to the attention of public authorities, police authorities and the judiciary as well as to make them available to journalists, the media and their professional organisations.

APPENDIX TO RECOMMENDATION NO. R (2000) 7
PRINCIPLES CONCERNING THE RIGHT OF
JOURNALISTS NOT TO DISCLOSE THEIR
SOURCES OF INFORMATION

Definitions

For the purposes of this Recommendation:

a. the term 'journalist' means any natural or legal person who is regularly or professionally engaged in the collection and dissemination of information to the public via any means of mass communication;

b. the term 'information' means any statement of fact, opinion or idea in the form of text, sound and/or picture;

c. the term 'source' means any person who provides information to a journalist;

d. the term 'information identifying a source' means, as far as this is likely to lead to the identification of a source:

    i. the name and personal data as well as voice and image of a source,

    ii. the factual circumstances of acquiring information from a source by a journalist,

    iii. the unpublished content of the information provided by a source to a journalist, and

    iv. personal data of journalists and their employers related to their professional work.

Principle 1 (Right of non-disclosure of journalists)

Domestic law and practice in member states should provide for explicit and clear protection of the right of journalists not to disclose information identifying a source in accordance with Article 10 of the Convention for the Protection of Human Rights and Fundamental Freedoms (hereinafter: the Convention) and the principles established herein, which are to be considered as minimum standards for the respect of this right.

Principle 2 (Right of non-disclosure of other persons)

Other persons who, by their professional relations with journalists, acquire knowledge of information identifying a source through the collection, editorial processing or dissemination of this information, should equally be protected under the principles established herein.

Principle 3 (Limits to the right of non-disclosure)

a. The right of journalists not to disclose information identifying a source must not be subject to other restrictions than those mentioned in Article 10, paragraph 2 of the Convention. In determining whether a legitimate interest in a disclosure falling within the scope of Article 10, paragraph 2 of the Convention outweighs the public interest in not disclosing information identifying a source, competent authorities of member states shall pay particular regard to the importance of the right of non-disclosure and the pre-eminence given to it in the case-law of the European Court of Human Rights, and may only order a disclosure if, subject to paragraph b, there exists an overriding requirement in the public interest and if circumstances are of a sufficiently vital and serious nature.

b. The disclosure of information identifying a source should not be deemed necessary unless it can be convincingly established that:

    i. reasonable alternative measures to the disclosure do not exist or have been exhausted by the persons or public authorities that seek the disclosure, and

    ii. the legitimate interest in the disclosure clearly outweighs the public interest in the non-disclosure, bearing in mind that:

      - an overriding requirement of the need for disclosure is proved,
      - the circumstances are of a sufficiently vital and serious nature,
      - the necessity of the disclosure is identified as responding to a pressing social need, and
      - member states enjoy a certain margin of appreciation in assessing this need, but this margin goes hand in hand with the supervision by the European Court of Human Rights.

c. The above requirements should be applied at all stages of any proceedings where the right of non-disclosure might be invoked.

Principle 4 (Alternative evidence to journalists' sources)

In legal proceedings against a journalist on grounds of an alleged infringement of the honour or reputation of a person, authorities should consider, for the purpose of establishing the truth or otherwise of the allegation, all evidence which is available to them under national procedural law and may not require for that purpose the disclosure of information identifying a source by the journalist.

Principle 5 (Conditions concerning disclosures)

a. The motion or request for initiating any action by competent authorities aimed at the disclosure of information identifying a source should only be introduced by persons or public authorities that have a direct legitimate interest in the disclosure.

b. Journalists should be informed by the competent authorities of their right not to disclose information identifying a source as well as of the limits of this right before a disclosure is requested.

c. Sanctions against journalists for not disclosing information identifying a source should only be imposed by judicial authorities during court proceedings which allow for a hearing of the journalists concerned in accordance with Article 6 of the Convention.

d. Journalists should have the right to have the imposition of a sanction for not disclosing their information identifying a source reviewed by another judicial authority.

e. Where journalists respond to a request or order to disclose information identifying a source, the competent authorities should consider applying measures to limit the extent of a disclosure, for example by excluding the public from the disclosure with due respect to Article 6 of the Convention, where relevant, and by themselves respecting the confidentiality of such a disclosure.

Principle 6 (Interception of communication, surveillance and judicial search and seizure)

a. The following measures should not be applied if their purpose is to circumvent the right of journalists, under the terms of these principles, not to disclose information identifying a source:

    i. interception orders or actions concerning communication or correspondence of journalists or their employers,

    ii. surveillance orders or actions concerning journalists, their contacts or their employers, or

    iii. search or seizure orders or actions concerning the private or business premises, belongings or correspondence of journalists or their employers or personal data related to their professional work.

b. Where information identifying a source has been properly obtained by police or judicial authorities by any of the above actions, although this might not have been the purpose of these actions, measures should be taken to prevent the subsequent use of this information as evidence before courts, unless the disclosure would be justified under Principle 3.

Principle 7 (Protection against self-incrimination)
The principles established herein shall not in any way limit national laws on the protection against self-incrimination in criminal proceedings, and journalists should, as far as such laws apply, enjoy such protection with regard to the disclosure of information identifying a source.

Terrorism Act 2000

(2000, c. 11)

19   Disclosure of information: duty

(1) This section applies where a person—

(a) believes or suspects that another person has committed an offence under any of sections 15 to 18, and

(b) bases his belief or suspicion on information which comes to his attention—

(i)   in the course of a trade, profession or business, or

(ii) in the course of his employment (whether or not in the course of a trade profession or business).

(1A) But this section does not apply if the information came to the person in the course of a business in the regulated sector.

(2) The person commits an offence if he does not disclose to a constable as soon as is reasonably practicable—

(a) his belief or suspicion, and

(b) the information on which it is based.

(3) It is a defence for a person charged with an offence under subsection (2) to prove that he had a reasonable excuse for not making the disclosure.

(4) Where—

(a) a person is in employment,

(b) his employer has established a procedure for the making of disclosures of the matters specified in subsection (2), and

(c) he is charged with an offence under that subsection,

it is a defence for him to prove that he disclosed the matters specified in that subsection in accordance with the procedure.

(5) Subsection (2) does not require disclosure by a professional legal adviser of—

(a) information which he obtains in privileged circumstances, or

(b) a belief or suspicion based on information which he obtains in privileged circumstances.

(6) For the purpose of subsection (5) information is obtained by an adviser in privileged circumstances if it comes to him, otherwise than with a view to furthering a criminal purpose—

(a) from a client or a client's representative, in connection with the provision of legal advice by the adviser to the client,

(b) from a person seeking legal advice from the adviser, or from the person's representative, or

(c) from any person, for the purpose of actual or contemplated legal proceedings.

(7) For the purposes of subsection (1)(a) a person shall be treated as having committed an offence under one of sections 15 to 18 if—

(a) he has taken an action or been in possession of a thing, and

(b) he would have committed an offence under one of those sections if he had been in the United Kingdom at the time when he took the action or was in possession of the thing.

(7A) The reference to a business in the regulated sector must be construed in accordance with Schedule 3A.

(7B) The reference to a constable includes a reference to a member of staff of the Serious Organised Crime Agency authorised for the purposes of this section by the Director of that Agency.

(8) A person guilty of an offence under this section shall be liable—

    (a) on conviction on indictment, to imprisonment for a term not exceeding five years, to a fine or to both, or

    (b) on summary conviction, to imprisonment for a term not exceeding six months, or to a fine not exceeding the statutory maximum or to both.

38B   Information about acts of terrorism

(1) This section applies where a person has information which he knows or believes might be of material assistance—

    (a) in preventing the commission by another person of an act of terrorism, or

    (b) in securing the apprehension, prosecution or conviction of another person, in the United Kingdom, for an offence involving the commission, preparation or instigation of an act of terrorism.

(2) The person commits an offence if he does not disclose the information as soon as reasonably practicable in accordance with subsection (3).

(3) Disclosure is in accordance with this subsection if it is made—

    (a) in England and Wales, to a constable,

    (b) in Scotland, to a constable, or

    (c) in Northern Ireland, to a constable or a member of Her Majesty's forces.

(4) It is a defence for a person charged with an offence under subsection (2) to prove that he had a reasonable excuse for not making the disclosure.

(5) A person guilty of an offence under this section shall be liable—

    (a) on conviction on indictment, to imprisonment for a term not exceeding five years, or to a fine or to both, or

    (b) on summary conviction, to imprisonment for a term not exceeding six months, or to a fine not exceeding the statutory maximum or to both.

(6) Proceedings for an offence under this section may be taken, and the offence may for the purposes of those proceedings be treated as having been committed, in any place where the person to be charged is or has at any time been since he first knew or believed that the information might be of material assistance as mentioned in subsection (1).

Part VI

Freedom of information and data protection

Freedom of Information Act 2000

(2000, c. 36)

PART I ACCESS TO INFORMATION HELD BY PUBLIC AUTHORITIES

Right to information

1 General right of access to information held by public authorities

(1) Any person making a request for information to a public authority is entitled—

    (a) to be informed in writing by the public authority whether it holds information of the description specified in the request, and

    (b) if that is the case, to have that information communicated to him.

(2) Subsection (1) has effect subject to the following provisions of this section and to the provisions of sections 2, 9, 12 and 14.

(3) Where a public authority—

    (a) reasonably requires further information in order to identify and locate the information requested, and

    (b) has informed the applicant of that requirement,

the authority is not obliged to comply with subsection (1) unless it is supplied with that further information.

(4) The information—

    (a) in respect of which the applicant is to be informed under subsection (1)(a), or

    (b) which is to be communicated under subsection (1)(b),

is the information in question held at the time when the request is received, except that account may be taken of any amendment or deletion made between that time and the time when the information is to be communicated under subsection (1)(b), being an amendment or deletion that would have been made regardless of the receipt of the request.

(5) A public authority is to be taken to have complied with subsection (1)(a) in relation to any information if it has communicated the information to the applicant in accordance with subsection (1)(b).

(6) In this Act, the duty of a public authority to comply with subsection (1)(a) is referred to as 'the duty to confirm or deny'.

2 Effect of the exemptions in Part II

(1) Where any provision of Part II states that the duty to confirm or deny does not arise in relation to any information, the effect of the provision is that where either—

    (a) the provision confers absolute exemption, or

(b) in all the circumstances of the case, the public interest in maintaining the exclusion of the duty to confirm or deny outweighs the public interest in disclosing whether the public authority holds the information,

section 1(1)(a) does not apply.

(2) In respect of any information which is exempt information by virtue of any provision of Part II, section 1(1)(b) does not apply if or to the extent that—

(a) the information is exempt information by virtue of a provision conferring absolute exemption, or

(b) in all the circumstances of the case, the public interest in maintaining the exemption outweighs the public interest in disclosing the information.

(3) For the purposes of this section, the following provisions of Part II (and no others) are to be regarded as conferring absolute exemption—

(a)   section 21,

(b)   section 23,

(c)   section 32,

(d)   section 34,

(e)   section 36 so far as relating to information held by the House of Commons or the House of Lords,

(ea)   in section 37 paragraphs (a) to (ab) of subsection (1), and subsection (2) so far as relating to those paragraphs,

(f)   in section 40—

(i)   subsection (1), and

(ii)   subsection (2) so far as relating to cases where the first condition referred to in that subsection is satisfied by virtue of subsection (3)(a)(i) or (b) of that section,

(g)   section 41, and

(h)   section 44.

3   Public authorities

(1) In this Act 'public authority' means—

(a) subject to section 4(4), any body which, any other person who, or the holder of any office which—

(i)   is listed in Schedule 1, or

(ii)   is designated by order under section 5, or

(b) a publicly-owned company as defined by section 6.

(2) For the purposes of this Act, information is held by a public authority if—

(a) it is held by the authority, otherwise than on behalf of another person, or

(b) it is held by another person on behalf of the authority.

4   Amendment of Schedule 1

(1) The Secretary of State may by order amend Schedule 1 by adding to that Schedule a reference to any body or the holder of any office which (in either case) is not for the time being listed in that Schedule but as respects which both the first and the second conditions below are satisfied.

(2) The first condition is that the body or office—

(a) is established by virtue of Her Majesty's prerogative or by an enactment or by subordinate legislation, or

(b) is established in any other way by a Minister of the Crown in his capacity as Minister, by a government department or the Welsh Ministers, the First Minister for Wales or the Counsel General to the Welsh Assembly Government.

(3) The second condition is—

(a) in the case of a body, that the body is wholly or partly constituted by appointment made by the Crown, by a Minister of the Crown, by a government department or the Welsh Ministers, the First Minister for Wales or the Counsel General to the Welsh Assembly Government, or

(b) in the case of an office, that appointments to the office are made by the Crown, by a Minister of the Crown, by a government department or by the Welsh Ministers, the First Minister for Wales or the Counsel General to the Welsh Assembly Government.

(4) If either the first or the second condition above ceases to be satisfied as respects any body or office which is listed in Part VI or VII of Schedule 1, that body or the holder of that office shall cease to be a public authority by virtue of the entry in question.

(5) The Secretary of State may by order amend Schedule 1 by removing from Part VI or VII of that Schedule an entry relating to any body or office—

(a) which has ceased to exist, or

(b) as respects which either the first or the second condition above has ceased to be satisfied.

(6) An order under subsection (1) may relate to a specified person or office or to persons or offices falling within a specified description.

(7) Before making an order under subsection (1), the Secretary of State shall—

(a) if the order adds to Part II, III, IV or VI of Schedule 1 a reference to—

(i)   a body whose functions are exercisable only or mainly in or as regards Wales, or

(ii) the holder of an office whose functions are exercisable only or mainly in or as regards Wales,

consult the the Welsh Ministers, and

(b) if the order relates to a body which, or the holder of any office who, if the order were made, would be a Northern Ireland public authority, consult the First Minister and deputy First Minister in Northern Ireland.

(8) This section has effect subject to section 80.

(9) In this section 'Minister of the Crown' includes a Northern Ireland Minister.

5   Further power to designate public authorities

(1) The Secretary of State may by order designate as a public authority for the purposes of this Act any person who is neither listed in Schedule 1 nor capable of being added to that Schedule by an order under section 4(1), but who—

(a) appears to the Secretary of State to exercise functions of a public nature, or

(b) is providing under a contract made with a public authority any service whose provision is a function of that authority.

(2) An order under this section may designate a specified person or office or persons or offices falling within a specified description.

(3) Before making an order under this section, the Secretary of State shall consult every person to whom the order relates, or persons appearing to him to represent such persons.

(4) This section has effect subject to section 80.

6   Publicly-owned companies

(1) A company is a 'publicly-owned company' for the purposes of section 3(1)(b) if—

(a) it is wholly owned by the Crown, or

(b) it is wholly owned by any public authority listed in Schedule 1 other than—

(i)   a government department, or

(ii) any authority which is listed only in relation to particular information.

(2) For the purposes of this section—

(a) a company is wholly owned by the Crown if it has no members except—

(i)   Ministers of the Crown, government departments or companies wholly owned by the Crown, or

(ii) persons acting on behalf of Ministers of the Crown, government departments or companies wholly owned by the Crown, and

(b) a company is wholly owned by a public authority other than a government department if it has no members except—

(i)   that public authority or companies wholly owned by that public authority, or

(ii) persons acting on behalf of that public authority or of companies wholly owned by that public authority.

(3) In this section—

'company' includes any body corporate;

'Minister of the Crown' includes a Northern Ireland Minister.

7 Public authorities to which Act has limited application

(1) Where a public authority is listed in Schedule 1 only in relation to information of a specified description, nothing in Parts I to V of this Act applies to any other information held by the authority.

(2) An order under section 4(1) may, in adding an entry to Schedule 1, list the public authority only in relation to information of a specified description.

(3) The Secretary of State may by order amend Schedule 1—

  (a) by limiting to information of a specified description the entry relating to any public authority, or

  (b) by removing or amending any limitation to information of a specified description which is for the time being contained in any entry.

(4) Before making an order under subsection (3), the [Secretary of State] shall—

  (a) if the order relates to the National Assembly for Wales or a Welsh public authority referred to in section 83(1)(b)(ii) (subsidiary of the Assembly Commission), consult the Presiding Officer of the National Assembly for Wales,

  (aa) if the order relates to the Welsh Assembly Government or a Welsh public authority other than one referred to in section 83(1)(b)(ii), consult the First Minister for Wales

  (b) if the order relates to the Northern Ireland Assembly, consult the Presiding Officer of that Assembly, and

  (c) if the order relates to a Northern Ireland department or a Northern Ireland public authority, consult the First Minister and deputy First Minister in Northern Ireland.

(5) An order under section 5(1)(a) must specify the functions of the public authority designated by the order with respect to which the designation is to have effect; and nothing in Parts I to V of this Act applies to information which is held by the authority but does not relate to the exercise of those functions.

(6) An order under section 5(1)(b) must specify the services provided under contract with respect to which the designation is to have effect; and nothing in Parts I to V of this Act applies to information which is held by the public authority designated by the order but does not relate to the provision of those services.

(7) Nothing in Parts I to V of this Act applies in relation to any information held by a publicly-owned company which is excluded information in relation to that company.

(8) In subsection (7) 'excluded information', in relation to a publicly-owned company, means information which is of a description specified in relation to that company in an order made by the Secretary of State for the purposes of this subsection.

(9) In this section 'publicly-owned company' has the meaning given by section 6.

8 Request for information

(1) In this Act any reference to a 'request for information' is a reference to such a request which—

  (a) is in writing,

  (b) states the name of the applicant and an address for correspondence, and

  (c) describes the information requested.

(2) For the purposes of subsection (1)(a), a request is to be treated as made in writing where the text of the request—

  (a) is transmitted by electronic means,

  (b) is received in legible form, and

  (c) is capable of being used for subsequent reference.

9 Fees

(1) A public authority to whom a request for information is made may, within the period for complying with section 1(1), give the applicant a notice in writing (in this Act referred to as a 'fees notice') stating that a fee of an amount specified in the notice is to be charged by the authority for complying with section 1(1).

(2) Where a fees notice has been given to the applicant, the public authority is not obliged to comply with section 1(1) unless the fee is paid within the period of three months beginning with the day on which the fees notice is given to the applicant.

(3) Subject to subsection (5), any fee under this section must be determined by the public authority in accordance with regulations made by the Secretary of State.

(4) Regulations under subsection (3) may, in particular, provide—

    (a) that no fee is to be payable in prescribed cases,

    (b) that any fee is not to exceed such maximum as may be specified in, or determined in accordance with, the regulations, and

    (c) that any fee is to be calculated in such manner as may be prescribed by the regulations.

(5) Subsection (3) does not apply where provision is made by or under any enactment as to the fee that may be charged by the public authority for the disclosure of the information.

10   Time for compliance with request

(1) Subject to subsections (2) and (3), a public authority must comply with section 1(1) promptly and in any event not later than the twentieth working day following the date of receipt.

(2) Where the authority has given a fees notice to the applicant and the fee is paid in accordance with section 9(2), the working days in the period beginning with the day on which the fees notice is given to the applicant and ending with the day on which the fee is received by the authority are to be disregarded in calculating for the purposes of subsection (1) the twentieth working day following the date of receipt.

(3) If, and to the extent that—

    (a) section 1(1)(a) would not apply if the condition in section 2(1)(b) were satisfied, or

    (b) section 1(1)(b) would not apply if the condition in section 2(2)(b) were satisfied,

the public authority need not comply with section 1(1)(a) or (b) until such time as is reasonable in the circumstances; but this subsection does not affect the time by which any notice under section 17(1) must be given.

(4) The Secretary of State may by regulations provide that subsections (1) and (2) are to have effect as if any reference to the twentieth working day following the date of receipt were a reference to such other day, not later than the sixtieth working day following the date of receipt, as may be specified in, or determined in accordance with, the regulations.

(5) Regulations under subsection (4) may—

    (a) prescribe different days in relation to different cases, and

    (b) confer a discretion on the Commissioner.

(6) In this section—

'the date of receipt' means—

    (a) the day on which the public authority receives the request for information, or

    (b) if later, the day on which it receives the information referred to in section 1(3);

'working day' means any day other than a Saturday, a Sunday, Christmas Day, Good Friday or a day which is a bank holiday under the Banking and Financial Dealings Act 1971 in any part of the United Kingdom.

11   Means by which communication to be made

(1) Where, on making his request for information, the applicant expresses a preference for communication by any one or more of the following means, namely—

    (a) the provision to the applicant of a copy of the information in permanent form or in another form acceptable to the applicant,

    (b) the provision to the applicant of a reasonable opportunity to inspect a record containing the information, and

    (c) the provision to the applicant of a digest or summary of the information in permanent form or in another form acceptable to the applicant,

the public authority shall so far as reasonably practicable give effect to that preference.

(1A) Where—

    (a) an applicant makes a request for information to a public authority in respect of information that is, or forms part of, a dataset held by the public authority, and

    (b) on making the request for information, the applicant expresses a preference for communication by means of the provision to the applicant of a copy of the information in electronic form, the public authority must, so far as reasonably practicable, provide the information to the applicant in an electronic form which is capable of re-use.

(2) In determining for the purposes of this section whether it is reasonably practicable to communicate information by particular means, the public authority may have regard to all the circumstances, including the cost of doing so.

(3) Where the public authority determines that it is not reasonably practicable to comply with any preference expressed by the applicant in making his request, the authority shall notify the applicant of the reasons for its determination.

(4) Subject to subsection (1), a public authority may comply with a request by communicating information by any means which are reasonable in the circumstances.

(5) In this Act 'dataset' means information comprising a collection of information held in electronic form where all or most of the information in the collection—

    (a) has been obtained or recorded for the purpose of providing a public authority with information in connection with the provision of a service by the authority or the carrying out of any other function of the authority,

    (b) is factual information which—

        (i) is not the product of analysis or interpretation other than calculation, and

        (ii) is not an official statistic (within the meaning given by section 6(1) of the Statistics and Registration Service Act 2007), and

    (c) remains presented in a way that (except for the purpose of forming part of the collection) has not been organised, adapted or otherwise materially altered since it was obtained or recorded.

12   Exemption where cost of compliance exceeds appropriate limit

(1) Section 1(1) does not oblige a public authority to comply with a request for information if the authority estimates that the cost of complying with the request would exceed the appropriate limit.

(2) Subsection (1) does not exempt the public authority from its obligation to comply with paragraph (a) of section 1(1) unless the estimated cost of complying with that paragraph alone would exceed the appropriate limit.

(3) In subsections (1) and (2) 'the appropriate limit' means such amount as may be prescribed, and different amounts may be prescribed in relation to different cases.

(4) The Secretary of State may by regulations provide that, in such circumstances as may be prescribed, where two or more requests for information are made to a public authority—

    (a) by one person, or

    (b) by different persons who appear to the public authority to be acting in concert or in pursuance of a campaign,

the estimated cost of complying with any of the requests is to be taken to be the estimated total cost of complying with all of them.

(5) The Secretary of State may by regulations make provision for the purposes of this section as to the costs to be estimated and as to the manner in which they are to be estimated.

13   Fees for disclosure where cost of compliance exceeds appropriate limit

(1) A public authority may charge for the communication of any information whose communication—

    (a) is not required by section 1(1) because the cost of complying with the request for information exceeds the amount which is the appropriate limit for the purposes of section 12(1) and (2), and

    (b) is not otherwise required by law,

such fee as may be determined by the public authority in accordance with regulations made by the Secretary of State.

(2) Regulations under this section may, in particular, provide—

(a) that any fee is not to exceed such maximum as may be specified in, or determined in accordance with, the regulations, and

(b) that any fee is to be calculated in such manner as may be prescribed by the regulations.

(3) Subsection (1) does not apply where provision is made by or under any enactment as to the fee that may be charged by the public authority for the disclosure of the information.

14 Vexatious or repeated requests

(1) Section 1(1) does not oblige a public authority to comply with a request for information if the request is vexatious.

(2) Where a public authority has previously complied with a request for information which was made by any person, it is not obliged to comply with a subsequent identical or substantially similar request from that person unless a reasonable interval has elapsed between compliance with the previous request and the making of the current request.

15 Special provisions relating to public records transferred to Public Record Office, etc.

(1) Where—

(a) the appropriate records authority receives a request for information which relates to information which is, or if it existed would be, contained in a transferred public record, and

(b) either of the conditions in subsection (2) is satisfied in relation to any of that information,

that authority shall, within the period for complying with section 1(1), send a copy of the request to the responsible authority.

(2) The conditions referred to in subsection (1)(b) are—

(a) that the duty to confirm or deny is expressed to be excluded only by a provision of Part II not specified in subsection (3) of section 2, and

(b) that the information is exempt information only by virtue of a provision of Part II not specified in that subsection.

(3) On receiving the copy, the responsible authority shall, within such time as is reasonable in all the circumstances, inform the appropriate records authority of the determination required by virtue of subsection (3) or (4) of section 66.

(4) In this Act 'transferred public record' means a public record which has been transferred—

(a) to the Public Record Office,

(b) to another place of deposit appointed by the Lord Chancellor under the Public Records Act 1958, or

(c) to the Public Record Office of Northern Ireland.

(5) In this Act—

'appropriate records authority', in relation to a transferred public record, means—

(a) in a case falling within subsection (4)(a), the Public Record Office,

(b) in a case falling within subsection (4)(b), the Lord Chancellor, and

(c) in a case falling within subsection (4)(c), the Public Record Office of Northern Ireland;

'responsible authority', in relation to a transferred public record, means—

(a) in the case of a record transferred as mentioned in subsection (4)(a) or (b) from a government department in the charge of a Minister of the Crown, the Minister of the Crown who appears to the Lord Chancellor to be primarily concerned,

(b) in the case of a record transferred as mentioned in subsection (4)(a) or (b) from any other person, the person who appears to the Lord Chancellor to be primarily concerned,

(c) in the case of a record transferred to the Public Record Office of Northern Ireland from a government department in the charge of a Minister of the Crown, the Minister of the Crown who appears to the appropriate Northern Ireland Minister to be primarily concerned,

(d) in the case of a record transferred to the Public Record Office of Northern Ireland from a Northern Ireland department, the Northern Ireland Minister who appears to the appropriate Northern Ireland Minister to be primarily concerned, or

(e) in the case of a record transferred to the Public Record Office of Northern Ireland from any other person, the person who appears to the appropriate Northern Ireland Minister to be primarily concerned.

16   Duty to provide advice and assistance

(1) It shall be the duty of a public authority to provide advice and assistance, so far as it would be reasonable to expect the authority to do so, to persons who propose to make, or have made, requests for information to it.

(2) Any public authority which, in relation to the provision of advice or assistance in any case, conforms with the code of practice under section 45 is to be taken to comply with the duty imposed by subsection (1) in relation to that case.

Refusal of request

17   Refusal of request

(1) A public authority which, in relation to any request for information, is to any extent relying on a claim that any provision of Part II relating to the duty to confirm or deny is relevant to the request or on a claim that information is exempt information must, within the time for complying with section 1(1), give the applicant a notice which—

(a) states that fact,

(b) specifies the exemption in question, and

(c) states (if that would not otherwise be apparent) why the exemption applies.

(2) Where—

(a) in relation to any request for information, a public authority is, as respects any information, relying on a claim—

(i)   that any provision of Part II which relates to the duty to confirm or deny and is not specified in section 2(3) is relevant to the request, or

(ii) that the information is exempt information only by virtue of a provision not specified in section 2(3), and

(b) at the time when the notice under subsection (1) is given to the applicant, the public authority (or, in a case falling within section 66(3) or (4), the responsible authority) has not yet reached a decision as to the application of subsection (1)(b) or (2)(b) of section 2,

the notice under subsection (1) must indicate that no decision as to the application of that provision has yet been reached and must contain an estimate of the date by which the authority expects that such a decision will have been reached.

(3) A public authority which, in relation to any request for information, is to any extent relying on a claim that subsection (1)(b) or (2)(b) of section 2 applies must, either in the notice under subsection (1) or in a separate notice given within such time as is reasonable in the circumstances, state the reasons for claiming—

(a) that, in all the circumstances of the case, the public interest in maintaining the exclusion of the duty to confirm or deny outweighs the public interest in disclosing whether the authority holds the information, or

(b) that, in all the circumstances of the case, the public interest in maintaining the exemption outweighs the public interest in disclosing the information.

(4) A public authority is not obliged to make a statement under subsection (1)(c) or (3) if, or to the extent that, the statement would involve the disclosure of information which would itself be exempt information.

(5) A public authority which, in relation to any request for information, is relying on a claim that section 12 or 14 applies must, within the time for complying with section 1(1), give the applicant a notice stating that fact.

(6) Subsection (5) does not apply where—

    (a) the public authority is relying on a claim that section 14 applies,

    (b) the authority has given the applicant a notice, in relation to a previous request for information, stating that it is relying on such a claim, and

    (c) it would in all the circumstances be unreasonable to expect the authority to serve a further notice under subsection (5) in relation to the current request.

(7) A notice under subsection (1), (3) or (5) must—

    (a) contain particulars of any procedure provided by the public authority for dealing with complaints about the handling of requests for information or state that the authority does not provide such a procedure, and

    (b) contain particulars of the right conferred by section 50.

The Information Commissioner

18   The Information Commissioner and the Information Tribunal

(1) The Data Protection Commissioner shall be known instead as the Information Commissioner.

(3) In this Act—

    (a) the Information Commissioner is referred to as 'the Commissioner', and

(4) Schedule 2 (which makes provision consequential on subsections (1) and (2) and amendments of the Data Protection Act 1998 relating to the extension by this Act of the functions of the Commissioner and the Tribunal) has effect.

Publication schemes

19   Publication schemes

(1) It shall be the duty of every public authority—

    (a) to adopt and maintain a scheme which relates to the publication of information by the authority and is approved by the Commissioner (in this Act referred to as a 'publication scheme'),

    (b) to publish information in accordance with its publication scheme, and

    (c) from time to time to review its publication scheme.

(2) A publication scheme must—

    (a) specify classes of information which the public authority publishes or intends to publish,

    (b) specify the manner in which information of each class is, or is intended to be, published, and

    (c) specify whether the material is, or is intended to be, available to the public free of charge or on payment.

(2A) A publication scheme must, in particular, include a requirement for the public authority concerned—

    (a) to publish—

        (i) any dataset held by the authority in relation to which a person makes a request for information to the authority, and

        (ii) any up-dated version held by the authority of such a dataset,

        unless the authority is satisfied that it is not appropriate for the dataset to be published,

    (b) where reasonably practicable, to publish any dataset the authority publishes by virtue of paragraph (a) in an electronic form which is capable of re-use,

    (c) where any information in a dataset published by virtue of paragraph (a) is a relevant copyright work in relation to which the authority is the only owner, to make the information available for re-use in accordance with the terms of the specified licence.

(3) In adopting or reviewing a publication scheme, a public authority shall have regard to the public interest—

(a) in allowing public access to information held by the authority, and

(b) in the publication of reasons for decisions made by the authority.

(4) A public authority shall publish its publication scheme in such manner as it thinks fit.

(5) The Commissioner may, when approving a scheme, provide that his approval is to expire at the end of a specified period.

(6) Where the Commissioner has approved the publication scheme of any public authority, he may at any time give notice to the public authority revoking his approval of the scheme as from the end of the period of six months beginning with the day on which the notice is given.

(7) Where the Commissioner—

(a) refuses to approve a proposed publication scheme, or

(b) revokes his approval of a publication scheme,

he must give the public authority a statement of his reasons for doing so.

20   Model publication schemes

(1) The Commissioner may from time to time approve, in relation to public authorities falling within particular classes, model publication schemes prepared by him or by other persons.

(2) Where a public authority falling within the class to which an approved model scheme relates adopts such a scheme without modification, no further approval of the Commissioner is required so long as the model scheme remains approved; and where such an authority adopts such a scheme with modifications, the approval of the Commissioner is required only in relation to the modifications.

(3) The Commissioner may, when approving a model publication scheme, provide that his approval is to expire at the end of a specified period.

(4) Where the Commissioner has approved a model publication scheme, he may at any time publish, in such manner as he thinks fit, a notice revoking his approval of the scheme as from the end of the period of six months beginning with the day on which the notice is published.

(5) Where the Commissioner refuses to approve a proposed model publication scheme on the application of any person, he must give the person who applied for approval of the scheme a statement of the reasons for his refusal.

(6) Where the Commissioner refuses to approve any modifications under subsection (2), he must give the public authority a statement of the reasons for his refusal.

(7) Where the Commissioner revokes his approval of a model publication scheme, he must include in the notice under subsection (4) a statement of his reasons for doing so.

PART II EXEMPT INFORMATION

21   Information accessible to applicant by other means

(1) Information which is reasonably accessible to the applicant otherwise than under section 1 is exempt information.

(2) For the purposes of subsection (1)—

(a) information may be reasonably accessible to the applicant even though it is accessible only on payment, and

(b) information is to be taken to be reasonably accessible to the applicant if it is information which the public authority or any other person is obliged by or under any enactment to communicate (otherwise than by making the information available for inspection) to members of the public on request, whether free of charge or on payment.

(3) For the purposes of subsection (1), information which is held by a public authority and does not fall within subsection (2)(b) is not to be regarded as reasonably accessible to the applicant merely because the information is available from the public authority itself on request, unless the information is made available in accordance with the authority's publication scheme and any payment required is specified in, or determined in accordance with, the scheme.

22   Information intended for future publication

(1) Information is exempt information if—

(a) the information is held by the public authority with a view to its publication, by the authority or any other person, at some future date (whether determined or not),

(b) the information was already held with a view to such publication at the time when the request for information was made, and

(c) it is reasonable in all the circumstances that the information should be withheld from disclosure until the date referred to in paragraph (a).

(2) The duty to confirm or deny does not arise if, or to the extent that, compliance with section 1(1)(a) would involve the disclosure of any information (whether or not already recorded) which falls within subsection (1).

23   Information supplied by, or relating to, bodies dealing with security matters

(1) Information held by a public authority is exempt information if it was directly or indirectly supplied to the public authority by, or relates to, any of the bodies specified in subsection (3).

(2) A certificate signed by a Minister of the Crown certifying that the information to which it applies was directly or indirectly supplied by, or relates to, any of the bodies specified in subsection (3) shall, subject to section 60, be conclusive evidence of that fact.

(3) The bodies referred to in subsections (1) and (2) are—

(a) the Security Service,

(b) the Secret Intelligence Service,

(c) the Government Communications Headquarters,

(d) the special forces,

(e) the Tribunal established under section 65 of the Regulation of Investigatory Powers Act 2000,

(f) the Tribunal established under section 7 of the Interception of Communications Act 1985,

(g) the Tribunal established under section 5 of the Security Service Act 1989,

(h) the Tribunal established under section 9 of the Intelligence Services Act 1994,

(i) the Security Vetting Appeals Panel,

(j) the Security Commission,

(k) the National Criminal Intelligence Service, and

(l) the Service Authority for the National Criminal Intelligence Service and

(m) the Serious Organised Crime Agency.

(4) In subsection (3)(c) 'the Government Communications Headquarters' includes any unit or part of a unit of the armed forces of the Crown which is for the time being required by the Secretary of State to assist the Government Communications Headquarters in carrying out its functions.

(5) The duty to confirm or deny does not arise if, or to the extent that, compliance with section 1(1)(a) would involve the disclosure of any information (whether or not already recorded) which was directly or indirectly supplied to the public authority by, or relates to, any of the bodies specified in subsection (3).

24   National security

(1) Information which does not fall within section 23(1) is exempt information if exemption from section 1(1)(b) is required for the purpose of safeguarding national security.

(2) The duty to confirm or deny does not arise if, or to the extent that, exemption from section 1(1)(a) is required for the purpose of safeguarding national security.

(3) A certificate signed by a Minister of the Crown certifying that exemption from section 1(1)(b), or from section 1(1)(a) and (b), is, or at any time was, required for the purpose of safeguarding national security shall, subject to section 60, be conclusive evidence of that fact.

(4) A certificate under subsection (3) may identify the information to which it applies by means of a general description and may be expressed to have prospective effect.

25   Certificates under ss. 23 and 24: supplementary provisions

(1) A document purporting to be a certificate under section 23(2) or 24(3) shall be received in evidence and deemed to be such a certificate unless the contrary is proved.

(2) A document which purports to be certified by or on behalf of a Minister of the Crown as a true copy of a certificate issued by that Minister under section 23(2) or 24(3) shall in any legal proceedings be evidence (or, in Scotland, sufficient evidence) of that certificate.

(3) The power conferred by section 23(2) or 24(3) on a Minister of the Crown shall not be exercisable except by a Minister who is a member of the Cabinet or by the Attorney General, the Advocate General for Scotland or the Attorney General for Northern Ireland.

26 Defence

(1) Information is exempt information if its disclosure under this Act would, or would be likely to, prejudice—

    (a) the defence of the British Islands or of any colony, or

    (b) the capability, effectiveness or security of any relevant forces.

(2) In subsection (1)(b) 'relevant forces' means—

    (a) the armed forces of the Crown, and

    (b) any forces co-operating with those forces,

or any part of any of those forces.

(3) The duty to confirm or deny does not arise if, or to the extent that, compliance with section 1(1)(a) would, or would be likely to, prejudice any of the matters mentioned in subsection (1).

27 International relations

(1) Information is exempt information if its disclosure under this Act would, or would be likely to, prejudice—

    (a) relations between the United Kingdom and any other State,

    (b) relations between the United Kingdom and any international organisation or international court,

    (c) the interests of the United Kingdom abroad, or

    (d) the promotion or protection by the United Kingdom of its interests abroad.

(2) Information is also exempt information if it is confidential information obtained from a State other than the United Kingdom or from an international organisation or international court.

(3) For the purposes of this section, any information obtained from a State, organisation or court is confidential at any time while the terms on which it was obtained require it to be held in confidence or while the circumstances in which it was obtained make it reasonable for the State, organisation or court to expect that it will be so held.

(4) The duty to confirm or deny does not arise if, or to the extent that, compliance with section 1(1)(a)—

    (a) would, or would be likely to, prejudice any of the matters mentioned in subsection (1), or

    (b) would involve the disclosure of any information (whether or not already recorded) which is confidential information obtained from a State other than the United Kingdom or from an international organisation or international court.

(5) In this section—

'international court' means any international court which is not an international organisation and which is established—

    (a) by a resolution of an international organisation of which the United Kingdom is a member, or

    (b) by an international agreement to which the United Kingdom is a party;

'international organisation' means any international organisation whose members include any two or more States, or any organ of such an organisation;

'State' includes the government of any State and any organ of its government, and references to a State other than the United Kingdom include references to any territory outside the United Kingdom.

28   Relations within the United Kingdom

(1) Information is exempt information if its disclosure under this Act would, or would be likely to, prejudice relations between any administration in the United Kingdom and any other such administration.

(2) In subsection (1) 'administration in the United Kingdom' means—

(a) the government of the United Kingdom,

(b) the Scottish Administration,

(c) the Executive Committee of the Northern Ireland Assembly, or

(d) the Welsh Assembly Government.

(3) The duty to confirm or deny does not arise if, or to the extent that, compliance with section 1(1)(a) would, or would be likely to, prejudice any of the matters mentioned in subsection (1).

29   The economy

(1) Information is exempt information if its disclosure under this Act would, or would be likely to, prejudice—

(a) the economic interests of the United Kingdom or of any part of the United Kingdom, or

(b) the financial interests of any administration in the United Kingdom, as defined by section 28(2).

(2) The duty to confirm or deny does not arise if, or to the extent that, compliance with section 1(1)(a) would, or would be likely to, prejudice any of the matters mentioned in subsection (1).

30   Investigations and proceedings conducted by public authorities

(1) Information held by a public authority is exempt information if it has at any time been held by the authority for the purposes of—

(a) any investigation which the public authority has a duty to conduct with a view to it being ascertained—

(i)   whether a person should be charged with an offence, or

(ii)   whether a person charged with an offence is guilty of it,

(b) any investigation which is conducted by the authority and in the circumstances may lead to a decision by the authority to institute criminal proceedings which the authority has power to conduct, or

(c) any criminal proceedings which the authority has power to conduct.

(2) Information held by a public authority is exempt information if—

(a) it was obtained or recorded by the authority for the purposes of its functions relating to—

(i)   investigations falling within subsection (1)(a) or (b),

(ii)   criminal proceedings which the authority has power to conduct,

(iii) investigations (other than investigations falling within subsection (1)(a) or (b)) which are conducted by the authority for any of the purposes specified in section 31(2) and either by virtue of Her Majesty's prerogative or by virtue of powers conferred by or under any enactment, or

(iv) civil proceedings which are brought by or on behalf of the authority and arise out of such investigations, and

(b) it relates to the obtaining of information from confidential sources.

(3) The duty to confirm or deny does not arise in relation to information which is (or if it were held by the public authority would be) exempt information by virtue of subsection (1) or (2).

(4) In relation to the institution or conduct of criminal proceedings or the power to conduct them, references in subsection (1)(b) or (c) and subsection (2)(a) to the public authority include references—

(a) to any officer of the authority,

(b) in the case of a government department other than a Northern Ireland department, to the Minister of the Crown in charge of the department, and

(c) in the case of a Northern Ireland department, to the Northern Ireland Minister in charge of the department.

(5) In this section—

'criminal proceedings' includes service law proceedings (as defined by section 324(5) of the Armed Forces Act 2006);

'offence' includes a service offence (as defined by section 50 of that Act).

(6) In the application of this section to Scotland—

(a) in subsection (1)(b), for the words from 'a decision' to the end there is substituted 'a decision by the authority to make a report to the procurator fiscal for the purpose of enabling him to determine whether criminal proceedings should be instituted',

(b) in subsections (1)(c) and (2)(a)(ii) for 'which the authority has power to conduct' there is substituted 'which have been instituted in consequence of a report made by the authority to the procurator fiscal', and

(c) for any reference to a person being charged with an offence there is substituted a reference to the person being prosecuted for the offence.

31   Law enforcement

(1) Information which is not exempt information by virtue of section 30 is exempt information if its disclosure under this Act would, or would be likely to, prejudice—

(a) the prevention or detection of crime,

(b) the apprehension or prosecution of offenders,

(c) the administration of justice,

(d) the assessment or collection of any tax or duty or of any imposition of a similar nature,

(e) the operation of the immigration controls,

(f) the maintenance of security and good order in prisons or in other institutions where persons are lawfully detained,

(g) the exercise by any public authority of its functions for any of the purposes specified in subsection (2),

(h) any civil proceedings which are brought by or on behalf of a public authority and arise out of an investigation conducted, for any of the purposes specified in subsection (2), by or on behalf of the authority by virtue of Her Majesty's prerogative or by virtue of powers conferred by or under an enactment, or

(i) any inquiry held under the Fatal Accidents and Sudden Deaths Inquiries (Scotland) Act 1976 to the extent that the inquiry arises out of an investigation conducted, for any of the purposes specified in subsection (2), by or on behalf of the authority by virtue of Her Majesty's prerogative or by virtue of powers conferred by or under an enactment.

(2) The purposes referred to in subsection (1)(g) to (i) are—

(a) the purpose of ascertaining whether any person has failed to comply with the law,

(b) the purpose of ascertaining whether any person is responsible for any conduct which is improper,

(c) the purpose of ascertaining whether circumstances which would justify regulatory action in pursuance of any enactment exist or may arise,

(d) the purpose of ascertaining a person's fitness or competence in relation to the management of bodies corporate or in relation to any profession or other activity which he is, or seeks to become, authorised to carry on,

(e) the purpose of ascertaining the cause of an accident,

(f) the purpose of protecting charities against misconduct or mismanagement (whether by trustees or other persons) in their administration,

(g) the purpose of protecting the property of charities from loss or misapplication,

(h) the purpose of recovering the property of charities,

(i) the purpose of securing the health, safety and welfare of persons at work, and

(j) the purpose of protecting persons other than persons at work against risk to health or safety arising out of or in connection with the actions of persons at work.

(3) The duty to confirm or deny does not arise if, or to the extent that, compliance with section 1(1)(a) would, or would be likely to, prejudice any of the matters mentioned in subsection (1).

32 Court records, etc.

(1) Information held by a public authority is exempt information if it is held only by virtue of being contained in—

    (a) any document filed with, or otherwise placed in the custody of, a court for the purposes of proceedings in a particular cause or matter,

    (b) any document served upon, or by, a public authority for the purposes of proceedings in a particular cause or matter, or

    (c) any document created by—

        (i) a court, or

        (ii) a member of the administrative staff of a court,

        for the purposes of proceedings in a particular cause or matter.

(2) Information held by a public authority is exempt information if it is held only by virtue of being contained in—

    (a) any document placed in the custody of a person conducting an inquiry or arbitration, for the purposes of the inquiry or arbitration, or

    (b) any document created by a person conducting an inquiry or arbitration, for the purposes of the inquiry or arbitration.

(3) The duty to confirm or deny does not arise in relation to information which is (or if it were held by the public authority would be) exempt information by virtue of this section.

(4) In this section—

    (a) 'court' includes any tribunal or body exercising the judicial power of the State,

    (b) 'proceedings in a particular cause or matter' includes any investigation under Part 1 of the Coroners and Justice Act 2009, any inquest under the Coroners Act (Northern Ireland) 1959 and any post-mortem examination,

    (c) 'inquiry' means any inquiry or hearing held under any provision contained in, or made under, an enactment, and

    (d) except in relation to Scotland, 'arbitration' means any arbitration to which Part I of the Arbitration Act 1996 applies.

33 Audit functions

(1) This section applies to any public authority which has functions in relation to—

    (a) the audit of the accounts of other public authorities, or

    (b) the examination of the economy, efficiency and effectiveness with which other public authorities use their resources in discharging their functions.

(2) Information held by a public authority to which this section applies is exempt information if its disclosure would, or would be likely to, prejudice the exercise of any of the authority's functions in relation to any of the matters referred to in subsection (1).

(3) The duty to confirm or deny does not arise in relation to a public authority to which this section applies if, or to the extent that, compliance with section 1(1)(a) would, or would be likely to, prejudice the exercise of any of the authority's functions in relation to any of the matters referred to in subsection (1).

34 Parliamentary privilege

(1) Information is exempt information if exemption from section 1(1)(b) is required for the purpose of avoiding an infringement of the privileges of either House of Parliament.

(2) The duty to confirm or deny does not apply if, or to the extent that, exemption from section 1(1)(a) is required for the purpose of avoiding an infringement of the privileges of either House of Parliament.

(3) A certificate signed by the appropriate authority certifying that exemption from section 1(1)(b), or from section 1(1)(a) and (b), is, or at anytime was, required for the purpose of avoiding an infringement of the privileges of either House of Parliament shall be conclusive evidence of that fact.

(4) In subsection (3) 'the appropriate authority' means—

    (a) in relation to the House of Commons, the Speaker of that House, and

    (b) in relation to the House of Lords, the Clerk of the Parliaments.

35   Formulation of government policy, etc.

   (1) Information held by a government department or by the Welsh Assembly Government is exempt information if it relates to—

     (a) the formulation or development of government policy,

     (b) Ministerial communications,

     (c) the provision of advice by any of the Law Officers or any request for the provision of such advice, or

     (d) the operation of any Ministerial private office.

   (2) Once a decision as to government policy has been taken, any statistical information used to provide an informed background to the taking of the decision is not to be regarded—

     (a) for the purposes of subsection (1)(a), as relating to the formulation or development of government policy, or

     (b) for the purposes of subsection (1)(b), as relating to Ministerial communications.

   (3) The duty to confirm or deny does not arise in relation to information which is (or if it were held by the public authority would be) exempt information by virtue of subsection (1).

   (4) In making any determination required by section 2(1)(b) or (2)(b) in relation to information which is exempt information by virtue of subsection (1)(a), regard shall be had to the particular public interest in the disclosure of factual information which has been used, or is intended to be used, to provide an informed background to decision-taking.

   (5) In this section—

'government policy' includes the policy of the Executive Committee of the Northern Ireland Assembly and the policy of the the Welsh Assembly Government;

'the Law Officers' means the Attorney General, the Solicitor General, the Advocate General for Scotland, the Lord Advocate, the Solicitor General for Scotland, the Counsel General to the Welsh Assembly Government and the Attorney General for Northern Ireland;

'Ministerial communications' means any communications—

     (a) between Ministers of the Crown,

     (b) between Northern Ireland Ministers, including Northern Ireland junior Ministers, or

     (c) between members of the Welsh Assembly Government,

and includes, in particular, proceedings of the Cabinet or of any committee of the Cabinet, proceedings of the Executive Committee of the Northern Ireland Assembly, the Cabinet or any committee of the Cabinet of the Welsh Assembly Government;

'Ministerial private office' means any part of a government department which provides personal administrative support to a Minister of the Crown, to a Northern Ireland Minister or a Northern Ireland junior Minister or any part of the administration of the Welsh Assembly Government providing personal administrative support to the members of the Welsh Assembly Government;

'Northern Ireland junior Minister' means a member of the Northern Ireland Assembly appointed as a junior Minister under section 19 of the Northern Ireland Act 1998.

36   Prejudice to effective conduct of public affairs

   (1) This section applies to—

     (a) information which is held by a government department or the Welsh Assembly Government and is not exempt information by virtue of section 35, and

     (b) information which is held by any other public authority.

   (2) Information to which this section applies is exempt information if, in the reasonable opinion of a qualified person, disclosure of the information under this Act—

     (a) would, or would be likely to, prejudice—

        (i)   the maintenance of the convention of the collective responsibility of Ministers of the Crown, or

        (ii) the work of the Executive Committee of the Northern Ireland Assembly, or

        (iii) the work of the Cabinet of the Welsh Assembly Government,

     (b) would, or would be likely to, inhibit—

        (i)   the free and frank provision of advice, or

  (ii) the free and frank exchange of views for the purposes of deliberation, or

 (c) would otherwise prejudice, or would be likely otherwise to prejudice, the effective conduct of public affairs.

 (3) The duty to confirm or deny does not arise in relation to information to which this section applies (or would apply if held by the public authority) if, or to the extent that, in the reasonable opinion of a qualified person, compliance with section 1(1)(a) would, or would be likely to, have any of the effects mentioned in subsection (2).

 (4) In relation to statistical information, subsections (2) and (3) shall have effect with the omission of the words 'in the reasonable opinion of a qualified person'.

 (5) In subsections (2) and (3) 'qualified person'—

  (a) in relation to information held by a government department in the charge of a Minister of the Crown, means any Minister of the Crown,

  (b) in relation to information held by a Northern Ireland department, means the Northern Ireland Minister in charge of the department,

  (c) in relation to information held by any other government department, means the commissioners or other person in charge of that department,

  (d) in relation to information held by the House of Commons, means the Speaker of that House,

  (e) in relation to information held by the House of Lords, means the Clerk of the Parliaments,

  (f) in relation to information held by the Northern Ireland Assembly, means the Presiding Officer,

  (g) in relation to information held by the Welsh Assembly Government, means the Welsh Ministers or the Counsel General to the Welsh Assembly Government,

 (ga) in relation to information held by the National Assembly for Wales, means the Presiding Officer of the National Assembly for Wales,

 (gb) in relation to information held by any Welsh public authority (other than one referred to in section 83(1)(b)(ii) (subsidiary of the Assembly Commission), the Auditor General for Wales or the Public Services Ombudsman for Wales), means—

  (i) the public authority, or

  (ii) any officer or employee of the authority authorised by the Welsh Ministers or the Counsel General to the Welsh Assembly Government,

 (gc) in relation to information held by a Welsh public authority referred to in section 83(1)(b)(ii), means—

  (i) the public authority, or

  (ii) any officer or employee of the authority authorised by the Presiding Officer of the National Assembly for Wales,

  (i) in relation to information held by the National Audit Office or the Comptroller and Auditor General, means the Comptroller and Auditor General,

  (j) in relation to information held by the Northern Ireland Audit Office, means the Comptroller and Auditor General for Northern Ireland,

  (k) in relation to information held by the Auditor General for Wales, means the Auditor General for Wales,

 (ka) in relation to information held by the Public Services Ombudsman for Wales, means the Public Services Ombudsman for Wales

  (l) in relation to information held by any Northern Ireland public authority other than the Northern Ireland Audit Office, means—

  (i) the public authority, or

  (ii) any officer or employee of the authority authorised by the First Minister and deputy First Minister in Northern Ireland acting jointly,

 (m) in relation to information held by the Greater London Authority, means the Mayor of London,

(n) in relation to information held by a functional body within the meaning of the Greater London Authority Act 1999, means the chairman of that functional body, and

(o) in relation to information held by any public authority not falling within any of paragraphs (a) to (n), means—

    (i)   a Minister of the Crown,

    (ii) the public authority, if authorised for the purposes of this section by a Minister of the Crown, or

    (iii) any officer or employee of the public authority who is authorised for the purposes of this section by a Minister of the Crown.

(6) Any authorisation for the purposes of this section—

(a) may relate to a specified person or to persons falling within a specified class,

(b) may be general or limited to particular classes of case, and

(c) may be granted subject to conditions.

(7) A certificate signed by the qualified person referred to in subsection (5)(d)or (e) above certifying that in his reasonable opinion—

(a) disclosure of information held by either House of Parliament, or

(b) compliance with section 1(1)(a) by either House,

would, or would be likely to, have any of the effects mentioned in subsection (2) shall be conclusive evidence of that fact.

37   Communications with Her Majesty, etc. and honours

(1) Information is exempt information if it relates to—

(a) communications with the Sovereign,

(aa) communications with the heir to, or the person who is for the time being second in line of succession to, the Throne,

(ab) communications with a person who has subsequently acceded to the Throne or become heir to, or second in line to, the Throne,

(ac) communications with other members of the Royal Family (other than communications which fall within any of paragraphs (a) to (ab) because they are made or received on behalf of a person falling within any of those paragraphs), and

(ad) communications with the Royal Household (other than communications which fall within any of paragraphs (a) to (ac) because they are made or received on behalf of a person falling within any of those paragraphs), or

(b) the conferring by the Crown of any honour or dignity.

(2) The duty to confirm or deny does not arise in relation to information which is (or if it were held by the public authority would be) exempt information by virtue of subsection (1).

38   Health and safety

(1) Information is exempt information if its disclosure under this Act would, or would be likely to—

(a) endanger the physical or mental health of any individual, or

(b) endanger the safety of any individual.

(2) The duty to confirm or deny does not arise if, or to the extent that, compliance with section 1(1)(a) would, or would be likely to, have either of the effects mentioned in subsection (1).

39   Environmental information

(1) Information is exempt information if the public authority holding it—

(a) is obliged by environmental information regulations to make the information available to the public in accordance with the regulations, or

(b) would be so obliged but for any exemption contained in the regulations.

(1A) In subsection (1) 'environmental information regulations' means—

(a) regulations made under section 74, or

(b) regulations made under section 2(2) of the European Communities Act 1972 for the purpose of implementing any EU obligation relating to public access to, and the dissemination of, information on the environment.

(2) The duty to confirm or deny does not arise in relation to information which is (or if it were held by the public authority would be) exempt information by virtue of subsection (1).

(3) Subsection (1)(a) does not limit the generality of section 21(1).

40 Personal information

(1) Any information to which a request for information relates is exempt information if it constitutes personal data of which the applicant is the data subject.

(2) Any information to which a request for information relates is also exempt information if—

    (a) it constitutes personal data which do not fall within subsection (1), and

    (b) either the first or the second condition below is satisfied.

(3) The first condition is—

    (a) in a case where the information falls within any of paragraphs (a) to (d) of the definition of 'data' in section 1(1) of the Data Protection Act 1998, that the disclosure of the information to a member of the public otherwise than under this Act would contravene—

        (i) any of the data protection principles, or

        (ii) section 10 of that Act (right to prevent processing likely to cause damage or distress), and

    (b) in any other case, that the disclosure of the information to a member of the public otherwise than under this Act would contravene any of the data protection principles if the exemptions in section 33A(1) of the Data Protection Act 1998 (which relate to manual data held by public authorities) were disregarded.

(4) The second condition is that by virtue of any provision of Part IV of the Data Protection Act 1998 the information is exempt from section 7(1)(c) of that Act (data subject's right of access to personal data).

(5) The duty to confirm or deny—

    (a) does not arise in relation to information which is (or if it were held by the public authority would be) exempt information by virtue of subsection (1), and

    (b) does not arise in relation to other information if or to the extent that either—

        (i) the giving to a member of the public of the confirmation or denial that would have to be given to comply with section 1(1)(a) would (apart from this Act) contravene any of the data protection principles or section 10 of the Data Protection Act 1998 or would do so if the exemptions in section 33A(1) of that Act were disregarded, or

        (ii) by virtue of any provision of Part IV of the Data Protection Act 1998 the information is exempt from section 7(1)(a) of that Act (data subject's right to be informed whether personal data being processed).

(6) In determining for the purposes of this section whether anything done before 24th October 2007 would contravene any of the data protection principles, the exemptions in Part III of Schedule 8 to the Data Protection Act 1998 shall be disregarded.

(7) In this section—

'the data protection principles' means the principles set out in Part I of Schedule 1 to the Data Protection Act 1998, as read subject to Part II of that Schedule and section 27(1) of that Act;

'data subject' has the same meaning as in section 1(1) of that Act;

'personal data' has the same meaning as in section 1(1) of that Act.

41 Information provided in confidence

(1) Information is exempt information if—

    (a) it was obtained by the public authority from any other person (including another public authority), and

    (b) the disclosure of the information to the public (otherwise than under this Act) by the public authority holding it would constitute a breach of confidence actionable by that or any other person.

(2) The duty to confirm or deny does not arise if, or to the extent that, the confirmation or denial that would have to be given to comply with section 1(1)(a) would (apart from this Act) constitute an actionable breach of confidence.

42   Legal professional privilege

(1) Information in respect of which a claim to legal professional privilege or, in Scotland, to confidentiality of communications could be maintained in legal proceedings is exempt information.

(2) The duty to confirm or deny does not arise if, or to the extent that, compliance with section 1(1)(a) would involve the disclosure of any information (whether or not already recorded) in respect of which such a claim could be maintained in legal proceedings.

43   Commercial interests

(1) Information is exempt information if it constitutes a trade secret.

(2) Information is exempt information if its disclosure under this Act would, or would be likely to, prejudice the commercial interests of any person (including the public authority holding it).

(3) The duty to confirm or deny does not arise if, or to the extent that, compliance with section 1(1)(a) would, or would be likely to, prejudice the interests mentioned in subsection (2).

44   Prohibitions on disclosure

(1) Information is exempt information if its disclosure (otherwise than under this Act) by the public authority holding it—

    (a) is prohibited by or under any enactment,

    (b) is incompatible with any Community obligation, or

    (c) would constitute or be punishable as a contempt of court.

(2) The duty to confirm or deny does not arise if the confirmation or denial that would have to be given to comply with section 1(1)(a) would (apart from this Act) fall within any of paragraphs (a) to (c) of subsection (1).

PART III   GENERAL FUNCTIONS OF SECRETARY OF STATE, LORD CHANCELLOR AND INFORMATION COMMISSIONER

45   Issue of code of practice by the Secretary of State

(1) The Secretary of State shall issue, and may from time to time revise, a code of practice providing guidance to public authorities as to the practice which it would, in his opinion, be desirable for them to follow in connection with the discharge of the authorities' functions under Part I.

(2) The code of practice must, in particular, include provision relating to—

    (a) the provision of advice and assistance by public authorities to persons who propose to make, or have made, requests for information to them,

    (b) the transfer of requests by one public authority to another public authority by which the information requested is or may be held,

    (c) consultation with persons to whom the information requested relates or persons whose interests are likely to be affected by the disclosure of information,

    (d) the inclusion in contracts entered into by public authorities of terms relating to the disclosure of information,

    (da) the disclosure by public authorities of datasets held by them, and

    (e) the provision by public authorities of procedures for dealing with complaints about the handling by them of requests for information.

(2A) Provision of the kind mentioned in subsection (2)(da) may, in particular, include provision relating to—

    (a) the giving of permission for datasets to be re-used,

    (b) the disclosure of datasets in an electronic form which is capable of re-use,

    (c) the making of datasets available for re-use in accordance with the terms of a licence,

    (d) other matters relating to the making of datasets available for re-use,

    (e) standards applicable to public authorities in connection with the disclosure of datasets.

(3) Any code under this section may make different provision for different public authorities.

(4) Before issuing or revising any code under this section, the Secretary of State shall consult the Commissioner.

(5) The Secretary of State shall lay before each House of Parliament any code or revised code made under this section.

46   Issue of code of practice by Lord Chancellor

(1) The Lord Chancellor shall issue, and may from time to time revise, a code of practice providing guidance to relevant authorities as to the practice which it would, in his opinion, be desirable for them to follow in connection with the keeping, management and destruction of their records.

(2) For the purpose of facilitating the performance by the Public Record Office, the Public Record Office of Northern Ireland and other public authorities of their functions under this Act in relation to records which are public records for the purposes of the Public Records Act 1958 or the Public Records Act (Northern Ireland) 1923, the code may also include guidance as to—

(a) the practice to be adopted in relation to the transfer of records under section 3(4) of the Public Records Act 1958 or section 3 of the Public Records Act (Northern Ireland) 1923, and

(b) the practice of reviewing records before they are transferred under those provisions.

(3) In exercising his functions under this section, the Lord Chancellor shall have regard to the public interest in allowing public access to information held by relevant authorities.

(4) The code may make different provision for different relevant authorities.

(5) Before issuing or revising any code under this section the Lord Chancellor shall consult—

(a) the Secretary of State,

(b) the Commissioner, and

(c) in relation to Northern Ireland, the appropriate Northern Ireland Minister.

(6) The Lord Chancellor shall lay before each House of Parliament any code or revised code made under this section.

(7) In this section 'relevant authority' means—

(a) any public authority, and

(b) any office or body which is not a public authority but whose administrative and departmental records are public records for the purposes of the Public Records Act 1958 or the Public Records Act (Northern Ireland) 1923.

47   General functions of Commissioner

(1) It shall be the duty of the Commissioner to promote the following of good practice by public authorities and, in particular, so to perform his functions under this Act as to promote the observance by public authorities of—

(a) the requirements of this Act, and

(b) the provisions of the codes of practice under sections 45 and 46.

(2) The Commissioner shall arrange for the dissemination in such form and manner as he considers appropriate of such information as it may appear to him expedient to give to the public—

(a) about the operation of this Act,

(b) about good practice, and

(c) about other matters within the scope of his functions under this Act,

and may give advice to any person as to any of those matters.

(3) The Commissioner may, with the consent of any public authority, assess whether that authority is following good practice.

(4) The Commissioner may charge such sums as he may determine for any relevant services provided by the Commissioner under this section.

(4A) In subsection (4) 'relevant services' means—

(a) the provision to the same person of more than one copy of any published material where each of the copies of the material is either provided on paper, a portable disk which stores the material electronically or a similar medium,

(b) the provision of training, or

(c)   the provision of conferences.

(4B) The Secretary of State may by order amend subsection (4A).

(4C) An order under subsection (4B) may include such transitional or saving provision as the Secretary of State considers appropriate.

(4D) The Secretary of State must consult the Commissioner before making an order under subsection (4B).

(5) The Commissioner shall from time to time as he considers appropriate—

    (a) consult the Keeper of Public Records about the promotion by the Commissioner of the observance by public authorities of the provisions of the code of practice under section 46 in relation to records which are public records for the purposes of the Public Records Act 1958, and

    (b) consult the Deputy Keeper of the Records of Northern Ireland about the promotion by the Commissioner of the observance by public authorities of those provisions in relation to records which are public records for the purposes of the Public Records Act (Northern Ireland) 1923.

(6) In this section 'good practice', in relation to a public authority, means such practice in the discharge of its functions under this Act as appears to the Commissioner to be desirable, and includes (but is not limited to) compliance with the requirements of this Act and the provisions of the codes of practice under sections 45 and 46.

48   Recommendations as to good practice

(1) If it appears to the Commissioner that the practice of a public authority in relation to the exercise of its functions under this Act does not conform with that proposed in the codes of practice under sections 45 and 46, he may give to the authority a recommendation (in this section referred to as a 'practice recommendation') specifying the steps which ought in his opinion to be taken for promoting such conformity.

(2) A practice recommendation must be given in writing and must refer to the particular provisions of the code of practice with which, in the Commissioner's opinion, the public authority's practice does not conform.

(3) Before giving to a public authority other than the Public Record Office a practice recommendation which relates to conformity with the code of practice under section 46 in respect of records which are public records for the purposes of the Public Records Act 1958, the Commissioner shall consult the Keeper of Public Records.

(4) Before giving to a public authority other than the Public Record Office of Northern Ireland a practice recommendation which relates to conformity with the code of practice under section 46 in respect of records which are public records for the purposes of the Public Records Act (Northern Ireland) 1923, the Commissioner shall consult the Deputy Keeper of the Records of Northern Ireland.

49   Reports to be laid before Parliament

(1) The Commissioner shall lay annually before each House of Parliament a general report on the exercise of his functions under this Act.

(2) The Commissioner may from time to time lay before each House of Parliament such other reports with respect to those functions as he thinks fit.

PART IV   ENFORCEMENT

50   Application for decision by Commissioner

(1) Any person (in this section referred to as 'the complainant') may apply to the Commissioner for a decision whether, in any specified respect, a request for information made by the complainant to a public authority has been dealt with in accordance with the requirements of Part I.

(2) On receiving an application under this section, the Commissioner shall make a decision unless it appears to him—

    (a) that the complainant has not exhausted any complaints procedure which is provided by the public authority in conformity with the code of practice under section 45,

    (b) that there has been undue delay in making the application,

    (c) that the application is frivolous or vexatious, or

    (d) that the application has been withdrawn or abandoned.

(3) Where the Commissioner has received an application under this section, he shall either—

    (a) notify the complainant that he has not made any decision under this section as a result of the application and of his grounds for not doing so, or

    (b) serve notice of his decision (in this Act referred to as a 'decision notice') on the complainant and the public authority.

(4) Where the Commissioner decides that a public authority—

    (a) has failed to communicate information, or to provide confirmation or denial, in a case where it is required to do so by section 1(1), or

    (b) has failed to comply with any of the requirements of sections 11 and 17,

the decision notice must specify the steps which must be taken by the authority for complying with that requirement and the period within which they must be taken.

(5) A decision notice must contain particulars of the right of appeal conferred by section 57.

(6) Where a decision notice requires steps to be taken by the public authority within a specified period, the time specified in the notice must not expire before the end of the period within which an appeal can be brought against the notice and, if such an appeal is brought, no step which is affected by the appeal need be taken pending the determination or withdrawal of the appeal.

(7) This section has effect subject to section 53.

51 Information notices

(1) If the Commissioner—

    (a) has received an application under section 50, or

    (b) reasonably requires any information—

      (i) for the purpose of determining whether a public authority has complied or is complying with any of the requirements of Part I, or

      (ii) for the purpose of determining whether the practice of a public authority in relation to the exercise of its functions under this Act conforms with that proposed in the codes of practice under sections 45 and 46,

he may serve the authority with a notice (in this Act referred to as 'an information notice') requiring it, within such time as is specified in the notice, to furnish the Commissioner, in such form as may be so specified, with such information relating to the application, to compliance with Part I or to conformity with the code of practice as is so specified.

(2) An information notice must contain—

    (a) in a case falling within subsection (1)(a), a statement that the Commissioner has received an application under section 50, or

    (b) in a case falling within subsection (1)(b), a statement—

      (i) that the Commissioner regards the specified information as relevant for either of the purposes referred to in subsection (1)(b), and

      (ii) of his reasons for regarding that information as relevant for that purpose.

(3) An information notice must also contain particulars of the right of appeal conferred by section 57.

(4) The time specified in an information notice must not expire before the end of the period within which an appeal can be brought against the notice and, if such an appeal is brought, the information need not be furnished pending the determination or withdrawal of the appeal.

(5) An authority shall not be required by virtue of this section to furnish the Commissioner with any information in respect of—

(a) any communication between a professional legal adviser and his client in connection with the giving of legal advice to the client with respect to his obligations, liabilities or rights under this Act, or

(b) any communication between a professional legal adviser and his client, or between such an adviser or his client and any other person, made in connection with or in contemplation of proceedings under or arising out of this Act (including proceedings before the Tribunal) and for the purposes of such proceedings.

(6) In subsection (5) references to the client of a professional legal adviser include references to any person representing such a client.

(7) The Commissioner may cancel an information notice by written notice to the authority on which it was served.

(8) In this section 'information' includes unrecorded information.

52   Enforcement notices

(1) If the Commissioner is satisfied that a public authority has failed to comply with any of the requirements of Part I, the Commissioner may serve the authority with a notice (in this Act referred to as 'an enforcement notice') requiring the authority to take, within such time as may be specified in the notice, such steps as may be so specified for complying with those requirements.

(2) An enforcement notice must contain—

(a) a statement of the requirement or requirements of Part I with which the Commissioner is satisfied that the public authority has failed to comply and his reasons for reaching that conclusion, and

(b) particulars of the right of appeal conferred by section 57.

(3) An enforcement notice must not require any of the provisions of the notice to be complied with before the end of the period within which an appeal can be brought against the notice and, if such an appeal is brought, the notice need not be complied with pending the determination or withdrawal of the appeal.

(4) The Commissioner may cancel an enforcement notice by written notice to the authority on which it was served.

(5) This section has effect subject to section 53.

53   Exception from duty to comply with decision notice or enforcement notice

(1) This section applies to a decision notice or enforcement notice which—

(a) is served on—

(i)   a government department,

(ii)   the Welsh Assembly Government,

(iii) any public authority designated for the purposes of this section by an order made by the Secretary of State, and

(b) relates to a failure, in respect of one or more requests for information—

(i)   to comply with section 1(1)(a) in respect of information which falls within any provision of Part II stating that the duty to confirm or deny does not arise, or

(ii)   to comply with section 1(1)(b) in respect of exempt information.

(2) A decision notice or enforcement notice to which this section applies shall cease to have effect if, not later than the twentieth working day following the effective date, the accountable person in relation to that authority gives the Commissioner a certificate signed by him stating that he has on reasonable grounds formed the opinion that, in respect of the request or requests concerned, there was no failure falling within subsection (1)(b).

(3) Where the accountable person gives a certificate to the Commissioner under subsection (2) he shall as soon as practicable thereafter lay a copy of the certificate before—

(a) each House of Parliament,

(b) the Northern Ireland Assembly, in any case where the certificate relates to a decision notice or enforcement notice which has been served on a Northern Ireland department or any Northern Ireland public authority, or

(c) the National Assembly for Wales, in any case where the certificate relates to a decision notice or enforcement notice which has been served on—

    (i)   the Welsh Assembly Government,

    (ii) the National Assembly for Wales, or

    (iii) any Welsh public authority.

(4) In subsection (2) 'the effective date', in relation to a decision notice or enforcement notice, means—

(a) the day on which the notice was given to the public authority, or

(b) where an appeal under section 57 is brought, the day on which that appeal (or any further appeal arising out of it) is determined or withdrawn.

(5) Before making an order under subsection (1)(a)(iii), the Secretary of State shall—

(a) if the order relates to a Welsh public authority, consult the Welsh Ministers,

(aa) if the order relates to the National Assembly for Wales, consult the Presiding Officer of that Assembly,

(b) if the order relates to the Northern Ireland Assembly, consult the Presiding Officer of that Assembly, and

(c) if the order relates to a Northern Ireland public authority, consult the First Minister and deputy First Minister in Northern Ireland.

(6) Where the accountable person gives a certificate to the Commissioner under subsection (2) in relation to a decision notice, the accountable person shall, on doing so or as soon as reasonably practicable after doing so, inform the person who is the complainant for the purposes of section 50 of the reasons for his opinion.

(7) The accountable person is not obliged to provide information under subsection (6) if, or to the extent that, compliance with that subsection would involve the disclosure of exempt information.

(8) In this section 'the accountable person'—

(a) in relation to a Northern Ireland department or any Northern Ireland public authority, means the First Minister and deputy First Minister in Northern Ireland acting jointly,

(b) in relation to the Welsh Assembly Government, the National Assembly for Wales or any Welsh public authority, means the First Minister for Wales, and

(c) in relation to any other public authority, means—

    (i)   a Minister of the Crown who is a member of the Cabinet, or

    (ii) the Attorney General, the Advocate General for Scotland or the Attorney General for Northern Ireland.

(9) In this section 'working day' has the same meaning as in section 10.

54   Failure to comply with notice

(1) If a public authority has failed to comply with—

(a) so much of a decision notice as requires steps to be taken,

(b) an information notice, or

(c) an enforcement notice,

the Commissioner may certify in writing to the court that the public authority has failed to comply with that notice.

(2) For the purposes of this section, a public authority which, in purported compliance with an information notice—

(a) makes a statement which it knows to be false in a material respect, or

(b) recklessly makes a statement which is false in a material respect, is to be taken to have failed to comply with the notice.

(3) Where a failure to comply is certified under subsection (1), the court may inquire into the matter and, after hearing any witness who may be produced against or on behalf of the public authority, and after hearing any statement that may be offered in defence, deal with the authority as if it had committed a contempt of court.

(4) In this section 'the court' means the High Court or, in Scotland, the Court of Session.

55 Powers of entry and inspection
Schedule 3 (powers of entry and inspection) has effect.

56 No action against public authority
(1) This Act does not confer any right of action in civil proceedings in respect of any failure to comply with any duty imposed by or under this Act.

(2) Subsection (1) does not affect the powers of the Commissioner under section 54.

PART V APPEALS

57 Appeal against notice served under Part IV
(1) Where a decision notice has been served, the complainant or the public authority may appeal to the Tribunal against the notice.

(2) A public authority on which an information notice or an enforcement notice has been served by the Commissioner may appeal to the Tribunal against the notice.

(3) In relation to a decision notice or enforcement notice which relates—
(a) to information to which section 66 applies, and
(b) to a matter which by virtue of subsection (3) or (4) of that section falls to be determined by the responsible authority instead of the appropriate records authority,

subsections (1) and (2) shall have effect as if the reference to the public authority were a reference to the public authority or the responsible authority.

58 Determination of appeals
(1) If on an appeal under section 57 the Tribunal considers—
(a) that the notice against which the appeal is brought is not in accordance with the law, or
(b) to the extent that the notice involved an exercise of discretion by the Commissioner, that he ought to have exercised his discretion differently,

the Tribunal shall allow the appeal or substitute such other notice as could have been served by the Commissioner; and in any other case the Tribunal shall dismiss the appeal.

(2) On such an appeal, the Tribunal may review any finding of fact on which the notice in question was based.

60 Appeals against national security certificate
(1) Where a certificate under section 23(2) or 24(3) has been issued—
(a) the Commissioner, or
(b) any applicant whose request for information is affected by the issue of the certificate, may appeal to the Tribunal against the certificate.

(2) If on an appeal under subsection (1) relating to a certificate under section 23(2), the Tribunal finds that the information referred to in the certificate was not exempt information by virtue of section 23(1), the Tribunal may allow the appeal and quash the certificate.

(3) If on an appeal under subsection (1) relating to a certificate under section 24(3), the Tribunal finds that, applying the principles applied by the court on an application for judicial review, the Minister did not have reasonable grounds for issuing the certificate, the Tribunal may allow the appeal and quash the certificate.

(4) Where in any proceedings under this Act it is claimed by a public authority that a certificate under section 24(3) which identifies the information to which it applies by means of a general description applies to particular information, any other party to the proceedings may appeal to the Tribunal on the ground that the certificate does not apply to the information in question and, subject to any determination under subsection (5), the certificate shall be conclusively presumed so to apply.

(5) On any appeal under subsection (4), the Tribunal may determine that the certificate does not so apply.

61 Appeal proceedings

The provisions of Schedule 6 to the Data Protection Act 1998 have effect (so far as applicable) in relation to appeals under this Part.

84 Interpretation

In this Act, unless the context otherwise requires—

'applicant', in relation to a request for information, means the person who made the request;

'appropriate Northern Ireland Minister' means the Northern Ireland Minister in charge of the Department of Culture, Arts and Leisure in Northern Ireland;

'appropriate records authority', in relation to a transferred public record, has the meaning given by section 15(5);

'body' includes an unincorporated association;

'the Commissioner' means the Information Commissioner;

'dataset' has the meaning given by section 11(5)

'decision notice' has the meaning given by section 50;

'the duty to confirm or deny' has the meaning given by section 1(6);

'enactment' includes an enactment contained in Northern Ireland legislation;

'enforcement notice' has the meaning given by section 52;

'exempt information' means information which is exempt information by virtue of any provision of Part II;

'fees notice' has the meaning given by section 9(1);

'government department' includes a Northern Ireland department and any other body or authority exercising statutory functions on behalf of the Crown, but does not include—

(a) any of the bodies specified in section 80(2),

(b) the Security Service, the Secret Intelligence Service or the Government Communications Headquarters, or

(c) the Welsh Assembly Government;

'information' (subject to sections 51(8) and 75(2)) means information recorded in any form;

'information notice' has the meaning given by section 51;

'Minister of the Crown' has the same meaning as in the Ministers of the Crown Act 1975;

'Northern Ireland Minister' includes the First Minister and deputy First Minister in Northern Ireland;

'Northern Ireland public authority' means any public authority, other than the Northern Ireland Assembly or a Northern Ireland department, whose functions are exercisable only or mainly in or as regards Northern Ireland and relate only or mainly to transferred matters;

'prescribed' means prescribed by regulations made by the Secretary of State;

'public authority' has the meaning given by section 3(1);

'public record' means a public record within the meaning of the Public Records Act 1958 or a public record to which the Public Records Act (Northern Ireland) 1923 applies;

'publication scheme' has the meaning given by section 19;

'request for information' has the meaning given by section 8;

'responsible authority', in relation to a transferred public record, has the meaning given by section 15(5);

'the special forces' means those units of the armed forces of the Crown the maintenance of whose capabilities is the responsibility of the Director of Special Forces or which are for the time being subject to the operational command of that Director;

'subordinate legislation' has the meaning given by subsection (1) of section 21 of the Interpretation Act 1978, except that the definition of that term in that subsection shall have effect as if 'Act' included Northern Ireland legislation;

'transferred matter', in relation to Northern Ireland, has the meaning given by section 4(1) of the Northern Ireland Act 1998;

'transferred public record' has the meaning given by section 15(4);

'the Tribunal' , in relation to any appeal under this Act, means—

    (a) the Upper Tribunal, in any case where it is determined by or under Tribunal Procedure Rules that the Upper Tribunal is to hear the appeal; or

    (b) the First-tier Tribunal, in any other case;

'Welsh public authority' has the meaning given by section 83.

88 Short title and extent

(1) This Act may be cited as the Freedom of Information Act 2000.

(2) Subject to subsection (3), this Act extends to Northern Ireland.

(3) The amendment or repeal of any enactment by this Act has the same extent as that enactment.

Data Protection Act 1998

(1998, c. 29)

PART I

Preliminary

1 Basic interpretative provisions

(1) In this Act, unless the context otherwise requires—

'data' means information which—

    (a) is being processed by means of equipment operating automatically in response to instructions given for that purpose,

    (b) is recorded with the intention that it should be processed by means of such equipment,

    (c) is recorded as part of a relevant filing system or with the intention that it should form part of a relevant filing system,

    (d) does not fall within paragraph (a), (b) or (c) but forms part of an accessible record as defined by section 68; or

    (e) is recorded information held by a public authority and does not fall within any of paragraphs (a) to (d);

'data controller' means, subject to subsection (4), a person who (either alone or jointly or in common with other persons) determines the purposes for which and the manner in which any personal data are, or are to be, processed;

'data processor', in relation to personal data, means any person (other than an employee of the data controller) who processes the data on behalf of the data controller;

'data subject' means an individual who is the subject of personal data;

'personal data' means data which relate to a living individual who can be identified—

(a) from those data, or

(b) from those data and other information which is in the possession of, or is likely to come into the possession of, the data controller,

and includes any expression of opinion about the individual and any indication of the intentions of the data controller or any other person in respect of the individual;

'processing', in relation to information or data, means obtaining, recording or holding the information or data or carrying out any operation or set of operations on the information or data, including—

(a) organisation, adaptation or alteration of the information or data,

(b) retrieval, consultation or use of the information or data,

(c) disclosure of the information or data by transmission, dissemination or otherwise making available, or

(d) alignment, combination, blocking, erasure or destruction of the information or data;

'public authority' means a public authority as defined by the Freedom of Information Act 2000 or a Scottish public authority as defined by the Freedom of Information (Scotland) Act 2002;

'relevant filing system' means any set of information relating to individuals to the extent that, although the information is not processed by means of equipment operating automatically in response to instructions given for that purpose, the set is structured, either by reference to individuals or by reference to criteria relating to individuals, in such a way that specific information relating to a particular individual is readily accessible.

(2) In this Act, unless the context otherwise requires—

(a) 'obtaining' or 'recording', in relation to personal data, includes obtaining or recording the information to be contained in the data, and

(b) 'using' or 'disclosing', in relation to personal data, includes using or disclosing the information contained in the data.

(3) In determining for the purposes of this Act whether any information is recorded with the intention—

(a) that it should be processed by means of equipment operating automatically in response to instructions given for that purpose, or

(b) that it should form part of a relevant filing system,

it is immaterial that it is intended to be so processed or to form part of such a system only after being transferred to a country or territory outside the European Economic Area.

(4) Where personal data are processed only for purposes for which they are required by or under any enactment to be processed, the person on whom the obligation to process the data is imposed by or under that enactment is for the purposes of this Act the data controller.

(5) In paragraph (e) of the definition of 'data' in subsection (1); the reference to information 'held' by a public authority shall be construed in accordance with section 3(2) of the Freedom of Information Act 2000 or section 3(2), (4) and (5) of the Freedom of Information (Scotland) Act 2002.

(6) Where —

(a) section 7 of the Freedom of Information Act 2000 prevents Parts I to V of that Act or

(b) section 7(1) of the Freedom of Information (Scotland) Act prevents that Act from applying to certain information held by a public authority,

that information is not to be treated for the purposes of paragraph (e) of the definition of 'data' in subsection (1) as held by a public authority.

2   Sensitive personal data

In this Act 'sensitive personal data' means personal data consisting of information as to—

(a) the racial or ethnic origin of the data subject,

(b) his political opinions,

(c) his religious beliefs or other beliefs of a similar nature,

(d) whether he is a member of a trade union (within the meaning of the Trade Union and Labour Relations (Consolidation) Act 1992),

(e) his physical or mental health or condition,

(f) his sexual life,

(g) the commission or alleged commission by him of any offence, or

(h) any proceedings for any offence committed or alleged to have been committed by him, the disposal of such proceedings or the sentence of any court in such proceedings.

3   The special purposes

In this Act 'the special purposes' means any one or more of the following—

(a) the purposes of journalism,

(b) artistic purposes, and

(c) literary purposes.

4   The data protection principles

(1) References in this Act to the data protection principles are to the principles set out in Part I of Schedule 1.

(2) Those principles are to be interpreted in accordance with Part II of Schedule 1.

(3) Schedule 2 (which applies to all personal data) and Schedule 3 (which applies only to sensitive personal data) set out conditions applying for the purposes of the first principle; and Schedule 4 sets out cases in which the eighth principle does not apply.

(4) Subject to section 27(1), it shall be the duty of a data controller to comply with the data protection principles in relation to all personal data with respect to which he is the data controller.

5   Application of Act

(1) Except as otherwise provided by or under section 54, this Act applies to a data controller in respect of any data only if—

(a) the data controller is established in the United Kingdom and the data are processed in the context of that establishment, or

(b) the data controller is established neither in the United Kingdom nor in any other EEA State but uses equipment in the United Kingdom for processing the data otherwise than for the purposes of transit through the United Kingdom.

(2) A data controller falling within subsection (1)(b) must nominate for the purposes of this Act a representative established in the United Kingdom.

(3) For the purposes of subsections (1) and (2), each of the following is to be treated as established in the United Kingdom—

(a) an individual who is ordinarily resident in the United Kingdom,

(b) a body incorporated under the law of, or of any part of, the United Kingdom,

(c) a partnership or other unincorporated association formed under the law of any part of the United Kingdom, and

(d) any person who does not fall within paragraph (a), (b) or (c) but maintains in the United Kingdom—

(i)   an office, branch or agency through which he carries on any activity, or

(ii)   a regular practice;

and the reference to establishment in any other EEA State has a corresponding meaning.

PART II RIGHTS OF DATA SUBJECTS AND OTHERS

7   Right of access to personal data

(1) Subject to the following provisions of this section and to sections 8, 9 and 9A, an individual is entitled—

    (a) to be informed by any data controller whether personal data of which that individual is the data subject are being processed by or on behalf of that data controller,

    (b) if that is the case, to be given by the data controller a description of—

        (i) the personal data of which that individual is the data subject,

        (ii) the purposes for which they are being or are to be processed, and

        (iii) the recipients or classes of recipients to whom they are or may be disclosed,

    (c) to have communicated to him in an intelligible form—

        (i) the information constituting any personal data of which that individual is the data subject, and

        (ii) any information available to the data controller as to the source of those data, and

    (d) where the processing by automatic means of personal data of which that individual is the data subject for the purpose of evaluating matters relating to him such as, for example, his performance at work, his credit worthiness, his reliability or his conduct, has constituted or is likely to constitute the sole basis for any decision significantly affecting him, to be informed by the data controller of the logic involved in that decision-taking.

(2) A data controller is not obliged to supply any information under subsection (1) unless he has received—

    (a) a request in writing, and

    (b) except in prescribed cases, such fee (not exceeding the prescribed maximum) as he may require.

(3) Where a data controller—

    (a) reasonably requires further information in order to satisfy himself as to the identity of the person making a request under this section and to locate the information which that person seeks, and

    (b) has informed him of that requirement,

the data controller is not obliged to comply with the request unless he is supplied with that further information.

(4) Where a data controller cannot comply with the request without disclosing information relating to another individual who can be identified from that information, he is not obliged to comply with the request unless—

    (a) the other individual has consented to the disclosure of the information to the person making the request, or

    (b) it is reasonable in all the circumstances to comply with the request without the consent of the other individual.

(5) In subsection (4) the reference to information relating to another individual includes a reference to information identifying that individual as the source of the information sought by the request; and that subsection is not to be construed as excusing a data controller from communicating so much of the information sought by the request as can be communicated without disclosing the identity of the other individual concerned, whether by the omission of names or other identifying particulars or otherwise.

(6) In determining for the purposes of subsection (4)(b) whether it is reasonable in all the circumstances to comply with the request without the consent of the other individual concerned, regard shall be had, in particular, to—

    (a) any duty of confidentiality owed to the other individual,

    (b) any steps taken by the data controller with a view to seeking the consent of the other individual,

    (c) whether the other individual is capable of giving consent, and

    (d) any express refusal of consent by the other individual.

(7) An individual making a request under this section may, in such cases as may be prescribed, specify that his request is limited to personal data of any prescribed description.

(8) Subject to subsection (4), a data controller shall comply with a request under this section promptly and in any event before the end of the prescribed period beginning with the relevant day.

(9) If a court is satisfied on the application of any person who has made a request under the foregoing provisions of this section that the data controller in question has failed to comply with the request in contravention of those provisions, the court may order him to comply with the request.

(10) In this section—

'prescribed' means prescribed by the Secretary of State by regulations;

'the prescribed maximum' means such amount as may be prescribed;

'the prescribed period' means forty days or such other period as may be prescribed;

'the relevant day', in relation to a request under this section, means the day on which the data controller receives the request or, if later, the first day on which the data controller has both the required fee and the information referred to in subsection (3).

(11) Different amounts or periods may be prescribed under this section in relation to different cases.

8 Provisions supplementary to section 7

(1) The Secretary of State may by regulations provide that, in such cases as may be prescribed, a request for information under any provision of subsection (1) of section 7 is to be treated as extending also to information under other provisions of that subsection.

(2) The obligation imposed by section 7(1)(c)(i) must be complied with by supplying the data subject with a copy of the information in permanent form unless—

(a) the supply of such a copy is not possible or would involve disproportionate effort, or

(b) the data subject agrees otherwise;

and where any of the information referred to in section 7(1)(c)(i) is expressed in terms which are not intelligible without explanation the copy must be accompanied by an explanation of those terms.

(3) Where a data controller has previously complied with a request made under section 7 by an individual, the data controller is not obliged to comply with a subsequent identical or similar request under that section by that individual unless a reasonable interval has elapsed between compliance with the previous request and the making of the current request.

(4) In determining for the purposes of subsection (3) whether requests under section 7 are made at reasonable intervals, regard shall be had to the nature of the data, the purposes for which the data are processed and the frequency with which the data are altered.

(5) Section 7(1)(d) is not to be regarded as requiring the provision of information as to the logic involved in any decision-taking if, and to the extent that, the information constitutes a trade secret.

(6) The information to be supplied pursuant to a request under section 7 must be supplied by reference to the data in question at the time when the request is received, except that it may take account of any amendment or deletion made between that time and the time when the information is supplied, being an amendment or deletion that would have been made regardless of the receipt of the request.

(7) For the purposes of section 7(4) and (5) another individual can be identified from the information being disclosed if he can be identified from that information, or from that and any other information which, in the reasonable belief of the data controller, is likely to be in, or to come into, the possession of the data subject making the request.

9A Unstructured personal data held by public authorities

(1) In this section 'unstructured personal data' means any personal data falling within paragraph (e) of the definition of 'data' in section 1(1), other than information which is recorded as part of, or with the intention that it should form part of, any set of information relating to individuals to the extent that the set is structured by reference to individuals or by reference to criteria relating to individuals.

(2) A public authority is not obliged to comply with subsection (1) of section 7 in relation to any unstructured personal data unless the request under that section contains a description of the data.

(3) Even if the data are described by the data subject in his request, a public authority is not obliged to comply with subsection (1) of section 7 in relation to unstructured personal data if the

authority estimates that the cost of complying with the request so far as relating to those data would exceed the appropriate limit.

(4) Subsection (3) does not exempt the public authority from its obligation to comply with paragraph (a) of section 7(1) in relation to the unstructured personal data unless the estimated cost of complying with that paragraph alone in relation to those data would exceed the appropriate limit.

(5) In subsections (3) and (4) 'the appropriate limit' means such amount as may be prescribed by the Secretary of State by regulations, and different amounts may be prescribed in relation to different cases.

(6) Any estimate for the purposes of this section must be made in accordance with regulations under section 12(5) of the Freedom of Information Act 2000.

10   Right to prevent processing likely to cause damage or distress

(1) Subject to subsection (2), an individual is entitled at any time by notice in writing to a data controller to require the data controller at the end of such period as is reasonable in the circumstances to cease, or not to begin, processing, or processing for a specified purpose or in a specified manner, any personal data in respect of which he is the data subject, on the ground that, for specified reasons—

   (a) the processing of those data or their processing for that purpose or in that manner is causing or is likely to cause substantial damage or substantial distress to him or to another, and

   (b) that damage or distress is or would be unwarranted.

(2) Subsection (1) does not apply—

   (a) in a case where any of the conditions in paragraphs 1 to 4 of Schedule 2 is met, or

   (b) in such other cases as may be prescribed by the Secretary of State by order.

(3) The data controller must within twenty-one days of receiving a notice under subsection (1) ('the data subject notice') give the individual who gave it a written notice—

   (a) stating that he has complied or intends to comply with the data subject notice, or

   (b) stating his reasons for regarding the data subject notice as to any extent unjustified and the extent (if any) to which he has complied or intends to comply with it.

(4) If a court is satisfied, on the application of any person who has given a notice under subsection (1) which appears to the court to be justified (or to be justified to any extent), that the data controller in question has failed to comply with the notice, the court may order him to take such steps for complying with the notice (or for complying with it to that extent) as the court thinks fit.

(5) The failure by a data subject to exercise the right conferred by subsection (1) or section 11(1) does not affect any other right conferred on him by this Part.

13   Compensation for failure to comply with certain requirements

(1) An individual who suffers damage by reason of any contravention by a data controller of any of the requirements of this Act is entitled to compensation from the data controller for that damage.

(2) An individual who suffers distress by reason of any contravention by a data controller of any of the requirements of this Act is entitled to compensation from the data controller for that distress if—

   (a) the individual also suffers damage by reason of the contravention, or

   (b) the contravention relates to the processing of personal data for the special purposes.

(3) In proceedings brought against a person by virtue of this section it is a defence to prove that he had taken such care as in all the circumstances was reasonably required to comply with the requirement concerned.

14   Rectification, blocking, erasure and destruction

(1) If a court is satisfied on the application of a data subject that personal data of which the applicant is the subject are inaccurate, the court may order the data controller to rectify, block, erase or destroy those data and any other personal data in respect of which he is the data controller and which contain an expression of opinion which appears to the court to be based on the inaccurate data ....

(3) Where the court—

   (a) makes an order under subsection (1), or

(b) is satisfied on the application of a data subject that personal data of which he was the data subject and which have been rectified, blocked, erased or destroyed were inaccurate,

it may, where it considers it reasonably practicable, order the data controller to notify third parties to whom the data have been disclosed of the rectification, blocking, erasure or destruction.

(4) If a court is satisfied on the application of a data subject—

(a) that he has suffered damage by reason of any contravention by a data controller of any of the requirements of this Act in respect of any personal data, in circumstances entitling him to compensation under section 13, and

(b) that there is a substantial risk of further contravention in respect of those data in such circumstances,

the court may order the rectification, blocking, erasure or destruction of any of those data.

PART IV

Exemptions

27 Preliminary

(1) References in any of the data protection principles or any provision of Parts II and III to personal data or to the processing of personal data do not include references to data or processing which by virtue of this Part are exempt from that principle or other provision.

(2) In this Part 'the subject information provisions' means—

(a) the first data protection principle to the extent to which it requires compliance with paragraph 2 of Part II of Schedule 1, and

(b) section 7.

(3) In this Part 'the non-disclosure provisions' means the provisions specified in subsection (4) to the extent to which they are inconsistent with the disclosure in question.

(4) The provisions referred to in subsection (3) are—

(a) the first data protection principle, except to the extent to which it requires compliance with the conditions in Schedules 2 and 3,

(b) the second, third, fourth and fifth data protection principles, and

(c) sections 10 and 14(1) to (3).

(5) Except as provided by this Part, the subject information provisions shall have effect notwithstanding any enactment or rule of law prohibiting or restricting the disclosure, or authorising the withholding, of information.

28 National security

(1) Personal data are exempt from any of the provisions of—

(a) the data protection principles,

(b) Parts II, III and V, and

(c) sections 54A and 55,

if the exemption from that provision is required for the purpose of safeguarding national security.

(2) Subject to subsection (4), a certificate signed by a Minister of the Crown certifying that exemption from all or any of the provisions mentioned in subsection (1) is or at any time was required for the purpose there mentioned in respect of any personal data shall be conclusive evidence of that fact.

(3) A certificate under subsection (2) may identify the personal data to which it applies by means of a general description and may be expressed to have prospective effect.

(4) Any person directly affected by the issuing of a certificate under subsection (2) may appeal to the Tribunal against the certificate.

(5) If on an appeal under subsection (4), the Tribunal finds that, applying the principles applied by the court on an application for judicial review, the Minister did not have reasonable grounds for issuing the certificate, the Tribunal may allow the appeal and quash the certificate.

(6) Where in any proceedings under or by virtue of this Act it is claimed by a data controller that a certificate under subsection (2) which identifies the personal data to which it applies by means of a general description applies to any personal data, any other party to the proceedings may appeal to the Tribunal on the ground that the certificate does not apply to the personal data in question and, subject to any determination under subsection (7), the certificate shall be conclusively presumed so to apply.

(7) On any appeal under subsection (6), the Tribunal may determine that the certificate does not so apply.

(8) A document purporting to be a certificate under subsection (2) shall be received in evidence and deemed to be such a certificate unless the contrary is proved.

(9) A document which purports to be certified by or on behalf of a Minister of the Crown as a true copy of a certificate issued by that Minister under subsection (2) shall in any legal proceedings be evidence (or, in Scotland, sufficient evidence) of that certificate.

(10) The power conferred by subsection (2) on a Minister of the Crown shall not be exercisable except by a Minister who is a member of the Cabinet or by the Attorney General or the Lord Advocate.

(11) No power conferred by any provision of Part V may be exercised in relation to personal data which by virtue of this section are exempt from that provision.

(12) Schedule 6 shall have effect in relation to appeals under subsection (4) or (6) and the proceedings of the Tribunal in respect of any such appeal.

29   Crime and taxation

(1) Personal data processed for any of the following purposes—

  (a) the prevention or detection of crime,

  (b) the apprehension or prosecution of offenders, or

  (c) the assessment or collection of any tax or duty or of any imposition of a similar nature,

are exempt from the first data protection principle (except to the extent to which it requires compliance with the conditions in Schedules 2 and 3) and section 7 in any case to the extent to which the application of those provisions to the data would be likely to prejudice any of the matters mentioned in this subsection.

(2) Personal data which—

  (a) are processed for the purpose of discharging statutory functions, and

  (b) consist of information obtained for such a purpose from a person who had it in his possession for any of the purposes mentioned in subsection (1),

are exempt from the subject information provisions to the same extent as personal data processed for any of the purposes mentioned in that subsection.

(3) Personal data are exempt from the non-disclosure provisions in any case in which—

  (a) the disclosure is for any of the purposes mentioned in subsection (1), and

  (b) the application of those provisions in relation to the disclosure would be likely to prejudice any of the matters mentioned in that subsection.

(4) Personal data in respect of which the data controller is a relevant authority and which—

  (a) consist of a classification applied to the data subject as part of a system of risk assessment which is operated by that authority for either of the following purposes—

    (i)   the assessment or collection of any tax or duty or any imposition of a similar nature, or

    (ii) the prevention or detection of crime, or apprehension or prosecution of offenders, where the offence concerned involves any unlawful claim for any payment out of, or any unlawful application of, public funds, and

  (b) are processed for either of those purposes,

are exempt from section 7 to the extent to which the exemption is required in the interests of the operation of the system.

(5) In subsection (4)—

'public funds' includes funds provided by any EU institution;
'relevant authority' means—
    (a) a government department,
    (b) a local authority, or
    (c) any other authority administering housing benefit or council tax benefit.

30   Health, education and social work

(1) The Secretary of State may by order exempt from the subject information provisions, or modify those provisions in relation to, personal data consisting of information as to the physical or mental health or condition of the data subject.

(2) The Secretary of State may by order exempt from the subject information provisions, or modify those provisions in relation to—
    (a) personal data in respect of which the data controller is the proprietor of, or a teacher at, a school, and which consist of information relating to persons who are or have been pupils at the school, or
    (b) personal data in respect of which the data controller is an education authority in Scotland, and which consist of information relating to persons who are receiving, or have received, further education provided by the authority.

(5) In this section—
'education authority' and 'further education' have the same meaning as in the Education (Scotland) Act 1980 ('the 1980 Act'), and
'proprietor'—
    (a) in relation to a school in England or Wales, has the same meaning as in the Education Act 1996,
    (b) in relation to a school in Scotland, means—
        (ii)   in the case of an independent school, the proprietor within the meaning of the 1980 Act,
        (iii) in the case of a grant-aided school, the managers within the meaning of the 1980 Act, and
        (iv)   in the case of a public school, the education authority within the meaning of the 1980 Act, and
    (c) in relation to a school in Northern Ireland, has the same meaning as in the Education and Libraries (Northern Ireland) Order 1986 and includes, in the case of a controlled school, the Board of Governors of the school.

31   Regulatory activity

(1) Personal data processed for the purposes of discharging functions to which this subsection applies are exempt from the subject information provisions in any case to the extent to which the application of those provisions to the data would be likely to prejudice the proper discharge of those functions.

(2) Subsection (1) applies to any relevant function which is designed—
    (a) for protecting members of the public against—
        (i)   financial loss due to dishonesty, malpractice or other seriously improper conduct by, or the unfitness or incompetence of, persons concerned in the provision of banking, insurance, investment or other financial services or in the management of bodies corporate,
        (ii)   financial loss due to the conduct of discharged or undischarged bankrupts, or
        (iii) dishonesty, malpractice or other seriously improper conduct by, or the unfitness or incompetence of, persons authorised to carry on any profession or other activity,
    (b) for protecting charities or community interest companies against misconduct or mismanagement (whether by trustees, directors or other persons) in their administration,
    (c) for protecting the property of charities or community interest companies from loss or misapplication,
    (d) for the recovery of the property of charities or community interest companies,

(e) for securing the health, safety and welfare of persons at work, or

(f) for protecting persons other than persons at work against risk to health or safety arising out of or in connection with the actions of persons at work.

(3) In subsection (2) 'relevant function' means—

(a) any function conferred on any person by or under any enactment,

(b) any function of the Crown, a Minister of the Crown or a government department, or

(c) any other function which is of a public nature and is exercised in the public interest.

(4B) Personal data processed for the purposes of discharging any function of the Legal Services Board are exempt from the subject information provisions in any case to the extent to which the application of those provisions to the data would be likely to prejudice the proper discharge of the function.

(4C) Personal data processed for the purposes of the function of considering a complaint under the scheme established under Part 6 of the Legal Services Act 2007 (legal complaints) are exempt from the subject information provisions in any case to the extent to which application of those provisions to the data would be likely to prejudice the proper discharge of the function.

32 Journalism, literature and art

(1) Personal data which are processed only for the special purposes are exempt from any provision to which this subsection relates if—

(a) the processing is undertaken with a view to the publication by any person of any journalistic, literary or artistic material,

(b) the data controller reasonably believes that, having regard in particular to the special importance of the public interest in freedom of expression, publication would be in the public interest, and

(c) the data controller reasonably believes that, in all the circumstances, compliance with that provision is incompatible with the special purposes.

(2) Subsection (1) relates to the provisions of—

(a) the data protection principles except the seventh data protection principle,

(b) section 7,

(c) section 10,

(d) section 12, and

(e) section 14(1) to (3).

(3) In considering for the purposes of subsection (1)(b) whether the belief of a data controller that publication would be in the public interest was or is a reasonable one, regard may be had to his compliance with any code of practice which—

(a) is relevant to the publication in question, and

(b) is designated by the Secretary of State by order for the purposes of this subsection.

(4) Where at any time ('the relevant time') in any proceedings against a data controller under section 7(9), 10(4), 12(8) or 14 or by virtue of section 13 the data controller claims, or it appears to the court, that any personal data to which the proceedings relate are being processed—

(a) only for the special purposes, and

(b) with a view to the publication by any person of any journalistic, literary or artistic material which, at the time twenty-four hours immediately before the relevant time, had not previously been published by the data controller,

the court shall stay the proceedings until either of the conditions in subsection (5) is met.

(5) Those conditions are—

(a) that a determination of the Commissioner under section 45 with respect to the data in question takes effect, or

(b) in a case where the proceedings were stayed on the making of a claim, that the claim is withdrawn.

(6) For the purposes of this Act 'publish', in relation to journalistic, literary or artistic material, means make available to the public or any section of the public.

33 Research, history and statistics

(1) In this section—

'research purposes' includes statistical or historical purposes;

'the relevant conditions', in relation to any processing of personal data, means the conditions—

>   (a) that the data are not processed to support measures or decisions with respect to particular individuals, and
>   (b) that the data are not processed in such a way that substantial damage or substantial distress is, or is likely to be, caused to any data subject.

(2) For the purposes of the second data protection principle, the further processing of personal data only for research purposes in compliance with the relevant conditions is not to be regarded as incompatible with the purposes for which they were obtained.

(3) Personal data which are processed only for research purposes in compliance with the relevant conditions may, notwithstanding the fifth data protection principle, be kept indefinitely.

(4) Personal data which are processed only for research purposes are exempt from section 7 if—

>   (a) they are processed in compliance with the relevant conditions, and
>   (b) the results of the research or any resulting statistics are not made available in a form which identifies data subjects or any of them.

(5) For the purposes of subsections (2) to (4) personal data are not to be treated as processed otherwise than for research purposes merely because the data are disclosed—

>   (a) to any person, for research purposes only,
>   (b) to the data subject or a person acting on his behalf,
>   (c) at the request, or with the consent, of the data subject or a person acting on his behalf, or
>   (d) in circumstances in which the person making the disclosure has reasonable grounds for believing that the disclosure falls within paragraph (a), (b) or (c).

33A   Manual data held by public authorities

(1) Personal data falling within paragraph (e) of the definition of 'data' in section 1(1) are exempt from—

>   (a) the first, second, third, fifth, seventh and eighth data protection principles,
>   (b) the sixth data protection principle except so far as it relates to the rights conferred on data subjects by sections 7 and 14,
>   (c) sections 10 to 12,
>   (d) section 13, except so far as it relates to damage caused by a contravention of section 7 or of the fourth data protection principle and to any distress which is also suffered by reason of that contravention,
>   (e) Part III, and
>   (f) section 55.

(2) Personal data which fall within paragraph (e) of the definition of 'data' in section 1(1) and relate to appointments or removals, pay, discipline, superannuation or other personnel matters, in relation to—

>   (a) service in any of the armed forces of the Crown,
>   (b) service in any office or employment under the Crown including a member of the staff of the National Assembly of Wales Commission or (as the case may be a person so employed) or under any public authority, or
>   (c) service in any office or employment, or under any contract for services, in respect of which power to take action, or to determine or approve the action taken, in such matters is vested in Her Majesty, any Minister of the Crown, the National Assembly for Wales, any Northern Ireland Minister (within the meaning of the Freedom of Information Act 2000) or any public authority,

are also exempt from the remaining data protection principles and the remaining provisions of Part II.

34   Information available to the public by or under enactment

Personal data are exempt from—

>   (a) the subject information provisions,

(b) the fourth data protection principle and sections 12A and 14(1) to (3), and

(c) the non-disclosure provisions,

if the data consist of information which the data controller is obliged by or under any enactment other than an enactment contained in the Freedom of Information Act 2000 to make available to the public, whether by publishing it, by making it available for inspection, or otherwise and whether gratuitously or on payment of a fee.

PART V

Enforcement

40   Enforcement notices

(1) If the Commissioner is satisfied that a data controller has contravened or is contravening any of the data protection principles, the Commissioners may serve him with a notice (in this Act referred to as 'an enforcement notice') requiring him, for complying with the principle or principles in question, to do either or both of the following—

(a) to take within such time as may be specified in the notice, or to refrain from taking after such time as may be so specified, such steps as are so specified, or

(b) to refrain from processing any personal data, or any personal data of a description specified in the notice, or to refrain from processing them for a purpose so specified or in a manner so specified, after such time as may be so specified.

(2) In deciding whether to serve an enforcement notice, the Commissioner shall consider whether the contravention has caused or is likely to cause any person damage or distress.

(6) An enforcement notice must contain—

(a) a statement of the data protection principle or principles which the Commissioner is satisfied have been or are being contravened and his reasons for reaching that conclusion, and

(b) particulars of the rights of appeal conferred by section 48.

(7) Subject to subsection (8), an enforcement notice must not require any of the provisions of the notice to be complied with before the end of the period within which an appeal can be brought against the notice and, if such an appeal is brought, the notice need not be complied with pending the determination or withdrawal of the appeal.

(8) If by reason of special circumstances the Commissioner considers that an enforcement notice should be complied with as a matter of urgency he may include in the notice a statement to that effect and a statement of his reasons for reaching that conclusion; and in that event subsection (7) shall not apply but the notice must not require the provisions of the notice to be complied with before the end of the period of seven days beginning with the day on which the notice is served.

(9) Notification regulations (as defined by section 16(2)) may make provision as to the effect of the service of an enforcement notice on any entry in the register maintained under section 19 which relates to the person on whom the notice is served.

(10) This section has effect subject to section 46(1).

41   Cancellation of enforcement notice

(1) If the Commissioner considers that all or any of the provisions of an enforcement notice need not be complied with in order to ensure compliance with the data protection principle or principles to which it relates, he may cancel or vary the notice by written notice to the person on whom it was served.

(2) A person on whom an enforcement notice has been served may, at any time after the expiry of the period during which an appeal can be brought against that notice, apply in writing to the Commissioner for the cancellation or variation of that notice on the ground that, by reason of a change of circumstances, all or any of the provisions of that notice need not be complied with in order to ensure compliance with the data protection principle or principles to which that notice relates.

41A Assessment notices

(1) The Commissioner may serve a data controller within subsection (2) with a notice (in this Act referred to as an 'assessment notice') for the purpose of enabling the Commissioner to determine whether the data controller has complied or is complying with the data protection principles.

(2) A data controller is within this subsection if the data controller is—

 (a) a government department,

 (b) a public authority designated for the purposes of this section by an order made by the Secretary of State, or

 (c) a person of a description designated for the purposes of this section by such an order.

(3) An assessment notice is a notice which requires the data controller to do all or any of the following—

 (a) permit the Commissioner to enter any specified premises;

 (b) direct the Commissioner to any documents on the premises that are of a specified description;

 (c) assist the Commissioner to view any information of a specified description that is capable of being viewed using equipment on the premises;

 (d) comply with any request from the Commissioner for—

  (i) a copy of any of the documents to which the Commissioner is directed;

  (ii) a copy (in such form as may be requested) of any of the information which the Commissioner is assisted to view;

 (e) direct the Commissioner to any equipment or other material on the premises which is of a specified description;

 (f) permit the Commissioner to inspect or examine any of the documents, information, equipment or material to which the Commissioner is directed or which the Commissioner is assisted to view;

 (g) permit the Commissioner to observe the processing of any personal data that takes place on the premises;

 (h) make available for interview by the Commissioner a specified number of persons of a specified description who process personal data on behalf of the data controller (or such number as are willing to be interviewed).

(4) In subsection (3) references to the Commissioner include references to the Commissioner's officers and staff.

(5) An assessment notice must, in relation to each requirement imposed by the notice, specify—

 (a) the time at which the requirement is to be complied with, or

 (b) the period during which the requirement is to be complied with.

(6) An assessment notice must also contain particulars of the rights of appeal conferred by section 48.

(7) The Commissioner may cancel an assessment notice by written notice to the data controller on whom it was served.

(8) Where a public authority has been designated by an order under subsection (2)(b) the Secretary of State must reconsider, at intervals of no greater than 5 years, whether it continues to be appropriate for the authority to be designated.

(9) The Secretary of State may not make an order under subsection (2)(c) which designates a description of persons unless—

 (a) the Commissioner has made a recommendation that the description be designated, and

 (b) the Secretary of State has consulted—

  (i) such persons as appear to the Secretary of State to represent the interests of those that meet the description;

  (ii) such other persons as the Secretary of State considers appropriate.

(10) The Secretary of State may not make an order under subsection (2)(c), and the Commissioner may not make a recommendation under subsection (9)(a), unless the Secretary of State or (as the case

may be) the Commissioner is satisfied that it is necessary for the description of persons in question to be designated having regard to—

(a) the nature and quantity of data under the control of such persons, and

(b) any damage or distress which may be caused by a contravention by such persons of the data protection principles.

(11) Where a description of persons has been designated by an order under subsection (2)(c) the Secretary of State must reconsider, at intervals of no greater than 5 years, whether it continues to be necessary for the description to be designated having regard to the matters mentioned in subsection (10).

(12) In this section—

'public authority' includes any body, office-holder or other person in respect of which—

(a) an order may be made under section 4 or 5 of the Freedom of Information Act 2000, or

(b) an order may be made under section 4 or 5 of the Freedom of Information (Scotland) Act 2002;

'specified' means specified in an assessment notice.

41B   Assessment notices: limitations

(1) A time specified in an assessment notice under section 41A(5) in relation to a requirement must not fall, and a period so specified must not begin, before the end of the period within which an appeal can be brought against the notice, and if such an appeal is brought the requirement need not be complied with pending the determination or withdrawal of the appeal.

(2) If by reason of special circumstances the Commissioner considers that it is necessary for the data controller to comply with a requirement in an assessment notice as a matter of urgency, the Commissioner may include in the notice a statement to that effect and a statement of the reasons for that conclusion; and in that event subsection (1) applies in relation to the requirement if for the words from 'within' to the end there were substituted 'of 7 days beginning with the day on which the notice is served'.

(3) A requirement imposed by an assessment notice does not have effect in so far as compliance with it would result in the disclosure of—

(a) any communication between a professional legal adviser and the adviser's client in con- nection with the giving of legal advice with respect to the client's obligations, liabilities or rights under this Act, or

(b) any communication between a professional legal adviser and the adviser's client, or be- tween such an adviser or the adviser's client and any other person, made in connection with or in contemplation of proceedings under or arising out of this Act (including pro- ceedings before the Tribunal) and for the purposes of such proceedings.

(4) In subsection (3) references to the client of a professional legal adviser include references to any person representing such a client.

(5) Nothing in section 41A authorises the Commissioner to serve an assessment notice on—

(a) a judge,

(b) a body specified in section 23(3) of the Freedom of Information Act 2000 (bodies dealing with security matters), or

(c) the Office for Standards in Education, Children's Services and Skills in so far as it is a data controller in respect of information processed for the purposes of functions exercisable by Her Majesty's Chief Inspector of Eduction, Children's Services and Skills by virtue of sec- tion 5(1)(a) of the Care Standards Act 2000.

(6) In this section 'judge' includes—

(a) a justice of the peace (or, in Northern Ireland, a lay magistrate),

(b) a member of a tribunal, and

(c) a clerk or other officer entitled to exercise the jurisdiction of a court or tribunal;

and in this subsection 'tribunal' means any tribunal in which legal proceedings may be brought.

41C   Code of practice about assessment notices

(1) The Commissioner must prepare and issue a code of practice as to the manner in which the Commissioner's functions under and in connection with section 41A are to be exercised.

(2) The code must in particular—

(a) specify factors to be considered in determining whether to serve an assessment notice on a data controller;

(b) specify descriptions of documents and information that—

(i) are not to be examined or inspected in pursuance of an assessment notice, or

(ii) are to be so examined or inspected only by persons of a description specified in the code;

(c) deal with the nature of inspections and examinations carried out in pursuance of an assessment notice;

(d) deal with the nature of interviews carried out in pursuance of an assessment notice;

(e) deal with the preparation, issuing and publication by the Commissioner of assessment reports in respect of data controllers that have been served with assessment notices.

(3) The provisions of the code made by virtue of subsection (2)(b) must, in particular, include provisions that relate to—

(a) documents and information concerning an individual's physical or mental health;

(b) documents and information concerning the provision of social care for an individual.

(4) An assessment report is a report which contains—

(a) a determination as to whether a data controller has complied or is complying with the data protection principles,

(b) recommendations as to any steps which the data controller ought to take, or refrain from taking, to ensure compliance with any of those principles, and

(c) such other matters as are specified in the code.

(5) The Commissioner may alter or replace the code.

(6) If the code is altered or replaced, the Commissioner must issue the altered or replacement code.

(7) The Commissioner must consult the Secretary of State before issuing the code (or an altered or replacement code).

(8) The Commissioner must arrange for the publication of the code (and any altered or replacement code) issued under this section in such form and manner as the Commissioner considers appropriate.

(9) In this section 'social care' has the same meaning as in Part 1 of the Health and Social Care Act 2008 (see section 9(3) of that Act).

42   Request for assessment

(1) A request may be made to the Commissioner by or on behalf of any person who is, or believes himself to be, directly affected by any processing of personal data for an assessment as to whether it is likely or unlikely that the processing has been or is being carried out in compliance with the provisions of this Act.

(2) On receiving a request under this section, the Commissioner shall make an assessment in such manner as appears to him to be appropriate, unless he has not been supplied with such information as he may reasonably require in order to—

(a) satisfy himself as to the identity of the person making the request, and

(b) enable him to identify the processing in question.

(3) The matters to which the Commissioner may have regard in determining in what manner it is appropriate to make an assessment include—

(a) the extent to which the request appears to him to raise a matter of substance,

(b) any undue delay in making the request, and

(c) whether or not the person making the request is entitled to make an application under section 7 in respect of the personal data in question.

(4) Where the Commissioner has received a request under this section he shall notify the person who made the request—

(a) whether he has made an assessment as a result of the request, and

(b) to the extent that he considers appropriate, having regard in particular to any exemption from section 7 applying in relation to the personal data concerned, of any view formed or action taken as a result of the request.

43   Information notices

(1) If the Commissioner—

(a) has received a request under section 42 in respect of any processing of personal data, or

(b) reasonably requires any information for the purpose of determining whether the data controller has complied or is complying with the data protection principles,

he may serve the data controller with a notice (in this Act referred to as 'an information notice') requiring the data controller to furnish the Commissioner with specified information relating to the request or to compliance with the principles.

(1A) In subsection (1) 'specified information' means information—

(a) specified, or described, in the information notice, or

(b) falling within a category which is specified, or described, in the information notice.

(1B) The Commissioner may also specify in the information notice—

(a) the form in which the information must be furnished;

(b) the period within which, or the time and place at which, the information must be furnished.

(2) An information notice must contain—

(a) in a case falling within subsection (1)(a), a statement that the Commissioner has received a request under section 42 in relation to the specified processing, or

(b) in a case falling within subsection (1)(b), a statement that the Commissioner regards the specified information as relevant for the purpose of determining whether the data controller has complied, or is complying, with the data protection principles and his reasons for regarding it as relevant for that purpose.

(3) An information notice must also contain particulars of the rights of appeal conferred by section 48.

(4) Subject to subsection (5), the time specified in an information notice shall not expire before the end of the period within which an appeal can be brought against the notice and, if such an appeal is brought, the information need not be furnished pending the determination or withdrawal of the appeal.

(5) If by reason of special circumstances the Commissioner considers that the information is required as a matter of urgency, he may include in the notice a statement to that effect and a statement of his reasons for reaching that conclusion; and in that event subsection (4) shall not apply, but the notice shall not require the information to be furnished before the end of the period of seven days beginning with the day on which the notice is served.

(6) A person shall not be required by virtue of this section to furnish the Commissioner with any information in respect of—

(a) any communication between a professional legal adviser and his client in connection with the giving of legal advice to the client with respect to his obligations, liabilities or rights under this Act, or

(b) any communication between a professional legal adviser and his client, or between such an adviser or his client and any other person, made in connection with or in contemplation of proceedings under or arising out of this Act (including proceedings before the Tribunal) and for the purposes of such proceedings.

(7) In subsection (6) references to the client of a professional legal adviser include references to any person representing such a client.

(8) A person shall not be required by virtue of this section to furnish the Commissioner with any information if the furnishing of that information would, by revealing evidence of the commission of

any offence, other than an offence under this Act or an offence within subsection (8A), expose him to proceedings for that offence.

(8A) The offences mentioned in subsection (8) are—

(a) an offence under section 5 of the Perjury Act 1911 (false statements made otherwise than on oath),

(b) an offence under section 44(2) of the Criminal Law (Consolidation) (Scotland) Act 1995 (false statements made otherwise than on oath), or

(c) an offence under Article 10 of the Perjury (Northern Ireland) Order 1979 (false statutory declarations and other false unsworn statements).

(8B) Any relevant statement provided by a person in response to a requirement under this section may not be used in evidence against that person on a prosecution for any offence under this Act (other than an offence under section 47) unless in the proceedings—

(a) in giving evidence the person provides information inconsistent with it, and

(b) evidence relating to it is adduced, or a question relating to it is asked, by that person or on that person's behalf.

(8C) In subsection (8B) 'relevant statement', in relation to a requirement under this section, means—

(a) an oral statement, or

(b) a written statement made for the purposes of the requirement.

(9) The Commissioner may cancel an information notice by written notice to the person on whom it was served.

(10) This section has effect subject to section 46(3).

44   Special information notices

(1) If the Commissioner—

(a) has received a request under section 42 in respect of any processing of personal data, or

(b) has reasonable grounds for suspecting that, in a case in which proceedings have been stayed under section 32, the personal data to which the proceedings relate—

(i)   are not being processed only for the special purposes, or

(ii)   are not being processed with a view to the publication by any person of any journalistic, literary or artistic material which has not previously been published by the data controller,

he may serve the data controller with a notice (in this Act referred to as a 'special information notice') requiring the data controller, to furnish the Commissioner with specified information for the purpose specified in subsection (2).

1(A) In subsection (1) 'specified information' means information—

(a) specified, or described, in the special information notice, or

(b) falling within a category which is specified, or described, in the special information notice.

(1B) The Commissioner may also specify in the special information notice—

(a) the form in which the information must be furnished;

(b) the period within which, or the time and place at which, the information must be furnished.

(2) That purpose is the purpose of ascertaining—

(a) whether the personal data are being processed only for the special purposes, or

(b) whether they are being processed with a view to the publication by any person of any journalistic, literary or artistic material which has not previously been published by the data controller.

(3) A special information notice must contain—

(a) in a case falling within paragraph (a) of subsection (1), a statement that the Commissioner has received a request under section 42 in relation to the specified processing, or

(b) in a case falling within paragraph (b) of that subsection, a statement of the Commissioner's grounds for suspecting that the personal data are not being processed as mentioned in that paragraph.

(4) A special information notice must also contain particulars of the rights of appeal conferred by section 48.

(7) A person shall not be required by virtue of this section to furnish the Commissioner with any information in respect of—

(a) any communication between a professional legal adviser and his client in connection with the giving of legal advice to the client with respect to his obligations, liabilities or rights under this Act, or

(b) any communication between a professional legal adviser and his client, or between such an adviser or his client and any other person, made in connection with or in contemplation of proceedings under or arising out of this Act (including proceedings before the Tribunal) and for the purposes of such proceedings.

(8) In subsection (7) references to the client of a professional legal adviser include references to any person representing such a client.

(9) A person shall not be required by virtue of this section to furnish the Commissioner with any information if the furnishing of that information would, by revealing evidence of the commission of any offence, other than an offence under this Act or an offence within subsection (9A), expose him to proceedings for that offence.

(9A) The offences mentioned in subsection (9) are—

(a) an offence under section 5 of the Perjury Act 1911 (false statements made otherwise than on oath),

(b) an offence under section 44(2) of the Criminal Law (Consolidation) (Scotland) Act 1995 (false statements made otherwise than on oath), or

(c) an offence under Article 10 of the Perjury (Northern Ireland) Order 1979 (false statutory declarations and other false unsworn statements).

(9B) Any relevant statement provided by a person in response to a requirement under this section may not be used in evidence against that person on a prosecution for any offence under this Act (other than an offence under section 47) unless in the proceedings—

(a) in giving evidence the person provides information inconsistent with it, and

(b) evidence relating to it is adduced, or a question relating to it is asked, by that person or on that person's behalf.

(9C) In subsection (9B) 'relevant statement', in relation to a requirement under this section, means—

(a) an oral statement, or

(b) a written statement made for the purposes of the requirement.

(10) The Commissioner may cancel a special information notice by written notice to the person on whom it was served.

45 Determination by Commissioner as to the special purposes

(1) Where at any time it appears to the Commissioner (whether as a result of the service of a special information notice or otherwise) that any personal data—

(a) are not being processed only for the special purposes, or

(b) are not being processed with a view to the publication by any person of any journalistic, literary or artistic material which has not previously been published by the data controller,

he may make a determination in writing to that effect.

(2) Notice of the determination shall be given to the data controller; and the notice must contain particulars of the right of appeal conferred by section 48.

(3) A determination under subsection (1) shall not take effect until the end of the period within which an appeal can be brought and, where an appeal is brought, shall not take effect pending the determination or withdrawal of the appeal.

46   Restriction on enforcement in case of processing for the special purposes

(1) The Commissioner may not at any time serve an enforcement notice on a data controller with respect to the processing of personal data for the special purposes unless—

(a) a determination under section 45(1) with respect to those data has taken effect, and

(b) the court has granted leave for the notice to be served.

(2) The court shall not grant leave for the purposes of subsection (1)(b) unless it is satisfied—

(a) that the Commissioner has reason to suspect a contravention of the data protection principles which is of substantial public importance, and

(b) except where the case is one of urgency, that the data controller has been given notice, in accordance with rules of court, of the application for leave.

(3) The Commissioner may not serve an information notice on a data controller with respect to the processing of personal data for the special purposes unless a determination under section 45(1) with respect to those data has taken effect.

47   Failure to comply with notice

(1) A person who fails to comply with an enforcement notice, an information notice or a special information notice is guilty of an offence.

(2) A person who, in purported compliance with an information notice or a special information notice—

(a) makes a statement which he knows to be false in a material respect, or

(b) recklessly makes a statement which is false in a material respect,

is guilty of an offence.

(3) It is a defence for a person charged with an offence under subsection (1) to prove that he exercised all due diligence to comply with the notice in question.

48   Rights of appeal

(1) A person on whom an enforcement notice, an assessment notice, an information notice or a special information notice has been served may appeal to the Tribunal against the notice.

(2) A person on whom an enforcement notice has been served may appeal to the Tribunal against the refusal of an application under section 41(2) for cancellation or variation of the notice.

(3) Where an enforcement notice, an assessment notice, an information notice or a special information notice contains a statement by the Commissioner in accordance with section 40(8), 41B(2), 43(5) or 44(6) then, whether or not the person appeals against the notice, he may appeal against—

(a) the Commissioner's decision to include the statement in the notice, or

(b) the effect of the inclusion of the statement as respects any part of the notice.

(4) A data controller in respect of whom a determination has been made under section 45 may appeal to the Tribunal against the determination.

(5) Schedule 6 has effect in relation to appeals under this section and the proceedings of the Tribunal in respect of any such appeal.

49   Determination of appeals

(1) If on an appeal under section 48(1) the Tribunal considers—

(a) that the notice against which the appeal is brought is not in accordance with the law, or

(b) to the extent that the notice involved an exercise of discretion by the Commissioner, that he ought to have exercised his discretion differently,

the Tribunal shall allow the appeal or substitute such other notice or decision as could have been served or made by the Commissioner; and in any other case the Tribunal shall dismiss the appeal.

(2) On such an appeal, the Tribunal may review any determination of fact on which the notice in question was based.

(3) If on an appeal under section 48(2) the Tribunal considers that the enforcement notice ought to be cancelled or varied by reason of a change in circumstances, the Tribunal shall cancel or vary the notice.

(4) On an appeal under subsection (3) of section 48 the Tribunal may direct—

    (a) that the notice in question shall have effect as if it did not contain any such statement as is mentioned in that subsection, or

    (b) that the inclusion of the statement shall not have effect in relation to any part of the notice,

and may make such modifications in the notice as may be required for giving effect to the direction.

(5) On an appeal under section 48(4), the Tribunal may cancel the determination of the Commissioner.

50   Powers of entry and inspection

Schedule 9 (powers of entry and inspection) has effect.

General

63   Application to Crown

(1) This Act binds the Crown.

(2) For the purposes of this Act each government department shall be treated as a person separate from any other government department.

(3) Where the purposes for which and the manner in which any personal data are, or are to be, processed are determined by any person acting on behalf of the Royal Household, the Duchy of Lancaster or the Duchy of Cornwall, the data controller in respect of those data for the purposes of this Act shall be—

    (a) in relation to the Royal Household, the Keeper of the Privy Purse,

    (b) in relation to the Duchy of Lancaster, such person as the Chancellor of the Duchy appoints, and

    (c) in relation to the Duchy of Cornwall, such person as the Duke of Cornwall, or the possessor for the time being of the Duchy of Cornwall, appoints.

(4) Different persons may be appointed under subsection (3)(b) or (c) for different purposes.

(5) Neither a government department nor a person who is a data controller by virtue of subsection (3) shall be liable to prosecution under this Act, but sections 54A and 55 and paragraph 12 of Schedule 9 shall apply to a person in the service of the Crown as they apply to any other person.

63A   Application to Parliament

(1) Subject to the following provisions of this section and to section 35A, this Act applies to the processing of personal data by or on behalf of either House of Parliament as it applies to the processing of personal data by other persons.

(2) Where the purposes for which and the manner in which any personal data are, or are to be, processed are determined by or on behalf of the House of Commons, the data controller in respect of those data for the purposes of this Act shall be the Corporate Officer of that House.

(3) Where the purposes for which and the manner in which any personal data are, or are to be, processed are determined by or on behalf of the House of Lords, the data controller in respect of those data for the purposes of this Act shall be the Corporate Officer of that House.

(4) Nothing in subsection (2) or (3) is to be taken to render the Corporate Officer of the House of Commons or the Corporate Officer of the House of Lords liable to prosecution under this Act, but section 55 and paragraph 12 of Schedule 9 shall apply to a person acting on behalf of either House as they apply to any other person.

SCHEDULE 1

THE DATA PROTECTION PRINCIPLES

PART I THE PRINCIPLES

1. Personal data shall be processed fairly and lawfully and, in particular, shall not be processed unless—

   (a) at least one of the conditions in Schedule 2 is met, and

   (b) in the case of sensitive personal data, at least one of the conditions in Schedule 3 is also met.

2. Personal data shall be obtained only for one or more specified and lawful purposes, and shall not be further processed in any manner incompatible with that purpose or those purposes.

3. Personal data shall be adequate, relevant and not excessive in relation to the purpose or purposes for which they are processed.

4. Personal data shall be accurate and, where necessary, kept up to date.

5. Personal data processed for any purpose or purposes shall not be kept for longer than is necessary for that purpose or those purposes.

6. Personal data shall be processed in accordance with the rights of data subjects under this Act.

7. Appropriate technical and organisational measures shall be taken against unauthorised or unlawful processing of personal data and against accidental loss or destruction of, or damage to, personal data.

8. Personal data shall not be transferred to a country or territory outside the European Economic Area unless that country or territory ensures an adequate level of protection for the rights and freedoms of data subjects in relation to the processing of personal data.

PART II INTERPRETATION OF THE PRINCIPLES IN PART I

The first principle

1—(1) In determining for the purposes of the first principle whether personal data are processed fairly, regard is to be had to the method by which they are obtained, including in particular whether any person from whom they are obtained is deceived or misled as to the purpose or purposes for which they are to be processed.

(2) Subject to paragraph 2, for the purposes of the first principle data are to be treated as obtained fairly if they consist of information obtained from a person who—

   (a) is authorised by or under any enactment to supply it, or

   (b) is required to supply it by or under any enactment or by any convention or other instrument imposing an international obligation on the United Kingdom.

2—(1) Subject to paragraph 3, for the purposes of the first principle personal data are not to be treated as processed fairly unless—

   (a) in the case of data obtained from the data subject, the data controller ensures so far as practicable that the data subject has, is provided with, or has made readily available to him, the information specified in sub-paragraph (3), and

   (b) in any other case, the data controller ensures so far as practicable that, before the relevant time or as soon as practicable after that time, the data subject has, is provided with, or has made readily available to him, the information specified in sub-paragraph (3).

(2) In sub-paragraph (1)(b) 'the relevant time' means—

   (a) the time when the data controller first processes the data, or

   (b) in a case where at that time disclosure to a third party within a reasonable period is envisaged—

      (i) if the data are in fact disclosed to such a person within that period, the time when the data are first disclosed,

      (ii) if within that period the data controller becomes, or ought to become, aware that the data are unlikely to be disclosed to such a person within that period, the time when the data controller does become, or ought to become, so aware, or

      (iii) in any other case, the end of that period.

  (3) The information referred to in sub-paragraph (1) is as follows, namely—

    (a) the identity of the data controller,

    (b) if he has nominated a representative for the purposes of this Act, the identity of that representative,

    (c) the purpose or purposes for which the data are intended to be processed, and

    (d) any further information which is necessary, having regard to the specific circumstances in which the data are or are to be processed, to enable processing in respect of the data subject to be fair.

  3—(1) Paragraph 2(1)(b) does not apply where either of the primary conditions in sub-paragraph (2), together with such further conditions as may be prescribed by the Secretary of State by order, are met.

  (2) The primary conditions referred to in sub-paragraph (1) are—

    (a) that the provision of that information would involve a disproportionate effort, or

    (b) that the recording of the information to be contained in the data by, or the disclosure of the data by, the data controller is necessary for compliance with any legal obligation to which the data controller is subject, other than an obligation imposed by contract.

  4—(1) Personal data which contain a general identifier falling within a description prescribed by the Secretary of State by order are not to be treated as processed fairly and lawfully unless they are processed in compliance with any conditions so prescribed in relation to general identifiers of that description.

  (2) In sub-paragraph (1) 'a general identifier' means any identifier (such as, for example, a number or code used for identification purposes) which—

    (a) relates to an individual, and

    (b) forms part of a set of similar identifiers which is of general application.

The second principle

  5. The purpose or purposes for which personal data are obtained may in particular be specified—

    (a) in a notice given for the purposes of paragraph 2 by the data controller to the data subject, or

    (b) in a notification given to the Commissioner under Part III of this Act.

  6. In determining whether any disclosure of personal data is compatible with the purpose or purposes for which the data were obtained, regard is to be had to the purpose or purposes for which the personal data are intended to be processed by any person to whom they are disclosed.

The fourth principle

  7. The fourth principle is not to be regarded as being contravened by reason of any inaccuracy in personal data which accurately record information obtained by the data controller from the data subject or a third party in a case where—

    (a) having regard to the purpose or purposes for which the data were obtained and further processed, the data controller has taken reasonable steps to ensure the accuracy of the data, and

    (b) if the data subject has notified the data controller of the data subject's view that the data are inaccurate, the data indicate that fact.

The sixth principle

  8. A person is to be regarded as contravening the sixth principle if, but only if—

    (a) he contravenes section 7 by failing to supply information in accordance with that section,

(b) he contravenes section 10 by failing to comply with a notice given under subsection (1) of that section to the extent that the notice is justified or by failing to give a notice under subsection (3) of that section,

(c) he contravenes section 11 by failing to comply with a notice given under subsection (1) of that section,

(d) he contravenes section 12 by failing to comply with a notice given under subsection (1) or (2)(b) of that section or by failing to give a notification under subsection (2)(a) of that section or a notice under subsection (3) of that section.

The seventh principle

9. Having regard to the state of technological development and the cost of implementing any measures, the measures must ensure a level of security appropriate to—

(a) the harm that might result from such unauthorised or unlawful processing or accidental loss, destruction or damage as are mentioned in the seventh principle, and

(b) the nature of the data to be protected.

10. The data controller must take reasonable steps to ensure the reliability of any employees of his who have access to the personal data.

11. Where processing of personal data is carried out by a data processor on behalf of a data controller, the data controller must in order to comply with the seventh principle—

(a) choose a data processor providing sufficient guarantees in respect of the technical and organisational security measures governing the processing to be carried out, and

(b) take reasonable steps to ensure compliance with those measures.

12. Where processing of personal data is carried out by a data processor on behalf of a data controller, the data controller is not to be regarded as complying with the seventh principle unless—

(a) the processing is carried out under a contract—

(i) which is made or evidenced in writing, and

(ii) under which the data processor is to act only on instructions from the data controller, and

(b) the contract requires the data processor to comply with obligations equivalent to those imposed on a data controller by the seventh principle.

The eighth principle

13. An adequate level of protection is one which is adequate in all the circumstances of the case, having regard in particular to—

(a) the nature of the personal data,

(b) the country or territory of origin of the information contained in the data,

(c) the country or territory of final destination of that information,

(d) the purposes for which and period during which the data are intended to be processed,

(e) the law in force in the country or territory in question,

(f) the international obligations of that country or territory,

(g) any relevant codes of conduct or other rules which are enforceable in that country or territory (whether generally or by arrangement in particular cases), and

(h) any security measures taken in respect of the data in that country or territory.

14. The eighth principle does not apply to a transfer falling within any paragraph of Schedule 4, except in such circumstances and to such extent as the Secretary of State may by order provide.

15—(1) Where—

(a) in any proceedings under this Act any question arises as to whether the requirement of the eighth principle as to an adequate level of protection is met in relation to the transfer of any personal data to a country or territory outside the European Economic Area, and

(b) a Community finding has been made in relation to transfers of the kind in question, that question is to be determined in accordance with that finding.

(2) In sub-paragraph (1) 'Community finding' means a finding of the European Commission, under the procedure provided for in Article 31(2) of the Data Protection Directive, that a country

or territory outside the European Economic Area does, or does not, ensure an adequate level of protection within the meaning of Article 25(2) of the Directive.

Section 4(3)
SCHEDULE 2

CONDITIONS RELEVANT FOR PURPOSES OF THE FIRST PRINCIPLE: PROCESSING OF ANY PERSONAL DATA

1. The data subject has given his consent to the processing.
2. The processing is necessary—
    (a) for the performance of a contract to which the data subject is a party, or
    (b) for the taking of steps at the request of the data subject with a view to entering into a contract.
3. The processing is necessary for compliance with any legal obligation to which the data controller is subject, other than an obligation imposed by contract.
4. The processing is necessary in order to protect the vital interests of the data subject.
5. The processing is necessary—
    (a) for the administration of justice,
    (aa) for the exercise of any functions of either House of Parliament,
    (b) for the exercise of any functions conferred on any person by or under any enactment,
    (c) for the exercise of any functions of the Crown, a Minister of the Crown or a government department, or
    (d) for the exercise of any other functions of a public nature exercised in the public interest by any person.
6—(1) The processing is necessary for the purposes of legitimate interests pursued by the data controller or by the third party or parties to whom the data are disclosed, except where the processing is unwarranted in any particular case by reason of prejudice to the rights and freedoms or legitimate interests of the data subject.
    (2) The Secretary of State may by order specify particular circumstances in which this condition is, or is not, to be taken to be satisfied.

Section 4(3)
SCHEDULE 3

CONDITIONS RELEVANT FOR PURPOSES OF THE FIRST PRINCIPLE: PROCESSING OF SENSITIVE PERSONAL DATA

1. The data subject has given his explicit consent to the processing of the personal data.
2—(1) The processing is necessary for the purposes of exercising or performing any right or obligation which is conferred or imposed by law on the data controller in connection with employment.
    (2) The Secretary of State may by order—
    (a) exclude the application of sub-paragraph (1) in such cases as may be specified, or
    (b) provide that, in such cases as may be specified, the condition in sub-paragraph (1) is not to be regarded as satisfied unless such further conditions as may be specified in the order are also satisfied.
3. The processing is necessary—
    (a) in order to protect the vital interests of the data subject or another person, in a case where—
        (i)   consent cannot be given by or on behalf of the data subject, or
        (ii) the data controller cannot reasonably be expected to obtain the consent of the data subject, or
    (b) in order to protect the vital interests of another person, in a case where consent by or on behalf of the data subject has been unreasonably withheld.

4. The processing—
   (a) is carried out in the course of its legitimate activities by any body or association which—
      (i)   is not established or conducted for profit, and
      (ii) exists for political, philosophical, religious or trade-union purposes,
   (b) is carried out with appropriate safeguards for the rights and freedoms of data subjects,
   (c) relates only to individuals who either are members of the body or association or have regular contact with it in connection with its purposes, and
   (d) does not involve disclosure of the personal data to a third party without the consent of the data subject.

5. The information contained in the personal data has been made public as a result of steps deliberately taken by the data subject.

6. The processing—
   (a) is necessary for the purpose of, or in connection with, any legal proceedings (including prospective legal proceedings),
   (b) is necessary for the purpose of obtaining legal advice, or
   (c) is otherwise necessary for the purposes of establishing, exercising or defending legal rights.

7—(1) The processing is necessary—
   (a) for the administration of justice,
   (aa) for the exercise of any functions of either House of Parliament,
   (b) for the exercise of any functions conferred on any person by or under an enactment, or
   (c) for the exercise of any functions of the Crown, a Minister of the Crown or a government department.

(2) The Secretary of State may by order—
   (a) exclude the application of sub-paragraph (1) in such cases as may be specified, or
   (b) provide that, in such cases as may be specified, the condition in sub-paragraph (1) is not to be regarded as satisfied unless such further conditions as may be specified in the order are also satisfied.

7A—(1) The processing—
   (a) is either—
      (i)   the disclosure of sensitive personal data by a person as a member of an anti-fraud organisation or otherwise in accordance with any arrangements made by such an organisation; or
      (ii) any other processing by that person or another person of sensitive personal data so disclosed; and
   (b) is necessary for the purposes of preventing fraud or a particular kind of fraud.

(2) In this paragraph 'an anti-fraud organisation' means any unincorporated association, body corporate or other person which enables or facilitates any sharing of information to prevent fraud or a particular kind of fraud or which has any of these functions as its purpose or one of its purposes.

8—(1) The processing is necessary for medical purposes and is undertaken by—
   (a) a health professional, or
   (b) a person who in the circumstances owes a duty of confidentiality which is equivalent to that which would arise if that person were a health professional.

(2) In this paragraph 'medical purposes' includes the purposes of preventative medicine, medical diagnosis, medical research, the provision of care and treatment and the management of health care services.

9—(1) The processing—
   (a) is of sensitive personal data consisting of information as to racial or ethnic origin,
   (b) is necessary for the purpose of identifying or keeping under review the existence or absence of equality of opportunity or treatment between persons of different racial or ethnic origins, with a view to enabling such equality to be promoted or maintained, and
   (c) is carried out with appropriate safeguards for the rights and freedoms of data subjects.

(2) The Secretary of State may by order specify circumstances in which processing falling within sub-paragraph (1)(a) and (b) is, or is not, to be taken for the purposes of sub-paragraph (1)(c) to be carried out with appropriate safeguards for the rights and freedoms of data subjects.

10. The personal data are processed in circumstances specified in an order made by the Secretary of State for the purposes of this paragraph.

Section 4(3)

SCHEDULE 4

CASES WHERE THE EIGHTH PRINCIPLE DOES NOT APPLY

1. The data subject has given his consent to the transfer.
2. The transfer is necessary—
   (a) for the performance of a contract between the data subject and the data controller, or
   (b) for the taking of steps at the request of the data subject with a view to his entering into a contract with the data controller.
3. The transfer is necessary—
   (a) for the conclusion of a contract between the data controller and a person other than the data subject which—
       (i)   is entered into at the request of the data subject, or
       (ii) is in the interests of the data subject, or
   (b) for the performance of such a contract.
4—(1) The transfer is necessary for reasons of substantial public interest.
(2) The Secretary of State may by order specify—
   (a) circumstances in which a transfer is to be taken for the purposes of sub-paragraph (1) to be necessary for reasons of substantial public interest, and
   (b) circumstances in which a transfer which is not required by or under an enactment is not to be taken for the purpose of sub-paragraph (1) to be necessary for reasons of substantial public interest.
5. The transfer—
   (a) is necessary for the purpose of, or in connection with, any legal proceedings (including prospective legal proceedings),
   (b) is necessary for the purpose of obtaining legal advice, or
   (c) is otherwise necessary for the purposes of establishing, exercising or defending legal rights.
6. The transfer is necessary in order to protect the vital interests of the data subject.
7. The transfer is of part of the personal data on a public register and any conditions subject to which the register is open to inspection are complied with by any person to whom the data are or may be disclosed after the transfer.
8. The transfer is made on terms which are of a kind approved by the Commissioner as ensuring adequate safeguards for the rights and freedoms of data subjects.
9. The transfer has been authorised by the Commissioner as being made in such a manner as to ensure adequate safeguards for the rights and freedoms of data subjects.

Section 37

SCHEDULE 7

MISCELLANEOUS EXEMPTIONS

Confidential references given by the data controller

1. Personal data are exempt from section 7 if they consist of a reference given or to be given in confidence by the data controller for the purposes of—
   (a) the education, training or employment, or prospective education, training or employment, of the data subject,

(b) the appointment, or prospective appointment, of the data subject to any office, or

(c) the provision, or prospective provision, by the data subject of any service.

Armed forces

2. Personal data are exempt from the subject information provisions in any case to the extent to which the application of those provisions would be likely to prejudice the combat effectiveness of any of the armed forces of the Crown.

Judicial appointments and honours

3. Personal data processed for the purposes of—

(a) assessing any person's suitability for judicial office or the office of Queen's Counsel, or

(b) the conferring by the Crown of any honour [or dignity], are exempt from the subject information provisions.

Crown employment and Crown or Ministerial appointments

4—(1) The Secretary of State may by order exempt from the subject information provisions personal data processed for the purposes of assessing any person's suitability for—

(a) employment by or under the Crown, or

(b) any office to which appointments are made by Her Majesty, by a Minister of the Crown or by a Northern Ireland authority.

(2) In this paragraph 'Northern Ireland authority' means the First Minister, the deputy First Minister, a Northern Ireland Minister or a Northern Ireland department.

Management forecasts etc.

5. Personal data processed for the purposes of management forecasting or management planning to assist the data controller in the conduct of any business or other activity are exempt from the subject information provisions in any case to the extent to which the application of those provisions would be likely to prejudice the conduct of that business or other activity.

Corporate finance

6—(1) Where personal data are processed for the purposes of, or in connection with, a corporate finance service provided by a relevant person—

(a) the data are exempt from the subject information provisions in any case to the extent to which either—

(i) the application of those provisions to the data could affect the price of any instrument which is already in existence or is to be or may be created, or

(ii) the data controller reasonably believes that the application of those provisions to the data could affect the price of any such instrument, and

(b) to the extent that the data are not exempt from the subject information provisions by virtue of paragraph (a), they are exempt from those provisions if the exemption is required for the purpose of safeguarding an important economic or financial interest of the United Kingdom.

(2) For the purposes of sub-paragraph (1)(b) the Secretary of State may by order specify—

(a) matters to be taken into account in determining whether exemption from the subject information provisions is required for the purpose of safeguarding an important economic or financial interest of the United Kingdom, or

(b) circumstances in which exemption from those provisions is, or is not, to be taken to be required for that purpose.

(3) In this paragraph—

'corporate finance service' means a service consisting in—

(a) underwriting in respect of issues of, or the placing of issues of, any instrument,

(b) advice to undertakings on capital structure, industrial strategy and related matters and advice and service relating to mergers and the purchase of undertakings, or

(c) services relating to such underwriting as is mentioned in paragraph (a);

'instrument' means any instrument listed in section B of the Annex to the Council Directive on investment services in the securities field (93/22/EEC);

'price' includes value;

'relevant person' means—

> (a) any person who, by reason of any permission he has under Part IV of the Financial Services and Markets Act 2000, is able to carry on a corporate finance service without contravening the general prohibition, within the meaning of section 19 of that Act;
>
> (b) an EEA firm of the kind mentioned in paragraph 5(a) or (b) of Schedule 3 to that Act which has qualified for authorisation under paragraph 12 of that Schedule, and may lawfully carry on a corporate finance service;
>
> (c) any person who is exempt from the general prohibition in respect of any corporate finance service—
>
>> (i) as a result of an exemption order made under section 38(1) of that Act, or
>>
>> (ii) by reason of section 39(1) of that Act (appointed representatives);
>
> (cc) any person, not falling within paragraph (a), (b) or (c) who may lawfully carry on a corporate finance service without contravening the general prohibition;
>
> (d) any person who, in the course of his employment, provides to his employer a service falling within paragraph (b) or (c) of the definition of 'corporate finance service', or
>
> (e) any partner who provides to other partners in the partnership a service falling within either of those paragraphs.

Negotiations

7. Personal data which consist of records of the intentions of the data controller in relation to any negotiations with the data subject are exempt from the subject information provisions in any case to the extent to which the application of those provisions would be likely to prejudice those negotiations.

Examination marks

8.—(1) Section 7 shall have effect subject to the provisions of sub-paragraphs (2) to (4) in the case of personal data consisting of marks or other information processed by a data controller—

> (a) for the purpose of determining the results of an academic, professional or other examination or of enabling the results of any such examination to be determined, or
>
> (b) in consequence of the determination of any such results.

(2) Where the relevant day falls before the day on which the results of the examination are announced, the period mentioned in section 7(8) shall be extended until—

> (a) the end of five months beginning with the relevant day, or
>
> (b) the end of forty days beginning with the date of the announcement, whichever is the earlier.

(3) Where by virtue of sub-paragraph (2) a period longer than the prescribed period elapses after the relevant day before the request is complied with, the information to be supplied pursuant to the request shall be supplied both by reference to the data in question at the time when the request is received and (if different) by reference to the data as from time to time held in the period beginning when the request is received and ending when it is complied with.

(4) For the purposes of this paragraph the results of an examination shall be treated as announced when they are first published or (if not published) when they are first made available or communicated to the candidate in question.

(5) In this paragraph—

'examination' includes any process for determining the knowledge, intelligence, skill or ability of a candidate by reference to his performance in any test, work or other activity;

'the prescribed period' means forty days or such other period as is for the time being prescribed under section 7 in relation to the personal data in question;

'relevant day' has the same meaning as in section 7.

Examination scripts etc.

9—(1) Personal data consisting of information recorded by candidates during an academic, professional or other examination are exempt from section 7.

(2) In this paragraph 'examination' has the same meaning as in paragraph 8.

Legal professional privilege

10. Personal data are exempt from the subject information provisions if the data consist of information in respect of which a claim to legal professional privilege or, in Scotland, to confidentiality of communications could be maintained in legal proceedings.

Self-incrimination

11—(1) A person need not comply with any request or order under section 7 to the extent that compliance would, by revealing evidence of the commission of any offence other than an offence under this Act or an offence within sub-paragraph (1A), expose him to proceedings for that offence.

(1A) The offences mentioned in sub-paragraph (1) are—

    (a) an offence under section 5 of the Perjury Act 1911 (false statements made otherwise than on oath),

    (b) an offence under section 44(2) of the Criminal Law (Consolidation) (Scotland) Act 1995 (false statements made otherwise than on oath), or

    (c) an offence under Article 10 of the Perjury (Northern Ireland) Order 1979 (false statutory declarations and other false unsworn statements).

(2) Information disclosed by any person in compliance with any request or order under section 7 shall not be admissible against him in proceedings for an offence under this Act.

Official Secrets Act 1989

(1989, c. 6)

1   Security and intelligence

(1) A person who is or has been—

    (a) a member of the security and intelligence services; or

    (b) a person notified that he is subject to the provisions of this subsection,

is guilty of an offence if without lawful authority he discloses any information, document or other article relating to security or intelligence which is or has been in his possession by virtue of his position as a member of any of those services or in the course of his work while the notification is or was in force.

(2) The reference in subsection (1) above to disclosing information relating to security or intelligence includes a reference to making any statement which purports to be a disclosure of such information or is intended to be taken by those to whom it is addressed as being such a disclosure.

(3) A person who is or has been a Crown servant or government contractor is guilty of an offence if without lawful authority he makes a damaging disclosure of any information, document or other article relating to security or intelligence which is or has been in his possession by virtue of his position as such but otherwise than as mentioned in subsection (1) above.

(4) For the purposes of subsection (3) above a disclosure is damaging if—

    (a) it causes damage to the work of, or of any part of, the security and intelligence services; or

    (b) it is of information or a document or other article which is such that its unauthorised disclosure would be likely to cause such damage or which falls within a class or description of information, documents or articles the unauthorised disclosure of which would be likely to have that effect.

(5) It is a defence for a person charged with an offence under this section to prove that at the time of the alleged offence he did not know, and had no reasonable cause to believe, that the

information, document or article in question related to security or intelligence or, in the case of an offence under subsection (3), that the disclosure would be damaging within the meaning of that subsection.

(6) Notification that a person is subject to subsection (1) above shall be effected by a notice in writing served on him by a Minister of the Crown; and such a notice may be served if, in the Minister's opinion, the work undertaken by the person in question is or includes work connected with the security and intelligence services and its nature is such that the interests of national security require that he should be subject to the provisions of that subsection.

(7) Subject to subsection (8) below, a notification for the purposes of subsection (1) above shall be in force for the period of five years beginning with the day on which it is served but may be renewed by further notices under subsection (6) above for periods of five years at a time.

(8) A notification for the purposes of subsection (1) above may at any time be revoked by a further notice in writing served by the Minister on the person concerned; and the Minister shall serve such a further notice as soon as, in his opinion, the work undertaken by that person ceases to be such as is mentioned in subsection (6) above.

(9) In this section 'security or intelligence' means the work of, or in support of, the security and intelligence services or any part of them, and references to information relating to security or intelligence include references to information held or transmitted by those services or by persons in support of, or of any part of, them.

2 Defence

(1) A person who is or has been a Crown servant or government contractor is guilty of an offence if without lawful authority he makes a damaging disclosure of any information, document or other article relating to defence which is or has been in his possession by virtue of his position as such.

(2) For the purposes of subsection (1) above a disclosure is damaging if—
   (a) it damages the capability of, or of any part of, the armed forces of the Crown to carry out their tasks or leads to loss of life or injury to members of those forces or serious damage to the equipment or installations of those forces; or
   (b) otherwise than as mentioned in paragraph (a) above, it endangers the interests of the United Kingdom abroad, seriously obstructs the promotion or protection by the United Kingdom of those interests or endangers the safety of British citizens abroad; or
   (c) it is of information or of a document or article which is such that its unauthorised disclosure would be likely to have any of those effects.

(3) It is a defence for a person charged with an offence under this section to prove that at the time of the alleged offence he did not know, and had no reasonable cause to believe, that the information, document or article in question related to defence or that its disclosure would be damaging within the meaning of subsection (1) above.

(4) In this section 'defence' means—
   (a) the size, shape, organisation, logistics, order of battle, deployment, operations, state of readiness and training of the armed forces of the Crown;
   (b) the weapons, stores or other equipment of those forces and the invention, development, production and operation of such equipment and research relating to it;
   (c) defence policy and strategy and military planning and intelligence;
   (d) plans and measures for the maintenance of essential supplies and services that are or would be needed in time of war.

3 International relations

(1) A person who is or has been a Crown servant or government contractor is guilty of an offence if without lawful authority he makes a damaging disclosure of—
   (a) any information, document or other article relating to international relations; or

(b) any confidential information, document or other article which was obtained from a State other than the United Kingdom or an international organisation,

being information or a document or article which is or has been in his possession by virtue of his position as a Crown servant or government contractor.

(2) For the purposes of subsection (1) above a disclosure is damaging if—

(a) it endangers the interests of the United Kingdom abroad, seriously obstructs the promotion or protection by the United Kingdom of those interests or endangers the safety of British citizens abroad; or

(b) it is of information or of a document or article which is such that its unauthorised disclosure would be likely to have any of those effects.

(3) In the case of information or a document or article within subsection (1)(b) above—

(a) the fact that it is confidential, or

(b) its nature or contents,

may be sufficient to establish for the purposes of subsection (2)(b) above that the information, document or article is such that its unauthorised disclosure would be likely to have any of the effects there mentioned.

(4) It is a defence for a person charged with an offence under this section to prove that at the time of the alleged offence he did not know, and had no reasonable cause to believe, that the information, document or article in question was such as is mentioned in subsection (1) above or that its disclosure would be damaging within the meaning of that subsection.

(5) In this section 'international relations' means the relations between States, between international organisations or between one or more States and one or more such organisations and includes any matter relating to a State other than the United Kingdom or to an international organisation which is capable of affecting the relations of the United Kingdom with another State or with an international organisation.

(6) For the purposes of this section any information, document or article obtained from a State or organisation is confidential at any time while the terms on which it was obtained require it to be held in confidence or while the circumstances in which it was obtained make it reasonable for the State or organisation to expect that it would be so held.

4   Crime and special investigation powers

(1) A person who is or has been a Crown servant or government contractor is guilty of an offence if without lawful authority he discloses any information, document or other article to which this section applies and which is or has been in his possession by virtue of his position as such.

(2) This section applies to any information, document or other article—

(a) the disclosure of which—

(i) results in the commission of an offence; or

(ii) facilitates an escape from legal custody or the doing of any other act prejudicial to the safekeeping of persons in legal custody; or

(iii) impedes the prevention or detection of offences or the apprehension or prosecution of suspected offenders; or

(b) which is such that its unauthorised disclosure would be likely to have any of those effects.

(3) This section also applies to—

(a) any information obtained by reason of the interception of any communication in obedience to a warrant issued under section 2 of the Interception of Communications Act 1985 or under the authority of an interception warrant under section 5 of the Regulation of Investigatory Powers Act 2000, any information relating to the obtaining of information by reason of any such interception and any document or other article which is or has been used or held for use in, or has been obtained by reason of, any such interception; and

(b) any information obtained by reason of action authorised by a warrant issued under section 3 of the Security Service Act 1989 or under section 5 of the Intelligence Services Act 1994 or by an authorisation given under section 7 of that Act, any information relating to the obtaining of information by reason of any such action and any document or other article which is or has been used or held for use in, or has been obtained by reason of, any such action.

(4) It is a defence for a person charged with an offence under this section in respect of a disclosure falling within subsection (2)(a) above to prove that at the time of the alleged offence he did not know, and had no reasonable cause to believe, that the disclosure would have any of the effects there mentioned.

(5) It is a defence for a person charged with an offence under this section in respect of any other disclosure to prove that at the time of the alleged offence he did not know, and had no reasonable cause to believe, that the information, document or article in question was information or a document or article to which this section applies.

(6) In this section 'legal custody' includes detention in pursuance of any enactment or any instrument made under an enactment.

5 Information resulting from unauthorised disclosures or entrusted in confidence

(1) Subsection (2) below applies where—

    (a) any information, document or other article protected against disclosure by the foregoing provisions of this Act has come into a person's possession as a result of having been—

        (i) disclosed (whether to him or another) by a Crown servant or government contractor without lawful authority; or

        (ii) entrusted to him by a Crown servant or government contractor on terms requiring it to be held in confidence or in circumstances in which the Crown servant or government contractor could reasonably expect that it would be so held; or

        (iii) disclosed (whether to him or another) without lawful authority by a person to whom it was entrusted as mentioned in sub-paragraph (ii) above; and

    (b) the disclosure without lawful authority of the information, document or article by the person into whose possession it has come is not an offence under any of those provisions.

(2) Subject to subsections (3) and (4) below, the person into whose possession the information, document or article has come is guilty of an offence if he discloses it without lawful authority knowing, or having reasonable cause to believe, that it is protected against disclosure by the foregoing provisions of this Act and that it has come into his possession as mentioned in subsection (1) above.

(3) In the case of information or a document or article protected against disclosure by sections 1 to 3 above, a person does not commit an offence under subsection (2) above unless—

    (a) the disclosure by him is damaging; and

    (b) he makes it knowing, or having reasonable cause to believe, that it would be damaging;

and the question whether a disclosure is damaging shall be determined for the purposes of this subsection as it would be in relation to a disclosure of that information, document or article by a Crown servant in contravention of section 1(3), 2(1) or 3(1) above.

(4) A person does not commit an offence under subsection (2) above in respect of information or a document or other article which has come into his possession as a result of having been disclosed—

    (a) as mentioned in subsection (1)(a)(i) above by a government contractor; or

    (b) as mentioned in subsection (1)(a)(iii) above,

unless that disclosure was by a British citizen or took place in the United Kingdom, in any of the Channel Islands or in the Isle of Man or a colony.

(5) For the purposes of this section information or a document or article is protected against disclosure by the foregoing provisions of this Act if—

    (a) it relates to security or intelligence, defence or international relations within the meaning of section 1, 2 or 3 above or is such as is mentioned in section 3(1)(b) above; or

    (b) it is information or a document or article to which section 4 above applies;

and information or a document or article is protected against disclosure by sections 1 to 3 above if it falls within paragraph (a) above.

(6) A person is guilty of an offence if without lawful authority he discloses any information, document or other article which he knows, or has reasonable cause to believe, to have come into his possession as a result of a contravention of section 1 of the Official Secrets Act 1911.

6   Information entrusted in confidence to other States or international organisations

(1) This section applies where—

    (a) any information, document or other article which—

        (i) relates to security or intelligence, defence or international relations; and

        (ii) has been communicated in confidence by or on behalf of the United Kingdom to another State or to an international organisation,

    has come into a person's possession as a result of having been disclosed (whether to him or another) without the authority of that State or organisation or, in the case of an organisation, of a member of it; and

    (b) the disclosure without lawful authority of the information, document or article by the person into whose possession it has come is not an offence under any of the foregoing provisions of this Act.

(2) Subject to subsection (3) below, the person into whose possession the information, document or article has come is guilty of an offence if he makes a damaging disclosure of it knowing, or having reasonable cause to believe, that it is such as is mentioned in subsection (1) above, that it has come into his possession as there mentioned and that its disclosure would be damaging.

(3) A person does not commit an offence under subsection (2) above if the information, document or article is disclosed by him with lawful authority or has previously been made available to the public with the authority of the State or organisation concerned or, in the case of an organisation, of a member of it.

(4) For the purposes of this section 'security or intelligence', 'defence' and 'international relations' have the same meaning as in section 1, 2 and 3 above and the question whether a disclosure is damaging shall be determined as it would be in relation to a disclosure of the information, document or article in question by a Crown servant in contravention of section 1(3), 2(1) and 3(1) above.

(5) For the purposes of this section information or a document or article is communicated in confidence if it is communicated on terms requiring it to be held in confidence or in circumstances in which the person communicating it could reasonably expect that it would be so held.

7   Authorised disclosures

(1) For the purposes of this Act a disclosure by—

    (a) a Crown servant; or

    (b) a person, not being a Crown servant or government contractor, in whose case a notification for the purposes of section 1(1) above is in force,

is made with lawful authority if, and only if, it is made in accordance with his official duty.

(2) For the purposes of this Act a disclosure by a government contractor is made with lawful authority if, and only if, it is made—

    (a) in accordance with an official authorisation; or

    (b) for the purposes of the functions by virtue of which he is a government contractor and without contravening an official restriction.

(3) For the purposes of this Act a disclosure made by any other person is made with lawful authority if, and only if, it is made—

    (a) to a Crown servant for the purposes of his functions as such; or

    (b) in accordance with an official authorisation.

(4) It is a defence for a person charged with an offence under any of the foregoing provisions of this Act to prove that at the time of the alleged offence he believed that he had lawful authority to make the disclosure in question and had no reasonable cause to believe otherwise.

(5) In this section 'official authorisation' and 'official restriction' mean, subject to subsection (6) below, an authorisation or restriction duly given or imposed by a Crown servant or government contractor or by or on behalf of a prescribed body or a body of a prescribed class.

(6) In relation to section 6 above 'official authorisation' includes an authorisation duly given by or on behalf of the State or organisation concerned or, in the case of an organisation, a member of it.

8   Safeguarding of information

(1) Where a Crown servant or government contractor, by virtue of his position as such, has in his possession or under his control any document or other article which it would be an offence under any of the foregoing provisions of this Act for him to disclose without lawful authority he is guilty of an offence if—

> (a) being a Crown servant, he retains the document or article contrary to his official duty; or
> (b) being a government contractor, he fails to comply with an official direction for the return or disposal of the document or article,

or if he fails to take such care to prevent the unauthorised disclosure of the document or article as a person in his position may reasonably be expected to take.

(2) It is a defence for a Crown servant charged with an offence under subsection (1)(a) above to prove that at the time of the alleged offence he believed that he was acting in accordance with his official duty and had no reasonable cause to believe otherwise.

(3) In subsections (1) and (2) above references to a Crown servant include any person, not being a Crown servant or government contractor, in whose case a notification for the purposes of section 1(1) above is in force.

(4) Where a person has in his possession or under his control any document or other article which it would be an offence under section 5 above for him to disclose without lawful authority, he is guilty of an offence if—

> (a) he fails to comply with an official direction for its return or disposal; or
> (b) where he obtained it from a Crown servant or government contractor on terms requiring it to be held in confidence or in circumstances in which that servant or contractor could reasonably expect that it would be so held, he fails to take such care to prevent its unauthorised disclosure as a person in his position may reasonably be expected to take.

(5) Where a person has in his possession or under his control any document or other article which it would be an offence under section 6 above for him to disclose without lawful authority, he is guilty of an offence if he fails to comply with an official direction for its return or disposal.

(6) A person is guilty of an offence if he discloses any official information, document or other article which can be used for the purpose of obtaining access to any information, document or other article protected against disclosure by the foregoing provisions of this Act and the circumstances in which it is disclosed are such that it would be reasonable to expect that it might be used for that purposes without authority.

(7) For the purposes of subsection (6) above a person discloses information or a document or article which is official if—

> (a) he has or has had it in his possession by virtue of his position as a Crown servant or government contractor; or
> (b) he knows or has reasonable cause to believe that a Crown servant or government contractor has or has had it in his possession by virtue of his position as such.

(8) Subsection (5) of section 5 above applies for the purposes of subsection (6) above as it applies for the purposes of that section.

(9) In this section 'official direction' means a direction duly given by a Crown servant or government contractor or by or on behalf of a prescribed body or a body of a prescribed class.

9   Prosecutions

(1) Subject to subsection (2) below, no prosecution for an offence under this Act shall be instituted in England and Wales or in Northern Ireland except by or with the consent of the Attorney General or, as the case may be, the Attorney General for Northern Ireland.

(2) Subsection (1) above does not apply to an offence in respect of any such information, document or article as is mentioned in section 4(2) above but no prosecution for such an offence shall be instituted in England and Wales or in Northern Ireland except by or with the consent of the Director of Public Prosecutions or, as the case may be, the Director of Public Prosecutions for Northern Ireland.

10   Penalties

(1) A person guilty of an offence under any provision of this Act other than section 8(1), (4) or (5) shall be liable—

    (a) on conviction on indictment, to imprisonment for a term not exceeding two years or a fine or both;

    (b) on summary conviction, to imprisonment for a term not exceeding six months or a fine not exceeding the statutory maximum or both.

(2) A person guilty of an offence under section 8(1), (4) or (5) above shall be liable on summary conviction to imprisonment for a term not exceeding 51 weeks or a fine not exceeding level 5 on the standard scale or both.

11   Arrest, search and trial

(1) [...]

(2) Offences under any provision of this Act other than section 8(1), (4) or (5) and attempts to commit them shall be arrestable offences within the meaning of section 2 of the Criminal Law Act (Northern Ireland) 1967.

(3) Section 9(1) of the Official Secrets Act 1911 (search warrants) shall have effect as if references to offences under that Act included references to offences under any provision of this Act other than section 8(1), (4) or (5); and the following provisions of the Police and Criminal Evidence Act 1984, that is to say—

    (a) section 9(2) (which excludes items subject to legal privilege and certain other material from powers of search conferred by previous enactments); and

    (b) paragraph 3(b) of Schedule 1 (which prescribes access conditions for the special procedure laid down in that Schedule),

shall apply to section 9(1) of the said Act of 1911 as extended by this subsection as they apply to that section as originally enacted.

(4) Section 8(4) of the Official Secrets Act 1920 (exclusion of public from hearing on grounds of national safety) shall have effect as if references to offences under that Act included references to offences under any provision of this Act other than section 8(1), (4) or (5).

(5) Proceedings for an offence under this Act may be taken in any place in the United Kingdom.

12   'Crown servant' and 'government contractor'

(1) In this Act 'Crown servant' means—

    (a) a Minister of the Crown;

    (aa) a member of the Scottish Executive or a junior Scottish Minister;

    (ab) the First Minister for Wales, a Welsh Minister appointed under section 48 of the Government of Wales Act 2006, the Counsel General to the Welsh Assembly Government or a Deputy Welsh Minister;

    (b) a person appointed under section 8 of the Northern Ireland Constitution Act 1973 (the Northern Ireland Executive etc.);

    (c) any person employed in the civil service of the Crown, including Her Majesty's Diplomatic Service, Her Majesty's Overseas Civil Service, the civil service of Northern Ireland and the Northern Ireland Court Service;

    (d) any member of the naval, military or air forces of the Crown, including any person employed by an association established for the purposes of Part XI of the Reserve Forces Act 1996;

    (e) any constable and any other person employed or appointed in or for the purposes of any police force (including a police force within the meaning of the Police Act (Northern Ireland) 1970) or of the Serious Organised Crime Agency;

(f) any person who is a member or employee of a prescribed body or a body of a prescribed class and either is prescribed for the purposes of this paragraph or belongs to a prescribed class of members or employees of any such body;

(g) any person who is the holder of a prescribed office or who is an employee of such a holder and either is prescribed for the purposes of this paragraph or belongs to a prescribed class of such employees.

(2) In this Act 'government contractor' means, subject to subsection (3) below, any person who is not a Crown servant but who provides, or is employed in the provision of, goods or services—

(a) for the purposes of any Minister or person mentioned in paragraph (a)[, (ab)] or (b) of subsection (1) above, of any office-holder in the Scottish Administration, of any of the services, forces or bodies mentioned in that subsection or of the holder of any office prescribed under that subsection;

(b) under an agreement or arrangement certified by the Secretary of State as being one to which the government of a State other than the United Kingdom or an international organisation is a party or which is subordinate to, or made for the purposes of implementing, any such agreement or arrangement.

(3) Where an employee or class of employees of any body, or of any holder of an office, is prescribed by an order made for the purposes of subsection (1) above—

(a) any employee of that body, or of the holder of that office, who is not prescribed or is not within the prescribed class; and

(b) any person who does not provide, or is not employed in the provision of, goods or services for the purposes of the performance of those functions of the body or the holder of the office in connection with which the employee or prescribed class of employees is engaged,

shall not be a government contractor for the purposes of this Act.

(4) In this section 'office-holder in the Scottish Administration' has the same meaning as in section 126(7)(a) of the Scotland Act 1998.

(4A) In this section the reference to a police force includes a reference to the Civil Nuclear Constabulary.

(5) This Act shall apply to the following as it applies to persons falling within the definition of Crown servant—

(a) the First Minister and deputy First Minister in Northern Ireland; and

(b) Northern Ireland Ministers and junior Ministers.

13 Other interpretation provisions

(1) In this Act—

'disclose' and 'disclosure', in relation to a document or other article, include parting with possession of it;

'international organisation' means, subject to subsections (2) and (3) below, an organisation of which only States are members and includes a reference to any organ of such an organisation;

'prescribed' means prescribed by an order made by the Secretary of State;

'State' includes the government of a State and any organ of its government and references to a State other than the United Kingdom include references to any territory outside the United Kingdom.

(2) In section 12(2)(b) above the reference to an international organisation includes a reference to any such organisation whether or not one of which only States are members and includes a commercial organisation.

(3) In determining for the purposes of subsection (1) above whether only States are members of an organisation, any member which is itself an organisation of which only States are members, or which is an organ of such an organisation, shall be treated as a State.

14 Orders

(1) Any power of the Secretary of State under this Act to make orders shall be exercisable by statutory instrument.

(2) No order shall be made by him for the purposes of section 7(5), 8(9) or 12 above unless a draft of it has been laid before, and approved by a resolution of, each House of Parliament.

(3) If, apart from the provisions of this subsection, the draft of an order under any of the provisions mentioned in subsection (2) above would be treated for the purposes of the Standing Orders of either House of Parliament as a hybrid instrument it shall proceed in that House as if it were not such an instrument.

15   Acts done abroad and extent

(1) Any act—

(a) done by a British citizen or Crown servant; or

(b) done by any person in any of the Channel Islands or the Isle of Man or any colony,

shall, if it would be an offence by that person under any provision of this Act other than section 8(1), (4) or (5) when done by him in the United Kingdom, be an offence under that provision.

(2) This Act extends to Northern Ireland.

(3) Her Majesty may by Order in Council provide that any provision of this Act shall extend, with such exceptions, adaptations and modifications as may be specified in the Order, to any of the Channel Islands or the Isle of Man or any colony.

16   Short title, citation, consequential amendments, repeals, revocation and commencement

(1) This Act may be cited as the Official Secrets Act 1989.

(2) This Act and the Official Secrets Acts 1911 to 1939 may be cited together as the Official Secrets Acts 1911 to 1989.

(3) Schedule 1 to this Act shall have effect for making amendments consequential on the provisions of this Act.

(4) The enactments and Order mentioned in Schedule 2 to this Act are hereby repealed or revoked to the extent specified in the third column of that Schedule.

(5) Subject to any Order under subsection (3) of section 15 above the repeals in the Official Secrets Act 1911 and the Official Secrets Act 1920 do not extend to any of the territories mentioned in that subsection.

(6) This Act shall come into force on such day as the Secretary of State may by order appoint.

Security Service Act 1989

(1989, c. 5)

2   The Director-General

(1) The operations of the Service shall continue to be under the control of a Director-General appointed by the Secretary of State.

(2) The Director-General shall be responsible for the efficiency of the Service and it shall be his duty to ensure—

(a) that there are arrangements for securing that no information is obtained by the Service except so far as necessary for the proper discharge of its functions or disclosed by it except so far as necessary for that purpose or for the purpose of the [prevention or detection] of serious crime or for the purpose of any criminal proceedings; and

(b) that the Service does not take any action to further the interests of any political party; and

(c) that there are arrangements, agreed with the Director General of the Serious Organised Crime Agency, for co-ordinating the activities of the Service in pursuance of section 1(4) of this Act with the activities of police forces, the Serious Organised Crime Agency and other law enforcement agencies.

(3) The arrangements mentioned in subsection (2)(a) above shall be such as to ensure that information in the possession of the Service is not disclosed for use in determining whether a person should be employed, or continue to be employed, by any person, or in any office or capacity, except in accordance with provisions in that behalf approved by the Secretary of State.

(3A) Without prejudice to the generality of subsection 2(a) above, the disclosure of information shall be regarded as necessary for the proper discharge of the functions of the Security Service if it consists of—

(a) the disclosure of records subject to and in accordance with the Public Records Act 1958; or

(b) the disclosure, subject to and in accordance with arrangements approved by the Secretary of State, of information to the Comptroller and Auditor General for the purposes of his functions.

(4) The Director-General shall make an annual report on the work of the Service to the Prime Minister and the Secretary of State and may at any time report to either of them on any matter relating to its work.

Criminal Justice and Immigration Act 2008

(2008, c.2)

77 Power to alter penalty for unlawfully obtaining etc. personal data

(1) The Secretary of State may by order provide for a person who is guilty of an offence under section 55 of the Data Protection Act 1998 (c. 29) (unlawful obtaining etc. of personal data) to be liable—

(a) on summary conviction, to imprisonment for a term not exceeding the specified period or to a fine not exceeding the statutory maximum or to both,

(b) on conviction on indictment, to imprisonment for a term not exceeding the specified period or to a fine or to both.

(2) In subsection (1)(a) and (b) 'specified period' means a period provided for by the order but the period must not exceed—

(a) in the case of summary conviction, 12 months (or, in Northern Ireland, 6 months), and

(b) in the case of conviction on indictment, two years.

(3) The Secretary of State must ensure that any specified period for England and Wales which, in the case of summary conviction, exceeds 6 months is to be read as a reference to 6 months so far as it relates to an offence committed before the commencement of section 282(1) of the Criminal Justice Act 2003 (c. 44) (increase in sentencing powers of magistrates' courts from 6 to 12 months for certain offences triable either way).

(4) Before making an order under this section, the Secretary of State must consult—

(a) the Information Commissioner,

(b) such media organisations as the Secretary of State considers appropriate, and

(c) such other persons as the Secretary of State considers appropriate.

(5) An order under this section may, in particular, amend the Data Protection Act 1998.

Part VII

Privacy and media intrusion

Protection from Harassment Act 1997

(1997, c. 40)

England and Wales

1   Prohibition of harassment

(1) A person must not pursue a course of conduct—

   (a) which amounts to harassment of another, and

   (b) which he knows or ought to know amounts to harassment of the other.

(1A) A person must not pursue a course of conduct—

   (a) which involves harassment of two or more persons, and

   (b) which he knows or ought to know involves harassment of those persons, and

   (c) by which he intends to persuade any person (whether or not one of those mentioned above)—

      (i)   not to do something that he is entitled or required to do, or

      (ii) to do something that he is not under any obligation to do.

(2) For the purposes of this section or section 2A(2)(c), the person whose course of conduct is in question ought to know that it amounts to or involves harassment of another if a reasonable person in possession of the same information would think the course of conduct amounted to or involved harassment of the other.

(3) Subsection (1) [or (1A)] does not apply to a course of conduct if the person who pursued it shows—

   (a) that it was pursued for the purpose of preventing or detecting crime,

   (b) that it was pursued under any enactment or rule of law or to comply with any condition or requirement imposed by any person under any enactment, or

   (c) that in the particular circumstances the pursuit of the course of conduct was reasonable.

2   Offence of harassment

(1) A person who pursues a course of conduct in breach of [section 1(1) or (1A)] is guilty of an offence.

(2) A person guilty of an offence under this section is liable on summary conviction to imprisonment for a term not exceeding six months, or a fine not exceeding level 5 on the standard scale, or both.

2A   Offence of stalking

(1) A person is guilty of an offence if—

   (a) the person pursues a course of conduct in breach of section 1(1), and

   (b) the course of conduct amounts to stalking.

(2) For the purposes of subsection (1)(b) (and section 4A(1)(a)) a person's course of conduct amounts to stalking of another person if—

    (a) it amounts to harassment of that person,

    (b) the acts or omissions involved are ones associated with stalking, and

    (c) the person whose course of conduct it is knows or ought to know that the course of conduct amounts to harassment of the other person.

(3) The following are examples of acts or omissions which, in particular circumstances, are ones associated with stalking—

    (a) following a person,

    (b) contacting, or attempting to contact, a person by any means,

    (c) publishing any statement or other material—

        (i)   relating or purporting to relate to a person, or

        (ii) purporting to originate from a person,

    (d) monitoring the use by a person of the internet, email or any other form of electronic communication,

    (e) loitering in any place (whether public or private),

    (f) interfering with any property in the possession of a person,

    (g) watching or spying on a person.

(4) A person guilty of an offence under this section is liable on summary conviction to imprisonment for a term not exceeding 51 weeks, or a fine not exceeding level 5 on the standard scale, or both.

(5) In relation to an offence committed before the commencement of section 281(5) of the Criminal Justice Act 2003, the reference in subsection (4) to 51 weeks is to be read as a reference to six months.

(6) This section is without prejudice to the generality of section 2.

2B   Power of entry in relation to offence of stalking

(1) A justice of the peace may, on an application by a constable, issue a warrant authorising a constable to enter and search premises if the justice of the peace is satisfied that there are reasonable grounds for believing that—

    (a) an offence under section 2A has been, or is being, committed,

    (b) there is material on the premises which is likely to be of substantial value (whether by itself or together with other material) to the investigation of the offence,

    (c) the material—

        (i)   is likely to be admissible in evidence at a trial for the offence, and

        (ii) does not consist of, or include, items subject to legal privilege, excluded material or special procedure material (within the meanings given by sections 10, 11 and 14 of the Police and Criminal Evidence Act 1984), and

    (d) either—

        (i)   entry to the premises will not be granted unless a warrant is produced, or

        (ii) the purpose of a search may be frustrated or seriously prejudiced unless a constable arriving at the premises can secure immediate entry to them.

(2) A constable may seize and retain anything for which a search has been authorised under subsection (1).

(3) A constable may use reasonable force, if necessary, in the exercise of any power conferred by virtue of this section.

(4) In this section 'premises' has the same meaning as in section 23 of the Police and Criminal Evidence Act 1984.

3   Civil remedy

(1) An actual or apprehended breach of [section 1(1)] may be the subject of a claim in civil proceedings by the person who is or may be the victim of the course of conduct in question.

(2) On such a claim, damages may be awarded for (among other things) any anxiety caused by the harassment and any financial loss resulting from the harassment.

(3) Where—

(a) in such proceedings the High Court or a county court grants an injunction for the purpose of restraining the defendant from pursuing any conduct which amounts to harassment, and

(b) the plaintiff considers that the defendant has done anything which he is prohibited from doing by the injunction,

the plaintiff may apply for the issue of a warrant for the arrest of the defendant.

(4) An application under subsection (3) may be made—

(a) where the injunction was granted by the High Court, to a judge of that court, and

(b) where the injunction was granted by a county court, to a judge or district judge of that or any other county court.

(5) The judge or district judge to whom an application under subsection (3) is made may only issue a warrant if—

(a) the application is substantiated on oath, and

(b) the judge or district judge has reasonable grounds for believing that the defendant has done anything which he is prohibited from doing by the injunction.

(6) Where—

(a) the High Court or a county court grants an injunction for the purpose mentioned in subsection (3)(a), and

(b) without reasonable excuse the defendant does anything which he is prohibited from doing by the injunction, he is guilty of an offence.

(7) Where a person is convicted of an offence under subsection (6) in respect of any conduct, that conduct is not punishable as a contempt of court.

(8) A person cannot be convicted of an offence under subsection (6) in respect of any conduct which has been punished as a contempt of court.

(9) A person guilty of an offence under subsection (6) is liable—

(a) on conviction on indictment, to imprisonment for a term not exceeding five years, or a fine, or both, or

(b) on summary conviction, to imprisonment for a term not exceeding six months, or a fine not exceeding the statutory maximum, or both.

3A Injunctions to protect persons from harassment within section 1(1A)

(1) This section applies where there is an actual or apprehended breach of section 1(1A) by any person ('the relevant person').

(2) In such a case—

(a) any person who is or may be a victim of the course of conduct in question, or

(b) any person who is or may be a person falling within section 1(1A)(c),

may apply to the High Court or a county court for an injunction restraining the relevant person from pursuing any conduct which amounts to harassment in relation to any person or persons mentioned or described in the injunction.

(3) Section 3(3) to (9) apply in relation to an injunction granted under subsection (2) above as they apply in relation to an injunction granted as mentioned in section 3(3)(a).

4 Putting people in fear of violence

(1) A person whose course of conduct causes another to fear, on at least two occasions, that violence will be used against him is guilty of an offence if he knows or ought to know that his course of conduct will cause the other so to fear on each of those occasions.

(2) For the purposes of this section, the person whose course of conduct is in question ought to know that it will cause another to fear that violence will be used against him on any occasion if a reasonable person in possession of the same information would think the course of conduct would cause the other so to fear on that occasion.

(3) It is a defence for a person charged with an offence under this section to show that—
  (a) his course of conduct was pursued for the purpose of preventing or detecting crime,
  (b) his course of conduct was pursued under any enactment or rule of law or to comply with any condition or requirement imposed by any person under any enactment, or
  (c) the pursuit of his course of conduct was reasonable for the protection of himself or another or for the protection of his or another's property.
(4) A person guilty of an offence under this section is liable—
  (a) on conviction on indictment, to imprisonment for a term not exceeding five years, or a fine, or both, or
  (b) on summary conviction, to imprisonment for a term not exceeding six months, or a fine not exceeding the statutory maximum, or both.
(5) If on the trial on indictment of a person charged with an offence under this section the jury find him not guilty of the offence charged, they may find him guilty of an offence under section 2 or 2A.
(6) The Crown Court has the same powers and duties in relation to a person who is by virtue of subsection (5) convicted before it of an offence under section 2 or 2A as a magistrates' court would have on convicting him of the offence.

4A   Stalking involving fear of violence or serious alarm or distress

(1) A person ('A') whose course of conduct—
  (a) amounts to stalking, and
  (b) either—
    (i) causes another ('B') to fear, on at least two occasions, that violence will be used against B, or
    (ii) causes B serious alarm or distress which has a substantial adverse effect on B's usual day-to-day activities,
is guilty of an offence if A knows or ought to know that A's course of conduct will cause B so to fear on each of those occasions or (as the case may be) will cause such alarm or distress.
(2) For the purposes of this section A ought to know that A's course of conduct will cause B to fear that violence will be used against B on any occasion if a reasonable person in possession of the same information would think the course of conduct would cause B so to fear on that occasion.
(3) For the purposes of this section A ought to know that A's course of conduct will cause B serious alarm or distress which has a substantial adverse effect on B's usual day-to-day activities if a reasonable person in possession of the same information would think the course of conduct would cause B such alarm or distress.
(4) It is a defence for A to show that—
  (a) A's course of conduct was pursued for the purpose of preventing or detecting crime,
  (b) A's course of conduct was pursued under any enactment or rule of law or comply with any condition or requirement imposed by any person under any enactment, or
  (c) the pursuit of A's course of conduct was reasonable for the protection of A or another or for the protection of A's or another's property.
(5) A person guilty of an offence under this section is liable—
  (a) on conviction on indictment, to imprisonment for a term not exceeding five years, or a fine, or both, or
  (b) on summary conviction, to imprisonment for a term not exceeding twelve months, or a fine not exceeding the statutory maximum, or both.
(6) In relation to an offence committed before the commencement of section 154(1) of the Criminal Justice Act 2003, the reference in subsection (5)(b) to twelve months is to be read as a reference to six months.
(7) If on the trial on indictment of a person charged with an offence under this section the jury find the person not guilty of the offence charged, they may find the person guilty of an offence under section 2 or 2A.

(8) The Crown Court has the same powers and duties in relation to a person who is by virtue of subsection (7) convicted before it of an offence under section 2 or 2A as a magistrates' court would have on convicting the person of the offence.

(9) This section is without prejudice to the generality of section 4.

5   Restraining orders on conviction

(1) A court sentencing or otherwise dealing with a person ('the defendant') convicted of an offence ... may (as well as sentencing him or dealing with him in any other way) make an order under this section.

(2) The order may, for the purpose of protecting the victim [or victims] of the offence, or any other person mentioned in the order, from [...] conduct which—

    (a) amounts to harassment, or

    (b) will cause a fear of violence,

prohibit the defendant from doing anything described in the order.

(3) The order may have effect for a specified period or until further order.

[(3A) In proceedings under this section both the prosecution and the defence may lead, as further evidence, any evidence that would be admissible in proceedings for an injunction under section 3.]

(4) The prosecutor, the defendant or any other person mentioned in the order may apply to the court which made the order for it to be varied or discharged by a further order.

[(4A) Any person mentioned in the order is entitled to be heard on the hearing of an application under subsection (4).]

(5) If without reasonable excuse the defendant does anything which he is prohibited from doing by an order under this section, he is guilty of an offence.

(6) A person guilty of an offence under this section is liable—

    (a) on conviction on indictment, to imprisonment for a term not exceeding five years, or a fine, or both, or

    (b) on summary conviction, to imprisonment for a term not exceeding six months, or a fine not exceeding the statutory maximum, or both.

[(7) A court dealing with a person for an offence under this section may vary or discharge the order in question by a further order.]

5A   Restraining orders on acquittal

(1) A court before which a person ('the defendant') is acquitted of an offence may, if it considers it necessary to do so to protect a person from harassment by the defendant, make an order prohibiting the defendant from doing anything described in the order.

(2) Subsections (3) to (7) of section 5 apply to an order under this section as they apply to an order under that one.

(3) Where the Court of Appeal allow an appeal against conviction they may remit the case to the Crown Court to consider whether to proceed under this section.

(4) Where—

    (a) the Crown Court allows an appeal against conviction, or

    (b) a case is remitted to the Crown Court under subsection (3),

the reference in subsection (1) to a court before which a person is acquitted of an offence is to be read as referring to that court.

(5) A person made subject to an order under this section has the same right of appeal against the order as if—

    (a) he had been convicted of the offence in question before the court which made the order, and

    (b) the order had been made under section 5.

6   Limitation

In section 11 of the Limitation Act 1980 (special time limit for actions in respect of personal injuries), after subsection (1) there is inserted—

'(1A) This section does not apply to any action brought for damages under section 3 of the Protection from Harassment Act 1997.'

7 Interpretation of this group of sections

(1) This section applies for the interpretation of [sections 1 to 5A].

(2) References to harassing a person include alarming the person or causing the person distress.

(3) A 'course of conduct' must involve—

    (a) in the case of conduct in relation to a single person (see section 1(1)), conduct on at least two occasions in relation to that person, or

    (b) in the case of conduct in relation to two or more persons (see section 1(1A)), conduct on at least one occasion in relation to each of those persons.

(3A) A person's conduct on any occasion shall be taken, if aided, abetted, counselled or procured by another—

    (a) to be conduct on that occasion of the other (as well as conduct of the person whose conduct it is); and

    (b) to be conduct in relation to which the other's knowledge and purpose, and what he ought to have known, are the same as they were in relation to what was contemplated or reasonably foreseeable at the time of the aiding, abetting, counselling or procuring.

(4) 'Conduct' includes speech.

[(5) References to a person, in the context of the harassment of a person, are references to a person who is an individual.]

Scotland

8 Harassment

(1) Every individual has a right to be free from harassment and, accordingly, a person must not pursue a course of conduct which amounts to harassment of another and—

    (a) is intended to amount to harassment of that person; or

    (b) occurs in circumstances where it would appear to a reasonable person that it would amount to harassment of that person.

(1A) Subsection (1) is subject to section 8A.

(2) An actual or apprehended breach of subsection (1) may be the subject of a claim in civil proceedings by the person who is or may be the victim of the course of conduct in question; and any such claim shall be known as an action of harassment.

(3) For the purposes of this section—

    'conduct' includes speech;

    'harassment' of a person includes causing the person alarm or distress;

and a course of conduct must involve conduct on at least two occasions.

(4) It shall be a defence to any action of harassment to show that the course of conduct complained of—

    (a) was authorised by, under or by virtue of any enactment or rule of law;

    (b) was pursued for the purpose of preventing or detecting crime; or

    (c) was, in the particular circumstances, reasonable.

(5) In an action of harassment the court may, without prejudice to any other remedies which it may grant—

    (a) award damages;

    (b) grant—

        (i) interdict or interim interdict;

        (ii) if it is satisfied that it is appropriate for it to do so in order to protect the person from further harassment, an order, to be known as a 'non-harassment order', requiring the defender to refrain from such conduct in relation to the pursuer as may be specified in the order for such period (which includes an indeterminate period) as may be so specified, but a person may not be subjected to the same prohibitions in an interdict or interim interdict and a non-harassment order at the same time.

(6) The damages which may be awarded in an action of harassment include damages for any anxiety caused by the harassment and any financial loss resulting from it.

(7) Without prejudice to any right to seek review of any interlocutor, a person against whom a non-harassment order has been made, or the person for whose protection the order was made, may apply to the court by which the order was made for revocation of or a variation of the order and, on any such application, the court may revoke the order or vary it in such manner as it considers appropriate.

9   Breach of non-harassment order

(1) Any person who is in breach of a non-harassment order made under section 8 is guilty of an offence under section 8 or section 8A and liable—

  (a) on conviction on indictment, to imprisonment for a term not exceeding five years or to a fine, or to both such imprisonment and such fine; and

  (b) on summary conviction, to imprisonment for a period not exceeding six months or to a fine not exceeding the statutory maximum, or to both such imprisonment and such fine.

(2) A breach of a non-harassment order shall not be punishable other than in accordance with subsection (1).

(3) A constable may arrest without warrant any person he reasonably believes is committing or has committed an offence under subsection (1).

(4) Subsection (3) is without prejudice to any power of arrest conferred by law apart from that subsection.

10   Limitation

(1) After section 18A of the Prescription and Limitation (Scotland) Act 1973 there is inserted the following section—

'18B   Actions of harassment

(1) This section applies to actions of harassment (within the meaning of section 8 of the Protection from Harassment Act 1997) which include a claim for damages.

(2) Subject to subsection (3) below and to section 19A of this Act, no action to which this section applies shall be brought unless it is commenced within a period of 3 years after—

  (a) the date on which the alleged harassment ceased; or

  (b) the date, (if later than the date mentioned in paragraph (a) above) on which the pursuer in the action became, or on which, in the opinion of the court, it would have been reasonably practicable for him in all the circumstances to have become, aware, that the defender was a person responsible for the alleged harassment or the employer or principal of such a person.

(3) In the computation of the period specified in subsection (2) above there shall be disregarded any time during which the person who is alleged to have suffered the harassment was under legal disability by reason of nonage or unsoundness of mind.'

(2) In subsection (1) of section 19A of that Act (power of court to override time-limits), for 'section 17 or section 18 and section 18A' there is substituted 'section 17, 18, 18A or 18B'.

11   Non-harassment order following criminal offence

After section 234 of the Criminal Procedure (Scotland) Act 1995 there is inserted the following section—

'234A   Non-harassment orders

(1) Where a person is convicted of an offence involving harassment of a person ('the victim'), the prosecutor may apply to the court to make a non-harassment order against the offender requiring him to refrain from such conduct in relation to the victim as may be specified in the order for such period (which includes an indeterminate period) as may be so specified, in addition to any other disposal which may be made in relation to the offence.

(2) On an application under subsection (1) above the court may, if it is satisfied on a balance of probabilities that it is appropriate to do so in order to protect the victim from further harassment, make a non-harassment order.

(3) A non-harassment order made by a criminal court shall be taken to be a sentence for the purposes of any appeal and, for the purposes of this subsection 'order' includes any variation or revocation of such an order made under subsection (6) below.

(4) Any person who is found to be in breach of a non-harassment order shall be guilty of an offence and liable—

(a) on conviction on indictment, to imprisonment for a term not exceeding 5 years or to a fine, or to both such imprisonment and such fine; and

(b) on summary conviction, to imprisonment for a period not exceeding 6 months or to a fine not exceeding the statutory maximum, or to both such imprisonment and such fine.

(5) The Lord Advocate, in solemn proceedings, and the prosecutor, in summary proceedings, may appeal to the High Court against any decision by a court to refuse an application under subsection (1) above; and on any such appeal the High Court may make such order as it considers appropriate.

(6) The person against whom a non-harassment order is made, or the prosecutor at whose instance the order is made, may apply to the court which made the order for its revocation or variation and, in relation to any such application the court concerned may, if it is satisfied on a balance of probabilities that it is appropriate to do so, revoke the order or vary it in such manner as it thinks fit, but not so as to increase the period for which the order is to run.

For the purposes of this section "harassment" shall be construed in accordance with section 8 of the Protection from Harassment Act 1997'.

General

12   National security, etc.

(1) If the Secretary of State certifies that in his opinion anything done by a specified person on a specified occasion related to—

(a) national security,

(b) the economic well-being of the United Kingdom, or

(c) the prevention or detection of serious crime, and was done on behalf of the Crown,

the certificate is conclusive evidence that this Act does not apply to any conduct of that person on that occasion.

(2) In subsection (1), 'specified' means specified in the certificate in question.

(3) A document purporting to be a certificate under subsection (1) is to be received in evidence and, unless the contrary is proved, be treated as being such a certificate.

13   Corresponding provision for Northern Ireland

An Order in Council made under paragraph 1(1)(b) of Schedule 1 to the Northern Ireland Act 1974 which contains a statement that it is made only for purposes corresponding to those of sections 1 to 7 and 12 of this Act—

(a) shall not be subject to sub-paragraphs (4) and (5) of paragraph 1 of that Schedule (affirmative resolution of both Houses of Parliament), but

(b) shall be subject to annulment in pursuance of a resolution of either House of Parliament.

14   Extent

(1) Sections 1 to 7 extend to England and Wales only.

(2) Sections 8 to 11 extend to Scotland only.

(3) This Act (except section 13) does not extend to Northern Ireland.

15 Commencement

(1) Sections 1, 2, 4, 5 and 7 to 12 are to come into force on such day as the Secretary of State may by order made by statutory instrument appoint.

(2) Sections 3 and 6 are to come into force on such day as the Lord Chancellor may by order made by statutory instrument appoint.

(3) Different days may be appointed under this section for different purposes.

16 Short title

This Act may be cited as the Protection from Harassment Act 1997.

Data Protection Act 1998

(1998, c. 29)

17 Prohibition on processing without registration

(1) Subject to the following provisions of this section, personal data must not be processed unless an entry in respect of the data controller is included in the register maintained by the Commissioner under section 19 (or is treated by notification regulations made by virtue of section 19(3) as being so included).

(2) Except where the processing is assessable processing for the purposes of section 22, subsection (1) does not apply in relation to personal data consisting of information which falls neither within paragraph (a) of the definition of 'data' in section 1(1) nor within paragraph (b) of that definition.

(3) If it appears to the Secretary of State that processing of a particular description is unlikely to prejudice the rights and freedoms of data subjects, notification regulations may provide that, in such cases as may be prescribed, subsection (1) is not to apply in relation to processing of that description.

(4) Subsection (1) does not apply in relation to any processing whose sole purpose is the maintenance of a public register.

18 Notification by data controllers

(1) Any data controller who wishes to be included in the register maintained under section 19 shall give a notification to the Commissioner under this section.

(2) A notification under this section must specify in accordance with notification regulations—
  (a) the registrable particulars, and
  (b) a general description of measures to be taken for the purpose of complying with the seventh data protection principle.

(3) Notification regulations made by virtue of subsection (2) may provide for the determination by the Commissioner, in accordance with any requirements of the regulations, of the form in which the registrable particulars and the description mentioned in subsection (2)(b) are to be specified, including in particular the detail required for the purposes of section 16(1)(c), (d), (e) and (f) and subsection (2)(b).

(4) Notification regulations may make provisions as to the giving of notification—
  (a) by partnerships, or
  (b) in other cases where two or more persons are the data controllers in respect of any personal data.

(5) The notification must be accompanied by such fee as may be prescribed by fees regulations.

(5A) Notification regulations may prescribe the information about the data controller which is required for the purpose of verifying the fee payable under subsection (5).

(6) Notification regulations may provide for any fee paid under subsection (5) or section 19(4) to be refunded in prescribed circumstances.

19   Register of notifications

(1) The Commissioner shall—

    (a) maintain a register of persons who have given notification under section 18, and

    (b) make an entry in the register in pursuance of each notification received by him under that section from a person in respect of whom no entry as data controller was for the time being included in the register.

(2) Each entry in the register shall consist of—

    (a) the registrable particulars notified under section 18 or, as the case requires, those particulars as amended in pursuance of section 20(4), and

    (b) such other information as the Commissioner may be authorised or required by notification regulations to include in the register.

(3) Notification regulations may make provision as to the time as from which any entry in respect of a data controller is to be treated for the purposes of section 17 as having been made in the register.

(4) No entry shall be retained in the register for more than the relevant time except on payment of such fee as may be prescribed by fees regulations.

(5) In subsection (4) 'the relevant time' means twelve months or such other period as may be prescribed by notification regulations; and different periods may be prescribed in relation to different cases.

(6) The Commissioner—

    (a) shall provide facilities for making the information contained in the entries in the register available for inspection (in visible and legible form) by members of the public at all reasonable hours and free of charge, and

    (b) may provide such other facilities for making the information contained in those entries available to the public free of charge as he considers appropriate.

(7) The Commissioner shall, on payment of such fee, if any, as may be prescribed by fees regulations, supply any member of the public with a duly certified copy in writing of the particulars contained in any entry made in the register.

(8) Nothing in subsection (6) or (7) applies to information which is included in an entry in the register only by reason of it falling within section 16(1)(h).

20   Duty to notify changes

(1) For the purpose specified in subsection (2), notification regulations shall include provision imposing on every person in respect of whom an entry as a data controller is for the time being included in the register maintained under section 19 a duty to notify to the Commissioner, in such circumstances and at such time or times and in such form as may be prescribed, such matters relating to the registrable particulars and measures taken as mentioned in section 18(2)(b) as may be prescribed.

(2) The purpose referred to in subsection (1) is that of ensuring, so far as practicable—

    (a) that at any time the entries in the register maintained under section 19 contain current names and addresses and describe the current practice or intentions of the data controller with respect to the processing of personal data, and

    (b) that at any time the Commissioner is provided with a general description of measures currently being taken as mentioned in section 18(2)(b).

(3) Subsection (3) of section 18 has effect in relation to notification regulations made by virtue of subsection (1) as it has effect in relation to notification regulations made by virtue of subsection (2) of that section.

(4) On receiving any notification under notification regulations made by virtue of subsection (1), the Commissioner shall make such amendments of the relevant entry in the register maintained under section 19 as are necessary to take account of the notification.

21   Offences

(1) If section 17(1) is contravened, the data controller is guilty of an offence.

(2) Any person who fails to comply with the duty imposed by notification regulations made by virtue of section 20(1) is guilty of an offence.

(3) It shall be a defence for a person charged with an offence under subsection (2) to show that he exercised all due diligence to comply with the duty.

22   Preliminary assessment by Commissioner

(1) In this section 'assessable processing' means processing which is of a description specified in an order made by the Secretary of State as appearing to him to be particularly likely—

(a) to cause substantial damage or substantial distress to data subjects, or

(b) otherwise significantly to prejudice the rights and freedoms of data subjects.

(2) On receiving notification from any data controller under section 18 or under notification regulations made by virtue of section 20 the Commissioner shall consider—

(a) whether any of the processing to which the notification relates is assessable processing, and

(b) if so, whether the assessable processing is likely to comply with the provisions of this Act.

(3) Subject to subsection (4), the Commissioner shall, within the period of twenty-eight days beginning with the day on which he receives a notification which relates to assessable processing, give a notice to the data controller stating the extent to which the Commissioner is of the opinion that the processing is likely or unlikely to comply with the provisions of this Act.

(4) Before the end of the period referred to in subsection (3) the Commissioner may, by reason of special circumstances, extend that period on one occasion only by notice to the data controller by such further period not exceeding fourteen days as the Commissioner may specify in the notice.

(5) No assessable processing in respect of which a notification has been given to the Commissioner as mentioned in subsection (2) shall be carried on unless either—

(a) the period of twenty-eight days beginning with the day on which the notification is received by the Commissioner (or, in a case falling within subsection (4), that period as extended under that subsection) has elapsed, or

(b) before the end of that period (or that period as so extended) the data controller has received a notice from the Commissioner under subsection (3) in respect of the processing.

(6) Where subsection (5) is contravened, the data controller is guilty of an offence.

(7) The Secretary of State may by order amend subsections (3), (4) and (5) by substituting for the number of days for the time being specified there a different number specified in the order.

35   Disclosures required by law or made in connection with legal proceedings etc.

(1) Personal data are exempt from the non-disclosure provisions where the disclosure is required by or under any enactment, by any rule of law or by the order of a court.

(2) Personal data are exempt from the non-disclosure provisions where the disclosure is necessary—

(a) for the purpose of, or in connection with, any legal proceedings (including prospective legal proceedings), or

(b) for the purpose of obtaining legal advice, or is otherwise necessary for the purposes of establishing, exercising or defending legal rights.

35A   Parliamentary privilege

Personal data are exempt from—

(a) the first data protection principle, except to the extent to which it requires compliance with the conditions in Schedules 2 and 3,

(b) the second, third, fourth and fifth data protection principles,

(c) section 7, and

(d) sections 10 and 14(1) to (3),

if the exemption is required for the purpose of avoiding an infringement of the privileges of either House of Parliament.

36 Domestic purposes
Personal data processed by an individual only for the purposes of that individual's personal, family or household affairs (including recreational purposes) are exempt from the data protection principles and the provisions of Parts II and III.

37 Miscellaneous exemptions
Schedule 7 (which confers further miscellaneous exemptions) has effect.

38 Powers to make further exemptions by order
(1) The Secretary of State may by order exempt from the subject information provisions personal data consisting of information the disclosure of which is prohibited or restricted by or under any enactment if and to the extent that he considers it necessary for the safeguarding of the interests of the data subject or the rights and freedoms of any other individual that the prohibition or restriction ought to prevail over those provisions.

(2) The Secretary of State may by order exempt from the non-disclosure provisions any disclosures of personal data made in circumstances specified in the order, if he considers the exemption is necessary for the safeguarding of the interests of the data subject or the rights and freedoms of any other individual.

Unlawful obtaining etc. of personal data

55 Unlawful obtaining etc. of personal data
(1) A person must not knowingly or recklessly, without the consent of the data controller—
  (a) obtain or disclose personal data or the information contained in personal data, or
  (b) procure the disclosure to another person of the information contained in personal data.
(2) Subsection (1) does not apply to a person who shows—
  (a) that the obtaining, disclosing or procuring—
    (i) was necessary for the purpose of preventing or detecting crime, or
    (ii) was required or authorised by or under any enactment, by any rule of law or by the order of a court,
  (b) that he acted in the reasonable belief that he had in law the right to obtain or disclose the data or information or, as the case may be, to procure the disclosure of the information to the other person,
  (c) that he acted in the reasonable belief that he would have had the consent of the data controller if the data controller had known of the obtaining, disclosing or procuring and the circumstances of it, or
(3) A person who contravenes subsection (1) is guilty of an offence.
(4) A person who sells personal data is guilty of an offence if he has obtained the data in contravention of subsection (1).
(5) A person who offers to sell personal data is guilty of an offence if—
  (a) he has obtained the data in contravention of subsection (1), or
  (b) he subsequently obtains the data in contravention of that subsection.
(6) For the purposes of subsection (5), an advertisement indicating that personal data are or may be for sale is an offer to sell the data.
(7) Section 1(2) does not apply for the purposes of this section; and for the purposes of subsections (4) to (6), 'personal data' includes information extracted from personal data.
(8) References in this section to personal data do not include references to personal data which by virtue of section 28 or 33A are exempt from this section.

55A Power of Commissioner to impose monetary penalty
(1) The Commissioner may serve a data controller with a monetary penalty notice if the Commissioner is satisfied that—
  (a) there has been a serious contravention of section 4(4) by the data controller,

(b) the contravention was of a kind likely to cause substantial damage or substantial distress, and

(c) subsection (2) or (3) applies.

(2) This subsection applies if the contravention was deliberate.

(3) This subsection applies if the data controller—

(a) knew or ought to have known—

(i) that there was a risk that the contravention would occur, and

(ii) that such a contravention would be of a kind likely to cause substantial damage or substantial distress, but

(b) failed to take reasonable steps to prevent the contravention.

(3A) The Commissioner may not be satisfied as mentioned in subsection (1) by virtue of any matter which comes to the Commissioner's attention as a result of anything done in pursuance of—

(a) an assessment notice;

(b) an assessment under section 51(7).

(4) A monetary penalty notice is a notice requiring the data controller to pay to the Commissioner a monetary penalty of an amount determined by the Commissioner and specified in the notice.

(5) The amount determined by the Commissioner must not exceed the prescribed amount.

(6) The monetary penalty must be paid to the Commissioner within the period specified in the notice.

(7) The notice must contain such information as may be prescribed.

(8) Any sum received by the Commissioner by virtue of this section must be paid into the Consolidated Fund.

(9) In this section—

'data controller' does not include the Crown Estate Commissioners or a person who is a data controller by virtue of section 63(3);

'prescribed' means prescribed by regulations made by the Secretary of State.

55B   Monetary penalty notices: procedural rights

(1) Before serving a monetary penalty notice, the Commissioner must serve the data controller with a notice of intent.

(2) A notice of intent is a notice that the Commissioner proposes to serve a monetary penalty notice.

(3) A notice of intent must—

(a) inform the data controller that he may make written representations in relation to the Commissioner's proposal within a period specified in the notice, and

(b) contain such other information as may be prescribed.

(4) The Commissioner may not serve a monetary penalty notice until the time within which the data controller may make representations has expired.

(5) A person on whom a monetary penalty notice is served may appeal to the Tribunal against—

(a) the issue of the monetary penalty notice;

(b) the amount of the penalty specified in the notice.

(6) In this section, 'prescribed' means prescribed by regulations made by the Secretary of State.

55C   Guidance about monetary penalty notices

(1) The Commissioner must prepare and issue guidance on how he proposes to exercise his functions under sections 55A and 55B.

(2) The guidance must, in particular, deal with—

(a) the circumstances in which he would consider it appropriate to issue a monetary penalty notice, and

(b) how he will determine the amount of the penalty.

(3) The Commissioner may alter or replace the guidance.

(4) If the guidance is altered or replaced, the Commissioner must issue the altered or replacement guidance.

(5) The Commissioner must consult the Secretary of State before issuing any guidance under this section.

(6) The Commissioner must lay any guidance issued under this section before each House of Parliament.

(7) The Commissioner must arrange for the publication of any guidance issued under this section in such form and manner as he considers appropriate.

(8) In subsections (5) to (7), 'guidance' includes altered or replacement guidance.

55D Monetary penalty notices: enforcement

(1) This section applies in relation to any penalty payable to the Commissioner by virtue of section 55A.

(2) In England and Wales, the penalty is recoverable—
   (a) if a county court so orders, as if it were payable under an order of that court;
   (b) if the High Court so orders, as if it were payable under an order of that court.

(3) In Scotland, the penalty may be enforced in the same manner as an extract registered decree arbitral bearing a warrant for execution issued by the sheriff court of any sheriffdom in Scotland.

(4) In Northern Ireland, the penalty is recoverable—
   (a) if a county court so orders, as if it were payable under an order of that court;
   (b) if the High Court so orders, as if it were payable under an order of that court.

55E Notices under sections 55A and 55B: supplemental

(1) The Secretary of State may by order make further provision in connection with monetary penalty notices and notices of intent.

(2) An order under this section may in particular—
   (a) provide that a monetary penalty notice may not be served on a data controller with respect to the processing of personal data for the special purposes except in circumstances specified in the order;
   (b) make provision for the cancellation or variation of monetary penalty notices;
   (c) confer rights of appeal to the Tribunal against decisions of the Commissioner in relation to the cancellation or variation of such notices;
   (e) make provision for the determination of appeals by virtue of paragraph (c);

(3) An order under this section may apply any provision of this Act with such modifications as may be specified in the order.

(4) An order under this section may amend this Act.

Information provided to Commissioner or Tribunal

58 Disclosure of information

No enactment or rule of law prohibiting or restricting the disclosure of information shall preclude a person from furnishing the Commissioner or the Tribunal with any information necessary for the discharge of their functions under this Act [or the Freedom of Information Act 2000].

59 Confidentiality of information

(1) No person who is or has been the Commissioner, a member of the Commissioner's staff or an agent of the Commissioner shall disclose any information which—
   (a) has been obtained by, or furnished to, the Commissioner under or for the purposes of the information Acts.
   (b) relates to an identified or identifiable individual or business, and
   (c) is not at the time of the disclosure, and has not previously been, available to the public from other sources, unless the disclosure is made with lawful authority.

(2) For the purposes of subsection (1) a disclosure of information is made with lawful authority only if, and to the extent that—

(a) the disclosure is made with the consent of the individual or of the person for the time being carrying on the business,

(b) the information was provided for the purpose of its being made available to the public (in whatever manner) under any provision of the information Acts,

(c) the disclosure is made for the purposes of, and is necessary for, the discharge of—

(i)   any functions under the information Acts, or

(ii) any EU obligation,

(d) the disclosure is made for the purposes of any proceedings, whether criminal or civil and whether arising under, or by virtue of, the information Acts or otherwise, or

(e) having regard to the rights and freedoms or legitimate interests of any person, the disclosure is necessary in the public interest.

(3) Any person who knowingly or recklessly discloses information in contravention of subsection (1) is guilty of an offence.

(4) In this section 'the information Acts' means this Act and the Freedom of Information Act 2000.

Copyright, Designs and Patents Act 1988

(1988, c. 48)

Right to privacy of certain photographs and films

85   Right to privacy of certain photographs and films

(1) A person who for private and domestic purposes commissions the taking of a photograph or the making of a film has, where copyright subsists in the resulting work, the right not to have—

(a) copies of the work issued to the public,

(b) the work exhibited or shown in public, or

(c) the work communicated to the public;

and, except as mentioned in subsection (2), a person who does or authorises the doing of any of those acts infringes that right.

(2) The right is not infringed by an act which by virtue of any of the following provisions would not infringe the copyright in the work—

(a) section 31 (incidental inclusion of work in an artistic work, film or broadcast),

(b) section 45 (parliamentary and judicial proceedings);

(c) section 46 (Royal Commissions and statutory inquiries);

(d) section 50 (acts done under statutory authority);

(e) section 57 or 66A (acts permitted on assumptions as to expiry of copyright, &c.).

88   Application of provisions to joint works

(6) The right conferred by section 85 (right to privacy of certain photographs and films) is, in the case of a work made in pursuance of a joint commission, a right of each person who commissioned the making of the work, so that—

(a) the right of each is satisfied if he consents to the act in question, and

(b) a waiver under section 87 by one of them does not affect the rights of the others.

Criminal Justice and Immigration Act 2008

(2008, c. 4)

140 Disclosure of information about convictions etc. of child sex offenders to members of the public

(1) After section 327 of the Criminal Justice Act 2003 (c. 44) insert—

'327A Disclosure of information about convictions etc. of child sex offenders to members of the public.

(1) The responsible authority for each area must, in the course of discharging its functions under arrangements established by it under section 325, consider whether to disclose information in its possession.

(2) In the case mentioned in subsection (3) there is a presumption that the responsible authority should disclose information in its possession about the relevant previous convictions of the offender to the particular member of the public.

(3) The case is where the responsible authority for the area has reasonable cause to believe that—

    (a) a child sex offender managed by it poses a risk in that or any other area of causing serious harm to any particular child or children or to children of any particular description, and

    (b) the disclosure of information about the relevant previous convictions of the offender to the particular member of the public is necessary for the purpose of protecting the particular child or children, or the children of that description, from serious harm caused by the offender.

(4) The presumption under subsection (2) arises whether or not the person to whom the information is disclosed requests the disclosure.

(5) Where the responsible authority makes a disclosure under this section—

    (a) it may disclose such information about the relevant previous convictions of the offender as it considers appropriate to disclose to the member of the public concerned, and

    (b) it may impose conditions for preventing the member of the public concerned from disclosing the information to any other person.

(6) Any disclosure under this section must be made as soon as is reasonably practicable having regard to all the circumstances.

(7) The responsible authority for each area must compile and maintain a record about the decisions it makes in relation to the discharge of its functions under this section.

(8) The record must include the following information—

    (a) the reasons for making a decision to disclose information under this section,

    (b) the reasons for making a decision not to disclose information under this section, and

    (c) the information which is disclosed under this section, any conditions imposed in relation to its further disclosure and the name and address of the person to whom it is disclosed.

(9) Nothing in this section requires or authorises the making of a disclosure which contravenes the Data Protection Act 1998.

(10) This section is not to be taken as affecting any power of any person to disclose any information about a child sex offender.

327B   Section 327A: interpretation

(1) This section applies for the purposes of section 327A.

(2) 'Child' means a person under 18.

(3) 'Child sex offence' means an offence listed in Schedule 34A, whenever committed.

(4) 'Child sex offender' means any person who—

    (a) has been convicted of such an offence,

    (b) has been found not guilty of such an offence by reason of insanity,

    (c) has been found to be under a disability and to have done the act charged against the person in respect of such an offence, or

    (d) has been cautioned in respect of such an offence.

(5) In relation to a responsible authority, references to information about the relevant previous convictions of a child sex offender are references to information about—

     (a) convictions, findings and cautions mentioned in subsection (4)(a) to (d) which relate to the offender, and

     (b) anything under the law of any country or territory outside England and Wales which in the opinion of the responsible authority corresponds to any conviction, finding or caution within paragraph (a) (however described).

(6) References to serious harm caused by a child sex offender are references to serious physical or psychological harm caused by the offender committing any offence listed in any paragraph of Schedule 34A other than paragraphs 1 to 6 (offences under provisions repealed by Sexual Offences Act 2003).

(7) A responsible authority for any area manages a child sex offender if the offender is a person who poses risks in that area which fall to be managed by the authority under the arrangements established by it under section 325.

(8) For the purposes of this section the provisions of section 4 of, and paragraph 3 of Schedule 2 to, the Rehabilitation of Offenders Act 1974 (protection for spent convictions and cautions) are to be disregarded.

(9) In this section "cautioned", in relation to any person and any offence, means—

     (a) cautioned after the person has admitted the offence, or

     (b) reprimanded or warned within the meaning given by section 65 of the Crime and Disorder Act 1998.

(10) Section 135(1), (2)(a) and (c) and (3) of the Sexual Offences Act 2003 (mentally disordered offenders) apply for the purposes of this section as they apply for the purposes of Part 2 of that Act.'

(2) After Schedule 34 to that Act insert the Schedule 34A set out in Schedule 24 to this Act.

Part VIII

Self-regulation of the print media

Press Complaints Commission Code of Practice

(July 2013)

The Press Complaints Commission is charged with enforcing the following Code of Practice which was framed by the newspaper and periodical industry and was ratified by the PCC in December 2011 to include changes taking effect from January 2012.

All members of the press have a duty to maintain the highest professional standards. The Code, which includes this preamble and the public interest exceptions below, sets the benchmark for those ethical standards, protecting both the rights of the individual and the public's right to know. It is the cornerstone of the system of self-regulation to which the industry has made a binding commitment.

It is essential that an agreed code be honoured not only to the letter but in the full spirit. It should not be interpreted so narrowly as to compromise its commitment to respect the rights of the individual, nor so broadly that it constitutes an unnecessary interference with freedom of expression or prevents publication in the public interest.

It is the responsibility of editors and publishers to apply the Code to editorial material in both printed and online versions of publications. They should take care to ensure it is observed rigorously by all editorial staff and external contributors, including non-journalists, in printed and online versions of publications.

Editors should co-operate swiftly with the PCC in the resolution of complaints. Any publication judged to have breached the Code must print the adjudication in full and with due prominence, agreed by the Commission's director, including a headline reference to the PCC.

1 Accuracy
  (i) The Press must take care not to publish inaccurate, misleading or distorted information, including pictures.
 (ii) A significant inaccuracy, misleading statement or distortion once recognised must be corrected, promptly and with due prominence, and—where appropriate—an apology published. In cases involving the Commission prominence should be agreed with the PCC in advance.
(iii) The Press, whilst free to be partisan, must distinguish clearly between comment, conjecture and fact.
 (iv) A publication must report fairly and accurately the outcome of an action for defamation to which it has been a party, unless an agreed settlement states otherwise, or an agreed statement is published.

2 Opportunity to reply
A fair opportunity for reply to inaccuracies must be given when reasonably called for.

3 *Privacy

(i) Everyone is entitled to respect for his or her private and family life, home, health and correspondence, including digital communications.

(ii) Editors will be expected to justify intrusions into any individual's private life without consent. Account will be taken of the complaint's own public disclosures of information.

(iii) It is unacceptable to photograph individuals in a private place without their consent.

Note: Private places are public or private property where there is a reasonable expectation of privacy.

4 *Harassment

(i) Journalists must not engage in intimidation, harassment or persistent pursuit.

(ii) They must not persist in questioning, telephoning, pursuing or photographing individuals once asked to desist; nor remain on their property when asked to leave and must not follow them. If requested, they must identify themselves and whom they represent.

(iii) Editors must ensure these principles are observed by those working for them and take care not to use non-compliant material from other sources.

5 Intrusion into grief or shock

(i) In cases involving personal grief or shock, enquiries and approaches must be made with sympathy and discretion and publication handled sensitively. This should not restrict the right to report legal proceedings, such as inquests.

*(ii) When reporting suicide, care should be taken to avoid excessive detail about the method used.

6 *Children

(i) Young people should be free to complete their time at school without unnecessary intrusion.

(ii) A child under 16 must not be interviewed or photographed on issues involving their own or another child's welfare unless a custodial parent or similarly responsible adult consents.

(iii) Pupils must not be approached or photographed at school without the permission of the school authorities.

(iv) Minors must not be paid for material involving children's welfare, nor parents or guardians for material about their children or wards, unless it is clearly in the child's interest.

(v) Editors must not use the fame, notoriety or position of a parent or guardian as sole justification for publishing details of a child's private life.

7 *Children in sex cases

1. The press must not, even if legally free to do so, identify children under 16 who are victims or witnesses in cases involving sex offences.

2. In any press report of a case involving a sexual offence against a child –

(i) The child must not be identified.

(ii) The adult may be identified.

(iii) The word 'incest' must not be used where a child victim might be identified.

(iv) Care must be taken that nothing in the report implies the relationship between the accused and the child.

8 *Hospitals

(i) Journalists must identify themselves and obtain permission from a responsible executive before entering non-public areas of hospitals or similar institutions to pursue enquiries.

(ii) The restrictions on intruding into privacy are particularly relevant to enquiries about individuals in hospitals or similar institutions.

9   *Reporting of crime

(i)   Relatives or friends of persons convicted or accused of crime should not generally be identified without their consent, unless they are genuinely relevant to the story.

(ii)   Particular regard should be paid to the potentially vulnerable position of children who witness, or are victims of, crime. This should not restrict the right to report legal proceedings.

10   *Clandestine devices and subterfuge

(i)   The press must not seek to obtain or publish material acquired by using hidden cameras or clandestine listening devices; or by intercepting private or mobile telephone calls, messages or emails; or by the unauthorised removal of documents or photographs; or by accessing digitally-held private information without consent.

(ii)   Engaging in misrepresentation or subterfuge, including by agents or intermediaries, can generally be justified only in the public interest and then only when the material cannot be obtained by other means.

11   Victims of sexual assault

The press must not identify victims of sexual assault or publish material likely to contribute to such identification unless there is adequate justification and they are legally free to do so.

12   Discrimination

(i)   The press must avoid prejudicial or pejorative reference to an individual's race, colour, religion, gender, sexual orientation or to any physical or mental illness or disability.

(ii)   Details of an individual's race, colour, religion, sexual orientation, physical or mental illness or disability must be avoided unless genuinely relevant to the story.

13   Financial journalism

(i)   Even where the law does not prohibit it, journalists must not use for their own profit financial information they receive in advance of its general publication, nor should they pass such information to others.

(ii)   They must not write about shares or securities in whose performance they know that they or their close families have a significant financial interest without disclosing the interest to the editor or financial editor.

(iii) They must not buy or sell, either directly or through nominees or agents, shares or securities about which they have written recently or about which they intend to write in the near future.

14   Confidential sources

Journalists have a moral obligation to protect confidential sources of information.

15   Witness payments in criminal trials

(i)   No payment or offer of payment to a witness—or any person who may reasonably be expected to be called as a witness—should be made in any case once proceedings are active as defined by the Contempt of Court Act 1981.

This prohibition lasts until the suspect has been freed unconditionally by police without charge or bail or the proceedings are otherwise discontinued; or has entered a guilty plea to the court; or, in the event of a not guilty plea, the court has announced its verdict.

*(ii) Where proceedings are not yet active but are likely and foreseeable, editors must not make or offer payment to any person who may reasonably be expected to be called as a witness, unless the information concerned ought demonstrably to be published in the public

interest and there is an over-riding need to make or promise payment for this to be done; and all reasonable steps have been taken to ensure no financial dealings influence the evidence those witnesses give. In no circumstances should such payment be conditional on the outcome of a trial.

*(iii) Any payment or offer of payment made to a person later cited to give evidence in proceedings must be disclosed to the prosecution and defence. The witness must be advised of this requirement.

16   *Payment to criminals

(i)   Payment or offers of payment for stories, pictures or information, which seek to exploit a particular crime or to glorify or glamorise crime in general, must not be made directly or via agents to convicted or confessed criminals or to their associates—who may include family, friends and colleagues.

(ii) Editors invoking the public interest to justify payment or offers would need to demonstrate that there was good reason to believe the public interest would be served. If, despite payment, no public interest emerged, then the material should not be published.

The public interest

There may be exceptions to the clauses marked * where they can be demonstrated to be in the public interest.

1. The public interest includes, but is not confined to:
   (i)   Detecting or exposing crime or serious impropriety.
   (ii)   Protecting public health and safety.
   (iii) Preventing the public from being misled by an action or statement of an individual or organisation.
2. There is a public interest in freedom of expression itself.
3. Whenever the public interest is invoked, the PCC will require editors to demonstrate fully that they reasonably believed that publication, or journalistic activity undertaken with a view to publication, would be in the public interest.
4. The PCC will consider the extent to which material is already in the public domain, or will become so.
5. In cases involving children under 16, editors must demonstrate an exceptional public interest to over-ride the normally paramount interest of the child.

National Union of Journalists Code of Conduct*

[2011 Version]

Members of the National Union of Journalists are expected to abide by the following professional principles:

A journalist:

1. At all times upholds and defends the principle of media freedom, the right of freedom of expression and the right of the public to be informed
2. Strives to ensure that information disseminated is honestly conveyed, accurate and fair
3. Does her/his utmost to correct harmful inaccuracies
4. Differentiates between fact and opinion
5. Obtains material by honest, straightforward and open means, with the exception of investigations that are both overwhelmingly in the public interest and which involve evidence that cannot be obtained by straightforward means

* Reproduced with permission from the National Union of Journalists, http://www.nuj.org.uk.

6. Does nothing to intrude into anybody's private life, grief or distress unless justified by overriding consideration of the public interest

7. Protects the identity of sources who supply information in confidence and material gathered in the course of her/his work

8. Resists threats or any other inducements to influence, distort or suppress information and takes no unfair personal advantage of information gained in the course of her/his duties before the information is public knowledge

9. Produces no material likely to lead to hatred or discrimination on the grounds of a person's age, gender, race, colour, creed, legal status, disability, marital status, or sexual orientation

10. Does not by way of statement, voice or appearance endorse by advertisement any commercial product or service save for the promotion of her/his own work or of the medium by which she/he is employed

11. A journalist shall normally seek the consent of an appropriate adult when interviewing or photographing a child for a story about her/his welfare.

12. Avoids plagiarism.

The NUJ believes a journalist has the right to refuse an assignment or be identified as the author of editorial that would break the letter or spirit of the code. The NUJ will fully support any journalist disciplined for asserting her/his right to act according to the code.

Enterprise and Regulatory Reform Act 2013

(2013, c. 24)

96 Royal Charters: requirements for Parliamentary approval
Where a body is established by Royal Charter after 1 March 2013 with functions relating to the carrying on of an industry, no recommendation may be made to Her Majesty in Council to amend the body's Charter or dissolve the body unless any requirements included in the Charter on the date it is granted for Parliament to approve the amendment or dissolution have been met.

Crime and Courts Act 2013

(2013, c. 22)

Publishers of news-related material: damages and costs

34 Awards of exemplary damages
(1) This section applies where—
  (a) a relevant claim is made against a person ('the defendant'),
  (b) the defendant was a relevant publisher at the material time,
  (c) the claim is related to the publication of news-related material, and
  (d) the defendant is found liable in respect of the claim.
(2) Exemplary damages may not be awarded against the defendant in respect of the claim if the defendant was a member of an approved regulator at the material time.
(3) But the court may disregard subsection (2) if—
  (a) the approved regulator imposed a penalty on the defendant in respect of the defendant's conduct or decided not to do so,
  (b) the court considers, in light of the information available to the approved regulator when imposing the penalty or deciding not to impose one, that the regulator was manifestly irrational in imposing the penalty or deciding not to impose one, and

(c) the court is satisfied that, but for subsection (2), it would have made an award of exemplary damages under this section against the defendant.

(4) Where the court is not prevented from making an award of exemplary damages by subsection (2) (whether because that subsection does not apply or the court is permitted to disregard that subsection as a result of subsection (3)), the court—

(a) may make an award of exemplary damages if it considers it appropriate to do so in all the circumstances of the case, but

(b) may do so only under this section.

(5) Exemplary damages may be awarded under this section only if they are claimed.

(6) Exemplary damages may be awarded under this section only if the court is satisfied that—

(a) the defendant's conduct has shown a deliberate or reckless disregard of an outrageous nature for the claimant's rights,

(b) the conduct is such that the court should punish the defendant for it, and

(c) other remedies would not be adequate to punish that conduct.

(7) Exemplary damages may be awarded under this section whether or not another remedy is granted.

(8) The decision on the question of—

(a) whether exemplary damages are to be awarded under this section, or

(b) the amount of such damages,

must not be left to a jury.

35 Relevant considerations

(1) This section applies where the court is deciding whether the circumstances of the case make it appropriate for exemplary damages to be awarded under section 34.

(2) The court must have regard to the principle that exemplary damages must not usually be awarded if, at any time before the decision comes to be made, the defendant has been convicted of an offence involving the conduct complained of.

(3) The court must take account of the following—

(a) whether membership of an approved regulator was available to the defendant at the material time;

(b) if such membership was available, the reasons for the defendant not being a member;

(c) so far as relevant in the case of the conduct complained of, whether internal compliance procedures of a satisfactory nature were in place and, if so, the extent to which they were adhered to in that case.

(4) The reference in subsection (3)(c) to 'internal compliance procedures' being in place is a reference to any procedures put in place by the defendant for the purpose of ensuring that—

(a) material is not obtained by or on behalf of the defendant in an inappropriate way, and

(b) material is not published by the defendant in inappropriate circumstances.

(5) The court may regard deterring the defendant and others from similar conduct as an object of punishment.

(6) This section is not to be read as limiting the power of the court to take account of any other matters it considers relevant to its decision.

36 Amount of exemplary damages

(1) This section applies where the court decides to award exemplary damages under section 34.

(2) The court must have regard to these principles in determining the amount of exemplary damages—

(a) the amount must not be more than the minimum needed to punish the defendant for the conduct complained of;

(b) the amount must be proportionate to the seriousness of the conduct.

(3) The court must take account of these matters in determining the amount of exemplary damages—

(a) the nature and extent of any loss or harm caused, or intended to be caused, by the defendant's conduct;

(b) the nature and extent of any benefit the defendant derived or intended to derive from such conduct.

(4) The court may regard deterring the defendant and others from similar conduct as an object of punishment.

(5) This section is not to be read as limiting the power of the court to take account of any other matters it considers relevant to its decision.

37 Multiple claimants

(1) This section applies where a relevant publisher—

(a) is a defendant to a relevant claim, and

(b) is found liable to two or more persons in respect of the claim ('the persons affected').

(2) In deciding whether to award exemplary damages under section 34 or the amount of such damages to award (whether to one or more of the persons affected), the court must take account of any settlement or compromise by any persons of a claim in respect of the conduct.

(3) But the court may take account of any such settlement or compromise only if the defendant agrees.

(4) If the court awards exemplary damages under section 34 to two or more of the persons affected, the total amount awarded must be such that it does not punish the defendant excessively

(5) If the court awards exemplary damages under section 34 to one or more of the persons affected, no later claim may be made for exemplary damages as regards the conduct.

38 Multiple defendants

(1) Any liability of two or more persons for exemplary damages awarded under section 34 is several (and not joint or joint and several).

(2) Subsection (1) has effect subject to the law relating to the liability of a partner for the conduct of another partner.

(3) Where the liability of two or more persons for exemplary damages is several, no contribution in respect of the damages may be recovered by any of them under section 1 of the Civil Liability (Contribution) Act 1978.

39 Awards of aggravated damages

(1) This section applies where—

(a) a relevant claim is made against a person ('the defendant'),

(b) the defendant was a relevant publisher at the material time,

(c) the claim is related to the publication of news-related material, and

(d) the defendant is found liable in respect of the claim.

(2) Aggravated damages may be awarded against the defendant only to compensate for mental distress and not for purposes of punishment.

(3) In this section, 'aggravated damages' means damages that were commonly called aggravated before the passing of this Act and which—

(a) are awarded against a person in respect of the person's motive or exceptional conduct, but

(b) are not exemplary damages or restitutionary damages.

(4) Nothing in this section is to be read as implying that, in cases where this section does not apply, aggravated damages may be awarded for purposes of punishment.

40 Awards of costs

(1) This section applies where—

(a) a relevant claim is made against a person ('the defendant'),

(b) the defendant was a relevant publisher at the material time, and

(c) the claim is related to the publication of news-related material.

(2) If the defendant was a member of an approved regulator at the time when the claim was commenced (or was unable to be a member at that time for reasons beyond the defendant's control or it

would have been unreasonable in the circumstances for the defendant to have been a member at that time), the court must not award costs against the defendant unless satisfied that—

    (a) the issues raised by the claim could not have been resolved by using an arbitration scheme of the approved regulator, or

    (b) it is just and equitable in all the circumstances of the case to award costs against the defendant.

(3) If the defendant was not a member of an approved regulator at the time when the claim was commenced (but would have been able to be a member at that time and it would have been reasonable in the circumstances for the defendant to have been a member at that time), the court must award costs against the defendant unless satisfied that—

    (a) the issues raised by the claim could not have been resolved by using an arbitration scheme of the approved regulator (had the defendant been a member), or

    (b) it is just and equitable in all the circumstances of the case to make a different award of costs or make no award of costs.

(4) The Secretary of State must take steps to put in place arrangements for protecting the position in costs of parties to relevant claims who have entered into agreements under section 58 of the Courts and Legal Services Act 1990.

(5) This section is not to be read as limiting any power to make rules of court.

(6) This section does not apply until such time as a body is first recognised as an approved regulator.

41 Meaning of 'relevant publisher'

(1) In sections 34 to 40, 'relevant publisher' means a person who, in the course of a business (whether or not carried on with a view to profit), publishes news-related material—

    (a) which is written by different authors, and

    (b) which is to any extent subject to editorial control.

This is subject to subsections (5) and (6).

(2) News-related material is 'subject to editorial control' if there is a person (whether or not the publisher of the material) who has editorial or equivalent responsibility for—

    (a) the content of the material,

    (b) how the material is to be presented, and

    (c) the decision to publish it.

(3) A person who is the operator of a website is not to be taken as having editorial or equivalent responsibility for the decision to publish any material on the site, or for content of the material, if the person did not post the material on the site.

(4) The fact that the operator of the website may moderate statements posted on it by others does not matter for the purposes of subsection (3).

(5) A person is not a 'relevant publisher' if the person is specified by name in Schedule 15.

(6) A person is not a 'relevant publisher' in so far as the person's publication of news-related material is in a capacity or case of a description specified in Schedule 15.

(7) But a person who is not a 'relevant publisher' as a result of paragraph 8 of that Schedule (micro-businesses) is nevertheless to be regarded as such if the person was a member of an approved regulator at the material time.

42 Other interpretative provisions

(1) This section applies for the purposes of sections 34 to 41.

(2) 'Approved regulator' means a body recognised as a regulator of relevant publishers.

(3) For the purposes of subsection (2), a body is 'recognised' as a regulator of relevant publishers if it is so recognised by any body established by Royal Charter (whether established before or after the

coming into force of this section) with the purpose of carrying on activities relating to the recognition of independent regulators of relevant publishers.

    (4) 'Relevant claim' means a civil claim made in respect of any of the following—

        (a) libel;

        (b) slander;

        (c) breach of confidence;

        (d) misuse of private information;

        (e) malicious falsehood;

        (f) harassment.

    (5) For the purposes of subsection (4)—

        (a) the reference to a claim made in respect of the misuse of private information does not include a reference to a claim made by virtue of section 13 of the Data Protection Act 1998 (damage or distress suffered as a result of a contravention of a requirement of that Act);

        (b) the reference to a claim made in respect of harassment is a reference to a claim made under the Protection from Harassment Act 1997.

    (6) The 'material time', in relation to a relevant claim, is the time of the events giving rise to the claim.

    (7) 'News-related material' means—

        (a) news or information about current affairs,

        (b) opinion about matters relating to the news or current affairs, or

        (c) gossip about celebrities, other public figures or other persons in the news.

    (8) A relevant claim is related to the publication of news-related material if the claim results from—

        (a) the publication of news-related material, or

        (b) activities carried on in connection with the publication of such material (whether or not the material is in fact published).

    (9) A reference to the 'publication' of material is a reference to publication—

        (a) on a website,

        (b) in hard copy, or

        (c) by any other means;

and references to a person who 'publishes' material are to be read accordingly.

    (10) A reference to 'conduct' includes a reference to omissions; and a reference to a person's conduct includes a reference to a person's conduct after the events giving rise to the claim concerned.

Draft Royal Charter on Self-Regulation of the Press

(March 2013)

Department of Culture, Media and Sport

EXTRACTS

AND WHEREAS the [Leveson] Report of the Inquiry recommended that for an effective system of self-regulation to be established, all those parts of the press which are significant news publishers should become members of an independent regulatory body:

    AND WHEREAS the independent regulatory body which is intended to be the successor to the Press Complaints Commission should put forward the Editors' Code of Practice as its initial code of standards:

AND WHEREAS the Report of the Inquiry recommended that there should be a mechanism to recognise and certify an independent regulatory body or bodies for the press, and that the responsibility for such recognition and certification should rest with a recognition body:

AND WHEREAS the Report of the Inquiry recommended that such a recognition body should not be involved in the regulation of the press:

1. Incorporation

1.1. There shall be a body corporate known as the Recognition Panel.

1.2. There shall be a Board of the Recognition Panel which shall be responsible for the conduct and management of the Recognition Panel's business and affairs, in accordance with the further terms of this Charter.

1.3. The members of the Board of the Recognition Panel shall be the only Members of the body corporate, but membership of the body corporate shall not enable any individual to act otherwise than through the Board to which he belongs.

2. Term of Charter

2.1. This Charter shall take effect from [date subsequent to the date of sealing].

2.2. This Charter shall continue in force unless and until it is dissolved, in accordance with Article 10, by Us, Our Heirs or Successors in Council, or otherwise.

3. Purpose

3.1. The Purpose for which the Recognition Panel is established and incorporated is to carry on activities relating to the recognition of Regulators in accordance with the terms of this Charter.

3.2. Provisions and definitions to assist in the interpretation of this Charter are contained in Schedule 4 (Interpretation).

4. Functions

4.1. The Recognition Panel has the general functions, in accordance with the terms of this Charter, of:

   a) determining applications for recognition from Regulators;
   b) reviewing whether a Regulator which has been granted recognition shall continue to be recognised;
   c) withdrawing recognition from a Regulator where the Recognition Panel is satisfied that the Regulator ceases to be entitled to recognition; and
   d) reporting on any success or failure of the recognition system.

4.2. In performing the general functions in Article 4.1 the Board shall apply the Scheme of Recognition set out in Schedule 2 (Scheme of Recognition).

4.3. The Board shall manage the assets of the Recognition Panel efficiently and effectively so as to best achieve the Recognition Panel's Purpose.

4.4. The functions of the Recognition Panel shall be public functions.

5. Appointments and Membership

5.1. The Board of the Recognition Panel shall consist of a Chair and no fewer than 4 and no more than 8 other Members.

5.2. Appointments to the Board of the Recognition Panel, and the terms of such appointments, shall be regulated by Schedule 1 (Appointments and Terms of Membership).

6. Governance

6.1. Subject to the terms of this Article, the Board shall determine and regulate its own procedures for conducting its business and discharging its functions under this Charter.

6.2. The Board shall not delegate the following decisions:

a) A decision to recognise or withdraw recognition from a Regulator in accordance with the Scheme of Recognition;

b) A decision to undertake an ad hoc review in accordance with the Scheme of Recognition.

6.3. The Board shall put in place arrangements by which a Member can:

a) register his interests or any other matter he considers relevant to the Purpose of the Recognition Panel;

b) determine whether any interest he holds, directly or indirectly, gives rise to a conflict of interest;

c) declare such conflicts to the Board; and

d) absent himself from decision-making where the Board determines it is appropriate so to do.

6.4. The Board shall publish its procedures.

7. Staff

. . .

7.3. None of the following may be a member of staff employed by the Recognition Panel or be otherwise engaged by the Recognition Panel in a similar capacity (whether on a full-time or part-time basis):

a) a relevant publisher or someone otherwise involved in the publication of news or current affairs in the United Kingdom;

b) a person who is part of the governing body of a relevant publisher;

c) the chair or member of the Board of a Regulator;

d) a member of staff working for a Regulator or relevant publisher;

e) a civil servant; or

f) a serving or former member of the House of Commons, the House of Lords, the Scottish Parliament, the Northern Ireland Assembly or the National Assembly for Wales.

8. Powers

8.1. The Recognition Panel, acting through the Board, may do all things that are lawful as may further the Purpose of the Recognition Panel . . .

9. Charter Amendment

9.1. A provision of this Charter may be added to, supplemented, varied or omitted (in whole or in part) if, and only if the requirements of Article 9.2 are met.

9.2. Before any proposal (made by any person) to add to, supplement, vary or omit (in whole or in part) a provision of this Charter ('proposed change') can take effect a draft of the proposed change must have been laid before Parliament, and approved by a resolution of each House. For this purpose 'approved' means that at least two- thirds of the members of the House in question who vote on the motion do so in support of it.

9.3. The Recognition Panel may only propose a change to the terms of this Charter if a resolution has been passed unanimously by all of the Members of the Board, who shall determine the matter at a meeting duly convened for that purpose.

9.4. The provisions of Article 9.2 do not apply to a proposed change to the Charter that is required merely to correct a clerical or typographical error.

9.5. Provided the terms of Article 9.2 have been met, any such addition, supplement, variation or omission shall, when approved by Us, Our Heirs or Successors in Council, become effective so that this Charter shall thenceforth continue and operate as though it had been originally granted and made accordingly.

10. Dissolution

10.1. This Charter, and the Recognition Panel created by it, shall not be dissolved unless information about the proposed dissolution has been presented to Parliament, and that proposal has been approved by a resolution of each House. For this purpose 'approved' means that at least two-thirds of the members of the House in question who vote on the motion do so in support of it.

10.2. The Recognition Panel may, if it appears necessary to the Board (acting unanimously) to do so:

  (a) surrender this Charter (and, provided the terms of Article 10.1 have been complied with, thereafter dissolve the Recognition Panel) with the permission of Us, Our Heirs or Successors in Council and upon such terms as We or They consider fit . . .

11. Money

11.1. The Exchequer shall grant to the Recognition Panel such sums of money as are sufficient to enable the Board to commence its operations and thereafter fulfil its Purpose for the first three years after the date upon which this Charter becomes effective. The grant of such monies shall be on such terms as Managing Public Money requires . . .

11.3. The Board shall prepare, consult publicly upon, and publish a scheme for charging fees to Regulators in relation to the functions of recognition and review, to come into force from the third anniversary of the date upon which this Charter becomes effective. Any fee charged shall comply with Article 11.4. The aim of the scheme shall be for the Recognition Panel to recover its full costs in determining applications for recognition and for conducting cyclical reviews, as appropriate . . .

11.7. In the event that the Board considers that its income (from whatever source received) is likely to be insufficient to meet its expenditure relating to (a) legal or other expenses arising from litigation or threatened litigation, (b) ad hoc reviews or (c) wholly unforeseen events, it shall have the right to request further reasonable sums from the Exchequer. In response to such a request, the Exchequer shall grant such sums to the Recognition Panel as it considers necessary to ensure that the Purpose of the Recognition Panel is not frustrated by a lack of funding . . .

13. Reports

13.1. As soon as practicable after the end of each financial year the Board must prepare and publish a report about the activities of the Recognition Panel during that year, including whether it has granted recognition to, or withdrawn it from a Regulator. The Board shall make arrangements for the Report to be laid before Parliament.

15. Liabilities

15.1. Each and every Member of the Board and of the Appointments Committee shall be indemnified from the assets of the Recognition Panel against any liability incurred by him by reason of any act or thing done by him in the proper discharge of his responsibilities, office or duty under this Charter.
IN WITNESS whereof . . . .

SCHEDULE 1

APPOINTMENTS AND TERMS OF MEMBERSHIP

1.   Initial Appointments to the Board of the Recognition Panel

1.1. This paragraph regulates the manner in which the initial appointments to the Board shall be made. Thereafter, upon any further appointment being required (whether of a successor or additional Member) the terms of paragraph 7 (further appointments) shall apply.

1.2. The appointment of the first Chair of the Board together with at least 4 initial other Members shall follow a fair and open process, to be conducted in the manner, and by the persons, described in this paragraph, and paragraphs 2 (appointments committee) 3 (criteria for appointment) and 4 (commissioner for public appointments).

1.3. The responsibility for identifying and thereafter appointing the Chair of the Board shall be that of an Appointments Committee, constituted in accordance with paragraph 2, and the Appointments Committee shall ensure that the Chair is identified and appointed first, before the appointment of any other Members of the Board.

1.4. The other initial Members of the Board shall be identified and appointed by the Appointments Committee, acting together with the Chair of the Board.

2. Appointments Committee [subject to approval of CPA]

2.1. The Commissioner for Public Appointments shall appoint the Appointments Committee, which shall consist of four people.

2.2. The Chair of the Committee shall be a Public Appointments Assessor (appointed pursuant to the Public Appointments Order in Council 2002 or a succeeding Order).

2.3. In order to ensure the independence of the Appointments Committee, a person shall be ineligible to be appointed if he:

a) is a serving editor of a publication of a relevant publisher;

b) is a relevant publisher or otherwise involved in the publication of news or current affairs in the United Kingdom;

c) is a member of the House of Commons, the Scottish Parliament, the Northern Ireland Assembly, the National Assembly for Wales the European Parliament or the House of Lords (but only if, in the case of the House of Lords, the member holds or has held within the previous 5 years an official affiliation with a political party); or

d) is a Minister of the Crown, a Scottish Minister, a Northern Ireland Executive Minister, or a Welsh Government Minister.

3. Criteria for Appointment to the Board of the Recognition Panel

3.1. In making any appointment to the Board under this Schedule, the matters set out in this paragraph shall be used for:

a) determining the overall nature of the membership of the Board; and

b) assessing the suitability of any particular person to be appointed as the Chair or a Member of the Board.

3.2. The criteria for appointment as a Member of the Board are:

a) That every Member shall have:

i. senior board level experience in a public or private sector organisation, including significant leadership responsibility, or equivalent; and

ii. an understanding of the context within which a Regulator will operate.

b) That at least one Member shall have:

i. legal qualifications and skills, together with an understanding of the legal framework within which the Board must operate;

ii. financial skills, including experience of delivering value for money; or

iii. experience of public policy making, particularly in the context of consumer rights.

3.3. In order to ensure the independence of the Board, a person shall be ineligible to be appointed, or to remain as, a Member of the Board if he:

a) is or has been an editor of a publication of a relevant publisher;

b) is a relevant publisher or otherwise involved in the publication of news or current affairs in the United Kingdom;

c) is a member of the House of Commons, the Scottish Parliament, the Northern Ireland Assembly, the National Assembly for Wales, the European Parliament or the House of Lords (but only if, in the case of the House of Lords, the member holds or has held within the previous 5 years an official affiliation with a political party); or

d) is a Minister of the Crown, a Scottish Minister, a Northern Ireland Executive Minister, or a Welsh Government Minister.

4.   Commissioner for Public Appointments [subject to approval of CPA]

4.1. After the initial appointments made by the Appointments Committee, and where further appointments to the Board are contemplated, pursuant to paragraph 7, the requirements of paragraph 4.2 shall apply.

4.2. Before a person selected for appointment to the Board (other than by the Appointments Committee) can be appointed formally, the Commissioner for Public Appointments shall be asked to consider whether the process followed in the selection of that person was fair and open, and, if he considers that it was, to confirm that this was the case, in writing. In order to be in a position to give such confirmation, the Commissioner may specify terms to the Board as to how it conducts a further appointments process.

4.3. No appointment to the Board shall be valid unless (a) it has been made by the Appointments Committee or (b) the confirmation described in paragraph 4.2 has been published by the Commissioner.

5.   Terms of Membership

5.1. Each Member, including the Chair, shall hold and vacate his office in accordance with the terms of this Charter.

5.2. Each Member shall be eligible to serve for an initial term of 5 years and shall be eligible to reappointment for a further period of up to 3 years. The Board shall have regard to the importance of staggering the reappointment and retirement of Members to deliver appropriate continuity in the performance of its functions.

5.3. The Board may make arrangements to pay or make provision for paying, in respect of any Member, such amounts by way of allowances or gratuities as the Board determines. The amount of any such allowances or gratuities shall be set having regard to the prevailing rates payable to the members of boards of public sector bodies.

6.   Termination

6.1. Any Member of the Board may resign by giving notice in writing to the Recognition Panel.

6.2. If the Board is satisfied (which shall require a majority of two thirds of the Members entitled to vote to concur), that a Member is unwilling, unable or unfit to discharge the functions of a Member of the Board under this Charter, that Member shall be duly dismissed and notified in writing of this fact, together with reasons. The Member concerned shall not be entitled to vote on this matter and the Board may make further provision as to the operation of this paragraph under Article 6 (governance) of this Charter.

7.   Further Appointments

7.1. Upon:

a)   any person, including the Chair, ceasing to be a Member of the Board, for any reason, or

b)   the Board determining that the appointment of an additional Member is desirable (having regard to the limitation on numbers imposed by Article 5.1) the process for appointing a successor or additional Member (as appropriate) shall be fair and open, and meet the requirements of paragraphs 3 (criteria for appointments) and 4 (commissioner for public appointments). The responsibility for making such an appointment (including selection) shall lie with the serving Members of the Board, and not the Appointments Committee. The Commissioner for Public Appointments shall be consulted by the Board about the process for making further appointments under this paragraph.

8.   Interpretation

8.1. Schedule 4 to this Charter shall be used in interpreting this Schedule. 8.2. A reference to a paragraph means to a paragraph in this Schedule.

SCHEDULE 2

SCHEME OF RECOGNITION

In the exercise of the functions set out in Article 4 of this Charter the following Scheme of Recognition shall apply:

Recognition

1. The Board of the Recognition Panel shall grant recognition to a Regulator if the Board is satisfied that the Regulator meets the recognition criteria numbered 1 to 23 in Schedule 3, and in making its decision on whether the Regulator meets those criteria it shall consider the concepts of effectiveness, fairness and objectivity of standards, independence and transparency of enforcement and compliance, credible powers and remedies, reliable funding and effective accountability, as articulated in the Leveson Report, Part K, Chapter 7, Section 4 ('Voluntary independent self-regulation').

2. The 'recognition criteria' means the requirements set out in Schedule 3 to this Charter.

3. Nothing in the recognition criteria shall be interpreted in a manner which conflicts with any regulatory obligation imposed on a Regulator. A regulatory obligation is one that (a) regulates the manner in which the Regulator is required to operate, (b) is contained in legislation and (c) applies as a matter of general law to bodies of the legal class to which the Regulator belongs.

4. The Board of the Recognition Panel, in determining an application by a Regulator for recognition, may but need not, take into account any of recommendations 34 to 36 (inclusive), 38, 43, 44 to 45 (inclusive) and 47 in the Summary of Recommendations of the Leveson Report. Where the Recognition Panel is satisfied that a Regulator meets the recognition criteria it shall not refuse to grant recognition to that Regulator by reason of a failure to comply with any of these specified recommendations.

Cyclical Reviews

5. The Board of the Recognition Panel must review the recognition of a Regulator as soon as practicable after:

    a. the end of the period of two years beginning with the day of the recognition,

    b. the end of the period of three years after that period, and

    c. the end of each subsequent period of three years.

6. As part of its cyclical review of a Regulator the Board of the Recognition Panel may:

    a. call for (or receive voluntarily from a Regulator) evidence from that Regulator about the fairness, effectiveness and sustainability of its arbitral process and its complaints handling (to the extent that this interacts with the arbitral process), including from any assessment of these arrangements that the Regulator has undertaken, and

    b. seek evidence on the matter from third parties.

7. Where the Board has received such evidence as part of a cyclical review, it shall consider that evidence, and publish its conclusions on the fairness, effectiveness and sustainability of the Regulator's arbitral process. Such conclusions may include recommendations about or revisions to the Recognition Panel's policies and guidance on the operation of criterion 22 (published in accordance with paragraph 13 (policies and guidance) of this Schedule).

Ad hoc Reviews

8. The Board of the Recognition Panel may review the recognition of a Regulator at any other time if it thinks that:

    a. there are exceptional circumstances that make it necessary so to do, having regard, in particular, to whether there have been serious breaches of the recognition criteria; and

    b. there is a significant public interest in a review of the Regulator's recognition being undertaken.

9. Where the Board proposes to carry out a review in such exceptional circumstances it must give reasonable notice in writing of its proposal to the Regulator, and must specify its reasons for the proposal.

General

10. The Board of the Recognition Panel must:

    a. prepare and publish a report of any review it conducts, whether of a cyclical or exceptional nature; and

    b. inform Parliament and the public as soon as practicable if, on the first anniversary of the commencement of this Charter and thereafter annually if:

        i. there is no recognised regulator for a continuous period of 3 months after the first anniversary of the commencement of this Charter; or

        ii. in the opinion of the Recognition Panel, the system of regulation does not cover all significant news publishers.

Withdrawal

11. The Board of the Recognition Panel may withdraw recognition from a Regulator at that body's request, or where, following a review, the Board is satisfied that:

    a. the Regulator is not meeting the recognition criteria; or

    b. the Board has insufficient information to determine whether or to what extent the Regulator is meeting those criteria.

12. The Board of the Recognition Panel may not withdraw recognition from a Regulator unless the Board has given the Regulator at least three months' notice in writing of its proposal to do so. Any such notice may be cancelled before the expiry of the period of 3 months.

Policies and Guidance

13. The Board of the Recognition Panel shall from time to time publish policies, guidance and information, as it thinks appropriate, about the manner in which it proposes to conduct the Scheme of Recognition, including material relating to:

    a. the making, processing and administration of applications (including for cyclical reviews);

    b. the conduct of ad hoc reviews; and

    c. the payment of any relevant fees.

SCHEDULE 3

RECOGNITION CRITERIA

The following requirements are the recognition criteria for the Scheme of Recognition established under Article 4 of, and Schedule 2 to, this Charter:

1. An independent self-regulatory body should be governed by an independent Board. In order to ensure the independence of the body, the Chair and members of the Board must be appointed in a genuinely open, transparent and independent way, without any influence from industry or Government. For the avoidance of doubt, the industry's activities in establishing a self-regulatory body, and its participation in making appointments to the Board in accordance with criteria 2 to 5; or its financing of the self- regulatory body, shall not constitute influence by the industry in breach of this criterion.

2. The Chair of the Board (who is subject to the restrictions of criterion 5(d), (e) and (f)) can only be appointed if nominated by an appointment panel. The selection of that panel must itself be conducted in an appropriately independent way and must, itself, be independent of the industry and of Government.

3. The appointment panel:

    a) should be appointed in an independent, fair and open way;

    b) should contain a substantial majority of members who are demonstrably independent of the press;

    c) should include at least one person with a current understanding and experience of the press;

    d) should include no more than one current editor of a publication that could be a member of the body.

4. The nomination process for the appointment of the Board should also be an independent process, and the composition of the Board should include people with relevant expertise. The appointment panel may only nominate as many people as there are vacancies on the Board (including the Chair), and the Board shall accept all nominations. The requirement for independence means that there should be no serving editors on the Board.

5. The members of the Board should be appointed only following nomination by the same appointment panel that nominates the Chair, together with the Chair (once appointed), and should:

a) be nominated by a process which is fair and open;

b) comprise a majority of people who are independent of the press;

c) include a sufficient number of people with experience of the industry who may include former editors and senior or academic journalists;

d) not include any serving editor;

e) not include any serving member of the House of Commons, the Scottish Parliament, the Northern Ireland Assembly, the National Assembly for Wales, the European Parliament or the House of Lords (but only if, in the case of the House of Lords, the member holds or has held within the previous 5 years an official affiliation with a political party) or a Minister of the Crown, a Scottish Minister, a Northern Ireland Executive Minister or a Welsh Government Minister; and

f) in the view of the appointment panel, be a person who can act fairly and impartially in the decision-making of the Board.

6. Funding for the system should be settled in agreement between the industry and the Board, taking into account the cost of fulfilling the obligations of the regulator and the commercial pressures on the industry. There should be an indicative budget which the Board certifies is adequate for the purpose. Funding settlements should cover a four or five year period and should be negotiated well in advance.

7. The standards code which is the responsibility of the Code Committee, must be approved by the Board or remitted to the Code Committee with reasons. The Code Committee will be appointed by the Board, in accordance with best practices for public appointments, and comprised of equal proportions of independent members, serving journalists (being national or regional journalists, or, where relevant to the membership of the self-regulatory body, local or on-line journalists) and serving editors. There will be a biennial public consultation by the Code Committee, the results of which must be considered openly with the Board.

8. The code must take into account the importance of freedom of speech, the interests of the public (including but not limited to the public interest in detecting or exposing crime or serious impropriety, protecting public health and safety and preventing the public from being seriously misled), the need for journalists to protect confidential sources of information, and the rights of individuals. Specifically, it must cover standards of:

a) conduct, especially in relation to the treatment of other people in the process of obtaining material;

b) appropriate respect for privacy where there is no sufficient public interest justification for breach; and

c) accuracy, and the need to avoid misrepresentation.

8A. A self-regulatory body should provide advice to the public in relation to issues concerning the press and the standards code, along with a service to warn the press, and other relevant parties such as broadcasters and press photographers, when an individual has made it clear that they do not welcome press intrusion.

8B. A self-regulatory body should make it clear that subscribers will be held strictly accountable under the standards code for any material that they publish, including photographs, however sourced. This criterion does not include advertising content.

8C. A self-regulatory body should provide non-binding guidance on the interpretation of the public interest that justifies what would otherwise constitute a breach of the standards code. This must be framed in the context of the different provisions of the code relating to the public interest.

8D. A self-regulatory body should establish a whistleblowing hotline for those who feel that they are being asked to do things which are contrary to the standards code.

9. The Board should require, of those who subscribe, appropriate internal governance processes (for dealing with complaints and compliance with the standards code), transparency on what governance processes they have in place, and notice of any failures in compliance, together with details of steps taken to deal with failures in compliance.

10. The Board should require all those who subscribe to have an adequate and speedy complaint handling mechanism; it should encourage those who wish to complain to do so through that mechanism and should not receive complaints directly unless or until the internal complaints system has been engaged without the complaint being resolved in an appropriate time.

11. The Board should have the power to hear and decide on complaints about breach of the standards code by those who subscribe. The Board will need to have the discretion not to look into complaints if they feel that the complaint is without justification, is an attempt to argue a point of opinion rather than a standards code breach, or is simply an attempt to lobby. The Board should have the power (but not necessarily the duty) to hear complaints:

   a) from anyone personally and directly affected by the alleged breach of the standards code, or

   b) where there is an alleged breach of the code and there is public interest in the Board giving consideration to the complaint from a representative group affected by the alleged breach, or

   c) from a third party seeking to ensure accuracy of published information.

In the case of third party complaints the views of the party most closely involved should be taken into account.

12. Decisions on complaints should be the ultimate responsibility of the Board, advised by complaints handling officials to whom appropriate delegations may be made.

12A. The Board should be prepared to allow a complaint to be brought prior to legal proceedings being commenced. Challenges to that approach (and applications to stay) can be decided on the merits.

13. Serving editors should not be members of any Committee advising the Board on complaints and should not play any role in determining the outcome of an individual complaint. Any such Committee should have a composition broadly reflecting that of the main Board, with a majority of people who are independent of the press.

14. It should continue to be the case that complainants are able to bring complaints free of charge.

15. In relation to complaints, where a negotiated outcome between a complainant and a subscriber (pursuant to criterion 10) has failed, the Board should have the power to direct appropriate remedial action for breach of standards and the publication of corrections and apologies. Although remedies are essentially about correcting the record for individuals, the power to direct a correction and an apology must apply equally in relation to:

   a. individual standards breaches; and

   b. groups of people as defined in criterion 11 where there is no single identifiable individual who has been affected; and

   c. matters of fact where there is no single identifiable individual who has been affected.

16. In the event of no agreement between a complainant and a subscriber (pursuant to criterion 10), the power to direct the nature, extent and placement of corrections and apologies should lie with the Board.

17. The Board should not have the power to prevent publication of any material, by anyone, at any time although (in its discretion) it should be able to offer a service of advice to editors of subscribing publications relating to code compliance.

18. The Board, being an independent self-regulatory body, should have authority to examine issues on its own initiative and have sufficient powers to carry out investigations both into suspected serious or systemic breaches of the code and failures to comply with directions of the Board. The

investigations process must be simple and credible and those who subscribe must be required to co-operate with any such investigation.

19. The Board should have the power to impose appropriate and proportionate sanctions (including but not limited to financial sanctions up to 1% of turnover attributable to the publication concerned with a maximum of £1,000,000) on any subscriber found to be responsible for serious or systemic breaches of the standards code or governance requirements of the body. The Board should have sufficient powers to require appropriate information from subscribers in order to ascertain the turnover that is attributable to a publication irrespective of any particular accounting arrangements of the publication or subscriber. The sanctions that should be available should include power to require publication of corrections, if the breaches relate to accuracy, or apologies if the breaches relate to other provisions of the code.

19A. The Board should establish a ring-fenced enforcement fund, into which receipts from financial sanctions could be paid, for the purpose of funding investigations.

20. The Board should have both the power and a duty to ensure that all breaches of the standards code that it considers are recorded as such and that proper data is kept that records the extent to which complaints have been made and their outcome; this information should be made available to the public in a way that allows understanding of the compliance record of each title.

21. The Board should publish an Annual Report identifying:
   a) the body's subscribers, identifying any significant changes in subscriber numbers;
   b) the number of:
      (i) complaints it has handled, making clear how many of them are multiple complaints,
      (ii) articles in respect of which it has considered complaints to be without merit, and
      (iii) articles in respect of which it has considered complaints to be with merit, and the outcomes reached, in aggregate for all subscribers and individually in relation to each subscriber;
   c) a summary of any investigations carried out and the result of them;
   d) a report on the adequacy and effectiveness of compliance processes and procedures adopted by subscribers; and
   e) information about the extent to which the arbitration service has been used.

22. The Board should provide an arbitral process for civil legal claims against subscribers which:
   a) complies with the Arbitration Act 1996 ('the Act');
   b) provides suitable powers for the arbitrator to ensure the process operates fairly and quickly, and on an inquisitorial basis (so far as possible);
   c) contains transparent arrangements for claims to be struck out, for legitimate reasons (including on frivolous or vexatious grounds);
   d) directs appropriate pre-publication matters to the courts;
   e) operates under the principle that arbitration should be free for complainants to use;
   f) ensures that the parties should each bear their own costs, subject to a successful complainant's costs being recoverable (having regard to section 60[1] of the Act and any applicable caps on recoverable costs); and
   g) overall, is inexpensive for all parties.

23. The membership of a regulatory body should be open to all publishers on fair, reasonable and non-discriminatory terms, including making membership potentially available on different terms for different types of publisher.

---

[1] Section 60 (Agreement to pay costs in any event): An agreement which has the effect that a party is to pay the whole or part of the costs of the arbitration in any event is only valid if made after the dispute in question has arisen.

SCHEDULE 4

INTERPRETATION

Key definitions

1. For the purposes of this Charter:
   a) 'Regulator' means an independent body formed by or on behalf of relevant publishers for the purpose of conducting regulatory activities in relation to their publications;
   b) 'relevant publisher' means a person (other than a broadcaster) who publishes in the United Kingdom:
       i. a newspaper or magazine containing news-related material, or
       ii. a website containing news-related material (whether or not related to a newspaper or magazine);
   c) 'broadcaster' means:
       i.   the holder of a licence under the Broadcasting Act 1990 or 1996;
       ii. the British Broadcasting Corporation; or
       iii. Sianel Pedwar Cymru;
   d) a person 'publishes in the United Kingdom' if the publication takes place in the United Kingdom or is targeted primarily at an audience in the United Kingdom;
   e) 'news-related material' means:
       i.   news or information about current affairs;
       ii. opinion about matters relating to the news or current affairs; or
       iii. gossip about celebrities, other public figures or other persons in the news.

Other definitions

2. In this Charter:
   a) 'ad hoc review' means a review conducted pursuant to paragraph 8 of Schedule 2 (scheme of recognition);
   b) 'Appointments Committee' means the committee established to make appointments to the Board of the Recognition Panel under paragraph 2 of Schedule 1 (appointments and terms of membership);
   c) a reference to 'the Board' means the governing body of the Recognition Panel (except in Schedule 3 (recognition criteria) where it means the Board of the Regulator);
   d) 'cyclical review' means a review conducted pursuant to paragraph 5 of Schedule 2 (scheme of recognition);
   e) 'editor', in relation to a publication, includes any person who acts in an editorial capacity in relation to the publication;
   f) a reference in any article to the date upon which this Charter becomes effective means the date the Charter takes effect in accordance with Article 2 (term of charter);
   g) 'Leveson Report' means the Report of an Inquiry into the Culture, Practices and Ethics of the Press, ordered by the House of Commons to be printed on 29 November 2012 (HC 779);
   h) a reference to 'Managing Public Money' means the document entitled 'Managing Public Money' last published by Our Treasury in October 2007 (including any amendments made by Our Treasury to that document, or any document that replaces or incorporates it);
   i) a reference to a 'Member' of the Board in the articles of this Charter (including Schedule 1 (appointment and terms of membership)), includes a reference to the Chair of the Board, unless the context otherwise requires;

j) 'Scheme of Recognition' means the arrangements described in Schedule 2 (scheme of recognition);

k) 'Standards Code' means the code established by a Regulator in accordance with Schedule 3 (recognition criteria).

3. In interpreting this Charter, and except where the context requires otherwise, words importing the masculine gender include the feminine, and vice versa, and words in the singular include the plural, and vice versa.

4. In this Charter a reference to an article refers to a provision of the main body of the Charter and a reference to a paragraph means a provision in a Schedule to this Charter.

5. In this Charter a reference to an Act of Parliament or an Order in Council includes any Act or Order that replaces or incorporates it.

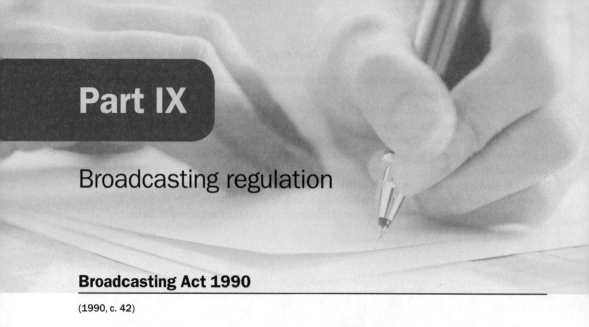

Part IX

Broadcasting regulation

Broadcasting Act 1990

(1990, c. 42)

PART I INDEPENDENT TELEVISION SERVICES

Chapter 1 Regulation by OFCOM Television Services Generally

General provisions about licences

3 Licences under Part I

(1) Any licence granted by OFCOM under this Part shall be in writing and (subject to the provisions of this Part) shall continue in force for such period as is provided, in relation to a licence of the kind in question, by the relevant provision of Chapter 2 or 5 of this Part or section 235 of the Communications Act 2003.

(2) A licence may be so granted for the provision of such a service as is specified in the licence or for the provision of a service of such a description as is so specified.

(3) OFCOM shall—

    (a) not grant a licence to any person unless they are satisfied that he is a fit and proper person to hold it; and

    (b) shall do all that they can to secure that, if they cease to be so satisfied in the case of any person holding a licence, that person does not remain the holder of the licence;

and nothing in this Part shall be construed as affecting the operation of this subsection or of section 5(1) or (2)(b) or (c).

(3A) Where OFCOM are not satisfied that a BBC company which has applied for a licence is a fit and proper person to hold it, they shall, before refusing the application, notify the Secretary of State that they are not so satisfied.

(4) OFCOM may vary a licence by a notice served on the licence holder if—

    (a) in the case of a variation of the period for which the licence is to continue in force, the licence holder consents; or

    (b) in the case of any other variation, the licence holder has been given a reasonable opportunity of making representations to OFCOM about the variation.

(5) Paragraph (a) of subsection (4) does not affect the operation of section 41(1)(b); and that subsection shall not authorise the variation of any conditions included in a licence in pursuance of section 19(1) or 52(1) or in pursuance of any other provision of this Part which applies section 19(1).

(6) A licence granted to any person under this Part shall not be transferable to any other person without the previous consent in writing of OFCOM.

(7) Without prejudice to the generality of subsection (6), OFCOM shall not give their consent for the purposes of that subsection unless they are satisfied that any such other person would be in a

position to comply with all of the conditions included in the licence which would have effect during the period for which it is to be in force.

(8) The holding by a person of a licence under this Part shall not relieve him of—

    (a) any liability in respect of a failure to hold a licence under section 8 of the Wireless Telegraphy Act 2006; or

    (b) any obligation to comply with requirements imposed by or under Chapter 1 of Part 2 of the Communications Act 2003 (electronic communications networks and electronic communications services).

4 General licence conditions

(1) A licence may include—

    (a) such conditions as appear to OFCOM to be appropriate having regard to any duties which are or may be imposed on them, or on the licence holder, by or under this Act, the Broadcasting Act 1996 or the Communications Act 2003;

    (b) conditions requiring the payment by the licence holder to OFCOM (whether on the grant of the licence or at such times thereafter as may be determined by or under the licence, or both) of a fee or fees of an amount or amounts so determined;

    (c) conditions requiring the licence holder to provide OFCOM, in such manner and at such times as they may reasonably require, with such information as they may require for the purpose of exercising the functions assigned to them by or under this Act, the Broadcasting Act 1996 or the Communications Act 2003;

    (d) conditions providing for such incidental and supplemental matters as appear to OFCOM to be appropriate.

(2) A licence may in particular include conditions requiring the licence holder—

    (a) to comply with any direction given by OFCOM as to such matters as are specified in the licence or are of a description so specified; or

    (b) (except to the extent that OFCOM consent to his doing or not doing them) not to do or to do such things as are specified in the licence or are of a description so specified.

(3) The fees required to be paid to OFCOM by virtue of subsection (1)(b) shall be in accordance with such tariff as may from time to time be fixed by OFCOM.

(4) A tariff fixed under subsection (3) may specify different fees in relation to different cases or circumstances; and OFCOM shall publish every such tariff in such manner as they consider appropriate.

(5) Where the holder of any licence—

    (a) is required by virtue of any condition [contained in the licence] to provide OFCOM with any information, and

    (b) in purported compliance with that condition provides them with information which is false in a material particular,

he shall be taken for the purposes of sections 41 and 42 or (as the case may be) sections 237 and 238 of the Communications Act 2003 (enforcement of television licensable content service licences) to have failed to comply with that condition.

(6) Nothing in this Act which authorises or requires the inclusion in a licence of conditions relating to any particular matter or having effect for any particular purpose shall be taken as derogating from the generality of subsection (1).

5 Restrictions on the holding of licences

(1) OFCOM shall do all that they can to secure—

    (a) that a person does not become or remain the holder of a licence if he is a person who is a disqualified person in relation to that licence by virtue of Part II of Schedule 2 to this Act;

    (b) that a person does not become the holder of a licence if requirements imposed by or under Schedule 14 to the Communications Act 2003 would be contravened were he to do so; and

(c) that those requirements are not contravened in the case of a person who already holds a licence.

(2) OFCOM may accordingly—

(a) require any applicant for a licence to provide them with such information as they may reasonably require for the purpose of determining—

   (i) whether he is such a disqualified person as is mentioned in subsection (1)(a),

   (ii) whether any such requirements as are mentioned in subsection (1)(b) would preclude them from granting a licence to him, and

   (iii) if so, what steps would be required to be taken by or in relation to him in order for any such requirements to be complied with;

(b) revoke the award of a licence to a body where a relevant change takes place after the award, but before the grant, of the licence;

(c) make the grant of a licence to any person conditional on the taking of any specified steps that appear to them to be required to be taken as mentioned in paragraph (a)(iii);

(d) impose conditions in any licence enabling them to require the licence holder, if a body corporate, to give to them advance notice of proposals affecting—

   (i) shareholdings in the body, or

   (ii) the directors of the body,

where such proposals are known to the body;

(da) impose conditions in a licence requiring the licence holder, if a body corporate, to give OFCOM notice, after they have occurred and irrespective of whether proposals for them have fallen to be notified, of changes, transactions or events affecting—

   (i) shareholdings in the body; or

   (ii) the directors of the body;

(db) impose conditions in a licence enabling OFCOM to require the licence holder to provide them with such information as they may reasonably require for determining—

   (i) whether the licence holder is a disqualified person in relation to that licence by virtue of Part 2 of Schedule 2; or

   (ii) whether any such requirements as are mentioned in subsection (1)(b) have been and are being complied with by or in relation to the licence holder;

(e) impose conditions in any licence enabling them to give the licence holder directions requiring him to take, or arrange for the taking of, any specified steps appearing to them to be required to be taken in order for any such requirements as are mentioned in subsection (1)(b) to be complied with.

(2A) Before revoking in pursuance of subsection (2)(b) the award of a licence to a BBC company, OFCOM shall give the Secretary of State notice of their intention to do so, specifying the relevant change.

(3) Where OFCOM—

(a) revoke the award of any licence in pursuance of subsection (2)(b), or

(b) determine that any condition imposed by them in relation to any licence in pursuance of subsection (2)(c) has not been satisfied,

any provisions of this Part relating to the awarding of licences of the kind in question shall (subject to subsection (4)) have effect as if the person to whom the licence was awarded or granted had not made an application for it.

(4) Those provisions shall not so have effect if OFCOM decide that it would be desirable to publish a fresh notice under this Part in respect of the grant of a licence, or (as the case may be) a further licence, to provide the service in question.

(5) Every licence shall include such conditions as OFCOM consider necessary or expedient to ensure that where—

(a) the holder of the licence is a body, and

(b) a relevant change takes place after the grant of the licence,

OFCOM may revoke the licence by notice served on the holder of the licence and taking effect forthwith or on a date specified in the notice.

(6) OFCOM shall not serve any such notice on the licence holder unless—

(a) OFCOM have notified him of the matters constituting their grounds for revoking the licence and given him a reasonable opportunity of making representations to them about those matters, and

(b) in a case where the relevant change is one falling within subsection (6A)—

(i) they have also given him an opportunity of complying with the requirements imposed by or under Schedule 14 to the Communications Act 2003, within a period specified in the notification, and

(ii) the period specified in the notification has elapsed.

(6A) A relevant change falls within this subsection if it consists only in one or more of the following—

(a) a change in the national market share (within the meaning of Part 1 of Schedule 14 to the Communications Act 2003) of one or more national newspapers (within the meaning of that Part of that Schedule);

(b) a change in the local market share (within the meaning of that Part of that Schedule in a particular area of one or more local newspapers (within the meaning of that Part of that Schedule).

(6AA) For the purposes of this section, the local market share of a local newspaper in any area at any time is the percentage of the total number of copies of all local newspapers sold in that area in the relevant six months which is represented by the total number of copies of that newspaper sold in that area in that six months.

(6AB) In subsection (6AA) 'the relevant six months' means the six months ending with the last whole calendar month to end before the time in question.

(6AC) For the purposes of subsection (6AA), the number of copies of a newspaper sold in a particular area during any period may be taken to be such number as is estimated by OFCOM—

(a) in such manner, or

(b) by reference to such statistics prepared by any other person,

as they think fit.

(6AD) In relation to a newspaper which is distributed free of charge (rather than sold), references in this section to the number of copies sold include references to the number of copies distributed.

(6C) OFCOM shall not serve any such notice as is mentioned in subsection (5) on a BBC company unless they have given the Secretary of State notice of their intention to do so, specifying the relevant change.

(6D) Where OFCOM receive any written representations from a BBC company under subsection (6), they shall send a copy of the representations to the Secretary of State.

(7) In this section 'relevant change', in relation to a body to which a licence has been awarded or granted, means—

(a) any change affecting the nature or characteristics of the body, or

(b) any change in the persons having control over or interests in the body, or

(c) any other change giving rise to a disqualification under Part 2 of Schedule 2 to this Act or a contravention of a requirement imposed by or under Schedule 14 to the Communications Act 2003 being (in any case) a change which is such that, if it fell to OFCOM to determine whether to award the licence to the body in the new circumstances of the case, they would be induced by the change to refrain from so awarding it.

General provisions about licensed services

6–12   [...]

Prohibition on providing unlicensed television services

13   Prohibition on providing television services without a licence

(1) Subject to subsection (2), any person who provides any relevant regulated television service without being authorised to do so by or under a licence under this Part or Part I of the Broadcasting Act 1996 shall be guilty of an offence.

(1A) In subsection (1) 'relevant regulated television service' means a service falling, in pursuance of section 211(1) of the Communications Act 2003, to be regulated by OFCOM, other than a television multiplex service.

(2) The Secretary of State may, after consultation with OFCOM, by order provide that subsection (1) shall not apply to such services or descriptions of services as are specified in the order.

(3) A person guilty of an offence under this section shall be liable—

    (a) on summary conviction, to a fine not exceeding the statutory maximum;

    (b) on conviction on indictment, to a fine.

(4) No proceedings in respect of an offence under this section shall be instituted—

    (a) in England and Wales, except by or with the consent of the Director of Public Prosecutions;

    (b) in Northern Ireland, except by or with the consent of the Director of Public Prosecutions for Northern Ireland.

(5) Without prejudice to subsection (3), compliance with this section shall be enforceable by civil proceedings by the Crown for an injunction or interdict or for any other appropriate relief.

(6) Any order under this section shall be subject to annulment in pursuance of a resolution of either House of Parliament.

Chapter II Television broadcasting on Channel 3, 4 and 5

Channel 3

14   Establishment of Channel 3

(1) OFCOM shall do all that they can to secure the provision, in accordance with this Chapter, of a nationwide system of television broadcasting services to be known as Channel 3.

(2) Subject to subsection (5), Channel 3 shall be structured on a regional basis, with each of the services comprised within it ('Channel 3 services') being provided for such area in the United Kingdom as OFCOM may determine in the case of that service.

(3) If it appears to OFCOM that it would be appropriate for a particular Channel 3 service to do so, they may determine that the service shall include the provision of different programmes—

    (a) for such different parts of the area for which it is provided, or

    (b) for such different communities living within that area, as they may determine.

(4) If OFCOM so determine in the case of a particular Channel 3 service, that service shall be provided for a particular area only between such times of the day or on such days of the week (or both) as OFCOM may determine.

(5) If OFCOM so determine, a Channel 3 service may be provided for two or more areas for which regional Channel 3 services are provided, but any such service may only be so provided between particular times of the day.

(6) In this Part—

'regional Channel 3 service' means a Channel 3 service provided for a particular area determined under subsection (2); and

'national Channel 3 service' means a Channel 3 service provided as mentioned in subsection (5).

(7A) The areas mentioned in subsection (2) must at all times include at least one area that comprises, or falls entirely within, Scotland.

(8) In this section and section 15 'programme' does not include an advertisement.

15   Applications for Channel 3 licences

(2) OFCOM shall, when publishing a notice under subsection (1), publish with the notice general guidance to applicants for the licence in question which contains examples of the kinds of programme whose inclusion in the service proposed by any such applicant under subsection (3)(b) would be likely to result in a finding by OFCOM that the service would comply with the requirements that have to be imposed under Chapter 4 of Part 3 of the Communications Act 2003 by conditions relating to—

(a) the public service remit for that service,

(b) programming quotas,

(c) news and current affairs programmes, and

(d) programme production and regional programming.

(3) Any application made in pursuance of a notice under this section must be in writing and accompanied by—

(a) the fee specified in the notice under subsection (1)(d)(i);

(b) the applicant's proposals for providing a service that would comply with the requirements that have to be imposed under Chapter 4 of Part 3 of the Communications Act 2003 by conditions relating to—

(i)   the public service remit for that service,

(ii) programming quotas,

(iii) news and current affairs programmes, and

(iv) programme production and regional programming;

(c) the applicant's cash bid in respect of the licence;

(d) such information as OFCOM may reasonably require as to the applicant's present financial position and his projected financial position during the period for which the licence would be in force; and

(e) such other information as OFCOM may reasonably require for the purpose of considering the application.

17A   Award of Channel 3 licence subject to conditions

(1) OFCOM may, when awarding a Channel 3 licence to any person, make the grant of the licence to him conditional on his compliance before the grant with such specified requirements relating to the financing of the service as appear to them to be appropriate, having regard to—

(a) any duties which are or may be imposed on them, or on the licence holder, by or under this Act, and

(b) any information provided to them under section 15(3)(g) by the person to whom the licence is awarded as to his projected financial position during the period for which the licence would be in force.

20   [...]

21   Restriction on changes in control over Channel 3 licence holder

(1) Where—

(a) any change in the persons having control over—

(i)   a body to which a Channel 3 licence has been awarded or transferred in accordance with this Part of this Act, or

(ii) an associated programme provider,

takes place within the relevant period, and

(b) that change takes place without having been previously approved for the purposes of this section by OFCOM, then

(subject to subsection (4)) OFCOM, if the licence has not yet been granted, refuse to grant it to the body referred to in paragraph (a)(i) above or, if it has already been granted, serve on that body a notice revoking it...

(3) OFCOM shall refuse to approve for the purposes of this section such a change as is mentioned in subsection (1)(a)—

    (a) if it appears to them that the change would be prejudicial to the provision under the licence, by the body referred to in subsection (1)(a)(i), of a service which accords with the proposals submitted under section 15(3)(b) by that body (or, as the case may be, by the person to whom the licence was originally awarded), or

    (b) it appears to them that the change would be prejudicial to the provision of Channel 3 as such a nationwide system of services as is mentioned in section 14(1);

and OFCOM may refuse so to approve any such change if, in any circumstances not falling within paragraph (a) or (b) above, they consider it appropriate to do so.

21A [...]

23   The Channel Four Television Corporation

(1) There shall be a corporation to be called the Channel Four Television Corporation (in this Part referred to as 'the Corporation').

24   Channel 4 to be provided by Corporation as licensed service

(1) The Corporation must secure the continued provision (subject to and in accordance with the provisions of this Part) of the television broadcasting service known as Channel 4 . . .

(3) Channel 4 shall be provided by the Corporation under a licence granted to them by OFCOM, and shall be so provided for so much of England, Scotland and Northern Ireland as may from time to time be reasonably practicable.

(4)–(6) [...]

25–27 [...]

Channel 5

28   Channel 5

(1) OFCOM shall do all that they can to secure the provision of a television broadcasting service for any such minimum area of the United Kingdom as may be determined by them in accordance with subsection (2); and any such service shall be known as Channel 5.

(2) In determining the minimum area of the United Kingdom for which Channel 5 is to be provided OFCOM shall have regard to the following consideration, namely that the service should, so far as is reasonably practicable, make the most effective use of the frequencies on which it is to be provided.

(3) If OFCOM so determine, Channel 5 shall be provided under a particular licence only between such times of the day or on such days of the week (or both) as they may determine.

(4) Where OFCOM have granted a licence to provide Channel 5, they may, if it appears to them to be appropriate to do so in view of any lack of facilities available for transmitting the service, dispense with any requirement to provide the service for such part of the area referred to in subsection (2) as they may determine; and any such dispensation shall have effect for such period as they may determine.

29   Application to Channel 5 of provisions relating to Channel 3

(1) Subject to subsections (2) and (3), sections 15 to 21 shall apply in relation to a Channel 5 licence as they apply in relation to a regional Channel 3 licence.

(2) In its application in relation to a Channel 5 licence—

    (a) section 15(1)(b)(i) shall be read as referring to any such minimum area of the United Kingdom as is determined by OFCOM in accordance with section 28(2).

(3) [...]

30 [...]

Provision of news programmes

31–32 […]

Miscellaneous provisions relating to Channels 3, 4 and 5

33–36 […]

37 Announcements of programme schedules

(1) Any Channel 3 licence or licence to provide Channel 4 may include conditions requiring the licence holder to include in the licensed service such announcements concerning relevant programme schedules as [OFCOM] may determine.

38–39 […]

Enforcement of licences

40 Power to direct licensee to broadcast correction or a statement of findings or not to repeat programme

(1) If OFCOM are satisfied—

  (a) that the holder of a Channel 3 or Channel 5 licence has failed to comply with any condition of the licence, and

  (b) that that failure can be appropriately remedied by the inclusion in the licensed service of a correction or a statement of findings (or both) under this subsection,

they may (subject to subsection (2)) direct the licence holder to include in the licensed service a correction or a statement of findings (or both) in such form, and at such time or times, as they may determine.

(2) OFCOM shall not give any person a direction under subsection (1) unless they have given him a reasonable opportunity of making representations to them about the matters complained of.

(3) Where the holder of a licence includes a correction or a statement of findings in the licensed service in pursuance of a direction under subsection (1), he may announce that he is doing so in pursuance of such a direction.

(4) If OFCOM are satisfied that the inclusion by the holder of a Channel 3 or Channel 5 licence of any programme in the licensed service involved a failure by him to comply with any condition of the licence, they may direct him not to include that programme in that service on any future occasion.

(5) This section shall apply in relation to Channel 4 as if any reference to a Channel 3 licence were a reference to the licence to provide Channel 4.

(6) For the purposes of this section a statement of findings, in relation to a case in which OFCOM are satisfied that the holder of a licence has contravened the conditions of his licence, is a statement of OFCOM's findings in relation to that contravention.

41 Power to impose financial penalty or shorten licence period

(1) If OFCOM are satisfied that the holder of a Channel 3 or Channel 5 licence has failed to comply with any condition of the licence or with any direction given by OFCOM under or by virtue of any provision of this Part, Part 5 of the Broadcasting Act 1996 or Part 3 of the Communications Act 2003 they may (subject to the following provisions of this section) serve on him—

  (a) a notice requiring him to pay, within a specified period, a specified financial penalty to OFCOM; or

  (b) a notice reducing the period for which the licence is to be in force by a specified period not exceeding two years.

(1A) The amount of a financial penalty imposed on a person in pursuance of subsection (1)(a) shall not exceed 5 per cent. of the qualifying revenue for the licence holder's last complete accounting period falling within the period for which his licence has been in force ('the relevant period').

(1B) In relation to a person whose first complete accounting period falling within the relevant period has not ended when the penalty is imposed, subsection (1A) is to be construed as referring to 5 per cent. of the amount which OFCOM estimate to be the qualifying revenue for that accounting period.

(1C) Section 19(2) to (6) applies for determining or estimating qualifying revenue for the purposes of subsection (1A) or (1B) above.

(2) [...]

(3) OFCOM shall not serve on any person such a notice as is mentioned in subsection (1)(a) or (b) unless they have given him a reasonable opportunity of making representations to them about the matters complained of.

(4) Where a licence is due to expire on a particular date by virtue of a notice served on any person under subsection (1)(b), OFCOM may, on the application of that person, revoke that notice by a further notice served on him at any time before that date, if they are satisfied that, since the date of the earlier notice, his conduct in relation to the operation of the licensed service has been such as to justify the revocation of that notice.

(5) It is hereby declared that any exercise by OFCOM of their powers under subsection (1) of this section in respect of any failure to comply with any condition of a licence shall not preclude any exercise by them of their powers under section 40 in respect of that failure.

(6) This section shall apply in relation to Channel 4 as if—

    (a) any reference to a Channel 3 licence were a reference to the licence to provide Channel 4; and

    (b) subsection (1)(b) were omitted.

42   Power to revoke Channel 3 or 5 licence

(1) If OFCOM are satisfied—

    (a) that the holder of a Channel 3 or Channel 5 licence is failing to comply with any condition of the licence or with any direction given by them under or by virtue of any provision of this Part, Part 5 of the Broadcasting Act 1996 or Part 3 of the Communications Act 2003 and

    (b) that that failure is such that, if not remedied, it would justify the revocation of the licence,

they shall (subject to subsection (8)) serve on the holder of the licence a notice under subsection (2).

(2) A notice under this subsection is a notice—

    (a) stating that OFCOM are satisfied as mentioned in subsection (1);

    (b) specifying the respects in which, in their opinion, the licence holder is failing to comply with any such condition or direction as is there mentioned; and

    (c) stating that, unless the licence holder takes, within such period as is specified in the notice, such steps to remedy the failure as are so specified, OFCOM will revoke his licence under subsection (3).

(3) If at the end of the period specified in a notice under subsection (2) OFCOM are satisfied—

    (a) that the person on whom the notice was served has failed to take the steps specified in it, and

    (b) that it is necessary in the public interest to revoke his licence, they shall (subject to subsection (8)) serve on that person a notice revoking his licence.

(4) If OFCOM are satisfied in the case of any Channel 3 or Channel 5 licence—

    (a) that the holder of the licence has ceased to provide the licensed service before the end of the period for which the licence is to continue in force, and

    (b) that it is appropriate for them to do so,

they shall (subject to subsection (8)) serve on him a notice revoking his licence.

(5) If OFCOM are satisfied—

    (a) that the holder of a Channel 3 or Channel 5 licence provided them, in connection with his application for the licence, with information which was false in a material particular, or

(b) that, in connection with his application for the licence, the holder of such a licence with-held any material information with the intention of causing them to be misled, they may (subject to subsection (8)) serve on him a notice revoking his licence.

(6) Subject to subsection (7), any notice served under subsection (3), (4) or (5) shall take effect as from the time when it is served on the licence holder.

(7) If it appears to OFCOM to be appropriate to do so for the purpose of preserving continuity in the provision of the service in question, they may provide in any such notice for it to take effect as from a date specified in it.

(8) OFCOM shall not serve any notice on a person under this section unless they have given him a reasonable opportunity of making representations to them about the matters complained of.

Chapter III Satellite television services

43–45A [...]

Chapter IV Licensable programme services

46–47 [...]

Chapter VI Television broadcasting by Welsh authority

56 Welsh Authority to continue in existence as Sianel Pedwar Cymru

(1) The authority which at the commencement of this section is called the Welsh Fourth Channel Authority shall continue in existence as a body corporate but—
   (a) shall be known as Sianel Pedwar Cymru (or S4C); and
   (b) shall be constituted in accordance with [...] this Act; and in this Act references to the Welsh Authority are references to that authority.

(2) The Welsh Authority shall consist of—
   (a) a chairman appointed by the Secretary of State; and
   (b) such number of other members appointed by the Secretary of State, not being less than four nor more than eight, as he may from time to time determine.

(3) Schedule 6 to this Act shall have effect with respect to the Welsh Authority.

57 [...]

58 Sources of programmes for S4C

(1) For the purpose mentioned in subsection (1A) the BBC shall—
   (a) provide to the Welsh Authority (free of charge) sufficient television programmes in Welsh to occupy not less than ten hours' transmission time per week; and
   (b) do so in a way which meets the reasonable requirements of the Authority.

(1A) The purpose is to enable the Welsh Authority to fulfil—
   (a) so much of the public service remit for S4C as is contained in paragraph 3(2)(a) and (b) of Schedule 12 to the Communications Act 2003; and
   (b) so much of the public service remit for S4C Digital as is contained in paragraph 3(3) of that Schedule.

(2) It shall be the duty of the Channel Four Television Corporation—
   (a) to provide the Welsh Authority with programme schedules for the programmes broadcast on Channel 4, including information as to the periods available for the broadcasting of advertisements, far enough in advance to enable the Welsh Authority to [fulfil so much of their public service remit in relation to S4C under paragraph 3 of Schedule 12 to the Communications Act 2003 as is contained in sub-paragraph (2)(c) of that paragraph]; and
   (b) to provide the Welsh Authority (free of charge) with any programmes which are required by the Authority for the purpose of complying with that provision.

(3) The programmes broadcast on S4C may, to the extent that they are not provided under subsection (1) or (2), be obtained by the Welsh Authority from such persons as they think fit.

59 [...]

60   Advertising on S4C

(4) The Welsh Authority shall—

    (a) from time to time consult the Secretary of State as to the classes and descriptions of advertisements which must not be broadcast on S4C and the methods of advertising or sponsorship which must not be employed in, or in connection with, the provision of S4C;

    (aa) from time to time consult the Secretary of State as to the forms and methods of product placement that should not be employed in the provision of S4C (including the description of products, services or trade marks for which product placement should not be employed); and

    (b) carry out any directions which he may give to them in respect of such matters.

(5) The Welsh Authority shall not act as an advertising agent.

(6) [...]

61   Funding of Welsh Authority

(1) The Secretary of State shall secure that in 2012 and each subsequent year the Welsh Authority are paid an amount which he considers sufficient to cover the cost to the Authority during that year of—

    (a) providing the Authority's public services (within the meaning of section 207 of the Communications Act 2003), and

    (b) arranging for the broadcasting or distribution of those services.

(2) The Secretary of State may discharge the duty in subsection (1) by making payments himself or entering into an agreement with another person for that person to do so (or both).

(3) If under this section the Welsh Authority are paid an amount for any year which exceeds the cost referred to in subsection (1), the Authority may pay the difference from the public service fund referred to in section 61A to the person (or pro rata to the persons) from whom payments were received.

(4) Any sums required by the Secretary of State under this section shall be paid out of money provided by Parliament.

62 [...]

63   Government control over S4C

(1) If it appears to him to be necessary or expedient to do so in connection with his functions as such, the Secretary of State or any other Minister of the Crown may at any time by notice require the Welsh Authority to broadcast, at such times as may be specified in the notice, any announcement specified in the notice, with or without visual images of any picture, scene or object mentioned in the announcement; and it shall be the duty of the Authority to comply with the notice.

(2) Where the Welsh Authority broadcast any announcement in pursuance of a notice under subsection (1), they may announce that they are doing so in pursuance of such a notice.

(3) The Secretary of State may at any time by notice require the Welsh Authority to refrain from broadcasting any matter or classes of matter specified in the notice; and it shall be the duty of the Authority to comply with the notice.

(4) Where the Secretary of State has given the Welsh Authority a notice under subsection (3), the Authority may broadcast an announcement of the giving of the notice or, when it has been revoked or has expired, of its revocation or expiration.

(5) The powers conferred by this section are in addition to any power specifically conferred on the Secretary of State by any other provision of this Act.

Chapter VII Supplemental

65 [...]

66A Enforcement of licences held by BBC companies
  (1) Where OFCOM—
    (a) give a direction to a BBC company under section 40(1),
    (b) serve a notice on a BBC company under any provision of section 41 or 42, or
    (c) receive any written representations from a BBC company under section 40(2), 41(3) or 42(8),
OFCOM shall send a copy of the direction, notice or representations to the Secretary of State.
  (2) References in subsection (1) to any of the provisions of sections 40 to 42 are references to that provision as applied—
    (a) by section 42B(2), in relation to a licence to provide a restricted service,
    (e) by section 55(4), in relation to an additional services licence.

PART V THE BROADCASTING COMPLAINTS COMMISSION

142–150 [...]

PART VI THE BROADCASTING STANDARDS COUNCIL

151–161 [...]

PART VII PROHIBITION ON INCLUSION OF OBSCENE AND OTHER MATERIAL IN PROGRAMME SERVICES

Defamation

166 Defamatory material
  (1) For the purposes of the law of libel and slander the publication of words in the course of any programme included in a programme service shall be treated as publication in permanent form.
  (2) Subsection (1) above shall apply for the purposes of section 3 of each of the Defamation Acts (slander of title etc.) as it applies for the purposes of the law of libel and slander.
  (3) [...]
  (4) In this section 'the Defamation Acts' means the Defamation Act 1952 and the Defamation Act (Northern Ireland) 1955.
  (5) Subsections (1) and (2) above do not extend to Scotland.

Supplementary

167 Power to make copies of recordings
  (1) If a justice of the peace is satisfied by information on oath laid by a constable that there is reasonable ground for suspecting that a relevant offence has been committed by any person in respect of a programme included in a programme service, he may make an order authorising any constable to require that person—
    (a) to produce to the constable a visual or sound recording of any matter included in that programme, if and so far as that person is able to do so; and
    (b) on the production of such a recording, to afford the constable an opportunity of causing a copy of it to be made.
  (2) An order made under this section shall describe the programme to which it relates in a manner sufficient to enable that programme to be identified.

(3) A person who without reasonable excuse fails to comply with any requirement of a constable made by virtue of subsection (1) shall be guilty of an offence and liable on summary conviction to a fine not exceeding the third level on the standard scale.

(4) No order shall be made under this section in respect of any recording in respect of which a warrant could be granted under any of the following provisions, namely—

    (a) section 3 of the Obscene Publications Act 1959;

    (b) section 24 or 29H of the Public Order Act 1986; and

    (c) Article 14 of the Public Order (Northern Ireland) Order 1987.

(5) In the application of subsection (1) to England and Wales 'relevant offence' means an offence under—

    (a) section 2 of the Obscene Publications Act 1959; or

    (b) section 22 or 29F of the Public Order Act 1986.

(6) In the application of subsection (1) to Scotland—

    (a) 'relevant offence' means an offence under—

        (i)   section 51 of the Civic Government (Scotland) Act 1982, or

        (ii) section 22 of the Public Order Act 1986;

    (b) the reference to a justice of the peace shall include a reference to the sheriff; and

    (c) for the reference to information on oath there shall be substituted a reference to evidence on oath.

(7) In the application of subsection (1) to Northern Ireland—

    (a) 'relevant offence' means an offence under Article 12 of the Public Order (Northern Ireland) Order 1987;

    (b) for the reference to a justice of the peace there shall be substituted a reference to a resident magistrate; and

    (c) for the reference to information on oath laid by a constable there shall be substituted a reference to a complaint on oath made by a constable.

PART X MISCELLANEOUS AND GENERAL

Foreign satellite services

177 Orders proscribing unacceptable foreign satellite services

(1) Subject to the following provisions of this section, the Secretary of State may make an order proscribing a foreign satellite service for the purposes of section 178.

(2) If OFCOM consider that the quality of any foreign satellite service which is brought to their attention is unacceptable and that the service should be the subject of an order under this section, they shall notify to the Secretary of State details of the service and their reasons why they consider such an order should be made.

(3) OFCOM shall not consider a foreign satellite service to be unacceptable for the purposes of subsection (2) unless they are satisfied that there is repeatedly contained in programmes included in the service matter which offends against good taste or decency or is likely to encourage or incite to crime or to lead to disorder or to be offensive to public feeling.

(4) Where the Secretary of State has been notified under subsection (2), he shall not make an order under this section unless he is satisfied that the making of the order—

    (a) is in the public interest; and

    (b) is compatible with any international obligations of the United Kingdom.

(5) An order under this section—

    (a) may make such provision for the purpose of identifying a particular foreign satellite service as the Secretary of State thinks fit; and

    (b) shall be subject to annulment in pursuance of a resolution of either House of Parliament.

(6) In this section and section 178—

'foreign satellite service' means—

(a) a service which is provided by a person who is not for the purposes of the Audiovisual Media Services Directive under the jurisdiction of the United Kingdom and which consists wholly or mainly in the transmission by satellite of television programmes which are capable of being received in the United Kingdom, or

(b) a service which consists wholly or mainly in the transmission by satellite from a place outside the United Kingdom of sound programmes which are capable of being received in the United Kingdom;

[...]

178   Offence of supporting proscribed foreign satellite services

(1) This section applies to any foreign satellite service which is proscribed for the purposes of this section by virtue of an order under section 177; and references in this section to a proscribed service are references to any such service.

(2) Any person who in the United Kingdom does any of the acts specified in subsection (3) shall be guilty of an offence.

(3) Those acts are—

(a) supplying any equipment or other goods for use in connection with the operation or day-to-day running of a proscribed service;

(b) supplying, or offering to supply, programme material to be included in any programme transmitted in the provision of a proscribed service;

(c) arranging for, or inviting, any other person to supply programme material to be so included;

(d) advertising, by means of programmes transmitted in the provision of a proscribed services, goods supplied by him or services provided by him;

(e) publishing the times or other details of any programmes which are to be transmitted in the provision of a proscribed service or (otherwise than by publishing such details) publishing an advertisement of matter calculated to promote a proscribed service (whether directly or indirectly);

(f) supplying or offering to supply any decoding equipment which is designed or adapted to be used primarily for the purpose of enabling the reception of programmes transmitted in the provision of a proscribed service.

(4) In any proceedings against a person for an offence under this section, it is a defence for him to prove that he did not know, and had no reasonable cause to suspect, that the service in connection with which the act was done was a proscribed service.

(5) A person who is guilty of an offence under this section shall be liable—

(a) on summary conviction, to imprisonment for a term not exceeding six months or to a fine not exceeding the statutory maximum, or both;

(b) on conviction on indictment, to imprisonment for a term not exceeding two years or to a fine, or both.

(6) For the purposes of this section a person exposing decoding equipment for supply or having such equipment in his possession for supply shall be deemed to offer to supply it.

(7) Section 46 of the Consumer Protection Act 1987 shall have effect for the purpose of construing references in this section to the supply of any thing as it has effect for the purpose of construing references in that Act to the supply of any goods.

(8) In this section 'programme material' includes—

(a) a film (within the meaning of Part I of the Copyright, Designs and Patents Act 1988);

(b) any other recording; and

(c) any advertisement or other advertising material.

Gaelic television programmes

183   Financing of programmes in Gaelic out of Gaelic Television Fund

(1) The Scottish Ministers must, for each financial year, pay to OFCOM such amount as they may determine to be appropriate for the purposes of this section.

(2) Any amount received by OFCOM under subsection (1) shall be carried by them to the credit of a fund established known as the Gaelic Broadcasting Fund (and any such amount shall accordingly not be regarded as forming part of the revenues of OFCOM).

(3) The Fund shall be under the management of a body established for the purposes of this section.

(3B) The functions of the Service shall be to secure that a wide and diverse range of high quality programmes in Gaelic are broadcast or otherwise transmitted so as to be available to persons in Scotland.

183A   Membership of the Gaelic Media Service

(1) The Service shall consist of not more than twelve members.

(2) The members of the Service are to be appointed by OFCOM.

(3) OFCOM must appoint one of the members to be the chairman of the Service.

(4) The approval of the Secretary of State and the Scottish Ministers is required for the appointment of a person as a member of the Service, and for the appointment of a member as their chairman.

(5) The members of the Service must include—

   (a) a member nominated by the BBC;

   (b) a member nominated by Highlands and Islands Enterprise; and

   (c) a member nominated by Bòrd na Gàidhlig.

(6) When appointing members of the Service, OFCOM must have regard to—

   (a) the desirability of having members of the Service who are proficient in written and spoken Gaelic; and

   (b) any guidance issued by the Secretary of State with the agreement of the Scottish Ministers for the purposes of this section

Power to give directions relating to international obligations

188   Power to give broadcasting bodies etc. directions relating to international obligations

(1) A body to which this section applies shall carry out any functions which the Secretary of State may by order direct them to carry out for the purpose of enabling Her Majesty's Government in the United Kingdom to give effect to any international obligations of the United Kingdom.

(2) This section applies to—

   (a) the BBC;

   (c) the Welsh Authority;

(3) An order under this section shall be subject to annulment in pursuance of a resolution of either House of Parliament.

202   General interpretation

(1) In this Act (unless the context otherwise requires)—

'advertising agent' shall be construed in accordance with subsection (7);

'the Audiovisual Media Services Directive' means Directive 2010/13/EU of the European Parliament and of the Council on the coordination of certain provisions laid down by law, regulation or administrative action in Member States concerning the provision of audiovisual media services;

'the BBC' means the British Broadcasting Corporation;

'a BBC company' means—

   (a) any body corporate which is controlled by the BBC, or

    (b) any body corporate in which the BBC or any body corporate falling within paragraph (a) above is (to any extent) a participant (as defined in paragraph 1(1) of Part I of Schedule 2);

'body', without more, means a body of persons whether incorporated or not, and includes a partnership;

'broadcast' means broadcast by wireless telegraphy;

'a Channel 4 company' means—

    (a) any body corporate which is controlled by the Channel Four Television Corporation, or

    (b) any body corporate in which the Corporation or any body corporate falling within paragraph (a) above is (to any extent) a participant (as defined in paragraph 1(1) of Part I of Schedule 2);

'connected', in relation to any person, shall be construed in accordance with paragraph 3 in Part I of Schedule 2;

'control', in relation to a body, has the meaning given by paragraph 1(1) in that Part of that Schedule;

'dwelling-house' includes a hotel, inn, boarding-house or other similar establishment;

'financial year' shall be construed in accordance with subsection (2);

'EEA Agreement' means the Agreement on the European Economic Area signed at Oporto on 2nd May 1992 as adjusted by the Protocol signed at Brussels on 17th March 1993;

'EEA State' means a State which is a contracting party to the EEA Agreement;

'frequency' includes frequency band;

'modifications' includes additions, alterations and omissions;

'OFCOM' means the Office of Communications;

'pension scheme' means a scheme for the payment of pensions, allowances or gratuities;

'product placement' has the meaning given by paragraph 1 of Schedule 11A to the Communications Act 2003

'programme' includes an advertisement and, in relation to any service, includes any item included in that service;

'an S4C company' means—

    (a) any body corporate which is controlled by the Welsh Authority, or

    (b) any body corporate in which the Welsh Authority or any body corporate falling within paragraph (a) above is (to any extent) a participant (as defined in paragraph 1(1) of Part I of Schedule 2);

'the Welsh Authority' means the authority renamed Sianel Pedwar Cymru by section 56(1);

'wireless telegraphy' and 'station for wireless telegraphy' have the same meaning as in the Wireless Telegraphy Act 2006.

    (5) It is hereby declared that, for the purpose of determining for the purposes of any provision of this Act whether a service is—

    (a) capable of being received, within the United Kingdom or elsewhere, or

    (b) for reception at any place or places, or in any area, in the United Kingdom, the fact that the service has been encrypted to any extent shall be disregarded.

    (6) Any reference in this Act, in relation to a service consisting of programmes transmitted by satellite—

    (a) to a person by whom the programmes are transmitted, or

    (b) to a place from which the programmes are transmitted, is a reference to a person by whom, or a place from which, the programmes are transmitted to the satellite by means of which the service is provided.

    (6A) Subsections (2) and (3) of section 362 of the Communications Act 2003 (persons by whom services provided) are to apply for the purposes of this Act as they apply for the purposes of Part 3 of that Act.

204 Short title, commencement and extent

(1) This Act may be cited as the Broadcasting Act 1990.

(2) This Act shall come into force on such day as the Secretary of State may by order appoint; and different days may be so appointed for different provisions or for different purposes.

(3) Subject to subsections (4) and (5), this Act extends to the whole of the United Kingdom.

Sections 5 and 88   SCHEDULE 2

RESTRICTIONS ON THE HOLDING OF LICENCE

PART I GENERAL

1.—(1) In this Schedule—

'the 1996 Act' means the Broadcasting Act 1996;

'advertising agency' means an individual or a body corporate who carries on business as an advertising agent (whether alone or in partnership) or has control over any body corporate which carries on business as an advertising agent, and any reference to an advertising agency includes a reference to an individual who—

(a) is a director or officer of any body corporate which carries on such a business, or

(b) is employed by any person who carries on such a business;

'associate'—

(a) in relation to a body corporate, shall be construed in accordance with paragraph (1A), and

(b) in relation to an individual, shall be construed in accordance with sub-paragraph (2);

'Broadcasting Act licence' means a licence under Part 1 or 3 of this Act or Part 1 or 2 of the Broadcasting Act 1996;

'control'—

(a) in relation to a body corporate, shall be construed in accordance with sub-paragraph (3), and

(b) in relation to any body other than a body corporate, means the power of a person to secure, by whatever means and whether directly or indirectly, that the affairs of the first-mentioned body are conducted in accordance with the wishes of that person;

'equity share capital' has the same meaning as in the Companies Acts (see section 548 of the Companies Act 2006)

'local authority'—

(a) in relation to England, means any of the following, that is to say, the council of a county, district or London borough, the Common Council of the City of London and the Council of the Isles of Scilly;

(aa) in relation to Wales, means a county council or county borough council;

(b) in relation to Scotland, means a council constituted under section 2 of the Local Government etc. (Scotland) Act 1994; and

(c) in relation to Northern Ireland, means a district council;

'participant', in relation to a body corporate, means a person who holds or is beneficially entitled to shares in that body or who possesses voting power in that body.

PART II DISQUALIFICATION FOR HOLDING LICENCES

General disqualification of non-EEC nationals and bodies having political connections

1.—(1) Subject to sub-paragraph (1A), the following persons are disqualified persons in relation to a Broadcasting Act licence—

    (c) a local authority;

    (d) a body whose objects are wholly or mainly of a political nature;

    (e) a body affiliated to a body falling within paragraph (d);

    (f) an individual who is an officer of a body falling within paragraph (d) or (e);

    (g) a body corporate which is an associate of a body corporate falling within paragraph (d) or (e);

    (h) a body corporate in which a body falling within any of paragraphs (c) to (e) and (g) is a participant with more than a 5 per cent interest;

    (hh) a body corporate which is controlled by a body corporate falling within paragraph (h);

    (i) a body which is controlled by a person falling within any of paragraphs (c) to (g) or by two or more such persons taken together; and

    (j) a body corporate in which a body falling within paragraph (i), other than one which is controlled—

        (i) by a person falling within paragraph (f), or

        (ii) by two or more such persons taken together,

    is a participant with more than a 5 per cent interest.

(1A) Where a service is provided exclusively for the purposes of the carrying out of the functions of a local authority under section 142 of the Local Government Act 1972 (provision by local authorities of information relating to their activities), a person is disqualified by virtue of sub-paragraph (1) in relation to a licence to provide that service only if he would be so disqualified disregarding paragraph (c) of that sub-paragraph.

Disqualification of religious bodies

2.—(1) The following persons are disqualified persons in relation only to licences falling within sub-paragraph (1A)—

    (a) a body whose objects are wholly or mainly of a religious nature;

    (b) a body which is controlled by a body falling within paragraph (a) or by two or more such bodies taken together;

    (c) a body which controls a body falling within paragraph (a);

    (d) a body corporate which is an associate of a body corporate falling within paragraph (a), (b) or (c);

    (e) a body corporate in which a body falling within any of paragraphs (a) to (d) is a participant with more than a 5 per cent interest;

    (f) an individual who is an officer of a body falling within paragraph (a);and

    (g) a body which is controlled by an individual falling within paragraph (f) or by two or more such individuals taken together.

(1A) A licence falls within this sub-paragraph if it is—

    (a) a Channel 3 licence;

    (b) a Channel 5 licence;

    (c) a national sound broadcasting licence;

    (d) a public teletext licence;

    (e) an additional television service licence;

    (f) a television multiplex licence; or

    (g) a radio multiplex licence.

(1B) In this paragraph—

'additional television service licence' means a licence under Part 1 of this Act to provide an additional television service within the meaning of Part 3 of the Communications Act 2003;

'Channel 3 licence' and 'Channel 5 licence' each has the same meaning as in Part 1 of this Act;

'national sound broadcasting licence' means a licence to provide a sound broadcasting service (within the meaning of Part 3 of this Act) which is a national service (within the meaning of that Part);

'public teletext licence' means a licence to provide the public teletext service (within the meaning of Part 3 of the Communications Act 2003);

'radio multiplex licence' means a licence under Part 2 of the Broadcasting Act 1996 to provide a radio multiplex service within the meaning of that Part; and

'television multiplex licence' means a licence under Part 1 of the Broadcasting Act 1996 to provide a multiplex service within the meaning of that Part.

General disqualification on grounds of undue influence

4—(1) A person is a disqualified person in relation to a Broadcasting Act licence if in the opinion of OFCOM—

    (a) any relevant body is, by the giving of financial assistance or otherwise, exerting influence over the activities of that person, and

    (b) that influence has led, is leading or is likely to lead to results which are adverse to the public interest.

  (2) In sub-paragraph (1) 'relevant body'—

    (a) in relation to a licence granted under Part 1 of this Act or Part 1 of the Broadcasting Act 1996, means a person falling within paragraph 1(1)(c) to (h) or (j) above or a body which is controlled—

      (i) by a person falling within paragraph 1(1)(c) to (g) above, or

      (ii) by two or more such persons taken together; and

    (b) in relation to a licence granted under Part 3 of this Act or Part 2 of the Broadcasting Act 1996, means a person falling within paragraph 1(1)(c) to (h) or (j) or 3 above or a body which is controlled—

      (i) by a person falling within paragraph 1(1)(c) to (g) above;

      (ii) by a person falling within paragraph 3 above; or

      (iii) by two or more persons taken together each of whom falls within sub-paragraph (i) or (ii) (whether or not they all fall within the same sub-paragraph).

General disqualification of broadcasting bodies

5. The following persons are disqualified persons in relation to [a Broadcasting Act licence]—

    (a) the BBC;

    (b) the Welsh Authority.

Disqualification of certain companies for certain licences

5A—(1) A BBC company, a Channel 4 company or an S4C company is a disqualified person in relation to—

    (a) any licence to provide regional or national Channel 3 services or Channel 5.

  (2) A BBC company is also a disqualified person in relation to any licence to provide a national, local or restricted service within the meaning of Part III of this Act.

  (3) [...]

General disqualification of advertising agencies

6. The following persons are disqualified persons in relation to a Broadcasting Act licence—

    (a) an advertising agency;

    (b) an associate of an advertising agency;

    (c) any body which is controlled by a person falling within sub-paragraph (a) or (b) or by two or more such persons taken together;

    (d) any body corporate in which a person falling within any of sub-paragraphs (a) to (c) is a participant with more than a 5 per cent. interest.

Broadcasting Act 1996

(1996, c. 55)

PART I DIGITAL TERRESTRIAL
TELEVISION BROADCASTING

Introductory

1 Multiplex services and digital programme services

(1) In this Part 'multiplex service' means (except where the context otherwise requires) a television multiplex service.

(2)–(3) [...]

(4) In this Part 'digital programme service' means a service consisting in the provision by any person of television programmes (together with any ancillary services, as defined by section 24(2)) with a view to their being broadcast in digital form so as to be available for reception by members of the public, whether by him or by some other person, but does not include—

  (za) a service provided under the authority of a licence under Part 1 of the 1990 Act to provide a television licensable content service,

  (a) a qualifying service,

  (b) a teletext service, or

  (c) any service in the case of which the visual images to be broadcast do not consist wholly or mainly of images capable of being seen as moving pictures,

except, in the case of a service falling within paragraph (b) or (c), to the extent that it is an ancillary service.

(4A) In subsection (4), 'available for reception by members of the public' means available for reception by members of the public (within the meaning of Part 3 of the Communications Act 2003) in the United Kingdom or another EEA State, or in an area of the United Kingdom or of such a State.

(5) The Secretary of State may, if having regard to developments in broadcasting technology he considers it appropriate to do so, by order amend the definition of 'digital programme service' in subsection (4).

(6) No order under subsection (5) shall be made unless a draft of the order has been laid before and approved by a resolution of each House of Parliament.

(7) In this section 'broadcast' means broadcast otherwise than from a satellite.

2 Meaning of 'independent analogue broadcaster' and 'qualifying service'

(1) [...]

(2) In this Part 'qualifying service' means any of the following, so far as they are provided with a view to their being broadcast in digital form—

  (a) a television broadcasting service included in Channel 3;

  (b) Channel 4;

  (c) Channel 5;

  (d) S4C Digital;

  (e) a television programme service provided by the Welsh Authority with the approval of the Secretary of State under section 205 of the Communications Act 2003;

  (f) the digital public teletext service.

(3)–(7) [...]

General provisions about licences

3   Licences under Part I

(1) Any licence granted by OFCOM under this Part shall be in writing and (subject to the provisions of this Part) shall continue in force for such period as is provided, in relation to a licence of the kind in question, by the relevant provision of this Part.

(2) A licence may be so granted for the provision of such a service as is specified in the licence or for the provision of a service of such a description as is so specified.

(3) OFCOM—

    (a) shall not grant a licence to any person unless they are satisfied that he is a fit and proper person to hold it, and

    (b) shall do all that they can to secure that, if they cease to be so satisfied in the case of any person holding a licence, that person does not remain the holder of the licence;

and nothing in this Part shall be construed as affecting the operation of this subsection or of section 5(1) or (2)(b) or (c).

(4) OFCOM may vary a licence by a notice served on the licence holder if—

    (a) in the case of a variation of the period for which a licence having effect for a specified period is to continue in force, the licence holder consents, or

    (b) in the case of any other variation, the licence holder has been given a reasonable opportunity of making representations to OFCOM about the variation.

(5) Paragraph (a) of subsection (4) does not affect the operation of section 17(1)(b); and that subsection shall not authorise the variation of any conditions included in a licence in pursuance of section 13(1).

(6) A licence granted to any person under this Part shall not be transferable to any other person without the previous consent in writing of OFCOM.

(7) Without prejudice to the generality of subsection (6), OFCOM shall not give their consent for the purposes of that subsection unless they are satisfied that any such other person would be in a position to comply with all of the conditions included in the licence which would have effect during the period for which it is to be in force.

(8) The holding by a person of a licence under this Part shall not relieve him of—

    (a) any liability in respect of a failure to hold a licence under section 1 of the Wireless Telegraphy Act 2006; or

    (b) any obligation to comply with requirements imposed by or under Chapter 1 of Part 2 of the Communications Act 2003 (electronic communications networks and electronic communications services).

4   General licence conditions

(1) A licence may include—

    (a) such conditions as appear to OFCOM to be appropriate having regard to any duties which are or may be imposed on them, or on the licence holder, by or under this Act, the 1990 Act or the Communications Act 2003;

    (b) conditions requiring the payment by the licence holder to OFCOM (whether on the grant of the licence or at such times thereafter as may be determined by or under the licence, or both) of a fee or fees of an amount or amounts so determined;

    (c) conditions requiring the licence holder to provide OFCOM, in such manner and at such times as they may reasonably require, with such information as they may require for the purpose of exercising the functions assigned to them by or under this Act, the 1990 Act or the Communications Act 2003;

    (d) conditions providing for such incidental and supplemental matters as appear to OFCOM to be appropriate.

(2) A licence may in particular include conditions requiring the licence holder—

    (a) to comply with any direction given by OFCOM as to such matters as are specified in the licence or are of a description so specified, or

(b) (except to the extent that OFCOM consent to his doing or not doing them) not to do or to do such things as are specified in the licence or are of a description so specified …

(6) Nothing in this Part which authorises or requires the inclusion in a licence of conditions relating to any particular matter or having effect for any particular purpose shall be taken as derogating from the generality of subsection (1).

5   Restrictions on holding of licences under Part I

(1) OFCOM shall do all that they can to secure—

(a) that a person does not become or remain the holder of a licence if he is a person who is a disqualified person in relation to that licence by virtue of Part II of Schedule 2 to the 1990 Act (as amended by this Act); and

(b) that a person does not become the holder of a licence if requirements imposed by or under Schedule 14 to the Communications Act 2003 would be contravened were he to do so; and

(c) that those requirements are not contravened in the case of a person who already holds a licence.

(2) OFCOM may accordingly—

(a) require any applicant for a licence to provide them with such information as they may reasonably require for the purpose of determining—

(i) whether he is such a disqualified person as is mentioned in subsection (1)(a),

(ii) whether any such requirements as are mentioned in subsection (1)(b) would preclude them from granting a licence to him, and

(iii) if so, what steps would be required to be taken by or in relation to him in order for any such requirements to be complied with;

(b) revoke the award of a licence to a body where a relevant change takes place after the award, but before the grant, of the licence;

(c) make the grant of a licence to any person conditional on the taking of any specified steps that appear to them to be required to be taken as mentioned in paragraph (a)(iii);

(d) impose conditions in any licence enabling them to require the licence holder, if a body corporate, to give to them advance notice of proposals affecting—

(i) shareholdings in the body, or

(ii) the directors of the body,

where such proposals are known to the body;

(da) impose conditions in a licence requiring the licence holder, if a body corporate, to give OFCOM notice, after they have occurred and irrespective of whether proposals for them have fallen to be notified, of changes, transactions or events affecting—

(i) shareholdings in the body; or

(ii) the directors of the body;

(db) impose conditions in a licence enabling OFCOM to require the licence holder to provide them with such information as they may reasonably require for determining—

(i) whether the licence holder is a disqualified person in relation to that licence by virtue of Part 2 of Schedule 2 to the 1990 Act; or

(ii) whether any such requirements as are mentioned in subsection (1)(b) have been and are being complied with by or in relation to the licence holder;

(e) impose conditions in any licence enabling them to give the licence holder directions requiring him to take, or arrange for the taking of, any specified steps appearing to them to be required to be taken in order for any such requirements as are mentioned in subsection (1)(b) to be complied with.

(3) Where OFCOM—

(a) revoke the award of any licence in pursuance of subsection (2)(b), or

(b) determine that any condition imposed by them in relation to any licence in pursuance of subsection (2)(c) has not been satisfied, any provisions of this Part relating to the awarding of licences of the kind in question shall (subject to subsection (4)) have effect as if the person to whom the licence was awarded or granted had not made an application for it.

(4) Those provisions shall not so have effect if OFCOM decide that it would be desirable to publish a fresh notice under this Part in respect of the grant of a licence, or (as the case may be) a further licence, to provide the service in question.

(5) Every licence shall include such conditions as OFCOM consider necessary or expedient to ensure that where—

      (a) the holder of the licence is a body, and

      (b) a relevant change takes place after the grant of the licence,

OFCOM may revoke the licence by notice served on the holder of the licence and taking effect forthwith or on a date specified in the notice.

(6) OFCOM shall not serve any such notice on the licence holder unless—

      (a) they have notified him of the matters constituting their grounds for revoking the licence and given him a reasonable opportunity of making representations to them about those matters, and

      (b) in a case where the relevant change is one falling within subsection (7)—

          (i) they have also given him an opportunity of complying with the requirements imposed by or under Schedule 14 to the Communications Act 2003 within a period specified in the notification, and

          (ii) the period specified in the notification has elapsed.

(7) A relevant change falls within this subsection if it consists only in one or more of the following—

      (a) [...]

      (b) a change in the national market share (within the meaning of Part 1 of Schedule 14 to the Communications Act 2003) of one or more national newspapers (within the meaning of that Part of that Schedule), or

      (c) a change in the local market share (within the meaning of section 5 of the Broadcasting Act 1990) in a particular area of one or more local newspapers (within the meaning of that Part I of Schedule 14 to the Communications Act 2003).

(8) In this section 'relevant change', in relation to a body to which a licence has been awarded or granted, means—

      (a) any change affecting the nature or characteristics of the body,

      (b) any change in the persons having control over or interests in the body, or

      (c) any other change giving rise to a disqualification under Part 2 of Schedule 2 to the 1990 Act or a contravention of a requirement imposed by or under Schedule 14 to the Communications Act 2003,

being (in any case) a change which is such that; if it fell to OFCOM to determine whether to award the licence to the body in the new circumstances of the case, they would be induced by the change to refrain from so awarding it.

Digital programme services

18 Licensing of digital programme services

(1) An application for a licence to provide digital programme services (in this Part referred to as a 'digital programme licence') shall—

      (a) be made in such manner as OFCOM may determine, and

      (b) be accompanied by such fee (if any) as they may determine.

(2) At any time after receiving such an application and before determining it, OFCOM may require the applicant to furnish such additional information as they may consider necessary for the purpose of considering the application.

(3) Any information to be furnished to OFCOM under this section shall, if they so require, be in such form or verified in such manner as they may specify.

(4) Where an application for a digital programme licence is made to OFCOM in accordance with the provisions of this section, they shall grant the licence unless precluded from doing so by section 3(3)(a) or 5(1).

(5)–(6) [...]

19 Duration and conditions of digital programme licence

(1) Subject to the provisions of this Part and to section 42 as applied by section 23(8), a digital programme licence shall continue in force until it is surrendered by its holder.

(3) A digital programme licence shall also include such conditions as appear to OFCOM to be appropriate for requiring the holder of the licence—

    (a) on entering into any agreement with the provider of a television multiplex service or general multiplex service for the provision of a digital programme service to be broadcast by means of that provider's service, to notify OFCOM—

        (i) of the identity of the service by means of which it will be broadcast,

        (ii) of the characteristics of the digital programme service to which the agreement relates,

        (iii) of the period during which it will be provided, and

        (iv) where under the agreement the holder of the digital programme licence will be entitled to the use of a specified amount of digital capacity, of that amount,

    (b) when any such agreement is varied so far as it relates to any of the matters mentioned in paragraph (a)(i), (ii), (iii) or (iv), to notify OFCOM of the variation so far as relating to those matters, and

    (c) where he is providing a digital programme service to the provider of a television multiplex service or general multiplex service in accordance with such an agreement as is mentioned in paragraph (a) but intends to cease doing so, to notify OFCOM of that fact.

(4)–(10) [...]

20–22 [...]

23 Enforcement of digital programme licences

(1) If OFCOM are satisfied that the holder of a digital programme licence has failed to comply with any condition of the licence or with any direction given by OFCOM under or by virtue of any provision of this Part, they may (subject to the following provisions of this section) serve on him—

    (a) a notice requiring him to pay, within a specified period, a specified financial penalty to OFCOM, or

    (b) a notice providing that the licence is to expire on a specified date, which shall be at least one year from the date of service of the notice.

(2) The amount of any financial penalty imposed on any person in pursuance of subsection (1)(a) shall not exceed the maximum penalty given by subsection (2A).

(2A) The maximum penalty is whichever is the greater of—

    (a) £250,000; and

    (b) 5 per cent of the aggregate amount of the shares of multiplex revenue attributable to him in relation to television multiplex services and general multiplex services in respect of relevant accounting periods.

Digital broadcasting of services provided by independent analogue broadcasters

28 [...]

29 The S4C digital service

(2) Sections 57(4), 58(5), 60 and 64 of the 1990 Act shall apply in relation to S4C Digital as they apply in relation to S4C.

30–31 [...]

Miscellaneous and supplemental

35   Enforcement of licences held by BBC companies

Where OFCOM—

    (a) give a direction to a BBC company under section 40(1) of the 1990 Act as applied by section 23(8) or 27(8),

    (b) serve a notice on a BBC company under any provision of section 17, 23 or 27, or

    (c) receive any representations from a BBC company under section 17(4), 23(6) or 27(6) or under section 42 of the 1990 Act as so applied,

OFCOM shall send a copy of the direction, notice or representations to the Secretary of State.

36   Power to vary amount of financial penalties

    (1) The Secretary of State may by order amend any of the provisions specified in subsection (2) by substituting a different sum for the sum for the time being specified there.

    (2) The provisions referred to in subsection (1) are—

    (a) section 11(5B)(a) and (5C)(a);

    (b) section 17(2A)(a);

    (c) section 23(2A)(a); and

    (d) section 27(2A)(a).

    (3) No order is to be made under subsection (1) unless a draft of the order has been laid before Parliament and approved by a resolution of each House.

38   [...]

Miscellaneous and supplemental

72   Interpretation of Part II

    (1) In this Part (unless the context otherwise requires)—

'ancillary service' has the meaning given by section 63(2);

    [...]

'digital additional service' has the meaning given by section 63(1), and 'digital additional services licence' means a licence to provide such services;

'digital sound programme service' has the meaning given by section 40(5), and 'digital sound programme licence' means a licence to provide such services;

'general multiplex service' has the same meaning as in Part 3 of the Communications Act 2003;

'independent national broadcaster' has the meaning given by section 41(1),

'licence' means a licence under this Part, and 'licensed' shall be construed accordingly;

'local digital sound programme service' and 'national digital sound programme service' shall be construed in accordance with section 60(1) and 'local digital sound programme licence' and 'national digital sound programme licence' mean a licence to provide local digital sound programme services and a licence to provide national digital sound programme services respectively;

'local radio multiplex service' and 'national radio multiplex service' shall be construed in accordance with section 40(4), and 'local radio multiplex licence' and 'radio multiplex licence' mean a licence to provide a local radio

    [...]

PART IV SPORTING AND OTHER EVENTS OF NATIONAL INTEREST

97   Listed events

    (1) The Secretary of State may, for the purposes of this Part, maintain a list of sporting and other events of national interest, and an event for the time being included in the list is referred to in this Part as a 'listed event'.

    (1A) A list maintained under subsection (1) must be divided into two categories, and those categories are referred to in this Part as 'Group A' and 'Group B'.

(1B) Each listed event must be allocated either to Group A or to Group B.

(2) Before drawing up such a list, or revising or ceasing to maintain it, the Secretary of State must consult—

    (a) OFCOM,

    (b) the BBC,

    (c) the Welsh Authority, and

    (d) in relation to a relevant event, the person from whom the rights to televise that event may be acquired.

(2A) For the purposes of subsection (2)(d), a relevant event is an event which the Secretary of State proposes—

    (a) to include in a list maintained under subsection (1),

    (b) to omit from such a list, or

    (c) to move from one category in such a list to the other.

(3) As soon as he has drawn up or revised such a list as is mentioned in subsection (1) the Secretary of State shall publish the list in such manner as he considers appropriate for bringing it to the attention of—

    (a) the persons mentioned in subsection (2), and

    (b) every person who is the holder of a licence granted [...] under Part I of the 1990 Act or a digital programme licence granted [...] under Part I of this Act.

(4) In this section 'national interest' includes interest within England, Scotland, Wales or Northern Ireland.

(5) The inclusion of any relevant event in such a list as is mentioned in subsection (1) shall not affect—

    (a) the validity of any contract entered into before the date on which the Secretary of State consulted the persons mentioned in subsection (2) in relation to the proposed inclusion, or

    (b) the exercise of any rights acquired under such a contract.

(5A) The allocation or transfer of an event to group A does not affect the validity of a contract entered into before the day on which the Secretary of State consulted the persons mentioned in subsection (2) in relation to the proposed allocation or transfer.

(5B) The Secretary of State may direct that, for the transitional purposes set out in the direction, the transfer of a Group B event to Group A is not to affect the application to that event of provisions of this Part relating to a Group B event.

(6) The list drawn up by the Secretary of State for the purposes of section 182 of the 1990 Act, as that list is in force immediately before the commencement of this section, shall be taken to have been drawn up for the purposes of this Part.

98 Categories of service

(1) For the purposes of this Part, television programme services and EEA satellite services shall be divided into two categories as follows—

    (a) those television programme services and EEA satellite services which for the time being satisfy the qualifying conditions, and

    (b) all other television programme services and EEA satellite services.

(2) In this section 'the qualifying conditions', in relation to a service, means the conditions—

    (a) that the service is provided without any consideration being required for reception of the service, and

    (b) that the service is received by at least 95 per cent of the population of the United Kingdom.

(3) There shall be disregarded for the purposes of subsection (2)(a) any fee payable in respect of a licence for the purposes of section 363 of the Communications Act 2003.

(4) The condition in subsection (2)(b)—

    (a) is to be taken to be satisfied in relation to a regional Channel 3 service if it is satisfied in relation to Channel 3 as a whole, and

    (b) is to be taken to be satisfied in relation to Channel 4 if it is satisfied in relation to Channel 4 and S4C taken together.

(5) OFCOM shall from time to time publish a list of the television programme services and EEA satellite services which appear to them to satisfy the qualifying conditions.

(6) In this section 'EEA satellite service' means any service which—

(a) consists in the broadcasting of television programmes from a satellite so as to be available for reception by members of the public (within the meaning of Part 3 of the Communications Act 2003), and

(b) is provided by a person who for the purposes of Council Directive 89/552/EEC is under the jurisdiction of an EEA State other than the United Kingdom.

99   Contract for exclusive right to televise listed event to be void

(1) Any contract entered into after the commencement of this section under which a television programme provider acquires rights to televise the whole or any part of a listed event live for reception in the United Kingdom, or in any area of the United Kingdom, shall be void so far as it purports, in relation to the whole or any part of the event or in relation to reception in the United Kingdom or any area of the United Kingdom, to grant those rights exclusively to any one television programme provider.

(2) In this Part 'television programme provider' means the BBC, the Welsh Authority or any person who is the holder of any licence under Part I of the 1990 Act or a digital programme licence under Part I of this Act.

(3) For the purpose of this section rights to televise the whole or any part of an event live for reception in any area granted to a television programme provider are granted exclusively if the person granting them—

(a) has not granted any right to televise the whole or, as the case may be, that part of the event live for reception in that area to any other television programme provider nor to any broadcaster who for the purposes of Council Directive 89/ 552/EEC is under the jurisdiction of an EEA State other than the United Kingdom, and

(b) is precluded by the terms of the contract from doing so.

100   Contract for televising listed event must specify category of service

(1) Any contract entered into after the commencement of this section shall be void so far as it purports to grant to a television programme provider rights to televise the whole or any part of a listed event live for reception in the United Kingdom, or any area of the United Kingdom, unless the contract complies with subsection (2).

(2) A contract complies with this subsection if the terms of the contract allow the television programme provider to include the live coverage of the listed event—

(a) only in a television programme service falling within paragraph (a) of subsection (1) of section 98, or

(b) only in a television programme service falling within paragraph (b) of the subsection.

101   Restriction on televising of listed event

(1) A television programme provider providing a service falling within either of the categories set out in subsection (1) of section 98 ('the first service') for reception in the United Kingdom or in any area of the United Kingdom shall not, without the previous consent of OFCOM, include in that service live coverage of the whole or any part of a listed event unless—

(a) another person, who is providing a service falling within the other category set out in that subsection ('the second service'), has acquired the right to include in the second service live coverage of the whole of the event or of that part of the event, and

(b) the area for which the second service is provided consists of or includes the whole, or substantially the whole, of the area for which the first service is provided.

(2) OFCOM may revoke any consent given by them under subsection (1).

(3) Failure to comply with subsection (1) shall not affect the validity of any contract.

(4) Subsection (1) shall not have effect where the television programme provider providing the first service is exercising rights acquired before the commencement of this section.

101A   Designated events in relation to other EEA States

For the purposes of this Part, a sporting or other event is a designated event, in relation to an EEA State other than the United Kingdom, if—

    (a) that State has designated the event in accordance with Article 3a(1) of Council Directive 89/552/EEC as being of major importance to its society, and

    (b) the designation forms part of measures—

        (i) which have been notified by that State to the European Commission for the purposes of Article 3a(2) of that Directive, and

        (ii) notice of which has been published by the European Commission in the Official Journal of the Communities.

101B   Restriction on televising of an event designated by other EEA State

(1) A television programme provider shall not, without the previous consent of OFCOM, exercise rights to televise the whole or part of an event which is a designated event, in relation to an EEA State other than the United Kingdom, for reception in that EEA State or any area of that EEA State, where a substantial proportion of the public in that EEA State is deprived of the possibility of following that event by live or deferred coverage on free television as determined by that State in accordance with Article 3a(1) of Council Directive 89/552/EEC.

(2) OFCOM may revoke any consent given by them under subsection (1).

(3) Failure to comply with subsection (1) shall not affect the validity of any contract.

(4) Subsection (1) shall not have effect where the rights were acquired before the day on which the event became a designated event.

102   Power of OFCOM to impose penalty

(1) If OFCOM—

    (a) are satisfied that the holder of a licence under Part I of the 1990 Act or a digital programme licence under Part I of this Act has failed to comply with subsection (1) of section 101 or subsection (1) of section 101B, and

    (b) are not satisfied that in all the circumstances it would be unreasonable to expect him to have complied with that subsection,

they may require him to pay, within a specified period, a specified financial penalty to OFCOM.

(2) If OFCOM are satisfied that, in connection with an application for consent under subsection (1) of section 101 or subsection (1) of section 101B, the holder of a licence under Part I of the 1990 Act or a digital programme licence under Part I of this Act has—

    (a) provided them with information which was false in a material particular, or

    (b) withheld any material information with the intention of causing OFCOM to be misled,

they may require him to pay, within a specified period, a specified financial penalty to OFCOM.

(2A) Before requiring any person to pay a financial penalty under subsection (1) on the ground that he has failed to comply with subsection (1) of section 101B, OFCOM shall consult such persons (who may include competent authorities in other EEA States) as appear to OFCOM to be appropriate.

(3) The amount of any financial penalty imposed on any person under subsection (1) or (2) shall not exceed the amount produced by multiplying the relevant consideration by the prescribed multiplier.

(4) In subsection (3)—

    (a) 'the relevant consideration' means an amount determined by OFCOM as representing so much of any consideration paid by the person on whom the penalty is being imposed as is attributable to the acquisition of the rights to televise the event in question, and

    (b) 'the prescribed multiplier' means such number as the Secretary of State may from time to time by order prescribe.

(5) An order under subsection (4)(b) shall be subject to annulment in pursuance of a resolution of either House of Parliament.

103   Report to Secretary of State
(1) If OFCOM—
  (a) are satisfied that a broadcasting body has failed to comply with subsection (1) of section 101 or subsection (1) of section 101B, and
  (b) are not satisfied that in all the circumstances it would be unreasonable to expect the body to have complied with that subsection,
they shall make a report on the matter to the Secretary of State.

104   Code of guidance
(1) OFCOM shall draw up, and may from time to time revise, a code giving guidance—
  (a) as to the matters which they will take into account in determining whether to give or to revoke their consent for the purposes of section 101(1B) or section 101B(1); and
  (b) as to the matters which they will take into account in determining for the purposes of section 102(1) or 103(1), whether in all the circumstances it is unreasonable to expect a television programme provider to comply with section 101(1) or section 101B(1).

(2) In exercising their powers under this Part, OFCOM shall have regard to the provisions of the code.

104ZA   Regulations about coverage of listed events
(1) OFCOM may make regulations for determining for the purposes of this Part—
  (a) the circumstances in which the televising of listed events generally, or of a particular listed event, is or is not to be treated as live;
  (b) what (whether generally or in relation to particular circumstances) is to be taken to represent the provision of adequate alternative coverage; and
  (c) the requirements that must be satisfied for the purposes of section 101(1C)(d) by persons who have acquired rights to provide adequate alternative coverage.

(2) The power conferred by subsection (1)(a) does not include power to define 'live' for the purposes of section 101B.

(3) Section 403 of the Communications Act 2003 (procedure for regulations and orders made by OFCOM) applies to the power of OFCOM to make regulations under this section.

104A   Provision of information
(1) A television programme provider shall, at the request of OFCOM, provide them with such information as OFCOM consider appropriate regarding any contract which he has entered into which relates to an event which, in relation to an EEA State other than the United Kingdom, is a designated event.

(2) If so requested by a competent authority in an EEA State other than the United Kingdom, OFCOM shall provide the authority with such information relating to rights to televise listed events or designated events as OFCOM consider it appropriate to provide.

105   Interpretation of Part IV and supplementary provisions
(1) In this Part (unless the context otherwise requires)—
'adequate alternative coverage' and 'live' are to be construed in accordance with any regulations under section 104ZA;
'Channel 4' has the same meaning as in Part I of the 1990 Act;
[...]
'designated event', in relation to an EEA State other than the United Kingdom, has the meaning given by section 101A;
'listed event' has the meaning given by section 97(1);
'national Channel 3 service' and 'regional Channel 3 service' have the same meaning as in Part I of the 1990 Act;
'S4C' has the same meaning as in Part I of the 1990 Act;
'television broadcasting service' has the same meaning as in Part I of the 1990 Act;

'television programme provider' has the meaning given by section 99(2);

'television programme service' has the same meaning as in Part I of the 1990 Act.

(2) Section 182 of the 1990 Act (certain events not to be shown on pay-per-view terms) shall cease to have effect.

PART V

106 [...]

Unjust or unfair treatment or unwarranted infringement of privacy

107 Preparation by OFCOM of code relating to avoidance of unjust or unfair treatment or interference with privacy

(1) It shall be the duty of OFCOM to draw up, and from time to time review; a code giving guidance as to principles to be observed, and practices to be followed, in connection with the avoidance of—

(a) unjust or unfair treatment in programmes to which this section applies, or

(b) unwarranted infringement of privacy in, or in connection with the obtaining of material included in, such programmes.

(3) OFCOM shall from time to time publish the code (as for the time being in force).

(4) Before drawing up or revising the code, OFCOM shall consult—

(a) each broadcasting body, and

(b) such other persons as appear to OFCOM to be appropriate.

(5) This section applies to—

(a) any programme broadcast by the BBC,

(b) any programme broadcast by the Welsh Authority or included in [any public service of the Welsh Authority (within the meaning of Part 2 of Schedule 12 to the Communications Act 2003), and

any programme included in a licensed service.

Complaints

110 General functions of OFCOM in relation to complaints

(1) Subject to the provisions of this Part, it shall be the duty of OFCOM to consider and adjudicate on complaints which are made to them in accordance with section 111 and 114 and relate—

(a) to unjust or unfair treatment in programmes to which section 107 applies, or

(b) to unwarranted infringement of privacy in, or in connection with the obtaining of material included in, such programmes.

(3) In exercising their functions under subsection (1), OFCOM shall take into account any relevant provisions of the code maintained by them under section 107.

(4) In this Part—

'a fairness complaint' means a complaint to OFCOM in respect of any of the matters referred to in subsection (1)(a) and (b)[.]

[...]

111 Complaints of unfair treatment etc.

(1) A fairness complaint may be made by an individual or by a body of persons, whether incorporated or not, but, subject to subsection (2), shall not be entertained by OFCOM unless made by the person affected or by a person authorised by him to make the complaint for him.

(2) Where the person affected is an individual who has died, a fairness complaint may be made by his personal representative or by a member of the family of the person affected, or by some other person or body closely connected with him (whether as his employer, or as a body of which he was at his death a member, or in any other way).

(3) Where the person affected is an individual who is for any reason both unable to make a complaint himself and unable to authorise another person to do so for him, a fairness complaint

may be made by a member of the family of the person affected, or by some other person or body closely connected with him (whether as his employer, or as a body of which he is a member, or in any other way).

(4) OFCOM shall not entertain, or proceed with the consideration of, a fairness complaint if it appears to them that the complaint relates to the broadcasting of the relevant programme, or to its inclusion in a licensed service, on an occasion more than five years after the death of the person affected, unless it appears to them that in the particular circumstances it is appropriate to do so.

(5) OFCOM may refuse to entertain a fairness complaint if it appears to them not to have been made within a reasonable time after the last occasion on which the relevant programme was broadcast or, as the case may be, included in a licensed service.

(6) Where, in the case of a fairness complaint, the relevant programme was broadcast or included in a licensed service after the death of the person affected, subsection (5) shall apply as if at the end there were added 'within five years (or such longer period as may be allowed by OFCOM in the particular case under subsection (4) after the death of the person affected'.

(7) OFCOM may refuse to entertain—

    (a) a fairness complaint which is a complaint of unjust or unfair treatment if the person named as the person affected was not himself the subject of the treatment complained of and it appears to OFCOM that he did not have a sufficiently direct interest in the subject-matter of that treatment to justify the making of a complaint with him as the person affected, or

    (b) a complaint made under subsection (2) or (3) by a person other than the person affected or a person authorised by him, if it appears to OFCOM that the complainant's connection with the person affected is not sufficiently close to justify the making of the complaint by him.

112–113   [...]

114   Supplementary provisions as to making of complaints of either kind

(1) A fairness complaint must be in writing, or in such other form as OFCOM may allow, and must give particulars of the matters complained of.

(2) OFCOM shall not entertain, or proceed with the consideration of, a fairness complaint if it appears to them—

    (a) that the matter complained of is the subject of proceedings in a court of law in the United Kingdom, or

    (b) that the matter complained of is a matter in respect of which the complainant or [...] the person affected has a remedy by way of proceedings in a court of law in the United Kingdom, and that in the particular circumstances it is not appropriate for OFCOM to consider a complaint about it, or

    (c) that the complaint is frivolous, or

    (d) that for any other reason it is inappropriate for them to entertain, or proceed with the consideration of, the complaint.

115   Consideration of fairness complaints

(1) Subject to the provisions of sections 111 and 114, every fairness complaint made to OFCOM shall be considered by them either at a hearing or, if they think fit, without a hearing.

(2) Hearings under this section shall be held in private; and where such a hearing is held in respect of a fairness complaint, each of the following persons shall be given an opportunity to attend and be heard, namely—

    (a) the complainant,

    (b) the relevant person,

    (d) any person not falling within any of paragraphs (a) or (b) who appears to OFCOM to have been responsible for the making or provision of that programme, and

    (e) any other person who OFCOM consider might be able to assist at the hearing.

(3) Before OFCOM proceed to consider a fairness complaint they shall send a copy of it—

    (a) to the relevant person.

(4) Where the relevant person receives from OFCOM a copy of the complaint, it shall be the duty of that person, if so required by OFCOM—

    (a) to provide OFCOM with a visual or sound recording of the relevant programme or of any specified part of it, if and so far as the relevant person has such a recording in his possession;

    (b) to make suitable arrangements for enabling the complainant to view or hear the relevant programme, or any specified part of it, if and so far as the relevant person has in his possession a visual or sound recording of it;

    (c) to provide OFCOM and the complainant with a transcript of so much of the relevant programme, or of any specified part of it, as consisted of speech, if and so far as the relevant person is able to do so;

    (d) to provide OFCOM and the complainant with copies of any documents in the possession of the relevant person, being the originals or copies of any correspondence between that person and the person affected or the complainant in connection with the complaint;

    (da) to provide OFCOM with such other things appearing to OFCOM to be relevant to their consideration of the complaint, and to be in the possession of the relevant person, as may be specified or described by OFCOM;

    (e) to furnish to OFCOM and the complainant a written statement in answer to the complaint.

(5) Where the relevant person receives from OFCOM a copy of a fairness complaint, it shall also be the duty of that person, if so required by OFCOM—

    (a) where the relevant person is a broadcasting body, to arrange for one or more of the governors, members or employees of the body to attend OFCOM and assist them in their consideration of the complaint, or

    (b) where the relevant person is a body other than a broadcasting body, to arrange for one or more of the following, namely—

        (i) the persons who take part in the management or control of the body, or

        (ii) the employees of the body, to attend OFCOM and assist them in their consideration of the complaint, or

    (c) where the relevant person is an individual, to attend, or to arrange for one or more of his employees to attend, OFCOM and assist them in their consideration of the complaint.

(6) Where the relevant person receives from OFCOM a copy of a fairness complaint and, in connection with the complaint, OFCOM make to any other person a request to which this subsection applies, it shall be the duty of the relevant person to take such steps as he reasonably can to ensure that the request is complied with.

(7) Subsection (6) applies to the following requests by OFCOM to any such other person as is there mentioned, namely—

    (a) a request to make suitable arrangements for enabling the complainant and any member or employee of OFCOM to view or hear the relevant programme, or any specified part of it, if and so far as the person requested has in his possession a visual or sound recording of it;

    (b) a request to provide OFCOM and the complainant with a transcript of so much of the relevant programme, or of any specified part of it, as consisted of speech, if and so far as the person requested is able to do so;

    (c) a request to provide OFCOM and the complainant with copies of any documents in the possession of the person requested, being the originals or copies of any correspondence between that person and the person affected or the complainant in connection with the complaint;

(ca) a request to provide OFCOM with such other things appearing to OFCOM to be relevant to their consideration of the complaint, and to be in the possession of the person requested, as may be specified or described by OFCOM;

(d) a request to furnish to OFCOM and the complainant a written statement in answer to the complaint;

(e) a request to attend, or (where the person requested is not an individual) to arrange for a representative to attend, OFCOM and assist them in their consideration of the complaint.

(8) Where OFCOM have adjudicated on a fairness complaint, OFCOM shall send a copy of their findings to the complainant.

(9) In this section 'the relevant person' means—

(a) in a case where the relevant programme was broadcast by a broadcasting body, that body, and

(b) in a case where the relevant programme was included in a licensed service, the licence holder providing the service.

116   [...]

117   Duty to retain recordings

For the purposes of section 115 of this Act and of section 167 of the 1990 Act (power to make copies of recordings in connection with certain offences) it shall be the duty of each broadcasting body to retain a recording of every television or sound programme which is broadcast by that body—

(a) where it is of a television programme, during the period of 90 days beginning with the day of the broadcast, and

(b) where it is of a sound programme, during the period of 42 days beginning with the day of the broadcast.

119   Publication of OFCOM's findings

(1) Where OFCOM have considered and adjudicated upon a fairness complaint, they may direct the relevant person to publish the matters mentioned in subsection (3) in such manner, and within such period, as may be specified in the directions.

(3) Those matters are—

(a) a summary of the complaint;

(b) OFCOM's findings on the complaint or a summary of them;

(4) References in subsection (1) to the publication of any matter are references to the publication of that matter without its being accompanied by any observations made by a person other than OFCOM and relating to the complaint.

(5) The form and content of any such summary as is mentioned in subsection (3)(a) or (b) shall be such as may be approved by OFCOM.

(6) A relevant person shall comply with any directions given to him under this section.

(7) The regulatory regime for every licensed service includes the conditions that OFCOM consider appropriate for securing that the licence holder complies with every direction given to him under this section.

(7A) Section 263 of the Communications Act 2003 applies in relation to conditions included by virtue of subsection (7) in the regulatory regime for a licensed service as it applies in relation to conditions which are so included by virtue of a provision of Chapter 4 of Part 3 of that Act.

(7B) It is hereby declared that, where—

(a) OFCOM exercise their powers under this Part to adjudicate upon a fairness complaint or to give a direction under subsection (1), and

(b) it appears to them that the matters to which the complaint in question relates consist in or include a contravention of the conditions of the licence for a licensed service,

the exercise by OFCOM of their powers under this Part is not to preclude the exercise by them of their powers under any other enactment in respect of the contravention.

(7C) Where OFCOM are proposing to exercise any of their powers in respect of a contravention of a licence condition in a case in which the contravention relates to matters that have been the subject-matter of a fairness complaint—

    (a) OFCOM may have regard, in the exercise of those powers, to any matters considered or steps taken by them for the purpose of adjudicating upon that complaint and to any direction given by them under this section; but

    (b) steps taken for the purposes of this Part do not satisfy a requirement to give the licence holder in relation to whom those powers are to be exercised a reasonable opportunity, before they are exercised, of making representations to OFCOM.

(8) OFCOM shall publish, monthly or at such other intervals as they think fit and in such manner as they think fit, reports each containing, as regards every fairness complaint which falls within this subsection and has been dealt with by them in the period covered by the report—

    (a) a summary of the complaint and the action taken by them on it,

    (b) where they have adjudicated on it, a summary of—

        (i) their findings,

        (ii) any direction given under subsection (1), or other action taken by them, in relation to the complaint, and

    (c) where a direction has been given under subsection (1) in relation to the complaint, a summary of any action taken by a broadcasting body or the holder of a licence to provide a licensed service in pursuance of the direction.

(9) A fairness complaint [...] made to OFCOM falls within subsection (8) unless it is one which under section 111(1), (4) or (5) or 114(2) they have refused to entertain.

(10) OFCOM may, if they think fit, omit from any summary which is included in a report under subsection (8) and relates to a fairness complaint any information which could lead to the disclosure of the identity of any person connected with the complaint in question other than a relevant person.

(11) The references in subsections (3)(b) and (8)(b) to OFCOM's findings on a complaint shall be construed, in relation to a fairness complaint which has been considered by them in two or more parts, as references to their findings on each part of the complaint.

(11A) In this section 'relevant person' means—

    (a) in a case where the relevant programme was broadcast by a broadcasting body, that body; and

    (b) in a case where the relevant programme was included in a licensed service, the licence holder providing that service.

121   Certain statements etc. protected by qualified privilege for purposes of defamation

(1) For the purposes of the law relating to defamation—

    (a) publication of any statement in the course of the consideration by OFCOM of, and their adjudication on, a fairness complaint,

    (b) publication by OFCOM of directions under section 119(1) relating to a fairness complaint, or

    (c) publication of a report of OFCOM, so far as the report relates to fairness complaints, is privileged unless the publication is shown to be made with malice.

(2) Nothing in subsection (1) shall be construed as limiting any privilege subsisting apart from that subsection.

Miscellaneous and general

130   Interpretation of Part V

(1) In this Part (unless the context otherwise requires)—

'broadcasting body' means the BBC or the Welsh Authority;

'fairness complaint' has the meaning given by section 110(4);

'licensed service' means—

    (a) any television programme service (within the meaning of Part I of the 1990 Act) which is licensed under that Part,

  (aa) the public teletext service,

    (b) any relevant independent radio service (within the meaning of section 85 of the 1990 Act),

    (c) any additional service (within the meaning of Part 1 of the 1990 Act) which is licensed under that Part,

    (d) any digital programme service (within the meaning of Part I of this Act) which is licensed under that Part,

    (e) any qualifying service (within the meaning of Part I of this Act) provided by a person other than the Welsh Authority,

    (f) any digital sound programme service (within the meaning of Part II of this Act) which is licensed under that Part,

    (g) any simulcast radio service (within the meaning of Part II of this Act), and

    (h) any digital additional service (within the meaning of Part I or II of this Act)

which is licensed under that Part;

'participant', in relation to a programme, means a person who appeared, or whose voice was heard, in the programme;

'the person affected'—

    (a) in relation to any such unjust or unfair treatment as is mentioned in section 110(1), means a participant in the programme in question who was the subject of that treatment or a person who, whether such a participant or not, had a direct interest in the subject-matter of that treatment, and

    (b) in relation to any such unwarranted infringement of privacy as is so mentioned, means a person whose privacy was infringed;

'programme' includes an advertisement and a teletext transmission and, in relation to a service, includes any item included in that service;

'the relevant programme', in relation to a complaint, means the programme to which the complaint relates;

'unjust or unfair treatment' includes treatment which is unjust or unfair because of the way in which material included in a programme has been selected or arranged.

  (2) In this Part—

    (a) any reference to programmes to which section 107 applies shall be construed in accordance with section 107(5), [. . .]

    (b) [. . .]

PART VII COPYRIGHT AND RELATED MATTERS

137 Avoidance of certain terms relating to use for purpose of news reporting of visual images from broadcast or cable programme

  (1) Any provision in an agreement is void in so far as it purports to prohibit or restrict relevant dealing with a broadcast in any circumstances where by virtue of section 30(2) of the Copyright, Designs and Patents Act 1988 (fair dealing for the purpose of reporting current events) copyright in the broadcast is not infringed.

  (2) In subsection (1)—

    (a) 'relevant dealing', in relation to a broadcast, means dealing by communicating to the public any visual images taken from that broadcast, and

    (b) 'broadcast' and 'communicating to the public' have the same meaning as in Part I of the Copyright, Designs and Patents Act 1988.

140–141 [. . .]

PART VIII MISCELLANEOUS AND GENERAL

Standards for transmission systems

142 [...]

Disqualification on grounds relating to political objects

143 Duties of OFCOM in cases involving disqualification on grounds related to political objects

(1) If it appears to OFCOM that there are grounds for suspecting that any person who is an applicant for a licence under Part 1 or 3 of the 1990 Act or Part 1 or 2 of this Act, is by virtue of any of the provisions specified in subsection (5) a disqualified person in relation to that licence, OFCOM shall be regarded as failing to discharge their duty under section 5(1) or 88(1) of the 1990 Act or section 5(1) or 44(1) of this Act, if they grant the licence to that person without being provided with information which satisfies them that he is not on those grounds a disqualified person by virtue of that provision.

(2) If it appears to OFCOM that there are grounds for suspecting that any person who is the holder of a licence under Part 1 or 3 of the 1990 Act or Part 1 or 2 of this Act, is by virtue of any of the provisions specified in subsection (5) a disqualified person in relation to that licence, OFCOM shall be regarded as failing to discharge their duty under section 5(1) or 88(1) of the 1990 Act or section 5(1) or 44(1) of this Act, unless—

    (a) they require him to provide them with information for the purpose of determining whether he is on those grounds a disqualified person by virtue of that provision, and

    (b) if they are satisfied that he is a disqualified person, they revoke the licence.

(5) The provisions referred to in subsections (1) and (2) are the following provisions of paragraph 1(1) of Part II of Schedule 2 to the 1990 Act—

    (a) paragraphs (d) to (g),

    (b) paragraph (h) so far as relating to participation by bodies falling within paragraph (d), (e) or (g),

    (c) paragraph (hh) so far as relating to a body corporate controlled by a body corporate in which a body falling within paragraph (d), (e), or (g) is a participant with more than a 5 per cent. interest,

    (d) paragraph (i) so far as relating to control by a person falling within any of paragraphs to (g) or by two or more such persons, and

    (e) paragraph (j) so far as relating to participation by a body corporate which is controlled by a person falling within any of paragraphs (d) to (g) or by two or more such persons.

(6) Nothing in subsections (1) to (5) shall be taken to limit the generality of the duties imposed on OFCOM by sections 5(1) and 88(1) of the 1990 Act and sections 5(1) and 44(1) of this Act.

    (a)–(b) [...]

Provision of false information, etc.

144 Offence of providing false information in certain circumstances

(1) A person who, in connection with an application by him for, or his continued holding of, a licence under the 1990 Act or this Act—

    (a) makes a statement to OFCOM which he knows to be false in a material particular, or

    (b) recklessly makes a statement to OFCOM which is false in a material particular, is guilty of an offence if the statement relates to a matter which would be relevant in determining whether he is by virtue of any of the provisions specified in subsection (3) a disqualified person, and he is by virtue of any of those provisions a disqualified person in relation to that licence.

(2) A person who, in connection with an application by him for, or his continued holding of, a licence under the 1990 Act or this Act, withholds any information with the intention of causing OFCOM to be misled is guilty of an offence if—

(a) the information would be relevant in determining whether he is by virtue of any of the provisions specified in subsection (3) a disqualified person, and

(b) he is by virtue of any of those provisions a disqualified person in relation to that licence.

(3) The provisions referred to in subsections (1) and (2) are the following provisions of paragraph 1(1) of Part II of Schedule 2 to the 1990 Act—

(a) paragraphs (d) to (g),

(b) paragraph (h) so far as relating to participation by bodies falling within paragraph (d), (e) or (g),

(c) paragraph (hh) so far as relating to a body corporate controlled by a body corporate in which a body falling within paragraph (d), (e) or (g) is a participant with more than a 5 per cent. interest,

(d) paragraph (i) so far as relating to control by a person falling within any of paragraphs (d) to (g) or by two or more such persons, and

(e) paragraph (j) so far as relating to participation by a body corporate which is controlled by a person falling within any of paragraphs (d) to (g) or by two or more such persons.

(4) A person guilty of an offence under this section is liable on summary conviction to a fine not exceeding level 5 on the standard scale.

(5) [...]

145   Disqualification for offence of supplying false information, etc.

(1) Where a person is convicted of an offence under section 144 the court by which he is convicted may make an order (in this section referred to as a 'disqualification order') disqualifying him from holding a licence during a period specified in the order.

(2) The period specified in a disqualification order shall not exceed five years beginning with the date on which the order takes effect.

(3) Where an individual is disqualified from holding a licence by virtue of a disqualification order, any body corporate—

(a) of which he is a director, or

(b) in the management of which he is directly or indirectly concerned, is also disqualified from holding a licence.

(4) Where the holder of a licence is disqualified by virtue of a disqualification order, the licence shall be treated as being revoked with effect from the time when the order takes effect.

(8) In this section—

'licence' means a licence under Part 1 or 3 of the 1990 Act or under Part 1 or 2 of this Act.

146   Supplementary provisions as to disqualification orders

(1) A person disqualified by a disqualification order may appeal against the order in the same manner as against a conviction.

General

147   General interpretation

(1) In this Act—

'the 1990 Act' means the Broadcasting Act 1990;

'the BBC' means the British Broadcasting Corporation;

'OFCOM' means the Office of Communications;

(2) The 1990 Act and the following provisions of this Act—

(a) Parts I and II and Schedule 1,

(b) Part IV,

(c) Part V and Schedules 3 and 4, and

(d) sections 142 to 146,

shall be construed as if those provisions were contained in that Act.

150 Short title and extent

(1) This Act may be cited as the Broadcasting Act 1996.

(2) This Act, except paragraph 27 of Schedule 10, extends to Northern Ireland.

(3) Section 204(6) of the 1990 Act (power to extend to Isle of Man and Channel Islands) applies to the provisions of this Act amending that Act.

(4) Her Majesty may by Order in Council direct that any of the other provisions of this Act shall extend to the Isle of Man or any of the Channel Islands with such modifications, if any, as appear to Her Majesty to be appropriate.

Communications Act 2003

(2003, c. 21)

PART 1 FUNCTIONS OF OFCOM

Transferred and assigned functions

1 Functions and general powers of OFCOM

(1) The Office of Communications ('OFCOM') shall have the following functions—

    (a) the functions transferred to OFCOM under section 2; and

    (b) such other functions as may be conferred on OFCOM by or under any enactment (including this Act)…….

(3) OFCOM may do anything which appears to them to be incidental or conducive to the carrying out of their functions, including borrow money.

(4) OFCOM are not to borrow money except with the consent of the Secretary of State, or in accordance with a general authorisation given by him.

(5) OFCOM's powers under subsection (3) include, in particular—

    (a) power to undertake research and development work in connection with any matter in relation to which they have functions;

    (b) power to promote the carrying out of such research and development by others, or otherwise to arrange for it to be carried out by others;

    (c) power to institute and carry on criminal proceedings in England and Wales or Northern Ireland for an offence relating to a matter in relation to which they have functions; and

    (d) power, in such cases and in such circumstances as they may think fit, to make payments (where no legal liability arises) to persons adversely affected by the carrying out by OFCOM of any of their functions.

(6) In exercise of their powers under subsection (3), OFCOM must establish and maintain separate offices in each of the following parts of the United Kingdom—

    (a) England;

    (b) Wales;

    (c) Scotland; and

    (d) Northern Ireland.

General duties in carrying out functions

3 General duties of OFCOM

(1) It shall be the principal duty of OFCOM, in carrying out their functions—

    (a) to further the interests of citizens in relation to communications matters; and

    (b) to further the interests of consumers in relevant markets, where appropriate by promoting competition.

(2) The things which, by virtue of subsection (1), OFCOM are required to secure in the carrying out of their functions include, in particular, each of the following—

(a) the optimal use for wireless telegraphy of the electro-magnetic spectrum;

(b) the availability throughout the United Kingdom of a wide range of electronic communications services;

(c) the availability throughout the United Kingdom of a wide range of television and radio services which (taken as a whole) are both of high quality and calculated to appeal to a variety of tastes and interests;

(d) the maintenance of a sufficient plurality of providers of different television and radio services;

(e) the application, in the case of all television and radio services, of standards that provide adequate protection to members of the public from the inclusion of offensive and harmful material in such services;

(f) the application, in the case of all television and radio services, of standards that provide adequate protection to members of the public and all other persons from both—

(i) unfair treatment in programmes included in such services; and

(ii) unwarranted infringements of privacy resulting from activities carried on for the purposes of such services.

(3) In performing their duties under subsection (1), OFCOM must have regard, in all cases, to—

(a) the principles under which regulatory activities should be transparent, accountable, proportionate, consistent and targeted only at cases in which action is needed; and

(b) any other principles appearing to OFCOM to represent the best regulatory practice.

(4) OFCOM must also have regard, in performing those duties, to such of the following as appear to them to be relevant in the circumstances—

(a) the desirability of promoting the fulfilment of the purposes of public service television broadcasting in the United Kingdom;

(b) the desirability of promoting competition in relevant markets;

(c) the desirability of promoting and facilitating the development and use of effective forms of self-regulation;

(d) the desirability of encouraging investment and innovation in relevant markets;

(e) the desirability of encouraging the availability and use of high speed data transfer services throughout the United Kingdom;

(f) the different needs and interests, so far as the use of the electro-magnetic spectrum for wireless telegraphy is concerned, of all persons who may wish to make use of it;

(g) the need to secure that the application in the case of television and radio services of standards falling within subsection (2)(e) and (f) is in the manner that best guarantees an appropriate level of freedom of expression;

(h) the vulnerability of children and of others whose circumstances appear to OFCOM to put them in need of special protection;

(i) the needs of persons with disabilities, of the elderly and of those on low incomes;

(j) the desirability of preventing crime and disorder;

(k) the opinions of consumers in relevant markets and of members of the public generally;

(l) the different interests of persons in the different parts of the United Kingdom, of the different ethnic communities within the United Kingdom and of persons living in rural and in urban areas;

(m) the extent to which, in the circumstances of the case, the furthering or securing of the matters mentioned in subsections (1) and (2) is reasonably practicable.

(5) In performing their duty under this section of furthering the interests of consumers, OFCOM must have regard, in particular, to the interests of those consumers in respect of choice, price, quality of service and value for money.

(6) Where it appears to OFCOM, in relation to the carrying out of any of the functions mentioned in section 4(1), that any of their general duties conflict with one or more of their duties under sections 4, 24 and 25, priority must be given to their duties under those sections.

(7) Where it appears to OFCOM that any of their general duties conflict with each other in a particular case, they must secure that the conflict is resolved in the manner they think best in the circumstances.

(8) Where OFCOM resolve a conflict in an important case between their duties under paragraphs (a) and (b) of subsection (1), they must publish a statement setting out—
- (a) the nature of the conflict;
- (b) the manner in which they have decided to resolve it; and
- (c) the reasons for their decision to resolve it in that manner.

(9) Where OFCOM are required to publish a statement under subsection (8), they must—
- (a) publish it as soon as possible after making their decision but not while they would (apart from a statutory requirement to publish) be subject to an obligation not to publish a matter that needs to be included in the statement; and
- (b) so publish it in such manner as they consider appropriate for bringing it to the attention of the persons who, in OFCOM's opinion, are likely to be affected by the matters to which the decision relates.

(11) A case is an important case for the purposes of subsection (8) or (10) only if—
- (a) it involved one or more of the matters mentioned in subsection (12); or
- (b) it otherwise appears to OFCOM to have been of unusual importance.

(12) Those matters are—
- (a) a major change in the activities carried on by OFCOM;
- (b) matters likely to have a significant impact on persons carrying on businesses in any of the relevant markets; or
- (c) matters likely to have a significant impact on the general public in the United Kingdom or in a part of the United Kingdom.

(13) This section is subject to sections 370(11) and 371(11) of this Act and to section 119A(4) of the Enterprise Act 2002 (c. 40) (which applies to functions conferred on OFCOM by Chapter 2 of Part 5 of this Act).

(14) In this section—

'citizens' means all members of the public in the United Kingdom;

'communications matters' means the matters in relation to which OFCOM have functions;

'general duties', in relation to OFCOM, means—
- (a) their duties under subsections (1) to (5);and
- (b) the duty which, under section 107(5), is to rank equally for the purposes of subsections (6) and (7) with their duties under this section;

'relevant markets' means markets for any of the services, facilities, apparatus or directories in relation to which OFCOM have functions.

4 Duties for the purpose of fulfilling EU obligations

(1) This section applies to the following functions of OFCOM—
- (a) their functions under Chapter 1 of Part 2;
- (b) their functions under the enactments relating to the management of the radio spectrum;
- (c) their functions under Chapter 3 of Part 2 in relation to disputes referred to them under section 185;
- (d) their functions under sections 24 and 25 so far as they relate to information required for purposes connected with matters in relation to which functions specified in this subsection are conferred on OFCOM; and
- (e) their functions under section 26 so far as they are carried out for the purpose of making information available to persons mentioned in subsection (2)(a) to (c) of that section...

(4) The second Community requirement is a requirement to secure that OFCOM's activities contribute to the development of the European internal market.

(5) The third Community requirement is a requirement to promote the interests of all persons who are citizens of the European Union (within the meaning of Article 20 of the Treaty on the Functioning of the European Union).

(11) Where it appears to OFCOM that any of the Community requirements conflict with each other, they must secure that the conflict is resolved in the manner they think best in the circumstances.

6   Duties to review regulatory burdens

(1) OFCOM must keep the carrying out of their functions under review with a view to securing that regulation by OFCOM does not involve—

    (a) the imposition of burdens which are unnecessary; or

    (b) the maintenance of burdens which have become unnecessary.

(2) In reviewing their functions under this section it shall be the duty of OFCOM—

    (a) to have regard to the extent to which the matters which they are required under section 3 to further or to secure are already furthered or secured, or are likely to be furthered or secured, by effective self-regulation; and

    (b) in the light of that, to consider to what extent it would be appropriate to remove or reduce regulatory burdens imposed by OFCOM.

(3) In determining for the purposes of this section whether procedures for self-regulation are effective OFCOM must consider, in particular—

    (a) whether those procedures are administered by a person who is sufficiently independent of the persons who may be subjected to the procedures; and

    (b) whether adequate arrangements are in force for funding the activities of that person in relation to those procedures.

8   Duty to publish and meet promptness standards

(1) It shall be the duty of OFCOM to publish a statement setting out the standards they are proposing to meet with respect to promptness in—

    (a) the carrying out of their different functions; and

    (b) the transaction of business for purposes connected with the carrying out of those functions.

(2) This section does not require standards to be set out with respect to anything which (apart from this section) is required to be done by a time, or within a period, provided for by or under an enactment.

(3) OFCOM may, if they think fit, at any time revise the statement for the time being in force under this section.

(4) It shall be the duty of OFCOM—

    (a) in carrying out their functions, and

    (b) in transacting business for purposes connected with the carrying out of their functions,

to have regard to the statement for the time being in force under this section.

9   Secretary of State's powers in relation to promptness standards

(1) Where the Secretary of State considers that the statement published by OFCOM under section 8 is not adequate for securing that they meet satisfactory promptness standards, he may give them a notification to that effect.

(2) If the period of three months after the date of the giving of a notification under subsection (1) expires without OFCOM taking steps which the Secretary of State is satisfied remedy the situation, he may give them a direction under this section.

(3) A direction under this section is one requiring OFCOM to issue a new or revised statement under section 8 in accordance with the direction.

Accessible domestic communications apparatus

10 Duty to encourage availability of easily usable apparatus

(1) It shall be the duty of OFCOM to take such steps, and to enter into such arrangements, as appear to them calculated to encourage others to secure—

    (a) that domestic electronic communications apparatus is developed which is capable of being used with ease, and without modification, by the widest possible range of individuals (including those with disabilities); and

    (b) that domestic electronic communications apparatus which is capable of being so used is as widely available as possible for acquisition by those wishing to use it.

Media literacy

11 Duty to promote media literacy

(1) It shall be the duty of OFCOM to take such steps, and to enter into such arrangements, as appear to them calculated—

    (a) to bring about, or to encourage others to bring about, a better public understanding of the nature and characteristics of material published by means of the electronic media;

    (b) to bring about, or to encourage others to bring about, a better public awareness and understanding of the processes by which such material is selected, or made available, for publication by such means;

    (c) to bring about, or to encourage others to bring about, the development of a better public awareness of the available systems by which access to material published by means of the electronic media is or can be regulated;

    (d) to bring about, or to encourage others to bring about, the development of a better public awareness of the available systems by which persons to whom such material is made available may control what is received and of the uses to which such systems may be put; and

    (e) to encourage the development and use of technologies and systems for regulating access to such material, and for facilitating control over what material is received, that are both effective and easy to use.

(2) In this section, references to the publication of anything by means of the electronic media are references to its being—

    (a) broadcast so as to be available for reception by members of the public or of a section of the public; or

    (b) distributed by means of an electronic communications network to members of the public or of a section of the public.

OFCOM's Content Board

12 Duty to establish and maintain Content Board

(1) It shall be the duty of OFCOM, in accordance with the following provisions of this section, to exercise their powers under paragraph 14 of the Schedule to the Office of Communications Act 2002 (c. 11) (committees of OFCOM) to establish and maintain a committee to be known as 'the Content Board'.

(2) The Content Board shall consist of—

    (a) a chairman appointed by OFCOM; and

    (b) such number of other members appointed by OFCOM as OFCOM think fit.

(3) The chairman of the Content Board must be a non-executive member of OFCOM but is not to be the chairman of OFCOM.

(4) At least one of the other members of the Content Board must also be a non-executive member of OFCOM other than the chairman of OFCOM.

(5) In appointing persons to be members of the Content Board, OFCOM must secure that, for each of the following parts of the United Kingdom—

(a) England,

(b) Scotland,

(c) Wales, and

(d) Northern Ireland,

there is a different member of the Board capable of representing the interests and opinions of persons living in that part of the United Kingdom.

(6) In appointing a person for the purposes of subsection (5)(a), OFCOM must have regard to the desirability of ensuring that the person appointed is able to represent the interests and opinions of persons living in all the different regions of England.

(7) The validity of any proceedings of the Content Board shall not be affected by any failure by OFCOM to comply with subsection (5) or (6).

(8) It shall be the duty of OFCOM when appointing members of the Content Board to secure, so far as practicable, that a majority of the members of the Board (counting the chairman) consists of persons who are neither members nor employees of OFCOM.

(9) The following shall be disqualified from being the chairman or another member of the Content Board—

(a) governors and employees of the BBC;

(b) members and employees of the Welsh Authority; and

(c) members and employees of C4C.

(10) Before appointing a person to be the chairman or another member of the Content Board, OFCOM must satisfy themselves that he will not have any financial or other interest which would be likely prejudicially to affect the carrying out by him of any of his functions as chairman or member of the Content Board.

(11) A person is not to be taken to have such an interest by reason only that he is or will be a member or employee of OFCOM.

(12) Every person whom OFCOM propose to appoint to be the chairman or another member of the Content Board, shall, whenever requested to do so by OFCOM, furnish OFCOM with any information they consider necessary for the performance of their duty under subsection (10).

13   Functions of the Content Board

(1) The Content Board shall have such functions as OFCOM, in exercise of their powers under the Schedule to the Office of Communications Act 2002 (c. 11), may confer on the Board.

(2) The functions conferred on the Board must include, to such extent and subject to such restrictions and approvals as OFCOM may determine, the carrying out on OFCOM's behalf of—

(a) functions in relation to matters that concern the contents of anything which is or may be broadcast or otherwise transmitted by means of electronic communications networks; and

(b) functions in relation to the promotion of public understanding or awareness of matters relating to the publication of matter by means of the electronic media.

(3) In determining what functions to confer on the Content Board, OFCOM must have particular regard to the desirability of securing that the Board have at least a significant influence on decisions which—

(a) relate to the matters mentioned in subsection (2); and

(b) involve the consideration of different interests and other factors as respects different parts of the United Kingdom.

(4) It shall be the duty of the Content Board to ensure, in relation to—

(a) the carrying out of OFCOM's functions under Part 3 of this Act, Parts 1 and 3 of the 1990 Act and Parts 1 and 2 of the 1996 Act,

(b) the matters with respect to which functions are conferred on the Board, and

(c) such other matters mentioned in subsection (2) as OFCOM may determine,

that OFCOM are aware of the different interests and other factors which, in the Board's opinion, need to be taken into account as respects the different parts of the United Kingdom in relation to the carrying out of OFCOM's functions.

(5) The power of OFCOM to determine the Content Board's functions includes power to authorise the Board to establish committees and panels to advise the Board on the carrying out of some or all of the Board's functions.

(6) The power of OFCOM to authorise the establishment of a committee or panel by the Content Board includes power to authorise the establishment of a committee or panel that includes persons who are not members of the Board.

(7) In this section references to the publication of anything by means of the electronic media are references to its being—

    (a) broadcast so as to be available for reception by members of the public or of a section of the public; or

    (b) distributed by means of an electronic communications network to members of the public or of a section of the public.

Functions for the protection of consumers

14 Consumer research

(1) OFCOM must make arrangements for ascertaining—

    (a) the state of public opinion from time to time about the manner in which electronic communications networks and electronic communications services are provided;

    (b) the state of public opinion from time to time about the manner in which associated facilities are made available;

    (c) the experiences of consumers in the markets for electronic communications services and associated facilities, in relation to the manner in which electronic communications networks and electronic communications services are provided and associated facilities made available;

    (d) the experiences of such consumers in relation to the handling, by communications providers and by persons making such facilities available, of complaints made to them by such consumers;

    (e) the experiences of such consumers in relation to the resolution of disputes with communications providers or with persons making associated facilities available; and

    (f) the interests and experiences of such consumers in relation to other matters that are incidental to, or are otherwise connected with, their experiences of the provision of electronic communications networks and electronic communications services or of the availability of associated facilities.

(3) The matters to which the arrangements must relate do not (except so far as authorised or required by subsections (4) to (6)) include public opinion with respect to—

    (a) the contents of anything broadcast or otherwise published by means of an electronic communications network; or

    (b) the experiences or interests of consumers in any market for electronic communications services with respect to anything so broadcast or published.

(4) OFCOM must make arrangements for ascertaining—

    (a) the state of public opinion from time to time concerning programmes included in television and radio services;

    (b) any effects of such programmes, or of other material published by means of the electronic media, on the attitudes or behaviour of persons who watch, listen to or receive the programmes or material; and

    (c) so far as necessary for the purpose mentioned in subsection (5), the types of programmes that members of the public would like to see included in television and radio services.

(6) OFCOM must make arrangements for the carrying out of research into the following—

    (a) the matters mentioned in section 11(1);

    (b) matters relating to, or connected with, the setting of standards under section 319 of this Act;

(c) matters relating to, or connected with, the observance of those standards by persons providing television and radio services;

(d) matters relating to, or connected with, the prevention of unjust or unfair treatment in programmes included in such services; and

(e) matters relating to, or connected with, the prevention of unwarranted infringements of privacy resulting from activities carried on for the purposes of such services.

15   Duty to publish and take account of research

(1) It shall be the duty of OFCOM—

(a) to publish the results of any research carried out by them or on their behalf under section 14; and

(b) to consider and, to such extent as they think fit, to take account of the results of such research in the carrying out of their functions.

16   Consumer consultation

(1) It shall be the duty of OFCOM to establish and maintain effective arrangements for consultation about the carrying out of their functions with—

(a) consumers in the markets for the services and facilities in relation to which OFCOM have functions;

(b) consumers in the markets for apparatus used in connection with any such services or facilities;

(c) consumers in the markets for directories capable of being used in connection with the use of an electronic communications network or electronic communications service.

(2) The arrangements must include the establishment and maintenance of a panel of persons (in this Act referred to as 'the Consumer Panel') with the function of advising both—

(a) OFCOM; and

(b) such other persons as the Panel think fit.

(5) The matters about which the Consumer Panel are to be able to give advice do not include any matter that concerns the contents of anything which is or may be broadcast or otherwise transmitted by means of electronic communications networks.

(7) It shall be the duty of OFCOM, in the carrying out of their functions, to consider and, to such extent as they think appropriate, to have regard to—

(a) any advice given to OFCOM by the Consumer Panel; and

(b) any results notified to OFCOM of any research undertaken by that Panel.

(8) It shall also be the duty of OFCOM (subject to subsection (9))—

(a) to provide the Consumer Panel with all such information as, having regard, in particular, to the need to preserve commercial confidentiality, OFCOM consider appropriate to disclose to the Panel for the purpose of enabling the Panel to carry out their functions; and

(b) to provide the Panel with all such further information as the Panel may require.

(9) OFCOM are not required to provide information by virtue of subsection (8)(b) if, having regard to—

(a) the need to preserve commercial confidentiality, and

(b) any other matters that appear to OFCOM to be relevant,

it is reasonable for OFCOM to refuse to disclose it to the Panel.

(10) It shall be the duty of OFCOM, in the case of any advice or opinion received from and published by the Panel which OFCOM propose to disregard in whole or in part, or with which OFCOM disagree in whole or in part—

(a) to ensure that the Panel know OFCOM's reasons for disregarding or disagreeing with the advice or opinion; and

(b) to ensure that those reasons are or have been published in such manner as OFCOM consider appropriate for bringing them to the attention of persons who are aware of the Panel's advice or opinion.

Advisory committees

20 Advisory committees for different parts of the United Kingdom

(1) It shall be the duty of OFCOM, in accordance with the following provisions of this section, to exercise their powers under paragraph 14 of the Schedule to the Office of Communications Act 2002 (c. 11) (committees of OFCOM) to establish and maintain a committee for each of the following parts of the United Kingdom—

    (a) England;

    (b) Wales;

    (c) Scotland; and

    (d) Northern Ireland.

(2) Each committee shall consist of—

    (a) a chairman appointed by OFCOM; and

    (b) such number of other members appointed by OFCOM as OFCOM think fit.

(3) In appointing a person in accordance with this section to be a member of a committee, OFCOM must have regard to the desirability of ensuring that the person appointed is able to represent the interests and opinions, in relation to communications matters, of persons living in the part of the United Kingdom for which the committee has been established.

(4) The function of each committee shall be to provide advice to OFCOM (including other committees established by OFCOM) about the interests and opinions, in relation to communications matters, of persons living in the part of the United Kingdom for which the committee has been established.

(5) A committee established under this section may also, at the request of the Consumer Panel, provide advice about those interests and opinions to the Consumer Panel.

(6) The consent of OFCOM is required for the giving of advice under subsection (5).

(7) In this section 'communications matters' has the same meaning as in section 3.

21 Advisory committee on elderly and disabled persons

(1) It shall be the duty of OFCOM, in accordance with the following provisions of this section, to exercise their powers under paragraph 14 of the Schedule to the Office of Communications Act 2002 (c. 11) (committees of OFCOM) to establish and maintain a committee to provide the advice specified in this section.

(3) In appointing persons to be members of the committee, OFCOM must have regard to the desirability of ensuring that the members of the committee include—

    (a) persons who are familiar with the needs of the elderly; and

    (b) persons who are familiar with the needs of persons with disabilities.

(4) The function of the committee shall be to provide advice to OFCOM (including other committees established by OFCOM) about the interests, in relation to communications matters, of—

    (a) the elderly; and

    (b) persons with disabilities.

General information functions

24 Provision of information to the Secretary of State

(1) It shall be the duty of OFCOM to comply with a direction by the Secretary of State to provide him with information falling within subsection (2).

(2) The information that may be the subject of a direction under this section is any information reasonably required by the Secretary of State for the purpose of enabling him to secure compliance with an international obligation of the United Kingdom.

(3) Information that is required to be provided by a direction under this section must be provided in such manner and at such times as may be required by the direction.

26 Publication of information and advice for consumers etc.

(1) OFCOM may arrange for the publication of such information and advice about matters in relation to which they have functions as it appears to them to be appropriate to make available to the persons mentioned in subsection (2).

(2) Those persons are—

  (d) persons to whom radio and television services are provided or who are otherwise able or likely to take advantage of any of those services.

(3) In arranging for the publication of information or advice under this section, OFCOM must have regard to the need to exclude from publication, so far as that is practicable, the matters which are confidential in accordance with subsections (4) and (5).

PART 3 TELEVISION AND RADIO SERVICES

Chapter 1 The BBC, C4C The Welsh Authority and The Gaelic Media Service etc.

The BBC

198 Functions of OFCOM in relation to the BBC

(1) It shall be a function of OFCOM, to the extent that provision for them to do so is contained in—

  (a) the BBC Charter and Agreement, and

  (b) the provisions of this Act and of Part 5 of the 1996 Act,

to regulate the provision of the BBC's services and the carrying on by the BBC of other activities for purposes connected with the provision of those services.

(2) For the purposes of the carrying out of that function OFCOM—

  (a) are to have such powers and duties as may be conferred on them by or under the BBC Charter and Agreement; and

  (b) are entitled, to the extent that they are authorised to do so by the Secretary of State or under the terms of that Charter and Agreement, to act on his behalf in relation to that Charter and Agreement.

(3) The BBC must pay OFCOM such penalties in respect of contraventions by the BBC of provision made by or under—

  (a) this Part,

  (aa) Part 4A or

  (b) the BBC Charter and Agreement, as are imposed by OFCOM in exercise of powers conferred on them by that Charter and Agreement.

(4) The BBC are also to be liable to pay OFCOM such sums in respect of the carrying out by OFCOM of their functions in relation to the BBC as may be—

  (a) agreed from time to time between the BBC and OFCOM; or

  (b) (in default of agreement) fixed by the Secretary of State.

(5) The maximum penalty that may be imposed on the BBC on any occasion by OFCOM in exercise of a power conferred by virtue of the BBC Charter and Agreement is £250,000.

(6) The Secretary of State may by order substitute a different sum for the sum for the time being specified in subsection (5).

(7) No order is to be made containing provision authorised by subsection (6) unless a draft of the order has been laid before Parliament and approved by a resolution of each House.

(8) It shall be the duty of OFCOM to have regard to their functions under this section when carrying out their functions under the 1990 Act, the 1996 Act and this Part in relation to services provided by persons other than the BBC.

(9) In this section 'the BBC's services' means such of the services provided by the BBC (excluding the services comprised in the World Service) as are of a description of service which, if provided by a BBC company, would fall to be regulated by OFCOM by virtue of section 211 or 245 or by the appropriate regulatory authority by virtue of section 368C.

C4C

198A C4C's functions in relation to media content

(1) C4C must participate in—

    (a) the making of a broad range of relevant media content of high quality that, taken as a whole, appeals to the tastes and interests of a culturally diverse society,

    (b) the making of high quality films intended to be shown to the general public at the cinema in the United Kingdom, and

    (c) the broadcasting and distribution of such content and films.

(2) C4C must, in particular, participate in—

    (a) the making of relevant media content that consists of news and current affairs,

    (b) the making of relevant media content that appeals to the tastes and interests of older children and young adults,

    (c) the broadcasting or distribution by means of electronic communications networks of feature films that reflect cultural activity in the United Kingdom (including third party films), and

    (d) the broadcasting or distribution of relevant media content by means of a range of different types of electronic communications networks.

(3) In performing their duties under subsections (1) and (2) C4C must—

    (a) promote measures intended to secure that people are well-informed and motivated to participate in society in a variety of ways, and

    (b) contribute towards the fulfilment of the public service objectives (as defined in section 264A).

(4) In performing their duties under subsections (1) to (3) C4C must—

    (a) support the development of people with creative talent, in particular—

        (i)   people at the beginning of their careers in relevant media content or films, and

        (ii) people involved in the making of innovative content and films,

    (b) support and stimulate well-informed debate on a wide range of issues, including by providing access to information and views from around the world and by challenging established views,

    (c) promote alternative views and new perspectives, and

    (d) provide access to material that is intended to inspire people to make changes in their lives.

(5) In performing those duties C4C must have regard to the desirability of—

    (a) working with cultural organisations,

    (b) encouraging innovation in the means by which relevant media content is broadcast or distributed, and

    (c) promoting access to and awareness of services provided in digital form.

(6) In this section—

'participate in' includes invest in or otherwise procure;

'relevant media content' means material, other than advertisements, which is included in any of the following services that are available to members of the public in all or part of the United Kingdom—

    (a) television programme services, additional television services or digital additional television services,

    (b) on-demand programme services, or

    (c) other services provided by means of the internet where there is a person who exercises editorial control over the material included in the service;

and a film is a 'third party film' if C4C did not participate in making it.

(7) The services that are to be taken for the purposes of this section to be available to members of the public include any service which—

    (a) is available for reception by members of the public (within the meaning of section 361); or

    (b) is available for use by members of the public (within the meaning of section 368R(4)).

198B   Statement of media content policy

(1) C4C must prepare a statement of media content policy—

(a) at the same time as they prepare the first statement of programme policy that is prepared under section 266 after this section comes into force, and

(b) subsequently at annual intervals.

(2) C4C must monitor their performance in carrying out the proposals contained in their statements of media content policy.

(3) A statement of media content policy must—

(a) set out C4C's proposals for securing that, during the following year, they will discharge their duties under section 198A, and

(b) include a report on their performance in carrying out the proposals contained in the previous statement.

(4) In preparing the statement, C4C must—

(a) have regard to guidance given by OFCOM, and

(b) consult OFCOM.

(5) C4C must publish each statement of media content policy—

(a) as soon as practicable after its preparation is complete, and

(b) in such manner as they consider appropriate, having regard to any guidance given by OFCOM.

(6) OFCOM must—

(a) from time to time review the guidance for the time being in force for the purposes of this section, and

(b) revise that guidance as they think fit.

198C   OFCOM reports on C4C's media content duties

(1) For each relevant period, OFCOM must—

(a) carry out a review of the extent to which C4C have discharged their duties under section 198A, and

(b) prepare a report on the matters found on the review.

(2) OFCOM must publish each report under this section—

(a) as soon as practicable after its preparation is complete, and

(b) in such manner as they consider appropriate.

(3) 'Relevant period' means each period selected by OFCOM for the purposes of section 264(1)(b) that ends after this section comes into force.

198D   Directions in relation to C4C's media content duties

(1) This section applies if OFCOM—

(a) are of the opinion that C4C have failed to perform one or more of their duties under section 198A or section 198B(1), (3) or (5),

(b) are of the opinion that the failure is serious and is not excused by economic or market conditions, and

(c) determine that the situation requires the exercise of their functions under this section.

(2) In making a determination under subsection (1)(c), OFCOM must have regard, in particular, to—

(a) C4C's statements of media content policy,

(b) C4C's effectiveness and efficiency in monitoring their own performance, and

(c) general economic and market conditions affecting the provision of relevant media content (as defined in section 198A).

(3) OFCOM may give directions to C4C to do one or both of the following—

(a) to revise the latest statement of media content policy in accordance with the direction;

(b) to take such steps for remedying the failure as OFCOM specify in the direction.

(4) A direction given under this section must set out—

(a) a reasonable timetable for complying with it, and

(b) the factors that OFCOM will take into account in determining whether or not a failure has been remedied.

(5) OFCOM must consult C4C before giving a direction under this section.

199   Functions of C4C

(1) The activities that C4C are able to carry on include any activities which appear to them—

(a) to be activities that it is appropriate for them to carry on in association with the carrying out of their primary functions; and

(b) to be connected, otherwise than merely in financial terms, with activities undertaken by them for the carrying out of those functions.

(2) In subsection (1) 'primary functions' means—

(za) the performance of C4C's duties under section 198A;

(a) securing the continued provision of Channel 4; and

(b) the fulfilment of the public service remit for that Channel under section 265.

The Welsh Authority

203   Function of OFCOM in relation to the Welsh Authority

It shall be a function of OFCOM, to the extent that provision for them to do so is contained in this Act and Part 5 of the 1996 Act, to regulate the services provided by the Welsh Authority.

204   Welsh Authority's function of providing S4C and S4C Digital

(1) The Welsh Authority shall continue in existence with the substitution of the following function for their functions under section 57 of the 1990 Act.

(2) The Welsh Authority shall have the function of providing television programme services of high quality with a view to their being available for reception wholly or mainly by members of the public in Wales.

(3) The carrying out of that function—

(a) must include the continuing provision of the service provided in digital form and known as S4C Digital; and

(b) may include the continuing provision of the television broadcasting service known as Sianel Pedwar Cymru ('S4C').

(4) The duty of the Welsh Authority to provide S4C Digital includes a duty to secure that arrangements are made and remain in force for it to be broadcast in digital form.

(5) It shall be the duty of the Welsh Authority to secure that S4C and S4C Digital each represents a public service for the dissemination of information, education and entertainment.

(6) The Welsh Authority may use part of the signals carrying S4C to provide—

(a) subtitling in relation to programmes included in the service; and

(b) other services which are ancillary to programmes included in S4C and which are directly related to their contents.

(7) In providing S4C Digital the Welsh Authority may also provide—

(a) assistance for disabled people in relation to programmes included in the service; and

(b) any other service (other than one mentioned in paragraph (a)) which is an ancillary service in relation to S4C Digital.

(8) The Secretary of State may by order modify this Act and such other enactments as he thinks fit for the purpose of—

(a) replacing the requirement of the Welsh Authority to provide S4C with a requirement to provide a service in digital form;

(b) requiring the Welsh Authority to secure that arrangements are made for that service and S4C Digital to be merged and provided as one service (also to be known as 'S4C Digital'); and

(c) applying enactments relating to the provision of S4C or S4C Digital to the provision of the merged service.

(9) An order under subsection (8) may require the Welsh Authority to ensure that, from the coming into force of a requirement to provide a merged service in digital form until a time determined

in the manner described in the order, the whole or a part of the merged service is also to be provided for broadcasting in analogue form.

(10) In this section 'programme' does not include an advertisement.

205   Powers to provide other services

(1) The Welsh Authority are not, in the carrying out of their function under section 204, to provide any television programme service (apart from S4C and S4C Digital) unless—

  (a) the service appears to them to satisfy the requirements of subsection (3); and

  (b) the provision by them of the service has been approved by an order made by the Secretary of State.

(2) The functions of the Welsh Authority include the provision of services that are neither television programme services nor sound services but—

  (a) are provided with a view to being made available for reception wholly or mainly by members of the public in Wales or otherwise to be received or used by persons in Wales;

  (b) are services appearing to them to satisfy the requirements of subsection (3); and

  (c) are services the provision of which by the Authority has been approved by an order made by the Secretary of State.

(3) A service provided under this section must be a public service of high quality for the dissemination of information, education or entertainment (or a combination of them) wholly or mainly to members of the public in Wales.

(4) The Welsh Authority are not to provide a television programme service under this section unless it is one the provision of which by them broadens the range of television programme services available for reception by members of the public in Wales.

(5) The Welsh Authority must ensure, in the case of every television programme service provided with the approval of the Secretary of State under this section, that a substantial proportion of the programmes included in the service consists of programmes in Welsh.

206   Other activities of Welsh Authority

(1) The activities that the Welsh Authority are able to carry on include activities which appear to them—

  (a) to be activities that it is appropriate for them to carry on in association with the carrying out of their function of providing S4C, S4C Digital or a service the provision of which is approved under section 205; and

  (b) to be connected, otherwise than merely in financial terms, with activities undertaken by them for the carrying out of that function.

(2) The approval of the Secretary of State is required for the carrying on by the Welsh Authority of activities authorised only by subsection (1).

(3) The approval of the Secretary of State—

  (a) must be contained in an order made by him; and

  (b) may be a general approval in relation to a description of activities or a specific approval in relation to particular activities.

(4) The activities capable of being authorised under subsection (1)—

  (a) do not include the provision of a licensable service; but

  (b) do include activities for securing the provision of such a service by an S4C company and other activities connected with the provision of such a service by such a company.

(5) The activities referred to in subsection (4)(b) include—

  (a) the formation of a company to provide a programme service;

  (b) the taking of steps by means of which a company that is providing such a service becomes an S4C company.

(7) In this section 'licensable service' means a service that would fall to be regulated under section 211 or 245 if provided by an S4C company.

(8) Section 57(1A)(b) and (1B) of the 1990 Act (power of Welsh Authority to establish, acquire an interest in or assist a qualifying company) shall cease to have effect.

207 Welsh Authority finances

(1) The Welsh Authority must not, whether directly or indirectly, impose charges on persons—

(a) in respect of their reception or use in Wales of any of the Authority's public services;

(b) in respect of their reception in Wales of any service consisting in the provision of assistance for disabled people in relation to programmes included in any one or more of those services; or

(c) in respect of their reception in Wales of any service (other than one mentioned in paragraph (b)) which is an ancillary service in relation to any of the Authority's public services provided in digital form.

Chapter 2 Regulatory Structure for Independent Television Services

Preliminary

211 Regulation of independent television services

(1) It shall be a function of OFCOM to regulate the following services in accordance with this Act, the 1990 Act and the 1996 Act—

(a) services falling within subsection (2) that are provided otherwise than by the BBC or the Welsh Authority; and

(b) services falling within subsection (3) that are provided otherwise than by the BBC.

(2) The services referred to in subsection (1)(a) are—

(a) television broadcasting services that are provided from places in the United Kingdom with a view to their being broadcast otherwise than only from a satellite;

(b) television licensable content services that are provided by persons under the jurisdiction of the United Kingdom for the purposes of the Television without Frontiers Directive;

(c) digital television programme services that are provided by persons under the jurisdiction of the United Kingdom for the purposes of that Directive;

(d) restricted television services that are provided from places in the United Kingdom; and

(e) additional television services that are provided from places in the United Kingdom.

(3) The services referred to in subsection (1)(b) are—

(a) television multiplex services that are provided from places in the United Kingdom; and

(b) digital additional television services that are provided by persons under the jurisdiction of the United Kingdom for the purposes of the Audiovisual Media Services Directive.

Channels 3 and 5

216 Renewal of Channel 3 and 5 licences

(1) The holder of—

(a) a licence to provide a Channel 3 service, or

(b) a licence to provide Channel 5,

may apply to OFCOM for the renewal of his licence for a period of ten years from the end of the licensing period current at the time of the application.

(2) An application for renewal may only be made in the period which—

(a) begins four years before the end of the current licensing period; and

(b) ends three months before the day that OFCOM have determined to be the day by which they would need to publish a tender notice if they were proposing to grant a fresh licence to take effect from the end of that period.

(3) A determination for the purposes of subsection (2)(b)—

(a) must be made at least one year before the day determined; and

(b) must be notified by OFCOM to every person who, at the time of the determination, holds a licence in respect of which there is right to apply for renewal under this section.

(4) Where OFCOM receive an application under this section for the renewal of a licence they must—

      (a) decide whether to renew the licence; and

      (b) notify the applicant of their decision.

(4A) If OFCOM decide to renew the licence they must—

      (a) in the case of a licence to provide a Channel 3 service, determine in accordance with section 216A the area for which the licence will be renewed;

      (b) in every case, determine in accordance with section 217 the financial terms on which the licence will be renewed; and

      (c) notify the applicant of their determinations.

(6) OFCOM may decide not to renew the licence if they are not satisfied that the applicant (if his licence were renewed) would provide a service complying with the requirements imposed under Chapter 4 of this Part by conditions relating to—

      (a) the public service remit for the licensed service;

      (b) programming quotas;

      (c) news and current affairs programmes; and

      (d) programme production and regional programming.

(6A) OFCOM may also decide not to renew a licence to provide a Channel 3 service if, for the licensing period in question, they have renewed or propose to renew one or more other licences to provide a Channel 3 service for all of the area to which the licence relates.

(7) OFCOM may also decide not to renew the licence if they propose to grant a fresh licence for a service replacing the licensed service which would differ from the licensed service in—

      (a) the area for which it would be provided; or

      (b) the times of the day, or days of the week, between or on which it would be provided.

(8) In all cases in which—

      (a) the applicant notifies OFCOM that he accepts the terms notified to him under subsection (4A)(c), and

      (b) they are not required or allowed by subsections (5) to (7) to refuse a renewal,

they must grant the renewal as soon as reasonably practicable.

(9) But OFCOM must not grant a renewal under this section more than eighteen months before the end of the licensing period from the end of which the renewal will take effect.

(10) Where a licence is renewed under this section, it must be renewed on the same terms and conditions, subject only to such modifications as are required to give effect,

      (a) to any determination under subsection (4A)(a);

      (b) in accordance with the determination under subsection (4A)(b), to the requirements imposed by section 217(4).

(11) Nothing in this section requires OFCOM, following the receipt of an application for the renewal of a licence—

      (a) to make a decision or determination, or

      (b) to take any other step under this section,

at any time after an order under section 230 has come into force preventing the renewal of the licence.

(12) For the purposes of this section a licensing period in relation to a licence is—

      (a) the period beginning with the commencement of this section and ending with the initial expiry date for that type of licence; or

      (b) any subsequent period of ten years beginning with the end of the previous licensing period for that type of licence.

(13) In this section 'tender notice' means a notice under section 15 of the 1990 Act.

216A   Renewal of Channel 3 licences: determination of licence areas

(1) This section applies if OFCOM decide under section 216(4) to renew a licence to provide a Channel 3 service.

(2) The area determined under section 216(4A)(a) for the licence—

   (a) must include all or part of the area to which the licence being renewed currently relates, and

   (b) may include all or part of another area if the holder of the licence to provide a Channel 3 service for the other area gives (and does not withdraw) consent before the determination is made.

The public teletext service

218   Power to secure the provision of a public teletext service

(1) OFCOM may secure the provision, in accordance with this Chapter and Part 1 of the 1996 Act, of a teletext service that is available nationwide and complies with this section.

(2) The service must consist of—

   (a) a single teletext service provided in digital form with a view to its being broadcast by means of a television multiplex service . . .

(7) OFCOM must exercise their powers—

   (a) to make frequencies available for the purposes of Channel 3 services, Channel 4 and S4C; and

   (b) to make determinations for the purposes of section 48(2)(b) of the 1990 Act (determinations of spare capacity),

in a manner that takes account of their duty under this section.

Meaning of initial expiry date

224   Meaning of 'initial expiry date'

(1) Subject to any postponement under this section, for the purposes of this Part the initial expiry date for the following types of licence is 31 December 2014—

   (a) a licence to provide a Channel 3 service;

   (b) a licence to provide Channel 5;

   (c) the licence to provide the public teletext service.

(2) The Secretary of State may (on one or more occasions) by order postpone the initial expiry date for one or more of the types of licence mentioned in subsection (1).

Reviews relating to licensing of Channels 3 & 5 and teletext

229   Report in anticipation of new licensing round

(1) OFCOM must, in anticipation of the end of each licensing period for a type of relevant licence—

   (a) prepare a report under this section; and

   (b) submit it to the Secretary of State no later than thirty months before the end of that period.

(2) A report under this section must set out OFCOM's opinion on the effect of each of the matters mentioned in subsection (3) on the capacity of the holder or holders of that type of licence to contribute, in the next licensing period, to the fulfilment of the purposes of public service television broadcasting in the United Kingdom at a cost to the licence holder or holders that is commercially sustainable.

(3) Those matters are—

   (a) the arrangements that (but for an order under section 230) would allow for the renewal of that type of licence from the end of the current licensing period; and

   (b) the conditions included in the regulatory regimes for the services provided under that type of licence.

(4) A report under this section must also include the recommendations (if any) which OFCOM consider, in the light of the opinion set out in the report, should be made to the Secretary of State for the exercise by him of—

   (a) his power under section 230; or

(b) any of the powers to make statutory instruments that are conferred on him by

(6) In this section—

'licensing period' means—

(a) the period beginning with the commencement of this section and ending with the initial expiry date for that type of licence; or

(b) any subsequent period of ten years beginning with the end of the previous licensing period for that type of licence;

'relevant licence' means—

(a) a licence to provide a Channel 3 service;

(b) a licence to provide Channel 5; or

(c) the licence to provide the public teletext service.

230   Orders suspending rights of renewal

(1) This section applies where the Secretary of State has received and considered a report submitted to him by OFCOM under section 229.

(2) If—

(a) the report contains a recommendation by OFCOM for the making of an order under this section, or

(b) the Secretary of State considers, notwithstanding the absence of such a recommendation, that it would be appropriate to do so,

he may by order provide that a licence for the time being in force that is of a description specified in the order is not to be renewable under section 216 or 222 from the end of the licensing period in which he received the report but see subsection (7).

(3) An order under this section preventing the renewal of a licence from the end of a licensing period must be made at least eighteen months before the end of that period.

(7) An order under this section with respect to a Channel 3 licence must be an order of one of the following descriptions—

(a) an order applying to every licence to provide a Channel 3 service;

(b) an order applying to every licence to provide a national Channel 3 service; or

(c) an order applying to every licence to provide a regional Channel 3 service.

Replacement of Channel 4 licence

231   Replacement of Channel 4 licence

(1) On the commencement of this subsection—

(a) Channel 4 shall cease to be licensed under the licence in force for the purposes of section 24(3) of the 1990 Act immediately before the commencement of this subsection; and

(b) a licence granted for those purposes in accordance with the following provisions of this section shall come into force as the licence under which Channel 4 is licensed.

(2) It shall be the duty of OFCOM, as soon as practicable after the television transfer date—

(a) to prepare a draft of a licence under Part 1 of the 1990 Act to replace the licence that is likely to be in force for the purposes of section 24(3) of the 1990 Act when subsection (1) of this section comes into force;

(b) to notify C4C of the terms and conditions of the replacement licence they propose; and

(c) after considering any representations made by C4C, to grant such a replacement licence to C4C so that it takes effect in accordance with paragraph (b) of subsection (1) of this section.

(3) A replacement licence proposed or granted under this section—

(a) must be a licence to provide a service with a view to its being broadcast in digital form;

(6) The terms of a replacement licence proposed or granted under this section must provide for it to continue in force until the end of 2014.

(7) But—

(a) such a licence may be renewed, on one or more occasions, for such period as OFCOM may think fit in relation to the occasion in question; and

(b) the provisions of this section (apart from subsections (1), (2) and (6)) are to apply in the case of a licence granted by way of a renewal of a licence granted under this section as they apply in the case of the replacement licence.

(8) The conditions of a replacement licence proposed or granted under this section must include the conditions that OFCOM consider appropriate for the purpose of performing their duty under section 263.

(9) The conditions of such a licence must also include a condition prohibiting the imposition, whether directly or indirectly, of the following—

(a) charges on persons in respect of their reception in the United Kingdom of Channel 4;

(b) charges on persons in respect of their reception in the United Kingdom of any service consisting in the provision of assistance for disabled people in relation to programmes included in Channel 4; and

(c) charges on persons in respect of their reception in the United Kingdom of any service (other than one mentioned in paragraph (b)) which is an ancillary service in relation to so much of Channel 4 as is provided in digital form.

(10) It shall be unlawful to impose a charge in contravention of a condition falling within subsection (9).

Television licensable content services

232 Meaning of 'television licensable content service'

(1) In this Part 'television licensable content service' means (subject to section 233) any service falling within subsection (2) in so far as it is provided with a view to its availability for reception by members of the public being secured by one or more of the following means—

(a) the broadcasting of the service (whether by the person providing it or by another) from a satellite;

(aa) the broadcasting of the service (whether by that person or by another) by means of a radio multiplex service; or

(b) the distribution of the service (whether by that person or by another) by any means involving the use of an electronic communications network.

(2) A service falls within this subsection if it—

(a) is provided (whether in digital or in analogue form) as a service that is to be made available for reception by members of the public; and

(b) consists of or has its principal purpose the provision of television programmes or electronic programme guides, or both.

(3) Where—

(a) a service consisting of television programmes, an electronic programme guide or both ('the main service') is provided by a person as a service to be made available for reception by members of the public, and

(b) that person provides the main service with other services or facilities that are ancillary to, or otherwise relate to, the main service and are also provided so as to be so available or in order to make a service so available,

subsection (1) has effect as if the main service and such of the other services or facilities as are relevant ancillary services and are not two-way services constituted a single service falling within subsection (2).

(4) Where a person providing the main service provides it with a facility giving access to another service, the other service shall also be taken for the purposes of this section as provided by that person with the main service only if what is comprised in the other service is something over which that person has general control.

(5) A service is a two-way service for the purposes of this section if it is provided by means of an electronic communications network and an essential feature of the service is that the purposes for which it is provided involve the use of that network, or a part of it, both—

(a) for the transmission of visual images or sounds (or both) by the person providing the service to users of the service; and

(b) for the transmission of visual images or sounds (or both) by those users for reception by the person providing the service or by other users of the service.

(6) In this section—

'electronic programme guide' means a service which consists of—

(a) the listing or promotion, or both the listing and the promotion, of some or all of the programmes included in any one or more programme services the providers of which are or include persons other than the provider of the guide; and

(b) a facility for obtaining access, in whole or in part, to the programme service or services listed or promoted in the guide;

'relevant ancillary service', in relation to the main service, means a service or facility provided or made available by the provider of the main service that consists of or gives access to—

(a) assistance for disabled people in relation to some or all of the programmes included in the main service;

(b) a service (apart from advertising) which is not an electronic programme guide but relates to the promotion or listing of programmes so included; or

(c) any other service (apart from advertising) which is ancillary to one or more programmes so included and relates directly to their contents.

233 Services that are not television licensable content services

(1) A service is not a television licensable content service to the extent that it is provided with a view to its being broadcast by means of television multiplex service or a general multiplex service.

(2) A service is not a television licensable content service to the extent that it consists of a service the provision of which is authorised by—

(a) a licence to provide a television broadcasting service;

(b) the licence to provide the public teletext service; or

(c) a licence to provide additional television services.

(4) A service is not a television licensable content service if it is a two-way service (within the meaning of section 232).

(5) A service is not a television licensable content service if—

(a) it is distributed by means of an electronic communications network only to persons all of whom are on a single set of premises; and

(b) that network is wholly within those premises and is not connected to an electronic communications network any part of which is outside those premises.

(6) For the purposes of subsection (5)—

(a) a set of premises is a single set of premises if, and only if, the same person is the occupier of all the premises; and

(b) two or more vehicles are capable of constituting a single set of premises if, and only if, they are coupled together.

(7) A service is not a television licensable content service if it is provided for the purpose only of being received by persons who have qualified as users of the service by reason of being—

(a) persons who have a business interest in the programmes included in the service; or

(b) persons who are to receive the programmes for the purpose only of showing them to persons falling within sub-paragraph (a) or to persons all of whom are on the business premises of the person receiving them.

(8) For the purposes of subsection (7) a person has a business interest in programmes if he has an interest in receiving or watching them—

(a) for the purposes of a business carried on by him; or

(b) for the purposes of his employment.

(9) In this section—

'business premises', in relation to a person, means premises at or from which any business of that person is carried on;

'premises' includes a vehicle;

'vehicle' includes a vessel, aircraft or hovercraft.

(10) References in this section, in relation to a person, to a business include references to—

    (a) any business or other activities carried on by a body of which he is a member and the affairs of which are managed by its members; and

    (b) the carrying out of any functions conferred on that person, or on any such body, by or under any enactment.

234 Modification of ss. 232 and 233

(1) The Secretary of State may by order modify any of the provisions of section 232 or 233 if it appears to him appropriate to do so having regard to any one or more of the following—

    (a) the protection which, taking account of the means by which the programmes and services are received or may be accessed, is expected by members of the public as respects the contents of television programmes;

    (b) the extent to which members of the public are able, before television programmes are watched or accessed, to make use of facilities for exercising control, by reference to the contents of the programmes, over what is watched or accessed;

    (c) the practicability of applying different levels of regulation in relation to different services;

    (d) the financial impact for providers of particular services of any modification of the provisions of that section; and

    (e) technological developments that have occurred or are likely to occur.

(2) The Secretary of State may also by order provide, in cases where it otherwise appears to him appropriate to do so, that a description of service specified in the order is not to be treated as a television licensable content service for the purposes of the provisions of this Act that are so specified.

(3) No order is to be made containing provision authorised by this section unless a draft of the order has been laid before Parliament and approved by a resolution of each House.

235 Licensing of television licensable content services

(1) The licence that is required for the purposes of section 13 of the 1990 Act in respect of a television licensable content service is a licence granted under Part 1 of that Act on an application complying with this section.

(2) An application for a licence to provide a television licensable content service—

    (a) must be made in such manner,

    (b) must contain such information about the applicant, his business and the service he proposes to provide, and

    (c) must be accompanied by such fee (if any),

as OFCOM may determine.

(3) Where an application is made to OFCOM in accordance with subsection (2) for a licence to provide a television licensable content service, OFCOM are entitled to refuse the application only if—

    (a) they are required to do so by section 3(3) of the 1990 Act (licences to be held only by fit and proper persons);

    (b) they are required to do so by section 5 of the 1990 Act (restrictions on the holding of licences); or

    (c) they are satisfied that, if the application were to be granted, the provision of the service would be likely to involve contraventions of—

        (i) standards set under section 319 of this Act; or

        (ii) the provisions of a code of practice in force under Part 5 of the 1996 Act (fairness).

(4) The provision of more than one television licensable content service shall require a separate licence under Part 1 of the 1990 Act to be granted and held in respect of each service.

(5) A single licence to provide a television licensable content service may authorise the provision of a service which consists (to any extent) of different programmes to be broadcast simultaneously, or virtually so.

(6) A licence to provide a television licensable content service shall continue in force until such time as it is surrendered or is revoked in accordance with any of the provisions of this Chapter or of the 1990 Act.

(7) A licence to provide a television licensable content service must contain such conditions as OFCOM consider appropriate for requiring the licence holder—

(a) on entering into any agreement with the provider of a radio multiplex service for the provision of a television licensable content service to be broadcast by means of that multiplex service, to notify OFCOM—

    (i) of the identity of the radio multiplex service;

    (ii) of the period during which the service will be provided; and

    (iii) where under the agreement he will be entitled to the use of a specified amount of digital capacity, of that amount;

(b) when any such agreement is varied so far as it relates to any of the matters mentioned in paragraph (a)(i), (ii) or (iii), to notify OFCOM of the variation so far as relating to those matters; and

(c) where he is providing a television licensable content service to the provider of a radio multiplex service in accordance with such an agreement as is mentioned in paragraph (a) but intends to cease doing so, to notify OFCOM of that fact.

236   Direction to licensee to take remedial action

(1) This section applies if OFCOM are satisfied—

(a) that the holder of a licence to provide a television licensable content service has contravened a condition of the licence; and

(b) that the contravention can be appropriately remedied by the inclusion in the licensed service of a correction or a statement of findings (or both).

(2) OFCOM may direct the licence holder to include a correction or a statement of findings (or both) in the licensed service.

(3) A direction may require the correction or statement of findings to be in such form, and to be included in programmes at such time or times, as OFCOM may determine.

(4) OFCOM are not to give a person a direction under this section unless they have given him a reasonable opportunity of making representations to them about the matters appearing to them to provide grounds for the giving of the direction.

(5) Where the holder of a licence includes a correction or a statement of findings in the licensed service in pursuance of a direction under this section, he may announce that he is doing so in pursuance of such a direction.

(6) If OFCOM are satisfied that the inclusion of a programme in a television licensable content service involved a contravention of a condition of the licence to provide that service, they may direct the holder of the licence not to include that programme in that service on any future occasion.

(7) Where OFCOM—

(a) give a direction to a BBC company under subsection (2), or

(b) receive representations from a BBC company by virtue of subsection (4),

they must send a copy of the direction or representations to the Secretary of State.

(8) For the purposes of this section a statement of findings, in relation to a case in which OFCOM are satisfied that the holder of a licence has contravened the conditions of his licence, is a statement of OFCOM's findings in relation to that contravention.

237   Penalties for contravention of licence condition or direction

(1) If OFCOM are satisfied that the holder of a licence to provide a television licensable content service—

(a) has contravened a condition of the licence, or

(b) has failed to comply with a direction given by OFCOM under or by virtue of a provision of this Part, Part 1 of the 1990 Act or Part 5 of the 1996 Act, they may serve on him a notice requiring him to pay them, within a specified period, a specified penalty.

(2) The amount of the penalty under this section must not exceed the maximum penalty given by subsection (3).

(3) The maximum penalty is whichever is the greater of—

(a) £250,000; and

(b) 5 per cent of the qualifying revenue for the licence holder's last complete accounting period falling within the period for which his licence has been in force ('the relevant period').

(4) In relation to a person whose first complete accounting period falling within the relevant period has not ended when the penalty is imposed, subsection (3) is to be construed as referring to 5 per cent of the amount which OFCOM estimate will be the qualifying revenue for that accounting period.

(5) Section 19(2) to (6) of the 1990 Act and Part 1 of Schedule 7 to that Act (calculation of qualifying revenue), with any necessary modifications, are to apply for the purposes of subsection (3) as they apply for the purposes of Part 1 of that Act.

(6) OFCOM are not to serve a notice on a person under subsection (1) unless they have given him a reasonable opportunity of making representations to them about the matters appearing to them to provide grounds for the service of the notice.

(7) Where OFCOM—

(a) serve a notice on a BBC company under subsection (1), or

(b) receive representations from a BBC company by virtue of subsection (6),

they must send a copy of the notice or representations to the Secretary of State.

(8) An exercise by OFCOM of their powers under subsection (1) does not preclude any exercise by them of their powers under section 236 in respect of the same contravention.

(9) The Secretary of State may by order substitute a different sum for the sum for the time being specified in subsection (3)(a).

(10) No order is to be made containing provision authorised by subsection (9) unless a draft of the order has been laid before Parliament and approved by a resolution of each House.

238   Revocation of television licensable content service licence

(1) OFCOM must serve a notice under subsection (2) on the holder of a licence to provide a television licensable content service if they are satisfied—

(a) that the holder of the licence is in contravention of a condition of the licence or is failing to comply with a direction given by them under or by virtue of any provision of this Part, Part 1 of the 1990 Act or Part 5 of the 1996 Act; and

(b) that the contravention or failure, if not remedied, would justify the revocation of the licence.

(2) A notice under this subsection must—

(a) state that OFCOM are satisfied as mentioned in subsection (1);

(b) specify the respects in which, in their opinion, the licence holder is contravening the condition or failing to comply with the direction; and

(c) state that OFCOM will revoke the licence unless the licence holder takes, within such period as is specified in the notice, such steps to remedy the failure as are so specified.

(3) If, at the end of the period specified in a notice under subsection (2), OFCOM are satisfied—

(a) that the person on whom the notice was served has failed to take the steps specified in it, and

(b) that it is necessary in the public interest to revoke his licence,

they shall serve a notice on him revoking his licence.

(4) If OFCOM are satisfied in the case of a licence to provide a television licensable content service—

(a) that the holder of the licence has ceased to provide the licensed service, and

(b) that it is appropriate for them to do so,

they shall serve a notice on him revoking his licence.

(5) If OFCOM are satisfied—

(a) that the holder of a licence to provide a television licensable content service has provided them, in connection with his application for the licence, with information which was false in a material particular, or

(b) that, in connection with his application for the licence, the holder of such a licence withheld any material information with the intention of causing them to be misled,

they may serve a notice on him revoking his licence.

(6) A notice under this section revoking a licence to provide a television licensable content service takes effect as from the time when it is served on the licence holder.

(7) OFCOM are not to serve a notice on a person under this section unless they have given him a reasonable opportunity of making representations to them about the matters in respect of which it is served.

(8) Where OFCOM—

(a) serve a notice on a BBC company under this section, or

(b) receive representations from a BBC company by virtue of subsection (7),

they must send a copy of the notice or representations to the Secretary of State.

(9) Nothing in this section applies to the revocation of a licence in exercise of the power conferred by section 239.

239 Action against licence holders who incite crime or disorder

(1) OFCOM must serve a notice under subsection (2) on the holder of a licence to provide a television licensable content service if they are satisfied—

(a) that the holder of the licence has included in the service one or more programmes containing material likely to encourage or to incite the commission of crime, or to lead to disorder;

(b) that, in doing so, he has contravened conditions contained by virtue of Chapter 4 of this Part in the licence to provide that service; and

(c) that the contravention is such as to justify the revocation of the licence.

(2) A notice under this subsection must—

(a) state that OFCOM are satisfied as mentioned in subsection (1);

(b) specify the respects in which, in their opinion, the licence holder has contravened the condition mentioned in paragraph (b) of that subsection;

(c) state that OFCOM may revoke the licence after the end of the period of twenty-one days beginning with the day on which the notice is served on the licence holder; and

(d) inform the licence holder of his right to make representations to OFCOM within that period about the matters appearing to OFCOM to provide grounds for revoking the licence.

(3) The effect of a notice under subsection (2) shall be to suspend the licence as from the time when the notice is served on the licence holder until either—

(a) the revocation of the licence takes effect; or

(b) OFCOM decide not to revoke the licence.

(4) If, after considering any representations made to them by the licence holder within the period specified for the purposes of subsection (2)(c), OFCOM are satisfied that it is necessary in the public interest to revoke the licence, they shall serve a notice of revocation on the licence holder.

(5) The revocation of a licence by a notice under subsection (4) takes effect from such time as may be specified in the notice.

(6) A notice of revocation under subsection (4) must not specify a time for it to take effect that falls before the end of the period of twenty-eight days beginning with the day on which the notice is served on the licence holder.

263 Application of regulatory regimes

(1) It shall be the duty of OFCOM, by exercising—

(a) their powers under the 1990 Act and the 1996 Act, and

(b) their powers under this Part,

to secure that the holder of every Broadcasting Act licence at all times holds his licence on the conditions which are for the time being included, under this Chapter and Chapter 5 of this Part, in the regulatory regime for the licensed service.

(2) It shall also be the duty of OFCOM to do all that they can to secure that the holder of every such licence complies, in relation to the licensed service, with the conditions so included in the regulatory regime for that service.

(4) The Secretary of State may by order provide for—

> (a) a condition included by virtue of this Act in a regulatory regime to be excluded from the regime;
>
> (b) a condition excluded from a regulatory regime by an order under this subsection to be included in the regime again.

(4A) An order under subsection (4) may, in particular, provide for a condition to be included or excluded for a period specified in the order.

(5) No order is to be made containing provision authorised by subsection (4) unless a draft of the order has been laid before Parliament and approved by a resolution of each House.

(6) This section does not restrict OFCOM's powers and duties apart from this section to impose obligations by means of the inclusion of conditions in a Broadcasting Act licence.

The public service remit for television

264   OFCOM reports on the fulfilment of the public service remit

(1) It shall be the duty of OFCOM—

> (a) as soon as practicable after the end of the period of twelve months beginning with the commencement of this section, and
>
> (b) as soon as practicable after the end of each such subsequent period as may be selected by OFCOM for the purposes of this section,

to satisfy, for that period, the review and reporting obligations of subsection (3).

(2) The period selected by OFCOM for the purposes of subsection (1)(b) must be a period of not more than five years beginning with the end of the previous period for which OFCOM have satisfied those review and reporting obligations.

(3) The review and reporting obligations for a period are—

> (a) an obligation to carry out a review of the extent to which the public service broadcasters have, during that period, provided relevant television services which (taking them all together over the period as a whole) fulfil the purposes of public service television broadcasting in the United Kingdom; and
>
> (b) an obligation, with a view to maintaining and strengthening the quality of public service television broadcasting in the United Kingdom, to prepare a report on the matters found on the review.

(4) The purposes of public service television broadcasting in the United Kingdom are—

> (a) the provision of relevant television services which secure that programmes dealing with a wide range of subject-matters are made available for viewing;
>
> (b) the provision of relevant television services in a manner which (having regard to the days on which they are shown and the times of day at which they are shown) is likely to meet the needs and satisfy the interests of as many different audiences as practicable;
>
> (c) the provision of relevant television services which (taken together and having regard to the same matters) are properly balanced, so far as their nature and subject-matters are concerned, for meeting the needs and satisfying the interests of the available audiences; and
>
> (d) the provision of relevant television services which (taken together) maintain high general standards with respect to the programmes included in them, and, in particular with respect to—
>
> > (i)   the contents of the programmes;
> >
> > (ii) the quality of the programme making; and

(iii) the professional skill and editorial integrity applied in the making of the programmes.

(5) When—

(a) determining the extent to which any of the purposes of public service television broadcasting in the United Kingdom are fulfilled, and

(b) reviewing and reporting on that matter,

OFCOM must have regard to the desirability of those purposes being fulfilled in a manner that is compatible with subsection (6).

(6) A manner of fulfilling the purposes of public service television broadcasting in the United Kingdom is compatible with this subsection if it ensures—

(a) that the relevant television services (taken together) comprise a public service for the dissemination of information and for the provision of education and entertainment;

(b) that cultural activity in the United Kingdom, and its diversity, are reflected, supported and stimulated by the representation in those services (taken together) of drama, comedy and music, by the inclusion of feature films in those services and by the treatment of other visual and performing arts;

(c) that those services (taken together) provide, to the extent that is appropriate for facilitating civic understanding and fair and well-informed debate on news and current affairs, a comprehensive and authoritative coverage of news and current affairs in, and in the different parts of, the United Kingdom and from around the world;

(d) that those services (taken together) satisfy a wide range of different sporting and other leisure interests;

(e) that those services (taken together) include what appears to OFCOM to be a suitable quantity and range of programmes on educational matters, of programmes of an educational nature and of other programmes of educative value;

(f) that those services (taken together) include what appears to OFCOM to be a suitable quantity and range of programmes dealing with each of the following, science, religion and other beliefs, social issues, matters of international significance or interest and matters of specialist interest;

(g) that the programmes included in those services that deal with religion and other beliefs include—

(i) programmes providing news and other information about different religions and other beliefs;

(ii) programmes about the history of different religions and other beliefs; and

(iii) programmes showing acts of worship and other ceremonies and practices (including some showing acts of worship and other ceremonies in their entirety);

(h) that those services (taken together) include what appears to OFCOM to be a suitable quantity and range of high quality and original programmes for children and young people;

(i) that those services (taken together) include what appears to OFCOM to be a sufficient quantity of programmes that reflect the lives and concerns of different communities and cultural interests and traditions within the United Kingdom, and locally in different parts of the United Kingdom;

(j) that those services (taken together), so far as they include programmes made in the United Kingdom, include what appears to OFCOM to be an appropriate range and proportion of programmes made outside the M25 area.

(7) In carrying out a review under this section OFCOM must consider—

(a) the costs to persons providing relevant television services of the fulfilment of the purposes of public service television broadcasting in a manner compatible with subsection (6); and

(b) the sources of income available to each of them for meeting those costs.

(8) Every report under this section must—

(a) specify, and comment on, whatever changes appear to OFCOM to have occurred, during the period to which the report relates, in the extent to which the purposes of public service television broadcasting in the United Kingdom have been satisfied;

(b) specify, and comment on, whatever changes appear to OFCOM to have occurred, during that period, in the manner in which those purposes are fulfilled;

(c) set out the findings of OFCOM on their consideration of the matters mentioned in subsection (7) and any conclusions they have arrived at in relation to those findings; and

(d) set out OFCOM's conclusions on the current state of public service television broadcasting in the United Kingdom.

(9) In performing their duties under this section, OFCOM must have regard, in particular, to—

(a) every statement of programme or service policy which has been made by virtue of this Chapter by a public service broadcaster, or which is treated as such a statement;

(b) every equivalent statement of policy made by the BBC in pursuance of the BBC Charter and Agreement; and

(c) such matters arising at times before the coming into force of this section as OFCOM consider material.

(10) Every report prepared by OFCOM under this section must be published by them—

(a) as soon as practicable after its preparation is complete; and

(b) in such manner as they consider appropriate.

(11) The following are relevant television services for the purposes of this section—

(a) the television broadcasting services provided by the BBC;

(b) the television programme services that are public services of the Welsh Authority (within the meaning of section 207);

(c) every Channel 3 service;

(d) Channel 4;

(e) Channel 5;

(f) the public teletext service.

(12) The following are public service broadcasters for the purposes of this section—

(a) the BBC;

(b) the Welsh Authority;

(c) the providers of the licensed public service channels; and

(d) the public teletext provider.

(13) In this section—

'belief' means a collective belief in, or other adherence to, a systemised set of ethical or philosophical principles or of mystical or transcendental doctrines; and

'drama' includes contemporary and other drama in a variety of different formats.

264A   OFCOM reports: wider review and reporting obligations

(1) When carrying out a review under section 264 for a period, OFCOM must also carry out a review of the extent to which material included in media services during that period (taken together over the period as a whole) contributed towards the fulfilment of the public service objectives.

(2) Every report under section 264 must—

(a) include a report on the matters found on the review under this section,

(b) specify, and comment on, whatever changes appear to OFCOM to have occurred, during the period to which the report relates, in the extent to which the public service objectives have been fulfilled,

(c) specify, and comment on, whatever changes appear to OFCOM to have occurred, during that period, in the manner in which those objectives are fulfilled, and

(d) set out OFCOM's conclusions on the current state of material included in media services.

(3) 'The public service objectives' are the objectives set out in paragraphs (b) to (j) of section 264(6)(as modified by subsection (4)).

(4) Paragraphs (b) to (j) of section 264(6) have effect for the purposes of subsection (3) as if—

(a) references to the relevant television services were to media services, and

(b) references to programmes were to material included in such services.

(5) In this section—

'material' does not include advertisements;

'media services' means any of the following services that are available to members of the public in all or part of the United Kingdom—

(a) television and radio services,

(b) on-demand programme services, and

(c) other services provided by means of the internet where there is a person who exercises editorial control over the material included in the service.

(6) The services that are to be taken for the purposes of this section to be available to members of the public include any service which—

(a) is available for reception by members of the public (within the meaning of section 361); or

(b) is available for use by members of the public (within the meaning of section 368R(4)).

265 Public service remits of licensed providers

(1) The regulatory regime for every licensed public service channel, and for the public teletext service, includes a condition requiring the provider of the channel or service to fulfil the public service remit for that channel or service.

(2) The public service remit—

(a) for every Channel 3 service, and

(b) for Channel 5,

is the provision of a range of high quality and diverse programming.

(3) The public service remit for Channel 4 is the provision of a broad range of high quality and diverse programming which, in particular—

(a) demonstrates innovation, experiment and creativity in the form and content of programmes;

(b) appeals to the tastes and interests of a culturally diverse society;

(c) makes a significant contribution to meeting the need for the licensed public service chan-nels to include programmes of an educational nature and other programmes of educative value; and

(d) exhibits a distinctive character.

(4) The public service remit for the public teletext service is the provision of a range of high quality and diverse text material.

266 Statements of programme policy

(1) The regulatory regime for every licensed public service channel includes a condition re-quiring the provider of the channel—

(a) as soon as practicable after the coming into force of this section and subsequently at annual intervals, to prepare a statement of programme policy; and

(b) to monitor his own performance in the carrying out of the proposals contained in the statements made in pursuance of the condition.

(2) The condition must require every statement of programme policy prepared in accordance with the condition to set out the proposals of the provider of the channel for securing that, during the following year—

(a) the public service remit for the channel will be fulfilled; and

(b) the duties imposed on the provider by virtue of sections 277 to 296 will be performed.

(3) The condition must also require every such statement to contain a report on the performance of the provider of the channel in the carrying out, during the period since the previous statement, of the proposals contained in that statement.

(4) The condition must also provide that every such statement—

(a) must be prepared having regard to guidance given by OFCOM;

(b) must be prepared taking account of the reports previously published by OFCOM under sections 264 and 358;

(c) must take special account of the most recent such reports;

(d) must be published by the provider of the channel in question as soon as practicable after its preparation is complete; and

(e) must be published in such manner as, having regard to any guidance given by OFCOM, the provider considers appropriate.

(5) In preparing guidance about the preparation of such a statement, OFCOM must have regard, in particular, to the matters which, in the light of the provisions of section 264(4) and (6), they consider should be included in statements of programme policy.

(6) It shall be the duty of OFCOM—

(a) from time to time to review the guidance for the time being in force for the purposes of this section; and

(b) to make such revisions of that guidance as they think fit.

(7) The conditions of a licence to provide a licensed public service channel may provide that a previous statement of policy made by the provider of the channel is to be treated for the purposes of this Part—

(a) as if it were a statement made in relation to such period as may be so specified; and

(b) were a statement of programme policy for the purposes of a condition imposed under this section.

(8) The reference in subsection (7) to a previous statement of policy is a reference to any statement made by the provider of the channel—

(a) whether before or after the commencement of this section, for the purposes of his application for a Broadcasting Act licence for the channel; or

(b) at any time before the commencement of this section, for any other purpose.

(9) A condition under subsection (7) cannot contain provision the effect of which is to postpone the time at which a licence holder is required to make the first statement of programme policy which (apart from that subsection) he is required to make in pursuance of a condition imposed under this section.

267 Changes of programme policy

(1) The regulatory regime for every licensed public service channel includes a condition requiring compliance with subsection (2) in the case of a statement of programme policy containing proposals for a significant change.

(2) This subsection requires the provider of the channel—

(a) to consult OFCOM before preparing the statement; and

(b) to take account, in the preparation of the statement, of any opinions expressed to the provider of the channel by OFCOM.

(3) A condition imposed under this section must further provide that, if it appears to OFCOM that a statement of programme policy has been prepared by the provider of the channel in contravention of a condition imposed under subsection (1), the provider is—

(a) to revise that statement in accordance with any directions given to him by OFCOM; and

(b) to publish a revision of the statement in accordance with any such directions only after the revision has been approved by OFCOM.

(4) A change is a significant change for the purposes of this section if it is a change as a result of which the channel would in any year be materially different in character from in previous years.

(5) In determining for the purposes of any condition under this section whether a change is a significant change—

(a) regard must be had to any guidance issued by OFCOM;

(b) the changes to be considered include any changes that, together with any proposed change for a particular year, would constitute a change occurring gradually over a period of not more than three years; and

(c) the previous years with which a comparison is to be made must be those immediately preceding the year in which the change is made, or in which the changes comprised in it began to occur.

(6) It shall be the duty of OFCOM—

(a) from time to time to review the guidance for the time being in force for the purposes of this section; and

(b) to make such revisions of that guidance as they think fit.

268   Statements of service policy by the public teletext provider

(1) The regulatory regime for the public teletext service includes a condition requiring the public teletext provider—

(a) as soon as practicable after the coming into force of this section and subsequently at annual intervals, to prepare a statement of service policy; and

(b) to monitor his own performance in the carrying out of the proposals contained in statements made in pursuance of the condition.

(2) The condition must require every statement of service policy prepared in accordance with the condition to set out the proposals of the public teletext provider for securing that, during the following year, the public service remit for the public teletext service will be fulfilled.

(3) The condition must also require every such statement to contain a report on the performance of the public teletext provider in the carrying out, during the period since the previous statement, of the proposals contained in that statement.

(5) The condition must also provide that every statement in pursuance of the condition—

(a) must be prepared having regard to guidance given by OFCOM;

(b) must be prepared taking account of the reports previously published by OFCOM under sections 264 and 358;

(c) must take special account of the most recent such reports;

(d) must be published by the public teletext provider as soon as practicable after its preparation is complete; and

(e) must be published in such manner as, having regard to any guidance given by OFCOM, that provider considers appropriate.

(6) In preparing guidance about the preparation of such a statement, OFCOM must have regard, in particular, to the matters which, in the light of the provisions of section 264(4) and (6), they consider should be included in statements of service policy by the public teletext provider.

(7) It shall be the duty of OFCOM—

(a) from time to time to review the guidance for the time being in force for the purposes of this section; and

(b) to make such revisions of that guidance as they think fit.

(8) The conditions of the licence to provide the public teletext service may provide that a previous statement of policy made by the public teletext provider is to be treated for the purposes of this Part—

(a) as if it were a statement made in relation to such period as may be so specified; and

(b) were a statement of service policy for the purposes of a condition imposed under this section.

269   Changes of service policy

(1) The regulatory regime for the public teletext service includes a condition requiring compliance with subsection (2) in the case of a statement of service policy containing proposals for a significant change.

(2) This subsection requires the provider of the service—

(a) to consult OFCOM before preparing the statement; and

(b) to take account, in the preparation of the statement, of any opinions expressed to the provider of the service by OFCOM.

(3) A condition imposed under this section must further provide that, if it appears to OFCOM that a statement of service policy has been prepared by the public teletext provider in contravention of a condition imposed under subsection (1), that provider is—

(a) to revise that statement in accordance with any directions given to him by OFCOM; and

(b) to publish a revision of the statement in accordance with any such directions only after the revision has been approved by OFCOM.

(4) A change is a significant change for the purposes of this section if it is a change as a result of which the service would in any year be materially different in character from in previous years.

(5) In determining for the purposes of any condition under this section whether a change is a significant change—

(a) regard must be had to any guidance issued by OFCOM;

(b) the changes to be considered include any changes that, together with any proposed change for a particular year, would constitute a change occurring gradually over a period of not more than three years;

(c) the previous years with which a comparison is to be made must be those immediately preceding the year in which the change is made, or in which the changes comprised in it began to occur; and

(d) any change that is a significant change in relation to so much of the public teletext service as is provided in digital form or in relation to so much of it as is provided in analogue form is to be regarded as a significant change in relation to the whole service.

(6) It shall be the duty of OFCOM—

(a) from time to time to review the guidance for the time being in force for the purposes of this section; and

(b) to make such revisions of that guidance as they think fit.

270   Enforcement of public service remits

(1) This section applies if OFCOM are of the opinion that the provider of a licensed public service channel or the public teletext provider—

(a) has failed to fulfil the public service remit for that channel or the public teletext service; or

(b) has failed, in any respect, to make an adequate contribution towards the fulfilment of the purposes of public service television broadcasting in the United Kingdom.

(2) This section does not apply unless—

(a) OFCOM are of the opinion that the failure of the provider is serious and is not excused by economic or market conditions; and

(b) OFCOM determine that the situation requires the exercise of their powers under this section.

(3) In making a determination under subsection (2)(b), OFCOM must have regard, in particular, to—

(a) the public service remit of that provider;

(b) the statements of programme policy or statements of service policy made (or treated as made) by the provider under section 266 or 268;

(c) the record generally of the provider in relation to the carrying out of obligations imposed by conditions of licences under the 1990 Act and the 1996 Act (including past obligations);

(d) the effectiveness and efficiency of the provider in monitoring his own performance; and

(e) general economic and market conditions affecting generally the providers of television programme services or the providers of television multiplex services, or both of them.

(4) OFCOM shall have power to give directions to the provider to do one or both of the following—

(a) to revise the provider's latest statement of programme policy, or statement of service policy, in accordance with the directions; and

(b) to take such steps for remedying the provider's failure as OFCOM may specify in the direction as necessary for that purpose.

(5) A direction given under this section must set out—

    (a) a reasonable timetable for complying with it; and

    (b) the factors that will be taken into account by OFCOM in determining—

        (i) whether or not a failure of the provider has been remedied; and

        (ii) whether or not to exercise their powers under subsection (6).

(6) If OFCOM are satisfied—

    (a) that the provider of a public service channel or the public teletext provider has failed to comply with a direction under this section,

    (b) that that provider is still failing to fulfil the public service remit for that channel or service or adequately to contribute to the fulfilment of the purposes of public service television broadcasting in the United Kingdom, and

    (c) that it would be both reasonable and proportionate to the seriousness of that failure to vary the provider's licence in accordance with this subsection,

OFCOM may, by notice to the provider, vary that licence so as to replace self-regulation with detailed regulation.

(7) For the purposes of subsection (6) a variation replacing self-regulation with detailed regulation is a variation which—

    (a) omits the conditions imposed by virtue of sections 265 to 269; and

    (b) replaces those conditions with such specific conditions as OFCOM consider appropriate for securing that the provider—

        (i) fulfils the public service remit for his service; and

        (ii) makes an adequate contribution towards the fulfilment of the purposes of public service television broadcasting in the United Kingdom.

(8) If, at any time following a variation in accordance with subsection (6) of a provider's licence, OFCOM consider that detailed regulation is no longer necessary, they may again vary the licence so as, with effect from such time as they may determine—

    (a) to provide for the conditions required by virtue of sections 265 to 269 again to be included in the regulatory regime for the service provided by that provider; and

    (b) to remove or modify some or all of the specific conditions inserted under that subsection.

(9) Before giving a direction under this section to a provider or exercising their power under this section to vary a provider's licence, OFCOM must consult that provider.

(10) In accordance with section 265(5), the reference in subsection (1) to a failure to fulfil the public service remit for the public teletext service includes a failure to fulfil that remit as respects only one of the services comprised in that service.

271 Power to amend public service remits

(1) The Secretary of State may by order modify any one or more of the following—

    (a) the public service remit for any licensed public service channel or for the public teletext service;

    (b) the purposes of public service television broadcasting in the United Kingdom (within the meaning given by subsection (4) of section 264);

    (c) the matters to which OFCOM are to have regard under subsections (5) and (6) of that section.

(2) The Secretary of State is not to make an order under this section except where—

    (a) OFCOM have made a recommendation for the making of such an order in their most recent report under section 229 or 264; or

    (b) subsection (3) applies to the order.

(3) This subsection applies to an order if—

    (a) it is made by the Secretary of State less than twelve months after the date on which he has received a report under section 229;

    (b) he has considered that report; and

(c) he is satisfied that the making of the order is required, notwithstanding the absence of a recommendation by OFCOM, by circumstances or other matters which are dealt with in that report or which (in his opinion) should have been.

(4) Before including a recommendation for the making of an order under this section in a report under section 229 or 264, OFCOM must consult—

(a) members of the public in the United Kingdom;

(b) such public service broadcasters as they consider are likely to be affected if the Secretary of State gives effect to the recommendation they are proposing to make; and

(c) such of the other persons providing television and radio services as OFCOM consider appropriate.

(5) Before making an order under this section, the Secretary of State must consult the persons mentioned in subsection (6) about its terms (even if the order is the one recommended by OFCOM).

(6) Those persons are—

(a) OFCOM;

(b) such public service broadcasters as they consider are likely to be affected by the order; and

(c) such of the other persons providing television and radio services as he considers appropriate.

(7) No order is to be made containing provision authorised by this section unless a draft of the order has been laid before Parliament and approved by a resolution of each House.

(8) In this section 'public service broadcaster' means any of the persons who are public service broadcasters for the purposes of section 264.

271A   Remedying failure by C4C to perform media content duties

(1) This section applies if OFCOM are satisfied—

(a) that C4C have failed to comply with a direction under section 198D in respect of a failure to perform one or more of their duties under section 198A,

(b) that C4C are still failing to perform that duty or those duties, and

(c) that it would be both reasonable and proportionate to the seriousness of the failure to vary the licence under which Channel 4 is licensed ('the Channel 4 licence') in accordance with this section.

(2) OFCOM may, by notice to C4C, vary the Channel 4 licence by adding such conditions, or making such modifications of conditions, as OFCOM consider appropriate for remedying (entirely or partly) C4C's failure to perform the duty or duties under section 198A.

(3) If, at any time following such a variation, OFCOM consider that any of the additional conditions or modifications is no longer necessary, they may again vary the licence with effect from such time as they may determine.

(4) OFCOM must consult C4C before exercising their power under this section to vary the Channel 4 licence.

Must-offer obligations etc. affecting public service television

272   Must-offer obligations in relation to networks

(1) The regulatory regime for—

(a) every licensed public service channel,

(b) the public teletext service, and

(c) every licensed television service added by order under section 64 to the list of must-carry services,

includes the conditions that OFCOM consider appropriate for securing the three objectives set out in this section (so far as they are not secured by provision made under section 243).

(2) The first objective is that the channel or other service, so far as it is provided in digital form, is at all times offered as available (subject to the need to agree terms) to be broadcast or distributed by means of every appropriate network.

(3) The second objective is that the person providing the channel or other service does his best to secure that arrangements are entered into, and kept in force, that ensure—

    (a) that the channel or other service, so far as it is provided in digital form, is broadcast or distributed on appropriate networks; and

    (b) that the broadcasting and distribution of the channel or other service, in accordance with those arrangements, result in its being available for reception, by means of appropriate networks, by as many members of its intended audience as practicable.

(4) The third objective is that the arrangements entered into and kept in force for the purpose of securing the second objective prohibit the imposition, for or in connection with the provision of an appropriate network, of any charge that is attributable (whether directly or indirectly) to the conferring of an entitlement to receive the channel or other service in question in an intelligible form by means of that network.

(5) The three objectives apply only in relation to times when the channel or other service in its digital form is included in the list of must-carry services in section 64.

(6) Conditions imposed under this section in relation to a channel or other service must, to such extent as OFCOM consider appropriate—

    (a) require arrangements made or kept in force for the purpose of securing the second objective to apply in the case of every service which is an ancillary service by reference to the channel or other service in question as they apply to the channel or other service itself; and

    (b) provide for the channel or other service to which the conditions apply to be treated, in relation to particular appropriate networks, as constituting such services comprised in or provided with that channel or other service as may be determined by OFCOM.

(7) In this section—

'appropriate network' means (subject to subsection (8)) an electronic communications network by means of which public electronic communications services are provided that are used by a significant number of end-users as their principal means of receiving television programmes;

'intended audience', in relation to a channel or other service, means—

    (a) if the channel or other service is one provided only for a particular area or locality of the United Kingdom, members of the public in that area or locality;

    (b) if the channel or other service is one provided for members of a particular community, members of that community; and

    (c) in any other case, members of the public in the United Kingdom;

'licensed television service' means a service falling to be licensed under Part 1 of the 1990 Act or Part 1 of the 1996 Act.

(8) For the purposes of this section an electronic communications network is not an appropriate network in relation to so much of a channel or other service as is provided only for a particular area or locality of the United Kingdom unless it is a network by means of which electronic communications services are provided to persons in that area or locality

(9) In subsection (7) 'public electronic communications service' and 'end-user' each has the same meaning as in Part 2.

(10) An order under section 411 must not appoint a day for provisions of this section to come into force that falls less than six months after the day on which the order is made.

273   Must-offer obligations in relation to satellite services

(1) The regulatory regime for—

    (a) every licensed public service channel,

    (b) the public teletext service, and

    (c) every other licensed television service specified for the purposes of this section in an order made by the Secretary of State,

includes the conditions that OFCOM consider appropriate for securing the three objectives set out in this section (so far as they are not secured by conditions imposed under section 272).

(2) The first objective is that the channel or other service, so far as it is provided in digital form, is at all times offered as available (subject to the need to agree terms) to be broadcast by means of every satellite television service that is available for reception by members of the public in the whole or a part of the United Kingdom.

(3) The second objective is that the person providing the channel or other service does his best to secure that arrangements are entered into, and kept in force, that ensure—

    (a) that the channel or other service, so far as it is provided in digital form, is broadcast by means of satellite television services that are broadcast so as to be available for reception by members of the public in the United Kingdom; and

    (b) that the broadcasting, in accordance with those arrangements, of the channel or other service by means of those satellite television services results in its being available for reception in an intelligible form and by means of those services by as many members of its intended audience as practicable.

(4) The third objective is that the arrangements entered into and kept in force for the purpose of securing the second objective prohibit the imposition, for or in connection with the provision of a satellite television service, of any charge that is attributable (whether directly or indirectly) to the conferring of an entitlement to receive the channel or other service in question in an intelligible form by means of that service.

(5) The three objectives apply only in relation to a time when the channel or service is included, in its digital form, in the list of services that are must-provide services for the purposes of section 274.

(6) Conditions imposed under this section in relation to a channel or other service must, to such extent as OFCOM consider appropriate—

    (a) require arrangements made or kept in force for the purpose of securing the second objective to apply in the case of every service which is an ancillary service by reference to the channel or other service in question as they apply to the channel or other service itself; and

    (b) provide for the channel or other service to which the conditions apply to be treated, in relation to particular satellite television services, as constituting such services comprised in or provided with the channel or other service as may be determined by OFCOM.

(7) In this section—

'intended audience', in relation to a channel or other service, means—

    (a) if the channel or other service is one provided only for a particular area or locality of the United Kingdom, members of the public in that area or locality;

    (b) if the channel or other service is one provided for members of a particular community, members of that community; and

    (c) in any other case, members of the public in the United Kingdom;

'licensed television service' means a service falling to be licensed under Part 1 of the 1990 Act or Part 1 of the 1996 Act; and

'satellite television service' means a service which—

    (a) consists in or involves the broadcasting of television programme services from a satellite; and

    (b) is used by a significant number of the persons by whom the broadcasts are received in an intelligible form as their principal means of receiving television programmes.

(8) An order under section 411 must not appoint a day for provisions of this section to come into force that falls less than six months after the day on which the order is made.

274 Securing reception of must-provide services in certain areas

(1) The regulatory regime for—

    (a) every licensed public service channel,

    (b) the public teletext service, and

(c) every licensed television service added by order under section 275 to the list of must-provide services,

includes the conditions that OFCOM consider appropriate for securing that arrangements satisfying the requirements of this section are entered into and maintained by all the persons who provide must-provide services.

(2) The conditions imposed on a person under this section may include the conditions that OFCOM consider appropriate for securing, in a case where—

(a) the persons providing must-provide services fail to enter into or maintain arrangements satisfying the requirements of this section, and

(b) OFCOM make and impose arrangements of their own instead,

that the person bound by the conditions is required to act in accordance with arrangements imposed by OFCOM.

(3) The arrangements that are to be entered into, or may be imposed, are arrangements that secure—

(a) that a facility for receiving each must-provide service is made available to every member of the intended audience for that service who is unable, without the use of that facility, to receive it in an intelligible form and free of charge;

(b) that the facility is one under which every such member of the intended audience for a must-provide service is entitled, free of charge, to receive in an intelligible form so much of a service broadcast from a satellite as includes that must-provide service;

(c) that the cost of making that facility available is shared, in appropriate proportions, by all the persons providing must-provide services;

(d) that procedures are established and maintained for dealing with complaints from persons claiming to be entitled, in accordance with the arrangements, to receive a service free of charge, and for resolving disputes about the existence or extent of such an entitlement;

(e) that the availability of those procedures is adequately publicised in accordance with guidance given from time to time by OFCOM.

(4) Arrangements entered into by the providers of must-provide services for the purposes of subsection (3), and any modifications of such arrangements made by the parties to them, are to have effect only if approved by OFCOM.

(5) Before imposing any arrangements for the purposes of a condition under subsection (2), OFCOM must consult all the persons who provide must-provide services.

(6) For the purposes of this section the reception of a service is not free of charge—

(a) if reception of the service is made conditional on the acceptance of an entitlement to receive another service in relation to which a charge is imposed (whether directly or indirectly);

(b) if a charge is made for or in connection with the provision of a service which is an ancillary service in relation to the service in question;

(c) if any consideration is required from the persons to whom it is made available for the provision of assistance for disabled people in respect of programmes included in the service; or

(d) if any other consideration is required to be given, by the person entitled to receive it, for or in connection with its provision or availability.

(7) A service is not prevented from being free of charge by a requirement to pay sums in accordance with regulations under section 365.

(8) The quality of reception that is required before someone is to be treated for the purposes of any conditions imposed under this section as able to receive a service in an intelligible form is to be determined by OFCOM.

(9) References in this section to a facility for receiving a must-provide service include references to—

    (a) software to be used in giving effect to the entitlement to receive a must-provide service in an intelligible form, and

    (b) apparatus to be used in associating apparatus capable of being used for receiving such a service, or for putting it into an intelligible form, with a person having such an entitlement,

but do not otherwise include references to apparatus.

    (10) In this section—

'intended audience', in relation to a must-provide service, means—

    (a) if the service is one provided only for a particular area or locality of the United Kingdom, members of the public in that area or locality;

    (b) if the service is one provided for members of a particular community, members of that community; and

    (c) in any other case, members of the public in the United Kingdom;

'licensed television service' means a service falling to be licensed under Part 1 of the 1990 Act or Part 1 of the 1996 Act;

'must-provide service' means a service for the time being included in the list of must-provide services in section 275.

    (11) An order under section 411 must not appoint a day for provisions of this section to come into force that falls less than six months after the day on which the order is made.

275 Must-provide services for the purposes of s. 274

    (1) For the purposes of section 274 the list of must-provide services is as follows—

    (a) every service of television programmes provided by the BBC so far as it is provided in digital form and is a service in relation to which OFCOM have functions;

    (b) the Channel 3 services so far as provided in digital form;

    (c) Channel 4 so far as provided in digital form;

    (d) Channel 5 so far as provided in digital form;

    (e) S4C Digital;

    (f) the digital public teletext service.

    (2) The Secretary of State may by order modify the list of must-provide services in sub-section (1).

    (3) In determining whether it is appropriate, by an order under subsection (2), to add a service to the list of must-provide services or to remove a service from that list, the Secretary of State must have regard, in particular, to—

    (a) the public benefit to be secured by the addition of the service to the list, or by its retention in the list;

    (b) the likely effect of the proposed modification as respects the costs to be borne, under arrangements entered into or imposed under section 274, by the persons who, after the coming into force of the modification, would have to be parties to those arrangements; and

    (c) the extent to which that effect is proportionate to the benefit mentioned in paragraph (a).

Programming quotas for public service television

277 Programming quotas for independent productions

    (1) The regulatory regime for every licensed public service channel includes the conditions that OFCOM consider appropriate for securing that, in each year, not less than 25 per cent. of the total amount of time allocated to the broadcasting of qualifying programmes included in the channel is allocated to the broadcasting of a range and diversity of independent productions.

    (2) In this section—

    (a) a reference to qualifying programmes is a reference to programmes of such description as the Secretary of State may by order specify as describing the programmes that are to be qualifying programmes for the purposes of this section;

(b) a reference to independent productions is a reference to programmes of such description as the Secretary of State may by order specify as describing the programmes that are to be independent productions for the purposes of this section; and

(c) a reference to a range of independent productions is a reference to a range of such productions in terms of cost of acquisition as well as in terms of the types of programme involved.

(3) The Secretary of State may by order amend subsection (1) by substituting a different percentage for the percentage for the time being specified in that subsection.

(4) The Secretary of State may also by order provide for the regulatory regime for every licensed public service channel to include conditions falling within subsection (5), either instead of or as well as those falling within subsection (1).

(5) The conditions falling within this subsection are those that OFCOM consider appropriate for securing that, in each year, not less than the percentage specified in the order of the programming budget for that year for that channel is applied in the acquisition of independent productions.

(6) The power to make an order under subsection (4) includes power to provide that conditions that have previously ceased under such an order to be included in the regulatory regime for every licensed public service channel are again so included, in addition to or instead of the conditions already so included (apart from the exercise of that power) by virtue of this section.

(7) The Secretary of State is not to make an order for the regulatory regime of every licensed public service channel to include or exclude conditions falling within subsection (1) or conditions falling within subsection (5) unless—

(a) OFCOM have made a recommendation to him for those conditions to be included or excluded; and

(b) the order gives effect to that recommendation.

(8) The regulatory regime for every licensed public service channel also includes a condition requiring the provider of the channel to comply with directions given to him by OFCOM for the purpose of—

(a) carrying forward to one or more subsequent years determined in accordance with the direction any shortfall for any year in his compliance with the requirements of conditions imposed by virtue of subsection (1) or (4);and

(b) thereby increasing the percentage applicable for the purposes of those conditions to the subsequent year or years.

(9) For the purposes of conditions imposed by virtue of this section—

(a) the amount of the programming budget for a licensed public service channel for a year, and

(b) the means of determining the amount of that budget that is applied for any purpose,

are to be computed in accordance with such provision as may be set out in an order made by the Secretary of State, or as may be determined by OFCOM in accordance with such an order.

(10) The powers of the Secretary of State to make orders under this section do not include—

(a) power to specify different percentages for the purposes of subsection (1), or of a condition falling within subsection (5), for different regional Channel 3 services or for different national Channel 3 services; or

(b) power to make different provision for different licensed public service channels as to whether conditions falling within subsection (1) or conditions falling within subsection (5), or both, are included in the regulatory regimes for those services.

(11) Before making an order under this section the Secretary of State must consult OFCOM, the BBC and the Welsh Authority.

(12) No order is to be made containing provision authorised by this section unless a draft of the order has been laid before Parliament and approved by a resolution of each House.

(13) In this section—

'acquisition', in relation to a programme, includes commissioning and the acquisition of a right to include it in a service or to have it broadcast;

'programme' does not include an advertisement; and

'programming budget' means the budget for the production and acquisition of qualifying programmes.

278 Programming quotas for original productions

(1) The regulatory regime for every licensed public service channel includes the conditions that OFCOM consider appropriate for securing—

(a) that the time allocated, in each year, to the broadcasting of original productions included in that channel is no less than what appears to them to be an appropriate proportion of the total amount of time allocated to the broadcasting of all the programmes included in the channel; and

(b) that the time allocated to the broadcasting of original productions is split in what appears to them to be an appropriate manner between peak viewing times and other times.

(2) The proportion determined by OFCOM for the purposes of subsection (1)—

(a) must, in the case of each licensed public service channel, be such proportion as OFCOM consider appropriate for ensuring that the channel is consistently of a high quality; and

(b) may, for the purposes of paragraph (b) of that subsection, be expressed as the cumulative effect of two different minimum proportions, one applying to peak viewing times and the other to other times.

(3) A condition contained in a licence by virtue of this section may provide—

(a) that specified descriptions of programmes are to be excluded in determining the programmes a proportion of which is to consist of original productions;

(b) that, in determining for the purposes of the condition whether a programme is of a description of programmes excluded by virtue of paragraph (a), regard is to be had to any guidance prepared and published, and from to time revised, by OFCOM.

(4) Before imposing a condition under this section, OFCOM must consult the person on whom it is to be imposed.

(5) The requirement to consult is satisfied, in the case of the imposition of a condition by way of a variation of a licence, by compliance with section 3(4)(b) of the 1990 Act (obligation to give opportunity to make representations about variation).

(6) References in this section, in relation to a licensed public service channel, to original productions are references to programmes of such description as the Secretary of State may by order specify as describing the programmes that are to be original productions for the purposes of this section.

(7) The power to specify descriptions of programmes by order under subsection (6) includes power to confer such discretions on OFCOM as the Secretary of State thinks fit.

(8) Before making an order under this section the Secretary of State must consult OFCOM, the BBC and the Welsh Authority.

(9) No order is to be made containing provision authorised by this section unless a draft of the order has been laid before Parliament and approved by a resolution of each House.

(10) In this section—

'peak viewing time', in relation to a licensed public service channel, means a time that appears to OFCOM to be, or to be likely to be, a peak viewing time for that channel; and

'programme' does not include an advertisement.

(11) Before determining for the purposes of this section what constitutes a peak viewing time for a channel, OFCOM must consult the provider of the channel.

News provision etc. on public service television

279   News and current affairs programmes

(1) The regulatory regime for every licensed public service channel includes the conditions that OFCOM consider appropriate for securing—

  (a) that the programmes included in the channel include news programmes and current affairs programmes;

  (b) that the news programmes and current affairs programmes included in the service are of high quality and deal with both national and international matters; and

  (c) that the news programmes so included are broadcast for viewing at intervals throughout the period for which the channel is provided.

(2) That regime also includes the conditions that OFCOM consider appropriate for securing that, in each year—

  (a) the time allocated to the broadcasting of news programmes included in the service, and

  (b) the time allocated to the broadcasting of current affairs programmes so included,

each constitutes no less than what appears to OFCOM to be an appropriate proportion of the time allocated to the broadcasting of all the programmes included in the channel.

(3) It further includes the conditions that OFCOM consider appropriate for securing that the time allocated—

  (a) to the broadcasting of news programmes included in the service, and

  (b) to the broadcasting of current affairs programmes so included,

is, in each case, split in what appears to OFCOM to be an appropriate manner between peak viewing times and other times.

(4) The proportion determined by OFCOM for the purposes of subsection (2) may, for the purposes of subsection (3), be expressed as the cumulative effect of two different minimum proportions, one applying to peak viewing times and the other to other times.

(5) In this section 'peak viewing time', in relation to a licensed public service channel, means a time determined by OFCOM to be, or to be likely to be, a peak viewing time for that channel.

(6) Before determining for the purposes of this section—

  (a) the proportion of time to be allocated to the broadcasting of news programmes or current affairs programmes; or

  (b) what constitutes a peak viewing time for a channel,

OFCOM must consult the provider of the channel or (as the case may be) the person who is proposing to provide it.

(7) The requirement to consult is satisfied, in the case of the imposition of a condition by way of a variation of a licence, by compliance with section 3(4)(b) of the 1990 Act (obligation to give opportunity to make representations about variation).

280   Appointed news providers for Channel 3

(1) The regulatory regime for every regional Channel 3 service includes the conditions that OFCOM consider appropriate for securing the nationwide broadcasting, on the regional Channel 3 services (taken together), of news programmes that are able to compete effectively with other television news programmes broadcast nationwide in the United Kingdom.

(2) The conditions imposed under this section must include a condition requiring the holder of a regional Channel 3 licence to do all that he can to ensure—

  (a) that arrangements for the appointment of a single body corporate as the appointed news provider are maintained between all the holders of regional Channel 3 licences; and

  (b) that, at all times while he is providing a regional Channel 3 service, there is in force an appointment made in accordance with those arrangements.

(3) The arrangements that are required to be maintained by virtue of conditions imposed under subsection (2) must provide—

    (a) for the terms on which a body is appointed as the appointed news provider to include the terms appearing to OFCOM to be appropriate for securing that the body's finances are adequate, throughout the period of its appointment, to ensure that the Channel 3 news obligations are capable of being met; and

    (b) for the approval of OFCOM to be required for the purposes of paragraph (a) to the terms on which an appointment is made.

(4) The conditions imposed under this section must include the conditions that OFCOM consider appropriate for securing that arrangements maintained between—

    (a) the holders of regional Channel 3 licences, and

    (b) the body which is the appointed news provider,

ensure that that body is subject to an obligation, enforceable by OFCOM, to provide OFCOM with all such information as they may require for the purpose of carrying out their functions.

(5) The conditions imposed under this section must include a condition requiring the news programmes included in a regional Channel 3 service—

    (a) to be programmes provided by the body which is for the time being the appointed news provider for the purposes of this section; and

    (b) to be so included in that service as to be broadcast simultaneously with the broadcasting of news programmes included, in accordance with conditions imposed under this subsection, in other regional Channel 3 services.

(6) Those conditions must also require the news programmes provided by the appointed news provider which, in accordance with a condition imposed under subsection (5), are included in a regional Channel 3 service to be programmes that are presented live.

(7) OFCOM—

    (a) may issue guidance as to the terms that will satisfy requirements imposed by virtue of subsection (3)(a); and

    (b) must have regard to guidance for the time being in force under this subsection when considering whether to give an approval for the purposes of provision made by virtue of subsection (3)(b).

(8) For the purposes of this section the Channel 3 news obligations are—

    (a) the requirements of any conditions imposed in relation to regional Channel 3 services under section 279; and

    (b) the nationwide broadcasting on the regional Channel 3 services (taken together) of news programmes that are able to compete effectively with other television news programmes broadcast nationwide in the United Kingdom.

(9) Conditions imposed under this section are not to require arrangements to make provision falling within subsection (3)(a) or (b) or (4) in relation to appointments made before the commencement of this section.

(10) Section 32 of the 1990 Act (nomination of bodies eligible for appointment as news providers) shall cease to have effect.

281 Disqualification from appointment as news provider

(1) The regulatory regime for every regional Channel 3 service includes the conditions that OFCOM consider appropriate for securing—

    (a) that a body is not appointed as the appointed news provider if it falls within subsection (2); and

    (b) that the appointment of a body as the appointed news provider ceases to have effect if it becomes a body falling within that subsection.

(2) A body falls within this subsection if—

    (a) it is a disqualified person under Part 2 of Schedule 2 to the 1990 Act in relation to a Channel 3 licence; or

    (b) there would be a contravention of Part 1 of Schedule 14 to this Act (whether by that body or by another person) if that body held a licence to provide a Channel 3 service, or held a licence to provide such a service for a particular area for which such a service is provided.

(3) The reference in subsection (2)(a) to a body which is a disqualified person under Part 2 of Schedule 2 to the 1990 Act in relation to a Channel 3 licence includes a reference to a person who is disqualified by virtue of a disqualification order under section 145 of the 1996 Act.

282   Power to repeal or modify Channel 3 news provider provisions

(1) If it appears to the Secretary of State appropriate to do so, he may by order repeal or otherwise modify any of the provisions of section 280 or 281.

(2) Except in a case to which subsection (3) applies, the Secretary of State must consult OFCOM before making an order under this section.

(3) Consultation with OFCOM is not required if the order is confined to giving effect to recommendations by OFCOM that are contained in a report of a review under section 391.

(4) No order is to be made containing provision authorised by this section unless a draft of the order has been laid before Parliament and approved by a resolution of each House.

283   News providers for Channel 5

(1) If it appears to the Secretary of State appropriate to do so, he may by order make provision requiring news programmes included in Channel 5 to be provided by a person appointed as a news provider in accordance with the order.

(2) An order under this section may make provision in relation to Channel 5 that corresponds, with such modifications as the Secretary of State thinks fit, to any provision made in relation to regional Channel 3 services by section 280 or 281.

(3) Subsection (2) applies irrespective of any repeal or other modification by an order under this Act of section 280 or 281.

(4) An order under this section may include provision for section 194A of the 1990 Act (application of Competition Act 1998 to Channel 3 news provision) to have effect (with such modifications as may be specified in the order) in relation to the appointment of a person as a news provider for Channel 5 as it has effect in relation to the appointment of a body as a news provider for Channel 3.

(5) The Secretary of State is not to make an order under this section for the imposition of obligations in relation to Channel 5 unless he is satisfied that Channel 5's share of the audience for television broadcasting services is broadly equivalent to that of the services comprising Channel 3.

(6) An order under this section must require a licence holder to have a reasonable opportunity of making representations to OFCOM before his licence is varied in pursuance of the order.

(7) Except in a case to which subsection (8) applies, the Secretary of State must consult OFCOM before making an order under this section.

(8) Consultation with OFCOM is not required if the order is confined to giving effect to recommendations by OFCOM that are contained in a report of a review under section 391.

(9) No order is to be made containing provision authorised by this section unless a draft of the order has been laid before Parliament and approved by a resolution of each House.

284   News provision on the public teletext service

(1) The regulatory regime for the public teletext service includes the conditions that OFCOM consider appropriate for securing—

   (a) that the service includes what appears to OFCOM to be a suitable quantity and variety of news items; and

   (b) that the news items included in the service are up to date and regularly revised.

(2) Conditions imposed under this section in relation to a time when the public teletext service comprises both—

   (a) an analogue teletext service, and

   (b) a teletext service provided in digital form,

must apply to both services but may make different provision for each of them.

Independent and regional productions and programmes for
public service television

285 Code relating to programme commissioning

(1) The regulatory regime for every licensed public service channel includes the conditions that OFCOM consider appropriate for securing that the provider of the channel draws up and from time to time revises a code of practice setting out the principles he will apply when agreeing terms for the commissioning of independent productions.

(2) That regime also includes the conditions that OFCOM consider appropriate for securing that the provider of every licensed public service channel—

    (a) at all times complies with a code of practice which has been drawn up by him by virtue of this section and is for the time being in force; and

    (b) exercises his power to revise his code to take account of revisions from time to time of the guidance issued by OFCOM for the purposes of this section.

(3) The conditions imposed under this section must ensure that the code for the time being in force in the case of every licensed public service channel secures, in the manner described in guidance issued by OFCOM—

    (a) that a reasonable timetable is applied to negotiations for the commissioning of an independent production and for the conclusion of a binding agreement;

    (b) that there is what appears to OFCOM to be sufficient clarity, when an (b) independent production is commissioned, about the different categories of rights to broadcast or otherwise to make use of or exploit the commissioned production that are being disposed of;

    (c) that there is what appears to OFCOM to be sufficient transparency about the amounts to be paid in respect of each category of rights;

    (d) that what appear to OFCOM to be satisfactory arrangements are made about the duration and exclusivity of those rights;

    (e) that procedures exist for reviewing the arrangements adopted in accordance with the code and for demonstrating compliance with it;

    (f) that those procedures include requirements for the monitoring of the application of the code and for the making of reports to OFCOM;

    (g) that provision is made for resolving disputes arising in respect of the provisions of the code (by independent arbitration or otherwise) in a manner that appears to OFCOM to be appropriate.

(4) The conditions imposed under this section must also ensure that the drawing up or revision of a code by virtue of this section is in accordance with guidance issued by OFCOM as to—

    (a) the times when the code is to be drawn up or reviewed with a view to revision;

    (b) the consultation to be undertaken before a code is drawn up or revised; and

    (c) the publication of every code or revised code.

(5) The provision that may be included in a condition imposed under this section includes—

    (a) provision requiring a draft of a code or of any revision of a code to be submitted to OFCOM for approval;

    (b) provision for the code or revision to have effect only if approved by OFCOM; and

    (c) provision for a code or revision that is approved by OFCOM subject to modifications to have effect with those modifications.

(6) OFCOM—

    (a) must issue and may from time to time revise guidance for the purposes of this section;

    (b) must ensure that there is always guidance for those purposes in force;

    (c) must, before issuing their guidance or revised guidance, consult the providers of licensed public service channels, persons who make independent productions (or persons appearing to OFCOM to represent them), the BBC and the Welsh Authority; and

(d) must publish their guidance or revised guidance in such manner as they think appropriate.

(7) Guidance issued by OFCOM for the purposes of this section must be general guidance and is not to specify particular terms to be included in agreements to which the guidance relates.

(8) Conditions imposed under this section requiring a code to be drawn up or approved may include transitional provision for treating a code drawn up before the imposition of the condition—

(a) as satisfying the requirements of that condition; and

(d) as a code approved by OFCOM for the purposes of conditions so imposed.

(9) In this section 'independent production' has the same meaning as in section 277.

286   Regional programme-making for Channels 3 and 5

(1) The regulatory regime for every Channel 3 service includes the conditions (if any) that OFCOM consider appropriate in the case of that service for securing—

(a) that what appears to OFCOM to be a suitable proportion of Channel 3 programmes made in the United Kingdom are programmes made in the United Kingdom outside the M25 area;

(b) that the Channel 3 programmes that are made in the United Kingdom outside the M25 area (taken together) constitute what appears to OFCOM to be a suitable range of programmes;

(c) that what appears to OFCOM to be a suitable proportion of the expenditure of the providers of Channel 3 services on Channel 3 programmes made in the United Kingdom is referable to programme production at different production centres outside the M25 area; and

(d) that the different programme production centres to which that expenditure is referable constitute what appears to OFCOM to be a suitable range of such production centres.

(2) In the case of a national Channel 3 service, subsection (1) requires the inclusion of conditions in the licence for the service only where OFCOM consider, having regard to the nature of the service, that it would be appropriate for conditions falling within that subsection to be so included.

(3) The regulatory regime for Channel 5 includes the conditions that OFCOM consider appropriate for securing—

(a) that what appears to OFCOM to be a suitable proportion of the programmes made in the United Kingdom for viewing on that Channel are programmes made in the United Kingdom outside the M25 area;

(b) that the programmes for such viewing that are made in the United Kingdom outside the M25 area (taken together) constitute what appears to OFCOM to be a suitable range of programmes;

(c) that what appears to OFCOM to be a suitable proportion of the expenditure of the provider of Channel 5 on programmes made in the United Kingdom for viewing on that Channel is referable to programme production at different production centres outside the M25 area; and

(d) that the different programme production centres to which that expenditure is referable constitute what appears to OFCOM to be a suitable range of such production centres.

(4) Before imposing a condition under this section, OFCOM must consult the person on whom it is to be imposed.

(5) The requirement to consult is satisfied, in the case of the imposition of a condition by way of a variation of a licence, by compliance with section 3(4)(b) of the 1990 Act (obligation to give opportunity to make representations about variation).

(6) A proportion is not to be regarded by OFCOM as suitable for the purposes of a provision of this section if it constitutes less than a significant proportion of the programmes or expenditure in question.

(7) In this section—

'Channel 3 programmes' means programmes made for viewing on Channel 3 in more than one area for which regional Channel 3 services are provided, including any programme made for viewing on a national Channel 3 service other than a regional programme;

'expenditure', in relation to a programme, means—

    (a) expenditure which constitutes an investment in or is otherwise attributable to the making of the programme; or

    (b) expenditure on the commissioning or other acquisition of the programme or on the acquisition of a right to include it in a service or to have it broadcast;

'programme' does not include an advertisement; and

'regional programme' means a programme made with a view to its inclusion in a national Channel 3 service as a programme of particular interest to persons living within a particular area of the United Kingdom.

287 Regional programmes on Channel 3

(1) The regulatory regime for every regional Channel 3 service includes the conditions that OFCOM consider appropriate for securing—

    (a) that what appears to OFCOM, in the case of that service, to be a sufficient amount of time is given in the programmes included in the service to what appears to them to be a suitable range of programmes (including regional news programmes) which are of particular interest to persons living within the area for which the service is provided;

    (b) that the regional programmes included in the service are of high quality;

    (c) that what appears to OFCOM, in the case of that service, to be a suitable proportion of the regional programmes included in the service consists of programmes made in that area;

    (d) that the regional news programmes included in the service are broadcast for viewing at intervals throughout the period for which the service is provided and, in particular, at peak viewing times;

    (e) that what appears to OFCOM, in the case of that service, to be a suitable proportion of the other regional programmes that are included in the service consists of programmes broadcast for viewing—

      (i) at peak viewing times; and

      (ii) at times immediately preceding or following those times.

(2) The regulatory regime for every local Channel 3 service includes the conditions that OFCOM consider appropriate for securing—

    (a) that what appears to OFCOM, in the case of that service, to be a sufficient amount of time is given in the programmes included in the service to what appears to them to be a suitable range of local programmes;

    (b) that, in the case of each part of an area or each community for which the service is provided, the range of local programmes is a range of programmes (including news programmes) which are of particular interest to persons living within that part of that area or to that community;

    (c) that the local programmes included in the service are of high quality;

    (d) that what appears to OFCOM, in the case of that service, to be a suitable proportion of the local programmes included in the service consists of programmes made in the area for which the service is provided;

    (e) that the local news programmes included in the service are broadcast for viewing at intervals throughout the period for which the service is provided and, in particular, at peak viewing times;

    (f) that what appears to OFCOM, in the case of that service, to be a suitable proportion of the other local programmes that are included in the service consists of programmes broadcast for viewing—

      (i) at peak viewing times; and

      (ii) at times immediately preceding or following those times.

(3) In the case of a local Channel 3 service, the conditions included in the regulatory regime for the service include conditions falling within subsection (1) to the extent only that it appears to OFCOM that the requirements of subsection (1) are not adequately met by conditions falling within subsection (2).

(4) In the case of a national Channel 3 service in the case of which OFCOM consider that it would be appropriate to impose conditions under this subsection, the regulatory regime for the service includes the conditions that OFCOM consider appropriate for securing—

    (a) that what appears to OFCOM, in the case of that service, to be a sufficient amount of time is given in the programmes included in the service to what appears to them to be a suitable range of programmes (including regional news programmes) which are of particular interest to persons living within particular areas of the United Kingdom;

    (b) that the regional programmes included in the service are of high quality;

    (c) that what appears to OFCOM, in the case of that service, to be a suitable proportion of the regional programmes included in the service consists of programmes made in the area by reference to which they are regional programmes;

    (d) that the regional news programmes included in the service are broadcast for viewing at intervals throughout the period for which the service is provided and, in particular, at peak viewing times;

    (e) that what appears to OFCOM, in the case of that service, to be a suitable proportion of the other regional programmes that are included in the service consists of programmes broadcast for viewing—

        (i)   at peak viewing times; and

        (ii) at times immediately preceding or following those times.

(5) Before imposing a condition under this section, OFCOM must consult the person on whom it is to be imposed.

(6) The requirement to consult is satisfied, in the case of the imposition of a condition by way of a variation of a licence, by compliance with section 3(4)(b) of the 1990 Act (obligation to give opportunity to make representations about variation).

(7) A proportion is not to be regarded by OFCOM as suitable for the purposes of a provision of this section if it constitutes less than a significant proportion of the programmes in question.

(8) In this section—

'local Channel 3 service' means a regional Channel 3 service the provision of which includes the provision (in pursuance of a determination under section 14(3) of the 1990 Act) of different programmes for different parts of an area or for different communities living within an area;

'local programme', in relation to a service provided for different parts of an area or for different communities, means a programme included in that service for any of the parts of that area or for any of those communities, and 'local news programme' is to be construed accordingly;

'peak viewing time', in relation to a service, means a time determined by OFCOM to be, or to be likely to be, a peak viewing time for that service;

'programme' does not include an advertisement;

'regional programme'—

    (a) in relation to a regional Channel 3 service, means a programme included in that service with a view to its being of particular interest to persons living within the area for which the service is provided;

    (b) in relation to a national Channel 3 service, means a programme included in that service with a view to its being of particular interest to persons living within a particular area of the United Kingdom;

and 'regional news programme' is to be construed accordingly.

288   Regional programme-making for Channel 4

(1) The regulatory regime for Channel 4 includes the conditions that OFCOM consider appropriate for securing—

    (a) that what appears to OFCOM to be a suitable proportion of programmes made in the United Kingdom for viewing on Channel 4 are programmes made in the United Kingdom outside the M25 area;

    (b) that the programmes for such viewing that are made in the United Kingdom outside the M25 area (taken together) constitute what appears to OFCOM to be a suitable range of programmes;

   (c) that what appears to OFCOM to be a suitable proportion of the expenditure of C4C
       on programmes made in the United Kingdom for viewing on Channel 4 is referable to
       programme production at different production centres outside the M25 area; and
   (d) that the different programme production centres to which that expenditure is
       referable constitute what appears to OFCOM to be a suitable range of such production
       centres.

(2) Before imposing a condition under this section, OFCOM must consult C4C.

(3) The requirement to consult is satisfied, in the case of the imposition of a condition by way of
a variation of a licence, by compliance with section 3(4)(b) of the 1990 Act (obligation to give opportunity to make representations about variation).

(4) A proportion is not to be regarded by OFCOM as suitable for the purposes of a provision of this
section if it constitutes less than a significant proportion of the programmes or expenditure in question.

(5) In this section—
'expenditure', in relation to a programme, means—
   (a) expenditure which constitutes an investment in or is otherwise attributable to the making
       of the programme; or
   (b) expenditure on the commissioning or other acquisition of the programme or on the acqui-
       sition of a right to include it in a service or to have it broadcast; and
'programme' does not include an advertisement.

289   Regional matters in the public teletext service

(1) The regulatory regime for the public teletext service includes the conditions that OFCOM
consider appropriate for securing that the service includes what appears to them to be an appropriate
proportion of material that is of particular interest to persons living in different parts of the United
Kingdom.

(2) Conditions imposed under this section in relation to a time when the public teletext service
comprises . . .
   (b) a teletext service provided in digital form . . .

Networking arrangements for Channel 3

290   Proposals for arrangements

(1) An application for a regional Channel 3 licence, in addition to being accompanied by the
proposals mentioned in section 15(3)(b) of the 1990 Act, must be accompanied by the applicant's
proposals for participating in networking arrangements.

(2) OFCOM may publish general guidance to applicants for regional Channel 3 licences as to the
kinds of proposals which they are likely to consider satisfactory.

(3) The publication of guidance under subsection (2) is to be in such manner as OFCOM consider
appropriate.

(4) Arrangements are networking arrangements for the purposes of this Part if they—
   (a) apply to all the holders of regional Channel 3 licences;
   (b) provide for programmes made, commissioned or acquired by or on behalf of one or more
       of the holders of such licences to be available for broadcasting in all regional Channel 3
       services; and
   (c) are made for the purpose of enabling regional Channel 3 services (taken as a whole) to be
       a nationwide system of services which is able to compete effectively with other television
       programme services provided in the United Kingdom.

291   Obligation as to making and continuance of approved arrangements

(1) The regulatory regime for every regional Channel 3 service includes the conditions that
OFCOM consider appropriate for securing that the licence holder does all that he can to ensure that
approved networking arrangements are in force whenever—
   (a) the licence holder is providing the licensed service; and
   (b) no networking arrangements imposed by OFCOM under section 292 are in force.

(2) In this section 'approved networking arrangements' means networking arrangements which are for the time being approved by OFCOM in accordance with Schedule 11.

(3) In paragraph 5 of Schedule 2 to the Competition Act 1998 (c. 41) (exclusion of networking arrangements from Chapter I prohibition), for sub-paragraph (1) there shall be substituted—

'(1) The Chapter I prohibition does not apply in respect of any networking arrangements to the extent that they—

  (a) have been approved for the purposes of licence conditions imposed under section 291 of the Communications Act 2003; or

  (b) are arrangements that have been considered under Schedule 4 to the Broadcasting Act 1990 and fall to be treated as so approved;

nor does that prohibition apply in respect of things done with a view to arrangements being entered into or approved to the extent that those things have effect for purposes that are directly related to, and necessary for compliance with, conditions so imposed.'

(4) For sub-paragraph (4) of that paragraph there shall be substituted—

'(4) In this paragraph 'networking arrangements' has the same meaning as in Part 3 of the Communications Act 2003.'

292   OFCOM's power to impose arrangements

(1) This section applies on each occasion on which OFCOM—

  (a) are proposing to award one or more regional Channel 3 licences; and

  (b) for that purpose publish a notice under section 15(1) of the 1990 Act.

(2) OFCOM must—

  (a) determine the date by which the holders of the licences awarded and all other regional Channel 3 providers (if any) must have entered into networking arrangements (the 'networking date'); and

  (b) set out that date in that notice.

(3) The networking date must be the date by which, in OFCOM's opinion, the networking arrangements must have been entered into if approved networking arrangements are to be fully in force before the persons awarded licences begin to provide their licensed services.

(4) If—

  (a) no suitable networking arrangements exist by the networking date, or

  (b) the suitable networking arrangements that exist at that date cease to apply to all regional Channel 3 providers on or after that date,

OFCOM may impose on all regional Channel 3 providers the networking arrangements that OFCOM consider appropriate.

(5) For the purposes of subsection (4) arrangements are suitable networking arrangements if it appears to OFCOM that they—

  (a) have been submitted to them for approval or have been approved by them; and

  (b) will be in force as approved networking arrangements when the persons awarded licences begin to provide their licensed services.

(6) Arrangements imposed under this section come into force on the date determined by OFCOM.

(7) The regulatory regime for every regional Channel 3 service includes the conditions that OFCOM consider appropriate for securing that the licence holder complies with the provisions of any networking arrangements imposed under this section.

(8) Where—

  (a) networking arrangements are imposed under this section,

  (b) other networking arrangements are entered into between the licence holders bound by the imposed arrangements, and

  (c) the other arrangements entered into are approved by OFCOM,

the imposed arrangements shall cease to have effect on the coming into force of the other arrangements as approved networking arrangements.

(9) In this section—

'approved networking arrangements' has the same meaning as in section 291; and

'regional Channel 3 providers' means persons who will be licensed to provide regional Channel 3 services and will be providing such services when the licences to be awarded come into force.

293   Review of approved networking arrangements etc.

(1) It shall be the duty of OFCOM from time to time to carry out general reviews of the networking arrangements (whether approved or imposed by OFCOM) that are in force.

(2) The first such review must be carried out no later than six months after the date on which the offers made under section 215(1) close or (if those offers close on different dates) the latest of those dates.

(3) Every subsequent review must be carried out no more than one year after the previous one.

(4) OFCOM may also, at any other time, carry out a review of whether those arrangements continue to satisfy one of the two competition tests set out in paragraph 6 of Schedule 11.

(5) If, on a review under this section, OFCOM are satisfied that modifications are required of the networking arrangements for the time being in force, they may—

   (a) require the holders of regional Channel 3 licences to give effect to the modifications proposed by OFCOM; or

   (b) in the case of arrangements imposed by OFCOM, make those modifications themselves.

(6) OFCOM must not exercise any of their powers under this Act or the 1990 Act so as to modify the requirements imposed on the holder of a regional Channel 3 licence by approved networking arrangements that are already in force except—

   (a) following a review under this section; or

   (b) with the consent of the licence holder.

(7) The regulatory regime for every Channel 3 service includes the conditions that OFCOM consider appropriate for securing that the licence holder does all that he can to ensure that modifications proposed by OFCOM under this section are given effect to.

(8) In this section 'approved networking arrangements' has the same meaning as in section 291.

294   Supplemental provision about networking arrangements

(1) Schedule 11 (which makes provision about the approval of networking arrangements and the imposition or modification of such arrangements) shall have effect.

(2) The obligations arising under conditions imposed in accordance with sections 291 to 293 are subject to the rights of appeal conferred by that Schedule.

Special obligations for Channel 4

295   Involvement of C4 Corporation in programme-making

(1) The regulatory regime for Channel 4 includes a condition requiring C4C not to be involved, except to such extent as OFCOM may allow, in the making of programmes to be broadcast on Channel 4.

(2) In this section 'programme' does not include an advertisement.

296   Schools programmes on Channel 4

(1) The regulatory regime for Channel 4 includes the conditions that OFCOM consider appropriate for securing that what appears to them to be a suitable proportion of the programmes which are included in Channel 4 are schools programmes.

(2) A licence under the 1990 Act to provide Channel 4 may also include conditions authorised by the following provisions of this section.

(3) The conditions authorised by this section include conditions requiring C4C—

   (a) to finance the production of schools programmes; and

   (b) to acquire schools programmes provided by other persons.

(4) The conditions authorised by this section include conditions requiring C4C to ensure that schools programmes on Channel 4—

(a) are of high quality; and

(b) are suitable to meet the needs of schools throughout the United Kingdom.

(5) The conditions authorised by this section include conditions specifying the minimum number of hours in term time, or within normal school hours, that are to be allocated to the broadcasting of schools programmes on Channel 4.

(6) The conditions authorised by this section include conditions requiring C4C to provide such material for use in connection with the schools programmes broadcast by them as may be necessary to secure that effective use is made of those programmes in schools.

(7) The conditions authorised by this section include conditions requiring C4C from time to time to consult such persons who—

(a) are concerned with schools or with the production of schools programmes, or

(b) have an interest in schools or in the production of schools programmes, as OFCOM think fit.

(8) Before imposing a condition under this section, OFCOM must consult C4C.

(9) The requirement to consult is satisfied, in the case of the imposition of a condition by way of a variation of a licence, by compliance with section 3(4)(b) of the 1990 Act (obligation to give opportunity to make representations about variation).

(10) In determining for the purposes of subsection (1) what proportion of the programmes included in Channel 4 should be schools programmes, OFCOM must take into account services, facilities and materials which C4C provide to schools, or make available for schools, otherwise than by the inclusion of programmes in Channel 4.

(11) Section 34 of the 1990 Act (requirement as to schools programmes in relation to all licensed public service channels taken together) shall cease to have effect.

(12) In this section 'schools programmes' means programmes which are intended for use in schools.

Special obligation for the public teletext provider

298 Conditions prohibiting interference with other services

The regulatory regime for the public teletext service includes the conditions that OFCOM consider appropriate for securing that the provision of so much of the public teletext service as is provided in analogue form does not cause interference with—

(a) the television broadcasting service or services on whose frequency or frequencies it is provided; or

(b) any other wireless telegraphy transmissions.

Television services for the deaf and visually impaired

303 Code relating to provision for the deaf and visually impaired

(1) It shall be the duty of OFCOM to draw up, and from time to time to review and revise, a code giving guidance as to—

(a) the extent to which the services to which this section applies should promote the understanding and enjoyment by—

(i)   persons who are deaf or hard of hearing,

(ii) persons who are blind or partially-sighted, and

(iii) persons with a dual sensory impairment,

of the programmes to be included in such services; and

(b) the means by which such understanding and enjoyment should be promoted.

(2) The code must include provision for securing that every provider of a service to which this section applies ensures that adequate information about the assistance for disabled people that is provided in relation to that service is made available to those who are likely to want to make use of it.

(5) The obligations to be fulfilled from the tenth anniversary of the relevant date are—

(a) that at least 90 per cent. of so much of a Channel 3 service or of Channel 4 as consists of programmes that are not excluded programmes must be accompanied by subtitling;

(b) that at least 80 per cent. of so much of every other service to which this section applies as consists of programmes that are not excluded programmes must be accompanied by subtitling;

(c) that at least 10 per cent. of so much of every service to which this section applies as consists of programmes that are not excluded programmes must be accompanied by audio-description for the blind; and

(d) that at least 5 per cent. of so much of every service to which this section applies as consists of programmes that are not excluded programmes must be presented in, or translated into, sign language.

304 Procedure for issuing and revising code under s. 303

(1) Before drawing up a code under section 303 or reviewing or revising it in pursuance of that section, OFCOM must consult—

(a) such persons appearing to them to represent the interests of persons falling within subsection (1)(a)(i), (ii) or (iii) of that section as OFCOM think fit; and

(b) such persons providing services to which that section applies as OFCOM think fit.

(2) OFCOM must publish the code drawn up under section 303, and every revision of it, in such manner as, having regard to the need to make the code or revision accessible to—

(a) persons who are deaf or hard of hearing,

(b) persons who are blind or partially sighted, and

(c) persons with a dual sensory impairment,

they consider appropriate.

306 Power to modify targets in s. 303

(1) Where it appears to the Secretary of State, in the case of services of a particular description, that the obligation specified in section 303(4) has been or is likely to be fulfilled in their case before the anniversary so specified, he may by order modify section 303 so as to do one or both of the following—

(a) increase the percentage so specified in relation to services of that description;

(b) substitute a different anniversary for the anniversary by which that obligation must be fulfilled in the case of such services.

307 Observance of code under s. 303

(1) The regulatory regime for every service to which this section applies includes the conditions that OFCOM consider appropriate for securing that the code maintained by them under section 303 is observed in the provision of those services.

(2) This section applies to every service to which section 303 applies which is licensed by a Broadcasting Act licence.

308 Assistance for the visually impaired with the public teletext service

The regulatory regime for the public teletext service includes the conditions that OFCOM consider appropriate for securing, so far as it is reasonable and practicable, by the inclusion of features in that service, to do so, that persons with disabilities affecting their sight are able to make use of the service.

Programming quotas for digital television programme services

309 Quotas for independent programmes

(1) The regulatory regime for every digital television programme service that is not comprised in a licensed public service channel includes the conditions that OFCOM consider appropriate for securing that, in each year, not less than 10 per cent. of the total amount of time allocated to the broadcasting of qualifying programmes included in the service is allocated to the broadcasting of a range and diversity of independent productions.

(2) In subsection (1)—

(a) the reference to qualifying programmes is a reference to programmes of such description as the Secretary of State may by order specify as describing the programmes that are to be qualifying programmes for the purposes of that subsection;

(b) the reference to independent productions is a reference to programmes of such description as the Secretary of State may by order specify as describing the programmes that are to be independent productions for the purposes of that subsection; and

(c) the reference to a range of independent productions is a reference to a range of such productions in terms of cost of acquisition as well as in terms of the types of programme involved.

(3) The Secretary of State may by order amend subsection (1) by substituting a different percentage for the percentage for the time being specified in that subsection.

(4) Before making an order under this section the Secretary of State must consult OFCOM.

(5) No order is to be made containing provision authorised by this section unless a draft of the order has been laid before Parliament and approved by a resolution of each House.

(6) In this section 'programme' does not include an advertisement.

Regulation of electronic programme guides

310   Code of practice for electronic programme guides

(1) It shall be the duty of OFCOM to draw up, and from time to time to review and revise, a code giving guidance as to the practices to be followed in the provision of electronic programme guides.

(2) The practices required by the code must include the giving, in the manner provided for in the code, of such degree of prominence as OFCOM consider appropriate to—

(a) the listing or promotion, or both the listing and promotion, for members of its intended audience, of the programmes included in each public service channel; and

(b) the facilities, in the case of each such channel, for members of its intended audience to select or access the programmes included in it.

(3) The practices required by the code must also include the incorporation of such features in electronic programme guides as OFCOM consider appropriate for securing that persons with disabilities affecting their sight or hearing or both—

(a) are able, so far as practicable, to make use of such guides for all the same purposes as persons without such disabilities; and

(b) are informed about, and are able to make use of, whatever assistance for disabled people is provided in relation to the programmes listed or promoted.

(4) Subject to subsection (5), in subsection (2) the reference to the public service channels is a reference to any of the following—

(a) any service of television programmes provided by the BBC in digital form so as to be available for reception by members of the public;

(b) any Channel 3 service in digital form;

(c) Channel 4 in digital form;

(d) Channel 5 in digital form;

(e) S4C Digital;

(f) the digital public teletext service.

(8) In this section 'electronic programme guide' means a service which consists of—

(a) the listing or promotion, or both the listing and the promotion, of some or all of the programmes included in any one or more programme services the providers of which are or include persons other than the provider of the guide; and

(b) a facility for obtaining access, in whole or in part, to the programme service or services listed or promoted in the guide.

311 Conditions to comply with code under s. 310

(1) The regulatory regime for every service consisting in or including an electronic programme guide includes whatever conditions (if any) OFCOM consider appropriate for securing that the code maintained by them under section 310 is observed in the provision of those services.

(2) In this section 'electronic programme guide' has the same meaning as in section 310.

Competition between licensed providers etc.

316 Conditions relating to competition matters

(1) The regulatory regime for every licensed service includes the conditions (if any) that OFCOM consider appropriate for ensuring fair and effective competition in the provision of licensed services or of connected services.

(2) Those conditions must include the conditions (if any) that OFCOM consider appropriate for securing that the provider of the service does not—

(a) enter into or maintain any arrangements, or

(b) engage in any practice,

which OFCOM consider, or would consider, to be prejudicial to fair and effective competition in the provision of licensed services or of connected services.

(3) A condition imposed under this section may require a licence holder to comply with one or both of the following—

(a) a code for the time being approved by OFCOM for the purposes of the conditions; and

(b) directions given to him by OFCOM for those purposes.

(4) In this section—

'connected services', in relation to licensed services, means the provision of programmes for inclusion in licensed services and any other services provided for purposes connected with, or with the provision of, licensed services; and

'licensed service' means a service licensed by a Broadcasting Act licence.

317 Exercise of Broadcasting Act powers for a competition purpose

(1) This section applies to the following powers of OFCOM (their 'Broadcasting Act powers')—

(a) their powers under this Part of this Act and under the 1990 Act and the 1996 Act to impose or vary the conditions of a Broadcasting Act licence;

(b) every power of theirs to give an approval for the purposes of provision contained in the conditions of such a licence;

(c) every power of theirs to give a direction to a person who is required to comply with it by the conditions of such a licence; and

(d) every power of theirs that is exercisable for the purpose of enforcing an obligation imposed by the conditions of such a licence.

(2) Before exercising any of their Broadcasting Act powers for a competition purpose, OFCOM must consider whether a more appropriate way of proceeding in relation to some or all of the matters in question would be under the Competition Act 1998 (c. 41).

(3) If OFCOM decide that a more appropriate way of proceeding in relation to a matter would be under the Competition Act 1998, they are not, to the extent of that decision, to exercise their Broadcasting Act powers in relation to that matter.

(4) If OFCOM have decided to exercise any of their Broadcasting Act powers for a competition purpose, they must, on or before doing so, give a notification of their decision.

(5) A notification under subsection (4) must—

(a) be given to such persons, or published in such manner, as appears to OFCOM to be appropriate for bringing it to the attention of the persons who, in OFCOM's opinion, are likely to be affected by their decision; and

(b) must describe the rights conferred by subsection (6) on the persons affected by that decision.

(6) A person affected by a decision by OFCOM to exercise any of their Broadcasting Act powers for a competition purpose may appeal to the Competition Appeal Tribunal against so much of that decision as relates to the exercise of that power for that purpose.

(7) Sections 192(3) to (8), 195 and 196 apply in the case of an appeal under subsection (6) as they apply in the case of an appeal under section 192(2).

(8) The jurisdiction of the Competition Appeal Tribunal on an appeal under subsection (6) excludes—

(a) whether OFCOM have complied with subsection (2); and

(b) whether any of OFCOM's Broadcasting Act powers have been exercised in contravention of subsection (3);

and, accordingly, those decisions by OFCOM on those matters fall to be questioned only in proceedings for judicial review.

(9) For the purposes of this section a power is exercised by OFCOM for a competition purpose if the only or main reason for exercising it is to secure that the holder of a Broadcasting Act licence does not—

(a) enter into or maintain arrangements, or

(b) engage in a practice, which OFCOM consider, or would consider, to be prejudicial to fair and effective competition in the provision of licensed services or of connected services.

(10) Nothing in this section applies to—

(a) the exercise by OFCOM of any of their powers under sections 290 to 294 or Schedule 11;

(b) the exercise by them of any power for the purposes of any provision of a condition included in a licence in accordance with any of those sections;

(c) the exercise by them of any power for the purpose of enforcing such a condition.

(11) In subsection (9) 'connected services' and 'licensed service' each has the same meaning as in section 316.

(12) References in this section to the exercise of a power include references to an exercise of a power in pursuance of a duty imposed on OFCOM by or under an enactment.

Programme and fairness standards for television and radio

319   OFCOM's standards code

(1) It shall be the duty of OFCOM to set, and from time to time to review and revise, such standards for the content of programmes to be included in television and radio services as appear to them best calculated to secure the standards objectives.

(2) The standards objectives are—

(a) that persons under the age of eighteen are protected;

(b) that material likely to encourage or to incite the commission of crime or to lead to disorder is not included in television and radio services;

(c) that news included in television and radio services is presented with due impartiality and that the impartiality requirements of section 320 are complied with;

(d) that news included in television and radio services is reported with due accuracy;

(e) that the proper degree of responsibility is exercised with respect to the content of programmes which are religious programmes;

(f) that generally accepted standards are applied to the contents of television and radio services so as to provide adequate protection for members of the public from the inclusion in such services of offensive and harmful material;

(fa) that the product placement requirements referred to in section 321(3A) are met in relation to programmes included in a television programme service (other than advertisements);

(g) that advertising that contravenes the prohibition on political advertising set out in section 321(2) is not included in television or radio services;

(h) that the inclusion of advertising which may be misleading, harmful or offensive in television and radio services is prevented;

(i) that the international obligations of the United Kingdom with respect to advertising included in television and radio services are complied with;

(j) that the unsuitable sponsorship of programmes included in television and radio services is prevented;

(k) that there is no undue discrimination between advertisers who seek to have advertisements included in television and radio services; and

(l) that there is no use of techniques which exploit the possibility of conveying a message to viewers or listeners, or of otherwise influencing their minds, without their being aware, or fully aware, of what has occurred.

(3) The standards set by OFCOM under this section must be contained in one or more codes.

(4) In setting or revising any standards under this section, OFCOM must have regard, in particular and to such extent as appears to them to be relevant to the securing of the standards objectives, to each of the following matters—

(a) the degree of harm or offence likely to be caused by the inclusion of any particular sort of material in programmes generally, or in programmes of a particular description;

(b) the likely size and composition of the potential audience for programmes included in television and radio services generally, or in television and radio services of a particular description;

(c) the likely expectation of the audience as to the nature of a programme's content and the extent to which the nature of a programme's content can be brought to the attention of potential members of the audience;

(d) the likelihood of persons who are unaware of the nature of a programme's content being unintentionally exposed, by their own actions, to that content;

(e) the desirability of securing that the content of services identifies when there is a change affecting the nature of a service that is being watched or listened to and, in particular, a change that is relevant to the application of the standards set under this section; and

(f) the desirability of maintaining the independence of editorial control over programme content.

(5) OFCOM must ensure that the standards from time to time in force under this section include—

(a) minimum standards applicable to all programmes included in television and radio services; and

(b) such other standards applicable to particular descriptions of programmes, or of television and radio services, as appear to them appropriate for securing the standards objectives.

(6) Standards set to secure the standards objective specified in subsection (2)(e) shall, in particular, contain provision designed to secure that religious programmes do not involve—

(a) any improper exploitation of any susceptibilities of the audience for such a programme; or

(b) any abusive treatment of the religious views and beliefs of those belonging to a particular religion or religious denomination.

(7) In setting standards under this section, OFCOM must take account of such of the international obligations of the United Kingdom as the Secretary of State may notify to them for the purposes of this section.

(8) In this section 'news' means news in whatever form it is included in a service.

(9) Subsection (2)(fa) applies only in relation to programmes the production of which begins after 19th December 2009.

320 Special impartiality requirements

(1) The requirements of this section are—

(a) the exclusion, in the case of television and radio services (other than a restricted service within the meaning of section 245), from programmes included in any of those services of all expressions of the views or opinions of the person providing the service on any of the matters mentioned in subsection (2);

 (b) the preservation, in the case of every television programme service, teletext service, national radio service and national digital sound programme service, of due impartiality, on the part of the person providing the service, as respects all of those matters;

 (c) the prevention, in the case of every local radio service, local digital sound programme service or radio licensable content service, of the giving of undue prominence in the programmes included in the service to the views and opinions of particular persons or bodies on any of those matters.

(2) Those matters are—

 (a) matters of political or industrial controversy; and

 (b) matters relating to current public policy.

(3) Subsection (1)(a) does not require—

 (a) the exclusion from television programmes of views or opinions relating to the provision of programme services; or

 (b) the exclusion from radio programmes of views or opinions relating to the provision of programme services.

(4) For the purposes of this section—

 (a) the requirement specified in subsection (1)(b) is one that (subject to any rules under subsection (5)) may be satisfied by being satisfied in relation to a series of programmes taken as a whole;

 (b) the requirement specified in subsection (1)(c) is one that needs to be satisfied only in relation to all the programmes included in the service in question, taken as a whole.

(5) OFCOM's standards code shall contain provision setting out the rules to be observed in connection with the following matters—

 (a) the application of the requirement specified in subsection (1)(b);

 (b) the determination of what, in relation to that requirement, constitutes a series of programmes for the purposes of subsection (4)(a);

 (c) the application of the requirement in subsection (1)(c).

(6) Any provision made for the purposes of subsection (5)(a) must, in particular, take account of the need to ensure the preservation of impartiality in relation to the following matters (taking each matter separately)—

 (a) matters of major political or industrial controversy, and

 (b) major matters relating to current public policy,

as well as of the need to ensure that the requirement specified in subsection (1)(b) is satisfied generally in relation to a series of programmes taken as a whole.

(7) In this section 'national radio service' and 'local radio service' mean, respectively, a sound broadcasting service which is a national service within the meaning of section 245 and a sound broadcasting service which is a local service within the meaning of that section.

321 Objectives for advertisements and sponsorship

(1) Standards set by OFCOM to secure the objectives mentioned in section 319(2)(a) and (fa) to (j)—

 (a) must include general provision governing standards and practice in advertising and in the sponsoring of programmes and, in relation to television programme services, general provision governing standards and practice in product placement;

 (b) may include provision prohibiting advertisements and forms and methods of advertising or sponsorship (whether generally or in particular circumstances).

 (c) in relation to television programme services, may include provision prohibiting forms and methods of product placement (including product placement of products, services, or trade marks of any description) (whether generally or in particular circumstances).

(2) For the purposes of section 319(2)(g) an advertisement contravenes the prohibition on political advertising if it is—

(a) an advertisement which is inserted by or on behalf of a body whose objects are wholly or mainly of a political nature;

(b) an advertisement which is directed towards a political end; or

(c) an advertisement which has a connection with an industrial dispute.

(3) For the purposes of this section objects of a political nature and political ends include each of the following—

(a) influencing the outcome of elections or referendums, whether in the United Kingdom or elsewhere;

(b) bringing about changes of the law in the whole or a part of the United Kingdom or elsewhere, or otherwise influencing the legislative process in any country or territory;

(c) influencing the policies or decisions of local, regional or national governments, whether in the United Kingdom or elsewhere;

(d) influencing the policies or decisions of persons on whom public functions are conferred by or under the law of the United Kingdom or of a country or territory outside the United Kingdom;

(e) influencing the policies or decisions of persons on whom functions are conferred by or under international agreements;

(f) influencing public opinion on a matter which, in the United Kingdom, is a matter of public controversy;

(g) promoting the interests of a party or other group of persons organised, in the United Kingdom or elsewhere, for political ends.

(3A) For the purposes of section 319(2)(fa) the product placement requirements are set out in Schedule 11A.

(4) OFCOM—

(a) shall—

(i) in relation to programme services, have a general responsibility with respect to advertisements and methods of advertising and sponsorship; and

(ii) in relation to television programme services, have a general responsibility with respect to methods of product placement; and

(b) in the discharge of that responsibility may include conditions in any licence which is granted by them for any such service that enable OFCOM to impose requirements with respect to any of those matters that go beyond the provisions of OFCOM's standards code.

(5) OFCOM must, from time to time, consult the Secretary of State about—

(a) the descriptions of advertisements that should not be included in programme services; and

(b) the forms and methods of advertising and sponsorship that should not be employed in, or in connection with, the provision of such services.

(c) the forms and methods of product placement that should not be employed in the provision of a television programme service (including descriptions of products, services or trade marks for which product placement should not be employed).

(6) The Secretary of State may give OFCOM directions as to the matters mentioned in subsection (5); and it shall be the duty of OFCOM to comply with any such direction.

(7) Provision included by virtue of this section in standards set under section 319 is not to apply to, or to be construed as prohibiting the inclusion in a programme service of—

(a) an advertisement of a public service nature inserted by, or on behalf of, a government department; or

(b) a party political or referendum campaign broadcast the inclusion of which is required by a condition imposed under section 333 or by paragraph 18 of Schedule 12 to this Act.

(8) In this section 'programme service' does not include a service provided by the BBC (except in the expression 'television programme service').

322 Supplementary powers relating to advertising

(1) The regulatory regime for each of the following—

(a) every television programme service licensed by a Broadcasting Act licence,

(b) the public teletext service, and

(c) every other teletext service so licensed that consists in an additional television service or a digital additional television service,

includes a condition requiring the person providing the service to comply with every direction given to him by OFCOM with respect to any of the matters mentioned in subsection (2).

(2) Those matters are—

(a) the maximum amount of time to be given to advertisements in any hour or other period;

(b) the minimum interval which must elapse between any two periods given over to advertisements;

(c) the number of such periods to be allowed in any programme or in any hour or day; and

(d) the exclusion of advertisements from a specified part of a licensed service.

(3) Directions under this section—

(a) may be either general or specific;

(b) may be qualified or unqualified; and

(c) may make different provision for different parts of the day, different days of the week, different types of programmes or for other differing circumstances.

(4) In giving a direction under this section, OFCOM must take account of such of the international obligations of the United Kingdom as the Secretary of State may notify to them for the purposes of this section.

323 Modification of matters to be taken into account under s. 319

(1) The Secretary of State may by order modify the list of matters in section 319(4) to which OFCOM are to have regard when setting or revising standards.

(2) Before making an order under this section, the Secretary of State must consult OFCOM.

(3) No order is to be made containing provision authorised by subsection (1) unless a draft of the order has been laid before Parliament and approved by a resolution of each House.

324 Setting and publication of standards

(1) Before setting standards under section 319, OFCOM must publish, in such manner as they think fit, a draft of the proposed code containing those standards.

(2) After publishing the draft code and before setting the standards, OFCOM must consult every person who holds a relevant licence and such of the following as they think fit—

(a) persons appearing to OFCOM to represent the interests of those who watch television programmes;

(b) persons appearing to OFCOM to represent the interests of those who make use of teletext services; and

(c) persons appearing to OFCOM to represent the interests of those who listen to sound programmes.

(3) After publishing the draft code and before setting the standards, OFCOM must also consult—

(a) the Welsh Authority, about so much of the draft code as relates to television programme services;

(b) the BBC, about so much of the draft code as contains standards other than those for advertising or sponsorship or for product placement; and

(c) such of the persons mentioned in subsection (4) as OFCOM think fit, about so much of the draft code as contains standards for advertising or sponsorship.

(4) Those persons are—

(a) persons appearing to OFCOM to represent the interests of those who will have to take account of the contents of the proposed standards for advertising or sponsorship;

(b) bodies and associations appearing to OFCOM to be concerned with the application of standards of conduct in advertising; and

    (c) professional organisations appearing to OFCOM to be qualified to give relevant advice in relation to the advertising of particular products.

(5) If it appears to OFCOM that a body exists which represents the interests of a number of the persons who hold relevant licences, they may perform their duty under subsection (2) of consulting such persons, so far as it relates to the persons whose interests are so represented, by consulting that body.

(6) OFCOM may set standards under section 319 either—

    (a) in the terms proposed in a draft code published under subsection (1); or

    (b) with such modifications as OFCOM consider appropriate in the light of the consultation carried out as a result of subsections (2) to (5).

(7) Subsections (1) to (6) apply to a proposal by OFCOM to revise standards set under section 319 as they apply to a proposal to set such standards.

(8) Where OFCOM set standards under section 319, they must publish the code containing the standards in such manner as they consider appropriate for bringing it to the attention of the persons who, in their opinion, are likely to be affected by the standards.

(9) Where OFCOM revise standards set under section 319, they shall so publish the code containing the standards as revised.

(10) Where OFCOM publish a code under subsection (8) or (9), they shall send a copy of it—

    (a) to the Secretary of State;

    (b) except in the case of a code containing standards for advertising or sponsorship, to the BBC; and

    (c) if the code relates to television programme services, to the Welsh Authority.

(11) A code (or draft code) contains standards for advertising or sponsorship for the purposes of this section to the extent that it sets standards under section 319 for securing any of the objectives mentioned in any of paragraphs (g) to (k) of subsection (2) of that section.

(11A) A code (or draft code) contains standards for product placement for the purposes of this section to the extent that it sets standards under section 319 for securing the objective mentioned in paragraph (fa) of subsection (2) of that section.

(12) In this section 'relevant licence', in relation to a draft code, means—

    (a) to the extent that the draft code relates to

        (i)   television programme services,

        (ii) the public teletext service, or

        (iii) an additional television service,

        a licence under Part 1 of the 1990 Act (independent television services), under section 18 of the 1996 Act (digital television programme services) under section 25 of that Act (digital additional television services) or under section 219 of this Act; and

    (b) to the extent that the draft code relates to radio programme services, any licence under Part 3 of the 1990 Act (independent radio services), under section 60 of the 1996 Act (digital sound programme service) or under section 64 of that Act (digital additional services).

325 Observance of standards code

(1) The regulatory regime for every programme service licensed by a Broadcasting Act licence includes conditions for securing—

    (a) that standards set under section 319 are observed in the provision of that service; and

    (b) that procedures for the handling and resolution of complaints about the observance of those standards are established and maintained.

(2) It shall be the duty of OFCOM themselves to establish procedures for the handling and resolution of complaints about the observance of standards set under section 319.

(3) OFCOM may from time to time make a report to the Secretary of State on any issues with respect to OFCOM's standards code which—

    (a) have been identified by them in the course of carrying out their functions; and

    (b) appear to them to raise questions of general broadcasting policy.

(4) The conditions of a licence which is granted by OFCOM for a programme service must, for the purpose of securing compliance—

    (a) with OFCOM's standards code, so far as it relates to advertising, the sponsorship of programmes and product placement, and

    (b) with any such requirements as are mentioned in section 321(4) which relate to advertising, sponsorship and product placement but go beyond that code,

include a condition requiring the licence holder to comply with every direction given to him by OFCOM with respect to any of the matters mentioned in subsection (5).

(5) Those matters are—

    (a) the exclusion from the service of a particular advertisement, or its exclusion in particular circumstances;

    (b) the descriptions of advertisements and methods of advertising to be excluded from the service (whether generally or in particular circumstances); and

    (c) the forms and methods of sponsorship to be excluded from the service (whether generally or in particular circumstances); and

    (d) in the case of a television programme service, the forms and methods of product placement to be excluded from the service (including descriptions of products, services or trade marks product placement of which is to be excluded) (whether generally or in particular circumstances).

(6) OFCOM's powers and duties under this section are not to be construed as restricting any power of theirs, apart from this section—

    (a) to include conditions with respect to the content of programmes included in any service in the licence to provide that service; or

    (b) to include conditions in a licence requiring the holder of a licence to comply with directions given by OFCOM or by any other person.

326 Duty to observe fairness code

The regulatory regime for every programme service licensed by a Broadcasting Act licence includes the conditions that OFCOM consider appropriate for securing observance—

    (a) in connection with the provision of that service, and

    (b) in relation to the programmes included in that service,

of the code for the time being in force under section 107 of the 1996 Act (the fairness code).

327 Standards with respect to fairness

(1) Part 5 of the 1996 Act (functions of the Broadcasting Standards Commission which are transferred to OFCOM so far as they relate to codes of practice and complaints with respect to fairness and privacy) shall be amended as follows.

(2) No person shall be entitled to make a standards complaint under that Part at any time after the coming into force of this section, and no person shall be required to entertain any such complaint that is so made.

328 Duty to publicise OFCOM's functions in relation to complaints

(1) The regulatory regime for every programme service licensed by a Broadcasting Act licence includes the conditions that OFCOM consider appropriate for securing that—

    (a) the procedures which, by virtue of section 325, are established and maintained for handling and resolving complaints about the observance of standards set under section 319, and

    (b) their functions under Part 5 of the 1996 Act in relation to that service,

are brought to the attention of the public (whether by means of broadcasts or otherwise).

(2) Conditions included in a licence by virtue of subsection (1) may require the holder of the licence to comply with every direction given to him by OFCOM for the purpose mentioned in that subsection.

Power to proscribe unacceptable foreign television and radio services

329 Proscription orders

(1) Where—

    (a) a foreign service to which this section applies comes to OFCOM's attention, and

    (b) they consider that the service is unacceptable and should be the subject of an order under this section,

they must send a notification to the Secretary of State giving details of the service and their reasons for considering that an order should be made.

(2) A service is not to be considered unacceptable by OFCOM unless they are satisfied that—

    (a) programmes containing objectionable matter are included in the service; and

    (b) that the inclusion of objectionable matter in programmes so included is occurring repeatedly.

(3) Matter is objectionable for the purposes of subsection (2) only if—

    (a) it offends against taste or decency;

    (b) it is likely to encourage or to incite the commission of crime;

    (c) it is likely to lead to disorder; or

    (d) it is likely to be offensive to public feeling.

(4) Where the Secretary of State has received a notification under this section in the case of a service, he may make an order—

    (a) identifying the service in such manner as he thinks fit; and

    (b) proscribing it.

(5) The Secretary of State is not to make an order proscribing a service unless he is satisfied that the making of the order is—

    (a) in the public interest; and

    (b) compatible with the international obligations of the United Kingdom.

(6) The television and sound services to which this section applies are—

    (a) television licensable content services provided otherwise than by broadcasting from a satellite;

    (b) digital television programme services;

    (c) digital additional television services;

    (d) radio licensable sound services provided otherwise than by being broadcast from a satellite;

    (e) digital sound programme services; and

    (f) digital additional sound services.

(7) A service to which this section applies is a foreign service if it—

    (a) is a service capable of being received in the United Kingdom for the provision of which no Broadcasting Act licence is either in force or required to be in force; but

    (b) is also a service for the provision of which such a licence would be required—

        (i)   in the case of a service falling within subsection (6)(a) to (c), if the person providing it were under the jurisdiction of the United Kingdom for the purposes of the Audiovisual Services Media Directive; and

        (ii) in any other case, if the person providing it provided it from a place in the United Kingdom or were a person whose principal place of business is in the United Kingdom.

330 Effect of proscription order

(1) This section applies where a service is for the time being proscribed by an order under section 329.

(2) The proscribed service is not to be included in—

    (a) a multiplex service; or

    (b) a cable package.

(3) In this section 'multiplex service' means a television multiplex service, a radio multiplex service or a general multiplex service.

(4) In this section 'cable package' means (subject to subsection (5)) a service by means of which programme services are packaged together with a view to their being distributed—

    (a) by means of an electronic communications service;

    (b) so as to be available for reception by members of the public in the United Kingdom; and

    (c) without the final delivery of the programme services to the persons to whom they are distributed being by wireless telegraphy.

(5) Programme services distributed by means of an electronic communications service do not form part of a cable package if—

    (a) the distribution of those services forms only part of a service provided by means of that electronic communications service; and

    (b) the purposes for which the service of which it forms a part is provided do not consist wholly or mainly in making available television programmes or radio programmes (or both) for reception by members of the public.

331 Notification for enforcing proscription

(1) Where OFCOM determine that there are reasonable grounds for believing that there has been a contravention of section 330 in relation to a multiplex service or a cable package, they may give a notification under this section to—

    (a) the provider of that multiplex service; or

    (b) the person providing the cable package.

(2) A notification under this section is one which—

    (a) sets out the determination made by OFCOM; and

    (b) requires the person to whom it is given to secure that the proscribed service (so long as it remains proscribed) is not—

        (i)   included in the notified person's multiplex service, or

        (ii)   distributed as part of his cable package,

at any time more than seven days after the day of the giving of the notification.

(3) If it is reasonably practicable for a person to whom a notification is given under this section to secure that the proscribed service ceases to be included in that person's multiplex service, or to be distributed as part of his cable package, before the end of that seven days, then he must do so.

(4) It shall be the duty of a person to whom a notification is given under this section to comply with the requirements imposed by the notification and by subsection (3).

(5) That duty shall be enforceable in civil proceedings by OFCOM—

    (a) for an injunction;

    (b) for specific performance of a statutory duty under section 45 of the Court of Session Act 1988 (c. 36); or

    (c) for any other appropriate remedy or relief.

(6) In this section 'cable package' and 'multiplex service' each has the same meaning as in section 330.

332 Penalties for contravention of notification under s. 331

(1) OFCOM may impose a penalty on a person who contravenes a requirement imposed on him by or under section 331.

(2) Before imposing a penalty on a person under this section OFCOM must give him a reasonable opportunity of making representations to them about their proposal to impose the penalty.

(3) The amount of the penalty imposed on a person is to be such amount not exceeding £5,000 as OFCOM determine to be—

    (a) appropriate; and

    (b) proportionate to the contravention in respect of which it is imposed.

(4) In making that determination OFCOM must have regard to—

(a) any representations made to them by the person notified under section 331; and

(b) any steps taken by him for complying with the requirements imposed on him under that section.

(5) Where OFCOM impose a penalty on a person under this section, they shall—

(a) notify the person penalised; and

(b) in that notification, fix a reasonable period after it is given as the period within which the penalty is to be paid.

(6) A penalty imposed under this section must be paid to OFCOM within the period fixed by them.

(7) The Secretary of State may by order amend this section so as to substitute a different maximum penalty for the maximum penalty for the time being specified in subsection (3).

(8) No order is to be made containing provision authorised by subsection (7) unless a draft of the order has been laid before Parliament and approved by a resolution of each House.

(9) For the purposes of this section there is a separate contravention in respect of every day on which the proscribed service is at any time included in a person's multiplex service or distributed as part of his cable package.

(10) In this section 'multiplex service' and 'cable package' each has the same meaning as in section 330.

Party political broadcasts on television and radio

333   Party political broadcasts

(1) The regulatory regime for every licensed public service channel, and the regulatory regime for every national radio service, includes—

(a) conditions requiring the inclusion in that channel or service of party political broadcasts and of referendum campaign broadcasts; and

(b) conditions requiring that licence holder to observe such rules with respect to party political broadcasts and referendum campaign broadcasts as may be made by OFCOM.

(2) The rules made by OFCOM for the purposes of this section may, in particular, include provision for determining—

(a) the political parties on whose behalf party political broadcasts may be made;

(b) in relation to each political party on whose behalf such broadcasts may be made, the length and frequency of the broadcasts; and

(c) in relation to each designated organisation on whose behalf referendum campaign broadcasts are required to be broadcast, the length and frequency of such broadcasts.

(3) Those rules are to have effect subject to sections 37 and 127 of the Political Parties, Elections and Referendums Act 2000 (c. 41) (only registered parties and designated organisations to be entitled to party political broadcasts or referendum campaign broadcasts).

(4) Rules made by OFCOM for the purposes of this section may make different provision for different cases.

(5) Before making any rules for the purposes of this section, OFCOM must have regard to any views expressed by the Electoral Commission.

(6) In this section—

'designated organisation', in relation to a referendum, means a person or body designated by the Electoral Commission under section 108 of the Political Parties, Elections and Referendums Act 2000 (c. 41) in respect of that referendum;

'national radio service' means a national service within the meaning of section 245 of this Act; and

'referendum campaign broadcast' has the meaning given by section 127 of that Act.

Monitoring of programmes

334   Retention and production of recordings

(1) The regulatory regime for every programme service licensed by a Broadcasting Act licence includes conditions imposing on the provider of the service—

    (a) a requirement in respect of every programme included in the service to retain a recording of the programme in a specified form and for a specified period after its inclusion;

    (b) a requirement to comply with any request by OFCOM to produce to them for examination or reproduction a recording retained in pursuance of the conditions in the licence; and

    (c) a requirement, if the provider is able to do so, to comply with any request by OFCOM to produce to them a script or transcript of a programme included in the programme service.

(2) The period specified for the purposes of a condition under subsection (1)(a) must be—

    (a) in the case of a programme included in a television programme service, a period not exceeding ninety days; and

    (b) in the case of a programme included in a radio programme service, a period not exceeding forty-two days.

(3) For the purpose of maintaining supervision of the programmes included in programme services, OFCOM may themselves make and use recordings of those programmes or any part of them.

(4) Nothing in this Part is to be construed as requiring OFCOM, in the carrying out of their functions under this Part as respects programme services and the programmes included in them, to view or listen to programmes in advance of their being included in such services.

International obligations

335 Conditions securing compliance with international obligations

(1) The regulatory regime for every service to which this section applies includes the conditions that OFCOM consider appropriate for securing that the relevant international obligations of the United Kingdom are complied with.

(2) In this section 'relevant international obligations of the United Kingdom' means the international obligations of the United Kingdom which have been notified to OFCOM by the Secretary of State for the purposes of this section.

(3) This section applies to the following services—

    (a) any Channel 3 service;

    (b) Channel 4;

    (c) Channel 5;

    (d) the public teletext service;

    (e) any television licensable content service;

    (f) any digital television programme service;

    (g) any additional television service;

    (h) any digital additional television service;

    (i) any restricted television service.

(4) The conditions included in any licence in accordance with the other provisions of this Chapter are in addition to any conditions included in that licence in pursuance of this section and have effect subject to them.

335A Co-operation with other Member States

(1) Where OFCOM—

    (a) receive under Article 4 of the Audiovisual Media Services Directive a request from another member State relating to a relevant broadcaster, and

    (b) consider that the request is substantiated, they must ask the broadcaster to comply with the rule identified in that request.

(2) In this section 'relevant broadcaster' means —

    (a) the BBC;

    (b) C4C;

    (c) the Welsh Authority; or

    (d) the holder of—

        (i) a Channel 3 licence;

        (ii) a Channel 5 licence; or

        (iii) a licence to provide any relevant regulated television service within the meaning of section 13(1) of the Broadcasting Act 1990.

Government requirements for licensed services

336   Government requirements for licensed services

(1) If it appears to the Secretary of State or any other Minister of the Crown to be appropriate to do so in connection with any of his functions, the Secretary of State or that Minister may at any time by notice require OFCOM to give a direction under subsection (2).

(2) A direction under this subsection is a direction to the holders of the Broadcasting Act licences specified in the notice under subsection (1) to include an announcement so specified in their licensed services.

(3) The direction may specify the times at which the announcement is to be broadcast or otherwise transmitted.

(4) Where the holder of a Broadcasting Act licence includes an announcement in his licensed service in pursuance of a direction under this section, he may announce that he is doing so in pursuance of such a direction.

(5) The Secretary of State may, at any time, by notice require OFCOM to direct the holders of the Broadcasting Act licences specified in the notice to refrain from including in their licensed services any matter, or description of matter, specified in the notice.

(6) Where—

    (a) OFCOM have given the holder of a Broadcasting Act licence a direction in accordance with a notice under subsection (5),

    (b) in consequence of the revocation by the Secretary of State of such a notice, OFCOM have revoked such a direction, or

    (c) such a notice has expired,

the holder of the licence in question may include in the licensed service an announcement of the giving or revocation of the direction or of the expiration of the notice, as the case may be.

(7) OFCOM must comply with every requirement contained in a notice under this section.

(8) The powers conferred by this section are in addition to any powers specifically conferred on the Secretary of State by or under this Act or any other enactment.

(9) In this section 'Minister of the Crown' includes the Treasury.

Enforcement against the Welsh Authority

339   Review of fulfilment by Welsh Authority of public service remits

(1) The Secretary of State may carry out a review of the performance by the Welsh Authority of their duty to secure that each of the following public service remits—

    (a) that for S4C;

    (b) that for S4C Digital; and

    (c) that for each of the television programme services provided by them with the approval of the Secretary of State under section 205,

is fulfilled in relation the services to which it applies.

(2) The first review carried out under this section—

    (a) shall be a review relating to the period since the passing of this Act; and

    (b) must not be carried out before the end of the period of five years beginning with the day of the passing of this Act.

(3) A subsequent review—

    (a) shall be a review relating to the period since the end of the period to which the previous review related; and

    (b) must not be carried out less than five years after the day of the publication of the report of the previous review.

(4) On a review under this section the Secretary of State—

    (a) shall consult the National Assembly for Wales and the Welsh Authority on the matters under review; and

    (b) shall have regard to their opinions when reaching his conclusions.

(5) The Secretary of State shall also consult such other persons as he considers are likely to be affected by whether, and in what manner, the Welsh Authority perform the duty mentioned in subsection (1).

(6) As soon as practicable after the conclusion of a review under this section the Secretary of State must publish a report of his conclusions.

340 Directions to Welsh Authority to take remedial action

(1) This section applies if the Secretary of State's conclusions on a review under section 339 include a finding—

  (a) that the Welsh Authority has failed in any respect to perform their duty to secure that the public service remit for a service mentioned in that section is fulfilled; and

  (b) that there is no reasonable excuse for the failure.

(2) The Secretary of State may give the Welsh Authority general or specific directions requiring them to take the steps that he considers will ensure that the Authority perform their duty properly in future.

(3) The Secretary of State is not to give a direction under this section unless a draft of the proposed direction has been laid before Parliament and approved by a resolution of each House.

(4) Before laying a proposed direction before Parliament, the Secretary of State must consult the Welsh Authority.

(5) It shall be the duty of the Welsh Authority to comply with every direction under this section.

341 Imposition of penalties on the Welsh Authority

(1) This section applies to the following requirements so far as they are imposed on the Welsh Authority in relation to services provided by them—

  (a) the requirements imposed by or under paragraphs 7 and 8 of Schedule 12 (programme quotas);

  (b) the requirements imposed by paragraph 9(1) and (3) of that Schedule (news and current affairs);

  (c) the requirements imposed by paragraph 10 of that Schedule (code relating to programme commissioning) or by a direction under sub-paragraph (3)(d) of that paragraph;

  (d) the requirement imposed by virtue of paragraph 12 of that Schedule to comply with standards set under section 319, so far as that requirement relates to standards set otherwise than for the purpose of securing the objectives set out in subsection (2)(c) or (d) of that section;

  (e) the requirements imposed by paragraphs 14 and 16 of that Schedule (advertising or sponsorship) to comply with a direction under those paragraphs;

  (f) the requirement imposed by paragraph 17 of that Schedule (observance of the fairness code);

  (g) the requirement imposed by paragraph 19 of that Schedule (publicising complaints procedure);

  (h) the requirement imposed by paragraph 20 of that Schedule (monitoring of programmes);

  (i) the requirement imposed by paragraph 21 of that Schedule (international obligations) to comply with a direction under that paragraph;

  (j) the requirement under paragraph 22 of that Schedule (assistance for disabled people) to comply with the code for the time being in force under section 303;

  (ja) the requirement imposed by paragraph 23A of that Schedule (complaints procedures for on-demand programme services) to comply with a direction under that paragraph;

  (jb) the requirements imposed by section 368D and section 368Q(3) (on-demand programme services), except the requirement imposed by section 368D(1) so far as it relates to advertising[and the requirement imposed by section 368D(3)(za);

  (k) the requirement to comply with a direction under section 119(1) of the 1996 Act (directions in respect of fairness matters).

(2) If OFCOM are satisfied that there has been a contravention of a requirement to which this section applies, they may serve on the Welsh Authority a notice requiring the Authority, within the specified period, to pay OFCOM a specified penalty.

(3) The amount of the penalty must not exceed £250,000.

(4) OFCOM are not to serve a notice on the Welsh Authority under this section unless they have given them a reasonable opportunity of making representations to OFCOM about the matters appearing to OFCOM to provide grounds for the service of the notice.

(5) An exercise by OFCOM of their powers under this section does not preclude any exercise by them of their powers under paragraph 15 of Schedule 12 in respect of the same contravention.

(6) The Secretary of State may by order substitute a different sum for the sum for the time being specified in subsection (3).

(7) No order is to be made containing provision authorised by subsection (6) unless a draft of the order has been laid before Parliament and approved by a resolution of each House.

343 Provision of information by Welsh Authority

(1) It shall be the duty of the Welsh Authority to comply with every direction given to them by OFCOM to provide OFCOM with information falling within subsection (2).

(2) The information that the Welsh Authority may be directed to provide is any information which OFCOM may reasonably require for the purposes of carrying out their functions in relation to the Welsh Authority under this Act, the 1990 Act or the 1996 Act.

(3) Information that is required to be provided by a direction under this section must be provided in such manner and at such times as may be required by the direction.

Enforcement of licence conditions

344 Transmission of statement of findings

(1) Sections 40 and 109 of the 1990 Act (power to direct licensee to broadcast correction or apology) shall be amended as follows.

(2) For 'apology', wherever occurring, there shall be substituted 'a statement of findings'.

(3) After subsection (5), there shall be inserted—

'(6) For the purposes of this section a statement of findings, in relation to a case in which OFCOM are satisfied that the holder of a licence has contravened the conditions of his licence, is a statement of OFCOM's findings in relation to that contravention.'

345 Financial penalties imposable on licence holders

Schedule 13 (which modifies the maximum penalties that may be imposed on the holders of Broadcasting Act licences) shall have effect.

Chapter 6 Other Provisions about Television and Radio Services

362 Interpretation of Part 3

(1) In this Part—

'additional radio service' means an additional service within the meaning given by section 114(1) of the 1990 Act for the purposes of Part 3 of that Act;

'additional television service' (except in the expression 'digital additional television service') means an additional service within the meaning given by section 48 of the 1990 Act for the purposes of Part 1 of the 1990 Act;

'analogue teletext service' is to be construed in accordance with section 218(4);

'ancillary service' has the same meaning as it has, by virtue of section 24(2) of the 1996 Act, in Part 1 of that Act;

'assistance for disabled people' means any of the following—

(a) subtitling;

(b) audio-description for the blind and partially sighted; and

(c) presentation in, or translation into, sign language;

'available for reception by members of the public' is to be construed in accordance with section 361;

'the BBC Charter and Agreement' means the following documents, or any one or more of them, so far as they are for the time being in force—

(a) a Royal Charter for the continuance of the BBC;

(b) supplemental Charters obtained by the BBC under such a Royal Charter;

(c) an agreement between the BBC and the Secretary of State entered into (whether before or after the passing of this Act) for purposes that include the regulation of activities carried on by the BBC;

'BBC company' means—

(a) a body corporate which is controlled by the BBC; or

(b) a body corporate in which the BBC or a body corporate controlled by the BBC is (to any extent) a participant;

'C4 company' means—

(a) a body corporate which is controlled by C4C; or

(b) a body corporate in which C4C or a body corporate controlled by C4C is (to any extent) a participant;

'Channel 3', 'Channel 4' and 'Channel 5' each has the same meaning as in Part 1 of the 1990 Act (see section 71 of that Act);

'Channel 3 licence' means a licence to provide a Channel 3 service;

'a Channel 3 service' means a television broadcasting service comprised in Channel 3;

'digital additional sound service' means a digital additional service within the meaning given by section 63 of the 1996 Act for the purposes of Part 2 of that Act;

'digital additional television service' means a digital additional service within the meaning given by section 24(1) of the 1996 Act for the purposes of Part 1 of that Act;

'the digital public teletext service' means so much of the public teletext service as consists of a service provided in digital form;

'digital sound programme licence' and 'digital sound programme service' each has the same meaning as in Part 2 of the 1996 Act (see sections 40 and 72 of that Act);

'digital television programme service' means a digital programme service within the meaning given by section 1(4) of the 1996 Act for the purposes of Part 1 of that Act;

'EEA State' means the United Kingdom or any other State that is a contracting party to the Agreement on the European Economic Area signed at Oporto on 22nd May 1992, as adjusted by the Protocol signed at Brussels on 17th March 1993, and 'another EEA State' means an EEA State other than the United Kingdom;

'general multiplex service' means a multiplex service within the meaning of section 175 which is neither a television multiplex service nor a radio multiplex service;

'initial expiry date' has the meaning given by section 224;

'licensed public service channel' means any of the following services (whether provided for broadcasting in digital or in analogue form) —

(a) any Channel 3 service;

(b) Channel 4;

(c) Channel 5;

'local digital sound programme licence' and 'local digital sound programme service' each has the same meaning as in Part 2 of the 1996 Act (see sections 60 and 72 of that Act);

'local radio multiplex licence' and 'local radio multiplex service' each has the same meaning as in Part 2 of the 1996 Act (see sections 40 and 72 of that Act);

'local sound broadcasting licence' means a licence under Part 3 of the 1990 Act to provide a local sound broadcasting service;

'local sound broadcasting service' means a sound broadcasting service which, under subsection (4)(b) of section 245, is a local service for the purposes of that section;

'the M25 area' means the area the outer boundary of which is represented by the London Orbital Motorway (M25);

'national Channel 3 service' means a Channel 3 service provided between particular times of the day for more than one area for which regional Channel 3 services are provided;

'national digital sound programme service' has the same meaning as in Part 2 of the 1996 Act;

'national radio multiplex licence' and 'national radio multiplex service' each has the same meaning as in Part 2 of the 1996 Act (see sections 40 and 72 of that Act);

'networking arrangements' has the meaning given by section 290;

'OFCOM's standards code' means any code or codes for the time being in force containing standards set by OFCOM under section 319 (whether originally or by way of any revision of any standards previously so set);

'product placement' has the meaning given by paragraph 1 of Schedule 11A;

'provision', in relation to a service, is to be construed (subject to subsection (3)) in accordance with subsection (2), and cognate expressions are to be construed accordingly;

'the public teletext provider' means—

(a) subject to paragraph (b), the person holding the licence under section 219 to provide the public teletext service; and

(b) in relation to a time before the grant of the first licence to be granted under that section, the person holding the Broadcasting Act licence to provide the existing service (within the meaning of section 221);

'the public teletext service' means the service the provision of which is or may be required to be secured in accordance with section 218;

'qualifying service' has the same meaning as in Part 1 of the 1996 Act (see section 2(2) of that Act);

'radio licensable content service' has the meaning given by section 247;

'radio multiplex service' has the same meaning as (by virtue of section 258 of this Act) it has in Part 2 of the 1996 Act;

'radio programme service' means any of the following—

(a) a service the provision of which is licensed under Part 3 of the 1990 Act;

(b) a digital sound programme service the provision of which is licensed under Part 2 of the 1996 Act;

(c) a digital additional sound service the provision of which is licensed under section 64 of the 1996 Act;

'regional Channel 3 licence' means a licence under Part 1 of the 1990 Act to provide a regional Channel 3 service;

'regional Channel 3 service' means a Channel 3 service provided for a particular area determined under section 14(2) of the 1990 Act;

'restricted television service' means any restricted service within the meaning given by section 42A of the 1990 Act for the purposes of Part 1 of that Act;

'S4C' and 'S4C Digital' means the services so described in section 204(3);

'S4C company' means—

(a) a body corporate which is controlled by the Welsh Authority; or

(b) a body corporate in which that Authority or a body corporate controlled by that Authority is (to any extent) a participant;

'simulcast radio service' means any simulcast radio service within the meaning given by section 41(2) of the 1996 Act for the purposes of Part 2 of that Act;

'sound broadcasting service' has the same meaning as in Part 3 of the 1990 Act (see section 126 of that Act);

'standards objectives' has the meaning given by section 319(2);

'subtitling' means subtitling for the deaf or hard of hearing, whether provided by means of a teletext service or otherwise;

'television broadcasting service' means (subject to subsection (4)) a service which—

    (a) consists in a service of television programmes provided with a view to its being broadcast (whether in digital or in analogue form);

    (b) is provided so as to be available for reception by members of the public; and

    (c) is not—

        (i) a restricted television service;

        (ii) a television multiplex service;

        (iii) a service provided under the authority of a licence under Part 1 of the 1990 Act to provide a television licensable content service; or

        (iv) a service provided under the authority of a licence under Part 1 of the 1996 Act to provide a digital television programme service;

'television licensable content service' has the meaning given by section 232 of this Act;

'television multiplex service' has meaning given by section 241(1) of this Act to a multiplex service within the meaning of Part 1 of the 1996 Act;

'television programme service' means any of the following—

    (a) a television broadcasting service;

    (b) a television licensable content service;

    (c) a digital television programme service;

    (d) a restricted television service;

'text service' means any teletext service or other service in the case of which the visual images broadcast or distributed by means of the service consist wholly or mainly of non-representational images.

(2) In the case of any of the following services—

    (a) a television broadcasting service or sound broadcasting service,

    (b) the public teletext service;

    (c) a television licensable content service or radio licensable content service,

    (d) a digital television programme service or digital sound programme service,

    (e) a restricted television service,

    (f) an additional television service or additional radio service,

    (g) a digital additional television service or a digital additional sound service,

the person, and the only person, who is to be treated for the purposes of this Part as providing the service is the person with general control over which programmes and other services and facilities are comprised in the service (whether or not he has control of the content of individual programmes or of the broadcasting or distribution of the service).

(3) For the purposes of this Part—

    (a) the provision of a service by the BBC does not include its provision by a BBC company;

    (b) the provision of a service by C4C does not include its provision by a C4 company;

    (c) the provision of a service by the Welsh Authority does not include its provision by an S4C company;

and, accordingly, control that is or is capable of being exercised by the BBC, C4C or the Welsh Authority over decisions by a BBC company, C4 company or S4C company about what is to be comprised in a service shall be disregarded for the purposes of subsection (2).

(4) References in this Part to a television broadcasting service do not include references to any text service.

(5) References in this Part to imposing a charge on a person in respect of his reception of a service in, or in a part of, the United Kingdom include references to imposing charges—

    (a) for his use of the service at a place in the United Kingdom or in that part of it;

    (b) for an entitlement of his to receive it at such place;

(c) for the use of a facility by means of which he exercises such an entitlement; or

(d) for the service's being made available for reception by him at such a place.

(6) In subsection (1) 'controlled' and 'participant' each has the same meaning as in Schedule 2 to the 1990 Act.

(7) In this section 'non-representational images' means visual images which are neither still pictures nor comprised within sequences of visual images capable of being seen as moving pictures.

PART 4A   ON-DEMAND PROGRAMME SERVICES

Preliminary

368A   Meaning of 'on-demand programme service'

(1) For the purposes of this Act, a service is an 'on-demand programme service' if—

(a) its principal purpose is the provision of programmes the form and content of which are comparable to the form and content of programmes normally included in television programme services;

(b) access to it is on-demand;

(c) there is a person who has editorial responsibility for it;

(d) it is made available by that person for use by members of the public; and

(e) that person is under the jurisdiction of the United Kingdom for the purposes of the Audiovisual Media Services Directive.

(2) Access to a service is on-demand if—

(a) the service enables the user to view, at a time chosen by the user, programmes selected by the user from among the programmes included in the service; and

(b) the programmes viewed by the user are received by the user by means of an electronic communications network (whether before or after the user has selected which programmes to view).

(3) For the purposes of subsection (2)(a), the fact that a programme may be viewed only within a period specified by the provider of the service does not prevent the time at which it is viewed being one chosen by the user.

(4) A person has editorial responsibility for a service if that person has general control—

(a) over what programmes are included in the range of programmes offered to users; and

(b) over the manner in which the programmes are organised in that range;

and the person need not have control of the content of individual programmes or of the broadcasting or distribution of the service (and see section 368R(6)).

(5) If an on-demand programme service ('the main service') offers users access to a relevant ancillary service, the relevant ancillary service is to be treated for the purposes of this Part as a part of the main service.

(6) In subsection (5), 'relevant ancillary service' means a service or facility that consists of or gives access to assistance for disabled people in relation to some or all of the programmes included in the main service.

(7) In this section 'assistance for disabled people' has the same meaning as in Part 3.

368B   The appropriate regulatory authority

(1) OFCOM may designate any body corporate to be, to the extent provided by the designation, the appropriate regulatory authority for the purposes of any provision of this Part, subject to subsection (9).

(2) To the extent that no body is designated for a purpose, OFCOM is the appropriate regulatory authority for that purpose.

(3) Where a body is designated for a purpose, OFCOM may act as the appropriate regulatory authority for that purpose concurrently with or in place of that body.

(4) OFCOM may provide a designated body with assistance in connection with any of the functions of the body under this Part.

(5) A designation may in particular—

   (a) provide for a body to be the appropriate regulatory authority in relation to on-demand programme services of a specified description;

   (b) provide that a function of the appropriate regulatory authority is exercisable by the designated body—

      (i) to such extent as may be specified;

      (ii) either generally or in such circumstances as may be specified; and

      (iii) either unconditionally or subject to such conditions as may be specified.

(6) The conditions that may be specified pursuant to subsection (5)(b)(iii) include a condition to the effect that a function may, generally or in specified circumstances, be exercised by the body only with the agreement of OFCOM.

(7) A designation has effect for such period as may be specified and may be revoked by OFCOM at any time.

(8) OFCOM must publish any designation in such manner as they consider appropriate for bringing it to the attention of persons who, in their opinion, are likely to be affected by it.

(9) OFCOM may not designate a body unless, as respects that designation, they are satisfied that the body—

   (a) is a fit and proper body to be designated;

   (b) has consented to being designated;

   (c) has access to financial resources that are adequate to ensure the effective performance of its functions as the appropriate regulatory authority;

   (d) is sufficiently independent of providers of on-demand programme services; and

   (e) will, in performing any function to which the designation relates, have regard in all cases—

      (i) to the principles under which regulatory activities should be transparent, accountable, proportionate, consistent and targeted only at cases in which action is needed; and

      (ii) to such of the matters mentioned in section 3(4) as appear to the body to be relevant in the circumstances.

(10) Subject to any enactment or rule of law restricting the disclosure or use of information by OFCOM or by a designated body—

   (a) a designated body may supply information to another designated body for use by that other body in connection with any of its functions as the appropriate regulatory authority;

   (b) a designated body may supply information to OFCOM for use by OFCOM in connection with any of their functions under this Part;

   (c) OFCOM may supply information to a designated body for use by that body in connection with any of its functions as the appropriate regulatory authority.

(11) In carrying out their functions as the appropriate regulatory authority, a designated body may carry out, commission or support (financially or otherwise) research.

(12) In this section—

'designation' means a designation under this section and cognate expressions are to be construed accordingly;

'specified' means specified in a designation.

368BA   Advance notification to appropriate regulatory authority

(1) A person must not provide an on-demand programme service unless, before beginning to provide it, that person has given a notification to the appropriate regulatory authority of the person's intention to provide that service.

(2) A person who has given a notification for the purposes of subsection (1) must, before—

   (a) providing the notified service with any significant differences; or

   (b) ceasing to provide it,

give a notification to the appropriate regulatory authority of the differences or (as the case may be) of an intention to cease to provide the service.

(3) A notification for the purposes of this section must—

    (a) be sent to the appropriate regulatory authority in such manner as the authority may require; and

    (b) contain all such information as the authority may require.

368BB　Enforcement of section 368BA

(1) Where the appropriate regulatory authority determine that the provider of an on-demand programme service has contravened section 368BA, they may do one or both of the following—

    (a) give the provider an enforcement notification under this section;

    (b) impose a penalty on the provider in accordance with section 368J.

(2) The appropriate regulatory authority must not make a determination as mentioned in subsection (1) unless there are reasonable grounds for believing that a contravention of section 368BA has occurred and they have allowed the provider an opportunity to make representations about that apparent contravention.

(3) An enforcement notification under this section is a notification which specifies the determination made as mentioned in subsection (1) and imposes a requirement on the provider to take all such steps for remedying the contravention of section 368BA as may be specified in the notification.

(4) An enforcement notification must—

    (a) include reasons for the appropriate regulatory authority's decision to give the enforcement notification, and

    (b) fix a reasonable period for taking the steps required by the notification.

(5) It is the duty of a person to whom an enforcement notification has been given to comply with it.

(6) That duty is enforceable in civil proceedings by the appropriate regulatory authority—

    (a) for an injunction;

    (b) for specific performance of a statutory duty under section 45 of the Court of Session Act 1988; or

    (c) for any other appropriate remedy or relief.

368C　Duties of the appropriate regulatory authority

(1) It is the duty of the appropriate regulatory authority to take such steps as appear to them best calculated to secure that every provider of an on-demand programme service complies with the requirements of section 368D.

(2) The appropriate regulatory authority must encourage providers of on-demand programme services to ensure that their services are progressively made more accessible to people with disabilities affecting their sight or hearing or both.

(3) The appropriate regulatory authority must ensure that providers of on-demand programme services promote, where practicable and by appropriate means, production of and access to European works (within the meaning given in Article 1(n) of the Audiovisual Media Services Directive).

(4) The appropriate regulatory authority must encourage providers of on-demand programme services to develop codes of conduct regarding standards concerning the appropriate promotion of food or beverages by sponsorship of, or in advertising which accompanies or is included in, children's programmes.

368D　Duties of service providers

(1) The provider of an on-demand programme service must ensure that the service complies with the requirements of sections 368E to 368H.

(2) The provider of an on-demand programme service ('P') must supply the following information to users of the service—

    (a) P's name;

    (b) P's address;

    (c) P's electronic address;

(d) the name, address and electronic address of any body which is the appropriate regulatory authority for any purpose in relation to P or the service that P provides.

(3) The provider of an on-demand programme service must—

(za) pay to the appropriate regulatory authority such fee as that authority may require under section 368NA;

(zb) retain a copy of every programme included in the service for at least forty-two days after the day on which the programme ceases to be available for viewing;

(a) comply with any requirement under section 368O (provision of information);

(b) co-operate fully with the appropriate authority for any purpose within section 368O(2) or (3).

(3A) A copy of a programme retained for the purposes of subsection (3)(zb) must be of a standard and in a format which allows the programme to be viewed as it was made available for viewing.

(4) In this section 'electronic address' means an electronic address to which users may send electronic communications, and includes any number or address used for the purposes of receiving such communications.

368E Harmful material

(1) An on-demand programme service must not contain any material likely to incite hatred based on race, sex, religion or nationality.

(2) If an on-demand programme service contains material which might seriously impair the physical, mental or moral development of persons under the age of eighteen, the material must be made available in a manner which secures that such persons will not normally see or hear it.

368F Advertising

(1) Advertising of the following products is prohibited in on-demand programme services—

(a) cigarettes or other tobacco products;

(b) any prescription-only medicine.

(2) Advertising of alcoholic drinks is prohibited in on-demand programme services unless—

(a) it is not aimed at persons under the age of eighteen, and

(b) it does not encourage excessive consumption of such drinks.

(3) Advertising included in an on-demand programme service—

(a) must be readily recognisable as such, and

(b) must not use techniques which exploit the possibility of conveying a message subliminally or surreptitiously.

(4) Advertising included in an on-demand programme service must not—

(a) prejudice respect for human dignity;

(b) include or promote discrimination based on sex, racial or ethnic origin, nationality, religion or belief, disability, age or sexual orientation;

(c) encourage behaviour prejudicial to health or safety;

(d) encourage behaviour grossly prejudicial to the protection of the environment;

(e) cause physical or moral detriment to persons under the age of eighteen;

(f) directly exhort such persons to purchase or rent goods or services in a manner which exploits their inexperience or credulity;

(g) directly encourage such persons to persuade their parents or others to purchase or rent goods or services;

(h) exploit the trust of such persons in parents, teachers or others; or

(i) unreasonably show such persons in dangerous situations.

368G Sponsorship

(1) An on-demand programme service or a programme included in an on-demand programme service must not be sponsored—

(a) for the purpose of promoting cigarettes or other tobacco products, or

(b) by an undertaking whose principal activity is the manufacture or sale of cigarettes or other tobacco products.

(2) An on-demand programme service or a programme included in an on-demand programme service must not be sponsored for the purpose of promoting a prescription-only medicine.

(3) An on-demand programme service may not include a news programme or current affairs programme that is sponsored.

(4) Subsections (5) to (11) apply to an on-demand programme service that is sponsored or that includes any programme that is sponsored.

(5) The sponsoring of a service or programme must not influence the content of that service or programme in a way that affects the editorial independence of the provider of the service.

(6) Where a service or programme is sponsored for the purpose of promoting goods or services, the sponsored service or programme and sponsorship announcements relating to it must not directly encourage the purchase or rental of the goods or services, whether by making promotional reference to them or otherwise.

(7) Where a service or programme is sponsored for the purpose of promoting an alcoholic drink, the service or programme and sponsorship announcements relating to it must not—

(a) be aimed specifically at persons under the age of eighteen; or

(b) encourage the immoderate consumption of such drinks.

(8) A sponsored service must clearly inform users of the existence of a sponsorship agreement.

(9) The name of the sponsor and the logo or other symbol (if any) of the sponsor must be displayed at the beginning or end of a sponsored programme.

(10) Techniques which exploit the possibility of conveying a message subliminally or surreptitiously must not be used in a sponsorship announcement.

(11) A sponsorship announcement must not—

(a) prejudice respect for human dignity;

(b) include or promote discrimination based on sex, racial or ethnic origin, nationality, religion or belief, disability, age or sexual orientation;

(c) encourage behaviour prejudicial to health or safety;

(d) encourage behaviour grossly prejudicial to the protection of the environment;

(e) cause physical or moral detriment to persons under the age of eighteen;

(f) directly encourage such persons to persuade their parents or others to purchase or rent goods or services;

(g) exploit the trust of such persons in parents, teachers or others; or

(h) unreasonably show such persons in dangerous situations.

(12) For the purposes of this Part a programme included in an on-demand programme service is 'sponsored' if a person ('the sponsor') other than—

(a) the provider of that service, or

(b) the producer of that programme,

has met some or all of the costs of the programme for the purpose of promoting the name, trademark, image, activities, services or products of the sponsor or of another person.

(13) But a programme is not sponsored if it falls within this section only by virtue of the inclusion of product placement (see section 368H(1)) or prop placement (see section 368H(2)).

(14) For the purposes of subsection (12) a person meets some or all of the costs of a programme included in a service only if that person makes a payment or provides other resources for the purpose of meeting or saving some or all of the costs of—

(a) producing that programme;

(b) transmitting that programme; or

(c) making that programme available as part of the service.

(15) For the purposes of this Part an on-demand programme service is 'sponsored' if a person ('the sponsor') other than the provider of the service has met some or all of the costs of providing the service for the purpose of promoting the name, trademark, image, activities, services or products of the sponsor or another person.

(16) For the purposes of subsection (15) a person is not to be taken to have met some or all of the costs of providing a service only because a programme included in the service is sponsored by that person.

(17) In this section a 'sponsorship announcement' means —
  (a) anything included for the purpose of complying with subsection (8) or (9), and
  (b) anything included at the same time as or otherwise in conjunction with anything within paragraph (a).

368H   Prohibition of product placement and exceptions

(1) 'Product placement', in relation to a programme included in an on-demand programme service, means the inclusion in the programme of, or of a reference to, a product, service or trade mark, where the inclusion—
  (a) is for a commercial purpose,
  (b) is in return for the making of any payment, or the giving of other valuable consideration, to any relevant provider or any connected person, and
  (c) is not prop placement.

(2) 'Prop placement', in relation to a programme included in an on-demand programme service, means the inclusion in the programme of, or of a reference to, a product, service or trade mark where—
  (a) the provision of the product, service or trade mark has no significant value; and
  (b) no relevant provider, or person connected with a relevant provider, has received any payment or other valuable consideration in relation to its inclusion in, or the reference to it in, the programme, disregarding the costs saved by including the product, service or trademark, or a reference to it, in the programme.

(3) Product placement is prohibited in children's programmes included in on-demand programme services.

(4) Product placement is prohibited in on-demand programme services if—
  (a) it is of cigarettes or other tobacco products,
  (b) it is by or on behalf of an undertaking whose principal activity is the manufacture or sale of cigarettes or other tobacco products, or
  (c) it is of prescription-only medicines.

(5) Product placement of alcoholic drinks must not —
  (a) be aimed specifically at persons under the age of eighteen;
  (b) encourage immoderate consumption of such drinks.

(6) Product placement is otherwise permitted in programmes included in on-demand programme services provided that—
  (a) conditions A to F are met, and
  (b) if subsection (14) applies, condition G is also met.

(7) Condition A is that the programme in which the product, service or trademark, or the reference to it, is included is—
  (a) a film made for cinema;
  (b) a film or series made for a television programme service or for an on-demand programme service;
  (c) a sports programme; or
  (d) a light entertainment programme.

(8) Condition B is that the product placement has not influenced the content of the programme in a way that affects the editorial independence of the provider of the service.

(9) Condition C is that the product placement does not directly encourage the purchase or rental of goods or services, whether by making promotional reference to those goods or services or otherwise.

(10) Condition D is that the programme does not give undue prominence to the products, services or trade marks concerned.

(11) Condition E is that the product placement does not use techniques which exploit the possibility of conveying a message subliminally or surreptitiously.

(12) Condition F is that the way in which the product, service or trade mark, or the reference to it, is included in the programme by way of product placement does not—

    (a) prejudice respect for human dignity;

    (b) promote discrimination based on sex, racial or ethnic origin, nationality, religion or belief, disability, age or sexual orientation;

    (c) encourage behaviour prejudicial to health or safety;

    (d) encourage behaviour grossly prejudicial to the protection of the environment;

    (e) cause physical or moral detriment to persons under the age of eighteen;

    (f) directly encourage such persons to persuade their parents or others to purchase or rent goods or services;

    (g) exploit the trust of such persons in parents, teachers or others; or

    (h) unreasonably show such persons in dangerous situations.

(13) Condition G is that the on-demand programme service in question signals appropriately the fact that product placement is contained in a programme, no less frequently than—

    (a) at the start and end of such a programme, and

    (b) in the case of an on-demand programme service which includes advertising breaks within it, at the recommencement of the programme after each such advertising break.

(14) This subsection applies where the programme featuring the product placement has been produced or commissioned by the provider of the service or any connected person.

(15) This section applies only in relation to programmes the production of which begins after 19th December 2009.

(16) In this section—

'connected' has the same meaning as it has in the Broadcasting Act 1990 by virtue of section 202 of that Act;

'film made for cinema' means a film made with a view to its being shown to the general public first in a cinema;

'producer', in relation to a programme, means the person by whom the arrangements necessary for the making of the programme are undertaken;

'programme' does not include an advertisement;

'relevant provider', in relation to a programme, means —

    (a) the provider of the on-demand programme service in which the programme is included; and

    (b) the producer of the programme;

'residual value' means any monetary or other economic value in the hands of the relevant provider other than the cost saving of including the product, service or trademark, or a reference to it, in a programme;

'significant value' means a residual value that is more than trivial; and

'trade mark', in relation to a business, includes any image (such as a logo) or sound commonly associated with that business or its products or services.

368I Enforcement of section 368D

(1) Where the appropriate regulatory authority determine that a provider of an on-demand programme service is contravening or has contravened section 368D they may do one or both of the following—

    (a) give the provider an enforcement notification under this section;

    (b) impose a financial penalty on the provider in accordance with section 368J.

(2) The appropriate regulatory authority must not make a determination as mentioned in subsection (1) unless there are reasonable grounds for believing that a contravention of section 368D is occurring or has occurred and they have allowed the provider an opportunity to make representations about that apparent contravention.

(3) An enforcement notification under this section is a notification which specifies the determination made as mentioned in subsection (1) and imposes requirements on the provider to take such steps for complying with section 368D and for remedying the consequences of the contravention of that section as may be specified in the notification.

(4) The requirements specified in an enforcement notification may in particular include requirements to do one or more of the following—

    (a) cease providing or restrict access to—
        (i) a specified programme, or
        (ii) programmes of a specified description;
    (b) cease showing or restrict access to–
        (i) a specified advertisement, or
        (ii) advertisements of a specified description;
    (c) provide additional information to users of the service prior to the selection of a specified programme by the user for viewing;
    (d) show an advertisement only with specified modifications;
    (e) publish a correction in the form and place and at the time specified; or
    (f) publish a statement of the findings of the appropriate regulatory authority in the form and place and at the time specified.

(5) An enforcement notification must—

    (a) include reasons for the appropriate regulatory authority's decision to give the enforcement notification, and
    (b) fix a reasonable period for the taking of the steps required by the notification.

(6) Where a provider is required by an enforcement notification to publish a correction or a statement of findings, the provider may publish with the correction or statement of findings a statement that it is published in pursuance of the enforcement notification.

(7) It is the duty of a provider to whom an enforcement notification has been given to comply with it.

(8) That duty is enforceable in civil proceedings by the appropriate regulatory authority—

    (a) for an injunction;
    (b) for specific performance of a statutory duty under section 45 of the Court of Session Act 1988; or
    (c) for any other appropriate remedy or relief.

(9) If a provider to whom an enforcement notification has been given does not comply with it within the period fixed by the appropriate regulatory authority in that enforcement notification the appropriate regulatory authority may impose a financial penalty on that provider in accordance with section 368J.

368J   Financial penalties

(1) The amount of a penalty imposed on a provider under section 368BB or 368I is to be such amount not exceeding 5 per cent. of the provider's applicable qualifying revenue or £250,000 whichever is the greater amount, as the appropriate regulatory authority determine to be—

    (a) appropriate; and
    (b) proportionate to the contravention in respect of which it is imposed.

(2) In determining the amount of a penalty under subsection (1) the appropriate regulatory authority must have regard to any statement published by OFCOM under section 392 (guidelines to be followed in determining amount of penalties).

(3) The 'applicable qualifying revenue', in relation to a provider, means—

    (a) the qualifying revenue for the provider's last complete accounting period falling within the period during which the provider has been providing the service to which the contravention relates; or
    (b) in relation to a person whose first complete accounting period falling within that period has not ended when the penalty is imposed, the amount that the appropriate regulatory authority estimate to be the qualifying revenue for that period.

(4) For the purposes of subsection (3) the 'qualifying revenue' for an accounting period consists of the aggregate of all the amounts received or to be received by the provider of the service to which the contravention relates or by any connected person in the accounting period—

(a) for the inclusion in that service of advertisements, product placement and sponsorship; and

(b) in respect of charges made in that period for the provision of programmes included in that service.

(5) For the purposes of subsection (4), 'connected' has the same meaning as it has in the Broadcasting Act 1990 by virtue of section 202 of that Act.

(6) A financial penalty imposed under this section—

(a) must be paid into the appropriate Consolidated Fund; and

(b) if not paid within the period fixed by the appropriate regulatory authority, is to be recoverable by the appropriate regulatory authority as a debt due to them from the person obliged to pay it.

(7) For the purposes of subsections (3) and (6)—

(a) the amount of a person's qualifying revenue for an accounting period, or

(b) the amount of any payment to be made into the appropriate Consolidated Fund by any person in respect of any such revenue,

is, in the event of a disagreement between the appropriate regulatory authority and that person, the amount determined by the appropriate regulatory authority.

368K   Suspension or restriction of service for contraventions

(1) The appropriate regulatory authority must serve a notice under subsection (2) on a provider of an on-demand programme service if they are satisfied—

(a) that the provider is in contravention of section 368BA or 368D;

(b) that an attempt to secure compliance with section 368BA or 368D (as the case may be) by the imposition of one or more financial penalties or enforcement notifications under section 368BB or 368I has failed; and

(c) that the giving of a direction under this section would be appropriate and proportionate to the seriousness of the contravention.

(2) A notice under this subsection must—

(a) state that the appropriate regulatory authority are satisfied as mentioned in subsection (1);

(b) state the reasons why they are satisfied as mentioned in subsection (1);

(c) state that the appropriate regulatory authority will give a direction under this section unless the provider takes, within a period specified in the notice, such steps to remedy the contravention within subsection (1)(a) as are so specified;

(d) specify any conditions that the appropriate regulatory authority propose to impose in the direction under section 368M(5)(b); and

(e) inform the provider that the provider has the right to make representations to the appropriate regulatory authority about the matters appearing to the authority to provide grounds for giving the proposed direction within the period specified for the purposes of paragraph (c).

(3) If, after considering any representations made to them by the provider within that period, the appropriate regulatory authority are satisfied that the provider has failed to take the steps specified in the notice for remedying the contravention and that it is necessary in the public interest to give a direction under this section, the appropriate regulatory authority must give such of the following as appears to them appropriate and proportionate as mentioned in subsection (1)(c)—

(a) a direction that the entitlement of the provider to provide an on-demand programme service is suspended (either generally or in relation to a particular service);

(b) a direction that that entitlement is restricted in the respects set out in the direction.

368L   Suspension or restriction of service for inciting crime or disorder

(1) The appropriate regulatory authority must serve a notice under subsection (2) on a provider of an on-demand programme service if they are satisfied—

(a) that the service has failed to comply with any requirement of section 368E to 368H and that accordingly the provider has contravened section 368D(1);

(b) that the failure is due to the inclusion in the service of material likely to encourage or to incite the commission of crime, or to lead to disorder; and

(c) that the contravention is such as to justify the giving of a direction under this section.

(2) A notice under this subsection must—

(a) state that the appropriate regulatory authority are satisfied as mentioned in subsection (1);

(b) specify the respects in which, in their opinion, the provider has contravened section 368D;

(c) specify the effect of the notice in accordance with subsection (3);

(d) state that the appropriate regulatory authority may give a direction under this section after the end of the period of twenty-one days beginning with the day on which the notice is served on the provider; and

(e) inform the provider of the provider's right to make representations to the appropriate regulatory authority within that period about the matters appearing to the appropriate regulatory authority to provide grounds for giving a direction under this section.

(3) A notice under subsection (2) has the effect specified under subsection (2)(c), which may be either—

(a) that the entitlement of the provider to provide an on-demand programme service is suspended (either generally or in relation to a particular service), or

(b) that that entitlement is restricted in the respects set out in the notice.

(4) The suspension or restriction has effect as from the time when the notice is served on the provider until either—

(a) a direction given under this section takes effect; or

(b) the appropriate regulatory authority decide not to give such a direction.

(5) If, after considering any representations made to them by the provider within the period mentioned in subsection (2)(d), the appropriate regulatory authority are satisfied that it is necessary in the public interest to give a direction under this section, they must give such of the following as appears to them justified as mentioned in subsection (1)(c)—

(a) a direction that the entitlement of the provider to provide an on-demand programme service is suspended (either generally or in relation to a particular service);

(b) a direction that that entitlement is restricted in the respects set out in the direction.

368M   Supplementary provision about directions

(1) This section applies to a direction given to a provider under section 368K or 368L.

(2) A direction must specify the service to which it relates or specify that it relates to any on-demand programme service provided or to be provided by the provider.

(3) A direction, except so far as it otherwise provides, takes effect for an indefinite period beginning with the time at which it is notified to the provider.

(4) A direction under section 368L must specify a time for it to take effect, and that time must not fall before the end of twenty-eight days beginning with the day on which the direction is notified to the provider.

(5) A direction—

(a) may provide for the effect of a suspension or restriction to be postponed by specifying that it takes effect only at a time determined by or in accordance with the terms of the direction; and

(b) in connection with the suspension or restriction contained in the direction or with the postponement of its effect, may impose such conditions on the provider as appear to the appropriate regulatory authority to be appropriate for the purpose of protecting that provider's customers.

(6) If the appropriate regulatory authority consider it appropriate to do so (whether or not in consequence of representations or proposals made to them), they may revoke a direction or modify its conditions—

    (a) with effect from such time as they may direct;

    (b) subject to compliance with such requirements as they may specify; and

    (c) to such extent and in relation to such services as they may determine.

368N Enforcement of directions under section 368K or 368L

(1) A person ('P') is guilty of an offence if P provides an on-demand programme service—

    (a) while P's entitlement to do so is suspended by a direction under section 368K or 368L, or

    (b) in contravention of a restriction contained in such a direction.

(2) A person guilty of an offence under this section is liable—

    (a) on summary conviction, to a fine not exceeding the statutory maximum;

    (b) on conviction on indictment, to a fine.

368O Power to demand information

(1) The appropriate regulatory authority may require a person who appears to them to be or to have been a provider of an on-demand programme service and to have information that they require for a purpose within subsection (2) to provide them with all such information as they consider necessary for that purpose.

(2) The following are within this subsection—

    (a) the purposes of an investigation which the appropriate regulatory authority are carrying out in order for it to be determined whether a contravention of section 368BA or section 368D has occurred or is occurring, where—

      (i) the investigation relates to a matter about which they have received a complaint, or

      (ii) they otherwise have reason to suspect that there has been a contravention of either of those sections;

    (b) the purpose of ascertaining or calculating applicable qualifying revenue under section 368J.

(3) The appropriate regulatory authority may require a person who appears to them to be or to have been a provider of an on-demand programme service and to have information that they require for the purpose of securing compliance with the obligations of the United Kingdom under the Audiovisual Media Services Directive to provide them with all such information as they consider necessary for that purpose.

(4) The appropriate regulatory authority may not require the provision of information under this section unless they have given the person from whom it is required an opportunity of making representations to them about the matters appearing to them to provide grounds for making the request.

(5) The appropriate regulatory authority must not require the provision of information under this section except by a demand for the information contained in a notice served on the person from whom the information is required that describes the required information and sets out the appropriate regulatory authority's reasons for requiring it.

(6) A person who is required to provide information under this section must provide it in such manner and within such reasonable period as may be specified by the appropriate regulatory authority in the demand for information.

(7) Sections 368I and 368K apply in relation to a failure to comply with a demand for information imposed under this section as if that failure were a contravention of a requirement of section 368D.

(8) In this section 'information' includes copies of programmes.

368P Application of Part 4A in relation to the BBC

(A1) Section 368BA (advance notification) does not apply in relation to an on-demand programme service provided or to be provided by the BBC.

(1) The following provisions do not apply to the BBC—

(a) section 368D(3) (duties of providers of on-demand programme services);

(b) section 368F (advertising);

(c) section 368G (sponsorship);

(d) section 368NA (fees).

(2) In the following provisions references to a provider of an on-demand programme service do not include references to the BBC—

(a) section 368C (duties of appropriate regulatory authority).

. . .

(d) section 368I (enforcement by appropriate regulatory authority);

(e) section 368K (suspension or restriction of service for contravention);

(f) section 368L (suspension or restriction of service for inciting crime or disorder);

(g) section 368O (power to demand information).

368Q   Application of Part 4A in relation to the Welsh Authority

(A1) Section 368BA (advance notification) does not apply in relation to an on-demand programme service provided or to be provided by the Welsh Authority, other than a service that includes advertising.

(1) In section 368C (duties of appropriate regulatory authority) references to a provider of an on-demand programme service do not include references to the Welsh Authority.

(2) It is the duty of the appropriate regulatory authority—

(a) to take such steps as appear to them best calculated to secure that the requirements of sections 368E and 368F are complied with by the Welsh Authority in relation to advertising, and

(b) to encourage the Welsh Authority to develop the codes of conduct referred to in section 368C(4) so far as it relates to advertising.

(3) It is the duty of the Welsh Authority in the provision of any on-demand programme service to promote, where practicable and by appropriate means, production of and access to European works (within the meaning given in Article 1(n) of the Audiovisual Media Services Directive).

(4) Section 368D(3) (zb), (a), and (b) (duties of providers of on-demand programme services) do not apply to the Welsh Authority except in relation to advertising or in relation to the inclusion of advertising in on-demand programme services provided by the Welsh Authority.

(5) Section 368I (enforcement by appropriate regulatory authority), section 368K (suspension or restriction of service for contraventions) and section 368L (suspension or restriction of service for inciting crime or disorder) do not apply in relation to the contravention of section 368D by the Welsh Authority except in the case of a contravention of section 368E or 368F that relates to advertising or in the case of a contravention of section 368D(3)(za) .

(6) Section 368O does not apply in relation to information held by the Welsh Authority except where that information is required by the appropriate regulatory authority for the purposes of—

(a) an investigation which the appropriate regulatory authority are carrying out (whether or not following receipt by them of a complaint) into a matter relating to compliance by the Welsh Authority with section 368E or 368F in relation to advertising; or

(b) securing compliance with the international obligations of the United Kingdom under the Audio-visual Media Services Directive in relation to advertising.

(7) Part 2 of Schedule 12 includes provision imposing obligations on the Welsh Authority in relation to on-demand programme services.

368R   Interpretation of Part 4A

(1) In this Part—

'appropriate regulatory authority' is to be construed in accordance with 368B;

'children's programme' means a programme made—

(a) for a television programme service or for an on-demand programme service; and

(b) for viewing primarily by persons under the age of sixteen;

'prescription-only medicine' means a prescription only medicine within the meaning of regulation 5(3) of the Human Medicines Regulations 2012;

'product placement' has the meaning given by section 368H(1);

'sponsorship' is to be construed in accordance with section 368G;

'tobacco product' has the meaning given in section 1 of the Tobacco Advertising and Promotion Act 2002.

(2) For the purposes of this Part, a programme is included in an on-demand programme service if it is included in the range of programmes the service offers to users.

(3) For the purposes of this Part, advertising is included in an on-demand programme service if it can be viewed by a user of the service as a result of the user selecting a programme to view.

(4) The services that are to be taken for the purposes of this Part to be available for use by members of the public include any service which—

(a) is made available for use only to persons who subscribe to the service (whether for a period or in relation to a particular occasion) or who otherwise request its provision; but

(b) is a service the facility of subscribing to which, or of otherwise requesting its provision, is offered or made available to members of the public.

(5) The person, and the only person, who is to be treated for the purposes of this Part as providing an on-demand programme service is the person who has editorial responsibility for the service (see section 368A(4)).

(6) For the purposes of this Part—

(a) the provision of a service by the BBC does not include its provision by a BBC company;

(b) the provision of a service by the Welsh Authority does not include its provision by an S4C company;

and, accordingly, control that is or is capable of being exercised by the BBC or the Welsh Authority over decisions by a BBC company or an S4C company about what is to be comprised in a service is to be disregarded for the purposes of determining who has editorial responsibility for the service.

PART 6 MISCELLANEOUS AND SUPPLEMENTAL

Annual report

Review of media ownership

391 Review of media ownership

(1) It shall be the duty of OFCOM—

(a) to carry out regular reviews of the operation, taken together, of all the provisions to which this section applies; and

(b) to send a report on every such review to the Secretary of State.

(2) This section applies to—

(a) the provisions of Schedule 2 to the 1990 Act;

(b) the provision made by or under Schedule 14 to this Act;

(c) the provisions of sections 280 and 281 of this Act;

(d) whatever provision (if any) has been made under section 283 of this Act; and

(e) the provisions of Part 3 of the Enterprise Act 2002 (c. 40) so far as they relate to intervention by the Secretary of State in connection with newspapers or other media enterprises.

(3) The first review must be carried out no more than three years after the commencement of this section, and subsequent reviews must be carried out at intervals of no more than three years.

(4) The report to the Secretary of State on a review must set out OFCOM's recommendations, in consequence of their conclusions on the review, for the exercise by the Secretary of State of—

(a) his power to make an order under section 348(5);

(b) his powers to make orders under Schedule 14;

(c) his powers under sections 282 and 283; and

(d) his powers under sections 44(11), 58(3) and 59(6A) of the Enterprise Act 2002 (media mergers).

(5) OFCOM must publish every report sent by them to the Secretary of State under this section in such manner as they consider appropriate for bringing it to the attention of persons who, in their opinion, are likely to be affected by it.

405 General interpretation

(1) In this Act, except in so far as the context otherwise requires—

'the 1990 Act' means the Broadcasting Act 1990 (c. 42);

'the 1996 Act' means the Broadcasting Act 1996 (c. 55);

'access' is to be construed in accordance with subsection (4);

'apparatus' includes any equipment, machinery or device and any wire or cable and the casing or coating for any wire or cable;

'associated facility' has the meaning given by section 32;

'the Audiovisual Media Services Directive' means Directive 2010/13/EU of the European Parliament and of the Council on the coordination of certain provisions laid down by law, regulation or administrative action in Member States concerning the provision of audiovisual media services;

'the BBC' means the British Broadcasting Corporation;

'body' (without more) means any body or association of persons, whether corporate or unincorporate, including a firm;

'broadcast' means broadcast by wireless telegraphy, and cognate expressions are to be construed accordingly;

'Broadcasting Act licence' means a licence under Part 1 or 3 of the 1990 Act or under Part 1 or 2 of the 1996 Act;

'business' includes any trade or profession;

'C4C' means the Channel Four Television Corporation;

'communications provider' means a person who (within the meaning of section 32(4)) provides an electronic communications network or an electronic communications service;

'the Consumer Panel' means the panel established under section 16;

'consumers' has the meaning given by subsection (5);

'Content Board' means the committee of OFCOM established and maintained under section 12;

'contravention' includes a failure to comply, and cognate expressions are to be construed accordingly;

'customers', in relation to a communications provider or a person who makes an associated facility available, means the following (including any of them whose use or potential use of the network, service or facility is for the purposes of, or in connection with, a business)—

(a) the persons to whom the network, service or facility is provided or made available in the course of any business carried on as such by the provider or person who makes it available;

(b) the persons to whom the communications provider or person making the facility available is seeking to secure that the network, service or facility is so provided or made available;

(c) the persons who wish to be so provided with the network or service, or to have the facility so made available, or who are likely to seek to become persons to whom the network, service or facility is so provided or made available;

'distribute', in relation to a service, does not include broadcast, and cognate expressions shall be construed accordingly;

'electronic communications network' and 'electronic communications service' have the meanings given by section 32;

'enactment' includes any enactment comprised in an Act of the Scottish Parliament or in any Northern Ireland legislation;

'the enactments relating to the management of the radio spectrum' means—

(a) the Wireless Telegraphy Act 2006; and
   [...]
(g) the provisions of this Act so far as relating to that Act;

'frequency' includes frequency band;

'holder', in relation to a Broadcasting Act licence, is to be construed in accordance with subsection (7), and cognate expressions are to be construed accordingly;

'information' includes accounts, estimates and projections and any document;

'intelligible' is to be construed in accordance with subsection (9);

'international obligation of the United Kingdom' includes any Community obligation and any obligation which will or may arise under any international agreement or arrangements to which the United Kingdom is a party;

'modification' includes omissions, alterations and additions, and cognate expressions are to be construed accordingly;

'OFCOM' means the Office of Communications;

'on-demand programme service' has the meaning given by section 368A(1);

'other member State' means a member State other than the United Kingdom;

'pre-commencement regulator' means any of the following—
(a) the Broadcasting Standards Commission;
(b) the Director General of Telecommunications;
(c) the Independent Television Commission;
(d) the Radio Authority;

'programme' includes an advertisement and, in relation to a service, anything included in that service;

'programme service' means—
(a) a television programme service;
(b) the public teletext service;
(c) an additional television service;
(d) a digital additional television service;
(e) a radio programme service; or
(f) a sound service provided by the BBC;

and expressions used in this definition and in Part 3 have the same meanings in this definition as in that Part;

'provide' and cognate expressions, in relation to an electronic communications network, electronic communications service or associated facilities, are to be construed in accordance with section 32(4);

'purposes of public service television broadcasting in the United Kingdom' shall be construed in accordance with subsection (4) of section 264 and subsections (5) and (6) of that section shall apply for the purposes of any provision of this Act referring to such purposes as they apply for the purposes of a report under that section;

'the radio transfer date' means the date on which the Radio Authority's functions under Part 3 of the 1990 Act and Part 2 of the 1996 Act are transferred under this Act to OFCOM;

'representation', in relation to a proposal or the contents of any notice or notification, includes an objection to the proposal or (as the case may be) to the whole or any part of those contents;

'subordinate legislation' means—
(a) any subordinate legislation, within the meaning of the Interpretation Act 1978 (c. 30); or
(b) any statutory rules (within the meaning of the Statutory Rules (Northern Ireland) Order 1979 (S.I. 1979/1573 (N.I. 12));

'television and radio services' means—
(a) programme services apart from those provided by the BBC; and
(b) services provided by the BBC in relation to which OFCOM have functions;

'television programme' means any programme (with or without sounds) which—

    (a) is produced wholly or partly to be seen on television; and

    (b) consists of moving or still images or of legible text or of a combination of those things;

'the television transfer date' means the date on which the Independent Television Commission's functions under Part 1 of the 1990 Act and Part 1 of the 1996 Act are transferred under this Act to OFCOM;

'TV licence' means a licence for the purposes of section 363;

'the Welsh Authority' means the authority whose name is, by virtue of section 56(1) of the 1990 Act, Sianel Pedwar Cymru;

'wireless telegraphy' has the same meaning as in the Wireless Telegraphy Act 2006;

'wireless telegraphy licence' means a licence granted under section 8 of the Wireless Telegraphy Act 2006.

(2) Any power under this Act to provide for the manner in which anything is to be done includes power to provide for the form in which it is to be done.

(3) References in this Act to OFCOM's functions under an enactment include references to their power to do anything which appears to them to be incidental or conducive to the carrying out of their functions under that enactment.

(4) References in this Act to access—

    (a) in relation to an electronic communications network or electronic communications service, are references to the opportunity of making use of the network or service; and

    (b) in relation to a programme service, are references to the opportunity of viewing in an intelligible form the programmes included in the service or (as the case may be) of listening to them in such a form.

(5) For the purposes of this Act persons are consumers in a market for a service, facility or apparatus, if they are—

    (a) persons to whom the service, facility or apparatus is provided, made available or supplied (whether in their personal capacity or for the purposes of, or in connection with, their businesses);

    (b) persons for whose benefit the service, facility or apparatus is provided, made available or supplied or for whose benefit persons falling within paragraph (a) arrange for it to be provided, made available or supplied;

    (c) persons whom the person providing the service or making the facility available, or the supplier of the apparatus, is seeking to make into persons falling within paragraph (a) or (b); or

    (d) persons who wish to become persons falling within paragraph (a) or (b) or who are likely to seek to become persons falling within one or both of those paragraphs.

(6) References in this Act to services in relation to which OFCOM have functions include references to any services in relation to which OFCOM are required to set standards under section 319.

(7) In this Act references, in relation to a time or a period, to the holder of a Broadcasting Act licence or of a particular description of such licence are references to the person who held that licence at that time or (as the case may be) to every person who held that licence for the whole or a part of that period.

(8) For the purposes of this Act the fact that a service is not in an intelligible form shall be disregarded, except where express provision is made to the contrary, in determining whether it has been provided—

    (a) for general reception;

    (b) for reception by particular persons; or

    (c) for reception at a particular place or in a particular area.

(9) For the purposes of this Act something is not to be regarded as in an intelligible form if it cannot readily be understood without being decrypted or having some comparable process applied to it.

410   Application of enactments to territorial sea and other waters

(1) This section applies to—

(a) provision made by or under Part 2 of this Act;

(b) any provision of the enactments relating to the management of the radio spectrum that are not contained in that Part or the Wireless Telegraphy Act 2006 makes provision; and

(c) any provision of Chapter 1 of Part 5 of this Act so far as it relates to a matter as respects which provision falling within paragraph (a) or (b) is made.

(2) Her Majesty may by Order in Council provide—

(a) for an area of the territorial sea to be treated, for the purposes of any provision to which this section applies, as if it were situated in such part of the United Kingdom as may be specified in the Order; and

(b) for jurisdiction with respect to questions arising in relation to the territorial sea under any such provision to be conferred on courts in a part of the United Kingdom so specified.

(7) In this section—

'installation' includes any floating structure or device maintained on a station by whatever means, and installations in transit;

'the territorial sea' means the territorial sea adjacent to the United Kingdom.

411   Short title, commencement and extent

(1) This Act may be cited as the Communications Act 2003.

(5) This Act extends to Northern Ireland.

(6) Subject to subsection (7), Her Majesty may by Order in Council extend the provisions of this Act, with such modifications as appear to Her Majesty in Council to be appropriate, to any of the Channel Islands or to the Isle of Man.

SCHEDULES

SCHEDULE 11A

RESTRICTIONS ON PRODUCT PLACEMENT

Introductory

1.—(1) In this Part 'product placement', in relation to a programme included in a television programme service, means the inclusion in the programme of, or of a reference to, a product, service or trade mark, where the inclusion—

(a) is for a commercial purpose;

(b) is in return for the making of any payment, or the giving of other valuable consideration, to any relevant provider or any person connected with a relevant provider; and

(c) is not prop placement.

(2) 'Prop placement', in relation to such a programme, means the inclusion in the programme of, or of a reference to, a product, service or trade mark where—

(a) the provision of the product, service or trade mark has no significant value; and

(b) no relevant provider, or person connected with a relevant provider, has received any payment or other valuable consideration in relation to its inclusion in, or the reference to it in, the programme, disregarding the costs saved by including the product, service or trademark, or a reference to it, in the programme.

2. The product placement requirements are—

(a) that the product placement does not fall within any of paragraphs 3 to 6;

(b) that all of the conditions in paragraph 7 are met; and

(c) that, where paragraph 8 applies, the condition in that paragraph is also met.

Prohibitions of product placement

3.—(1) Product placement falls within this paragraph if it is in a children's programme.

(2) In sub-paragraph (1)'children's programme' means a programme made—

(a) for a television programme service or for an on-demand programme service, and

(b) for viewing primarily by persons under the age of sixteen.

4. Product placement falls within this paragraph if it is—

(a) of cigarettes or other tobacco products;

(b) by or on behalf of an undertaking whose principal activity is the manufacture or sale of cigarettes or other tobacco products; or

(c) of prescription-only medicines.

5. Product placement of alcoholic drinks falls within this paragraph if—

(a) it is aimed specifically at persons under the age of eighteen; or

(b) it encourages immoderate consumption of such drinks.

6.—(1) Product placement falls within this paragraph if it is in a programme to which this paragraph applies and—

(a) the programme is a religious, consumer affairs or current affairs programme;

(b) the product placement is of anything within sub-paragraph (2); or

(c) the product placement is otherwise unsuitable.

(2) The following are within this sub-paragraph—

(a) electronic or smokeless cigarettes, cigarette lighters, cigarette papers or pipes intended for smoking;

(b) medicinal products;

(c) alcoholic drinks;

(d) infant formulae or follow-on formulae;

(e) a food or drink high in fat, salt or sugar;

(f) gambling services.

(3) This paragraph applies to—

(a) a programme that has been produced or commissioned by the provider of the television programme service in which it is included, or by a person connected with that provider, and that is not a film made for cinema; and

(b) a programme that has been produced or commissioned by any other person with a view to its first showing taking place in a television programme service which is provided by a person under the jurisdiction of the United Kingdom for the purposes of the Audiovisual Media Services Directive.

Conditions applying to product placement

7.—(1) These are the conditions referred to in paragraph 2(b).

(2) Condition A is that the programme in which the product, service or trademark, or the reference to it, is included is—

(a) a film made for cinema;

(b) a film or series made for a television programme service or for an on-demand programme service;

(c) a sports programme; or

(d) a light entertainment programme.

(3) Condition B is that the product placement has not influenced the content or scheduling of the programme in a way that affects the editorial independence of the provider of the television programme service in which the programme is included.

(4) Condition C is that the product placement does not directly encourage the purchase or rental of goods or services, whether by making promotional reference to those goods or services or otherwise.

(5) Condition D is that the programme does not give undue prominence to the products, services or trade marks concerned.

(6) Condition E is that the product placement does not use techniques which exploit the possibility of conveying a message subliminally or surreptitiously.

(7) Condition F is that the way in which the product, service or trade mark, or the reference to it, is included in the programme by way of product placement does not—

(a) prejudice respect for human dignity;

(b) promote discrimination based on sex, racial or ethnic origin, nationality, religion or belief, disability, age or sexual orientation;

(c) encourage behaviour prejudicial to health or safety;

(d) encourage behaviour grossly prejudicial to the protection of the environment;

(e) cause physical or moral detriment to persons under the age of eighteen;

(f) directly encourage such persons to persuade their parents or others to purchase or rent goods or services;

(g) exploit the trust of such persons in parents, teachers or others; or

(h) unreasonably show such persons in dangerous situations.

8.—(1) This paragraph applies where the programme featuring the product placement has been produced or commissioned by the provider of the television programme service in which it is included or by a person connected with that provider.

(2) The condition referred to in paragraph 2(c) is that the television programme service in which the programme is included signals appropriately the fact that product placement is contained in a programme no less frequently than—

(a) at the start and end of such a programme; and

(b) in the case of a television programme service which includes advertising breaks within it, at the recommencement of the programme after each such advertising break.

Minor definitions

9. In this Schedule—

'connected' has the same meaning as it has in the Broadcasting Act 1990 by virtue of section 202 of that Act;

'film made for cinema' means a film made with a view to its being shown to the general public first in a cinema;

'follow-on formulae' has the meaning given in Article 2 of Commission Directive 2006/141/EC on infant formulae and follow-on formulae and amending Directive 1999/21/EC;

'infant formulae' has the meaning given in Article 2 of Commission Directive 2006/141/EC on infant formulae and follow-on formulae and amending Directive 1999/21/EC;

'medicinal product' has the meaning given in section 130 of the Medicines Act 1968;

'prescription-only medicine' means a medicinal product of a description or falling within a class specified in an order made under section 58 of the Medicines Act 1968;

'producer', in relation to a programme, means the person by whom the arrangements necessary for the making of the programme are undertaken;

'programme' does not include an advertisement;

'relevant provider', in relation to a programme, means—

(a) the provider of the television programme service in which the programme is included; and

(b) the producer of the programme;

'residual value' means any monetary or other economic value in the hands of the relevant provider other than the cost saving of including the product, service or trademark, or a reference to it, in a programme;

'significant value' means a residual value that is more than trivial;

'tobacco product' has the meaning given in section 1 of the Tobacco Advertising and Promotion Act 2002;

'trade mark', in relation to a business, includes any image (such as a logo) or sound commonly associated with that business or its products or services.

Directive 2010/13/EU of the European Parliament and of the Council

of 10 March 2010

on the coordination of certain provisions laid down by law, regulation or administrative action in Member States concerning the provision of audiovisual media services (Audiovisual Media Services Directive)

(Codified version)

Chapter I Definitions

Article 1

1. For the purposes of this Directive, the following definitions shall apply:
    (a) 'audiovisual media service' means:
        (i) a service as defined by Articles 56 and 57 of the Treaty on the Functioning of the European Union which is under the editorial responsibility of a media service provider and the principal purpose of which is the provision of programmes, in order to inform, entertain or educate, to the general public by electronic communications networks within the meaning of point (a) of Article 2 of Directive 2002/21/EC. Such an audiovisual media service is either a television broadcast as defined in point (e) of this paragraph or an on-demand audiovisual media service as defined in point (g) of this paragraph;
        (ii) audiovisual commercial communication;
    (b) 'programme' means a set of moving images with or without sound constituting an individual item within a schedule or a catalogue established by a media service provider and the form and content of which are comparable to the form and content of television broadcasting. Examples of programmes include feature-length films, sports events, situation comedies, documentaries, children's programmes and original drama;
    (c) 'editorial responsibility' means the exercise of effective control both over the selection of the programmes and over their organisation either in a chronological schedule, in the case of television broadcasts, or in a catalogue, in the case of on-demand audiovisual media services. Editorial responsibility does not necessarily imply any legal liability under national law for the content or the services provided;
    (d) 'media service provider' means the natural or legal person who has editorial responsibility for the choice of the audiovisual content of the audiovisual media service and determines the manner in which it is organised;
    (e) 'television broadcasting' or 'television broadcast' (i.e. a linear audiovisual media service) means an audiovisual media service provided by a media service provider for simultaneous viewing of programmes on the basis of a programme schedule;
    (f) 'broadcaster' means a media service provider of television broadcasts;
    (g) 'on-demand audiovisual media service' (i.e. a non-linear audiovisual media service) means an audiovisual media service provided by a media service provider for the viewing of programmes at the moment chosen by the user and at his individual request on the basis of a catalogue of programmes selected by the media service provider;
    (h) 'audiovisual commercial communication' means images with or without sound which are designed to promote, directly or indirectly, the goods, services or image of a natural or legal entity pursuing an economic activity. Such images accompany or are included in a programme in return for payment or for similar consideration or for self-promotional

purposes. Forms of audiovisual commercial communication include, inter alia, television advertising, sponsorship, teleshopping and product placement;

(i) 'television advertising' means any form of announcement broadcast whether in return for payment or for similar consideration or broadcast for self-promotional purposes by a public or private undertaking or natural person in connection with a trade, business, craft or profession in order to promote the supply of goods or services, including immovable property, rights and obligations, in return for payment;

(j) 'surreptitious audiovisual commercial communication' means the representation in words or pictures of goods, services, the name, the trade mark or the activities of a producer of goods or a provider of services in programmes when such representation is intended by the media service provider to serve as advertising and might mislead the public as to its nature. Such representation shall, in particular, be considered as intentional if it is done in return for payment or for similar consideration;

(k) 'sponsorship' means any contribution made by public or private undertakings or natural persons not engaged in providing audiovisual media services or in the production of audiovisual works, to the financing of audiovisual media services or programmes with a view to promoting their name, trade mark, image, activities or products;

(l) 'teleshopping' means direct offers broadcast to the public with a view to the supply of goods or services, including immovable property, rights and obligations, in return for payment;

(m) 'product placement' means any form of audiovisual commercial communication consisting of the inclusion of or reference to a product, a service or the trade mark thereof so that it is featured within a programme, in return for payment or for similar consideration;

(n) 'European works' means the following:

   (i)   works originating in Member States;

   (ii) works originating in European third States party to the European Convention on Transfrontier Television of the Council of Europe and fulfilling the conditions of paragraph 3;

   (iii) works co-produced within the framework of agreements related to the audiovisual sector concluded between the Union and third countries and fulfilling the conditions defined in each of those agreements.

2. The application of the provisions of points (n)(ii) and (iii) of paragraph 1 shall be conditional on works originating in Member States not being the subject of discriminatory measures in the third country concerned.

3. The works referred to in points (n)(i) and (ii) of paragraph 1 are works mainly made with authors and workers residing in one or more of the States referred to in those provisions provided that they comply with one of the following three conditions:

   (i)   they are made by one or more producers established in one or more of those States;

   (ii) the production of the works is supervised and actually controlled by one or more producers established in one or more of those States;

   (iii) the contribution of co-producers of those States to the total co-production costs is preponderant and the co-production is not controlled by one or more producers established outside those States.

4. Works that are not European works within the meaning of point (n) of paragraph 1 but that are produced within the framework of bilateral co-production agreements concluded between Member States and third countries shall be deemed to be European works provided that the co-producers from the Union supply a majority share of the total cost of production and that the production is not controlled by one or more producers established outside the territory of the Member States.

CHAPTER II GENERAL PROVISIONS

Article 2

1. Each Member State shall ensure that all audiovisual media services transmitted by media service providers under its jurisdiction comply with the rules of the system of law applicable to audiovisual media services intended for the public in that Member State.

2. For the purposes of this Directive, the media service providers under the jurisdiction of a Member State are any of the following:

    (a) those established in that Member State in accordance with paragraph 3;

    (b) those to whom paragraph 4 applies.

3. For the purposes of this Directive, a media service provider shall be deemed to be established in a Member State in the following cases:

    (a) the media service provider has its head office in that Member State and the editorial decisions about the audiovisual media service are taken in that Member State;

    (b) if a media service provider has its head office in one Member State but editorial decisions on the audiovisual media service are taken in another Member State, it shall be deemed to be established in the Member State where a significant part of the workforce involved in the pursuit of the audiovisual media service activity operates. If a significant part of the workforce involved in the pursuit of the audiovisual media service activity operates in each of those Member States, the media service provider shall be deemed to be established in the Member State where it has its head office. If a significant part of the workforce involved in the pursuit of the audiovisual media service activity operates in neither of those Member States, the media service provider shall be deemed to be established in the Member State where it first began its activity in accordance with the law of that Member State, provided that it maintains a stable and effective link with the economy of that Member State;

    (c) if a media service provider has its head office in a Member State but decisions on the audiovisual media service are taken in a third country, or vice versa, it shall be deemed to be established in the Member State concerned, provided that a significant part of the workforce involved in the pursuit of the audiovisual media service activity operates in that Member State.

4. Media service providers to whom the provisions of paragraph 3 are not applicable shall be deemed to be under the jurisdiction of a Member State in the following cases:

    (a) they use a satellite up-link situated in that Member State;

    (b) although they do not use a satellite up-link situated in that Member State, they use satellite capacity appertaining to that Member State.

5. If the question as to which Member State has jurisdiction cannot be determined in accordance with paragraphs 3 and 4, the competent Member State shall be that in which the media service provider is established within the meaning of Articles 49 to 55 of the Treaty on the Functioning of the European Union.

6. This Directive does not apply to audiovisual media services intended exclusively for reception in third countries and which are not received with standard consumer equipment directly or indirectly by the public in one or more Member States.

Article 3

1. Member States shall ensure freedom of reception and shall not restrict retransmissions on their territory of audiovisual media services from other Member States for reasons which fall within the fields coordinated by this Directive.

2. In respect of television broadcasting, Member States may provisionally derogate from paragraph 1 if the following conditions are fulfilled:

    (a) a television broadcast coming from another Member State manifestly, seriously and gravely infringes Article 27(1) or (2) and/or Article 6;

    (b) during the previous 12 months, the broadcaster has infringed the provision(s) referred to in point (a) on at least two prior occasions;

    (c) the Member State concerned has notified the broadcaster and the Commission in writing of the alleged infringements and of the measures it intends to take should any such infringement occur again;

    (d) consultations with the transmitting Member State and the Commission have not produced an amicable settlement within 15 days of the notification provided for in point (c), and the alleged infringement persists.

The Commission shall, within 2 months following notification of the measures taken by the Member State, take a decision on whether the measures are compatible with Union law. If it decides that they are not, the Member State will be required to put an end to the measures in question as a matter of urgency.

3. Paragraph 2 shall be without prejudice to the application of any procedure, remedy or sanction to the infringements in question in the Member State which has jurisdiction over the broadcaster concerned.

4. In respect of on-demand audiovisual media services, Member States may take measures to derogate from paragraph 1 in respect of a given service if the following conditions are fulfilled:

    (a) the measures are:

        (i) necessary for one of the following reasons:

            – public policy, in particular the prevention, investigation, detection and prosecution of criminal offences, including the protection of minors and the fight against any incitement to hatred on grounds of race, sex, religion or nationality, and violations of human dignity concerning individual persons,

            – the protection of public health,

            – public security, including the safeguarding of national security and defence,

            – the protection of consumers, including investors;

        (ii) taken against an on-demand audiovisual media service which prejudices the objectives referred to in point (i) or which presents a serious and grave risk of prejudice to those objectives;

        (iii) proportionate to those objectives;

    (b) before taking the measures in question and without prejudice to court proceedings, including preliminary proceedings and acts carried out in the framework of a criminal investigation, the Member State has:

        (i)   asked the Member State under whose jurisdiction the media service provider falls to take measures and the latter did not take such measures, or they were inadequate;

        (ii) notified the Commission and the Member State under whose jurisdiction the media service provider falls of its intention to take such measures.

5. Member States may, in urgent cases, derogate from the conditions laid down in point (b) of paragraph 4. Where this is the case, the measures shall be notified in the shortest possible time to the Commission and to the Member State under whose jurisdiction the media service provider falls, indicating the reasons for which the Member State considers that there is urgency.

6. Without prejudice to the Member State's possibility of proceeding with the measures referred to in paragraphs 4 and 5, the Commission shall examine the compatibility of the notified measures with Union law in the shortest possible time. Where it comes to the conclusion that the measures are incompatible with Union law, the Commission shall ask the Member State in question to refrain from taking any proposed measures or urgently to put an end to the measures in question.

Article 4

1. Member States shall remain free to require media service providers under their jurisdiction to comply with more detailed or stricter rules in the fields coordinated by this Directive provided that such rules are in compliance with Union law.

2. In cases where a Member State:

    (a) has exercised its freedom under paragraph 1 to adopt more detailed or stricter rules of general public interest; and

    (b) assesses that a broadcaster under the jurisdiction of another Member State provides a television broadcast which is wholly or mostly directed towards its territory;

it may contact the Member State having jurisdiction with a view to achieving a mutually satisfactory solution to any problems posed. On receipt of a substantiated request by the first Member State, the Member State having jurisdiction shall request the broadcaster to comply with the rules of general public interest in question. The Member State having jurisdiction shall inform the first Member State of the results obtained following this request within 2 months. Either Member State may invite the contact committee established pursuant to Article 29 to examine the case.

    3. The first Member State may adopt appropriate measures against the broadcaster concerned where it assesses that:

    (a) the results achieved through the application of paragraph 2 are not satisfactory; and

    (b) the broadcaster in question has established itself in the Member State having jurisdiction in order to circumvent the stricter rules, in the fields coordinated by this Directive, which would be applicable to it if it were established in the first Member State.

Such measures shall be objectively necessary, applied in a non-discriminatory manner and proportionate to the objectives which they pursue.

    4. A Member State may take measures pursuant to paragraph 3 only if the following conditions are met:

    (a) it has notified the Commission and the Member State in which the broadcaster is established of its intention to take such measures while substantiating the grounds on which it bases its assessment; and

    (b) the Commission has decided that the measures are compatible with Union law, and in particular that assessments made by the Member State taking those measures under paragraphs 2 and 3 are correctly founded.

    5. The Commission shall decide within 3 months following the notification provided for in point (a) of paragraph 4. If the Commission decides that the measures are incompatible with Union law, the Member State in question shall refrain from taking the proposed measures.

    6. Member States shall, by appropriate means, ensure, within the framework of their legislation, that media service providers under their jurisdiction effectively comply with the provisions of this Directive.

    7. Member States shall encourage coregulation and/or self-regulatory regimes at national level in the fields coordinated by this Directive to the extent permitted by their legal systems. These regimes shall be such that they are broadly accepted by the main stakeholders in the Member States concerned and provide for effective enforcement.

    8. Directive 2000/31/EC shall apply unless otherwise provided for in this Directive. In the event of a conflict between a provision of Directive 2000/31/EC and a provision of this Directive, the provisions of this Directive shall prevail, unless otherwise provided for in this Directive.

CHAPTER III PROVISIONS APPLICABLE TO ALL AUDIOVISUAL MEDIA SERVICES

Article 5

Member States shall ensure that audiovisual media service providers under their jurisdiction shall make easily, directly and permanently accessible to the recipients of a service at least the following information:

    (a) the name of the media service provider;

    (b) the geographical address at which the media service provider is established;

    (c) the details of the media service provider, including its electronic mail address or website, which allow it to be contacted rapidly in a direct and effective manner;

    (d) where applicable, the competent regulatory or supervisory bodies.

Article 6

Member States shall ensure by appropriate means that audiovisual media services provided by media service providers under their jurisdiction do not contain any incitement to hatred based on race, sex, religion or nationality.

Article 7

Member States shall encourage media service providers under their jurisdiction to ensure that their services are gradually made accessible to people with a visual or hearing disability.

Article 8

Member States shall ensure that media service providers under their jurisdiction do not transmit cinematographic works outside periods agreed with the rights holders.

Article 9

1. Member States shall ensure that audiovisual commercial communications provided by media service providers under their jurisdiction comply with the following requirements:
    (a) audiovisual commercial communications shall be readily recognisable as such. Surreptitious audiovisual commercial communication shall be prohibited;
    (b) audiovisual commercial communications shall not use techniques;
    (c) audiovisual commercial communications shall not:
        (i) prejudice respect for human dignity;
        (ii) include or promote any discrimination based on sex, racial or ethnic origin, nationality, religion or belief, disability, age or sexual orientation;
        (iii) encourage behaviour prejudicial to health or safety;
        (iv) encourage behaviour grossly prejudicial to the protection of the environment;
    (d) all forms of audiovisual commercial communications for cigarettes and other tobacco products shall be prohibited;
    (e) audiovisual commercial communications for alcoholic beverages shall not be aimed specifically at minors and shall not encourage immoderate consumption of such beverages;
    (f) audiovisual commercial communication for medicinal products and medical treatment available only on prescription in the Member State within whose jurisdiction the media service provider falls shall be prohibited;
    (g) audiovisual commercial communications shall not cause physical or moral detriment to minors. Therefore they shall not directly exhort minors to buy or hire a product or service by exploiting their inexperience or credulity, directly encourage them to persuade their parents or others to purchase the goods or services being advertised, exploit the special trust minors place in parents, teachers or other persons, or unreasonably show minors in dangerous situations.
2. Member States and the Commission shall encourage media service providers to develop codes of conduct regarding inappropriate audiovisual commercial communications, accompanying or included in children's programmes, of foods and beverages containing nutrients and substances with a nutritional or physiological effect, in particular those such as fat, transfatty acids, salt/sodium and sugars, excessive intakes of which in the over-all diet are not recommended.

Article 10

1. Audiovisual media services or programmes that are sponsored shall meet the following requirements:
    (a) their content and, in the case of television broadcasting, their scheduling shall in no circumstances be influenced in such a way as to affect the responsibility and editorial independence of the media service provider;
    (b) they shall not directly encourage the purchase or rental of goods or services, in particular by making special promotional references to those goods or services;
    (c) viewers shall be clearly informed of the existence of a sponsorship agreement. Sponsored programmes shall be clearly identified as such by the name, logo and/or any other symbol

of the sponsor such as a reference to its product(s) or service(s) or a distinctive sign thereof in an appropriate way for programmes at the beginning, during and/or at the end of the programmes.

2. Audiovisual media services or programmes shall not be sponsored by undertakings whose principal activity is the manufacture or sale of cigarettes and other tobacco products.

3. The sponsorship of audiovisual media services or programmes by undertakings whose activities include the manufacture or sale of medicinal products and medical treatment may promote the name or the image of the undertaking, but shall not promote specific medicinal products or medical treatments available only on prescription in the Member State within whose jurisdiction the media service provider falls.

4. News and current affairs programmes shall not be sponsored. Member States may choose to prohibit the showing of a sponsorship logo during children's programmes, documentaries and religious programmes.

Article 11

1. Paragraphs 2, 3 and 4 shall apply only to programmes produced after 19 December 2009.

2. Product placement shall be prohibited.

3. By way of derogation from paragraph 2, product placement shall be admissible in the following cases unless a Member State decides otherwise:

  (a) in cinematographic works, films and series made for audiovisual media services, sports programmes and light entertainment programmes;

  (b) where there is no payment but only the provision of certain goods or services free of charge, such as production props and prizes, with a view to their inclusion in a programme.

The derogation provided for in point (a) shall not apply to children's programmes.

Programmes that contain product placement shall meet at least all of the following requirements:

  (a) their content and, in the case of television broadcasting, their scheduling shall in no circumstances be influenced in such a way as to affect the responsibility and editorial independence of the media service provider;

  (b) they shall not directly encourage the purchase or rental of goods or services, in particular by making special promotional references to those goods or services;

  (c) they shall not give undue prominence to the product in question;

  (d) viewers shall be clearly informed of the existence of product placement. Programmes containing product placement shall be appropriately identified at the start and the end of the programme, and when a programme resumes after an advertising break, in order to avoid any confusion on the part of the viewer.

By way of exception, Member States may choose to waive the requirements set out in point (d) provided that the programme in question has neither been produced nor commissioned by the media service provider itself or a company affiliated to the media service provider.

4. In any event programmes shall not contain product placement of:

  (a) tobacco products or cigarettes or product placement from undertakings whose principal activity is the manufacture or sale of cigarettes and other tobacco products;

  (b) specific medicinal products or medical treatments available only on prescription in the Member State under whose jurisdiction the media service provider falls.

CHAPTER IV PROVISIONS APPLICABLE ONLY TO ON-DEMAND AUDIOVISUAL MEDIA SERVICES

Article 12

Member States shall take appropriate measures to ensure that on-demand audiovisual media services provided by media service providers under their jurisdiction which might seriously impair the physical, mental or moral development of minors are only made available in such a way as to ensure that minors will not normally hear or see such on-demand audiovisual media services.

Article 13

1. Member States shall ensure that on-demand audiovisual media services provided by media service providers under their jurisdiction promote, where practicable and by appropriate means, the production of and access to European works. Such promotion could relate, inter alia, to the financial contribution made by such services to the production and rights acquisition of European works or to the share and/or prominence of European works in the catalogue of programmes offered by the on-demand audiovisual media service.

2. Member States shall report to the Commission no later than 19 December 2011 and every 4 years thereafter on the implementation of paragraph 1.

3. The Commission shall, on the basis of the information provided by Member States and of an independent study, report to the European Parliament and to the Council on the application of paragraph 1, taking into account the market and technological developments and the objective of cultural diversity.

CHAPTER V PROVISIONS CONCERNING EXCLUSIVE RIGHTS AND SHORT NEWS REPORTS IN TELEVISION BROADCASTING

Article 14

1. Each Member State may take measures in accordance with Union law to ensure that broadcasters under its jurisdiction do not broadcast on an exclusive basis events which are regarded by that Member State as being of major importance for society in such a way as to deprive a substantial proportion of the public in that Member State of the possibility of following such events by live coverage or deferred coverage on free television. If it does so, the Member State concerned shall draw up a list of designated events, national or non-national, which it considers to be of major importance for society. It shall do so in a clear and transparent manner in due time. In so doing the Member State concerned shall also determine whether these events should be available by whole or partial live coverage or, where necessary or appropriate for objective reasons in the public interest, whole or partial deferred coverage.

2. Member States shall immediately notify to the Commission any measures taken or to be taken pursuant to paragraph 1. Within a period of 3 months from the notification, the Commission shall verify that such measures are compatible with Union law and communicate them to the other Member States. It shall seek the opinion of the contact committee established pursuant to Article 29. It shall forthwith publish the measures taken in the Official Journal of the European Union and at least once a year the consolidated list of the measures taken by Member States.

3. Member States shall ensure, by appropriate means within the framework of their legislation, that broadcasters under their jurisdiction do not exercise the exclusive rights purchased by those broadcasters after 18 December 2007 in such a way that a substantial proportion of the public in another Member State is deprived of the possibility of following events which are designated by that other Member State in accordance with paragraphs 1 and 2 by whole or partial live coverage or, where necessary or appropriate for objective reasons in the public interest, whole or partial deferred coverage on free television as determined by that other Member State in accordance with paragraph 1.

Article 15

1. Member States shall ensure that for the purpose of short news reports, any broadcaster established in the Union has access on a fair, reasonable and non-discriminatory basis to events of high interest to the public which are transmitted on an exclusive basis by a broadcaster under their jurisdiction.

2. If another broadcaster established in the same Member State as the broadcaster seeking access has acquired exclusive rights to the event of high interest to the public, access shall be sought from that broadcaster.

3. Member States shall ensure that such access is guaranteed by allowing broadcasters to freely choose short extracts from the transmitting broadcaster's signal with, unless impossible for reasons of practicality, at least the identification of their source.

4. As an alternative to paragraph 3, Member States may establish an equivalent system which achieves access on a fair, reasonable and non-discriminatory basis through other means.

5. Short extracts shall be used solely for general news programmes and may be used in on-demand audiovisual media services only if the same programme is offered on a deferred basis by the same media service provider.

6. Without prejudice to paragraphs 1 to 5, Member States shall ensure, in accordance with their legal systems and practices, that the modalities and conditions regarding the provision of such short extracts are defined, in particular, with respect to any compensation arrangements, the maximum length of short extracts and time limits regarding their transmission. Where compensation is provided for, it shall not exceed the additional costs directly incurred in providing access.

CHAPTER VI PROMOTION OF DISTRIBUTION AND PRODUCTION OF TELEVISION PROGRAMMES

Article 16

1. Member States shall ensure, where practicable and by appropriate means, that broadcasters reserve for European works a majority proportion of their transmission time, excluding the time allotted to news, sports events, games, advertising, teletext services and teleshopping. This proportion, having regard to the broadcaster's informational, educational, cultural and entertainment responsibilities to its viewing public, should be achieved progressively, on the basis of suitable criteria.

2. Where the proportion laid down in paragraph 1 cannot be attained, it must not be lower than the average for 1988 in the Member State concerned.

However, in respect of Greece and Portugal, the year 1988 shall be replaced by the year 1990.

3. Member States shall provide the Commission every 2 years, starting from 3 October 1991, with a report on the application of this Article and Article 17.

That report shall in particular include a statistical statement on the achievement of the proportion referred to in this Article and Article 17 for each of the television programmes falling within the jurisdiction of the Member State concerned, the reasons, in each case, for the failure to attain that proportion and the measures adopted or envisaged in order to achieve it.

The Commission shall inform the other Member States and the European Parliament of the reports, which shall be accompanied, where appropriate, by an opinion. The Commission shall ensure the application of this Article and Article 17 in accordance with the provisions of the Treaty on the Functioning of the European Union. The Commission may take account in its opinion, in particular, of progress achieved in relation to previous years, the share of first broadcast works in the programming, the particular circumstances of new television broadcasters and the specific situation of countries with a low audiovisual production capacity or restricted language area.

Article 17

Member States shall ensure, where practicable and by appropriate means, that broadcasters reserve at least 10 % of their transmission time, excluding the time allotted to news, sports events, games, advertising, teletext services and teleshopping, or alternately, at the discretion of the Member State, at least 10 % of their programming budget, for European works created by producers who are independent of broadcasters. This proportion, having regard to the broadcaster's informational, educational, cultural and entertainment responsibilities to its viewing public, should be achieved progressively, on the basis of suitable criteria. It must be achieved by earmarking an adequate proportion for recent works, that is to say works transmitted within 5 years of their production.

Article 18

This Chapter shall not apply to television broadcasts that are intended for local audiences and do not form part of a national network.

CHAPTER VII TELEVISION ADVERTISING AND TELESHOPPING

Article 19

1. Television advertising and teleshopping shall be readily recognisable and distinguishable from editorial content. Without prejudice to the use of new advertising techniques, television advertising and teleshopping shall be kept quite distinct from other parts of the programme by optical and/or acoustic and/or spatial means.

2. Isolated advertising and teleshopping spots, other than in transmissions of sports events, shall remain the exception.

Article 20

1. Member States shall ensure, where television advertising or teleshopping is inserted during programmes, that the integrity of the programmes, taking into account natural breaks in and the duration and the nature of the programme concerned, and the rights of the right holders are not prejudiced.

2. The transmission of films made for television (excluding series, serials and documentaries), cinematographic works and news programmes may be interrupted by television advertising and/or teleshopping once for each scheduled period of at least 30 minutes. The transmission of children's programmes may be interrupted by television advertising and/or teleshopping once for each scheduled period of at least 30 minutes, provided that the scheduled duration of the programme is greater than 30 minutes. No television advertising or teleshopping shall be inserted during religious services.

Article 21

Teleshopping for medicinal products which are subject to a marketing authorisation within the meaning of Directive 2001/83/EC, as well as teleshopping for medical treatment, shall be prohibited.

Article 22

Television advertising and teleshopping for alcoholic beverages shall comply with the following criteria:

(a) it may not be aimed specifically at minors or, in particular, depict minors consuming these beverages;

(b) it shall not link the consumption of alcohol to enhanced physical performance or to driving;

(c) it shall not create the impression that the consumption of alcohol contributes towards social or sexual success;

(d) it shall not claim that alcohol has therapeutic qualities or that it is a stimulant, a sedative or a means of resolving personal conflicts;

(e) it shall not encourage immoderate consumption of alcohol or present abstinence or moderation in a negative light;

(f) it shall not place emphasis on high alcoholic content as being a positive quality of the beverages.

Article 23

1. The proportion of television advertising spots and teleshopping spots within a given clock hour shall not exceed 20 %.

2. Paragraph 1 shall not apply to announcements made by the broadcaster in connection with its own programmes and ancillary products directly derived from those programmes, sponsorship announcements and product placements.

Article 24

Teleshopping windows shall be clearly identified as such by optical and acoustic means and shall be of a minimum uninterrupted duration of 15 minutes.

Article 25

This Directive shall apply mutatis mutandis to television channels exclusively devoted to advertising and teleshopping as well as to television channels exclusively devoted to self-promotion.

However, Chapter VI as well as Articles 20 and 23 shall not apply to these channels.

Article 26

Without prejudice to Article 4, Member States may, with due regard for Union law, lay down conditions other than those laid down in Article 20(2) and Article 23 in respect of television broadcasts intended solely for the national territory which cannot be received directly or indirectly by the public in one or more other Member States.

CHAPTER VIII PROTECTION OF MINORS IN TELEVISION BROADCASTING

Article 27

1. Member States shall take appropriate measures to ensure that television broadcasts by broadcasters under their jurisdiction do not include any programmes which might seriously impair the physical, mental or moral development of minors, in particular programmes that involve pornography or gratuitous violence.

2. The measures provided for in paragraph 1 shall also extend to other programmes which are likely to impair the physical, mental or moral development of minors, except where it is ensured, by selecting the time of the broadcast or by any technical measure, that minors in the area of transmission will not normally hear or see such broadcasts.

3. In addition, when such programmes are broadcast in unencoded form Member States shall ensure that they are preceded by an acoustic warning or are identified by the presence of a visual symbol throughout their duration.

CHAPTER IX RIGHT OF REPLY IN TELEVISION BROADCASTING

Article 28

1. Without prejudice to other provisions adopted by the Member States under civil, administrative or criminal law, any natural or legal person, regardless of nationality, whose legitimate interests, in particular reputation and good name, have been damaged by an assertion of incorrect facts in a television programme must have a right of reply or equivalent remedies. Member States shall ensure that the actual exercise of the right of reply or equivalent remedies is not hindered by the imposition of unreasonable terms or conditions. The reply shall be transmitted within a reasonable time subsequent to the request being substantiated and at a time and in a manner appropriate to the broadcast to which the request refers.

2. A right of reply or equivalent remedies shall exist in relation to all broadcasters under the jurisdiction of a Member State.

3. Member States shall adopt the measures needed to establish the right of reply or the equivalent remedies and shall determine the procedure to be followed for the exercise thereof. In particular, they shall ensure that a sufficient time span is allowed and that the procedures are such that the right or equivalent remedies can be exercised appropriately by natural or legal persons resident or established in other Member States.

4. An application for exercise of the right of reply or the equivalent remedies may be rejected if such a reply is not justified according to the conditions laid down in paragraph 1, would involve a punishable act, would render the broadcaster liable to civil-law proceedings or would transgress standards of public decency.

5. Provision shall be made for procedures whereby disputes as to the exercise of the right of reply or the equivalent remedies can be subject to judicial review.

CHAPTER X CONTACT COMMITTEE

Article 29

1. A contact committee is established under the aegis of the Commission. It shall be composed of representatives of the competent authorities of the Member States. It shall be chaired by a representative of the Commission and meet either on his initiative or at the request of the delegation of a Member State.

2. The tasks of the contact committee shall be:

(a) to facilitate effective implementation of this Directive through regular consultation on any practical problems arising from its application, and particularly from the application of Article 2, as well as on any other matters on which exchanges of views are deemed useful;

(b) to deliver own-initiative opinions or opinions requested by the Commission on the application by the Member States of this Directive;

(c) to be the forum for an exchange of views on what matters should be dealt with in the reports which Member States must submit pursuant to Article 16(3) and on their methodology;

(d) to discuss the outcome of regular consultations which the Commission holds with representatives of broadcasting organisations, producers, consumers, manufacturers, service providers and trade unions and the creative community;

(e) to facilitate the exchange of information between the Member States and the Commission on the situation and the development of regulatory activities regarding audiovisual media services, taking account of the Union's audiovisual policy, as well as relevant developments in the technical field;

(f) to examine any development arising in the sector on which an exchange of views appears useful.

CHAPTER XI COOPERATION BETWEEN REGULATORY BODIES OF THE MEMBER STATES

Article 30

Member States shall take appropriate measures to provide each other and the Commission with the information necessary for the application of this Directive, in particular Articles 2, 3 and 4, in particular through their competent independent regulatory bodies.

CHAPTER XII FINAL PROVISIONS

Article 31

In fields which this Directive does not coordinate, it shall not affect the rights and obligations of Member States resulting from existing conventions dealing with telecommunications or broadcasting.

Article 32

Member States shall communicate to the Commission the text of the main provisions of national law which they adopt in the field covered by this Directive.

Article 33

Not later than 19 December 2011, and every 3 years thereafter, the Commission shall submit to the European Parliament, to the Council and to the European Economic and Social Committee a report on the application of this Directive and, if necessary, make further proposals to adapt it to developments in the field of audiovisual media services, in particular in the light of recent technological developments, the competitiveness of the sector and levels of media literacy in all Member States.

That report shall also assess the issue of television advertising accompanying or included in children's programmes, and in particular whether the quantitative and qualitative rules contained in this Directive have afforded the level of protection required.

Article 34

Directive 89/552/EEC, as amended by the Directives listed in Annex I, Part A, is repealed, without prejudice to the obligations of the Member States relating to the time limits for transposition into national law of the Directives set out in Annex I, Part B.

References to the repealed Directive shall be construed as references to this Directive and shall be read in accordance with the correlation table in Annex II.

Article 35

This Directive shall enter into force on the 20th day following its publication in the Official Journal of the European Union.

Article 36

This Directive is addressed to the Member States.

OFCOM Broadcasting Code

[2013 Version]

Section 1 Protecting the under-eighteens

This section must be read in conjunction with Section Two: Harm and Offence.

Principle

To ensure that people under eighteen are protected.

Rules

Scheduling and content information

1.1 Material that might seriously impair the physical, mental or moral development of people under eighteen must not be broadcast.

1.2 In the provision of services, broadcasters must take all reasonable steps to protect people under eighteen. For television services, this is in addition to their obligations resulting from the Audiovisual Media Services Directive (in particular, Article 27, see Appendix 2).

1.3 Children must also be protected by appropriate scheduling from material that is unsuitable for them.

Meaning of 'children' Children are people under the age of fifteen years.

Meaning of 'appropriate scheduling' Appropriate scheduling should be judged according to:
- the nature of the content;
- the likely number and age range of children in the audience, taking into account school time, weekends and holidays;
- the start time and finish time of the programme;
- the nature of the channel or station and the particular programme; and
- the likely expectations of the audience for a particular channel or station at a particular time and on a particular day.

1.4 Television broadcasters must observe the watershed.

Meaning of the 'watershed' The watershed only applies to television. The watershed is at 2100. Material unsuitable for children should not, in general, be shown before 2100 or after 0530.

On premium subscription film services which are not protected as set out in Rule 1.24, the watershed is at 2000. There is no watershed on premium subscription film services or pay per view services which are protected as set out in Rule 1.24 and 1.25 respectively.

1.5 Radio broadcasters must have particular regard to times when children are particularly likely to be listening.

Meaning of 'when children are particularly likely to be listening' This phrase particularly refers to the school run and breakfast time, but might include other times.

1.6 The transition to more adult material must not be unduly abrupt at the watershed (in the case of television) or after the time when children are particularly likely to be listening (in the case of radio). For television, the strongest material should appear later in the schedule.

1.7 For television programmes broadcast before the watershed, or for radio programmes broadcast when children are particularly likely to be listening, clear information about content that may distress some children should be given, if appropriate, to the audience (taking into account the context). (For the meaning of 'context' see Section Two: Harm and Offence.)

The coverage of sexual and other offences in the UK involving the under-eighteens

1.8 Where statutory or other legal restrictions apply preventing personal identification, broadcasters should also be particularly careful not to provide clues which may lead to the identification of those who are not yet adult (the defining age may differ in different parts of the UK) and who are, or might be, involved as a victim, witness, defendant or other perpetrator in the case of sexual offences featured in criminal, civil or family court proceedings:

— by reporting limited information which may be pieced together with other information available elsewhere, for example in newspaper reports (the 'jigsaw effect');

— inadvertently, for example, by describing an offence as 'incest';

— or in any other indirect way.

(**Note:** Broadcasters should be aware that there may be statutory reporting restrictions that apply even if a court has not specifically made an order to that effect.)

1.9 When covering any pre-trial investigation into an alleged criminal offence in the UK, broadcasters should pay particular regard to the potentially vulnerable position of any person who is not yet adult who is involved as a witness or victim, before broadcasting their name, address, identity of school or other educational establishment, place of work, or any still or moving picture of them. Particular justification is also required for the broadcast of such material relating to the identity of any person who is not yet adult and who is involved in the defence as a defendant or potential defendant.

Drugs, smoking, solvents and alcohol

1.10 The use of illegal drugs, the abuse of drugs, smoking, solvent abuse and the misuse of alcohol:

— must not be featured in programmes made primarily for children unless there is strong editorial justification;

— must generally be avoided and in any case must not be condoned, encouraged or glamorised in other programmes broadcast before the watershed (in the case of television), or when children are particularly likely to be listening (in the case of radio), unless there is editorial justification;

— must not be condoned, encouraged or glamorised in other programmes likely to be widely seen or heard by under eighteens unless there is editorial justification.

Violence and dangerous behaviour

1.11 Violence, its after-effects and descriptions of violence, whether verbal or physical, must be appropriately limited in programmes broadcast before the watershed (in the case of television) or when children are particularly likely to be listening (in the case of radio) and must also be justified by the context.

1.12 Violence, whether verbal or physical, that is easily imitable by children in a manner that is harmful or dangerous:

— must not be featured in programmes made primarily for children unless there is strong editorial justification;

— must not be broadcast before the watershed (in the case of television) or when children are particularly likely to be listening (in the case of radio), unless there is editorial justification.

1.13 Dangerous behaviour, or the portrayal of dangerous behaviour, that is likely to be easily imitable by children in a manner that is harmful:

> — must not be featured in programmes made primarily for children unless there is strong editorial justification;
>
> — must not be broadcast before the watershed (in the case of television), or when children are particularly likely to be listening (in the case of radio), unless there is editorial justification.

(Regarding Rules 1.11 to 1.13 see Rules 2.4 and 2.5 in Section Two: Harm and Offence.)

Offensive language

1.14 The most offensive language must not be broadcast before the watershed (in the case of television) or when children are particularly likely to be listening (in the case of radio).

1.15 Offensive language must not be used in programmes made for younger children except in the most exceptional circumstances.

1.16 Offensive language must not be broadcast before the watershed (in the case of television), or when children are particularly likely to be listening (in the case of radio), unless it is justified by the context. In any event, frequent use of such language must be avoided before the watershed. (Regarding Rules 1.14 to 1.16 see Rule 2.3 in Section Two: Harm and Offence.)

Sexual material

1.17 Material equivalent to the British Board of Film Classification ('BBFC') R18-rating must not be broadcast at any time.

1.18 'Adult sex material'—material that contains images and/or language of a strong sexual nature which is broadcast for the primary purpose of sexual arousal or stimulation—must not be broadcast at any time other than between 2200 and 0530 on premium subscription services and pay per view/night services which operate with mandatory restricted access.

In addition, measures must be in place to ensure that the subscriber is an adult.

Meaning of 'mandatory restricted access' Mandatory restricted access means there is a PIN protected system (or other equivalent protection) which cannot be removed by the user, that restricts access solely to those authorised to view.

1.19 Broadcasters must ensure that material broadcast after the watershed which contains images and/or language of a strong or explicit sexual nature, but is not 'adult sex material' as defined in Rule 1.18 above, is justified by the context.

(See Rules 1.6 and 1.18 and Rule 2.3 in Section Two: Harm and Offence which includes meaning of 'context'.)

1.20 Representations of sexual intercourse must not occur before the watershed (in the case of television) or when children are particularly likely to be listening (in the case of radio), unless there is a serious educational purpose. Any discussion on, or portrayal of, sexual behaviour must be editorially justified if included before the watershed, or when children are particularly likely to be listening, and must be appropriately limited.

Nudity

1.21 Nudity before the watershed must be justified by the context.

Films, premium subscription film services, pay per view services

1.22 No film refused classification by the British Board of Film Classification (BBFC) may be broadcast unless it has subsequently been classified or the BBFC has confirmed that it would not be rejected according to the standards currently operating. Also, no film cut as a condition of classification by the BBFC may be transmitted in a version which includes the cut material unless:

- the BBFC has confirmed that the material was cut to allow the film to pass at a lower category; or

- the BBFC has confirmed that the film would not be subject to compulsory cuts according to the standards currently operating.

1.23 BBFC 18-rated films or their equivalent must not be broadcast before 2100 on any service (except for pay per view services), and even then they may be unsuitable for broadcast at that time.

1.24 Premium subscription film services may broadcast up to BBFC 15-rated films or their equivalent, at any time of day provided that mandatory restricted access is in place pre-2000 and post-0530.

In addition, those security systems which are in place to protect children must be clearly explained to all subscribers.

(See meaning of 'mandatory restricted access' under Rule 1.18 above.)

1.25 Pay per view services may broadcast up to BBFC 18-rated films or their equivalent, at any time of day provided that mandatory restricted access is in place pre-2100 and post-0530.

In addition:

- information must be provided about programme content that will assist adults to assess its suitability for children;

- there must be a detailed billing system for subscribers which clearly itemises all viewing including viewing times and dates; and

- those security systems which are in place to protect children must be clearly explained to all subscribers.

(See meaning of 'mandatory restricted access' under Rule 1.18 above.)

1.26 BBFC R18-rated films must not be broadcast.

Exorcism, the occult and the paranormal

1.27 Demonstrations of exorcisms, occult practices and the paranormal (which purport to be real), must not be shown before the watershed (in the case of television) or when children are particularly likely to be listening (in the case of radio). Paranormal practices which are for entertainment purposes must not be broadcast when significant numbers of children may be expected to be watching, or are particularly likely to be listening. (This rule does not apply to drama, film or comedy.) (See Rules 2.6 to 2.8 in Section Two: Harm and Offence and Rule 4.7 in Section Four: Religion.)

The involvement of people under eighteen in programmes

1.28 Due care must be taken over the physical and emotional welfare and the dignity of people under eighteen who take part or are otherwise involved in programmes. This is irrespective of any consent given by the participant or by a parent, guardian or other person over the age of eighteen in loco parentis.

1.29 People under eighteen must not be caused unnecessary distress or anxiety by their involvement in programmes or by the broadcast of those programmes.

1.30 Prizes aimed at children must be appropriate to the age range of both the target audience and the participants.

(See Rule 2.16 in Section Two: Harm and Offence.)

Section 2 Harm and offence

This section must be read in conjunction with Section One: Protecting the Under-Eighteens. The rules in this section are designed not only to provide adequate protection for adults but also to protect people under eighteen.

Principle

To ensure that generally accepted standards are applied to the contents of television and radio services so as to provide adequate protection for members of the public from the inclusion in such services of harmful and/or offensive material.

Rules

2.1 Generally accepted standards must be applied to the contents of television and radio services so as to provide adequate protection for members of the public from the inclusion in such services of harmful and/or offensive material.

2.2 Factual programmes or items or portrayals of factual matters must not materially mislead the audience.

(Note to Rule 2.2: News is regulated under Section Five of the Code.)

2.3 In applying generally accepted standards broadcasters must ensure that material which may cause offence is justified by the context (see meaning of 'context' below). Such material may include, but is not limited to, offensive language, violence, sex, sexual violence, humiliation, distress, violation of human dignity, discriminatory treatment or language (for example, on the grounds of age, disability, gender, race, religion, beliefs and sexual orientation). Appropriate information should also be broadcast where it would assist in avoiding or minimising offence.

Meaning of 'context' Context includes (but is not limited to):
— the editorial content of the programme, programmes or series;
— the service on which the material is broadcast;
— the time of broadcast;
— what other programmes are scheduled before and after the programme or programmes concerned;
— the degree of harm or offence likely to be caused by the inclusion of any particular sort of material in programmes generally or programmes of a particular description;
— the likely size and composition of the potential audience and likely expectation of the audience;
— the extent to which the nature of the content can be brought to the attention of the potential audience, for example, by giving information; and
— the effect of the material on viewers or listeners who may come across it unawares.

2.4 Programmes must not include material (whether in individual programmes or in programmes taken together) which, taking into account the context, condones or glamorises violent, dangerous or seriously antisocial behaviour and is likely to encourage others to copy such behaviour.

(See Rules 1.11 to 1.13 in Section One: Protecting the Under-Eighteens.)

2.5 Methods of suicide and self-harm must not be included in programmes except where they are editorially justified and are also justified by the context.

(See Rule 1.13 in Section one: Protecting the under-eighteens.)

2.6 Demonstrations of exorcism, the occult, the paranormal, divination, or practices related to any of these that purport to be real (as opposed to entertainment) must be treated with due objectivity.

(See Rule 1.27 in Section one: Protecting the under-eighteens, concerning scheduling restrictions.)

2.7 If a demonstration of exorcism, the occult, the paranormal, divination, or practices related to any of these is for entertainment purposes, this must be made clear to viewers and listeners.

2.8 Demonstrations of exorcism, the occult, the paranormal, divination, or practices related to any of these (whether such demonstrations purport to be real or are for entertainment purposes) must not contain life-changing advice directed at individuals. (Religious programmes are exempt from this rule but must, in any event, comply with the provisions in Section Four: Religion. Films, dramas and fiction generally are not bound by this rule.)

Meaning of 'life-changing' Life-changing advice includes direct advice for individuals upon which they could reasonably act or rely about health, finance, employment or relationships.

2.9 When broadcasting material featuring demonstrations of hypnotic techniques, broadcasters must exercise a proper degree of responsibility in order to prevent hypnosis and/or adverse reactions in viewers and listeners. The hypnotist must not broadcast his/her full verbal routine or be shown performing straight to camera.

2.10 Simulated news (for example, in drama or in documentaries) must be broadcast in such a way that there is no reasonable possibility of the audience being misled into believing that they are listening to, or watching, actual news.

2.11 Broadcasters must not use techniques which exploit the possibility of conveying a message to viewers or listeners, or of otherwise influencing their minds without their being aware, or fully aware, of what has occurred.

2.12 Television broadcasters must take precautions to maintain a low level of risk to viewers who have photosensitive epilepsy. Where it is not reasonably practicable to follow the Ofcom guidance (see the Ofcom website), and where broadcasters can demonstrate that the broadcasting of flashing lights and/or patterns is editorially justified, viewers should be given an adequate verbal and also, if appropriate, text warning at the start of the programme or programme item.

Broadcast competitions and voting

2.13 Broadcast competitions and voting must be conducted fairly.

2.14 Broadcasters must ensure that viewers and listeners are not materially misled about any broad-cast competition or voting.

2.15 Broadcasters must draw up rules for a broadcast competition or vote. These rules must be clear and appropriately made known. In particular, significant conditions that may affect a viewer's or listener's decision to participate must be stated at the time an invitation to participate is broadcast.

2.16 Broadcast competition prizes must be described accurately.

(See also Rule 1.30 in Section One: Protecting the Under-Eighteens, which concerns the provision of appropriate prizes for children.)

Note:

For broadcast competitions and voting that involve the use of premium rate telephony services (PRS), broadcasters should also refer to Rules 9.26 to 9.30. Radio Broadcasters should refer to Rules 10.9 and 10.10.

Meaning of 'broadcast competition' A competition or free prize draw featured in a programme in which viewers or listeners are invited to enter by any means for the opportunity to win a prize.

Meaning of 'voting' Features in a programme in which viewers or listeners are invited to register a vote by any means to decide or influence, at any stage, the outcome of a contest.

Section 3 Crime

Principle

To ensure that material likely to encourage or incite the commission of crime or to lead to disorder is not included in television or radio services.

Rules

3.1 Material likely to encourage or incite the commission of crime or to lead to disorder must not be included in television or radio services.

3.2 Descriptions or demonstrations of criminal techniques which contain essential details which could enable the commission of crime must not be broadcast unless editorially justified.

3.3 No payment, promise of payment, or payment in kind, may be made to convicted or confessed criminals whether directly or indirectly for a programme contribution by the criminal (or any other person) relating to his/her crimes. The only exception is where it is in the public interest.

3.4 While criminal proceedings are active, no payment or promise of payment may be made, directly or indirectly, to any witness or any person who may reasonably be expected to be called as a witness. Nor should any payment be suggested or made dependent on the outcome of the trial. Only actual expenditure or loss of earnings necessarily incurred during the making of a programme contribution may be reimbursed.

3.5 Where criminal proceedings are likely and foreseeable, payments should not be made to people who might reasonably be expected to be witnesses unless there is a clear public interest, such as investigating crime or serious wrongdoing, and the payment is necessary to elicit the information. Where such a payment is made it will be appropriate to disclose the payment to both defence and prosecution if the person becomes a witness in any subsequent trial.

3.6 Broadcasters must use their best endeavours so as not to broadcast material that could endanger lives or prejudice the success of attempts to deal with a hijack or kidnapping.

Section 4 Religion

The rules in this section apply to religious programmes.

Principles

To ensure that broadcasters exercise the proper degree of responsibility with respect to the content of programmes which are religious programmes.

To ensure that religious programmes do not involve any improper exploitation of any susceptibilities of the audience for such a programme.

To ensure that religious programmes do not involve any abusive treatment of the religious views and beliefs of those belonging to a particular religion or religious denomination.

Rules

4.1 Broadcasters must exercise the proper degree of responsibility with respect to the content of programmes which are religious programmes.

Meaning of a 'religious programme' A religious programme is a programme which deals with matters of religion as the central subject, or as a significant part, of the programme.

4.2 The religious views and beliefs of those belonging to a particular religion or religious denomination must not be subject to abusive treatment.

4.3 Where a religion or religious denomination is the subject, or one of the subjects, of a religious programme, then the identity of the religion and/or denomination must be clear to the audience.

4.4 Religious programmes must not seek to promote religious views or beliefs by stealth.

4.5 Religious programmes on television services must not seek recruits. This does not apply to specialist religious television services. Religious programmes on radio services may seek recruits.

Meaning of 'seek recruits' Seek recruits means directly appealing to audience members to join a religion or religious denomination.

4.6 Religious programmes must not improperly exploit any susceptibilities of the audience.

(Regarding charity appeals in programming and appeals for funds by broadcasters, television broadcasters should refer to Rules 9.33 and 9.34, and 9.36 and 9.39. Radio broadcasters should refer to Rules 10.11 and 10.12.)

4.7 Religious programmes that contain claims that a living person (or group) has special powers or abilities must treat such claims with due objectivity and must not broadcast such claims when significant numbers of children may be expected to be watching (in the case of television), or when children are particularly likely to be listening (in the case of radio).

Section 5 Due Impartiality and Due Accuracy and Undue Prominence of Views and Opinions

This section of the Code does not apply to BBC services funded by the licence fee or grant in aid, which are regulated on these matters by the BBC Governors.

Principles

To ensure that news, in whatever form, is reported with due accuracy and presented with due impartiality.

To ensure that the special impartiality requirements of the Act are complied with.

Rules

Meaning of 'due impartiality' 'Due' is an important qualification to the concept of impartiality. Impartiality itself means not favouring one side over another. 'Due' means adequate or appropriate to the subject and nature of the programme. So 'due impartiality' does not mean an equal division of time has to be given to every view, or that every argument and every facet of every argument has to be represented. The approach to due impartiality may vary according to the nature of the subject, the type of programme and channel, the likely expectation of the audience as to content, and the extent to which the content and approach is signalled to the audience. Context, as defined in Section Two: Harm and Offence of the Code, is important.

Due impartiality and due accuracy in news

5.1 News, in whatever form, must be reported with due accuracy and presented with due impartiality.

5.2 Significant mistakes in news should normally be acknowledged and corrected on air quickly. Corrections should be appropriately scheduled.

5.3 No politician may be used as a newsreader, interviewer or reporter in any news programmes unless, exceptionally, it is editorially justified. In that case, the political allegiance of that person must be made clear to the audience.

Special impartiality requirements: news and other programmes

Matters of political or industrial controversy and matters relating to current public policy

Meaning of 'matters of political or industrial controversy and matters relating to current public policy' Matters of political or industrial controversy are political or industrial issues on which politicians, industry and/or the media are in debate. Matters relating to current public policy need not be the subject of debate but relate to a policy under discussion or already decided by a local, regional or national government or by bodies mandated by those public bodies to make policy on their behalf, for example, non-governmental organisations, relevant European institutions, etc.

The exclusion of view or opinions
(Rule 5.4 applies to television and radio services except restricted services.)

5.4 Programmes in the services (listed above) must exclude all expressions of the views and opinions of the person providing the service on matters of political and industrial controversy and matters relating to current public policy (unless that person is speaking in a legislative forum or in a court of law). Views and opinions relating to the provision of programme services are also excluded from this requirement.

The preservation of due impartiality
(Rules 5.5 to 5.12 apply to television programme services, teletext services, national radio and national digital sound programme services.)

5.5 Due impartiality on matters of political or industrial controversy and matters relating to current public policy must be preserved on the part of any person providing a service (listed above). This may be achieved within a programme or over a series of programmes taken as a whole.

Meaning of 'series of programmes taken as a whole' This means more than one programme in the same service, editorially linked, dealing with the same or related issues within an appropriate period and aimed at a like audience. A series can include, for example, a strand, or two programmes (such as a drama and a debate about the drama) or a 'cluster' or 'season' of programmes on the same subject.

5.6 The broadcast of editorially linked programmes dealing with the same subject matter (as part of a 'series' in which the broadcaster aims to achieve due impartiality) should normally be made clear to the audience on air.

5.7 Views and facts must not be misrepresented. Views must also be presented with due weight over appropriate timeframes.

5.8 Any personal interest of a reporter or presenter, which would call into question the due impartiality of the programme, must be made clear to the audience.

5.9 Presenters and reporters (with the exception of news presenters and reporters in news programmes), presenters of 'personal view' or 'authored' programmes or items, and chairs of discussion programmes may express their own views on matters of political or industrial controversy or matters relating to current public policy. However, alternative viewpoints must be adequately represented either in the programme, or in a series of programmes taken as a whole. Additionally, presenters must not use the advantage of regular appearances to promote their views in a way that compromises the requirement for due impartiality. Presenter phone-ins must encourage and must not exclude alternative views.

5.10 A personal view or authored programme or item must be clearly signalled to the audience at the outset. This is a minimum requirement and may not be sufficient in all circumstances. (Personality phone-in hosts on radio are exempted from this provision unless their personal view status is unclear.)

Meaning of 'personal view' and 'authored' 'Personal view' programmes are programmes presenting a particular view or perspective. Personal view programmes can range from the outright expression of highly partial views, for example, by a person who is a member of a lobby group and is campaigning on the subject, to the considered 'authored' opinion of a journalist, commentator or academic, with professional expertise or a specialism in an area which enables her or him to express opinions which are not necessarily mainstream.

Matters of major political or industrial controversy and major matters relating to current public policy

5.11 In addition to the rules above, due impartiality must be preserved on matters of major political and industrial controversy and major matters relating to current public policy by the person providing a service (listed above) in each programme or in clearly linked and timely programmes.

Meaning of 'matters of major political or industrial controversy and major matters relating to current public policy' These will vary according to events but are generally matters of political or industrial controversy or matters of current public policy which are of national, and often international, importance, or are of similar significance within a smaller broadcast area.

5.12 In dealing with matters of major political and industrial controversy and major matters relating to current public policy an appropriately wide range of significant views must be included and given due weight in each programme or in clearly linked and timely programmes. Views and facts must not be misrepresented.

The prevention of undue prominence of views and opinions on matters of political or industrial controversy and matters relating to current public policy
(Rule 5.13 applies to local radio services (including community radio services), local digital sound programme services (including community digital sound programme services) and radio licensable content services.)

5.13 Broadcasters should not give undue prominence to the views and opinions of particular persons or bodies on matters of political or industrial controversy and matters relating to current public policy in all the programmes included in any service (listed above) taken as a whole.

Meaning of 'undue prominence of views and opinions' Undue prominence is a significant imbalance of views aired within coverage of matters of political or industrial controversy or matters relating to current public policy.

Meaning of 'programmes included in any service...taken as a whole' Programmes included in any service taken as a whole, means all programming on a service dealing with the same or related issues within an appropriate period.

Section 7 Fairness

Foreword

This section and the following section on privacy are different from other sections of the Code. They apply to how broadcasters treat the individuals or organisations directly affected by programmes, rather than to what the general public sees and/or hears as viewers and listeners.

As well as containing a principle and a rule this section contains 'practices to be followed' by broadcasters when dealing with individuals or organisations participating in or otherwise directly affected by programmes as broadcast. Following these practices will not necessarily avoid a breach of this section. However, failure to follow these practices will only constitute a breach of this section of the Code (Rule 7.1) where it results in unfairness to an individual or organisation in the programme. Importantly, the Code does not and cannot seek to set out all the 'practices to be followed' in order to avoid unfair treatment.

The following provisions in the next section on privacy are also relevant to this section:

— the explanation of public interest that appears in the meaning of 'warranted' under Rule 8.1 in Section Eight: Privacy;

— the meaning of surreptitious filming or recording that appears under 'practices to be followed' 8.13 in Section Eight: Privacy.

Principle

To ensure that broadcasters avoid unjust or unfair treatment of individuals or organisations in programmes.

Rule

7.1 Broadcasters must avoid unjust or unfair treatment of individuals or organisations in programmes.

Practices to be followed (7.2 to 7.14 below)

Dealing fairly with contributors and obtaining informed consent

7.2 Broadcasters and programme makers should normally be fair in their dealings with potential contributors to programmes unless, exceptionally, it is justified to do otherwise.

7.3 Where a person is invited to make a contribution to a programme (except when the subject matter is trivial or their participation minor) they should normally, at an appropriate stage:

— be told the nature and purpose of the programme, what the programme is about and be given a clear explanation of why they were asked to contribute and when (if known) and where it is likely to be first broadcast;

— be told what kind of contribution they are expected to make, for example, live, prerecorded, interview, discussion, edited, unedited, etc;

— be informed about the areas of questioning and, wherever possible, the nature of other likely contributions;

— be made aware of any significant changes to the programme as it develops which might reasonably affect their original consent to participate, and which might cause material unfairness;

— be told the nature of their contractual rights and obligations and those of the programme maker and broadcaster in relation to their contribution; and

— be given clear information, if offered an opportunity to preview the programme, about whether they will be able to effect any changes to it.

Taking these measures is likely to result in the consent that is given being 'informed consent' (referred to in this section and the rest of the Code as 'consent').

It may be fair to withhold all or some of this information where it is justified in the public interest or under other provisions of this section of the Code.

7.4 If a contributor is under sixteen, consent should normally be obtained from a parent or guardian, or other person of eighteen or over in loco parentis. In particular, persons under sixteen should not be asked for views on matters likely to be beyond their capacity to answer properly without such consent.

7.5 In the case of persons over sixteen who are not in a position to give consent, a person of eighteen or over with primary responsibility for their care should normally give it on their behalf. In particular, persons not in a position to give consent should not be asked for views on matters likely to be beyond their capacity to answer properly without such consent.

7.6 When a programme is edited, contributions should be represented fairly.

7.7 Guarantees given to contributors, for example relating to the content of a programme, confidentiality or anonymity, should normally be honoured.

7.8 Broadcasters should ensure that the re-use of material, i.e. use of material originally filmed or recorded for one purpose and then used in a programme for another purpose or used in a later or different programme, does not create unfairness. This applies both to material obtained from others and the broadcaster's own material.

Opportunity to contribute and proper consideration of facts

7.9 Before broadcasting a factual programme, including programmes examining past events, broadcasters should take reasonable care to satisfy themselves that:

— material facts have not been presented, disregarded or omitted in a way that is unfair to an individual or organisation; and

— anyone whose omission could be unfair to an individual or organisation has been offered an opportunity to contribute.

7.10 Programmes—such as dramas and factually-based dramas—should not portray facts, events, individuals or organisations in a way which is unfair to an individual or organisation.

7.11 If a programme alleges wrongdoing or incompetence or makes other significant allegations, those concerned should normally be given an appropriate and timely opportunity to respond.

7.12 Where a person approached to contribute to a programme chooses to make no comment or refuses to appear in a broadcast, the broadcast should make clear that the individual concerned has chosen not to appear and should give their explanation if it would be unfair not to do so.

7.13 Where it is appropriate to represent the views of a person or organisation that is not participating in the programme, this must be done in a fair manner.

Deception, set-ups and 'wind-up' calls

7.14 Broadcasters or programme makers should not normally obtain or seek information, audio, pictures or an agreement to contribute through misrepresentation or deception. (Deception includes surreptitious filming or recording.) However:

— it may be warranted to use material obtained through misrepresentation or deception without consent if it is in the public interest and cannot reasonably be obtained by other means;

— where there is no adequate public interest justification, for example some unsolicited wind-up calls or entertainment set-ups, consent should be obtained from the individual and/or organisation concerned before the material is broadcast;

— if the individual and/or organisation are not identifiable in the programme then consent for broadcast will not be required;

— material involving celebrities and those in the public eye can be used without consent for broadcast, but it should not be used without a public interest justification if it is likely to result in unjustified public ridicule or personal distress. (Normally, therefore such contributions should be pre-recorded.)

(See 'practices to be followed' 8.11 to 8.15 in Section Eight: Privacy.)

Section 8 Privacy

Foreword

This section and the preceding section on fairness are different from other sections of the Code. They apply to how broadcasters treat the individuals or organisations directly affected by programmes, rather than to what the general public sees and/or hears as viewers and listeners.

As well as containing a principle and a rule this section contains 'practices to be followed' by broadcasters when dealing with individuals or organisations participating or otherwise directly affected by programmes, or in the making of programmes. Following these practices will not necessarily avoid a breach of this section. However, failure to follow these practices will only constitute a breach of this section of the Code (Rule 8.1) where it results in an unwarranted infringement of privacy. Importantly, the Code does not and cannot seek to set out all the 'practices to be followed' in order to avoid an unwarranted infringement of privacy.

The Broadcasting Act 1996 (as amended) requires Ofcom to consider complaints about unwarranted infringements of privacy in a programme or in connection with the obtaining of material included in a programme. This may call for some difficult on-the-spot judgments about whether privacy is unwarrantably infringed by filming or recording, especially when reporting on emergency situations ('practices to be followed' 8.5 to 8.8 and 8.16 to 8.19). We recognise there may be a strong public interest in reporting on an emergency situation as it occurs and we understand there may be pressures on broadcasters at the scene of a disaster or emergency that may make it difficult to judge at the time whether filming or recording is an unwarrantable infringement of privacy. These are factors Ofcom will take into account when adjudicating on complaints.

Where consent is referred to in Section Eight it refers to informed consent. Please see 'practice to be followed' 7.3 in Section Seven: Fairness.

Principle

To ensure that broadcasters avoid any unwarranted infringement of privacy in programmes and in connection with obtaining material included in programmes.

Rule

8.1 Any infringement of privacy in programmes, or in connection with obtaining material included in programmes, must be warranted.

Meaning of 'warranted'   In this section 'warranted' has a particular meaning. It means that where broadcasters wish to justify an infringement of privacy as warranted, they should be able to demonstrate why in the particular circumstances of the case, it is warranted. If the reason is that it is in the public interest, then the broadcaster should be able to demonstrate that the public interest outweighs the right to privacy. Examples of public interest would include revealing or detecting crime, protecting public health or safety, exposing misleading claims made by individuals or organisations or disclosing incompetence that affects the public.

Practices to be followed (8.2 to 8.22)

Private lives, public places and legitimate expectation of privacy
Meaning of 'legitimate expectation of privacy'   Legitimate expectations of privacy will vary according to the place and nature of the information, activity or condition in question, the extent to which it is in the public domain (if at all) and whether the individual concerned is already in the public eye. There may be circumstances where people can reasonably expect privacy even in a public place. Some activities and conditions may be of such a private nature that filming or recording, even in a public place, could involve an infringement of privacy. People under investigation or in the public eye, and their immediate family and friends, retain the right to a private life, although private behaviour can raise issues of legitimate public interest.

8.2 Information which discloses the location of a person's home or family should not be revealed without permission, unless it is warranted.

8.3 When people are caught up in events which are covered by the news they still have a right to privacy in both the making and the broadcast of a programme, unless it is warranted to infringe it. This applies both to the time when these events are taking place and to any later programmes that revisit those events.

8.4 Broadcasters should ensure that words, images or actions filmed or recorded in, or broadcast from, a public place, are not so private that prior consent is required before broadcast from the individual or organisation concerned, unless broadcasting without their consent is warranted.

Consent

8.5 Any infringement of privacy in the making of a programme should be with the person's and/ or organisation's consent or be otherwise warranted.

8.6 If the broadcast of a programme would infringe the privacy of a person or organisation, consent should be obtained before the relevant material is broadcast, unless the infringement of privacy is warranted. (Callers to phone-in shows are deemed to have given consent to the broadcast of their contribution.)

8.7 If an individual or organisation's privacy is being infringed, and they ask that the filming, recording or live broadcast be stopped, the broadcaster should do so, unless it is warranted to continue.

8.8 When filming or recording in institutions, organisations or other agencies, permission should be obtained from the relevant authority or management, unless it is warranted to film or record without permission. Individual consent of employees or others whose appearance is incidental or where they are essentially anonymous members of the general public will not normally be required.

However, in potentially sensitive places such as ambulances, hospitals, schools, prisons or police stations, separate consent should normally be obtained before filming or recording and for broadcast from those in sensitive situations (unless not obtaining consent is warranted). If the individual will not be identifiable in the programme then separate consent for broadcast will not be required.

Gathering information, sound or images and the re-use of material

8.9 The means of obtaining material must be proportionate in all the circumstances and in particular to the subject matter of the programme.

8.10 Broadcasters should ensure that the reuse of material, i.e. use of material originally filmed or recorded for one purpose and then used in a programme for another purpose or used in a later or different programme, does not create an unwarranted infringement of privacy. This applies both to material obtained from others and the broadcaster's own material.

8.11 Doorstepping for factual programmes should not take place unless a request for an interview has been refused or it has not been possible to request an interview, or there is good reason to believe that an investigation will be frustrated if the subject is approached openly, and it is warranted to doorstep. However, normally broadcasters may, without prior warning interview, film or record people in the news when in public places.

(See 'practice to be followed' 8.15.)

Meaning of 'doorstepping' Doorstepping is the filming or recording of an interview or attempted interview with someone, or announcing that a call is being filmed or recorded for broadcast purposes, without any prior warning. It does not, however, include vox-pops (sampling the views of random members of the public).

8.12 Broadcasters can record telephone calls between the broadcaster and the other party if they have, from the outset of the call, identified themselves, explained the purpose of the call and that the call is being recorded for possible broadcast (if that is the case) unless it is warranted not to do one or more of these practices. If at a later stage it becomes clear that a call that has been recorded will be broadcast (but this was not explained to the other party at the time of the call) then the broadcaster must obtain consent before broadcast from the other party, unless it is warranted not to do so. (See 'practices to be followed' 7.14 and 8.13 to 8.15.)

8.13 Surreptitious filming or recording should only be used where it is warranted. Normally, it will only be warranted if:
- there is prima facie evidence of a story in the public interest; and
- there are reasonable grounds to suspect that further material evidence could be obtained; and
- it is necessary to the credibility and authenticity of the programme. (See 'practices to be followed' 7.14, 8.12, 8.14 and 8.15.)

Meaning of 'surreptitious filming or recording' Surreptitious filming or recording includes the use of long lenses or recording devices, as well as leaving an unattended camera or recording device on private property without the full and informed consent of the occupiers or their agent. It may also include recording telephone conversations without the knowledge of the other party, or deliberately continuing a recording when the other party thinks that it has come to an end.

8.14 Material gained by surreptitious filming and recording should only be broadcast when it is warranted.

(See also 'practices to be followed' 7.14 and 8.12 to 8.13 and 8.15.)

8.15 Surreptitious filming or recording, doorstepping or recorded 'wind-up' calls to obtain material for entertainment purposes may be warranted if it is intrinsic to the entertainment and does not amount to a significant infringement of privacy such as to cause significant annoyance, distress or embarrassment. The resulting material should not be broadcast without the consent of those involved. However, if the individual and/or organisation is not identifiable in the programme then consent for broadcast will not be required.

(See 'practices to be followed' 7.14 and 8.11 to 8.14.)

Suffering and distress

8.16 Broadcasters should not take or broadcast footage or audio of people caught up in emergencies, victims of accidents or those suffering a personal tragedy, even in a public place, where that results in an infringement of privacy, unless it is warranted or the people concerned have given consent.

8.17 People in a state of distress should not be put under pressure to take part in a programme or provide interviews, unless it is warranted.

8.18 Broadcasters should take care not to reveal the identity of a person who has died or of victims of accidents or violent crimes, unless and until it is clear that the next of kin have been informed of the event or unless it is warranted.

8.19 Broadcasters should try to reduce the potential distress to victims and/or relatives when making or broadcasting programmes intended to examine past events that involve trauma to individuals (including crime) unless it is warranted to do otherwise. This applies to dramatic reconstructions and factual dramas, as well as factual programmes.

In particular, so far as is reasonably practicable, surviving victims, and/or the immediate families of those whose experience is to feature in a programme, should be informed of the plans for the programme and its intended broadcast, even if the events or material to be broadcast have been in the public domain in the past.

People under sixteen and vulnerable people

8.20 Broadcasters should pay particular attention to the privacy of people under sixteen. They do not lose their rights to privacy because, for example, of the fame or notoriety of their parents or because of events in their schools.

8.21 Where a programme features an individual under sixteen or a vulnerable person in a way that infringes privacy, consent must be obtained from:
- a parent, guardian or other person of eighteen or over in loco parentis; and
- wherever possible, the individual concerned;

unless the subject matter is trivial or uncontroversial and the participation minor, or it is warranted to proceed without consent.

8.22 Persons under sixteen and vulnerable people should not be questioned about private matters without the consent of a parent, guardian or other person of eighteen or over in loco parentis (in the case of persons under sixteen), or a person with primary responsibility for their care (in the case of a vulnerable person), unless it is warranted to proceed without consent.

Meaning of 'vulnerable people'   This varies, but may include those with learning difficulties, those with mental health problems, the bereaved, people with brain damage or forms of dementia, people who have been traumatised or who are sick or terminally ill.

BBC Royal Charter for the Continuance of the British Broadcasting Corporation

(2006)

1.   Incorporation of the BBC

(1) The BBC shall continue to be a body corporate by the name of the British Broadcasting Corporation.

(2) The members of the BBC Trust and the Executive Board shall be the members of the Corporation, but membership of the Corporation shall not enable any individual to act otherwise than through the Trust or the Board to which he belongs (see article 8).

(3) Additional and technical provisions about the BBC's corporate nature and powers are contained in article 47.

2.   Term of Charter

(1) This Charter will for most practical purposes take effect as from the beginning of 1st January 2007, but that general statement must be read subject to paragraph (2).

(3) Subject to article 53, this Charter shall continue in force until the end of 31st December 2016.

3.   The BBC's public nature and its objects

(1) The BBC exists to serve the public interest.

(2) The BBC's main object is the promotion of its Public Purposes.

(3) In addition, the BBC may maintain, establish or acquire subsidiaries through which commercial activities may be undertaken to any extent permitted by a Framework Agreement. (The BBC's general powers enable it to maintain, establish or acquire subsidiaries for purposes sufficiently connected with its Public Purposes – see article 47(3) and (4)).

4.   The Public Purposes

The Public Purposes of the BBC are as follows—

      (a) sustaining citizenship and civil society;

      (b) promoting education and learning;

      (c) stimulating creativity and cultural excellence;

      (d) representing the UK, its nations, regions and communities;

      (e) bringing the UK to the world and the world to the UK;

      (f) in promoting its other purposes, helping to deliver to the public the benefit of emerging communications technologies and services and, in addition, taking a leading role in the switchover to digital television.

5.   How the BBC promotes its Public Purposes: the BBC's mission to inform, educate and entertain

(1) The BBC's main activities should be the promotion of its Public Purposes through the provision of output which consists of information, education and entertainment, supplied by means of—

(a) television, radio and online services;

(b) similar or related services which make output generally available and which may be in forms or by means of technologies which either have not previously been used by the BBC or which have yet to be developed.

(2) The BBC may also carry out other activities which directly or indirectly promote the Public Purposes, but such activities should be peripheral, subordinate or ancillary to its main activities. Overall, such peripheral, subordinate or ancillary activities of the BBC should bear a proper sense of proportion to the BBC's main activities, and each of them should be appropriate to be carried on by the BBC alongside its main activities.

(3) The means by which the BBC is, or is not, to promote its Public Purposes within the scope described in this Charter may be elaborated in a Framework Agreement (see article 49).

6.   The independence of the BBC

(1) The BBC shall be independent in all matters concerning the content of its output, the times and manner in which this is supplied, and in the management of its affairs.

(2) Paragraph (1) is subject to any provision made by or under this Charter or any Framework Agreement or otherwise by law.

Constitution

7.   Introduction

Within the BBC, there shall be a BBC Trust and an Executive Board of the BBC. These two bodies shall each play important, but different, roles within the BBC. In summary, the main roles of the Trust are in setting the overall strategic direction of the BBC, including its priorities, and in exercising a general oversight of the work of the Executive Board. The Trust will perform these roles in the public interest, particularly the interest of licence fee payers. The Executive Board has responsibility for delivering the BBC's services in accordance with the priorities set by the Trust and for all aspects of operational management, except that of the Trust's resources. Further details of the respective functions of the Trust and Executive Board are set out below and may also be addressed in a Framework Agreement.

8.   Trust and Executive Board to act separately

As described in article 1(2), the Corporation that is the BBC shall comprise all the members of the BBC Trust and the Executive Board. This reflects the importance of both the Trust and the Board, and the status and standing which their respective members are to enjoy. However, all the functions of the Corporation shall be exercised through either the Trust or the Board in accordance with the provisions set out in this Charter and any Framework Agreement. The members of the Trust and the members of the Board shall never act together as a single corporate body.

9.   Relationship between the Trust and the Executive Board

(1) The Trust must maintain its independence of the Executive Board.

(2) The Trust shall be the sovereign body within the BBC, in the sense that wherever it has a function under this Charter or any Framework Agreement, it may always fully exercise that function as it sees fit and require the Executive Board to act in ways which respect and are compatible with how the Trust has seen fit to exercise that function. In particular, where the Executive Board has operational responsibility for activities which are subject to a Trust function of approval, supervision, review or enforcement, any decision of the Trust in exercise of such a function shall be final within the BBC. (Of course, in certain areas, the activity in question may also be subject to regulation by external bodies, such as Ofcom.)

(3) However, the Trust must not exercise or seek to exercise the functions of the Executive Board.

10. The Chairman of the BBC

The Chairman of the Trust may also be known as the Chairman of the BBC. In view of article 8, this is an honorary title, as the members of the BBC will never act as a single corporate body, but only as members of the Trust or Board to which they belong.

11. Guidance and best practice

The Trust and the Executive Board, in performing their respective functions, must have regard—

    (a) to such general guidance concerning the management of the affairs of public bodies as they consider relevant and appropriate; and

    (b) to generally accepted principles of good corporate governance, but only—

        (i) where to do so would not be incompatible with sub-paragraph (a), and

        (ii) to the extent that such principles may reasonably be regarded as applicable in relation to their respective functions and within the particular constitution of the BBC as a chartered corporation.

The BBC Trust

12. Legal nature of the Trust

The word 'trust' is used in the name of the BBC Trust in a colloquial sense, to suggest a body which discharges a public trust as guardian of the public interest. The word is not used in its technical legal sense, and it is not intended to imply that the members of the Trust are to be treated as trustees of property or to be subject to the law relating to trusts or trustees.

Constitution of the Trust

13. Composition of the Trust

    (1) The Trust shall consist of a Chairman, a Vice-Chairman, and a number of ordinary members.

    (2) The number of ordinary members shall be ten (including those designated under article 14), unless a different number is fixed by Order in Council. It shall not be necessary to fix a lower number by Order in Council merely to reflect the existence of a vacancy which is intended to be filled by a further appointment in due course.

    (3) The Chairman, Vice-Chairman and ordinary members of the Trust shall be appointed by Order in Council. The selection of persons for appointment as ordinary members of the Trust shall take account of the need for designations to be made under article 14.

    (4) Whenever the office of Chairman is vacant, the Vice-Chairman shall be 'Acting Chairman' with all the powers of the Chairman until a new Chairman is appointed.

14. Trust members for the nations

    (1) Four ordinary members of the Trust shall respectively be designated—

    (a) the Trust member for England;

    (b) the Trust member for Scotland;

    (c) the Trust member for Wales; and

    (d) the Trust member for Northern Ireland.

    (2) Such designations shall be made by Order in Council. They may be made either at the same time that the person concerned is appointed to be an ordinary member of the Trust or at any time while he remains an ordinary member. A designation has effect until superseded by a fresh designation or until the designated person ceases to be a member of the Trust.

    (3) Each person to be designated under this article shall be suitably qualified by virtue of—

    (a) his knowledge of the culture, characteristics and affairs of the people in the nation for which he is to be designated, and

    (b) his close touch with opinion in that nation.

    (4) For the purposes of this article, 'England' includes the Channel Islands and the Isle of Man and references to 'nation' shall be interpreted accordingly.

15. Length of terms

(1) The Order in Council which appoints a Chairman, Vice-Chairman or ordinary member of the Trust shall specify the period for which he is being appointed. No period longer than five years may be specified.

(2) A serving Chairman, Vice-Chairman or ordinary member may at any time be re-appointed by Order in Council for any further period specified in the Order. Such a further period may not be longer than five years. This power may be exercised with effect from a date other than that on which the previous term would have expired.

16. Termination of office

A member of the Trust (whether Chairman, Vice-Chairman or ordinary member) shall cease to hold his office—

    (a) on the expiration of the period for which he had most recently been appointed (see article 15);

    (b) if he resigns by written notice to the Secretary of State;

    (c) if his appointment is terminated by Order in Council;

    (d) if—

        (i) he becomes bankrupt,

        (ii) his estate is sequestrated

        (iii) he grants a trust deed for his creditors, or

        (iv) he makes any arrangement or composition with his creditors generally;

    (e) if he is, or may be, suffering from mental disorder and either—

        (i) he is admitted to hospital in pursuance of an application for admission for treatment under the Mental Health Act 1983 or, in Scotland, an application for authorisation for detention in hospital under the Mental Health (Care and Treatment) (Scotland) Act 2003, or

        (ii) an order is made by a court having jurisdiction (whether in Our United Kingdom or elsewhere) in matters concerning mental disorder for his detention or for the appointment of a receiver, curator bonis, or other person to exercise powers with respect to his property or affairs; or

    (f) if—

        (i) he fails to attend meetings of the Trust continuously for three months or longer without the consent of the Trust, and

        (ii) the Trust resolves that his office be vacated.

Role of the Trust

22. Guardians of the licence fee and the public interest

The Trust is the guardian of the licence fee revenue and the public interest in the BBC. The Trust has the ultimate responsibility, subject to the provisions of this Charter, for—

    (a) the BBC's stewardship of the licence fee revenue and its other resources;

    (b) upholding the public interest within the BBC, particularly the interests of licence fee payers; and

    (c) securing the effective promotion of the Public Purposes.

23. General duties

In exercising all its functions, the Trust must act in the public interest and, in particular, it must—

    (a) represent the interests of licence fee payers;

    (b) secure that the independence of the BBC is maintained;

    (c) carefully and appropriately assess the views of licence fee payers;

    (d) exercise rigorous stewardship of public money;

    (e) have regard to the competitive impact of the BBC's activities on the wider market; and

    (f) ensure that the BBC observes high standards of openness and transparency.

24. Functions of the Trust

(1) The Trust has the general function of—

(a) setting the overall strategic direction for the BBC within the framework set by this Charter and any Framework Agreement;

(b) approving high-level strategy and budgets in respect of the BBC's services and activities in the UK and overseas; and

(c) assessing the performance of the Executive Board in delivering the BBC's services and activities and holding the Executive Board to account for its performance.

(2) In particular, the Trust has the following specific functions—

(a) setting multi-year purpose remits, and approving strategies which include high-level budgetary allocations;

(b) defining suitable performance criteria and measures against which the effective promotion of the Public Purposes will be judged;

(c) issuing service licences for BBC services and monitoring compliance with them;

(d) approving guidelines designed to secure appropriate standards in the content of the BBC's services;

(e) approving individual strategic or financial proposals where they stand to have significant implications for the fulfilment of the purpose remits and strategies referred to in sub-paragraph (a) or for the overall financial position of the BBC;

(f) discharging the regulatory functions accorded to the Trust and holding the Executive Board to account for the BBC's compliance with applicable regulatory requirements and the general law;

(g) setting the framework within which the BBC should handle complaints (and the framework must provide for the Trust to play a role as final arbiter in appropriate cases);

(h) where appropriate, conducting investigations into any activity of the BBC which it has grounds to suspect does not comply with requirements supervised by the Trust;

(i) commissioning value for money investigations into specific areas of BBC activity;

(j) ensuring the Executive Board addresses key operating risks for the BBC;

(k) adopting a statement of policy on fair trading and holding the Executive Board to account for compliance with it;

(l) setting an approvals framework within which the Trust will assess proposals from the Executive Board for new services, significant changes to existing services, commercial services and other activities; and

(m) ensuring that arrangements for the collection of the licence fee are efficient, appropriate and proportionate.

(3) The Trust shall play an executive role in relation to the Trust Unit (see articles 42 and 43).

(4) In addition, the Trust has all the functions expressly or impliedly conferred upon it elsewhere by or under this Charter or any Framework Agreement.

25. Protocols—their general role

The Trust must adopt and publish Protocols which—

(a) set out a detailed framework within which the Trust will (consistently with all specific requirements of this Charter or any Framework Agreement) discharge its functions, which may address the practical application of its functions and impose upon the Trust more specific obligations within the scope of its functions;

(b) address in greater detail the relationship between the Trust and the Executive Board, and what the division between their respective functions will mean in practice (which may include allocating as between the Trust and the Executive Board responsibility for anything which is not allocated by the Charter or any Framework Agreement).

26. Protocols on engaging with licence fee payers

(1) Protocols must (as an aspect of how the Trust will discharge its general duty under article 23(c) carefully and appropriately to assess the views of licence fee payers) make provision in appropriate detail—

(a) requiring the Trust actively to seek the views of, and engage with, licence fee payers, and

(b) setting out how the Trust will do so.

(2) The Trust must consult publicly before adopting any Protocol pursuant to this article.

27. Protocols on openness and transparency

(1) Protocols must (as an aspect of how the Trust will discharge its general duty under article 23(f) to ensure that the BBC observes high standards of openness and transparency) make provision in appropriate detail requiring the Trust to ensure, and setting out how it will ensure, as far as is reasonable, that the principal points of its proceedings and the reasons and key considerations behind important decisions (including decisions on proposals submitted by the Executive Board for the Trust's approval) are made public.

(2) This article imposes obligations which are separate from, and are not intended to detract from, any other requirements which apply to the Trust or the BBC, whether imposed by more specific provisions in this Charter, any Framework Agreement or otherwise. Nor do they imply that Protocols need not address other aspects of the Trust's general duty under article 23(f).

The Executive Board

Constitution of the Executive Board

28. Composition of the Executive Board

(1) The Executive Board shall consist of executive and non-executive members.

(2) Subject to the overarching requirements of paragraph (3), the total number of Board members, and the respective numbers of executive and non-executive members, shall, so far as practicable, be as determined by the Executive Board with the approval of the Trust.

(3) So far as practicable—

(a) there must always be at least four non-executive members, and

(b) the total number of non-executive members must never fall below one third nor be equal to or exceed one half of the total membership of the Board.

(4) In paragraphs (2) and (3), we say 'so far as practicable' to recognise the fact that sometimes a member might cease to hold office suddenly or at short notice (such as through death or resignation) and that it may take some time before a replacement can be appointed. As long as he is replaced as soon as is practicable, it does not matter that the composition of the Board deviates from the norm in the meanwhile.

Role of the Executive Board

38. Functions of the Executive Board

(1) The Executive Board is the executive body of the BBC and is responsible for—

(a) the delivery of the BBC's services in accordance with the priorities set by purpose remits and the framework set by service licences and any other strategies;

(b) the direction of the BBC's editorial and creative output;

(c) the operational management of the BBC (except the BBC Trust Unit);

(d) ensuring compliance with all legal and regulatory requirements placed upon the BBC (including the initial handling of complaints about the BBC) except to the extent that they relate to the affairs of the Trust or the BBC Trust Unit;

(e) ensuring compliance with requirements placed upon the Executive Board by the Trust (for example, through Protocols or the Trust's statement of policy on fair trading);

(f) making proposals to the Trust for anything which is for the Trust to approve under article 24(2)(a), (d) or (e);

(g) appointing, and holding to account, the management of the BBC and its subsidiaries;

(h) the conduct of the BBC's operational financial affairs (except those relating directly to the affairs of the Trust and the BBC Trust Unit) in a manner best designed to ensure value for money; and

(i) accounting to the Trust for its own performance and the performance of the BBC and its subsidiaries.

(2) In addition, the Executive Board has all the functions expressly or impliedly conferred upon it elsewhere by or under this Charter or any Framework Agreement.

(3) In the exercise of its functions, the Executive Board shall be subject to the Trust as set out in article 9.

Audience Councils

39. Audience Councils

(1) There shall be Audience Councils the purpose of which is to bring the diverse perspectives of licence fee payers to bear on the work of the Trust, through the Councils' links with diverse communities, including geographically-based communities and other communities of interest, within the UK.

(2) The Councils must use their engagement with and understanding of communities to advise the Trust on how well the BBC is promoting its Public Purposes from the perspective of licence fee payers, and serving licence fee payers, in different parts of the UK.

(3) There shall be four Councils, corresponding in geographical remit to the four nations for which Trust members are designated under article 14. Each Council shall be chaired by the designated Trust member for the nation concerned.

(4) In addition, there must be mechanisms for bringing together members from different Councils to consider how well the BBC is serving audiences in promoting the Public Purposes.

(5) The network of members across the four Councils must be recruited to ensure that they reflect the diversity of the UK, have connections with communities, and are able to take a view on how the Public Purposes should be promoted.

(6) The Councils have the following remit—

(a) to engage with licence fee payers including geographically-based communities and other communities of interest;

(b) to be consulted on all relevant proposals that are required to be subject to a Public Value Test by virtue of any Framework Agreement;

(c) to be consulted, as part of any review of service licences which the Trust undertakes in accordance with the requirements of any Framework Agreement, on the content of the service licences and the performance of the services to which the review relates;

(d) to be consulted on the BBC's performance in promoting the Public Purposes;

(e) to submit a report to the Trust each year on the BBC's performance in each nation and advise on issues arising; and

40. The Director General

(1) There shall be a Director General of the BBC.

(2) The Director General shall be the chief executive officer of the BBC. He shall be an executive member of the Executive Board and may be its chairman (see article 29).

(3) The Director General shall also be the editor-in-chief of the BBC. As such, he shall be accountable for the BBC's editorial and creative output.

(4) Where a vacancy is to be filled in the office of Director General and the Trust has determined that the person to be appointed shall also serve as the Chairman of the Executive Board in an executive capacity, the Director General shall be appointed, hold and vacate office in accordance with articles 29 and 32.

(5) In other circumstances, the Director General is appointed in accordance with article 30 and holds and vacates office in accordance with article 33.

49. Framework Agreements

(1) A 'Framework Agreement' is an agreement between the BBC and the Secretary of State which contains a statement to the effect that it is a Framework Agreement made for BBC Charter purposes.

[. . .]

(3) Framework Agreements may in principle impose obligations on the BBC in relation to particular topics which are addressed in this Charter, as well as in relation to topics which are not. A Framework Agreement may, for example, impose more detailed requirements. For example, article 24(2)(i) imposes a general requirement which is elaborated in clause 79 of the Agreement made on 30th June 2006. However, a Framework Agreement must be consistent with this Charter and, in the event of any contradiction, the terms of this Charter shall prevail. It is hereby declared that the content of the Framework Agreement as made on 30th June 2006 (mentioned in paragraph (2)) is fully compatible with the intentions of this Charter.

(4) The BBC must comply with any Framework Agreement, for so long as it is in force (see article 52).

(5) Whether the BBC should make any particular Framework Agreement with the Secretary of State is a matter to be decided by the Trust.

52. Compliance with Charter and Framework Agreements

(1) The BBC shall strictly and faithfully comply with this Charter and any Framework Agreement in force. This includes complying with requirements set out in other documents which have effect by virtue of provisions of this Charter or a Framework Agreement.

(2) Where the BBC fails to comply with paragraph (1) of this article in any respect, anyone who is aggrieved and/or adversely affected may be entitled to seek an appropriate remedy.

(3) Complaints to the BBC have an important role to play. The BBC's complaints handling framework (including appeals to the Trust) is intended to provide appropriate, proportionate and cost effective methods of securing that the BBC complies with its obligations and that remedies are provided which are proportionate and related to any alleged non-compliance.

(4) Complaints can sometimes also be made to other bodies with regulatory and law enforcement powers such as Ofcom and the Office of Fair Trading.

(5) The courts may have an appropriate role to play in exercising judicial review according to normal principles of public law.

(6) This article does not seek to exclude any other remedy which may be available but, so far as relevant, it is the intention of this Charter that remedies should be appropriate and proportionate to the issues at stake.

BBC Licence Agreement

(June 2010 as amended)

2. Status of this Agreement as a 'Framework Agreement'
for BBC Charter Purposes

This is a Framework Agreement for BBC Charter purposes. The significance of this is explained in the Charter (see in particular article 49)

4. The Independence of the BBC

The parties to this Agreement affirm their commitment to the independence of the BBC as stated in article 6 of the Charter. By entering into this Agreement, the BBC has voluntarily assumed obligations which restrict, to some extent, its future freedom of action.

The BBC's Public Purposes

5. Purpose remits

(1) Purpose remits set by the Trust under article 24(2)(a) of the Charter must comply with the requirements of this clause.

(2) There shall be a separate purpose remit for each of the six Public Purposes.

(3) Each remit must—

    (a) set out priorities, and

    (b) specify how the BBC's performance against them will be judged, in relation to how the BBC promotes its Public Purposes in accordance with article 5 of the Charter (the BBC's mission to inform, educate and entertain).

(4) The Trust must consult publicly in developing purpose remits.

(5) Once purpose remits have been adopted, the Trust must keep them under review and may amend them. Before an amendment is made, there must be a process of public consultation appropriate to the nature of the proposed change. For example, any substantial change to the priorities set within a purpose must be subject to a particularly thorough process of full consultation.

6. Sustaining citizenship and civil society

(1) In developing (and reviewing) the purpose remit for sustaining citizenship and civil society, the Trust must, amongst other things, seek to ensure that the BBC gives information about, and increases understanding of, the world through accurate and impartial news, other information, and analysis of current events and ideas.

(2) In doing so, the Trust must have regard amongst other things to—

    (a) the need to promote understanding of the UK political system (including Parliament and the devolved structures), including through dedicated coverage of Parliamentary matters, and the need for the purpose remit to require that the BBC transmits an impartial account day by day of the proceedings in both Houses of Parliament;

    (b) the need to promote media literacy; and

    (c) the importance of sustaining citizenship through the enrichment of the public realm.

7. Promoting education and learning

In developing (and reviewing) the purpose remit for promoting education and learning, the Trust must, amongst other things, seek to ensure that the BBC—

    (a) stimulates interest in, and knowledge of, a full range of subjects and issues through content that is accessible and can encourage either formal or informal learning; and

    (b) provides specialist educational content and accompanying material to facilitate learning at all levels and for all ages.

8. Stimulating creativity and cultural excellence

(1) In developing (and reviewing) the purpose remit for stimulating creativity and cultural excellence, the Trust must, amongst other things, seek to ensure that the BBC—

    (a) enriches the cultural life of the UK through creative excellence in distinctive and original content;

    (b) fosters creativity and nurtures talent; and

    (c) promotes interest, engagement and participation in cultural activity among new audiences.

(2) In doing so, the Trust must have regard amongst other things to—

    (a) the need for the BBC to have a film strategy; and

    (b) the need for appropriate coverage of sport, including sport of minority interest.

9. Representing the UK, its nations, regions and communities

(1) In developing (and reviewing) the purpose remit for representing the UK, its nations, regions and communities, the Trust must, amongst other things, seek to ensure that the BBC—

    (a) reflects and strengthens cultural identities through original content at local, regional and national level, on occasion bringing audiences together for shared experiences; and

    (b) promotes awareness of different cultures and alternative viewpoints, through content that reflects the lives of different people and different communities within the UK.

(2) In doing so, the Trust must have regard amongst other things to—

    (a) the importance of reflecting different religious and other beliefs; and

    (b) the importance of appropriate provision in minority languages.

10. Bringing the UK to the world and the world to the UK

In developing (and reviewing) the purpose remit for bringing the UK to the world and the world to the UK, the Trust must, amongst other things, seek to ensure that the BBC—

(a) makes people in the UK aware of international issues and of the different cultures and viewpoints of people living outside the UK through news and current affairs and other outputs such as drama, comedy, documentaries, educational output and sports coverage; and

(b) brings high-quality international news coverage to international audiences.

14. UK Public Service content characteristics

(1) The content of the UK Public Services taken as a whole must be high quality, challenging, original, innovative and engaging.

(2) Every programme included in the UK Public Broadcasting Services must exhibit at least one of those characteristics. In relation to other UK Public Services, each item of content must exhibit at least one of those characteristics.

15. The purposes of public service television

In performing its functions in relation to the UK Public Television Services, the Trust shall have regard to the purposes of public service television broadcasting set out in section 264(4) of the Communications Act 2003 and the desirability of those purposes being fulfilled in a manner that is compatible with section 264(6) of that Act.

Changes to the BBC's UK Public Services

23. Introduction

(1) During the lifetime of the Charter, the BBC will need to be able to modify its UK Public Services—for example, to respond to changes in technology, culture, market conditions, public expectations and views, etc.

(2) However, any significant proposal for change must be subject to full and public scrutiny.

The means by which this scrutiny will be brought about will be the Public Value Test. Clauses 24 to 31 below explain the Public Value Test and clause 33 explains the role of the Secretary of State.

24. The Public Value Test

(1) The Public Value Test is a means by which public value and market impact are taken into account.

(2) Clause 25 explains when the Public Value Test must be applied and clauses 26 to 31 explain what must happen when the Test is applied.

25. When the Public Value Test must be applied

(1) The Public Value Test must be applied before a decision is taken to make any significant change to the UK Public Services (which can include introducing a new service or discontinuing a service).

(2) Whether any proposals for change meet this criterion of significance is a matter for the judgment of the Trust. In exercising that judgment, the Trust must have regard to the following considerations (and to the presumption explained in paragraphs (3) and (4))—

(a) impact—the extent to which the change is likely to affect relevant users and others;

(b) the financial implications of the change;

(c) novelty—the extent to which the change would involve the BBC in a new area of activity for the BBC, as yet untested;

(d) duration—how long the activity will last.

(3) The Trust should presume that any change which requires a new service licence or any amendment of the key characteristics described as such in a service licence ought to be subject to a Public Value Test. Where this presumption applies, the Trust may still decide that there is no need for the Public Value Test to be applied, but in that case the onus is on the Trust to justify departing from the presumption. For example, the Trust may be satisfied that changes in circumstances since the

issue of a relevant existing service licence mean that a particular change to the key characteristics set out in the licence would not, contrary to what had been anticipated at the time, meet the criterion for a Public Value Test.

(4) Before exercising its judgment under this clause, the Trust must investigate or otherwise inform itself of any facts or considerations which it considers potentially relevant to the exercise of that judgment. What this means in practice will vary according to the circumstances. Sometimes, for example, the proposed change may be so manifestly significant that the Trust will not need to look beyond the nature of the proposed change itself before concluding that it would be a significant change. In other cases, which are less clear cut, the Trust may feel it appropriate to investigate more thoroughly competing arguments for and against the application of the Public Value Test.

26.   How the Public Value Test is applied

(1) The application of the Public Value Test involves several elements.

(2) The first is a public value assessment (see clause 28).

(3) The second is a market impact assessment (see clause 30).

(4) The Trust must consider the outcome of the public value assessment and the market impact assessment and reach provisional conclusions regarding the proposed change.

(5) Those assessments must be published.

(6) The Trust must consult about its provisional conclusions reached under paragraph (4) and then proceed to reach a final conclusion about whether the proposed change should be made. In particular, the Trust must be satisfied that any likely adverse impact on the market is justified by the likely public value of the change before concluding that the proposed change should be made.

27.   Time limits on Public Value Tests

(1) A Public Value Test must be completed within six months of the date on which the Trust determines that it is to be applied.

(2) At its discretion, where justified by the circumstances, the Trust may allow a longer period.

28.   Public value assessments

(1) The purpose of a public value assessment is to ascertain the likely public value of the proposed change.

(2) In general terms, a public value assessment should include an assessment of the following factors—

   (a) the value which licence fee payers would place on the proposed change as individuals;
   (b) the value which the proposed change would deliver to society as a whole through its contribution to the BBC's Public Purposes, but having regard to article 5 of the Charter and the contribution of the proposed change to the priorities set out in the BBC's purpose remits;
   (c) the value for money of the proposed change and its cost (including the potential financial implications if the proposed change were not to be made).

(3) As the nature of likely or potential public value may differ widely according to the nature of the change proposed, the Trust must at the outset consider very carefully—

   (a) the aspects of public value which may be relevant; and
   (b) how those aspects should be explored and evaluated (but always including public consultation).

(4) In this context, the concept of 'public value' means the public value of the change bearing in mind that the service or activities concerned involve the BBC, and the need for the BBC to comply with all applicable restrictions (for example, those in article 5(2) of the Charter).

29.   Joint Steering Group

(1) In respect of market impact assessments, the Trust and Ofcom must together establish a Joint Steering Group.

(2) The Trust and Ofcom must jointly make arrangements for the operation and constitution of the Group that are based on the principle of an equality of status and participation as between the Trust and Ofcom, and those arrangements must, in particular, provide that—

(a) the Group's membership must consist of an equal number of members drawn from the Trust and Ofcom respectively, but may also include some independent members;

(b) both the Trust and Ofcom are to have an equality of opportunities to appoint the Group's chairman from amongst the membership of the Group;

(c) accordingly, each successive market impact assessment is to be overseen by the Group under the chairmanship of an appointee of the Trust or (as the case may require) an appointee of Ofcom on an alternating basis, unless otherwise agreed; and

(d) the chairman is not to have a casting vote.

(3) Subject to sub-paragraph (2), the precise composition of the Group is to be agreed between the Trust and Ofcom.

(4) Where a Public Value Test is applied, the Trust must inform the Group of the need for a market impact assessment. The Group must then set and publish the terms of reference for the market impact assessment. The terms of reference may specify how the methodology set under clause 30 is to be applied.

(5) The Group will be responsible for agreeing the potential relevant markets for the assessment after considering advice from Ofcom. Where there are a number of potential markets identified by the Group, the market impact assessment shall report on each potential market in the absence of agreement to do otherwise.

(6) The Group will also be responsible for ensuring that the market impact assessment is conducted in a manner appropriate to the nature of the Public Value Test and to a suitable schedule.

(7) The Trust and Ofcom must make suitable arrangements for working together to ensure that market impact assessments are conducted in a timely manner.

(8) If, in respect of any matter arising under this clause, the Group is unable to reach agreement on suitable arrangements or their implementation, the matters in dispute may be referred to the Chairman of the Trust and the Chairman of Ofcom for resolution by them jointly (but this does not apply in the case of the matters mentioned in sub-paragraphs (2)(c) and (5), which make specific provision for the position in the absence of agreement to the contrary).

43.   Content standards

(1) The Trust must approve guidelines designed to secure appropriate standards in the content of the UK Public Services.

(2) The more specific obligations set out below are not intended to restrict the general scope of paragraph (1).

44.   Accuracy and impartiality

(1) The BBC must do all it can to ensure that controversial subjects are treated with due accuracy and impartiality in all relevant output.

(2) In applying paragraph (1), a series of programmes may be considered as a whole.

(3) The UK Public Services must not contain any output which expresses the opinion of the BBC or of its Trust or Executive Board on current affairs or matters of public policy other than broadcasting or the provision of online services.

(4) Paragraph (3) does not apply to output which consists of—

(a) proceedings in either House of Parliament;

(b) proceedings in the Scottish Parliament, the Welsh Assembly or the Northern Ireland Assembly; or

(c) proceedings of a local authority or a committee of two or more local authorities.

(5) The Trust must—

(a) draw up and from time to time review a code giving guidance as to the rules to be observed in connection with the application of paragraphs (1) to (4), and

(b) do all it can to secure that the code is complied with.

(6) The rules in the code must, in particular, take account of the following matters —

    (a) that due impartiality should be preserved by the BBC as respects major matters falling within paragraph (b) of the definition of 'relevant output' (in paragraph (8)) as well as matters falling within it taken as a whole; and

    (b) the need to determine what constitutes a series of programmes for the purposes of paragraph (2).

(7) The rules must, in addition, indicate to such extent as the Trust considers appropriate—

    (a) what due impartiality does and does not require, either generally or in relation to particular circumstances;

    (b) the ways in which due impartiality may be achieved in connection with programmes of particular descriptions;

    (c) the period within which a programme should be included in a service if its inclusion is intended to secure that due impartiality is achieved for the purposes of paragraph (1) in connection with that programme and any programme previously included in that service taken together; and

    (d) in relation to any inclusion in a service of a series of programmes which is of a description specified in the rules—

        (i) that the dates and times of the other programmes comprised in the series should be announced at the time when the first programme so comprised is included in that service, or

        (ii) if that is not practicable, that advance notice should be given by other means of subsequent programmes so comprised which include material intended to secure, or assist in securing, that due impartiality is achieved in connection with the series as a whole; and the rules must, in particular, indicate that due impartiality does not require absolute neutrality on every issue or detachment from fundamental democratic principles.

(8) For the purposes of this clause—

'relevant output' means the output of any UK Public Service which—

    (a) consists of news, or

    (b) deals with matters of public policy or of political or industrial controversy;

'programme', except in paragraph (7) and (d), includes any item of output in non-programme form; and

'series of programmes', except in paragraph (7) includes items of output in non-programme form which are analogously linked.

45. The Fairness Code

(1) The BBC must comply with the Fairness Code—

    (a) in connection with the provision of the UK Public Broadcasting Services, and

    (b) in relation to the programmes included in those services.

(2) 'The Fairness Code' means the code for the time being in force under section 107 of the Broadcasting Act 1996.

46. Programme Code Standards

(1) The BBC must observe Relevant Programme Code Standards in the provision of the UK Public Broadcasting Services.

(2) 'Relevant Programme Code Standards' means those standards for the time being set under section 319 of the Communications Act 2003—

    (a) which relate to the objectives set out in the following paragraphs of subsection (2) of that section, that is to say—

        (i) paragraph (a) (protection of persons under the age of eighteen);

        (ii) paragraph (b) (omission of material likely to encourage or incite any crime or disorder);

        (iii) paragraph (e) (exercise of responsibility with respect to the content of religious programmes);

(iv) paragraph (f) (application of generally accepted standards so as to provide adequate protection for members of the public from the inclusion of offensive and harmful material);

(iva) paragraph (fa) (product placement requirements in section 321(3A)); and

(v) paragraph (l) (refraining from use of techniques which exploit the possibility of conveying a message to viewers or listeners, or of otherwise influencing their minds, without their being aware, or fully aware, of what has occurred), but

(b) only to the extent that they do not concern the accuracy or impartiality of the content of any programme included in the UK Public Broadcasting Services.

47. News and current affairs

(1) The Trust must impose on the Executive Board the requirements it considers appropriate for securing—

(a) that, in relation to BBC One, news programmes are broadcast for viewing at intervals throughout the period for which the service is provided;

(b) that, in each year, the time allocated to the broadcasting of news programmes included in BBC One constitutes no less than what appears to the Trust to be an appropriate amount of time;

(c) that the time allocated to the broadcasting of news programmes included in BBC One is split in what appears to the Trust to be an appropriate manner between peak viewing times and other times;

(d) that, in each year, the time allocated to the broadcasting of current affairs programmes included in BBC One and BBC Two taken together constitutes no less than what appears to the Trust to be an appropriate amount of time;

(e) that the time allocated to the broadcasting of current affairs programmes included in BBC One and BBC Two taken together is split in what appears to the Trust to be an appropriate manner between peak viewing times and other times.

(2) Before imposing any requirements under paragraph (1), the Trust must consult Ofcom on its proposals for such requirements, and shall have regard to any comments made by Ofcom upon those proposals.

(3) Subject to paragraphs (4) and (5), the Trust must not, without first securing the agreement of Ofcom, impose requirements the effect of which would be to allow any of the following—

(a) the hours of news programmes included, in any year, in BBC One,

(b) the hours of news programmes included, in any year, in BBC One which are broadcast at peak viewing times,

(c) the hours of current affairs programmes included, in any year, in BBC One and BBC Two taken together,

(d) the hours of current affairs programmes included, in any year, in BBC One and BBC Two taken together which are broadcast at peak viewing times, to fall, respectively, below the number of hours which were included in each such category in the year 2002.

(4) A figure must be agreed to represent the number of hours which were included, in the year 2002, in each of the categories set out in sub-paragraphs (a) to (d) of paragraph (3) respectively, and that figure shall, subject to paragraph (5), be used for the purposes of paragraph (3).

(5) Where the agreed meaning of 'year' for the purposes of this clause includes any period which is longer or shorter than the year 2002, it must be agreed whether, and if so in what respect, the figures agreed under paragraph (4) shall be subject to any adjustment for the purpose of enabling them to relate fairly to any such period.

(6) For the purposes of this clause—'agreed' means agreed in accordance with clause 92; the meaning of 'current affairs' must be agreed; the meaning of 'news' must be agreed; 'peak viewing time', in relation to a service, means a time agreed to be, or to be likely to be, a peak viewing time for that service; and the meaning of 'year' must be agreed.

48. Party political broadcasts

(1) The BBC must include, in some or all of the UK Public Broadcasting Services, party political broadcasts and referendum campaign broadcasts.

(2) The Trust must determine—

(a) which of the UK Public Broadcasting Services are in principle to include party political broadcasts and referendum campaign broadcasts; and

(b) the basis on which, and the terms and conditions subject to which, such broadcasts are to be included in them.

(3) In particular, the Trust may determine, so far as they are permitted so to do by sections 37 and 127 of the Political Parties, Elections and Referendums Act 2000 (only registered parties and designated organisations to be entitled to party political broadcasts or referendum campaign broadcasts)—

(a) the political parties on whose behalf party political broadcasts may be made; and

(b) the length and frequency of party political broadcasts and referendum campaign broadcasts.

(4) In this clause, 'referendum campaign broadcast' has the meaning given by section 127 of the Political Parties, Elections and Referendums Act 2000.

49. Programming quotas for original productions

(1) In relation to each of the UK Public Television Services, the BBC must comply with agreed arrangements for securing—

(a) that the time allocated, in each year, to the broadcasting of original productions included in that service is no less than what appears to the parties to be an appropriate proportion of the total amount of time allocated to the broadcasting of all the programmes included in the service; and

(b) that the time allocated to the broadcasting of original productions is split in what appears to the parties to be an appropriate manner between peak viewing times and other times.

(2) The proportion determined by the parties for the purposes of paragraph (1) above—

(a) shall, in the case of each service, be such proportion as the parties consider appropriate for ensuring that the service is consistently of a high quality; and

(b) may, for the purposes of paragraph (1)(b), be expressed as the cumulative effect of two different minimum proportions, one applying to peak viewing times and the other to other times.

(3) The agreed arrangements may provide—

(a) that specified descriptions of programmes are to be excluded in determining the programmes a proportion of which is to consist of original productions;

(b) that, in determining for the purposes of the arrangements whether a programme is of a description of programmes excluded by virtue of sub-paragraph (a) of this paragraph, regard is to be had to any guidance prepared and published, and revised, by Ofcom.

(4) This clause must be interpreted in accordance with, and have effect subject to, clause 92, which explains such things as 'agreed' and 'the parties', and how the process of reaching agreement should work.

(5) For the purposes of this clause—

'original productions', in relation to the UK Public Television Services taken together, has the same meaning that is specified by order under section 278(6) of the Communications Act 2003 (programming quotas for original productions in relation to licensed public service channels) in relation to a licensed public service channel, except that—

(a) to any extent that such an order makes different provision for different cases, the agreed arrangements must determine which of those cases shall be taken to be relevant for the purposes of this clause; and

(b) to any extent that such an order makes provision in terms which are not apt to apply for the purposes of this clause, the agreed arrangements must determine whether, and if so what, necessary modifications are to be made so that such provision may apply, as analogously as practicable, for those purposes;

'peak viewing time', in relation to a service, means a time agreed to be, or to be likely to be, a peak viewing time for that service; and the meaning of 'year' must be agreed.

50. Programming for the nations and regions

(1) The Trust must impose on the Executive Board the requirements it considers appropriate for securing—

    (a) that what appears to the Trust to be a sufficient amount of time is given in the programmes included in the Relevant Services to what appears to it to be a suitable range of programmes (including, in the case of BBC One, regional news programmes) which are of regional interest;

    (b) that the regional programmes included in the Relevant Services are of high quality;

    (c) that what appears to the Trust to be a suitable proportion of the regional programmes included in the Relevant Services consists of programmes made in the relevant area;

    (d) that the regional news programmes included in BBC One are broadcast for viewing at intervals throughout the period for which the service is provided and, in particular, at peak viewing times; and

    (e) that what appears to the Trust to be a suitable number of the hours of regional programmes that—

        (i) are included in the relevant services, and

        (ii) are not regional news programmes included in BBC One, are broadcast for viewing—

            (i) at times which are peak viewing times in relation to any particular service in which they are in fact included; and

            (ii) at times immediately preceding or following those times.

(2) Before imposing any requirements under paragraph (1), the Trust must consult Ofcom on its proposals for such requirements, and must have regard to any comments made by Ofcom upon those proposals.

(3) Subject to paragraphs (4) and (5), the Trust must not, without first securing the agreement of Ofcom, impose requirements the effect of which would be to allow any of the following—

    (a) the hours of regional programmes included, in any year, in the Relevant Services,

    (b) the proportion of regional programmes included, in any year, in the Relevant Services which consist of programmes made in the relevant area,

    (c) the hours of regional news programmes included, in any year, in BBC One,

    (d) in relation to any year, the number of hours mentioned in paragraph (1)(e),

to fall, respectively, below the number of hours or, as the case may be, the proportion of programmes, which were included in each such category in the year 2002.

(4) A figure must be agreed to represent the number of hours or, as the case may be, the proportion of programmes which were included, in the year 2002, in each of the categories set out in sub-paragraphs (a) to (d) of paragraph (3) respectively, and that figure shall, subject to paragraph (5), be used for the purposes of paragraph (3).

(5) Where the agreed meaning of 'year' for the purposes of this clause includes any period which is longer or shorter than the year 2002, it must be agreed whether, and if so in what respect, the figures agreed under paragraph (4) shall be subject to any adjustment for the purpose of enabling them to relate fairly to any such period.

(6) For the purposes of this clause, a programme is of regional interest if—

    (a) it is of particular interest to persons living in any one of the following nations or regions—

        (i) Northern Ireland,

        (ii) Scotland,

        (iii) Wales,

        (iv) any region of England in relation to which there is a regional variation of the television service concerned; and

    (b) it is included in the variation of the service that relates to that nation or region.

(7) For the purposes of this clause—

'agreed' means agreed in accordance with clause 92;

'particular service' means any of the services which, together, form the Relevant Services;

'peak viewing time', in relation to a service, means a time agreed to be, or to be likely to be, a peak viewing time for that service;

'regional programme', in relation to BBC One or the Relevant Services, means a programme included in BBC One or, as the case may be, the Relevant Services, with a view to its being of regional interest, and 'regional news programmes' is to be interpreted accordingly;

'the relevant area', in relation to regional programmes, means the nation or region in relation to which those programmes are to be of regional interest;

'the Relevant Services' means BBC One and BBC Two, taken together; and the meaning of 'year' must be agreed.

Welsh Language Services

63A   Partnership and funding model for S4C Services

(1) From 1st April 2013 the provision of the S4C Services shall be organised and funded as a partnership between the BBC and S4C under arrangements that accord with the principles relating to the future of those Services contained in the Secretary of State's letter to the Chairman of the BBC dated 21st October 2010 ('the settlement letter').

(3) The arrangements must also contain—

(a) governance arrangements agreed between the BBC and the Secretary of State in a Framework Agreement to amend further this Agreement; and

(b) operational arrangements agreed (subsequent to the governance arrangements) between the BBC and S4C.

68.   Commercial services to be organisationally separate from the 'core' BBC

(1) The BBC as a corporation shall not directly provide any commercial services, but it may carry out other trading activities.

(2) Any commercial services must be provided through one or more commercial subsidiaries.

69.   The criteria for commercial services etc.

(1) Subject to paragraph (2), all of the BBC's commercial services must meet all the following criteria—

(a) they must fit with the BBC's Public Purpose activities (in the manner defined by paragraph (3));

(b) they must exhibit commercial efficiency;

(c) they must not jeopardise the good reputation of the BBC or the value of the BBC brand;

(d) they must comply with fair trading guidelines in force under clause 67(1)(a) and in particular avoid distorting the market.

(2) Where the commercial service consists of participation in a joint venture or other form of commercial partnership with a person or body other than the BBC or a subsidiary within the BBC's commercial arm (see the definition of 'commercial service' in clause 101 below), the BBC must use its best endeavours to ensure—

(a) that the participation complies with paragraph (1) and

(b) that any services provided, or activities undertaken, by way of or through the venture or partnership meet the criteria set out in sub-paragraphs (1)(a) to (d).

(3) A commercial service is to be considered to fit with the BBC's Public Purpose activities if—

(a) it is appropriate to be carried on in association with the promotion of the Public Purposes (albeit through the separate framework required by clause 68); and

(b) it is connected, otherwise than merely in financial terms, with the ways in which the BBC promotes its Public Purposes.

(4) A commercial service does not cease to be considered to fit with the BBC's Public Purposes just because the service includes activities which in themselves do not meet the requirements of

paragraph (3), provided such activities are peripheral, subordinate or ancillary to other activities that do meet those requirements.

(5) The application of these criteria is a matter of judgment for the Trust. The Trust must hold the BBC's Executive Board to account for ensuring that the BBC's commercial services are operated in a way which complies with these criteria.

79. Value for Money

(3) The subject-matter of [National Audit Office] reviews shall be determined by the Comptroller and Auditor General ('CAG'); and accordingly, each year, the CAG shall send the Trust a written list of the value for money reviews the CAG has decided the NAO should conduct in the following calendar year and indicate in the list when each review is expected to be conducted (but subject to paragraphs (4) to (7)).

(16) Nothing in this clause entitles the CAG to question the merits of any editorial or creative judgment which is made by or on behalf of the BBC, or of any policy objective of the BBC relating to the manner in which BBC services are made or distributed.

81. Defence and Emergency Arrangements

(1) Any Government Minister—
- (a) may request that the BBC broadcast or otherwise distribute any announcement, and
- (b) may, if that Minister has requested that the announcement be broadcast or otherwise distributed on television or by means of an online service, request that the BBC accompany that announcement with a visual image (moving or still) of anything mentioned in the announcement.

(2) If it appears to any Government Minister that an emergency has arisen, that Minister may request that the BBC broadcast or otherwise distribute any announcement or other programme.

(3) A request under paragraph (1) or (2) must be made in writing, and the BBC—
- (a) must comply with the request,
- (b) must meet the cost of doing so itself, and
- (c) may, when broadcasting or distributing the announcement or other programme, announce that it is doing so pursuant to such a request.

(4) The Secretary of State may give the BBC a direction in writing that the BBC must not broadcast or otherwise distribute any matter, or class of matter, specified in the direction, whether at a time or times so specified or at any time.

(5) The BBC may, if it wishes, announce that such a direction has been given, varied or revoked.

Complaints

89. Setting the framework and procedure for handling complaints

(1) The Trust must set and publish one or more frameworks within which the BBC and the commercial arm must handle complaints, and the procedures that are to apply to complaints.

(2) In particular, the Trust must establish and maintain procedures for the handling and resolution of complaints about standards in the content of the BBC's services, including complaints concerning the subject-matter of clauses 43 to 46 (BBC guidelines designed to secure appropriate standards; accuracy and impartiality; Ofcom's Fairness Code; and Relevant Programme Code Standards and those concerning section 368D of the Communications Act 2003 (requirements for on-demand programme services and their providers) so far as it applies to the BBC).

(3) The Trust must consult publicly on any framework and its associated procedures before setting them.

(4) Every framework and its associated procedures—
- (a) must reflect the principles set out in clause 90;
- (b) must ensure that all appeals that raise matters of substance are subject to a right of appeal to the Trust, and that the Trust is the final arbiter if any question arises as to whether an appeal is for the Trust to determine or not; and
- (c) may make different provision for different complaints or classes of complaint.

90.   Some overriding principles that must be respected in relation to complaints

(1) There must be a clear division of responsibilities between the Trust and the Executive Board.

(2) The Trust must ensure that, so far as practicable, the published framework and procedures place a complainant on an equal footing with the BBC, the Trust, the Executive Board or the commercial arm (as the case may require).

(3) The Trust should not have a role in handling or determining individual complaints in the first instance, except where the complaint relates to any act or omission of the Trust itself or of the Trust Unit.

(4) The published framework and procedures must give detailed information on how complainants can expect to be treated (including, for example, in terms of timescales).

(5) The published framework and procedures must provide for complainants and prospective complainants to be given, ad hoc, clear guidance explaining—

> (a) how the complaints system (including appeals) works; and
>
> (b) where relevant, the availability of other methods by which redress might be pursued in relation to the type of issues raised by the complainant or prospective complainant.

(6) Whenever the Trust determines a complaint or an appeal, adequate reasons must be given.

(7) The Trust must also ensure, in relation to any fair trading complaint, that—

> (a) any advice provided to the Trust (including any legal advice) is provided by advisers who are separate from, and independent of, any advisers providing advice in relation to that complaint to the Executive Board or the commercial arm; and
>
> (b) the published framework and procedures make clear what sanctions and other remedies the Trust has power to apply.

The BBC and Ofcom

91.   Co-operation with Ofcom

The BBC must co-operate with Ofcom, and provide them with such information and other assistance as they may reasonably require from the BBC, in connection with any function of Ofcom's under section 198 of the Communications Act 2003 (functions of Ofcom in relation to the BBC).

92.   Agreements between the BBC and Ofcom

(1) This clause applies to the interpretation of the following provisions of this Agreement which are referred to below as 'the relevant provisions')—

> (a) clause 47;
>
> (b) clause 49;
>
> (c) clause 50;
>
> (d) clause 51;
>
> (e) clause 52;
>
> (f) clause 59;
>
> (g) clause 61; and
>
> (h) clause 62.

(2) In those provisions—

'agreed' means agreed between the BBC and Ofcom; and

'the parties' means Ofcom and, subject to the obligations imposed upon it by paragraph (3), the BBC.

(3) The BBC shall do all it can to secure and maintain the agreement of Ofcom to anything which is, for any purposes of the relevant provisions, to be agreed, and shall for the purpose of securing or maintaining such agreement—

> (a) make proposals to Ofcom; and
>
> (b) liaise with Ofcom to such extent as may be necessary to secure or maintain such agreement.

93. Power of Ofcom to require remedial action

(1) If Ofcom are satisfied—

(a) that the BBC has, in relation to any of its services, contravened a Relevant Enforceable Requirement, and

(b) that the contravention can be appropriately remedied by the inclusion in that service of a correction or a statement of findings (or both),

Ofcom may direct the BBC to include a correction or statement of findings (or both) in the service.

(2) A direction may require the correction or statement of findings to be in such form, and to be included in programmes at such times, as Ofcom may determine.

(3) Ofcom are not to give the BBC a direction under this clause unless they have given it a reasonable opportunity of making representations to them about the matters appearing to them to provide grounds for the giving of the direction.

(4) Where the BBC includes a correction or a statement of findings in a service in pursuance of a direction under this clause, it may announce that it is doing so in pursuance of such a direction.

(5) If Ofcom are satisfied that the inclusion of a programme in a service involved a contravention of a Relevant Enforceable Requirement, they may direct the BBC not to include that programme in that service on any future occasion.

(6) Where Ofcom—

(a) give a direction to the BBC under paragraph (1), or

(b) receive representations from it by virtue of paragraph (3),

they shall send a copy of the notice or representations to the Secretary of State.

(7) 'Relevant Enforceable Requirement' is defined by clause 95.

94. Power of Ofcom to fine the BBC

(1) If Ofcom are satisfied that the BBC has contravened a Relevant Enforceable Requirement, they may serve on the BBC a notice requiring it to pay them, within a specified period, a specified penalty.

(2) The amount of the penalty that may be imposed on any occasion under this clause shall not exceed the maximum specified in section 198(5) of the Communications Act 2003.

(3) Ofcom are not to serve a notice on the Corporation under paragraph (1) unless they have given it a reasonable opportunity of making representations to them about the matters appearing to them to provide grounds for the service of the notice.

(4) Where Ofcom—

(a) serve a notice on the BBC under paragraph (1), or

(b) receive representations from it by virtue of paragraph (3),

they shall send a copy of the notice or representations to the Secretary of State.

(5) An exercise by Ofcom of their powers under paragraph (1) does not preclude any exercise by them of their powers under clause 93 in respect of the same contravention.

(6) 'Relevant Enforceable Requirement' is defined by clause 95.

95. Relevant Enforceable Requirements

(1) For the purposes of clauses 93 and 94, the Relevant Enforceable Requirements are all requirements imposed on the BBC by or under the following—

(a) clause 45 (the Fairness Code);

(b) clause 46 (Programme Code Standards);

(c) clause 47 (news and current affairs);

(d) clause 49 (programming quotas for original productions);

(e) clause 50 (programming for the nations and regions);

(f) clause 51 (programme-making in the nations and regions);

(g) clause 52 (quotas for independent productions);

(h) clause 59 (code relating to provision for the deaf and visually impaired);

(i) clause 60 (power to modify targets for the purposes of clause 59);

(j) clause 61 (code relating to programme commissioning);

(k) clause 62 (retention and production of recordings);

(l) clause 63 (international obligations);

(m) clause 91 (co-operation with Ofcom);

(ma) section 368D of the Communications Act 2003 (requirements for on-demand programme services and their providers) so far as it applies to the BBC, but only to the extent that the requirements in that section do not concern the accuracy or impartiality of the content of any programmes included in a UK Public On-demand Programme Service;

(n) paragraph 1 of Schedule 12 to the Communications Act 2003 (quotas for independent productions);

(o) paragraph 2 of Schedule 12 to the Communications Act 2003 (duty to publicise complaints procedures etc.).

(2) In addition, for the purposes of clause 94 only, the Relevant Enforceable Requirements include all requirements imposed on the BBC by direction under clause 93 (power of Ofcom to require remedial action).

95A. Local television

(1) With a view to the BBC supporting the provision of local television services by local media companies from 1st April 2013 (or such other date as the Secretary of State and the BBC may agree) to the end of the period of the Charter, the Secretary of State and the BBC must comply with arrangements ('local television arrangements') agreed between the BBC and the Secretary of State in accordance with this clause.

UN Convention on the Law of the Sea 1982*

(1833 UNTS 396)

Article 109

Unauthorized broadcasting from the high seas

1. All States shall co-operate in the suppression of unauthorized broadcasting from the high seas.

2. For the purposes of this Convention, 'unauthorized broadcasting' means the transmission of sound radio or television broadcasts from a ship or installation on the high seas intended for reception by the general public contrary to international regulations, but excluding the transmission of distress calls.

3. Any person engaged in unauthorized broadcasting may be prosecuted before the court of:

(a) the flag State of the ship;

(b) the State of registry of the installation;

(c) the State of which the person is a national;

(d) any State where the transmissions can be received; or

(e) any State where authorized radio communication is suffering interference.

4. On the high seas, a State having jurisdiction in accordance with paragraph 3 may, in conformity with article 110, arrest any person or ship engaged in unauthorized broadcasting and seize the broadcasting apparatus.

---

* Reproduced with the kind permission of the United Nations Publications, https//unp.un.org/.

Part X

Proscribed, offensive and indecent materials

Obscene Publications Act 1959

(1959, 7 and 8 Eliz., c. 66)

Test of obscenity

(1) For the purposes of this Act an article shall be deemed to be obscene if its effect or (where the article comprises two or more distinct items) the effect of any one of its items is, if taken as a whole, such as to tend to deprave and corrupt persons who are likely, having regard to all relevant circumstances, to read, see or hear the matter contained or embodied in it.

(2) In this Act 'article' means any description of article containing or embodying matter to be read or looked at or both, any sound record, and any film or other record of a picture or pictures.

(3) For the purposes of this Act a person publishes an article who—

(a) distributes, circulates, sells, lets on hire, gives, or lends it, or who offers it for sale or for letting on hire; or

(b) in the case of an article containing or embodying matter to be looked at or a record, shows, plays or projects it or, where the matter is data stored electronically, transmits that data.

(4) For the purposes of this Act a person also publishes an article to the extent that any matter recorded on it is included by him in a programme included in a programme service.

(5) Where the inclusion of any matter in a programme so included would, if that matter were recorded matter, constitute the publication of an obscene article for the purposes of this Act by virtue of subsection (4) above, this Act shall have effect in relation to the inclusion of that matter in that programme as if it were recorded matter.

(6) In this section 'programme' and 'programme service' have the same meaning as in the Broadcasting Act 1990.

2 Prohibition of publication of obscene matter

(1) Subject as hereinafter provided, any person who, whether for gain or not, publishes an obscene article or who has an obscene article for publication for gain (whether gain to himself or gain to another) shall be liable—

(a) on summary conviction to a fine not exceeding one hundred pounds or to imprisonment for a term not exceeding six months;

(b) on conviction on indictment to a fine or to imprisonment for a term not exceeding five years or both.

(3) A prosecution for an offence against this section shall not be commenced more than two years after the commission of the offence.

(3A) Proceedings for an offence under this section shall not be instituted except by or with the consent of the Director of Public Prosecutions in any case where the article in question is a moving picture film of a width of not less than sixteen millimetres and the relevant publication or the only other publication which followed or could reasonably have been expected to follow from the relevant publication took place or (as the case may be) was to take place in the course of an exhibition of a film; and in this subsection 'the relevant publication' means—

(a) in the case of any proceedings under this section for publishing an obscene article, the publication in respect of which the defendant would be charged if the proceedings were brought; and

(b) in the case of any proceedings under this section for having an obscene article for publication for gain, the publication which, if the proceedings were brought, the defendant would be alleged to have had in contemplation.

(4) A person publishing an article shall not be proceeded against for an offence at common law consisting of the publication of any matter contained or embodied in the article where it is of the essence of the offence that the matter is obscene.

(4A) Without prejudice to subsection (4) above, a person shall not be proceeded against for an offence at common law—

(a) in respect of an exhibition of a film or anything said or done in the course of an exhibition of a film, where it is of the essence of the common law offence that the exhibition or, as the case may be, what was said or done was obscene, indecent, offensive, disgusting or injurious to morality; or

(b) in respect of an agreement to give an exhibition of a film or to cause anything to be said or done in the course of such an exhibition where the common law offence consists of conspiring to corrupt public morals or to do any act contrary to public morals or decency.

(5) A person shall not be convicted of an offence against this section if he proves that he had not examined the article in respect of which he is charged and had no reasonable cause to suspect that it was such that his publication of it would make him liable to be convicted of an offence against this section.

(6) In any proceedings against a person under this section the question whether an article is obscene shall be determined without regard to any publication by another person unless it could reasonably have been expected that the publication by the other person would follow from publication by the person charged.

(7) In this section, 'exhibition of a film' has the meaning given in paragraph 15 of Schedule 1 to the Licensing Act 2003.

3   Powers of search and seizure

(1) If a justice of the peace is satisfied by information on oath that there is reasonable ground for suspecting that, in any premises or on any stall or vehicle, being premises or a stall or vehicle specified in the information, obscene articles are, or are from time to time, kept for publication for gain, the justice may issue a warrant under his hand empowering any constable to enter (if need be by force) and search the premises, or to search the stall or vehicle and to seize and remove any articles found therein or thereon which the constable has reason to believe to be obscene articles and to be kept for publication for gain.

(2) A warrant under the foregoing subsection shall, if any obscene articles are seized under the warrant, also empower the seizure and removal of any documents found in the premises or, as the case may be, on the stall or vehicle which relate to a trade or business carried on at the premises or from the stall or vehicle.

(3) Subject to subsection (3A) of this section any articles seized under subsection (1) of this section shall be brought before a justice of the peace acting in the local justice area in which the articles were seized, who may thereupon issue a summons to the occupier of the premises or, as the case may be, the user of the stall or vehicle to appear on a day specified in the summons before a magistrates' court acting in that local justice area to show cause why the articles or any of them should not be forfeited; and if the court is satisfied, as respects any of the articles, that at the time when they were

seized they were obscene articles kept for publication for gain, the court shall order those articles to be forfeited:

Provided that if the person summoned does not appear, the court shall not make an order unless service of the summons is proved. Provided also that this subsection does not apply in relation to any article seized under subsection (1) of this section which is returned to the occupier of the premises or, as the case may be, to the user of the stall or vehicle in or on which it was found.

(3A) Without prejudice to the duty of a court to make an order for the forfeiture of an article where section 1(4) of the Obscene Publications Act 1964 applies (orders made on conviction), in a case where by virtue of subsection (3A) of section 2 of this Act proceedings under the said section 2 for having an article for publication for gain could not be instituted except by or with the consent of the Director of Public Prosecutions, no order for the forfeiture of the article shall be made under this section unless the warrant under which the article was seized was issued on an information laid by or on behalf of the Director of Public Prosecutions.

(4) In addition to the person summoned, any other person being the owner, author or maker of any of the articles brought before the court, or any other person through whose hands they had passed before being seized, shall be entitled to appear before the court on the day specified in the summons to show cause why they should not be forfeited.

(5) Where an order is made under this section for the forfeiture of any articles, any person who appeared, or was entitled to appear, to show cause against the making of the order may appeal to the Crown Court, and no such order shall take effect until the expiration of the period within which notice of appeal to the Crown Court may be given against the order, or, if before the expiration thereof notice of appeal is duly given or application is made for the statement of a case for the opinion of the High Court, until the final determination or abandonment of the proceedings on the appeal or case.

(6) If as respects any articles brought before it the court does not order forfeiture, the court may if it thinks fit order the person on whose information the warrant for the seizure of the articles was issued to pay such costs as the court thinks reasonable to any person who has appeared before the court to show cause why those articles should not be forfeited; and costs ordered to be paid under this subsection shall be enforceable as a civil debt.

(7) For the purposes of this section the question whether an article is obscene shall be determined on the assumption that copies of it would be published in any manner likely having regard to the circumstances in which it was found, but in no other manner.

4   Defence of public good

(1) Subject to subsection (1A) of this section a person shall not be convicted of an offence against section two of this Act, and an order for forfeiture shall not be made under the foregoing section, if it is proved that publication of the article in question is justified as being for the public good on the ground that it is in the interests of science, literature, art or learning, or of other objects of general concern.

(1A) Subsection (1) of this section shall not apply where the article in question is a moving picture film or soundtrack, but—

    (a) a person shall not be convicted of an offence against section 2 of this Act in relation to any such film or soundtrack, and

    (b) an order for forfeiture of any such film or soundtrack shall not be made under section 3 of this Act,

if it is proved that publication of the film or soundtrack is justified as being for the public good on the ground that it is in the interests of drama, opera, ballet or any other art, or of literature or learning.

(2) It is hereby declared that the opinion of experts as to the literary, artistic, scientific or other merits of an article may be admitted in any proceedings under this Act either to establish or to negative the said ground.

[(3) In this section 'moving picture soundtrack' means any sound record designed for playing with a moving picture film, whether incorporated with the film or not.]

5   Citation, commencement and extent

(1) This Act may be cited as the Obscene Publications Act 1959.

(2) This Act shall come into operation on the expiration of one month beginning with the date of the passing thereof.

(3) This Act shall not extend to Scotland or to Northern Ireland.

Obscene Publications Act 1964

(1964, c. 74)

1   Obscene articles intended for publication for gain

(1) [...]

(2) For the purpose of any proceedings for an offence against the said section 2 a person shall be deemed to have an article for publication for gain if with a view to such publication he has the article in his ownership, possession or control.

(3) In proceedings brought against a person under the said section 2 for having an obscene article for publication for gain the following provisions shall apply in place of subsections (5) and (6) of that section, that is to say,—

  (a) he shall not be convicted of that offence if he proves that he had not examined the article and had no reasonable cause to suspect that it was such that his having it would make him liable to be convicted of an offence against that section; and

  (b) the question whether the article is obscene shall be determined by reference to such publication for gain of the article as in the circumstances it may reasonably be inferred he had in contemplation and to any further publication that could reasonably be expected to follow from it, but not to any other publication.

(4) Where articles are seized under section 3 of the Obscene Publications Act 1959 (which provides for the seizure and forfeiture of obscene articles kept for publication for gain), and a person is convicted under section 2 of that Act of having them for publication for gain, the court on his conviction shall order the forfeiture of those articles:

Provided that an order made by virtue of this subsection (including an order so made on appeal) shall not take effect until the expiration of the ordinary time within which an appeal in the matter of the proceedings in which the order was made may be instituted or, where such an appeal is duly instituted, until the appeal is finally decided or abandoned; and for this purpose—

  (a) an application for a case to be stated or for leave to appeal shall be treated as the institution of an appeal; and

  (b) where a decision on appeal is subject to a further appeal, the appeal shall not be deemed to be finally decided until the expiration of the ordinary time within which a further appeal may be instituted or, where a further appeal is duly instituted, until the further appeal is finally decided or abandoned.

(5) References in section 3 of the Obscene Publications Act 1959 and this section to publication for gain shall apply to any publication with a view to gain, whether the gain is to accrue by way of consideration for the publication or in any other way.

2   Negatives, etc. for production of obscene articles

(1) The Obscene Publications Act 1959 (as amended by this Act) shall apply in relation to anything which is intended to be used, either alone or as one of a set, for the reproduction or manufacture therefrom of articles containing or embodying matter to be read, looked at or listened to, as if it were an article containing or embodying that matter so far as that matter is to be derived from it or from the set.

(2) For the purposes of the Obscene Publications Act 1959 (as so amended) an article shall be deemed to be had or kept for publication if it is had or kept for the reproduction or manufacture

therefrom of articles for publication; and the question whether an article so had or kept is obscene shall—

(a) for purposes of section 2 of the Act be determined in accordance with section 1(3)(b) above as if any reference there to publication of the article were a reference to publication of articles reproduced or manufactured from it; and

(b) for purposes of section 3 of the Act be determined on the assumption that articles reproduced or manufactured from it would be published in any manner likely having regard to the circumstances in which it was found, but in no other manner.

3 Citation, commencement and extent

(1) This Act may be cited as the Obscene Publications Act 1964, and this Act and the Obscene Publications Act 1959 may be cited together as the Obscene Publications Acts 1959 and 1964.

(2) This Act shall come into operation on the expiration of one month beginning with the date of the passing thereof.

(3) This Act shall not extend to Scotland or to Northern Ireland.

Video Recordings Act 1984

(1984, c. 39)

Preliminary

1 Interpretation of terms

(1) The provisions of this section shall have effect for the interpretation of terms used in this Act.

(2) 'Video work' means any series of visual images (with or without sound)—

(a) produced electronically by the use of information contained on any disc . . . magnetic tape [or any other device capable of storing data electronically], and

(b) shown as a moving picture.

(3) 'Video recording' means any disc . . . magnetic tape [or any other device capable of storing data electronically] containing information by the use of which the whole or part of a video work may be produced.

(4) 'Supply' means supply in any manner, whether or not for reward, and, therefore, includes supply by way of sale, letting on hire, exchange or loan; and references to a supply are to be interpreted accordingly.

2 Exempted video works

(1) Subject to subsection (2) [or (3)] below, a video work [other than a video game] is for the purposes of this Act an exempted work if, taken as a whole—

(a) it is designed to inform, educate or instruct; or

(b) it is concerned with sport, religion or music; [. . .]

[(1A) Subject to subsection (2) or (3) below, a video game is for the purposes of this Act an exempted work if—

(a) it is, taken as a whole, designed to inform, educate or instruct;

(b) it is, taken as a whole, concerned with sport, religion or music; or

(c) it satisfies one or more of the conditions in section 2A.]

(2) A video work is not an exempted work for those purposes if, to any significant extent, it depicts—

(a) human sexual activity or acts of force or restraint associated with such activity;

(b) mutilation or torture of, or other acts of gross violence towards, humans or animals;

(c) human genital organs or human urinary or excretory functions;

[(d) techniques likely to be useful in the commission of offences;]

or is [likely] to any significant extent to stimulate or encourage anything falling within paragraph (a) or, in the case of anything falling within paragraph (b), is [likely] to any extent to do so.

(3) A video work is not an exempted work for those purposes if, to any significant extent, it depicts criminal activity which is likely to any significant extent to stimulate or encourage the commission of offences.

[(4) The Secretary of State may by regulations amend this section—

  (a) by adding or removing a case in which a video work is not an exempted work, or

  (b) by amending a description of such a case.

2A   Conditions relating to video games

(1) The conditions referred to in section 2(1A)(c) are as follows.

(2) The first condition is that the video game does not include any of the following—

  (a) depictions of violence towards human or animal characters, whether or not the violence looks realistic and whether or not the violence results in obvious harm,

  (b) depictions of violence towards other characters where the violence looks realistic,

  (c) depictions of criminal activity that are likely, to any extent, to stimulate or encourage the commission of offences,

  (d) depictions of activities involving illegal drugs or the misuse of drugs,

  (e) words or images that are likely, to any extent, to stimulate or encourage the use of alcohol or tobacco,

  (f) words or images that are intended to convey a sexual message,

  (g) swearing, or

  (h) words or images that are intended or likely, to any extent, to cause offence, whether on the grounds of race, gender, disability, religion or belief or sexual orientation or otherwise.

(3) In subsection (2) 'human or animal character' means a character that is, or whose appearance is similar to that of—

  (a) a human being, or

  (b) an animal that exists or has existed in real life,

but does not include a simple stick character or any equally basic representation of a human being or animal.

(4) The second condition is that the designated authority, or a person nominated by the designated authority for the purposes of this section, has confirmed in writing that the video game is suitable for viewing by persons under the age of 12.

(5) The Secretary of State may by regulations amend this section—

  (a) by amending the first condition, or

  (b) by adding a further condition (or by amending or removing such a condition).

(6) Regulations under this section may make provision by reference to documents produced by the designated authority.]

4   Authority to determine suitability of video works for classification

(1) The Secretary of State may by notice under this section designate any person as the authority responsible for making arrangements—

  (a) for determining for the purposes of this Act whether or not video works are suitable for classification certificates to be issued in respect of them, having special regard to the likelihood of video works in respect of which such certificates have been issued being viewed in the home,

  (b) in the case of works which are determined in accordance with the arrangements to be so suitable—

    [(ia) for assigning a unique title to each video work in respect of which a classification certificate is to be issued]

    (i)   for making such other determinations as are required for the issue [or revocation] of classification certificates, and

    (ii) for issuing [and revoking] such certificates, and

(c)　for maintaining a record of such determinations (whether determinations made in pursuance of arrangements made by that person or by any person previously designated under this section).

(1A)　A title assigned to a video work under subsection (1)(b)(ia) above shall consist of—

(a)　the title under which the video work was determined to be suitable for the issue of a classification certificate; and

(b)　a registration number (which may contain letters and other symbols as well as figures).

(1B)　The record maintained under subsection (1)(c) above shall include, in relation to each video work in respect of which a classification certificate has been issued, a video recording which—

(a)　contains the video work; and

(b)　shows, or shows on its spool, case or other thing on or in which the recording is kept—

(i)　the title assigned to the video work under subsection (1)(b)(ia) above; and

(ii)　the determination or determinations made in respect of the video work.

[(1C)　The arrangements made under this section may require a person requesting a classification certificate for a video work to agree to comply with a code of practice, which may, in particular, include provision relating to the labelling of video recordings.]

(2)　The power to designate any person by notice under this section includes power—

(a)　to designate two or more persons jointly as the authority responsible for making those arrangements, and

(b)　to provide that any person holding an office or employment specified in the notice is to be treated as designated while holding that office or employment.

(3)　The Secretary of State shall not make any designation under this section unless he is satisfied that adequate arrangements will be made for an appeal by any person against a determination that a video work submitted by him for the issue of a classification certificate—

(a)　is not suitable for a classification certificate to be issued in respect of it, or

(b)　is not suitable for viewing by persons who have not attained a particular age,

or against a determination that no video recording containing the work is to be supplied other than in a licensed sex shop.

[(3A)　The Secretary of State must not make a designation under this section unless satisfied that adequate arrangements will be made for taking account of public opinion in the United Kingdom.]

(4)　The Secretary of State may at any time designate another person in place of any person designated under this section and, if he does so, may give directions as to the transfer of any record kept in pursuance of the arrangements referred to in subsection (1) above; and it shall be the duty of any person having control of any such record or any part of it to comply with the directions.

[(5)　No fee is recoverable by, or in accordance with arrangements made by, the designated authority in connection with a determination in respect of a video work or the issue of a classification certificate unless the designated authority has consulted the Secretary of State about such fees.]

[. . .]

[(6A)　When making arrangements under this section, the designated authority must have regard to any guidance issued by the Secretary of State.

(6B)　The Secretary of State may not issue guidance about the matters to be taken into account when determining the suitability of a video work for the issue of a classification certificate or a classification certificate of a particular description.]

(7)　Any notice under this section shall be published in the London, Edinburgh and Belfast Gazettes.

[4A　Criteria for suitability to which special regard to be had

(1)　The designated authority shall, in making any determination as to the suitability of a video work, have special regard (among the other relevant factors) to any harm that may be caused to potential viewers or, through their behaviour, to society by the manner in which the work deals with—

(a)　criminal behaviour;

(b)　illegal drugs;

   (c)   violent behaviour or incidents;
   (d)   horrific behaviour or incidents; or
   (e)   human sexual activity.
   (2) For the purposes of this section—
'potential viewer' means any person (including a child or young person) who is likely to view the video work in question if a classification certificate or a classification certificate of a particular description were issued;
   'suitability' means suitability for the issue of a classification certificate or suitability for the issue of a certificate of a particular description;
   'violent behaviour' includes any act inflicting or likely to result in the infliction of injury;
and any behaviour or activity referred to in subsection (1)(a) to (e) above shall be taken to include behaviour or activity likely to stimulate or encourage it.

4B   Review of determinations as to suitability

   (1) The Secretary of State may by order make provision enabling the designated authority to review any determination made by them, before the coming into force of section 4A of this Act, as to the suitability of a video work.
   (2) The order may in particular provide—
   (a)   for the authority's power of review to be exercisable in relation to such determinations as the authority think fit;
   (b)   for the authority to determine, on any review, whether, if they were then determining the suitability of the video work to which the determination under review relates, they—
      (i)   would issue a classification certificate, or
      (ii)   would issue a different classification certificate;
   (c)   for the cancellation of a classification certificate, where they determine that they would not issue a classification certificate;
   (d)   for the cancellation of a classification certificate and issue of a new classification certificate, where they determine that they would issue a different classification certificate;
   (e)   for any such cancellation or issue not to take effect until the end of such period as may be determined in accordance with the order;
   (f)   for such persons as may appear to the authority to fall within a specified category of person to be notified of any such cancellation or issue in such manner as may be specified;
   (g)   for treating a classification certificate, in relation to any act or omission occurring after its cancellation, as if it had not been issued;
   (h)   for specified provisions of this Act to apply to determinations made on a review subject to such modifications (if any) as may be specified;
   (i)   for specified regulations made under section 8 of this Act to apply to a video work in respect of which a new classification certificate has been issued subject to such modifications (if any) as may be specified.
   (3) In subsection (2) above 'specified' means specified by an order made under this section.
   (4) The Secretary of State shall not make any order under this section unless he is satisfied that adequate arrangements will be made for an appeal against determinations made by the designated authority on a review.
   (5) The power to make an order under this section shall be exercisable by statutory instrument which shall be subject to annulment in pursuance of a resolution of either House of Parliament.
   (6) In this section 'suitability' has the same meaning as in section 4A of this Act.]

Coroners and Justice Act 2009

(2009, c. 25)

PART 2   CRIMINAL OFFENCES

[...]

Chapter 2   Images of children

Prohibited images

62   Possession of prohibited images of children

(1) It is an offence for a person to be in possession of a prohibited image of a child.

(2) A prohibited image is an image which—

(a) is pornographic,

(b) falls within subsection (6), and

(c) is grossly offensive, disgusting or otherwise of an obscene character.

(3) An image is 'pornographic' if it is of such a nature that it must reasonably be assumed to have been produced solely or principally for the purpose of sexual arousal.

(4) Where (as found in the person's possession) an image forms part of a series of images, the question whether the image is of such a nature as is mentioned in subsection (3) is to be determined by reference to—

(a) the image itself, and

(b) (if the series of images is such as to be capable of providing a context for the image) the context in which it occurs in the series of images.

(5) So, for example, where—

(a) an image forms an integral part of a narrative constituted by a series of images, and

(b) having regard to those images as a whole, they are not of such a nature that they must reasonably be assumed to have been produced solely or principally for the purpose of sexual arousal,

the image may, by virtue of being part of that narrative, be found not to be pornographic, even though it might have been found to be pornographic if taken by itself.

(6) An image falls within this subsection if it—

(a) is an image which focuses solely or principally on a child's genitals or anal region, or

(b) portrays any of the acts mentioned in subsection (7).

(7) Those acts are—

(a) the performance by a person of an act of intercourse or oral sex with or in the presence of a child;

(b) an act of masturbation by, of, involving or in the presence of a child;

(c) an act which involves penetration of the vagina or anus of a child with a part of a person's body or with anything else;

(d) an act of penetration, in the presence of a child, of the vagina or anus of a person with a part of a person's body or with anything else;

(e) the performance by a child of an act of intercourse or oral sex with an animal (whether dead or alive or imaginary);

(f) the performance by a person of an act of intercourse or oral sex with an animal (whether dead or alive or imaginary) in the presence of a child.

(8) For the purposes of subsection (7), penetration is a continuing act from entry to withdrawal.

(9) Proceedings for an offence under subsection (1) may not be instituted—

(a) in England and Wales, except by or with the consent of the Director of Public Prosecutions;

(b) in Northern Ireland, except by or with the consent of the Director of Public Prosecutions for Northern Ireland.

63   Exclusion of classified film etc.

(1) Section 62(1) does not apply to excluded images.

(2) An 'excluded image' is an image which forms part of a series of images contained in a recording of the whole or part of a classified work.

(3) But such an image is not an 'excluded image' if—

(a) it is contained in a recording of an extract from a classified work, and

(b) it is of such a nature that it must reasonably be assumed to have been extracted (whether with or without other images) solely or principally for the purpose of sexual arousal.

(4) Where an extracted image is one of a series of images contained in the recording, the question whether the image is of such a nature as is mentioned in subsection (3)(b) is to be determined by reference to—

(a) the image itself, and

(b) (if the series of images is such as to be capable of providing a context for the image) the context in which it occurs in the series of images;

and section 62(5) applies in connection with determining that question as it applies in connection with determining whether an image is pornographic.

(5) In determining for the purposes of this section whether a recording is a recording of the whole or part of a classified work, any alteration attributable to—

(a) a defect caused for technical reasons or by inadvertence on the part of any person, or

(b) the inclusion in the recording of any extraneous material (such as advertisements),

is to be disregarded.

(6) Nothing in this section is to be taken as affecting any duty of a designated authority to have regard to section 62 (along with other enactments creating criminal offences) in determining whether a video work is suitable for a classification certificate to be issued in respect of it.

(7) In this section—

'classified work' means (subject to subsection (8)) a video work in respect of which a classification certificate has been issued by a designated authority (whether before or after the commencement of this section);

'classification certificate' and 'video work' have the same meaning as in the Video Recordings Act 1984 (c. 39);

'designated authority' means an authority which has been designated by the Secretary of State under section 4 of that Act;

'extract' includes an extract consisting of a single image;

'pornographic' has the same meaning as in section 62;

'recording' means any disc, tape or other device capable of storing data electronically and from which images may be produced (by any means).

(8) Section 22(3) of the Video Recordings Act 1984 (effect of alterations) applies for the purposes of this section as it applies for the purposes of that Act.

64   Defences

(1) Where a person is charged with an offence under section 62(1), it is a defence for the person to prove any of the following matters—

(a) that the person had a legitimate reason for being in possession of the image concerned;

(b) that the person had not seen the image concerned and did not know, nor had any cause to suspect, it to be a prohibited image of a child;

(c) that the person—

(i)   was sent the image concerned without any prior request having been made by or on behalf of the person, and

(ii) did not keep it for an unreasonable time.

(2) In this section 'prohibited image' has the same meaning as in section 62.

65 Meaning of 'image' and 'child'

(1) The following apply for the purposes of sections 62 to 64.

(2) 'Image' includes—

  (a) a moving or still image (produced by any means), or

  (b) data (stored by any means) which is capable of conversion into an image within paragraph (a).

(3) 'Image' does not include an indecent photograph, or indecent pseudo-photograph, of a child.

(4) In subsection (3) 'indecent photograph' and 'indecent pseudo-photograph' are to be construed—

  (a) in relation to England and Wales, in accordance with the Protection of Children Act 1978 (c. 37), and

  (b) in relation to Northern Ireland, in accordance with the Protection of Children (Northern Ireland) Order 1978 (S.I. 1978/1047 (N.I. 17)).

(5) 'Child', subject to subsection (6), means a person under the age of 18.

(6) Where an image shows a person the image is to be treated as an image of a child if—

  (a) the impression conveyed by the image is that the person shown is a child, or

  (b) the predominant impression conveyed is that the person shown is a child despite the fact that some of the physical characteristics shown are not those of a child.

(7) References to an image of a person include references to an image of an imaginary person.

(8) References to an image of a child include references to an image of an imaginary child.

Racial and Religious Hatred Act 2006

(2006, c. 1)

1 Hatred against persons on religious grounds

The Public Order Act 1986 (c. 64) is amended in accordance with the Schedule to this Act, which creates offences involving stirring up hatred against persons on religious grounds.

2 Racial and religious hatred offences: powers of arrest

In section 24A of the Police and Criminal Evidence Act 1984 (c. 60) (arrest without warrant by persons other than constables) after subsection (4) add—

'(5) This section does not apply in relation to an offence under Part 3 or 3A of the Public Order Act 1986.'

3 Short title, commencement and extent

(1) This Act may be cited as the Racial and Religious Hatred Act 2006.

(2) This Act comes into force on such day as the Secretary of State may appoint by order made by statutory instrument.

(3) An order under subsection (2) may make—

  (a) such supplementary, incidental or consequential provision, or

  (b) such transitory, transitional or saving provision,

  (c) as the Secretary of State considers appropriate in connection with the coming into force of this Act.

(4) This Act extends to England and Wales only.

Public Order Act 1986

(1986, c. 64)

PART 3A HATRED AGAINST PERSONS ON RELIGIOUS GROUNDS

Meaning of 'religious hatred' [and 'hatred on the grounds of sexual orientation']

29A Meaning of 'religious hatred'

In this Part 'religious hatred' means hatred against a group of persons defined by reference to religious belief or lack of religious belief.

[29AB Meaning of 'hatred on the grounds of sexual orientation'

In this Part 'hatred on the grounds of sexual orientation' means hatred against a group of persons defined by reference to sexual orientation (whether towards persons of the same sex, the opposite sex or both).]

Acts intended to stir up religious hatred [or hatred on the grounds of sexual orientation]

29B Use of words or behaviour or display of written material

(1) A person who uses threatening words or behaviour, or displays any written material which is threatening, is guilty of an offence if he intends thereby to stir up religious hatred [or hatred on the grounds of sexual orientation].

(2) An offence under this section may be committed in a public or a private place, except that no offence is committed where the words or behaviour are used, or the written material is displayed, by a person inside a dwelling and are not heard or seen except by other persons in that or another dwelling.

[. . .]

(4) In proceedings for an offence under this section it is a defence for the accused to prove that he was inside a dwelling and had no reason to believe that the words or behaviour used, or the written material displayed, would be heard or seen by a person outside that or any other dwelling.

(5) This section does not apply to words or behaviour used, or written material displayed, solely for the purpose of being included in a programme service.

29C Publishing or distributing written material

(1) A person who publishes or distributes written material which is threatening is guilty of an offence if he intends thereby to stir up religious hatred [or hatred on the grounds of sexual orientation].

(2) References in this Part to the publication or distribution of written material are to its publication or distribution to the public or a section of the public.

29D Public performance of play

(1) If a public performance of a play is given which involves the use of threatening words or behaviour, any person who presents or directs the performance is guilty of an offence if he intends thereby to stir up religious hatred [or hatred on the grounds of sexual orientation].

(2) This section does not apply to a performance given solely or primarily for one or more of the following purposes—

(a) rehearsal,

(b) making a recording of the performance, or

(c) enabling the performance to be included in a programme service;

but if it is proved that the performance was attended by persons other than those directly connected with the giving of the performance or the doing in relation to it of the things mentioned in paragraph (b) or (c), the performance shall, unless the contrary is shown, be taken not to have been given solely or primarily for the purpose mentioned above.

(3) For the purposes of this section—

(a) a person shall not be treated as presenting a performance of a play by reason only of his taking part in it as a performer,

(b) a person taking part as a performer in a performance directed by another shall be treated as a person who directed the performance if without reasonable excuse he performs otherwise than in accordance with that person's direction, and

(c) a person shall be taken to have directed a performance of a play given under his direction notwithstanding that he was not present during the performance;

and a person shall not be treated as aiding or abetting the commission of an offence under this section by reason only of his taking part in a performance as a performer.

(4) In this section 'play' and 'public performance' have the same meaning as in the Theatres Act 1968.

(5) The following provisions of the Theatres Act 1968 apply in relation to an offence under this section as they apply to an offence under section 2 of that Act–

(a) section 9 (script as evidence of what was performed),

(b) section 10 (power to make copies of script),

(c) section 15 (powers of entry and inspection).

29E   Distributing, showing or playing a recording

(1) A person who distributes, or shows or plays, a recording of visual images or sounds which are threatening is guilty of an offence if he intends thereby to stir up religious hatred [or hatred on the grounds of sexual orientation].

(2) In this Part 'recording' means any record from which visual images or sounds may, by any means, be reproduced; and references to the distribution, showing or playing of a recording are to its distribution, showing or playing to the public or a section of the public.

(3) This section does not apply to the showing or playing of a recording solely for the purpose of enabling the recording to be included in a programme service.

29F   Broadcasting or including programme in programme service

(1) If a programme involving threatening visual images or sounds is included in a programme service, each of the persons mentioned in subsection (2) is guilty of an offence if he intends thereby to stir up religious hatred [or hatred on the grounds of sexual orientation].

(2) The persons are—

(a) the person providing the programme service,

(b) any person by whom the programme is produced or directed, and

(c) any person by whom offending words or behaviour are used.

Inflammatory material

29G   Possession of inflammatory material

(1) A person who has in his possession written material which is threatening, or a recording of visual images or sounds which are threatening, with a view to—

(a) in the case of written material, its being displayed, published, distributed, or included in a programme service whether by himself or another, or

(b) in the case of a recording, its being distributed, shown, played, or included in a programme service, whether by himself or another,

is guilty of an offence if he intends [thereby to stir up religious hatred or hatred on the grounds of sexual orientation].

(2) For this purpose regard shall be had to such display, publication, distribution, showing, playing, or inclusion in a programme service as he has, or it may be reasonably be inferred that he has, in view.

29H   Powers of entry and search

(1) If [. . .] a justice of the peace is satisfied by information on oath laid by a constable that there are reasonable grounds for suspecting that a person has possession of written material or a recording in contravention of section 29G, the justice may issue a warrant under his hand authorising any constable to enter and search the premises where it is suspected the material or recording is situated.

[. . .]

(3) A constable entering or searching premises in pursuance of a warrant issued under this section may use reasonable force if necessary.

(4) In this section 'premises' means any place and, in particular, includes—

(a) any vehicle, vessel, aircraft or hovercraft,

(b) any offshore installation as defined in section 12 of the Mineral Workings (Offshore Installations) Act 1971, and

(c) any tent or movable structure.

29I   Power to order forfeiture

(1) A court by or before which a person is convicted of—

(a) an offence under section 29B relating to the display of written material, or

(b) an offence under section 29C, 29E or 29G,

shall order to be forfeited any written material or recording produced to the court and shown to its satisfaction to be written material or a recording to which the offence relates.

(2) An order made under this section shall not take effect—

(a) [. . .] until the expiry of the ordinary time within which an appeal may be instituted or, where an appeal is duly instituted, until it is finally decided or abandoned;

[. . .]

(3) For the purposes of subsection (2)(a)—

(a) an application for a case stated or for leave to appeal shall be treated as the institution of an appeal, and

(b) where a decision on appeal is subject to a further appeal, the appeal is not finally determined until the expiry of the ordinary time within which a further appeal may be instituted or, where a further appeal is duly instituted, until the further appeal is finally decided or abandoned.

[. . .]

29J   Protection of freedom of expression

Nothing in this Part shall be read or given effect in a way which prohibits or restricts discussion, criticism or expressions of antipathy, dislike, ridicule, insult or abuse of particular religions or the beliefs or practices of their adherents, or of any other belief system or the beliefs or practices of its adherents, or proselytising or urging adherents of a different religion or belief system to cease practising their religion or belief system.

29JA   Protection of freedom of expression (sexual orientation)

In this Part, for the avoidance of doubt, the discussion or criticism of sexual conduct or practices or the urging of persons to refrain from or modify such conduct or practices shall not be taken of itself to be threatening or intended to stir up hatred.

Supplementary provisions

29K   Savings for reports of parliamentary or judicial proceedings

(1) Nothing in this Part applies to a fair and accurate report of proceedings in Parliament [in the Scottish Parliament or in the National Assembly for Wales].

(2) Nothing in this Part applies to a fair and accurate report of proceedings publicly heard before a court or tribunal exercising judicial authority where the report is published contemporaneously with the proceedings or, if it is not reasonably practicable or would be unlawful to publish a report of them contemporaneously, as soon as publication is reasonably practicable and lawful.

29L Procedure and punishment

(1) No proceedings for an offence under this Part may be instituted [. . .] except by or with the consent of the Attorney General.

(2) For the purposes of the rules [. . .] against charging more than one offence in the same count or information, each of sections 29B to 29G creates one offence.

(3) A person guilty of an offence under this Part is liable—

    (a) on conviction on indictment to imprisonment for a term not exceeding seven years or a fine or both;

    (b) on summary conviction to imprisonment for a term not exceeding [12] months or a fine not exceeding the statutory maximum or both.

[(4) In subsection (3)(b) the reference to 12 months shall be read as a reference to 6 months in relation to an offence committed before the commencement of section 154(1) of the Criminal Justice Act 2003.]

29M Offences by corporations

(1) Where a body corporate is guilty of an offence under this Part and it is shown that the offence was committed with the consent or connivance of a director, manager, secretary or other similar officer of the body, or a person purporting to act in any such capacity, he as well as the body corporate is guilty of the offence and liable to be proceeded against and punished accordingly.

(2) Where the affairs of a body corporate are managed by its members, subsection (1) applies in relation to the acts and defaults of a member in connection with his functions of management as it applies to a director.

29N Interpretation

In this Part—

'distribute', and related expressions, shall be construed in accordance with section 29C(2) (written material) and section 29E(2) (recordings);

'dwelling' means any structure or part of a structure occupied as a person's home or other living accommodation (whether the occupation is separate or shared with others) but does not include any part not so occupied, and for this purpose;

['hatred on the grounds of sexual orientation' has the meaning given by section 29AB;]

'structure' includes a tent, caravan, vehicle, vessel or other temporary or movable structure;

'programme' means any item which is included in a programme service;

'programme service' has the same meaning as in the Broadcasting Act 1990;

'publish', and related expressions, in relation to written material, shall be construed in accordance with section 29C(2);

'religious hatred' has the meaning given by section 29A;

'recording' has the meaning given by section 29E(2), and 'play' and 'show', and related expressions, in relation to a recording, shall be construed in accordance with that provision;

'written material' includes any sign or other visible representation.'

Terrorism Act 2006

(2006, c. 11)

PART 1 OFFENCES

Encouragement etc. of terrorism

1 Encouragement of terrorism

(1) This section applies to a statement that is likely to be understood by some or all of the members of the public to whom it is published as a direct or indirect encouragement or other inducement to them to the commission, preparation or instigation of acts of terrorism or Convention offences.

(2) A person commits an offence if—

    (a) he publishes a statement to which this section applies or causes another to publish such a statement; and

    (b) at the time he publishes it or causes it to be published, he—

        (i) intends members of the public to be directly or indirectly encouraged or otherwise induced by the statement to commit, prepare or instigate acts of terrorism or Convention offences; or

        (ii) is reckless as to whether members of the public will be directly or indirectly encouraged or otherwise induced by the statement to commit, prepare or instigate such acts or offences.

(3) For the purposes of this section, the statements that are likely to be understood by members of the public as indirectly encouraging the commission or preparation of acts of terrorism or Convention offences include every statement which—

    (a) glorifies the commission or preparation (whether in the past, in the future or generally) of such acts or offences; and

    (b) is a statement from which those members of the public could reasonably be expected to infer that what is being glorified is being glorified as conduct that should be emulated by them in existing circumstances.

(4) For the purposes of this section the questions how a statement is likely to be understood and what members of the public could reasonably be expected to infer from it must be determined having regard both—

    (a) to the contents of the statement as a whole; and

    (b) to the circumstances and manner of its publication.

(5) It is irrelevant for the purposes of subsections (1) to (3)—

    (a) whether anything mentioned in those subsections relates to the commission, preparation or instigation of one or more particular acts of terrorism or Convention offences, of acts of terrorism or Convention offences of a particular description or of acts of terrorism or Convention offences generally; and,

    (b) whether any person is in fact encouraged or induced by the statement to commit, prepare or instigate any such act or offence.

(6) In proceedings for an offence under this section against a person in whose case it is not proved that he intended the statement directly or indirectly to encourage or otherwise induce the commission, preparation or instigation of acts of terrorism or Convention offences, it is a defence for him to show—

    (a) that the statement neither expressed his views nor had his endorsement (whether by virtue of section 3 or otherwise); and

    (b) that it was clear, in all the circumstances of the statement's publication, that it did not express his views and (apart from the possibility of his having been given and failed to comply with a notice under subsection (3) of that section) did not have his endorsement.

(7) A person guilty of an offence under this section shall be liable—

    (a) on conviction on indictment, to imprisonment for a term not exceeding 7 years or to a fine, or to both;

    (b) on summary conviction in England and Wales, to imprisonment for a term not exceeding 12 months or to a fine not exceeding the statutory maximum, or to both;

    (c) on summary conviction in Scotland or Northern Ireland, to imprisonment for a term not exceeding 6 months or to a fine not exceeding the statutory maximum, or to both.

(8) In relation to an offence committed before the commencement of section 154(1) of the Criminal Justice Act 2003 (c. 44), the reference in subsection (7)(b) to 12 months is to be read as a reference to 6 months.

2   Dissemination of terrorist publications

(1) A person commits an offence if he engages in conduct falling within subsection (2) and, at the time he does so—

    (a) he intends an effect of his conduct to be a direct or indirect encouragement or other inducement to the commission, preparation or instigation of acts of terrorism;

    (b) he intends an effect of his conduct to be the provision of assistance in the commission or preparation of such acts; or

    (c) he is reckless as to whether his conduct has an effect mentioned in paragraph (a) or (b).

(2) For the purposes of this section a person engages in conduct falling within this subsection if he—

    (a) distributes or circulates a terrorist publication;

    (b) gives, sells or lends such a publication;

    (c) offers such a publication for sale or loan;

    (d) provides a service to others that enables them to obtain, read, listen to or look at such a publication, or to acquire it by means of a gift, sale or loan;

    (e) transmits the contents of such a publication electronically; or

    (f) has such a publication in his possession with a view to its becoming the subject of conduct falling within any of paragraphs (a) to (e).

(3) For the purposes of this section a publication is a terrorist publication, in relation to conduct falling within subsection (2), if matter contained in it is likely—

    (a) to be understood, by some or all of the persons to whom it is or may become available as a consequence of that conduct, as a direct or indirect encouragement or other inducement to them to the commission, preparation or instigation of acts of terrorism; or

    (b) to be useful in the commission or preparation of such acts and to be understood, by some or all of those persons, as contained in the publication, or made available to them, wholly or mainly for the purpose of being so useful to them.

(4) For the purposes of this section matter that is likely to be understood by a person as indirectly encouraging the commission or preparation of acts of terrorism includes any matter which—

    (a) glorifies the commission or preparation (whether in the past, in the future or generally) of such acts; and

    (b) is matter from which that person could reasonably be expected to infer that what is being glorified is being glorified as conduct that should be emulated by him in existing circumstances.

(5) For the purposes of this section the question whether a publication is a terrorist publication in relation to particular conduct must be determined—

    (a) as at the time of that conduct; and

    (b) having regard both to the contents of the publication as a whole and to the circumstances in which that conduct occurs.

(6) In subsection (1) references to the effect of a person's conduct in relation to a terrorist publication include references to an effect of the publication on one or more persons to whom it is or may become available as a consequence of that conduct.

(7) It is irrelevant for the purposes of this section whether anything mentioned in subsections (1) to (4) is in relation to the commission, preparation or instigation of one or more particular acts of terrorism, of acts of terrorism of a particular description or of acts of terrorism generally.

(8) For the purposes of this section it is also irrelevant, in relation to matter contained in any article whether any person—

    (a) is in fact encouraged or induced by that matter to commit, prepare or instigate acts of terrorism; or

    (b) in fact makes use of it in the commission or preparation of such acts.

(9) In proceedings for an offence under this section against a person in respect of conduct to which subsection (10) applies, it is a defence for him to show—

    (a) that the matter by reference to which the publication in question was a terrorist publication neither expressed his views nor had his endorsement (whether by virtue of section 3 or otherwise); and

    (b) that it was clear, in all the circumstances of the conduct, that that matter did not express his views and (apart from the possibility of his having been given and failed to comply with a notice under subsection (3) of that section) did not have his endorsement.

(10) This subsection applies to the conduct of a person to the extent that—

    (a) the publication to which his conduct related contained matter by reference to which it was a terrorist publication by virtue of subsection (3)(a); and

    (b) that person is not proved to have engaged in that conduct with the intention specified in subsection (1)(a).

(11) A person guilty of an offence under this section shall be liable—

    (a) on conviction on indictment, to imprisonment for a term not exceeding 7 years or to a fine, or to both;

    (b) on summary conviction in England and Wales, to imprisonment for a term not exceeding 12 months or to a fine not exceeding the statutory maximum, or to both;

    (c) on summary conviction in Scotland or Northern Ireland, to imprisonment for a term not exceeding 6 months or to a fine not exceeding the statutory maximum, or to both.

(12) In relation to an offence committed before the commencement of section 154(1) of the Criminal Justice Act 2003 (c. 44), the reference in subsection (11)(b) to 12 months is to be read as a reference to 6 months.

(13) In this section—

'lend' includes let on hire, and 'loan' is to be construed accordingly;

'publication' means an article or record of any description that contains any of the following, or any combination of them—

    (a) matter to be read;

    (b) matter to be listened to;

    (c) matter to be looked at or watched.

3   Application of ss1 and 2 to internet activity etc.

(1) This section applies for the purposes of sections 1 and 2 in relation to cases where—

    (a) a statement is published or caused to be published in the course of, or in connection with, the provision or use of a service provided electronically; or

    (b) conduct falling within section 2(2) was in the course of, or in connection with, the provision or use of such a service.

(2) The cases in which the statement, or the article or record to which the conduct relates, is to be regarded as having the endorsement of a person ('the relevant person') at any time include a case in which—

    (a) a constable has given him a notice under subsection (3);

    (b) that time falls more than 2 working days after the day on which the notice was given; and

    (c) the relevant person has failed, without reasonable excuse, to comply with the notice.

(3) A notice under this subsection is a notice which—

    (a) declares that, in the opinion of the constable giving it, the statement or the article or record is unlawfully terrorism-related;

    (b) requires the relevant person to secure that the statement or the article or record, so far as it is so related, is not available to the public or is modified so as no longer to be so related;

(c) warns the relevant person that a failure to comply with the notice within 2 working days will result in the statement, or the article or record, being regarded as having his endorsement; and

(d) explains how, under subsection (4), he may become liable by virtue of the notice if the statement, or the article or record, becomes available to the public after he has complied with the notice.

(4) Where—

(a) a notice under subsection (3) has been given to the relevant person in respect of a statement, or an article or record, and he has complied with it, but

(b) he subsequently publishes or causes to be published a statement which is, or is for all practical purposes, the same or to the same effect as the statement to which the notice related, or to matter contained in the article or record to which it related, (a 'repeat statement');

the requirements of subsection (2)(a) to (c) shall be regarded as satisfied in the case of the repeat statement in relation to the times of its subsequent publication by the relevant person.

(5) In proceedings against a person for an offence under section 1 or 2 the requirements of subsection (2)(a) to (c) are not, in his case, to be regarded as satisfied in relation to any time by virtue of subsection (4) if he shows that he—

(a) has, before that time, taken every step he reasonably could to prevent a repeat statement from becoming available to the public and to ascertain whether it does; and

(b) was, at that time, a person to whom subsection (6) applied.

(6) This subsection applies to a person at any time when he—

(a) is not aware of the publication of the repeat statement; or

(b) having become aware of its publication, has taken every step that he reasonably could to secure that it either ceased to be available to the public or was modified as mentioned in subsection (3)(b).

(7) For the purposes of this section a statement or an article or record is unlawfully terrorism-related if it constitutes, or if matter contained in the article or record constitutes—

(a) something that is likely to be understood, by any one or more of the persons to whom it has or may become available, as a direct or indirect encouragement or other inducement to the commission, preparation or instigation of acts of terrorism or Convention offences; or

(b) information which—

(i) is likely to be useful to any one or more of those persons in the commission or preparation of such acts; and

(ii) is in a form or context in which it is likely to be understood by any one or more of those persons as being wholly or mainly for the purpose of being so useful.

(8) The reference in subsection (7) to something that is likely to be understood as an indirect encouragement to the commission or preparation of acts of terrorism or Convention offences includes anything which is likely to be understood as—

(a) the glorification of the commission or preparation (whether in the past, in the future or generally) of such acts or such offences; and

(b) a suggestion that what is being glorified is being glorified as conduct that should be emulated in existing circumstances.

(9) In this section 'working day' means any day other than—

(a) a Saturday or a Sunday;

(b) Christmas Day or Good Friday; or

(c) a day which is a bank holiday under the Banking and Financial Dealings Act 1971 (c. 80) in any part of the United Kingdom.

Terrorism Act 2000

60 Northern Ireland

(1) A person commits an offence if—

(a) he incites another person to commit an act of terrorism wholly or partly outside the United Kingdom, and

(b) the act would, if committed in Northern Ireland, constitute one of the offences listed in subsection (2).

(2) Those offences are—

(a) murder,

(b) an offence under section 18 of the Offences against the Person Act 1861 (wounding with intent),

(c) an offence under section 23 or 24 of that Act (poison),

(d) an offence under section 28 or 29 of that Act (explosions), and

(e) an offence under Article 3(2) of the Criminal Damage (Northern Ireland) Order 1977 (endangering life by damaging property).

(4) For the purposes of subsection (1) it is immaterial whether or not the person incited is in the United Kingdom at the time of the incitement.

Criminal Justice and Immigration Act 2008

(2008, c. 4)

PART 5 CRIMINAL LAW

Pornography etc.

63 Possession of extreme pornographic images

(1) It is an offence for a person to be in possession of an extreme pornographic image.

(2) An 'extreme pornographic image' is an image which is both—

(a) pornographic, and

(b) an extreme image.

(3) An image is 'pornographic' if it is of such a nature that it must reasonably be assumed to have been produced solely or principally for the purpose of sexual arousal.

(4) Where (as found in the person's possession) an image forms part of a series of images, the question whether the image is of such a nature as is mentioned in subsection (3) is to be determined by reference to—

(a) the image itself, and

(b) (if the series of images is such as to be capable of providing a context for the image) the context in which it occurs in the series of images.

(5) So, for example, where—

(a) an image forms an integral part of a narrative constituted by a series of images, and

(b) having regard to those images as a whole, they are not of such a nature that they must reasonably be assumed to have been produced solely or principally for the purpose of sexual arousal,

the image may, by virtue of being part of that narrative, be found not to be pornographic, even though it might have been found to be pornographic if taken by itself.

(6) An 'extreme image' is an image which—

(a) falls within subsection (7), and

(b) is grossly offensive, disgusting or otherwise of an obscene character.

(7) An image falls within this subsection if it portrays, in an explicit and realistic way, any of the following—

(a) an act which threatens a person's life,

(b) an act which results, or is likely to result, in serious injury to a person's anus, breasts or genitals,

(c) an act which involves sexual interference with a human corpse, or

(d) a person performing an act of intercourse or oral sex with an animal (whether dead or alive),

and a reasonable person looking at the image would think that any such person or animal was real.

(8) In this section 'image' means—

(a) a moving or still image (produced by any means); or

(b) data (stored by any means) which is capable of conversion into an image within paragraph (a).

(9) In this section references to a part of the body include references to a part surgically constructed (in particular through gender reassignment surgery).

(10) Proceedings for an offence under this section may not be instituted—

(a) in England and Wales, except by or with the consent of the Director of Public Prosecutions; or

(b) in Northern Ireland, except by or with the consent of the Director of Public Prosecutions for Northern Ireland.

64 Exclusion of classified films etc.

(1) Section 63 does not apply to excluded images.

(2) An 'excluded image' is an image which forms part of a series of images contained in a recording of the whole or part of a classified work.

(3) But such an image is not an 'excluded image' if—

(a) it is contained in a recording of an extract from a classified work, and

(b) it is of such a nature that it must reasonably be assumed to have been extracted (whether with or without other images) solely or principally for the purpose of sexual arousal.

(4) Where an extracted image is one of a series of images contained in the recording, the question whether the image is of such a nature as is mentioned in subsection (3)(b) is to be determined by reference to—

(a) the image itself, and

(b) (if the series of images is such as to be capable of providing a context for the image) the context in which it occurs in the series of images;

and section 63(5) applies in connection with determining that question as it applies in connection with determining whether an image is pornographic.

(5) In determining for the purposes of this section whether a recording is a recording of the whole or part of a classified work, any alteration attributable to—

(a) a defect caused for technical reasons or by inadvertence on the part of any person, or

(b) the inclusion in the recording of any extraneous material (such as advertisements), is to be disregarded.

(6) Nothing in this section is to be taken as affecting any duty of a designated authority to have regard to section 63 (along with other enactments creating criminal offences) in determining whether a video work is suitable for a classification certificate to be issued in respect of it.

(7) In this section—

'classified work' means (subject to subsection (8)) a video work in respect of which a classification certificate has been issued by a designated authority (whether before or after the commencement of this section);

'classification certificate' and 'video work' have the same meanings as in the Video Recordings Act 1984 (c. 39);

'designated authority' means an authority which has been designated by the Secretary of State under section 4 of that Act;

'extract' includes an extract consisting of a single image;

'image' and 'pornographic' have the same meanings as in section 63;

'recording' means any disc, tape or other device capable of storing data electronically and from which images may be produced (by any means).

(8) Section 22(3) of the Video Recordings Act 1984 (effect of alterations) applies for the purposes of this section as it applies for the purposes of that Act.

65   Defences: general

(1) Where a person is charged with an offence under section 63, it is a defence for the person to prove any of the matters mentioned in subsection (2).

(2) The matters are—

(a) that the person had a legitimate reason for being in possession of the image concerned;

(b) that the person had not seen the image concerned and did not know, nor had any cause to suspect, it to be an extreme pornographic image;

(c) that the person—

(i)   was sent the image concerned without any prior request having been made by or on behalf of the person, and

(ii)   did not keep it for an unreasonable time.

(3) In this section 'extreme pornographic image' and 'image' have the same meanings as in section 63.

66   Defence: participation in consensual acts

(1) This section applies where—

(a) a person ('D') is charged with an offence under section 63, and

(b) the offence relates to an image that portrays an act or acts within paragraphs (a) to (c) (but none within paragraph (d)) of subsection (7) of that section.

(2) It is a defence for D to prove—

(a) that D directly participated in the act or any of the acts portrayed, and

(b) that the act or acts did not involve the infliction of any non-consensual harm on any person, and

(c) if the image portrays an act within section 63(7)(c), that what is portrayed as a human corpse was not in fact a corpse.

(3) For the purposes of this section harm inflicted on a person is 'non-consensual' harm if—

(a) the harm is of such a nature that the person cannot, in law, consent to it being inflicted on himself or herself; or

(b) where the person can, in law, consent to it being so inflicted, the person does not in fact consent to it being so inflicted.

67   Penalties etc. for possession of extreme pornographic images

(1) This section has effect where a person is guilty of an offence under section 63.

(2) Except where subsection (3) applies to the offence, the offender is liable—

(a) on summary conviction, to imprisonment for a term not exceeding the relevant period or a fine not exceeding the statutory maximum or both;

(b) on conviction on indictment, to imprisonment for a term not exceeding 3 years or a fine or both.

(3) If the offence relates to an image that does not portray any act within section 63(7)(a) or (b), the offender is liable—

(a) on summary conviction, to imprisonment for a term not exceeding the relevant period or a fine not exceeding the statutory maximum or both;

(b) on conviction on indictment, to imprisonment for a term not exceeding 2 years or a fine or both.

(4) In subsection (2)(a) or (3)(a) 'the relevant period' means—

(a) in relation to England and Wales, 12 months;

(b) in relation to Northern Ireland, 6 months.

Hatred on the grounds of sexual orientation

74   Hatred on the grounds of sexual orientation

Schedule 16—

(a) amends Part 3A of the Public Order Act 1986 (c. 64) (hatred against persons on religious grounds) to make provision about hatred against a group of persons defined by reference to sexual orientation, and

(b) makes minor amendments of that Part.

Blasphemy

79   Abolition of common law offences of blasphemy and blasphemous libel

(1) The offences of blasphemy and blasphemous libel under the common law of England and Wales are abolished.

(2) In section 1 of the Criminal Libel Act 1819 (60 Geo. 3 & 1 Geo. 4 c. 8) (orders for seizure of copies of blasphemous or seditious libel) the words 'any blasphemous libel, or' are omitted.

(3) In sections 3 and 4 of the Law of Libel Amendment Act 1888 (c. 64) (privileged matters) the words 'blasphemous or' are omitted.

(4) Subsections (2) and (3) (and the related repeals in Schedule 28) extend to England and Wales only.

Index

A

Access to Justice Act 1999
  s. 6, Sched. 2 *32–3*
Administration of Justice Act 1960
  s. 12 *104–5*

B

BBC Licence Agreement *373–86*
BBC Royal Charter *366–73*
Bill of Rights 1688
  s. 9 *1*
Broadcasting Act 1990
  ss. 3–5, 13–15, 17A, 21, 23, 24, 28, 29, 37, 40–2,
    56, 58, 60, 61, 63, 66A, 166, 167, 177, 178, 183,
    183A, 188, 202, 204, Sched. 2 *214–32*
  s. 166 *33*
Broadcasting Act 1996
  ss. 1–5, 18, 19, 23, 29, 33, 35, 36, 72, 97–105, 107,
    110, 111, 114, 115, 117, 119, 121, 130, 137,
    143–7, 150 *233–51*

C

Children Act 1989
  s. 97 *55*
Children and Young Persons Act 1933
  ss. 39, 49 *44–7*
Children, Schools and Families Act 2010
  ss. 11–18, 21 *55–61*
Children's Hearings (Scotland) Act 2011
  s. 182 *61–2*
Civil Evidence Act 1968
  ss. 11, 13 *33–4*
Communications Act 2003
  ss. 1, 3, 4, 6, 8–16, 20, 21, 24, 26, 198, 198A–D,
    199, 203–7, 211, 216, 218, 224, 229–39,
    263–75, 277–96, 298, 303, 304, 306–11, 316,
    317, 319–36, 339–41, 343–5, 362, 368A–R, 390,
    391, 405, 410, 411, Sched. 11A *251–340*
Contempt of Court Act 1981
  ss. 1–12, 14–21, Sched. 1 *97–104*
Copyright, Designs and Patents Act 1988
  ss. 80–4, 86–9, 103 *37–41*
  ss. 85, 88 *190*
Coroners and Justice Act 1996
  ss. 62–5 *395–7*
  ss. 86–9, 91–3, 97 *92–6*
Courts Act 2003
  s. 93 *105*
Courts and Legal Services Act 1990
  s. 8 *32*
Crime and Courts Act 2013
  ss. 34–42 *197–201*

Crime and Disorder Act 1998
  ss. 51, 52B *72–4*
Criminal Justice Act 1987
  ss. 11, 11A *74–6*
Criminal Justice Act 2003
  ss. 71, 72 *76–8*
Criminal Justice and Immigration Act 2008
  ss. 63–7, 74, 79 *406–9*
  s. 77 *175*
  ss. 140, 327B *190–2*
Criminal Procedure and Investigations Act 1996
  ss. 37–43 *78–82*
  ss. 58–61 *35–7*

D

Data Protection Act 1998
  ss. 1–5, 7, 8, 9A, 10, 13, 14, 27–34, 40–50 63, 63A,
    Scheds 1–4, 7 *138–66*
  ss. 17–22, 35–8, 55, 58, 59 *184–90*
Defamation Act 1952
  ss. 2, 3, 9–14, 16–18 *15–17*
Defamation Act 1996
  ss. 1–4, 7–15, 17–20, Sched. 1 *17–27*
Defamation Act 2013
  ss. 1–6, 8–10, 12–17 *10–15*

E

Electronic Commerce (EC Directive) Regulations
  2002/2013
  regs 2, 17–20 *41–3*
Employment Tribunals Act 1996
  ss. 10A–12, 31, 32 *85–90*
Enterprise and Regulatory Reform Act 2013
  s. 96 *197*
EU Law
  , Directive 2010/13/EU of the European Parliament
    and Council
      Arts 1–36 *340–52*
  Rec. No. R (2000) 7 (Disclosure of Journalists'
    Sources) *106–9*
European Convention for the Protection of Human
    Rights and Fundamental Freedoms 1950
    Arts 6, 8–10, 14, 16–17, Protocol *1–2*

F

Freedom of Information Act 2000
  ss. 1–58, 60, 61, 84, 88 *111–38*

H

Human Rights Act 1998
  ss. 1–13, 21, 22 *3–9*

I

Inquiries Act 2005
  ss. 18–20, 36 *90–1*

J

Judicial Proceedings (Regulation of Reports)
    Act 1926
  ss. 1, 2 *84*

L

Limitation Act 1980
  ss. 4A, 28, 32, 32A, 36 *29–32*

M

Magistrates' Courts Act 1980
  s. 8 *82–3*

N

National Union of Journalists Code of
    Conduct *196–7*

O

Obscene Publications Act 1959
  ss. 1–5 *387–90*
Obscene Publications Act 1964
  ss. 1–3 *390–1*
OFCOM Broadcasting Code *352–66*
Official Secrets Act 1989
  ss. 1–16 *166–74*

P

Parliamentary Standards Act 2009
  s. 1 *1*
Press Complaints Commission Code of
    Practice *193–6*
Protection from Harassment Act 1997
  ss. 1–16 *176–84*
Public Order Act 1986
  ss. 29A–N *398–401*

R

Racial and Religious Hatred Act 2006
  ss. 1–3 *397*
Rehabilitation of Offenders Act 1974
  ss. 8, 8A, Sched. 2 *28–9*
Royal Charter on Self-Regulation of the Press (Draft)
    2013 *201–13*

S

Security Service Act 1989
  s. 2 *174–5*
Senior Courts Act 1981
  s. 69 *35*
Sexual Offences (Amendment) Act 1976
  s. 7 *62*
Sexual Offences (Amendment) Act 1992
  ss. 2–6, 8 *63–8*
Sexual Offences (Protected Material) Act 1997
  ss. 1–4, 8, 11, Sched. *68–72*

T

Terrorism Act 2000
  ss. 19, 38B *109–10*
  s. 60 *406*
Terrorism Act 2006
  ss. 1–3 *401–5*

U

UN Convention on the Law of the Sea 1982
  Art. 109 *386*
United States Constitution 1787
  First Amendment *9*

V

Video Recordings Act 1984
  ss. 1, 2, 4–4B *391–4*

Y

Youth Justice and Criminal Evidence Act 1999
  ss. 44–50, 52 *47–55*